Lost Descendants of William Lee

By Jacqueli Finley

Table of Contents

Autosomal DNA is more accurate, especially in this under 8 generational timeframe which is applicable from Col Richard Lee descending downward - even more so for a lower generation such as Gen Robert E Lee.The sad fact is that in the Lee Y-DNA projects Haplogroups assigned to Lee descendants by these Y-DNA Project administrators and 'experts' are inconclusive and should have never been set as a precedent for discerning whether a Lee descendant is a Lee of Virginia Lee or not basically from a few 'well documented' but publicly non verifiable Lee descendants that are promoted by the Society and genealogy websites as the true Y-DNA male Haplogroup guideline to accept or deny Lee ancestor and lineages - when any or all of these Lee Y-DNA donors with or without well documented or accepted Lee descendant pedigrees can (and do per At DNA results) have Non-Parental Events making it unclear, unfair and dishonest that this has been even done in the first place as these claims that started the whole mess that created this false Haplogroup assignment to the LOV family:.....................................36

The DNA conundrum ... | The William Lee lineage is just one aspect of the disconnect and false claims because of wrongful assertions from Lee Y-DNA Projects that many genealogists and genealogy website promote unfairly. There are many Lee descendants from the children of our Lee ancestors who came from mixed race. Some Lee children from mixed marriages were soon forgotten as those Lee families were cut off from their lines, and some from the mistreatment of the slaves that they wrongfully held against their will by our lee ancestors, as the lines from these children of Gen Robert E Lee and his slave Nancy Ruffin, just to mention another one..40

Prologue

L ost Descendants of William Lee

For hundreds of years, the Lees of Virginia descendants of Col. Richard Lee's son, William Lee, have been denied their heritage- denied their birthright by historians and scholars that refuse to allow the truth to be known, referring to the descendants of William Lee and his wife Alice Felton as the "Lost Descendants of William Lee".

Because of past speculation that was considered as truths, and opinions that were published as facts by outdated references that have no proven documentation, as law that governs over who descends from Richard Lee and Anne Constable on 'majority rule' genealogy sites, and false Lee Y-DNA Project claims.

The denial of the William Lee line goes on even in these times because of false Lee Y-DNA Project claims, as the internet opens new frontiers of knowledge, as Federal Census records and documentation that was previously blocked from our view are now accessible - as birth, marriage and death publications are now available-making it possible to prove the existence of this lineage and that it does live on-through the thousands of GEDCOM files available on genealogy sites worldwide—and even though the facts are there, the denial of these proud descendants goes on ...

And the denial of descendants goes beyond William Lee, it goes on to all lines, except for those associated with Ditchley, Cobb's, or Stratford, of primarily white European descent, which seem to be the only lines recognized at this time because of tainted Y-DNA projects, prejudiced genealogy sites, and non-sourced references!

Part 1: William Lee Research

Many previous Lee researchers failed to note that William Lee the son of Col Richard Lee was of age to inherit when his father passed away in 1664 as Will and Last Testament does not stipulate William was not of age as his younger siblings were mentioned as when probated 1664/65. Most previous researchers and genealogy references have William's birth circa 1650 per Edmund J Lee's research in Lee of Virginia setting that stage William's birth would have been more of circa 1640, as men were to be age 21 to inherit without a legal guardian, yet he would have been legally able to wed at a younger age, as was customary at that time as it appears that he did just that. A practice of when giving a 'circa' date in genealogy research as EJ Lee had done usually gave a 10-year span in general understanding not to be taken literally. The math tells us William Lee would have been born around 1640 to be more accurate to his father's probate instructions which would also coincide with marriage record date for William Lee (Lea was a phonic spelling as was often the case in records of that time as with this record) to widow Alice Felton and land transactions that they had both witnessed as well.

NOTE: Regarding supposed research of Alice Felton having the surname FENTON, unfortunately about 20 years ago I had shared research information from a GEDCOM I had made that had a typo error of FENTON for Alice (as I had written an 'N' instead of 'L'). I had an acquaintance with a daughter with a name of Alice Fenton, so I did not catch it until after I submitted that GEDCOM to the LDS Library. This had been a typo that unfortunately some researchers have taken as a fact, even running amuck with the error by going as far as publishing books with the erroneous surname as if factual even after I had warned them it WAS A TYPO ... I have the evidence of the creation of the typo - the GEDCOM, messages and emails about the needed correction. I reached out and informed who I could that it had been just that - a typo mistake. It seems there are those who are trying to use this as evidence to dispute William Lee's wife as Alice

Felton. Again, I apologize, Fenton was my error which I did correct and it was limited to just one GEDCOM file at that time. It is unfortunate that some have and are trying to take advantage of this mistake.

Most seasoned researchers of family history and genealogy acknowledge that there are many variations of spellings that occur with a given surname such as Lee, Lea, Leigh, etc., as one surname example because of phonic spellings, enumerator errors and adaptations over time. Many times, the practice of using alternate phonic spellings of surnames can be helpful in finding archived records.

Unfortunately, Y-DNA projects and individuals who seem to wish to add to the misinformation and confusion in particularly the Lee lineage have used Y-DNA to dissect lines even more or separate one individual as two entities because a record may have a different spelling of a surname than another recording even though common sense and prior earlier research as in William Lee's case (Lea in this instance) were accepted as the same person. Then to add to the arguments it is claimed that his birth had to be about 1650 to 1655 so it would have been impossible for him to have married Alice Felton, widow of Thomas Felton, which conflicts what has been found on the marriage record and completely ignore the fact that William had to be at least 21 when his father WROTE his Last Will and Testament otherwise his being a minor would have been indicated. That was the law of that time. Too often words are used as 'probably, most likely, possibly, etc.,' to describe the reasoning behind what online genealogy sites argue for these dates. There are a lot of assumptions.

LAND GRANT SIGNED BY William Lee:

NO. 1-1
LEE

APPENDIX AC

EARLY REFERENCES IN VIRGINIA RECORDS TO PERSONS
WITH SURNAMES OF LEA, LEIGH, AND LEE

William Leigh - (1608)

William Dawkes, planter, 250 a. in upper part near the neck of
land commonly called Verinas. 20 June 1632, due in right of
his father Henry Dawke and his uncle William Leigh for their
personal adventure. 14 July 1608. (Cavaliers & Pioneers, p.
15)

William Lea (Charles City Co. & Surry Co. - 1654-60

William Lea, 500 acres Charles City Co. 6 Feb. 1654, ebg. opposite plantation of Thos. Felton for transportation of 10 persons among them Wm. Lea. (Cavaliers & Pioneers - Nugent, Land
Patents, p. 303)

William Lea, Feb. 6, 1654 - 500 acres on the south side of James
River and on the west side of an Indian Swamp (Wm. & Mary Quart.
- Vol. 10 - Book No. 3-322).

William Lea, 500 acs. Chas. City Co., 6 Feb. 1654. On s. side
of James River & W. side of an Indian Swamp called Choruk; beg.
opposite plantation of Thos. Felton. Trans. of 10 persons:
John Tredeskin, John Aires, Bertrum Obert, Thomas Austen, his
wife Jane Austen, Richard Austen, Edward Golbourn (Claibourne?
- WHE), Jane Glenn, William Lea. (Cavaliers and Pioneers,
Abstracts of Va. Land Patents and Grants, 1623-1800 by N. M.
Nugent - 1934, p. 322.)

1655, Mar. 17 - 500 acres - granted unto Wm. Lea, 6 Feb. 1654,
and assigned unto the above named patentees. (Ibid, p. 303)

4 Oct. 1660, between Wm. Lea & Alice his wife to Wm. Heath, 150
a. of land which was formerly Thos. Felton, dec. in Surry Co.,
Va. adjoining John Harris plantation which was formerly Robt.
Moselys between Surry & Chas. City Co. and was give by sd. Thos.
Felton to Alice his wife by his last will and testament. Alice
now wife of Wm. Lea. Nov. 10, 1660 (Surry Co. D.B. 1, p. 168).

Capt. William Leigh - York Co. (1640-C1653)

(Note: York Co. formed 1642, Formerly Charles River.)

Capt. Wm. Leigh was a justice in York Co. 1640 (Virginia Mag.
Vol. 32, p. 62).

Wm. Leigh patented 1000 acres on the north side of York River
in 1642 (Ibid).

67

ACTIONS MINORS COULD PERFORM EARLY COLONIAL VIRGINIA

There are those who argue that land grants and recordings signed by William Lee (or Lea) were not those of our William Lee, and wife Alice on some as they are both Witnesses, because of the given age of 'Circa 1650's' made him too young and state that he could not acquire, buy, sell land, or witness legal contracts because he was not 21 per the argument. That is not entirely true at all, age 21 was mainly about inheritance without a guardian under age 21, the rest is assumptive imposing limitations on the historical documentation signed by William Lee to create an argument not based on true facts:

Some legal actions did not require that a person be 21. For some legal actions, the law merely required that the person be judged capable of discretion. The age of 14 was generally accepted under common law as the age of discretion, and in rare individual cases (particularly females) it could be even lower. A minor could be judged by courts to be capable, just as an elderly person or an idiot could be judged to be incapable. Further, a father could give or withhold some or all of the rights of majority to a child, by "giving freedom", though actually finding such a record is quite rare.

Generally speaking, children aged 14 and over could legitimately perform a variety of legal actions:

Choose their guardian or replace an existing guardian.

Apprentice themselves without parental consent.

Bequeath personal property (but not real property) in a will.

Witness deeds and contracts.

Testify in court.

Boys aged 16 and over were obliged to serve in militias and could obligate themselves to military service without the consent of parents in most of the colonies.

Children aged 17 and over could act as an executor so long as other actions by adults were not required. (This is a relatively rare occurrence.) See: Legal Age | Bob's Genealogy Filing Cabinet (genfiles.com)

These actions by minors were accepted without question. For example, when we find record of a child selecting their own guardian or binding themselves as apprentices, it is a certainty that the minor was aged 14 or more. Further, if judged by the court to be of sufficient discretion, a child could make a will disposing of personal property (but not real property) at the age of 14 (age 12 for females). Children could also be witnesses in a court action. Children aged 14 or more could legally witness a deed, will, or contract. For a variety of practical reasons the parties to such acts might prefer to use adults, or at least older children, as witnesses. However, at one time it was common in England to select as a witness a young child who could be counted upon to outlive the parties to the transaction.

So strongly was this traditional common law embedded in American society that the Virginia colonial legislature deviated from it in only one circumstance. In 1727, after the Virginia legislature enacted a statute declaring slaves to be subject to the same treatments and laws as real estate, it recognized that real estate could not be devised in the will of a minor and amended the statute to permit a child aged 18 or more to bequeath slaves in a will. 2

Minors and Land

The case of land transactions deserves special attention. Minors could be landowners since they could acquire land by gift or inheritance. Land was never without title, so a fathers will devising land to a minor resulted in the minor's immediate ownership regardless of age. Likewise, the land of an intestate person fell immediately to a specific heir, even if a minor, under the law of succession.

Minors and Lawsuits

In the same manner, children were protected from lawsuits. A child under 21 could not be sued except in the name of his guardian. Conversely, an infant could initiate a suit only in the name of his guardian or next friend. A minor could, however, be charged with any crime at the age of 14.

For a detailed discussion of legal age, see Blackstone, Sir William, Commentaries on The Laws of England, Book 1, Chapter 17. Note that specific actions by minors could be altered by colonial legislatures, based on local needs.

See Hening, Vol. 4, page 223

Blackstone, Book 1, page 465.

Blackstone, Book 1, page 465.

Hening, Vol. 1, pp269-70.

So, they plant the seeds of doubt then over time and then that doubt is used to destroy our Lee lines.

It is a pattern of lineage destruction that has been used and is being implemented currently, as these latest claims that son of Richard Lee that married Mary Young was not related to William and Alice at all, but a random immigrant from England who voyaged over with his soon to be wife Mary.

This has been the way for the Lee lines, especially with William Lee.

First EJ Lee published William died without issue in his 'Lee of Virginia' book (EJ Lee's son published after EJ Lee's death a re-write correction that William had married and Alice and had four children). Then it was argued Mary Lee was not a child of William Lee's as the Lee Society still states this today and does not recognize the line using that argument even though William Lee's handwritten Will sat hidden within the Virginia State archives.

They have argued and dissected William's children one by one from William Lee, II and John Lee, now Richard Lee.

They have accepted for most part son Richard Lee until recently but had wrongly cut off many Lee descendants of the next generation descent down by claiming Richard Lee's son John Lee, Esquire was not the great grandson of Col Richard Lee and Anne Constable as previously claimed.

Using unverifiable Y-DNA they disputed, then divided John Lee, Esquire into three separate individuals as a John Lee, Esquire, John Lee from Johnston County and a John Lee from Nansemond, ignoring the facts that tell he was one individual - John Lee who was son of Richard Lee and Mary Young. They use unverified Y-DNA studies to discredit previous well researched and sourced published conclusions on these Lee ancestors and their lines.

They used the false Y-DNA claims to destroy our Lee lines beyond William Lee to most of our Lee descendant lineages and continue to sow the seeds of doubt and dissect our ancestry, ignoring factual evidence that the majority of Lee descendants DNA now shows us the truth of the matter and what has been occurring is wrong.

I have learned that when I see on these online genealogy sites that promote "collaborative consensus genealogy" that each site does mirror each other's verbiage on the biographies for ancestor profile reflecting the information on what they wish to present on the World stage as true and accurate regarding our Lee family ancestors and history. Seeing the words "In Dispute" on the ancestor profiles this eventually means that existing Lee lines from that ancestor profile will soon be separated from their rightful descents and lineages. This has happened repeatedly in this pattern.

THESE SITES AND INDIVIDUALS often give our ancestors different names, making our ancestors unrecognizable and impossible to find in research for future generations.

THESE SITES ALSO PROMOTE opinion and assumptions over facts and primary sourcing. Instead, they use the words "maybe, probably, possibly, could have been ... " often as well as all kinds of vocabulary that looks good on paper but if fact checked, cannot be verified. Many of the sources they use are not sources, not even a reference to a source and too often unverifiable.

Since the first publishing of Edmund Jennings Lee's book 'Lee of Virginia' that the Lee Society and many Lee researchers use as a guide on our Lee ancestry, the only Lee lines that mattered or 'accepted' are the all-male Lee lines of descent from the 'famous' Lees or IF a female Lee married into a wealthy affluent family. When DNA became a factor with genealogy by using only male Y-DNA the segregation and discrimination continued. It is rare if a mixed marriage, or partnership resulting in children of mixed race, or a gender switch in a Lee line from a male ancestor to a female child, these lines are rarely ever recognized and IF it once was, it is disputed then eliminated. Even though these female gender switches (meaning a female Lee child married and had descendants), or a mixed race descendancy occurred, represent 80% or more of Lee DNA that can be used to verify family and ancestral relationships. With accuracy, in spite of what they claim.

Fact: William Lee did have a handwritten Will which verified and named Mary Lee as his daughter when she was made Trustee of Estate by the Court:

Source: Northumberland County Court Transcript:

1687-1699 ORDER BOOK PART 2 - Northumberland Co Va; Hamrick: Pg 740 Northumberland County Court September 16, 1696 Upon the Petition of MARY SCREVER formerly HEATH Executrix of the Last Will and Testament of Capt. WILLIAM LEE the said Will here in Court produced, which in the Court's Opinion (being well acquainted with the hand of the said Capt. LEE) was written by his own hand but the Witnesses not forthcoming a Probate is granted her of the Last Will and Testament

BUT SOMEHOW WILLIAM Lee's Will and appointment of daughter Mary Lee as Executor was lost to researchers in the past ... one must visit the archives to view the microfilm which is a feat in itself as it is a difficult task to get the opportunity to with the bureaucracy involved. The Virginia State Library archives are full of historical public records yet a few years back the access to these public records was changed from the traditional process of viewing to a very limited process that has narrowed the access, even though these archives are for the public to view as containing public information that should be accessed freely.

Even past seasoned researchers and historical publishing's seemed to have ignored the existence of this record.

One Example:

William's daughter Mary Lee: William and Mary College quarterly historical magazine, Volume 9, page 274. - Caroline Jett wrote in her article "In the Shadow of the Chicacoan Oak": "It was in the 1680's that Thomas Heath came to Northumberland County. As he died soon after arriving there, the folks of Northumberland County knew little about him. His wife was Mary, and much effort has been made to discover her maiden name. Some believe that she was the daughter of Captain William Lee (son of Richard Lee.) However, as no clear evidence or proof that she was Captain Lee's daughter has ever been discovered, the Society of Lees of Virginia will not accept her descendants as members. Whether she was his daughter or not, she definitely was the executor of Capt. Lee's estate."

One would think if such statements were made as above years ago, there had to have been a Will for William Lee to have had made Mary an Executor of his estate ... and we are to believe they did not even think of it as possible a Will existed as is necessary to legally address a probate in court.

More recent research, documentation and using DNA has confirmed that William Lee and Alice Felton did have four children, Mary Lee Heath Schriever being their daughter. The court records verify that their sons did eventually have their day in court with Uncle Richard. They were awarded monies and land from their uncle, Richard Lee, years after the initial court battle, when they were not yet of adult age, where their uncle had taken their inheritance from their sister Mary's husband, Bart Schriever. It has been documented that Bart and Mary received her furniture and what money that Bart had saved up, then the land had been divided between Uncle Richard and his two brothers. This included the same land occupied by William and his family and the adjacent land which once had belonged to Thomas Felton, then Alice Felton, then sold to William Heath, then Mary and husband Bart.

UNCLE RICHARD LEE'S – meaning Richard Henry Lee son of Col Richard Lee and Anne Constable - distribution of brother William's inheritance to himself and two brothers – Charles and Hancock Lee. This was per 'the agreement' made by these three Lee brothers of William, as mentioned by Edmund Jennings Lee in 'Lee of Virginia':

COBBS HALL LINE, SECOND GENERATION.   559

[...] in a list of civil officers, dated in 1702, showing him to have been in [posses-]sion at the time of his death.

[As] previously stated (page 53), Colonel Richard Lee had taken up two [tracts] of land at the Dividing Creeks, in Northumberland; the first of these [contain-]ed six hundred acres, and was the plantation later known as "Cobbs [Hall." The] other tract contained eight hundred acres, two hundred of [which] were given to Charles by his brother Richard Lee, as shown by the [deed] given on page 521. No less than six deeds, with accompanying [papers,] are on record at Northumberland court-house, securing these lands [to the] two brothers. The following is the original patent for "Cobbs Hall."

[... &]ll &c Whereas &c now Knowe That I the said Edward Diggs Esq doe give and [grant unto] Collo Richard Lee six hundred Acres of Land Scituate in Northumberland [... and] upon the South side of the Dividing Creek abutting East upon the said Creek [and] southerly upon another Parcell of Land belonging to the said Lee divided from [... a small] Creek Called Andrews Creek, South West Westerly upon the Glade and high [... South] West northerly upon a run and small Creek Called freemans ford, The said [... being] due unto the said Collo Richard Lee by and for the Transportation of Twelve [... into] this Callony &c To Have and To Hold &c Yielding and paying &c Which [... &]c dated the 4th of March 1656.

[Next] after the patent, on the records, comes this brief deed:

[Richar]d Lee son and heir of Collo Richard Lee dec'd doe by these p'sents and out of [... af]fection I beare Cozen [nephew] Charles Lee assign over all my Right and Title [... intere]st to the Land contained in the Pattent on the other side to my Cozen Charles Lee [... his] heirs for Ever, In witness, etc. Dated 9th September, 1707.

[His] will was dated the 13th of July, 1700, and probated at Northum-[berland] court-house, on the 17th of December, 1701.

[Charl]es Lee being in perfect health and strength of memory do make this my last Will [and Tes]tament. First, I give and bequeath my soul to that good and gracious God yt gave [it, and] to my blessed redeemer Jesus Christ, assuredly trusting in and by his meritorious [death and] Passion to receive Salvation, and my Body to be disposed of as my loving Wife [shall desire?] not doubting but at the last both body and soul will be reunited and [... Next] I give and bequeath unto my son Thomas all my Land on Rappahannock River [given] by my wife as also 500 acres left me by Walter Jenkins, to him and his heirs male [... one] feather bed and further a child's part of my negroes, Cattel and household stuff [... in case] of his death without heirs, to be divided amongst my other children, the Land to [... Ch]arles and the heir male of his body. Next, I give and bequeath to my son Charles [... acres] whereon I now am, a feather bed and furniture, a childs part of my negroes [... and] wth other household stuff, and in case of his death before age to be equally divided [... my] other Children, the land to my son Thomas. Next, I give and bequeath to my [... Lee] Hannah Lee that 200 acres of land had out of Bro. Hancock's tract, a childs [part of my] negroes and cattle wth other houshold stuff, the sheep of her mark, which is two [... and] a slit in one ear, and in case of her death before age, to be divided amongst my [... Chil]dren, the land to my son Charles.

DITCHLEY ... SE, SECOND GENERATION.   521

The Northern Neck land records show that Hancock patented land as follows: 1,100 acres in Richmond county, the 18th April, 1704; 370 acres on both sides of Rappahannock Horsepen Run and adjoining his own land, 21st May, 1705; 1,353 acres in Richmond county, 6th June, 1704; 160 acres on north side of the Occoquan in Stafford county, 2d November, 1705; 1,750 acres at the heads of the branches of Chapowamsic in Stafford, adjoining the land of Capt. Thomas Harrison, 10th February, 1707. Hancock Lee, son of Hancock Lee, deceased, patented 1,025 acres on Wolf Run in Stafford, for which Hancock Lee the elder had obtained a warrant, 1708, and by a codicil to his will, 31st December, 1706, gave to his son the said Hancock, 6th March, 1709 to. In 1658, Hancock Lee, gent., obtained a patent for 568 acres in Accomac county.

The land formerly included in the Ditchley estate was patented the 21st of May, 1651, as shown by this patent:

To all &c. Whereas &c now Know you that I the said Sr William Berkeley Knight &c Do with the Consent of the Council of State accordingly give and grant unto Colo. Richard Lee Esq. Secretary of State for this Colony Eight hundred acres of Land Scituate in Northumberland County and upon the South side of a Creeke Commonly called the Dividing Creek . . . abutting North East and Northerly uppon the said Creeke Southeast and Southerly Upon a creeke which issueth forth of the said Dividing Creek Which divideth the Land and the land of Mr Thomas Wilson Marriner, Southwest into the maine Woods West and Northwest upon a small creek which divideth this Land and the Land of Colo Richard Lee. The said Land being due unto the said Colo Richard Lee by and for the Transportation of Sixteen persons and whose names are in the Records mentioned under this Patent &c To have and to hold &c To be held of Our Soveraigne Lord the King his Heirs and Successors forever as of his mannor of East Greenwich in free and Common Socage and not in Capite nor by Knights Service Yielding and paying unto our Soveraigne Lord the King his Heirs and Successors &c Which payment &c. yeeulded &c. Given att James City under my hand and the Seal of this Colony the 21st day of May, 1651.

Following this patent on the records of Northumberland are these two deeds:

Know all men by these presents that I Richard Lee of Lower Machotique in the Parish of Cople and County of Westmoreland upon the perusall of my good father Colo Richard Lee der'd his Will finding the Lands he left my Broth'r Hancock and Charles Lee are in Law but an Estate for Life out of the paternall affection I have to them and their heirs doe by these presents as heir to my good father der'd doe give the Land contained in this Pat'tent on the other side from me and my heirs to them and their heirs as followeth (viz.) 600 acres of the said Land to my Broth'r Hancock and his heirs and the other 200 acres to my Cozen [nephew] Charles Lee and his heirs according to the agreement made between my two Broth'rs Hancock and Charles and Recorded in Northumberland County Court Records, always provided that according to the Will made by my broth'r Charles my Cozen Loreanna Jones Enjoy and use and occupy the said 200 acres called Hickory Neck during her Life and when her deceasete to revert to the said Charles Lee and his heirs according to the dispo-

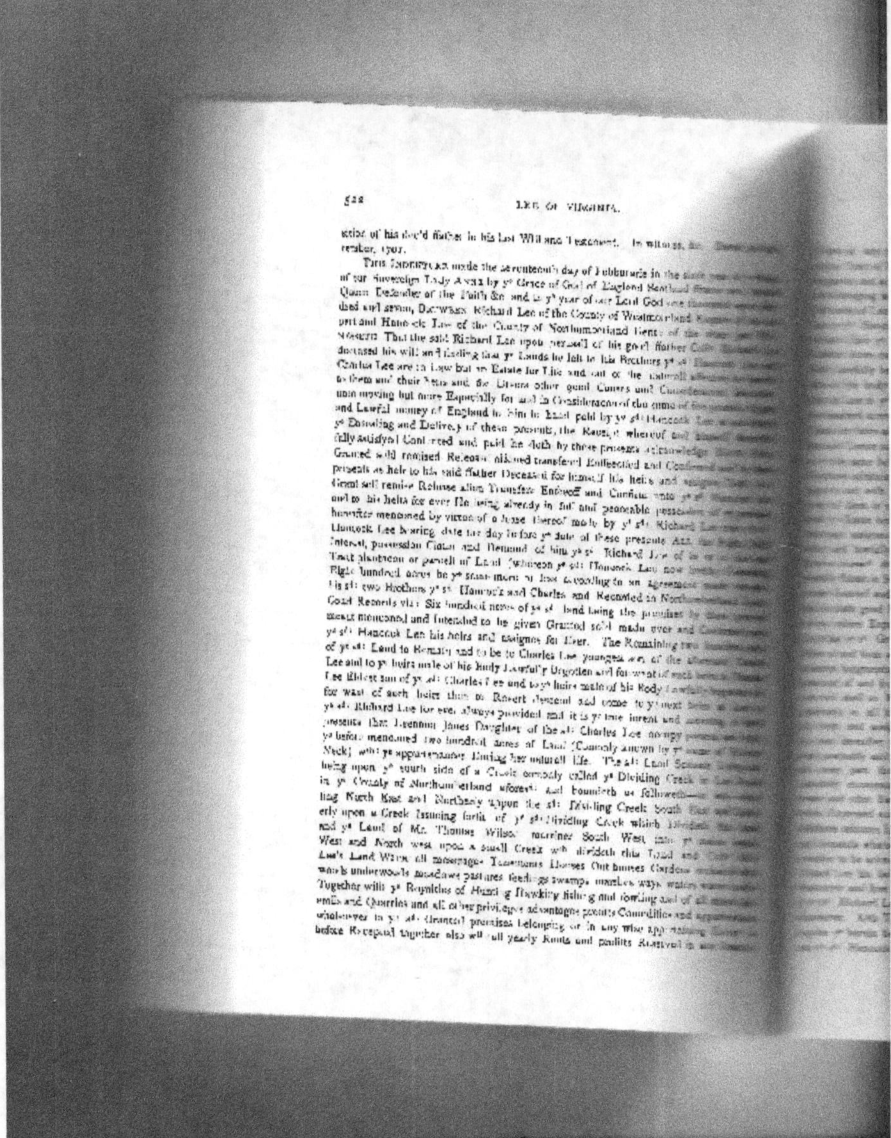

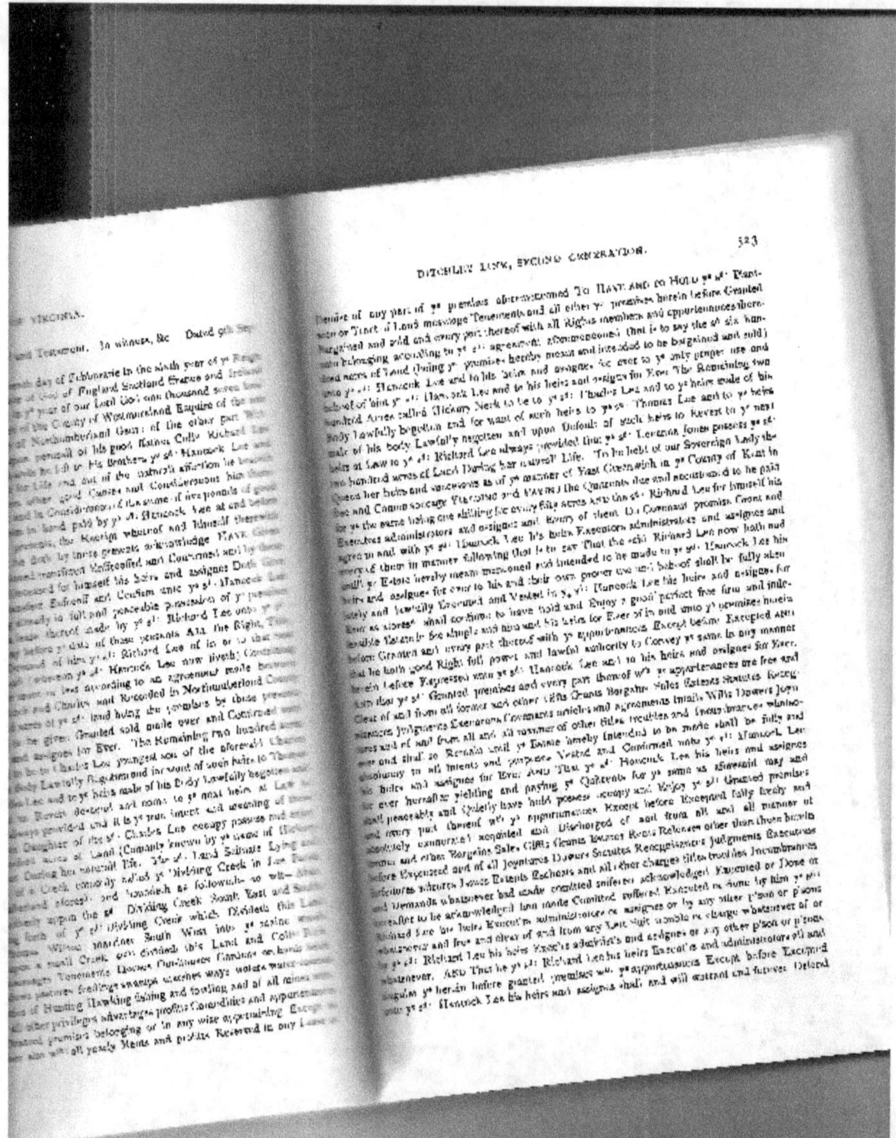

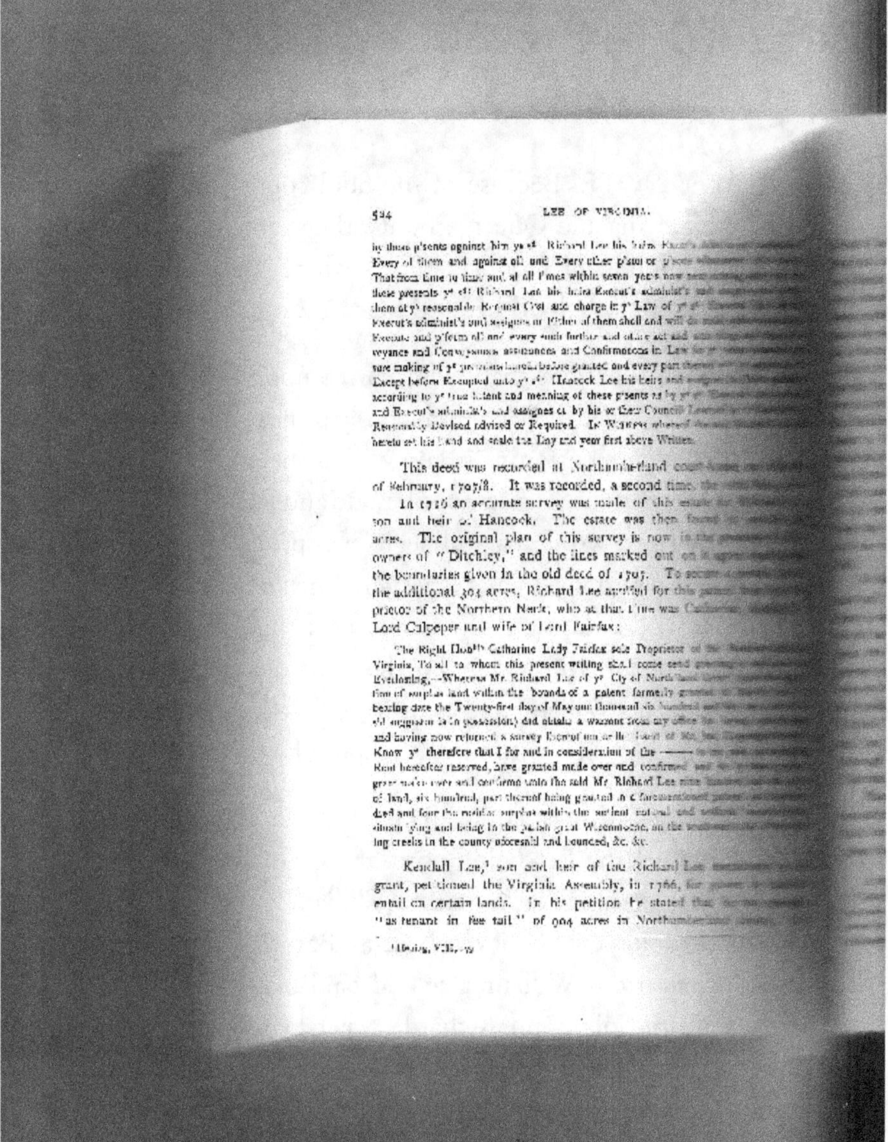

594   LEE OF VIRGINIA.

by these p'sents against him y.e s.d Richard Lee his heirs Execut's
Every of them and against all and Every other p'son or p'sons
That from time to time and at all t'mes within seven years now
these presents y.e s.d Richard Lee his heirs Execut's administ's
them at y.e reasonable Request Cost and charge in y.e Law of y.e s.d
Execut's administ's and assignes or Either of them shall and will
Execute and p'form all and every such further and other act and
veyance and Conveyances assurances and Confirmacons in Law
sure making of y.e p'misses herein before granted and every part
Except before Excepted unto y.e s.d Hancock Lee his heirs and
according to y.e true Intent and meaning of these p'sents as by y.e
and Execut's administ's and assignes or by his or their Councell
Reasonably Devised advised or Required. In Witness whereof
hereto set his hand and seale the Day and year first above Written.

This deed was recorded at Northumberland court
of February, 1707/8. It was recorded, a second time
In 1726 an accurate survey was made of this estate
son and heir of Hancock. The estate was then
acres. The original plan of this survey is now in
owners of "Ditchley," and the lines marked out on
the boundaries given in the old deed of 1705. To
the additional 304 acres, Richard Lee applied for this
prietor of the Northern Neck, who at that time was Ca
Lord Culpeper and wife of Lord Fairfax:

The Right Hon.ble Catharine Lady Fairfax sole Proprietor
Virginia, To all to whom this present writing shall come send
Everlasting,—Whereas Mr. Richard Lee of y.e City of North
tion of surplus land within the bounds of a patent formerly
bearing date the Twenty-first day of May one thousand six hun
(d mansion is in possession) did obtain a warrant from my office
and having now returned a survey thereof un.er the hand of
Know y.e therefore that I for and in consideration of the ———
Rent hereafter reserved, have granted made over and confirmed
gran make over and confirme unto the said Mr. Richard Lee
of land, six hundred, part thereof being granted in c forementioned
died and four the residue surplus within the antient natural and
situate lying and being in the parish great Wicomoco, on the
ing creeks in the county aforesaid and bounded, &c. &c.

Kendall Lee,[1] son and heir of the Richard Lee
grant, petitioned the Virginia Assembly, in 1766, for
entail on certain lands. In his petition he stated that
"as tenant in fee tail" of 904 acres in Northumber

[1] Hening, VIII, 72.

Part 2: UPON WILLIAM LEE'S DEATH

IMPORTANT NOTE: Because of the fluid county lines of that time, Surry Virginia, King and Queen County, then came to become parts of Nansemond, and Johnston County, NC – where John Lee, Esquire did reside as he was a son of Richard Lee and Mary Young.

A quick synopsis of situations that had occurred upon William Lee's death, as it appears his wife Alice died simultaneously or near the same time as her husband as there is no mentioning in his Will, if she was still alive when he wrote it, she would have been executor of estate and guardian of their minor children. He also hand wrote his Will as he was passing in haste as he had no time to make prior arrangements especially when one considers William's legal background and education - he would have done so in advance if he had known his passing was imminent. So, the assertions that Alice Felton Lee died after her husband William makes no sense at all as is what is currently promoted on genealogy sites without any record of why.

The daughter Mary had married William Heath at age 15 had two sons, Thomas, and Samuel the last being born after his father died. Mary and William Heath lived on the farm next to William and Alice's estate. Mary remarried to Bartholomew Schriever. Because Bart was of age, he over saw the inherited estate from William Lee and paid out a yearly living to the three boys: William, John, and Richard. What he paid was far less than the estate could manage; and they deserved more; but it was legally large enough that they could not sue their guardian until ALL of them were of age. But before this would occur, the uncle, Richard Lee, William's brother, took Mary Lee Heath Schriever and her husband Bart to court using an out of area circuit court that their uncle Richard had used many times prior as one can see if one researches Richard Lee's court records. It was through this judge Uncle Richard convinced the court to reverse his brother William's inheritance back to himself from missing verbiage that was not used in his father's Will when it came to son William Lee's mention.

Keep in mind this was all done not in probate court but in a common pleas court. And not in the original county Westmoreland but as the county had been split and then re-split in the meantime it was Surry County and worse the judge a VIP that Uncle Richard used for years for his legal issues, did not travel to them but they had to travel to him in King and Queen County.

William Lee's boys did sue the instant the youngest turned 21 which was 1710/11.

Here below is a record of a Land Grant record to Richard Lee (son of Wm Lee) from court battle with Uncle Richard Lee - Court Order to Richard Lee, son of Col Richard Lee, Immigrant to return certain land back to William Lee's sons John Lee and Richard Lee.

These appear to be the land Richard Lee had taken from Wm's sons after court battle over Col Richard Lee Will and Wm's inheritance (this land when traced William Lee had acquired with wife Alice outside of inheritance) Wm's son William took a cash settlement instead of land.

COURT ORDER FROM COURT TO UNCLE RICHARD LAND GRANT TO WILLIAM:

Source:

9 May 1711 Westmoreland County Grant: Author Link: Lee, Richard, Col., grantee.

Title Link: Land grant 9 May 1711.

Summary Location: Westmoreland County.

Description: 792 acres beginning &c being the 4th corner of a patent for 2200 acres of land belonging to the sd. Richd. Lee by patent granted to Colo. Richard Lee, decd.

Source: Northern Neck Grants No. 4, 1710-1712 , p. 33 (Reel 289).

Part of the index to recorded copies of land grants issued by the agents of the Fairfax Proprietary between 1690 and 1781 and by the Commonwealth between 1786 and 1874. Original and recorded surveys are also indexed when available. The collection is housed in the Archives at the Library of Virginia. Other Format Available on microfilm. Northern Neck Grants, reels 288-311.

Subject - Personal Link: Lee, Richard, Col., grantee. Link: Lee, Richd. Subject - Topical Link: Land titles.—Registration and transfer—Virginia—Westmoreland County Subject -Geographic Link: Westmoreland County Virginia—History—18th century. Genre/Form Link: Land grants—Virginia—Westmoreland County. Added Entry Link: Northern Neck Land Office. Northern Neck grants, 1690-1874. Link: Library of Virginia. Archives.

RESEARCH NOTE: GRANTEE COL Richard Henry Lee – from lawsuit 1711 – so lawsuit was recorded around that timetable not from Col Richard Lee probate as he died in 1664 and his probate distributed in 1665 ... not 1711 and the probate gave a detailed inventory of Col Richard Lee's vast estate and what William Lee had inherited. This land the court viewed as possible land Uncle Rich took back from William's sons and as inherited land from Col. Richard Lee.

By tracing land back to William and Alice Lee this land grant starts to make more sense as records show William and Alice owned land adjacent to William Heath and daughter Mary.

There are more court filings available to view as well in the VA archives regarding this matter. This one in particular holds some details to land that may be traced to future descendants from Richard Lee and his child John Lee, Esquire's estate.

John Lee, Esq – son of Richard Henry Lee and grandson of Wm Lee, appears to inherit portions of this same land from his father Richard Lee and by following the land John Lee, Esq distributes later on to his children via his Will, by reviewing inventory of the land William had inherited from his father, reviewing land his brother distributed to his two siblings after reversing William's inheritance, and noting that William, Alice acquired properties in what was the Westmoreland region and comparing to land divisions and renaming of that particular territory.

You can follow the land that Wm's boys got back from their Uncle Richard Henry Lee in court battle, following intricate territorial name changes – eventually to Nansemond then to Johnston County, North Carolina. This was what I label the "HEATH" land because the deeds and land grants make it a little easier to follow as this land was given back to the boys Richard and John from their Uncle Richard when the inheritance reversal occurred as he had confiscated the land on which Mary and her husband Bart had occupied at that time as well.

Part 3: DNA Does Prove William Lee Descendants Lees of Virginia Lines

Newer verifiable DNA studies from Lee descendants using GEDMatch and similar DNA comparison tools with Lee descendant collected linear DNA overrides previous Y-DNA controversial and incorrect data stating otherwise.

IT HAS BEEN AND CAN be determined by these new linear DNA comparisons confirmation of the relationships of lines for William Lee, son of Richard Lee and Anne Constable, their children, and descendants. This includes for their son Richard Lee who married Mary Young and their children, and descendants.

DESCENDANTS OF LEE lines from Richard Lee and Anne Constable can use linear DNA – which means using the raw data from Autosomal, Mitochondrial, and Y-DNA comparison results – to verify genetic relationships using GEDMatch type DNA tools regardless of Lee descendant donor sexual orientation using both male and female Lee descendant DNA.

BECAUSE Y-DNA IS LIMITED and cannot verify an NPE (Non-Parental Event), linear DNA studies are more comprehensive and when using a platform as GEDMatch the comparison results are fairer and more transparent.

AND WITH THESE NEW tools and advancement in DNA comparisons, especially for clarification where paper trails may not clear up Lee relationships and lineages, the DNA is able to confirm what has been in dispute.

Of course, there are family trees and GEDCOMs that may be incorrect or have NPEs, but in these cases there will not be DNA matches or discrepancies in what MRCAs may reflect. That is where the documentation and research can be complimented with the DNA results.

And if there are DEFINITIVE records of facts and not just an opinion of records of Lee ancestor relationships, please come forth with the factual evidence (not just research speculation) as many of us Lee descendants have confirming DNA matches with other confirmed Lee descendant lines from Richard Lee and Anne Constable, overwhelmingly so.

MANY OF US WHO ARE often told we are not related to the famous Lees are in fact related and not "Lee Wanna-Be's" as we have been erroneously called. Our DNA tells us the facts and evidence of our genetic relationships, not opinion.

Thanks to public DNA collective sites that give the DNA donor the control over their own DNA results, matches, and verification the process has become more transparent.

As we may have opinion and different interpretations of documents, records, and historical evidence: comprehensive DNA comparisons with significant segment matches do not lie to us.

Especially true when our DNA family trees and GEDCOMs can tell us EXACTLY what generation the DNA ancestral matches exist when we run DNA Generational Match reports.

Because this DNA evidence is so overwhelmingly present and by a great quantity of Lee descendant DNA donor contributions, it is hard to fathom the arguments that these DNA confirmations are not credible. Especially considering the real limitations to Y-DNA studies and the potential of NPE's existing in many of the documented male Lee lines they use in these Lee Y-DNA projects.

Many Lee descendants are getting confusing information and non-acceptance of DNA matches of descending lines from the Lees of Virginia. This may be happening even when DNA has been confirmed to match to documented ancestry to Col. Richard Lee and his wife Anne Constable.

Over 85% of Lee descendants are being denounced, and compared to DNA Haplogroups that may be questionable, or corrupted from a NPE within the DNA being used to compare the other descending lines.

AN IMPORTANT NOTE ABOUT LEE DNA PROJECTS AND GENEALOGY SITES AND LINEAGE HAPLOGROUP COMPARISONS:

The Lee Y-DNA Haplogroup claims for the Lees of Virginia lines from these Lee Y-DNA Projects Are NOT THE ABSOLUTE TRUTH!!!!!

What has been claimed by these Lee Y-DNA projects is 100% unverifiable and PROVABLY WRONG!!

THE CLAIMS THAT Col. Richard Lee, The Immigrant, progenitor of the Lees of Virginia lines are Y-DNA Haplogroup is M-253, or M-269, or ANY Y-DNA Haplogroup assigned to him or the LEE male ancestor lines - it is all speculative without his or the progenerating male Y-DNA available and publicly verifiable , regardless of what may be promoted - AND Y-DNA CAN NEVER TELL IF THERE HAS BEEN AN NON-PARENTAL EVENT (NPE) EVER IN AN ALL MALE LINE DESCENT REGARDLESS OF HOW WELL DOCUMENTED OR SOCIALLY ACCEPTED. That IS a scientific FACT.

UNLESS you have the patriarchal ancestor whose Y-DNA progenerates the male descending lines there is no way a Y-DNA Haplogroup can ever be assigned to that patriarch ancestor or his descendants because Y-DNA can never show a non-parental event regardless of how well the lines up to the male patriarch are documented. Regardless how the Y-DNA is analyzed, speculated on, referred to, etc., if any lab, administrator, DNA expert, or Y-DNA project does go outside the scientific facts they would be doing so without regard to the truth and based solely on guesswork, opinion, politics, agenda, and possibly unlawfully.

To explain why these Autosomal DNA results ARE DNA confirmations of the Lee relationship of these Lee/Ruffin descendants to Gen Robert E Lee and the Lees of Virginia ancestors is this article which mirrors my Y-DNA argument and why Autosomal is more accurate in identifying our common ancestral relationships.

Often it is pointed out in criticism that Autosomal DNA can only give accurate genetic matching from ancestor generations 8 gens or less - there is an ongoing assumption that when scrutinizing the results of these DNA test comparisons and confirmations that there is a limitation of a specific age group that does not reflect the participants DNA involved.

An important consideration is being overlooked such as the QUANTITY and VARIETY in the collected Lee descendant donor DNA involved in these confirmations.

These Lee descendant DNA donors collected are of a wide range of age groups. They include not just a current generational age group, but Lee descendant donor DNA from great grandparents, grandparents, parents, children, great grandchildren and in some cases gr-great grandparents and great-great grandchildren - and both female and male participants. By doing this it can give us a wider range of match accuracy. Everyone can benefit and verify the genetic connections and ancestor matches themselves, online, publicly, anytime.

Keep in mind as well that not all surnames will have the same issues with Y-DNA test results as our Lee ancestral lines The Lee lineages are complicated and a mess, especially since there have been Y-DNA Haplogroup assignments to Lee ancestors that are incorrect or are opinion based as the descrepencies between the two testing styles can be observed by comparing the resulting matches from tools available such as on GEDmatch to what the Lee Y-DNA projects have presented.

Not all of the Lee DNA descendant donors are of Lee ancestry that have been ruled out as not being related to the 'Famous' Lee's. The comparison match results also include male descendants of 'approved' Lee ancestral lines. That is where Lee descendants can see the genetic relationships to each other, regardless of being told that they are not related. Especially when compared with DNA of Lee/Carter descendant DNA of both male and female donors.

Imagine this for a moment: A group of 100 Lee male descendants that have documented lines from Col Richard Lee get Y-DNA tested.

Within this group are 4 males that have Y-DNA that share the same Y-DNA Haplogroup, the other 96 do not yet are denounce as Lee descendants of Col Richard Lee because they do not have similar Y-DNA to these other 4 male Lee descendants that have documented lineages descending from Gen R E Lee, Ditchley or Stratford, and are accepted by the Society of Lees as Lees of Virginia descendants, the other remaining Lee descendants are not.

The associated lines for those 96 other males are told they are not Lees of Virginia related because of these Y-DNA results. That is exactly what did occur and is still being promoted by many unscrupulously.

If there is a non-Parental event within the 4 male Lee descendants that have been accepted and deemed valid Lees of Virginia members, the NPE would not be detected or in any way be acknowledged, even though this NPE occurrence would nullify the authenticity of the accepted Lees of Virginia lineage of these 4 males.

THAT is an example in easy-to-understand terms of what has happened in these Lee Y-DNA projects as over 90% of the Lee descendant males have been denied their heritage - and the female descendants of these lines from Col Richard lee - because they do not share the similarities in their Y-DNA with the "R E Lee" crew as these 4 males have been nicknamed.

Y-DNA projects should not be limited as they have been. We learning as DNA testing improves and evolves, through this we are continuing to understand the limits of Y-DNA and the errors in the interpretations of the results.

This is a good read written by a DNA EXPERT Cheryl Lynn 'Herstory' who is stating on her Blog this same view about using Autosomal DNA because of the Y-DNA limitations and discrepancies:

https://cherielynnsherstory.com/2018/10/19/allow-autosomaldna-testers-into-y-dna-surname-groups-prove-expanded-lines-identify-non-paternity-events-why-oh-why-would-i-research-linear-duh/

"Allow Autosomal DNA Testers Into y-DNA (Surname) Projects? Prove Expanded Lines ~ Identify Non-Paternity Events ~ Why Oh Why Would I Research Linear? – Yes! | Cherie Lynn's Herstory (cherielynnsherstory.com)

OCTOBER 19, 2018/CHERIELYNNSHERSTORY

Two dozen, more or less, males all claim one patriarch. There are clearly two groups of men with two different haplogroups and so unrelated. But, what? Just sit on your hands and squabble about which is the rightful line to any patriarch? Or, fight and break up the DNA project and create a 2nd one and both claim the same ancestor and both proved with DNA? Both publish competing websites and both claim victory in genetic genealogy?

Folks who tested only for autosomal DNA, on the other hand, cannot as easily and assuredly learn their distant ancestors because autosomal reaches back only so far. To really take the lines back you need it all – the male line y-DNA signature, collect and compare as many mt-DNA haplogroups as you can, and with the au-DNA testing (aka at-DNA, whichever you like to use) when you test extended members of your family groups for autosomal, you can sometimes learn which family has the correct DNA connection to the patriarch through the additional ancestry.

One has to have male descendants of two brothers to prove any father. Whether they all were born in 1900 or 1600. (Good luck with 1600) And if you have any dispute with different results of two testers then you need to add more men to test to prove each of those family lines. There must be a match with two sons' descendant lines. We just cannot have one man to test and claim his results represent any patriarch father.

These wonderful charts are made on Ancestry.com an essential website in records, in many ways, for research – check to see if they have records for your areas of research. Make any tree private if you have a research and working theories with speculative ancestors your guesses might create false positives for matching in DNA trees.

Certainly, au-DNA aka at-DNA will not reach very far back in time, but this does not mean you should throw away and not use identifying relationships from 3, 4 maybe 7... generations ago. When two groups of men claiming the same patriarch have different y-DNA haplogroups, either one group is mistaken or there has been a non-paternity event. That's where the au-DNA can help. If you test enough of the family members, you begin to learn more about how they are related to each other and any anomalies give you clues to what's happening. Eventually you can build a genetic picture of a family and know where a line broke.

Another reason to let the au-DNA aka at-DNA person in the project is, it might be a girl, and she personally only has au-DNA (and possibly mt-DNA) and she might be the one willing to spend the money to pay for the y-DNA tests for the boys because she is the one who is keen on learning mamma's daddy's y-DNA Haplogroup (R1a), besides her own daddy's (I2a), and she wants her husband's (G2a), or husbands' (R1b), as the case might be, and her husband's mother's daddy's (R1b WAMH) and after she has those she might want daddy's mamma's daddy's (E1b) y-DNA Haplogroup. I would not be a snob about membership – I would verify what someone wants in joining, and hopefully people can use the great activity pages to post questions and ask for research ideas.

Sure, I get it, some of the projects are just too big to be part of fine tuned genealogy – but isn't this what the DNA for genealogy is all about, and the activity page is a place for project questions? And of course Facebook groups are taking people away from project participation and even introducing testers to new and other companies, websites and methods.

But over all I believe there is a large increase in y-DNA testing and now the new and also wonderful MyHeritage (see link below) is teaming with Family

Tree DNA and MyHeritage customers were offered a special price to add their haplogroups – which is fantastic!

MyHeritage, I read, I can't swear, has and will be having more and more testers from Europe and beyond. I hear also in the genetic genealogy groups and blogs that the great LivingDNA (see link below) will be expanding in Germany . Now since my mt-DNA H10a1 was from Saalfeld, Thurengia, Germany then I am beside myself to think there is a chance a relative might turn up.

The great discoveries of who a father might have been in a non-paternity event (or to use the new label, misattributed parentage) can often be seen in who the 'other' surnames are in a family group thatmatches genetically.

So a bunch of men — group A — all match each other and a bunch of men — group B — all match each other. Group A men and group B men are different, but all these men have thought they descend from the same patriarch.

Besides the autosomal DNA possibly answering some questions — if a male matches another group of men genetically but they have a different surname — then all may have the answer to why these Mr Smiths are not the Mr Smith's family they thought they were.

This is invaluable information for all families. Particularly if this is a misattributed parentage then family trees can be built in DNA and not just some guessing because someone married a so/n/so and they must be the same family.

I have an R1b family and the man needed his father's identity. He matches 37 for 37 and you can place the families nearby for a couple of places, so it looked like the guy. But an autosomal test turned up someone else as the father with a different surname. So now we have several members of the surname group who find out that they are descended from someone with a different surname. Are we going to throw them out of the group?

So, let just anybody in a project? Well, no, not just anybody. And since au-DNA is not yet seen anywhere in a project except for admin eyes only, I do not see the reasoning for not allowing other relatives.

With all the results for Senator Warren recently, you will also find in the contents, blogs and links about her and her stories, and the resulting DNA stories, including this one for one of my own Native ancestries. "Of Colors" "...There are a couple of stamps on envelopes – one she way overdid the postage so I bet all those are her. ..."

https://cherielynnsherstory.com/2018/10/16/of-colors-what-is-left-of-mamma-to-test/

Proving the ancestors with DNA and enjoying each family's all the families' haplogroups. This is my chart and will print like a regular copy paper page. I also have a size printed that fits fully into a 3-ring binder and with the larger page they do not slide and a touch more roomy for writing the names. – I still love hand written charts for all.

I tested autosomal DNA quite late – it was 2011. I wanted the kinks out first and in some respects I did not wait long enough. But it was a y-DNA project administrator that first got me to test the autosomal DNA of these men who matched but there were a couple of misses (35 out of 37) and I wanted to make triple sure. We knew the paper documentation should be proof enough for this man with the miss but the au-DNA (at-DNA) proved conclusively this man was related also with autosomal DNA.

The same autosomal was used and another two men did not match. They matched exactly 37 out of 37 and we could have kept adding more STR markers but decided to first add autosomal – they did not match. So although they will have had a common paternal line ancestor some where back in time it was not two families that genealogy would likely help.

Note a comment and answer: I should have noted it was a y-DNA project administrator that got me to test two men for their autosomal. They were both R1b and matched exactly 37 for 37. The finances were tight for both and the next sale we tested the two of them for autosomal and they did not match. We had our answer. Later on both men added more STRs then we saw 64 of 67 – so the added STRs would not have given us the answer – when the autosomal did. > > > > > And with our two families both competing for the same patriarch?

They may not be two families they may be a non-paternity event – we are still working to add more autosomal – but several of the men from the two groups are related via autosomal and not in any other explainable way and y-DNA can never prove this – ever. And one of their project administrators had told one family their research was wrong and they were just wannabes – but he was incorrect and I bet he is incorrect about which family actually represents that patriarch."

As Cherie honestly states in her conclusion in her article above:

"Note a comment and answer: I should have noted it was a y-DNA project administrator that got me to test two men for their autosomal. They were both R1b and matched exactly 37 for 37. The finances were tight for both and the next sale we tested the two of them for autosomal and they did not match. We had our answer. Later on both men added more STRs then we saw 64 of 67 – so the added STRs would not have given us the answer – when the autosomal did. >>>>> And with our two families both competing for the same patriarch? They may not be two families they may be a non-paternity event – we are still working to add more autosomal – but several of the men from the two groups are related via autosomal and not in any other explainable way and y-DNA can never prove this – ever. And one of their project administrators had told one family their research was wrong and they were just wannabes – but he was incorrect and I bet he is incorrect about which family actually represents that patriarch.

So - Simply by using common sense and logical approaches and not the 'forced' Y-DNA propaganda - we can see the whole DNA picture of the Lee ancestor/descendant relationship through Autosomal matching when the At DNA aspect is combined and given merit.

How To Solve The Biggest Problems In Your Genealogy Research – Ancestral Findings"

Allow Autosomal DNA Testers Into y-DNA (Surname) Projects? Prove Expanded Lines ~ Identify Non-Paternity Events ~ Why Oh Why Would I Research Linear? – Yes!

Two dozen, more or less, males all claim one patriarch. There are clearly two groups of men with two different haplogroups and so unrelated. But, what? Just sit on your hands and squabble about which is the rightful line to any patriarch? Or, fight and break up the DNA project and create a 2nd one and both claim the same ancestor and both prove with DNA? Both publish competing websites and both claim victory in genetic genealogy?

Folks who tested only for autosomal DNA, on the other hand, cannot as easily and assuredly learn their distant ancestors because autosomal reaches back only so far. To really take the lines back you need it all – the male line y-DNA signature, collect and compare as many mt-DNA haplogroups as you can, and with the au-DNA testing (also as-DNA, whichever you like to use) when you test extended members of your family group for autosomal, you can sometimes learn which family has the correct DNA connection to the patriarch through the additional ancestry.

One has to have male descendants of two brothers to prove any father. Whether they all were born in 1900 or 1600. Good luck with 1600! And if you have any dispute with different results of two testers then you need to add more men to test to prove each of those family lines. There must be a match with two sons' descendant lines. We just cannot have one man to test and claim his results represent any patriarch father.

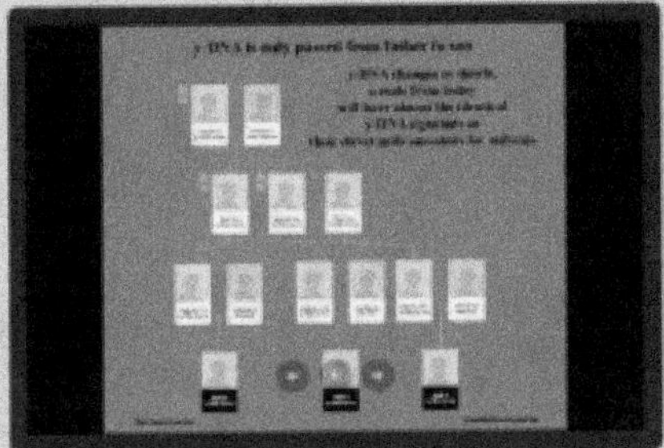

These wonderful charts are made on Ancestry.com an essential website in records, in many ways, for research – check to see if they have records for your areas of research. Make any tree private if you have a research and working theories with speculative ancestors your guesses might create false positives for matching in DNA trees.

Certainly, au-DNA also as-DNA will not reach very far back in time, but this does not mean you should throw away and not use identifying relationships from 3, 4 maybe 7 generations ago. When two groups of men claiming the same patriarch have different y-DNA haplogroups, either one group is mistaken or there has been a non-paternity event. That is where the au-DNA can help. If you test enough of the family members, you begin to learn more about how they are related to each other and any au-matches give you clues to what's happening. Eventually you can build a genetic picture of a family and know where a line broke.

Another reason to let the au-DNA also as-DNA person in the project is it might be a girl, and she personally only has au-DNA (and possibly mt-DNA) and she might be the one willing to spend the money to pay for the y-DNA tests for the boys because she is the one who is keen on learning mamma's daddy's y-DNA Haplogroup (R1a). Besides her own daddy's (I2a), and she wants her husband's (G2a), or husband's (R1b), as the case might be, and her husband's mother's daddy's (R1b VVNNN) and after she has those she might want daddy's mamma's daddy's (E1b) y-DNA Haplogroup. I would not be a snob about membership – I would verify what someone wants in joining, and hopefully people can use the great activity pages to post questions and ask for research ideas.

Sure, I get it, some of the projects are just too big to be part of fine tuned genealogy – but isn't this what the DNA for genealogy is all about, and the activity page is a place for project questions? And of course Facebook groups are taking people away from project participation and even introducing testers to new and other companies, websites and methods.

I tested autosomal DNA quite late – it was 2011. I wanted the kinks out first and in some respects I did not wait long enough. But it was a y-DNA project administrator that first got me to test the autosomal DNA of these men who matched but there were a couple of misses (35 out of 37) and I wanted to make triple sure. We knew the paper documentation should be proof enough for this man with the miss but the au-DNA (at-DNA) proved conclusively this man was related also with autosomal DNA.

The same autosomal was used and another two men did not match. They matched exactly 37 out of 37 and we could have kept adding more STR markers but decided to first add autosomal – they did not match. So although they will have had a common paternal line ancestor some where back in time it was not two families that genealogy would likely help.

Note a comment and answer: I should have noted it was a y-DNA project administrator that got me to test two men for their autosomal. They were both R1b and matched exactly 37 for 37. The finances were tight for both and the next sale we tested the two of them for autosomal and they did not match. We had our answer. Later on both men added more STRs then we saw 64 of 67 – so the added STRs would not have given us the answer – when the autosomal did. >>>>> And with our two families both competing for the same patriarch? They may not be two families they may be a non-paternity event – we are still working to add more autosomal – but several of the men from the two groups are related via autosomal and not in any other explainable way and y-DNA can never prove this – ever. And one of their project administrators had told one family their research was wrong and they were just wannabes – but he was incorrect and I bet he is incorrect about which family actually represents that patriarch.

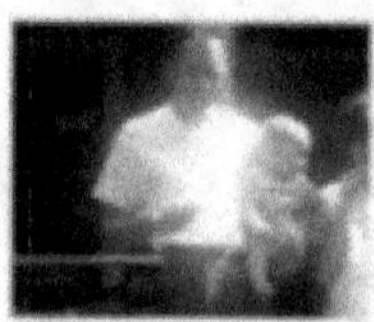

Surname Projects Missed The Point Of "Not" Matching ~ "1 in 10 is mistaken about father's identity"

This story has gone around the Facebook DNA groups like wildfire: 'One in 10 is mistaken about identity of father,' by Sarah Knapton from

https://www.theage.com.au/world/europe/one-in-10-is-mistaken-about-identity-of-father-20190601-p51tgf.html?

fbclid=IwAR1nGpQk8GNknr7du6sYrS2_hqj38n3_cz69y_Q8pRhUbP895fCoiSmaXCo It was 2004 when cousin Buddy first directed me to the trough of y-DNA-for-genealogy magic to read the results for the Lewis Surname y-DNA project. He and I both remarked ... Continue reading

 Cherie Lynn's Herstory

Share this:

5 thoughts on "Allow Autosomal DNA Testers Into Y-DNA (Surname) Projects? Prove Expanded Lines – Identify Non-Paternity Events – Why Oh Why Would I Research Linear? – Yes!"

jacquelfinley

MAY 6, 2019 AT 12:41 PM

Exactly what I have been trying to say for years, especially with the Lee Y-DNA projects and how wrong project administrators have been in assigning a Haplogroup for Lee descendants from brothers Y-DNA from Robert E. Lee as the Haplogroup 'STANDARD' for all male Lee descendants of Virginia Lees – as Y-DNA CANNOT identify an NPE (Non-Parental Event) in an all-male line ever even in WELL DOCUMENTED PEDIGREES ... but Autosomal DNA can! So many real Lee's of Virginia descendants that have been told they are Lee 'imposters' are now finding out they really are through Autosomal DNA matching even though they were told they were not related to the famous Lees of Virginia.

Thank you, Cherie, very much! Maybe someday someone will be listening to our commonsense logic and give more credence to the capabilities of Autosomal DNA and the limitations of Y-DNA, and not be thinking about profits only ... we can only hope as Autosomal DNA has evolved into a very useful genealogical tool in relationship confirmations were Y-DNA has not or has been used to dissect lineages.

Jacquel Finley
https://jacquelfinley.com/

Liked by 1 people

REPLY

jacquelfinley

MAY 7, 2019 AT 12:51 PM

Reblogged this on Lees of Virginia and commented:
Exactly what I have been trying to say for years, especially with the Lee Y-DNA projects and how wrong project administrators have been in assigning a Haplogroup for Lee descendants from brothers Y-DNA from Robert E. Lee as the Haplogroup 'STANDARD' for all male Lee descendants of Virginia Lees – as Y-DNA CANNOT identify an NPE (Non-Parental Event) in an all-male line ever even in WELL DOCUMENTED PEDIGREES ... but Autosomal DNA can! So many real Lee's of Virginia descendants that have been told they are Lee 'imposters' are now finding out they really are through Autosomal DNA matching even though they were told they were not related to the famous Lees of Virginia.

Thank you, Cherie, very much! Maybe someday someone will be listening to our commonsense logic and give more credence to the capabilities of Autosomal DNA and the limitations of Y-DNA, and not be thinking about profits only ... we can only hope as Autosomal DNA has evolved into a very useful genealogical tool in relationship confirmations were Y-DNA has not or has been used to dissect lineages.

Jacquel Finley
https://jacquelfinley.com/

Liked by 1 people

REPLY

cherielynnaherstory

MAY 10, 2019 AT 7:52 AM

Without multiple layers of research on the many Lees, there is no clue who could confirm which family group is the y-DNA line and which of the at-DNA matches to matching lineages and which are just a different family. But this is doable, Jacquel – great work to press this forward. We need this in all projects. We certainly need more historical DNA sequencing.

I have to pass the mantle for a while. I am a bit puny. But keep me posted!

Autosomal DNA is more accurate, especially in this under 8 generational timeframe which is applicable from Col Richard Lee descending downward - even more so for a lower generation such as Gen Robert E Lee.The sad fact is that in the Lee Y-DNA projects Haplogroups assigned to Lee descendants by these Y-DNA Project administrators and 'experts' are inconclusive and should have never been set as a precedent for discerning whether a Lee descendant is a Lee of Virginia Lee or not basically from a few 'well documented' but publicly non verifiable Lee descendants that are promoted by the Society and genealogy websites as the true Y-DNA male Haplogroup guideline to accept or deny Lee ancestor and lineages - when any or all of these Lee Y-DNA donors with or without well documented or accepted Lee descendant pedigrees can (and do per At DNA results) have Non-Parental Events making it unclear, unfair and dishonest that this has been even done in the first place as these claims that started the whole mess that created this false Haplogroup assignment to the LOV family:

I t is a scientific fact that Y-DNA CANNOT identify a non-parental event (NPE) in an all-male line - even well documented pedigrees."

IT IS A SCIENTIFIC fact that Autosomal (At) can identify if there is a NPE in a lineage because, especially under 8 generations which MOST of the Lee descendants Lee ancestors fall into this category. Yet they still wave around these Y-DNA results claiming this as the standard for acceptable Lee of Virginia lines.

SO, WHEN LOOKING AT such results on Lee Y-DNA projects as:

http://leedna.com/dnaresults.php?id=104

https://henryleesociety.com/leeancestry/familygroups.php

https://henryleesociety.com/leeancestry/index.php

You are looking at un-verifiable Y-DNA results based on assumptions and opinion as there could be and most likely are non-parental events especially since no ascending patriarch ancestor's Y-DNA ever obtained.

Autosomal results from most Lee descendants show different results than what has been promoted by these Y-DNA sites - these Y-DNA relationship comparison results are all SPECULATION and not FACT.

As 'Modern Day' DNA testing HAS evolved, and improvements now have proven that many of us Lee "WANNABES" as we have been labeled are now factually and publicly verifiable DNA confirmed Lee of Virginia descendants as we have claimed all along even though it has been promoted falsely by these same Lee Y-DNA project administrators and users on genealogy websites publicly the opposite through insulting methods so that many of us Lee descendants and ancestors would not be accepted.

Maybe someday they will stop the nonsense and correct their errors and assumptive genealogy assertions as it has only caused damage and harm to many people. Only time will tell who has the courage to be honest and do the right thing or keep being dishonest in doing the wrong because of 'peer' pressure ...Jacqueli

In response to my commenting of what DNA Expert Cherrie had stated on her blog I did hear back from her, and her response was a positive affirmation on my Autosomal research and arguments against why Lee Y-DNA were wrongful in their assertions of acceptance, and DENIALS, of Lee descendants and their ancestors based on the Y-DNA from one group of brothers that descended from Robert E Lee that the Lee Society approved - by the documented pedigree as the standard for matches and comparisons of acceptable male Lee descendants of the LOV lineages - whose Y-DNA and Haplogroup does match over 90% of the Male Lee Descendants from ancestors of adjacent Lees of Virginia lines, resulting in the majority of Lee descendants being told that they were not related to Col Richard Lee by their Lee ancestor, WRONGFULLY, as the Autosomal DNA does confirm most of these relationships:

New comment on Cherie Lynn's Herstory

jacquelifinley MAY 8, 2022 AT 12:40 PM

"Exactly what I have been trying to say for years, especially with the Lee Y-DNA projects and how wrong project administrators have been in assigning a Haplogroup for Lee descendants from brothers Y-DNA from Robert E. Lee as the Haplogroup 'STANDARD' for all male Lee descendants of Virginia Lees – as Y-DNA CANNOT identify an NPE (Non-Parental Event) in an all-male line, ever, even in WELL DOCUMENTED PEDIGREES ... but Autosomal DNA can!

So many real Lee's of Virginia descendants that have been told they are Lee 'wannabes' are now finding out they really are through Autosomal DNA matching even though they were told they were not related to the famous Lees of Virginia.

Thank you, Cherie, very much! Maybe someday someone will be listening to our commonsense logic and give more credence to the capabilities of Autosomal DNA and the limitations of Y-DNA, and not be thinking about profits only ... we can only hope as Autosomal DNA has evolved into a very useful genealogical tool in relationship confirmations were Y-DNA has not or has been used to dissect lineages."

Jacqueli Finley

https://jacquelifinley.com/

Liked by 2 peopleREPLY

cherielynnsherstory MAY 10, 2022 AT 7:32 AM

commented on Allow Autosomal DNA Testers Into y-DNA (Surname) Projects? Prove Expanded Lines ~ Identify Non-Paternity Events ~ Why Oh Why Would I Research Linear? - Yes!

In response to jacquelifinley:

"Without multiple layers of research on the many Lees, there is no one who could confirm which family group is the y-DNA line and which of the at-DNA multiple matching families and which are just a different family. But this is doable. Jacqueli – great work to press this forward. We need this in all projects. We certainly need more historical DNA sequencing.

I have to pass the mantle for a while. I am a bit puny. But keep me posted!"

The DNA conundrum ...

The William Lee lineage is just one aspect of the disconnect and false claims because of wrongful assertions from Lee Y-DNA Projects that many genealogists and genealogy website promote unfairly. There are many Lee descendants from the children of our Lee ancestors who came from mixed race. Some Lee children from mixed marriages were soon forgotten as those Lee families were cut off from their lines, and some from the mistreatment of the slaves that they wrongfully held against their will by our lee ancestors, as the lines from these children of Gen Robert E Lee and his slave Nancy Ruffin, just to mention another one.

———

Here are some examples of promoted claims by the Lee Y-DNA project administrators that have been use to disassociate Lee descendant lines and slandered anyone who disagreed with what they were promoting, while they profited off of this mis-information and harm they cause to many who were just researching their family history:

RE: COL. RICHARD LEE, THE IMMIGRANT

By **Dennis Lee** April 17, 2014 at 02:22:25
In reply to: **Re: Col. Richard Lee, The Immigrant**
Bill Davidson 4/01/14

The Society of the Lees of Virginia is the historical organization devoted to this particular family. They use the book LEE OF VIRGINIA by Edmund Jennings Lee as their reference, so any website that quotes this book faithfully should work. There have been some corrections to LEE OF VIRGINIA over the years, and these should be taken into account.

Please note that a lot of people have taken LEE OF VIRGINIA and tacked on their own beliefs and posted this on various websites and published it in books and such. That does not make the beliefs to be true, and in most cases, these add-ons have been disproved by modern DNA evidence.

You should look at the SOLVA website at
http://www.thesocietyoftheleesofva.org/http://www.thesocietyoftheleesofva.org/ and avoid wannabes like
http://www.leesofvirginia.org/http://www.leesofvirginia.org/ .

Dennis Lee
Wimberley, TX

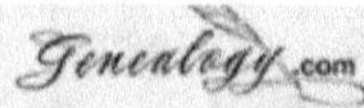

FORUM

RE: PROOF OF LINEAGE TO GEN. ROBERT E. LEE?

By **Dennis Lee** February 08, 2010 at 05:51:38
In reply to: **Proof of Lineage to Gen. Robert E. Lee?**
Nella Lee Raymer 2/07/10

Nella:

There are three known descendants of the Lees of Virginia line (Robert E. Lee's crew) that have been DNA tested.Their results are remarkably similar, as they should be.Yes, theirhaplotype is I1a, so if your participant is an R1a or R1b (as am I), any male-line-of-descent connection with the Lees of Virginia is far, far back in the mists of time.

Even other I1a haplotypes can be so distantly related as to be insignificant.For example, many Lees in the Southern USA are related to a fellow known as John Lee of Nansemond.These people have I1a haplotypes, but there is enough of a variation with the Lee of Virginia DNA profile as to put any connection between the lines back into the time period where surnames were not used.And just what would that mean?

One thing to remember is that this sort of testing only tracks the male line of descent.Your line MIGHT be related to The General via a female linkage someplace, e.g. his daughter or aunt or some maternal uncle or whatever.YDNA will tell you nothing about that sort of thing.

I advised you privately to have your male representative DNA tested.You can use Ancestry.com or FTDNA or one of several other reputable labs.Some folks, including myself, periodically take the participants of one lab's tests and compare it against that of other labs.Occasionally we find matches that don't show up in the individual labs' Family Studies.That said, I recommend strongly two things: Join one of the Studies (you'll get a discount and some help comparing your results, as well as some help connecting with fellow researchers), and purchase at least a 35-marker test (FDNA has a 37, Ancestry has a 46).Anything less is a waste of money.

When the results come back - from whatever lab - email me and I can tell you if you match with the Lees of VA.

Re some of the results that people have talked about for lineages leading back to Robert E. Lee: They're mostly garbage.Wishful thinking.Wild assumptions.Almost every Lee line out there has had a legend in the family that they were related to The General.Books have been written, websites have been created, DAR submissions made, etc. and all of that has reinforced some very bad research.Don't believe that you have a connection until you prove it yourself with original research.DNA testing is one of those tools to help you.

Good luck,
Dennis Lee
Wimberley, TX

RE: LEE DNA PROJECT--- PLEASE READ

By **Dennis Lee** July 14, 2005 at 12:18:48
In reply to: **Re: LEE DNA PROJECT--- PLEASE READ**
Donna Follin 7/13/05

Hi Donna:

I'm assuming your question was a general one and not specifically directed at Ms. Thomas.If I'm incorrect, please accept my apologies (both of you).

At present, the Lee Study at Relative Genetics has two confirmed participants that are members of the famous Lees of VA.I.e., they are confirmed kin to Robert E. Lee, the Confederate General.Comparing a Lee-surnamed male descendant's DNA against those individuals will tell one if that person is or is not kin to the Lees of VA - by the paternal line only.It is possible to be kin to Robert E. Lee via a maternal connection, yet not show up as so in the paternally-specific Y-chromosome tests offered by the various testing labs.

But, if you're a Lee from the South (like me, for instance) your family probably has legends about being kin to Robert E.Sounds like yours does.Mine did, but we proved them false both by standard genealogical research and by the fact that my DNA and the Lee of VA DNA samples are dramatically different.Ergo, in my case, the legend was flat-out wrong.Your results may be different.

The way to test this is for a Lee-surnamed male descendant of your line to submit their DNA for testing.It has to be a male; they have to have the Lee surname as Y-Chromosome DNA follows only father to son, just like the surname in our society.The results will tell you one of 3 things: 1) You're somehow kin, via your Lee family, to the Lees of VA and by extension Robert E. Lee.2) You are not kin to the Lees of VA in any statistically valid measure VIA THE LEE FAMILY LINE, but you are kin to one of the other Lee lines for which participants have been tested.3) You are not kin to any of the tested participants (there's about 60 to date in several different studies).

Option 1 is what you're hoping for, and expect to find.Option 2 may be a little disappointing, as you'll have to put away the old family legend, but at least you'll know that you're part of one of the known Lee lines, e.g. the John Lee Esquire line, the Hugh Lee line, the James Leigh of Bath line, the James and Mary Lee of MD line, the John Lee of Nansemond Line, or one of the other fragmentary lines.Option 3 is the Purgatory where I live.You're not kin to anyone else.You're a Space Alien, an Adoptee, an Illegitimate Child, or just someone waiting for enough people to join up in a DNA study so that you can connect to SOMEONE out there.

Please encourage your family to have a representative join one of the studies.The more we have from different lines, the more we can tie these various family fragments together.Contact Clint Lee at mclintlee@aol.com, and he'll give you the details.The process is simple: Email Clint; he gets RG to send your guy a test kit.Then, your guy fills out the form and a check, swabs his cheeks a couple times with an overgrown Q-Tip, stuffs the whole mess in an envelope, and mails it off.A few weeks later, the DNA info is posted and you can compare to everyone out there.

If I may help in any way, please do not hesitate to ask.I'm sure Ms. Thomas feels the same.But do please go through Clint to get the sample kit and get enrolled in the Lee Study.

Re: LEE DNA PROJECT--- PLEASE READ

By **Dennis Lee** July 20, 2005 at 09:01:59

In reply to: **Re: LEE DNA PROJECT--- PLEASE READ**

DEBBIE HANSON 7/19/05

Debbie:

One thing the whole issue MIGHT mean relates to the great Arthur Fernay Lee controversy.

We know:

1) The DNA of a Needham, Sr. descendant is incompatible with that of two Lee of VA descendants. Ergo, Needham, Sr. is not part of the Lees of VA.

2) The DNA of a Needham, Sr. descendant IS compatible with John Lee of Nansemond (and several MS Lee lines).

3) The DNA of a John Lee of Nansemond descendant is incompatible with the that of two Lee of VA descendants.

Ergo, if Needham, Sr. descends from the "Arthur Fernay" line, as stated by some, then "Arthur Fernay" and his antecedants and descendants CANNOT be directly related to the Lees of VA.

This effective disproves a contention many have held regarding the "Arthur Fernay Lee" line, and leaves two possible conclusions:

a) Needham, Sr. is not a descendant of "Arthur Fernay Lee".

or

b) "Arthur Fernay Lee" is part of the John Lee of Nansemond line, somewhere, somehow.

* Note: I quoted "Arthur Fernay Lee" because there is considerable discussion about whether such an individual actually existed. Someone obviously did, but he may have been named Arthur, Fernay, or both.

It'll be interesting to see how this all works out.

Part 4: The DNA Proof

IN THIS SECTION I AM presenting the Lee Descendants and associated lines DNA donor reports that confirm the William Lee descendant lines, as well as others, via GEDMatch.

Lee Descendant DNA Match Reports GEDMatch DNA Donor and Kit#

Stratford Lee/Ruffin Lines

James Harpe

DN3063060

Darick Hendrix

A520925

Katie Hendrix

M915799

Cobbs, Stratford, Ditchley, and William Lee Lines

Jacqueli Finley

NP070205C1

Lee Descendants of Lees of Virginia Lines Cobbs, Ditchley, and Stratford -

Society of Lee 'Accepted' Lee Lines Per Wikitree/GEDMatch

BY3843687

TB53738

A874114

T108846

TV9165492

M623536

LC9048688

AF7769802

A119796

A115245

T513362

ZD6573505

YU8300938

M963089

T560494

KF7937712

M925841

A516513

A069864

XM7101560

YC3676208

M510764

T509807

SL8354388

A692640

A527997

T108846

A284646

M269802

M220064

A286995

A544145

YT5630887

F135466

A638877

NJ9849252

LS9471102

William Lee Line Descendants per Wikitree/GEDMatch

FK8954624

GN9504264

A955589

A101494

69249EE0

A519809

A955589

A360019

T667077

A385721

A411128

HC6220885

A917655

John Lee, Esquire Descendants Per Wikitree/GEDmatch

ZM1414319

T490396

A124004

SE3864740

A020866

WY4645753

A372074

A783637

LF5473377

RY4826857

A162988

WC8749747

RE6684792

Mary Lee Heath Schiever Descendant Lines Per Wikitree/GEDMatch

PY9984568

A737803

HL3322133

A022886

FR7180885

Constable-Savage Descendant Lines Per Wikitree/GEDMatch – Sister of
Anne Constable that came to America and survived Plague

A835334

PE3075925

A745222

PQ8304100

A665196

GEDmatch®

Generations Matrix Comparison

GEDmatch®

Generations Matrix Comparison

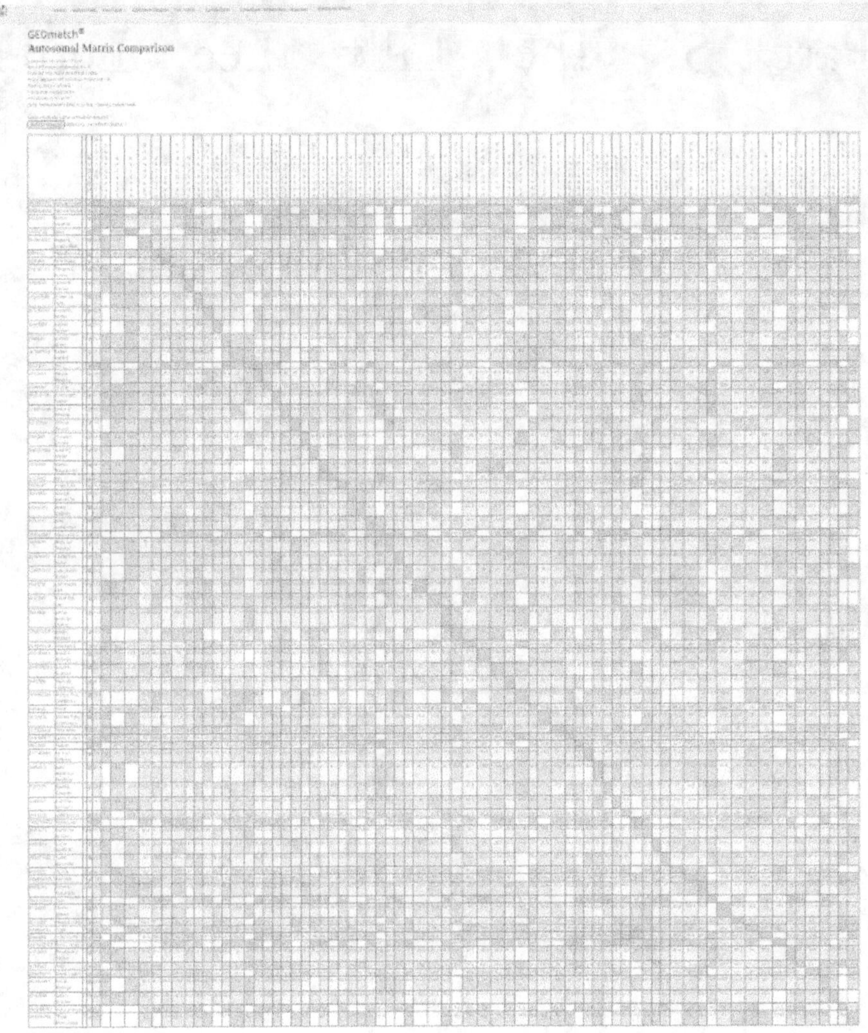

ONE WOULD BE HARD PRESSED to argue that these DNA match comparison results are anything other than 100% proof that what the Y-DNA projects claimed about these Lee lineages not being related to each other and all descendants of the Lees of Virginia lines were incorrect.

Obviously these DNA donors are Lee descendants and related.

Part 5: The Lilly Lee Letter

Here is a copy of a letter written by Narcissus Verlilia 'Lily' Lee, at age 66, explaining what was believed to be the family connection with Henry 'Light Horse Harry' Lee, and his son, Gen. Robert E Lee.

It is well known that some descendants of the 'Virginia Lees' went to Alabama at that time. I have found the connection, although not exactly as she thought.

The history of the
Lee family, to my
Harry Lee, and Jerry Lee,
were my fathers own
grandfathers. My father
were Robert Edward Lee's
own nephew,and he
is a son of Harry Lee.
My father were named
after two uncles of his
Robert, Washington Lee.
I am told that my
grandmother was a Lee,
and married his cousin
See that is why both our
grandfathers are named
Lee. This is a true history.
See I am a great grand
child of theirs and a

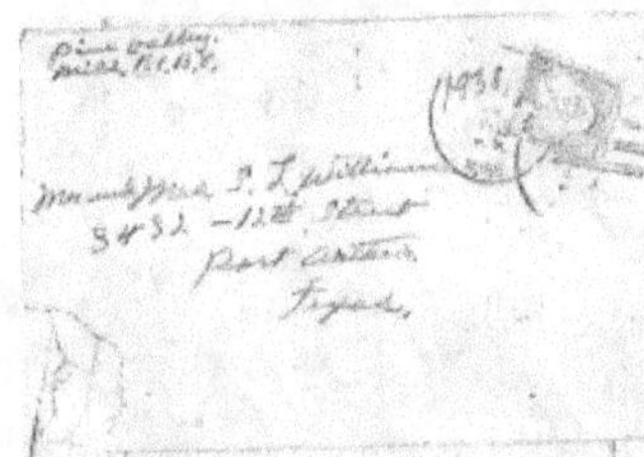

great neice of R. E. Lee.
My name is by birth
Narcissus Verlilia Lee,
but known now as
Mrs Lily Williams,
Patsy Jean Williams
grandmother.
Hope she can honor
the name.
He is her great great
great uncle.
I wish her all of the
honors can be bestowed
upon her for my
sake and Stanleys.
Respectfully,
Mrs Lillie Williams

Pine Valley, Miss
    to
Port Arthur, Tx
postmarked 1938
with a three cent stamp

Here is what research has shown:

Descendants of Richard Henry Lee I

1 Richard Henry Lee I   Abt. 1617 - 1664

..+Ann Constable   Abt. 1621 - Aft. 1664

2 Richard Lee   1647 - 1714

...+Laetitia Corbin   Abt. 1656 - 1706

3 Henry Lee   Abt. 1691 - 1747

....+Mary Bland

4 Henry Lee

......+Lucy Grymes

5 Henry "Light Horse Harry" Lee   1756 - 1818

.......+Matilda Lee

6 Robert Edward Lee, General   1807 - 1870

.........+Mary A R Custis

2 William C Lee   Abt. 1650 - 1696

...+Alice Felton   1648 -

3 Richard Lee   Abt. 1670 -

.....+Mary Young   - Aft. 1690

4 John Lee, Esquire   Abt. 1690 - 1766

......+Mary W Bryan   1704 - Bef. 1780

5 Edward Lee   1725 - 1775

.........+Mary Allen   Abt. 1730 - Abt. 1815

6 Jeremiah Lee   1771 - 1824

.........+Elizabeth Avera   Abt. 1771 - Aft. 1830

7 Henry 'Harry' Lee   1810 - 1835

...........+Elizabeth Jane Lee   1814 - 1877

Descendants of Hugh Lee I

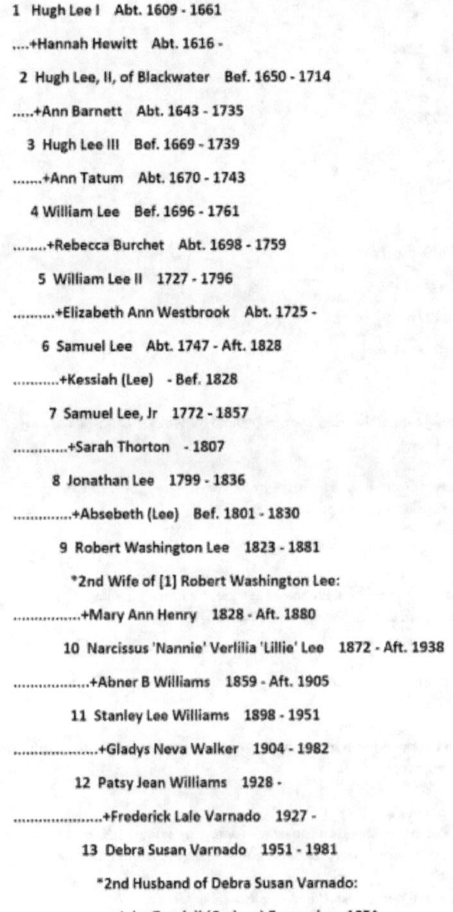

1 Hugh Lee I   Abt. 1609 - 1661

....+Hannah Hewitt   Abt. 1616 -

 2 Hugh Lee, II, of Blackwater   Bef. 1650 - 1714

.....+Ann Barnett   Abt. 1643 - 1735

  3 Hugh Lee III   Bef. 1669 - 1739

.......+Ann Tatum   Abt. 1670 - 1743

  4 William Lee   Bef. 1696 - 1761

........+Rebecca Burchet   Abt. 1698 - 1759

  5 William Lee II   1727 - 1796

..........+Elizabeth Ann Westbrook   Abt. 1725 -

  6 Samuel Lee   Abt. 1747 - Aft. 1828

...........+Kessiah (Lee)   - Bef. 1828

  7 Samuel Lee, Jr   1772 - 1857

............+Sarah Thorton   - 1807

  8 Jonathan Lee   1799 - 1836

.............+Absebeth (Lee)   Bef. 1801 - 1830

  9 Robert Washington Lee   1823 - 1881

    *2nd Wife of [1] Robert Washington Lee:

...............+Mary Ann Henry   1828 - Aft. 1880

  10 Narcissus 'Nannie' Verlilia 'Lillie' Lee   1872 - Aft. 1938

.................+Abner B Williams   1859 - Aft. 1905

  11 Stanley Lee Williams   1898 - 1951

...................+Gladys Neva Walker   1904 - 1982

  12 Patsy Jean Williams   1928 -

....................+Frederick Lale Varnado   1927 -

  13 Debra Susan Varnado   1951 - 1981

    *2nd Husband of Debra Susan Varnado:

......................+John Randall (Carlson) Farmacka   1951 -

                14 Sandra Gail Farmacka   1976 -

    ....+Marco Antonio Leal   1974 -

                15 Alana Nicole Leal   1998 -

                15 Alyssa Susan Leal   2001 -

        (7) *2nd Wife of Samuel Lee, Jr:

    ....+Mary Rhodes   Abt. 1789 - 1814

            8   Samuel Washington Lee   1811 - 1867

            8   Elizabeth Jane Lee   1814 - 1877

            *2nd Husband of [4] Elizabeth Jane Lee:

            +Henry 'Harry' Lee   1810 - 1835

Although there is probably some family connection way back in England between the families of John Lee and Hugh Lee, no proof has been found.

General Robert E Lee and Henry 'Harry' Lee are both decendants of Richard Henry Lee, I (the Imigrant, and son of John Lee).   They are 4th cousins, once removed.

Henry 'Harry' Lee married Elizabeth Jane Lee.

Elizabeth Jane Lee is a descendant of Hugh Lee, I (and his son of Blackwater River, Virginia).
Elizabeth Jane Lee is half-sister to Jonathan Lee, father of Robert Washington Lee.

The relation is:
    Jonathan Lee is the half-brother... of the wife... of the 4th cousin, once removed... of General Robert E Lee.

It is rare to find an actual connection between the two Lee lines, no matter how distant or remote. This one is done by half-siblings and marriage.

The letter of Lilly Lee is accurate up to a point.
From her letter, the 'Robert' part of Robert Washington Lee's name was from Robert Edward Lee that was the son of Henry 'Harry' Lee. But this Henry 'Harry' Lee was not the same person as the famous Henry 'Light Horse Harry' Lee, father of General Robert E Lee.
Also, Robert Washington was born before Henry 'Harry' had any known children.
Henry 'Harry' did have at least 3 brothers, but I have not verifed their names at this time. It's possible the name came from one of them.

The 'Washington' part of Robert Washington Lee's name possibly came from his uncle, Samuel Washington Lee, brother of Elizabeth Jane, and half-brother to Jonathan.
Or there may be another Washington that I have not found yet, such as the brothers of Henry 'Harry'.

The Jerry Lee is Jeremiah Lee, of Johnston county, North Carolina, and father of Henry 'Harry' Lee.
In one North Carolina census he is listed as Jerry Lee, and Jeremiah in others.

Elizabeth Jane Lee would be the grandmother that Lily was told married a cousin.

It should be noted that the mother of Elizabeth Jane Lee was Mary Rhodes, 2nd wife of Samuel Lee, Jr. Robert Washington Lee's first wife was Margaret Rhodes, and there is a strong probability she was a relation to Mary Rhodes, his step-grandmother. This could make for all kinds of other possible connections.
Starting in North Carolina and continuing through into Alabama, there were several families very closely associated that had many marriages among them. Just some of these were the Lee, Allen, Rhodes, Thigpen, and Williams.

With the way the names match, the locations, and the time period, it's easy to see how mistakes could be made. Lily was born in 1872, many years after most of these people had died, and was given handed down information.
Everyone in the South, then and now, looked to a 'family connection' with the famous 'Virginia Lees'.

I hope this makes sense, and you are able to follow the rationale.
It has taken a LOT of research to reach this point, and I believe these are the mostly likely conclusions, based on Lily's letter, and available facts.

The significance of the letter by Lilly Lee is that she was so compelled by the importance of the preservation of her own Lee family history that she had the mind to document what was known of her Lee family lines and ancestry, then posted this documentation using a legal timestamped envelope ensuring that this record would become available to all in the future as a valid source on record for these lees of Virginia lines and ancestors.

Part 4: William Lee Descendants

Below, I have created a 4-generation descendant report from William Lee and Alice Felton. This information includes research from James H L Lawler, my mentor, who dedicated most of his life researching his William Lee and Alice Felton line from their son William. The research listed also includes many other dedicated Lee researchers from over the past 40 years plus that have also made contributions. The documentation and sources also show the process of debunking "myths", bad genealogy information and the confirming of the descendants of William Lee and Alice Felton, and the MESS the LEE Y-DNA Projects have created with incorrect assignments of Haplogroups to Lee ancestors. I hope this is helpful to all of you.

Please note: On my research reports, such as these presented below, I include the individual 'arguments' and the 'ruling out' process used to eliminate fiction from facts.

I mention this as some people have tried to use the arguments eliminated shown as fact instead of resolved and eliminated, adding in

confusion. If it was a 'controversy', it was disproven or proven, thus why I show the process for better understand. At least that is my hope. Thank you, Jacqueli.

DESCENDANTS OF WILLIAM Lee

Generation 1

1.

WILLIAM LEE was born about 1650 in Charles City, Co, Virginia, Colony. He died about 1696 in

1696/1703 estate suit, King and Queen, Va. He married ALICE FELTON about 1675. She was

born about 1644 in of, Richmond, Co, Va. She died about 1703 in St Stephen Parsh, King and

Queen, Co, Va.

Notes for William Lee:

3. William Lee b. 1678 or 1682, Northampton, Northumberland Co, VA

m. Dorothy Taylor, ca 1703, Westmoreland Co, VA d/o Thomas Taylor & Elizabeth Harwood b.

1681, Surry,

King and Queen Co, VA

Information on Dorothy Taylor comes from "Log Cabins to White House" by Brewer. 13 Apr 1745

Dorothy was witness to will of Henry Williams in Richmond Co.,VA. signed as Dorothy Croucher.

Dorothy and her brother Thomas were administrators of her husband William Lee's estate. She

was left wearing apparel in her mother's will. "Dorothy to have my Coyas" d. 1717, Richmond Co,

VA (Source: Amelia Co. Order Book 7, p. 226, Letters of Administration of Estate of William Lee to

Dorothy Lee, relict of William Lee on 12/4/1717.).

Documentation from "Log Cabins to White House" by Brewer. On page 275 "On 19 Jan 1668

William and wife Alice acknowledged debt of 250 acres of land to William Heath.

On 5 Sep 1668 William and wife Alice sold their plantation to Thomas Adams (Surry Co. records

p.54).

From "Log Cabin" book on p.276 it gives William Lee(who married Dorothy Taylor) as one of his

children. On p.273, Richard Henry Lee and Anna Constable are given as the parents of William

(husband of Alice) but other sources state that Richard Lee's son William did not marry. Other

sources say he married and had a daughter Mary who married a Heath and that he left his estate

to her—which was contested by his brother and returned to the Lee family.

There is a William Lee and Mary Lee, witnesses in Richard Jesper's will, dated 1698 in North

Farnham Parish, VA. Need to identify them. Dorothy and brother Thomas Taylor were

administrators of his estate. They left to William's grandchildren (children of Wm.3rd) the legacy left

to him by his grandmother Elizabeth Taylor. Thomas Hanks received 9 lbs 11 shillings 8 pence;

Joseph Hanks 2 lbs2 shillings 6 pence; Richard Lee 4 shillings; none was listed for John Lee who

had probably died young.

———————

ALT VERSION BELOW PROBABLE error confused

ID: I16208 Name: William COLONEL Lee Leigh

Sex: M Birth: 1654 in Surry County, , Virginia

Death: 14 JUL 1703

Father: William Lee Leigh b: ABT 1588 in England

Mother: Catherine b: ABT 1592

Marriage 1 Mary Green b: ABT 1659 in King & Queen County, VA

Married: 1675 in King & Queen County, VA

Children

John CAPTAIN Lee Leigh b: 1677 in Of Leigh Hall, , Cheshire, England

William Lee Leigh b: 1682 in New Kent County, VA

Sources:

Title: Family Group Record FamilySearch™ Ancestral File v4.19

GENERATION 1 (CON'T)

: William Lee Leigh 1 Sex: M Birth: ABT 1588 in England Death: 1653 in , James, Virginia

Marriage 1 Mary Dawkes b: ABT 1578 in < , Charles City County, Virginia>

Marriage 2 Catherine b: ABT 1592

Children

William COLONEL Lee Leigh b: 1654 in Surry County, , Virginia

Sources:

Title: Family Group Record FamilySearch™ Ancestral File v4.19

EDMUND JENNINGS LEE had not found any record of what happened to one son William Lee and

blew it off finally saying he appears to have died young.

Weelllll sort of.

He did die earlier, 1694-5, than other siblings, leaving a 18 year old daughter and three younger

minor sons. The daughter Mary had married William Heath at age 15 had two sons, Thomas and

Samuel the last being born after his father died. She re married to Bartholomew Schriever who is the villain of this story. He was "of age" so grabbed the estate and paid out yearly " a gentleman's

living" to the three boys; Wm, John, and Richard. What he paid was far less than the estate could

manage; and they deserved more; but it was legally large enough that they could not sue their

"guardian" until ALL of them were of age. The instant the youngest turned 21 they did sue.

BUT

Not in probate court but common pleas court to recover their inheritance.

And not in the original county (Westmoreland) but the county had been split and then re-split in the

mean time (at this time it was Surry Co) and worse the judge (a VIP) did not travel to them he

stayed put and they had to come to him in King and Queen County. (This was a MAJOR estate

-and why they had a "superior" judge in a higher court-in today's terms it would be multi millionaire

stuff).

AND

It was 7-8 years out of time...7 -8 years later than expected.

Wrong place, wrong time, wrong court, and why E J Lee missed it.

Bart and Mary got her furniture and what money he had sequestered (the court knew he had milked estate, said so, but did not bother to try to find where he had squirreled money

away—{Bermuda}), just gave Mary HER furniture, and kicked them off land and divided it 3 ways

each boy getting roughly 1/3. Bart packed up in high dudgeon and went back to England (assume

they stopped at Bermuda where $$were) -and lived life of rich ex colonial gentleman.

OK first problem solved. This I got from two separate books /people who had done work

independently, and I cross-checked just to be sure. (A Weavin' and Log Cabin to White House

Next problem

William (ii) son Wm (i) and grandson of Co Richard died 1717 (about 13 years after court bruhoo);

leaving 4 sons. And I will stick to our line his son Charles b 1706 moved to new land at North

Farnham Parish, Richmond Co., Va.

Charles moves again dies 1799 at-really near just out of town-Leesburg, Cumberland Co., Va.

leaving cash to a son William (others got land) and just down the road, land adjoining Charles is a

William Lee that the previous genealogists had assumed was his son.

BooBoo!

It was a reasonable assumption. Just wrong. Charles died in 1799 Cumberland Co Va and had a son William. There is a William Lee (md Ave Noel) whose land adjoins Charles' land so they

assume he is the son. Unfortunately they happened to buy adjoining lands at about the same time

and they were cousins, but unwarranted assumption as to being his son.

Then I found the full name of James Garnett Early Lee b. 23 feb 1777 known as Garnett Lee

usually, AND known to be son of William and Ave Noel and that triggered my memory that James

Lee had md Mary Clark Garnett and I cross connected Wm and Ave to James Lee and Mary

Garnett who also had known son William but unknown what happened to him if we connect Wm

and Ave to Charles. To add to the surety I was right, Wm and Ave moved about 1788 to Evington

Generation 1 (con't)

Road Bedford Co Va. just a bit down the road from James and Mary Garnett—(Ah Ha!)———-so this

time making the assumption that the William who was close to James was his son works. James

died by the way 1791 Probate Bedford Co Va.

With that I was able to disconnect he wrong William (md Ave) and get him to correct papa-and so

was left connecting MY William (1738-1808) to Charles. Reason for cash was my William had gone on to Hardy Co Va. (now West Va) at the same time, abt 1760, his father Charles had moved from

Richmond Co where he was born (The residual of the original estate was now in Surry Co.-but had

been split up so much the land left to Charles was too small to make him well off -or as well off as

he wished) then on to Leesburgh in Cumberland Co and so our William had no use for land-he

had his own-but hundreds of miles away. SO cash.

Oh me oh my long story. I also jumped 4 years work in getting all of the above. I followed Loads of

dead ends.

Notes for Alice Mrs FELTON:

Subj: Alice Felton

Date: 10/23/2006 4:19:29 PM Central Daylight Time

From: dalell@earthlink.net (Eleanor Prieskorn) To: Corvid1@msn.com ('Marilyn Hutton'),

Jhlawr@wmconnect.com

->

Today I am tracking Alice Felton, I have found nothing on her in Virginia, and if she had married

Thomas Felton she would have been 7 years old.

From what I have found below she must have came to Virginia as a servant met William Lee (the

rogue that he was) and married him. Still found nothing on marriage though.

I have been doing census on Williams' and Richards' (Tax list) (census)

WM would have to be in Maryland; that is where his father left him a home and land. I found Col

Richard Lee's will he made in England when he and his family were in their home there, he went to

sell all and give up England for good. He had made many trips back and forth over the years and

owned 1/8 of 3 ships for transporting goods back and forth and people.

Francis Lee went back to England lived, raised his family and died there in 1714.

Col Lee left the ownership of the 3 ships to (Elizabeth-Mary-& Susan 1/8th eh.) to Francis and if he

dies first it goes to Charles and the two sisters, Elizabeth and Ann.

Jim, how do I go about getting Edmond Jennings Lee's book?

Did you find anything in there on Alice?

Talk to you two later

Ellie

Generation 1 (con't)

William Lee and Alice Mrs FELTON had the following children:

2.

i. MARY2

LEE was born about 1676 in Richmond Co, Westmoreland, Va, area. She

married (1) WILLIAM HEATH about 1692 in Westmoreland, Richmond, Va, area. He was born about 1668 in Richmond Co, Westmoreland, Va, area. He died before

1795 in Richmond, Co Va. She married (2) BARTHOLOMEW SCHREEVER about 1695

in Westmoreland, Richmond, second husband, area. He was born about 1670 in

Richmond, Westmoreland, Va, area.

3.

ii. RICHARD HENRY LEE was born about 1678 in Surry, County, , Va. He died on 10 Dec

1726 in N. Farnham, parish, Richmond Co. Va.. He married MARY YOUNG in 1695 in

King & Queens Co., Virginia. She was born about 1679 in King & Queens Co.,

Virginia.

4.

iii. WILLIAM LEE II was born on 1679/80 in b Northampton, Co, Va later Surry Co., Va.

He died on 04 Dec 1717 in will probate, Richmond, Co, Virginia. He married

DOROTHY TAYLOR about 1702 in of, Richmond, Co, Va, daughter of Thomas

TAYLOR and Elizabeth HARWOOD. She was born about 1681 in of, Surry, King

and Queen, Va. She died on 25 Feb 1754 in will probate, Amelia, County, Virginia.

5.

iv. JOHN LEE MAJOR was born about 1682 in Surry, County, , Va. He died on 05 Oct

1731 in of, Surry, King and Queen, Va. He married ANNE* TAYLOR TWIN about 1699

in Richmond, Co, , Va, daughter of James TAYLOR and MARY BISHOP

GREGORY. She was born on 12 Jan 1683/84 in Hare Forest, New Kent Co, Va.

She died in 1731 in St. George Parish, Spotsylvania Co., VA.

Generation 2

2.

MARY2

LEE (William1) was born about 1676 in Richmond Co, Westmoreland, Va, area. She married

(1) WILLIAM HEATH about 1692 in Westmoreland, Richmond, Va, area. He was born about 1668 in

Richmond Co, Westmoreland, Va, area. He died before 1795 in Richmond, Co Va. She married (2)

BARTHOLOMEW SCHREEVER about 1695 in Westmoreland, Richmond, second husband, area. He

was born about 1670 in Richmond, Westmoreland, Va, area.

William Heath and Mary Lee had the following children:

i.

THOMAS3

HEATH was born about 1693 in Richmond, Westmoreland, Va, area.

ii.

SAMUEL HEATH was born about 1694 in Richmond, Westmoreland, Va, area.

3.

RICHARD HENRY2

LEE (William1) was born about 1678 in Surry, County, , Va. He died on 10 Dec

1726 in N. Farnham, parish, Richmond Co. Va.. He married MARY YOUNG in 1695 in King &

Queens Co., Virginia. She was born about 1679 in King & Queens Co., Virginia.

Notes for Mary YOUNG:

Mary, (7grt-grndmthr) YOUNG Sex: F Birth: 1679 in Virginia,(See Notes/ Photo Coat-of-Arms)

Change Date: 1 AUG 2002 at 20:20:40

Marriage 1 Richard Sr., (7grt-grndfthr) LEE b: Abt 1677 in IMPORTED 1st Gresham Lee Line/Surry,Co.,VA (See Notes)

Children

Charles LEE

Thomas LEE b: in Buckingham Co,Virginia

Young LEE b: in Buckingham Co,Virginia

Richard H. II "ESQUIRE", (6grt-grndfthr) LEE

b: 1710 in Buckingham Co,VA (See Notes/LAND RECORD)

John, (6grt-grndfthr) ESQUIRE LEE b: Abt

1711 in VA to Craven Co,North Carolina later became Johnston Co.

William LEE b: in Buckinham Co,VA (Resided/Dupiln Co. North Carolina)

Richard Henry Lee and Mary YOUNG had the following children:

6.

i. JOHN [ESQ]3

LEE was born in 1696 in Richmond Co., Va , Of Johnston Co., Nc. He

died on 04 Dec 1766 in Mill Creek, Johnston county, NC. He married MARY BRYAN or BRYANT about 1725 in Nottoway Parish, Isle Of Wight, Virginia, daughter of William

BRYAN and Alice MCCLOUD. She was born in 1706 in , Isle Of Wight, Virginia.

She died in , Johnson, Nc.

7.

ii. RICHARD HENRY LEE was born about 1707 in Buckingham co., VA or

Northumberland, Va. He died after 1790 in , Jackson Co., Tenn. He married (1)

MARY GRESHAM OR GRISHAM about 1727. She was born about 1709 in , , Va. She

died in 1767 in Buckingham Co.,Va. He married (2) MARY ELIZABETH BETSY MILLER

in 1769 in Buckingham Co.,Va. She was born about 1746 in Delaware. She died in

Ballston,,Va.

iii.

MARY LEE was born in 1710 in , Northumberland, Va. She died after 1746
in , ,

Virginia.

iv.

CHARLES LEE was born about 1712 in Northumberland, Va.

v.

WILLIAM LEE was born about 1714 in Northumberland, Va.

vi.

YOUNG LEE was born about 1718 in Buckingham co., Va. He died in
1774.

Notes for Young LEE:

Name: Young LEE Given Name: Young Surname: Lee Sex: M Birth: in
Buckingham

Co, Virginia Death: 1774

Father: Richard Sr. LEE (7GRT-GRNDFTHR) b: Abt. 1677 in

IMPORTED 1st Gresham Lee Line/Surry, County, VA (See Notes)

Mother: Mary YOUNG (7GRT-GRNDMTHR)VA b: 1679 in Virginia,
(See Notes)

8.

vii. PETER LEE was born about 1724 in Washington Co., Va of Madison
Co., KY. He

married SARAH GREEN about 1758. She was born about 1738 in Northumbreland

Co., Va.

4.

WILLIAM2

LEE II (William1) was born on 1679/80 in b Northampton, Co, Va later Surry Co., Va. He

died on 04 Dec 1717 in will probate, Richmond, Co, Virginia. He married DOROTHY TAYLOR about

1702 in of, Richmond, Co, Va, daughter of Thomas TAYLOR and Elizabeth HARWOOD. She was

born about 1681 in of, Surry, King and Queen, Va. She died on 25 Feb 1754 in will probate,

Amelia, County, Virginia.

Notes for William Lee ii:

alt version

I21729 Name: William Lee Leigh

Sex: M

Birth: 1682 in New Kent County, VA

Death: 1784 in King & Queen County, VA

Father: William COLONEL Lee Leigh b: 1654 in Surry County, , Virginia

Mother: Mary Green b: ABT 1659 in King & Queen County, VA

Marriage 1 Frances Major

Children

James Lea Leigh < b: 1706 in King & Queen County, Virginia

Sources:

Title: Family Group Record FamilySearch™ Ancestral File v4.19

———————

POSTED BY: DENNIS W. Lee

Email:

Subject:Re: Peter Lee/Rebecca Taylor

Post Date: February 09, 2001 at 16:22:32

Message URL: <http://genforum.genealogy.com/lee/messages/10006.html>

Forum: Lee Family Genealogy Forum

Forum URL: <http://genforum.genealogy.com/lee/>

I have been following this exchange for a while now. We have discussed this family

several times in this Forum, and I have been compiling information regarding it, as John, the

brother of Peter Lee, may be my umpteenth great grandfather. Included here is my current file.

This information comes from numerous sources and may be in part inaccurate, so use it at your

own risk. Nonetheless, there's a lot of good data here and some hints for more. Ignore the

"Impossible" and other tags on the John Lees -that's just my notes.

Dennis

2. William C. Lee / Lea b. 1651 VA (or 1650 Northumberland, VA) d. 1687 ?? 1696??

m1.

m2. Mary

m3. Alice b: 1650 in Richmond, Co, VA (widow of Thomas Felton) John Bursage sued estate of

William Lee for note signed by Lee Nov. 17, 1694. The Leas sold land to William Heath of

Southwark Parish, Surry, in 1660.

The land was part Charles City Co, part Surry Co, originally granted to William in 1654.

3. John Lee IMPOSSIBLE b. ca 1682 in Surry Co, VA

3. Richard Lee b. ca. 1684 in Surry, Co, VA

3. William Lee b. 1678 or 1682, Northampton, Northumberland Co, VA

m. Dorothy Taylor, ca 1703, Westmoreland Co, VA d/o Thomas Taylor & Elizabeth Harwood b.

1681, Surry,

King and Queen Co, VA

Information on Dorothy Taylor comes from "Log Cabins to White House" by Brewer. 13 Apr

1745

Dorothy was witness to will of Henry Williams in Richmond Co.,VA. signed as Dorothy Croucher.

Dorothy and her brother Thomas were administrators of her husband William Lee's estate. She

was left wearing apparel in her mother's will. "Dorothy to have my Coyas" d. 1717, Richmond Co,

VA (Source: Amelia Co. Order Book 7, p. 226, Letters of Administration of Estate of William Lee to

Dorothy Lee, relict of William Lee on 12/4/1717.).

Documentation from "Log Cabins to White House" by Brewer. On page 275 "On 19 Jan 1668

William and wife Alice acknowledged debt of 250 acres of land to William Heath.

On 5 Sep 1668 William and wife Alice sold their plantation to Thomas Adams (Surry Co. records

p.54).

From "Log Cabin" book on p.276 it gives William Lee(who married Dorothy Taylor) as one of his

children. On p.273, Richard Henry Lee and Anna Constable are given as the parents of William

(husband of Alice) but other sources state that Richard Lee's son William did not marry. Other

sources say he married and had a daughter Mary who married a Heath and that he left his estate

to her—which was contested by his brother and returned to the Lee family.

There is a William Lee and Mary Lee, witnesses in Richard Jesper's will, dated 1698 in North

Farnham Parish, VA. Need to identify them. Dorothy and brother Thomas Taylor were

administrators of his estate. They left to William's grandchildren (children of Wm.3rd) the legacy left

to him by his grandmother Elizabeth Taylor. Thomas Hanks received 9 lbs 11 shillings 8 pence;

Joseph Hanks 2 lbs2 shillings 6 pence; Richard Lee 4 shillings; none was listed for John Lee who

had probably died young.

4. William Lee b. 14 May 1704, North Farnham Parish, Richmond Co, VA

(Source: Parish Registers of North Farnham Church, Richmond Co., VA and Parish Register of

Lunenburg Parish 1783-1800, p. 131-135.) Baptized 14 May 1704, N. Farnham Parish, Richmond

Co, VA. d. 2 Jul 1764, VA

This was a poor family, apparently either not related or distantly related to the Lees of Stratford

Hall. Barbara Vernon notes that Hannah Lee, of the same generation would have been likely to

hire a relative as overseer. This implies that there was a relationship between Hannah Lee and

Justice Thomas Barber, for whom William became a plantation overseer in Lunenberg Parish in the

1740's. William was charged with the felony death of a slave, but apparently not convicted. The

Richmond County Criminal Court minutes for May 18, 1743, give an almost verbatim account of

testimony concerning the incident. He appears in Richmond Co, VA in the 1740's and 1750's,

specifically in the North Farnham Parish. Late in life, he was poverty-stricken and jailed as a debtor.

Research done by Dr.Robert Stickley in the 1970's, DAR568969, DAR54156, "VA Calendar of

State Papers". Clara Funai of VA published a book "The Weaving" on the Lee family which included all she and Dr. Stickley had found. m1. Jane, ca. 1728, Londonderry, Ireland b. 1708 Londonderry, Ireland

5. William Lee (note half-brother of same name) b. 12 Oct 1729, Derry, Ulster, Ireland d.

Chatham Co, NC m2. Ann / Anne ???, 16 Dec 1728, Richmond Co, VA b. ca 1706, Richmond Co,

VA d. < 1764 5. Elizabeth / Eliza "Betty" Lee b. ca 1723 m. Thomas Hanks A Thomas Hanks is in

Michael Cresap's company along with some of the Lees -Richard, Mark, and John.

5. Sarah Lee b. 1 Jul 1732, North Farnham Parish, Richmond Co, VA m. Thomas Hanks

?????????

per Barbara Vernon and "The Lineage of Lincoln" by Barton.

See above notes for Thomas Hanks. Was Elizabeth and Sarah the same person? Did Thomas

marry both girls? Another source says that Sarah was unmarried.

5. Richard Lee b. ca 1731 ???, Richmond Co, VA m. Mary Rose b. 1725 d. 1764, MD A

Richard Lee is found along with Mark and John in Michael Cresap's Company in Lord Dunmore's

War of 1774.

6. John Lee IMPOSSIBLE b. 1745, St. Mary Co, MD *** Conflict: some say this

John was the s/o John Lee & Mary Stiles *** d. 1788 Nelson Co, KY/VA m. Elizabeth Thompson,

ca. 1769 b. 9 Apr 1752 d. ca. 1824, Nelson Co, KY Pvt VA, Revolutionary War patriot. John Lee's

few short years in Nelson Co, VA (formed in 1785) were inauspicious from the beginning. When he

settled along the Rolling Fork the region was inhospitable. Indian attacks were frequent and the

newly-arriving burdened frontiersmen often sought protection in stockaded Goodin's Fort two miles

to the north. In 1782 the peril was so great that a sentry guarded the cabins by night and the fields

by day. John Lee served in the autumn of 1782 under Col. Isaac Cox in General George Rogers

Clark's expedition against the Shawnee in southern Ohio. He probably rendered other military

service as every able bodied man was needed in the militia for defense against sporadic Indian

attack until the late 1780s. Despite his courageous struggle to establish a home on his own land,

John Lee's dream did not come true. A clear title was not forthcoming during his lifetime to either of

two tracts he attempted to acquire. He took possession of a 400-acre tract south of New Haven

that was allotted to him December 3, 1781, with the provision that full payment be made within two

and a half years, but Joseph Barnett steadfastly refused to relinquish a prior claim. In February

1787, John Lee sold 150 of the 400 acres on which he was living, received cash payment and

granted possession although a deed of transfer could not be drawn up. It was apparently at this

time that he bought 86 acres on the Beech Fork about four miles to the north, with the assurance of

clear title. Nevertheless, the deed to the latter tract was not recorded until five years after his death.

These were the unfortunate circumstances that denied John Lee the longed-for security of outright

land ownership, the goal of every settler. John Lee died in the summer of 1788. Elizabeth, the

widow, was left with seven children ranging in age from sixteen to a toddling infant. Daughter

Eleanor, the oldest child, had married the previous year, and Wilford, the oldest son, was fourteen.

The 400 acres of virgin soil had provided a livelihood during the family's occupancy and a small amount of movable property had been accumulated. Widow Elizabeth Lee was appointed executor

of the estate August 12, 1788. The inventory made April 13, 1790, listed one slave, about twenty

head of livestock, household goods and farming implements at a total value of a trifle over 105 pounds.

7. Eleanor Lee b. 1770 m. 1787, Bennett Hayden

7. Sarah Lee b.1772 m. Cornelius Brothers

7. Wilford Lee b. 1774 d. 24 Jan 1849, Bullitt Co, KY m1. Rebecca Hill, 8 Aug 1796, Nelson Co, KY

m2. Margaret Hill, 14 Jul 1821, Nelson Co, KY

7. Charles Lee b. 1776 d. 1819 m. Margaret Marraman / Maraman, 5 Jun 1799, Nelson Co, KY

7. Mary Lee b. ca 1778 d. 1839 m. Francis Marraman / Maraman, 8 Mar 1797, Nelson Co, KY

7. William Lee b. 1780 d. 1852 m. Sarah Younger, ca 1810

7. John Lee, Jr. (aka "Jacky") IMPOSSIBLE b. 1785 Nelson Co, KY d. 1835, Bullitt Co, KY m.

Elizabeth Hill, 30 Mar 1803, Nelson Co, KY *** Conflict *** d/o Atkinson Hill and Elizabeth Goodin

7. Henry Lee b. 1786 m. Ann Norris

6. Phillip Philmar Lee b. 1749 6. Charles Lee b. ca 1750 m. Abigail Crawford

7. John Lee IMPOSSIBLE b. ca 1770, Hardin Co, KY m. Mary LaFollet, 27 Jul

1790, Nelson Co, KY

5. Nancy Ann "Nanny" Lee b. 1736 or 1728 Richmond Co, VA d. > 18 Oct 1807 VA m.

Joseph Hanks, 1758 b. 20 Dec 1725, North Farnham Parish, Richmond Co, VA d. < 19 May 1793,

Nelson Co, KY s/o John Hanks (<21 in 1708, d. c. 1740) & Catherine (m. ca 1714, d. 1779) Lived

in Richmond Co, VA until the spring of 1782, then moved to Hampshire Co, WV (now Mineral Co.)

Lived in the Patterson Creek valley. Thomas (son) preceded Joseph there and was there as of

1780. They lived next to William Lee, who later moved to KY. Also nearby was Peter Lee. Joseph,

Peter, and William were all found in the 1782 census of Hampshire Co, WV, but no Hanks or Lees

are in the 1784 census there. Joseph and Ann Hanks later moved to Nelson Co, KY and bought

land there on 28 Feb 1787 (150 acres) from John Lee, possibly the brother of Anne. On 10 Jan

1794 widow Nannie and son Joseph entered into contract selling land to son William Hanks,

following which she and Joseph returned to Rockingham Virginia, where her family lived (Lees).

Joseph returned to Nelson Co, KY.

―――――

HERE CUT SOME HANKS data see under Joseph Hanks

―――――

5. WILLIAM LEE B. 1748/9 in Richmond Co, VA

A William Lee is found in the 1782 Tax rolls of Hampshire Co, WV. William supposedly moved on

to KY in 1784 and on to Natchez, MS. William is listed as Mary's kid, but note the birthdate and

marriage date.

5. Mark Lee b. 1752/3 in Richmond Co, VA (Opelousas Church records lists Marc as "of

MD"???)

m. Nancy Keeze / Quize / Kais / Quaze / Keys in Natchez, MS?. (a Marc Lee is shown as married

to an Anne Quaze, another is shown marrying a Nancy Hanks, both in the Opelousas Church,

Opelousas, LA between 1756 and 1810 according to SW LA Records, Volume 1, by Rev. Hebert.

Although these are not necessarily what they seem -the records may just be making a note that

these were married couples, married elsewhere)

b. ca 1754 MD

d. ca 1823, Opelousas, St. Landry Parish, LA

d. poss in Natchez

Mark Lee moved to western MD, with Clark in KY Indian wars, to Mason Co, KY ca 1780+, then to

Natchez in 1789, then to LA 1790. Mark and family settled in St. Landry Parish. There is also a record of a Nancy Hanks and a Marc Lee in the Opelousas Church with children born in the

1799-1810 timeframe. Could Nancy have been a Hanks from KY who was a widow of a Quaze /

Keys?

Served in Dunmore's War and during the American Revolution served in the Militia of Skipton

(Oldtown) in Western Maryland (Skipton/Oldtown was the home of Michael Cresap). He migrated

to Mercer and Nelson Counties in KY with Peter and William Lee, brothers. Also, sister "Nanny"

Ann Lee and Joseph Hanks were there about the same time. Records in LA show that Peter and

Mark made entries for land grants after 1790. Vol. III American State Paper, "Before Richard

Cocke 1809 in Attakapas, Peter Lee deposed that his brother Mark went in the fall of 1802 to

reside on land claimed as tenant of John Abshire, until fall of 1803." Page 145, "Mark Lee sold 400

acres he got in 1796 in Vermilion Bayou. Ben Hargrave stated that Mark Lee resided on land

claimed 1797-1801. Mark Lee was then head of a family."

On 23 Feb 1790, Don Carlos de Grand Pre noted that a flatboat from KY had arrived in the

Natchez District from the USA. One John Lee was a boatman in the employ of Mark Lee, who had descended the river with two flatboats, bringing a cargo of 1500 minots of lime, 18000 lbs. of salt

meat, 12 hogsheads of tobacco, and 800 lbs of salt.

Notice of people who arrived from KY at Natchez 23 Feb 1790...on the boats were Mark Lee, John

Lee, John Waziam, John Nuoy, William Gifford, Leonard Bocoman, Robert Fryel, Ramon

Bocoman. (These are translated from the Spanish and may not be the correct English names)

Americans who took the oath of allegiance to Spain...7-24 March 1789 Mark Lee

A "Marck Lea" is listed next to "Peter Lea" in the 1810 Attakapas District, LA census. Marck is

listed as 1m26-45, 2f<10, no wife...

6. William Lee Baptism: January 29, 1811, Opelousas Church, LA, as an

adult, sponsors were Ignatius Tear and Anne Lee Opel Ch. v.1-B p.517

m. Francoise "Fanny" Tear

7. Jean (John) Lee IMPOSSIBLE b. February 18, 1815, St. Landry Pa., La.

This may be the "John Lee" listed as an early settler of the Opelousas area.

7. Ann Francoise Lee b. July 17, 1819, St. Landry Pa., La.

6. James Lee b. KY d. ca Jan 1819 m1. marr license. 26 Dec 1809, Mary / Marie Tear (widow Neville), Opelousas court, Opelousas, LA marr: 20 Feb 1810, Opelousas

Church, Opelousas, LA (note baptism of their child Marie Anne)

In revised book of Fr. Hebert, p.459: Witnesses: Henry Hageland and Margret Cunningham. This is

a validation of a marraige already legitimately and civilly contracted according to the civil laws of

the state. Opel Ch v.1-A, p.198

7. Mary/Marie Anne Lee

bapt. 23 Sep 1810 at age 5 weeks, Opelousas Church, Opelousas, LA

m2. Eleanor Lee, 1800,

d/o Peter Lee and Rebecca Taylor.

7. Nancy Lee

6. George M. Lee

b. 15 Mar 1791

bapt. 7 Nov 1815, Opelousas Church, Opelousas, LA at age 24 years

d. 9 Sep 1843, Opelousas, St. Landry Parish, LA

m. Rachel Clark, November 07, 1815 in Opelousas Church, LA (Opelousas Church records)

b. Baltimore, MD.

7. Robert Elisha Lee

b. August 1863, Acadia Pa., LA

d. September 1934, St. Landry Pa., LA.

6. Elizabeth Lee

b. 1795

bapt. 29 Oct 1808 at age 13 years, Opelousas Church, Opelousas, LA

m1. John Smith, 30 Jun 1812, Opelousas, St. Landry, LA

b. PA

m2. 7 Dec 1818, Samuel Datton, Opelousas, St. Landry, LA ???

6. Rebecca Lee

b. 1799

bapt. 21 Mar 1808 at age 9 years, Opelousas Church, Opelousas, LA

m. Jacob Bougard, 31 Mar 1818

6. Nancy Ann/Anna Lee

b. 13 Oct 1792, St. Landry Parish, LA

bapt. 13 Oct 1807, Opelousas Church, Opelousas, LA at age 16

m. 13 Oct 1807, Ignatius John Tear of Opelousas, Opelousas Church, Opelousas, LA

d. 23 May 1818, Bayou Boeuf, LA (In Hebert's revised vol: died at age 26, buried the next day in

parish cemetery. Opel Ch.v.1, p 170)

5. Peter Lee

b: January 30, 1749/50 in Richmond Co, VA; (Christened in Mason Co, KY?)

m. Rebecca Taylor in Hampshire Co, WV/VA in 27 Jan 1778 (source FTM) (several records show

Pierre Lee m. Rebecca Taleur from St. Martin Church records, but these may just be indicating that

they were married elsewhere) From DAR Magazine, Aug 1950, pg.699 are"
The Records of the

Rev. Thaddeus Dod" contributed by Raymond M. Bell, Washington & Jefferson College,

Washington, PA. Among the marriages for Patterson Creek, WV is that of Peter Lee and Rebecca

Taylor.

b: ca 1763 in Richmond Co, VA

d/o Simon Taylor & Mary / Anna Maria Hite

b. 11 Mar 1727 d. 14 Mar 1786 b. 15 Dec 1738 d. 10 Mar 1784 m. wft est 1766-1781

d. 1 Oct 1831, Lafayette Parish (Vermillion), LA

d. 1823 in Lafayette Parish, LA -(Marian Hughlett has a copy of his succession records); burial in

Vermilion Parish, LA (then Lafayette Parish).Peter and his brother Mark traveled from VA, settled

briefly in frontier KY (Mason Co), then went down the Ohio and Mississippi to Natchez, and settled

in LA. Peter had land on the east side of the Vermillion River, just opposite the town of Perry, LA.

He had been there since 1798, at least. Possibly 1796. Peter ended up in St. Martin Parish. Check

SAR File 5911 -this may be the Rev War Vet. Two islands, bearing the names of Peter and Mark

Lee are located in the marsh S of Henry, LA and W of the Boston Canal. Neighbors include

Benjamin Hargrove of VA and Jacob Ryan of GA. On the E side of the Vermillion River, several

large tracts of land were held by the White Family: John White, Jesse White, another John White,

William White. The family is from VA.

William Lee ii and Dorothy TAYLOR had the following children:

9.

i. WILLIAM3

LEE III OR JR. was born on 14 May 1704 in N. Farnham, parish, Richmond

Co. Va.. He died on 02 Jul 1764 in will probate, Richmond, Co, Va Will Book 6, p.

361. He married (1) ANNE in of, Richmond, Co, Va. She was born about 1706 in

Richmond, Co, , Va. She died in Richmond, Co, , Va. He married (2) MARY OR

MARIE THORNTON on 1746/47 in Richmond, Co, , Va, daughter of James Thornton

and Anne. She was born on 13 Mar 1723/24 in MD of Richmond County, Virginia.

10.

ii. CHARLES LEE SR. was born on 18 Sep 1706 in Richmond, Co, N Farnham Parish,

Va. He died in 1799 in will probate, Cumberland, Co, Va. He married ANN DABBS about 1736 in Charlotte, Co, Va, daughter of Joseph Dabbs Sr. and Ann. She was

born about 1716 in of, Charlotte, Co, Va. She died in 1795 in will probate,

Cumberland, Co, Va.

iii.

ANNE LEE was born about 1707 in Richmond, Co, , Va. She died after 1747 in will,

grandmother, Elizabeth, TAYLOR.

iv.

RICHARD LEE was born in 1711 in Richmond, Co, , Va. He died after 1747 in will,

grandmother, Elizabeth, TAYLOR.

v.

JOHN LEE was born on 11 Oct 1713 in Richmond, Co, , Va. He died on 12 Dec 1722

in N. Farnham, parish, register, Richmond Co. Va.. He married ELIZABETH PAGE.

She was born about 1715 in of, Richmond, Co Va.

vi.

JOSEPH LEE was born on 1714/15 in York, Co, Va.

vii.

ELIZABETH BETSEY LEE was born about 1715 in Richmond, Co, , Va. She died after

1747 in will, grandmother, Elizabeth, TAYLOR.

viii.

SARAH LEE was born about 1716 in Richmond, Co, , Va. She died after 1747 in will,

grandmother, Elizabeth, TAYLOR.

5.

JOHN2

LEE MAJOR (William1) was born about 1682 in Surry, County, , Va. He died on 05 Oct 1731

in of, Surry, King and Queen, Va. He married ANNE* TAYLOR TWIN about 1699 in Richmond, Co, ,

Va, daughter of James TAYLOR and MARY BISHOP GREGORY. She was born on 12 Jan

1683/84 in Hare Forest, New Kent Co, Va. She died in 1731 in St. George Parish, Spotsylvania

Co., VA.

Notes for John Lee Major:

I07909 Name: John CAPTAIN -&-MAJOR Lee Leigh

Sex: M

Birth: 1677 in Of Leigh Hall, , Cheshire, England

Death: 5 OCT 1731 in Of Surry, King & Queen County, Virginia

Father: William COLONEL Lee Leigh b: 1654 in Surry County, , Virginia

Mother: Mary Green b: ABT 1659 in King & Queen County, VA

Marriage 1 Ann Taylor b: 12 JAN 1684/85 in Caroline Co., VA

Married: 1699 in Richmond County, Virginia

Children

John Lee Leigh b: 1 SEP 1700 in , King &

Queen County, Virginia

Catherine Lee Leigh b: ABT 1702 in King &

Queen County, Virginia

Ferdinand Lee Leigh b: ABT 1706

Elizabeth Lee Leigh b: 1709 in Westmoreland

County, Virginia

James Lee Leigh b: ABT 1711 in , King &

Queen County, Virginia

William Lee Leigh b: ABT 1711 in Richmond

County, Virginia

James Lee Leigh b: ABT 1714 in St.

Stephens Par., King & Queen County, VA

Betty Lee Leigh b: ABT 1716 in < , , Prob.

England>

William Lee Leigh b: 1716 in Richmond

County, Virginia

John Lee Leigh b: ABT 1717 in < , , Prob.

England>

Elizabeth Lee Leigh b: 1717 in Richmond

County, Virginia

James Lee Leigh b: ABT 1723 in Richmond

County, Virginia

Notes for Anne* TAYLOR twin:

: I07345 Name: Ann Taylor

Sex: F

Birth: 12 JAN 1684/85 in Caroline Co., VA

Death: 1731 in St. George Parish, Spotsylvania Co., VA

Immigration: 1635 On 'True Love' from London, England

Father: JAMES 1ST TAYLOR b: 12 FEB 1609/10 in Earl Hare, Carlisle, England

Mother: MARY BISHOP GREGORY b: 1665 in Of Essex, Rappahannock, County, VA

Marriage 1 John CAPTAIN Lee Leigh b: 1677 in Of Leigh Hall, , Cheshire, England

Married: 1699 in Richmond County, Virginia

Children

John Lee Leigh b: 1 SEP 1700 in , King & Queen County, Virginia

Catherine Lee Leigh b: ABT 1702 in King & Queen County, Virginia

Ferdinand Lee Leigh b: ABT 1706

Elizabeth Lee Leigh b: 1709 in Westmoreland County, Virginia

James Lee Leigh b: ABT 1711 in , King &

Queen County, Virginia

William Lee Leigh b: ABT 1711 in Richmond

County, Virginia

James Lee Leigh b: ABT 1714 in St.

Stephens Par., King & Queen County, VA

Betty Lee Leigh b: ABT 1716 in < , , Prob.

England>

William Lee Leigh b: 1716 in Richmond

County, Virginia

John Lee Leigh b: ABT 1717 in < , , Prob. England>

Elizabeth Lee Leigh b: 1717 in Richmond County, Virginia

James Lee Leigh b: ABT 1723 in Richmond County, Virginia

Marriage 2 George Edward Eastham b: ABT 1681 Married: 1704

Sources:

Title: Erasmus Taylor Bible from TaylorFamilyWebsite

Text: http://image.vtls.com/Bible/27558/index.html

John Lee Major and Anne* TAYLOR twin had the following children:

11.

i. JOHN3

LEE JR was born on 01 Sep 1700 in Richmond, Co, , Va. He died in Orange,

Co, , Va. He married ANN CARTER. She was born about 1695 in of,
Spotsylvania,

King and Queen, Va. She died in later, Orange, Co, Va.

ii.

CATHERINE LEE was born about 1702 in King and Queen Co., Va. She married (1)

GEORGE PRIDDY in 1725 in first husband. He was born about 1700 in King and

Queen Co., Va. She married (2) RICHARD SHACKLEFORD about 1730 in second

husband. He was born about 1710.

12.

iii. FERDINAND LEIGH LEE was born about 1704 in Surry Co., VA of Warwick Co., VA.

He died. He married MARY MARTHA COLE about 1731 in Surry Co., VA, daughter of

William Cole Jr. and Mary ROSCOW. She was born in 1711 in Boldrup, Warwick

County, VA. She died about 1750.

13.

iv. ELIZABETH LEE was born in 1706 in Richmond, Co, , Va. She died in Apr 1750 in

Orange Co., VA. She married BENJAMIN TAYLOR about 1736 in Northumberland Co.,

Va, son of John TAYLOR III and Ann VEZEY. He was born about 1699 in Wicomico

Pa. Northumberland Co. VA. He died on 18 Jul 1748 in Northumberland Co., Va.

14.

v. JAMES LEE was born about 1713 in Surry Co., Va. of Richmond, Co, ,
Va. He died in

1791 in Bedford, Co, , Va. He married MARY CLARKE GARNETT about
1737. She was

born in 1718 in daughter, William, Garnett, Essex Co., Va. She died in 1794.

15.

vi. WILLIAM LEE LEA was born in 1710 in King and Queen Co., Va of
Richmond, Co, ,

Va. He died on 10 Mar 1784 in Leesburg, Caswell Co., also Orange Co., NC
1755

moved, Leesburg, NC. He married (1) FRANCES WHITE about 1737 in
Spotsylvania,

King and Queen, Richmond, Va. She was born about 1717 in Richmond,
Co, , Va.

She died after 1758 in South Hico, Caswell, Co, NC. He married (2)
CATHERINE

after 1758 in Caswell, NC. She was born in second wife, Caswell, NC.

16.

vii. JAMES LEE was born in 1715 in King and Queen Co., Va of Richmond,
Co, , Va. He

died in Caswell, Co, , NC. He married ANN TOLBERT HERNDON
about 1739 in

Caswell Co., NC. She was born about 1717 in Richmond, Co, , Va. She died
in

1777 in Caswell, Co, , NC.

Generation 3

6.

JOHN [ESQ]3

LEE (Richard Henry2

Lee, William1

Lee) was born in 1696 in Richmond Co., Va , Of

Johnston Co., Nc. He died on 04 Dec 1766 in Mill Creek, Johnston county, NC. He married MARY

BRYAN BRYANT about 1725 in Nottoway Parish, Isle Of Wight, Virginia, daughter of William BRYAN

and Alice MCCLOUD. She was born in 1706 in , Isle Of Wight, Virginia. She died in , Johnson, Nc.

Notes for John [Esq] LEE:

This was where his will was probated, per Kay G.

NC records of numerous land transactions. His will shows that he was a slave owner.

From "John Lee Esq. of Johnston Co, NC & Some of His Descendants, May 1975", copy on file in

Burkett/Lee file folder. NC Archives #27602, Oct. 29, 1720, lists John Lee among the "Roanoke

River Settlers, 1720".

Change Date: 27 Jul 2002 at 16:03:55

Father: Richard LEE b: ABT 1677 in Surry Co., Virginia

Mother: Mary YOUNG b: AFT 1679 in Virginia

Marriage 1 Mary BRYAN b: 1704 in Isle of Wright, Virginia

Married: ABT 1725 in Virginia

Children

John [Esq] LEE and Mary BRYAN Bryant had the following children:

17.

i. BARTHANIA ELIZABETH4

LEE was born about 1725 in <Chester Co, Sc>. She died

after 1755 in Johnston Co., North Carolina,. She married WILLIAM
INGRAM about

1748. He was born about 1727 in Johnston Co., North Carolina.

18.

ii. ROBERT LEE was born in 1726 in Isle of W ight Co., , Virginia. He died
on 28 Oct

1782 in Winton, Barnwell Co., South Carolina. He married ELIZABETH
STEVENS. She

was born about 1728 in Va..

19.

iii. EDWARD LEE was born in 1728 in , Buckingham, Va. He died on 05
Jun 1775 in ,

Johnson, Nc. He married about 1749. He married (2) MARY ALLEN OR
GREEN in

1747 in , Buckingham, Va. She was born in 1730 in , , Va. She died in 1810
in

Johnston Co., Nc.

20.

iv. THOMAS LEE was born on 03 Dec 1729 in Nottaway Parish, Isle Of Wight, Virginia.

He died on 02 Jul 1816 in Hawkins County,TN. He married (1) MARY BRYAN on 15

Mar 1761 in second wife, in, , NC, daughter of WIlliam Bryan and Elizabeth SMITH.

She was born on 04 Nov 1745 in , Johnson,North Carolina. She died in 1818 in ,

Hawkins, Co, Tenn. He married (2) MARY INGRAM-RAINS about 1773 in ,

Johnston,North Carolina. She was born on 04 Nov 1745 in , Johnston,North

Carolina. She died on 03 Mar 1824 in Hawkins County, TN.

21.

v. JOHN LEE JR. was born in 1730 in , Buckingham, Va. He died on 22 Aug 1809 in Lee

Valley, Hawkins, Ten. He married (1) ELIZABETH HOCUTT about 1753. She was born

about 1735 in Children also other wife. She died in 1794. He married (2) ELIZABETH

UNKNOWN about 1767.

22.

vi. WALTER WASHINGTON LEE was born about 1732 in Johnston Co., North Carolina. He

married SUSANNAH.

vii. MISS LEE was born about 1734 in Nottaway Parish, Isle Of Wight, Virginia.

23.

viii. FREDERICK LEE was born in 1736 in Nottaway Parish, Isle Of Wight, Virginia. He

died on 28 Jan 1814 in Chester Co, Sc. He married SUSANNA. She was born about

1741 in <, , Va>.

24.

ix. RACHEL LEE was born about 1738 in Nottaway Parish, Isle Of Wight, Virginia. She

died after 1768. She married JOHN POWELL. He was born about 1735 in Johnston

Co., North Carolina.

25.

x. SABRAY SABRA LEE was born about 1742 in Nottaway Parish, Isle Of Wight, Virginia.

She married JOHN GREEN.

26.

xi. MARY LEE was born in 1743 in Nottaway Parish, Isle Of Wight, Virginia. She died after 1797 in Johnston Co., North Carolina. She married EDWARD BALLINGER about

1757 in Johnston Co., North Carolina. He was born about 1738 in Prince William,

Virginia. He died on 30 Aug 1772 in Johnston Co., North Carolina.

7.

RICHARD HENRY3

LEE (Richard Henry2

Lee, William1

Lee) was born about 1707 in Buckingham co.,

VA or Northumberland, Va. He died after 1790 in , Jackson Co., Tenn. He married (1) MARY

GRESHAM OR GRISHAM about 1727. She was born about 1709 in , , Va. She died in 1767 in

Buckingham Co.,Va. He married (2) MARY ELIZABETH BETSY MILLER in 1769 in Buckingham

Co.,Va. She was born about 1746 in Delaware. She died in Ballston,,Va.

Generation 3 (con't)

Notes for Mary GRESHAM or Grisham:

Sister to JOhn Gresham(Grisham)

Richard Henry LEE and Mary GRESHAM or Grisham had the following children:

27.

i. AGNES4

LEE was born on 15 Mar 1728 in , Buckingham, Va.. She died on 12 Nov

1774 in Lee Valley, Hawkins, Ten. She married WILLIAM LEE about 1748. He was

born about 1727 in Meherrin Parish, Brunswick Co., VA. He died on 12 Sep 1796 in

, Union Co, Sc.

28.

ii. JOHN LEE was born about 1733 in Buckingham Co.,Va. He died in Feb 1756 in

Reed Creek,Washington Co.,Va.

iii.

DOROTHY DOLLY LEE was born about 1740 in , , Va. She died in TN. She married

THORNTON. He was born in lived in TN.

29.

iv. GEORGE LEE was born about 1743 in , , Va. He died in 1803 in National Rd between

Vandalia & Urebar RIver in ILL. He married NANCY PINKSTON on Unknown date in ?.

She was born about 1753.

30.

v. GRESHAM LEE SR. was born about 1745 in Fishpond Creek,Goochland Co,V. He

died about 1829 in Buckingham co., Va. He married (1) PRISCILLA PRICILEY STAPLES about 1774 in Buckingham Co. Va.. She was born about 1747 in Buckingham co.,

Va. She died before 1808. He married (2) JUNE.

vi.

JESSEE LEE was born about 1746 in , , Va. He died in , Oglethorp, Ga..

vii.

ARCHIBALD ARCHER LEE was born about 1748 in Buckingham Co. Va of Smith Co.,

TN. He died about 1777 in Smith Co., TN. He married DRUTHILLA SMITH on 28 Apr

1799 in Washington Co., Va. She was born about 1779 in Washington Co., Va.

Notes for Archibald Archer LEE:

***********jhll died 1777 and md 1799 + of Smith Co Tn are major conflict ****to say the least**

Name: Archibald, (Revolution 4th Reg.) LEE

Given Name: Archibald, (Revolution 4th Reg.)

Surname: Lee

Sex: M

Birth: Abt 1758 in

(Note) Resided in Smith County, Tennessee

Death: Abt 1777 in Revolutionary War

Note:

Probably "Archibald". Tithable as of 1774, so probably 16 then. Serv

ed in the Revolution in the 4th Reg of the Continental Line.

An Archer Lee listed as married to Druthilla Smith, 4/28/1799, in Washington Co.,

VA.

January 26, 2002

Peggy,

In my notes I have a Archibald Lee was appointed a messenger to carry disp

atches to England. May 13, 1809 Vol. 1, No. 25 (976.8 D2e Vol2) Genealogi

cal Abstracts from Tenn Newspaper.

Lisa Haug

buggs@softcom.net

Father: Richard H. II "Esquire", LEE b: 1710 in (Note-Land) "Richard Henry Lee" -

Buckingham County, Virginia. Land owner of Fishpond Creek area. Later moved to

Jackson, Tennessee.Mother: Mary, GRESHAM b: 1704 in (Note) Prince Edward,

Virginia -Across the Appomattox River

Marriage 1 Druthilla SMITH b: Abt 1758

Married: 28 Apr 1799 in Washington County, Virginia

========

NAME: ARCHIBALD, (REVOLUTION 4th Reg.) LEE Sex: M Birth: Abt 1758 in Resided in

Smith Co,TN (See Notes) Death: Abt 1777 in Died in the Revolutionary War

Change Date: 1 AUG 2002 at 20:20:40

Father: Richard H. II "ESQUIRE", (6grt-grndfthr) LEE b: 1710 in Buckingham Co,VA

(See Notes/LAND RECORD)

Mother: Mary, (6grt-grndmthr) GRESHAM b: Abt 1715 in Prince

Edward,VA -Across the Appomattox River (See Note)

Marriage 1 Spouse Unknown

Married: 28 APR 1799 in Washington County,Virginia

31.

viii. ABNER LEE was born in Aug 1750 in Jackson Co,Tennessee (Buckingham Co,VA

-Moved). He died on 06 Oct 1852 in Jackson Co,Tennessee. He married (1)

CATHERINE WILSON on 20 Sep 1785 in Green County, Tennessee.

Part 5: Outline Descendant Report for William Lee

The next 'Outline Descendant Report for William Lee' is what I have been able to compile as accurately up to current day from my Lees of Virginia data files. There may be more descendants that connect to these branches that I am unaware of but hopefully this gives a good 'map' of where they connect to the William Lee lineage from the branches that I show.

All these lines from have been well researched and vetted. Many of the descendants have done their DNA as well – both male and female descendants, both Autosomal, Y-DNA and Mitochondrial. I hope this all clarifies that William Lee was the son of Colonel Richard lee as claimed, his children and descendants as listed here in this book are descendants of Colonel Richard Lee as well, regardless of what has been said against this truth.

═══

I suggest all descendants of the Lees of Virginia lines, or those who suspect they may be, get your DNA tested at a reputable laboratory, upload your DNA results onto a reputable DNA genealogy analytic site such as

GEDMatch that even the Department of Justice uses for DNA forensics, and use the tools there that are publicly available and verifiable to confirm your ancestry. Don't depend on others outside opinions and analysis of your DNA to verify your important family history research.

Outline Descendant Report for William Lee

1 William Lee b: Abt. 1644 in Charles City, Co, Virginia, Colony; Wm Lee was adult at time of father's Will probated, d: Abt. 1696 in 1696/1703 estate suit, King and Queen, Va; Source: Northumberland County Court Transcript: 1687-1699 Order Book Part 2 - Northumberland Co Va; Hamrick: Pg 740 Northumberland County Court September 16, 1696 Upon the Petition of MARY SCREVER formerly HEATH Executrix of the Last Will and Testament of Capt. WILLIAM LEE the said Will here in Court produced, which in the Court's Opinion (being well acquainted with the hand of the said Capt. LEE) was written by his own hand but the Witnesses not forthcoming a Probate is granted her of the Last Will and Testament

+ Alice FELTON b: Abt. 1644 in of, Richmond, Co, Va, m: Abt. 1675, d: Abt. 1703 in St Stephen Parsh, King and Queen, Co, Va; Y

...2 Mary Lee b: Abt. 1676 in Richmond Co, Westmoreland, Va, area

+ William Heath b: Abt. 1668 in Richmond Co, Westmoreland, Va, area, m: Abt. 1692 in Westmoreland, Richmond, Va, area, d: Bef. 1795 in Richmond, Co Va; Y

......3 Thomas Heath b: Abt. 1693 in Richmond, Westmoreland, Va, area

......3 Samuel Heath b: Abt. 1694 in Richmond, Westmoreland, Va, area

+ Bartholomew Schreever b: Abt. 1670 in Richmond, Westmoreland, Va, area, m: Abt. 1695 in Westmoreland, Richmond, second husband, area

...2 Richard Henry Lee b: Abt. 1678 in Surry, County, Va, d: 10 Dec 1726 in N. Farnham, parish, Richmond Co. Va.; Y

+ Mary YOUNG b: Abt. 1679 in King & Queens Co., Virginia, m: 1695 in King & Queens Co., Virginia, d: Buckingham, Virginia, USA; Y

......3 Richard Henry LEE b: Abt. 1707 in Buckingham co., VA or Northumberland, Va, d: Aft. 1790 in Jackson Co., Tenn; Y

+ Mary GRESHAM or Grisham b: Abt. 1709 in Va, m: Abt. 1727, d: 1767 in Buckingham Co., Va; Y

.........4 Agnes LEE b: 15 Mar 1728 in Buckingham, Va., d: 12 Nov 1774 in Lee Valley, Hawkins, Ten; Y

+ William LEE b: Abt. 1727 in Meherrin Parish, Brunswick Co., VA, m: Abt. 1748, d: 12 Sep 1796 in Union Co, Sc; Y

...........5 Thomas LEE b: Abt. 1749 in Meherrin Parish, Brunswick Co., VA, d: Bedford, Tennessee; Y

+ Hannah MURPHY b: 1752 in Union, Sc, m: 1770 in Union, Sc, d: 07 Oct 1787 in Union, Sc; Y

...............6 William LEE b: 1772 in Union, Sc, d: 1838 in Union, Sc; Y

...............6 Amos LEE b: 1774 in Of, Virginia, d: Bef. 04 Dec 1843 in Union, Sc; Y

...............6 Drucilla LEE b: 1776 in Union, Sc

...............6 Mirian LEE b: 1778 in Union, Sc

...............6 Miriam LEE b: 1778 in Virginia

...............6 Sarah LEE b: 1780 in Union, Sc

...............6 Joseph LEE b: 1782 in Union, Sc

...............6 Thomas LEE b: 1784 in Union, Sc

...............6 Michael Byrd LEE b: 07 Oct 1787 in Union, Sc, d: 13 Dec 1837 in Union, Sc; Y

+ Mary Willard b: 21 Jan 1793 in Union, Union County, South, m: 1810 in Union, Union County, South

...................7 Catherine LEE b: 11 Oct 1811 in Union, Union County, South

...................7 Sarah LEE b: 09 Mar 1813 in Union, Union County, South

...................7 Berry Willard LEE b: 18 Jul 1814 in Union, Union County, South

...................7 Drucilla LEE b: 16 Feb 1816 in Union, Union County, South

...................7 Elizabeth LEE b: 08 Mar 1818 in Union, Union County, South

...................7 Elena LEE b: 14 Nov 1819 in Union, Union County, South

...................7 Mary Frances LEE b: 30 Nov 1821 in Union, Union County, South

...................7 Robert Byrd LEE b: 22 Dec 1822 in Union, Union County, South

...................7 John Thomas LEE b: 26 Apr 1826 in Union, Union County, South

...................7 Martha Jane LEE b: 12 Aug 1828 in Union, Union County, South

...................7 Eveline LEE b: 15 Nov 1831 in Union, Union County, South

...................7 Mairian Caroline LEE b: 22 Jul 1834 in Union, Union County, South

+ Sarah SMITH b: 04 Jun 1769 in Of, South Carolina, m: 26 May 1789, d: 19 Feb 1813 ; Y

...............6 William LEE b: 15 Jan 1791 in Of, Virginia, d: 01 Jun 1818 ; Y

............6 Jeremiah LEE b: 08 May 1793 in Of, Virginia, d: 08 Apr 1795 ; Y
............6 Hannah LEE b: 28 Mar 1795 in Of, Virginia, d: 06 Apr 1795 ; Y
............6 Sarah LEE b: 03 May 1796 in Of, Virginia
............6 Catherine Breed LEE b: 20 Feb 1799 in Of, Virginia
............6 David Lewis LEE b: 04 Apr 1801 in Of, Virginia
............6 Ann Susannah LEE b: 23 Jan 1803 in Of, Virginia
............6 Green Thomas LEE b: 19 Oct 1805 in Union Dist, South Carolina, d: 01 Jul 1889 ; Y
       + Henrietta Charlotte JACKSON b: Abt. 1807 in Union Co., Sc
............6 Charlotte LEE b: 06 Feb 1808 in Of, Virginia
............6 Margaret LEE b: 21 Feb 1810 in Of, Virginia, d: 20 Nov 1872 ; Y
............6 Lavinia Olivia LEE b: 23 Feb 1812 in Of, Virginia, d: 03 Oct 1862 in Union, Union, South
       Carolina; Y
............6 Macey LEE b: 17 Feb 1813 in Of, Virginia, d: 12 Sep 1813 ; Y
..........5 William LEE b: Abt. 1751 in Meherrin Parish, Brunswick Co., VA, d: 1838 in Union Co, Sc; Y
..........5 Jean (Jane) LEE b: Abt. 1755 in Meherrin Parish, Brunswick Co., VA
       + Daniel HOWELL b: Abt. 1755 in Union Co., Sc, m: Abt. 1795 in Union Co., Sc
..........5 Catherine LEE b: Abt. 1757 in Meherrin Parish, Brunswick Co., VA, d: Abt. 1807 in Warren Co.,
       GA; Y
       + Joseph BREED' b: 1738 in Union, South Carolina, d: 1807 ; Y
..........5 Nancy Anna LEE b: 24 Feb 1760 in Meherrin Parish, Brunswick Co., VA, d: Dec 1834 in St.
       Helena Parish, LA; Y
       + James JACKSON b: Abt. 1758, m: Abt. 1788 in Union Co., Sc
............6 Sarah JACKSON b: 1789 in Union Co., Sc, d: Livingston, LA; Y
............6 ELizabeth JACKSON b: 04 Jun 1800 in Union Co., Sc, d: 05 Jun 1885 in St. Helena,
       Louisiana; Y
............6 Nancy JACKSON b: Abt. 1803
............6 Lavina JACKSON b: Abt. 1805
..........5 Oliviah LEE b: Abt. 1761 in Meherrin Parish, Brunswick Co., VA, d: Aft. 1830 in Rapides Parish,
       LA; Y
       + Isaac FRAZIER b: Abt. 1760, m: Abt. 1879
..........5 Sarah LEE b: Abt. 1763 in <, Easternshore, Tn>
       + Ephraim BATES m: 06 May 1773 in Litchfield, CT
..........5 Joseph LEE b: Abt. 1765 in <, Union Co, Sc>, d: 1812 in Union Co, Sc; Y
..........5 John LEE b: 25 Nov 1770 in Goshen Hill, Union, South Carolina, d: 23 Nov 1823 in Union Co,
       Sc; Y
       + Hannah COOPER b: 06 Jan 1775 in Goshen Hill, Union, South Carolina, m: Abt. 1795, d: 14
       May 1830 ; Y
............6 William Calhoon LEE b: 28 Feb 1796 in Goshen Hill, Union, South Carolina, d: 06 May 1864
       in Paulding, Union, South Carolina; Y
............6 John LEE b: 12 Dec 1797 in Goshen Hill, Union, South Carolina, d: 23 Nov 1823 ; Y
............6 Lydria LEE b: 03 Aug 1800 in Goshen Hill, Union, Sc, d: 23 Oct 1871 ; Y
............6 Sarah Ann LEE b: 19 May 1803 in Union, Union, Sc, d: 09 Oct 1840 in Union, Union, Sc; Y
............6 Hannah LEE b: 20 Jan 1804 in Goshen Hill, Union, South Carolina, d: 17 Dec 1883 ; Y
............6 Persilla Ann LEE b: 25 Nov 1805 in Goshen Hill, Union, South Carolina, d: 07 Nov 1822 ; Y
............6 Jonathan LEE b: 19 Jun 1809 in Goshen Hill, Union, South Carolina, d: 20 Sep 1882 ; Y
............6 Lydia LEE b: 30 Aug 1810 in Goshen Hill, Union, South Carolina, d: 23 Oct 1871 ; Y
............6 Margaret Elizabeth LEE b: 12 Mar 1811 in Goshen Hill, Union, South Carolina, d: 09 Sep
       1877 ; Y
............6 Jeremiah Sampson LEE b: 16 Jan 1814 in Goshen Hill, Union, South Carolina, d: 25 Sep
       1875 ; Y
............6 Jeremiah E. LEE b: Goshen Hill, Union, Sc, d: Bef. 1875 in Paulding, Ga; Y
..........5 Michael LEE b: Union Co., Sc, d: 1807 in Union Co. Sc; Y
       + Drucilla MURPHY b: Abt. 1759 in Union, South Carolina, m: Abt. 1779 in Cross Keys, Union
       County, Sc, d: 05 Sep 1814 in Union, South Carolina; Y
............6 Holly LEE b: Abt. 1780 in Union Co, Sc

..............6 Mariam LEE b: Abt. 1786 in Union Co, Sc, d: Aft. 1854 ; Y
..............6 Robert LEE b: Abt. 1788 in Union Co, Sc, d: 1832 in Union Co, Sc; Y
..............6 Michael LEE b: Abt. 1790 in Union Co, Sc, d: Bef. 1853 ; Y
..............6 Joseph LEE b: Abt. 1792 in Union Co, Sc
..............6 Catherine LEE b: Abt. 1794 in Union Co, Sc
..............6 Thomas LEE b: Abt. 1796 in Union Co, Sc, d: Bef. 1853 ; Y
..............6 Drucila LEE twin b: Union Co, Sc, d: 1953 ; Y
..............6 Delila LEE twin b: Union Co, Sc
.........4 John Lee b: Abt. 1733 in Buckingham Co., Va, d: Feb 1756 in Reed Creek, Washington Co., Va;
        Y

        + [unknown spouse]
..............5 Mary WEBB Lee b: Abt. 1757 in VA, d: 1791 in Saltville, Washington Co., Va; Y
          + John Jackie Lee b: 1748 in Albemarle Co., Va, m: 27 Apr 1787 in Saltville, Washington Co.,
            Va, d: Aft. 16 May 1797 in Saltville, Washington Co., Va; Y
..............6 Henry Lee b: 1788 in Washington Co., Va, d: Abt. 1870 in Wayne Co. TN; Y
            + Darcus COPELAND b: Abt. 1790 in Chatham Co. NC, m: Sep 1808 in Overton Co., Tn, d:
              Wayne Co. TN; Y
..............6 Martha Patsey Lee b: 1789 in Washington Co., Va, d: Abt. 1877 in Oak Hill, Overton CO, TN;
        Y
            + Thomas CANNON b: Abt. 1784 in Overton Co., Tn, m: 1809 in Overton Co., Tn, d: 24 Oct
              1863 in Overton CO, TN; Y
..................7 Catherine Cannon b: 1810 in Overton Co., Tn
..................7 Elizabeth Cannon b: 1811 in Overton CO, TN, d: 27 Sep 1876 in Overton CO, TN; Y
                + Edward Sisco b: 16 May 1809 in Overton CO, TN, m: Abt. 1838 in Overton CO, TN, d: 01
                  Mar 1898 in Overton CO, TN; Y
....................8 Sarah J. Sisco b: Abt. 1838 in Dry Hollow, Overton CO, Tn
....................8 Thomas "Tommy" Sisco b: 15 Jul 1839 in Dry Hollow, Overton CO, Tn, d: 26 Nov 1911 in
                    Dry Hollow, Overton CO, Tn; Y
....................8 Mary "Polly" Sisco b: Abt. 1842 in Overton CO, TN
....................8 Delilah "Patsy" Sisco b: Abt. 1844 in Dry Hollow, Overton CO, Tn
....................8 Catherine Elizabeth Sisco b: 08 May 1850 in Dry Hollow, Overton CO, Tn, d: 18 Jan 1890
                    in Overton CO, TN; Y
....................8 Lillie Anne Sisco b: 14 Jul 1854 in Dry Hollow, Overton CO, Tn, d: 20 Dec 1912 in Dry
                    Hollow, Overton CO, Tn; Y
..................7 Sarah "Sallie" Cannon b: 1812 in Overton CO, TN
                + Archibald Qualls b: 12 Feb 1806 in VA, d: 22 Nov 1861 in Overton CO, TN; Y
....................8 Henry Qualls b: Abt. 1828 in Overton CO, TN
....................8 Thomas Qualls b: Abt. 1830 in Overton CO, TN
....................8 George Qualls b: Abt. 1838 in Overton CO, TN
..................7 John Cannon b: 1816 in Overton CO, TN
                + Jemima Fite b: Abt. 1816
....................8 Benjamin Cannon b: Abt. 1835 in Overton CO, TN
....................8 Martha Cannon b: Sep 1835 in Overton CO, TN, d: 30 Mar 1930 in Overton CO, TN; Y
....................8 Arminta Cannon b: Mar 1838 in Overton CO, TN, d: 1907 in Overton CO, TN; Y
....................8 Delila Cannon b: Abt. 1840 in Overton CO, TN
....................8 William J. Cannon b: Abt. 1841 in Overton CO, TN
....................8 Christopher C. Cannon b: Abt. 1842 in Overton CO, TN
....................8 James K. P. Cannon b: 27 Oct 1844 in Overton CO, TN
....................8 Nancy J. Cannon b: Abt. 1846 in Overton CO, TN
....................8 Catharine Cannon b: Abt. 1848 in Overton CO, TN
....................8 Sarah Cannon b: Mar 1850 in Overton CO, TN
....................8 John Cannon b: 15 Mar 1851 in Overton CO, TN, d: 1934 ; Y
....................8 Elizabeth Cannon b: Abt. 1852 in Overton CO, TN
....................8 Thomas B. Cannon b: Abt. 1854 in Overton CO, TN, d: Bef. 1899 in Overton CO, TN; Y
....................8 Margaret Cannon b: 15 Feb 1856 in Overton CO, TN, d: 26 Oct 1922 ; Y

...............8 Elmira C. Cannon b: Abt. 1859 in Overton CO, TN
...............7 William M. Cannon b: 07 Dec 1818 in Algood, OvertonCO, TN, d: 18 Apr 1908 in Roaring
          River, Overton CO, TN; Y
          + Catherine Oga Copeland b: 11 Apr 1814 in Overton CO, TN, m: 19 Jan 1835 in Overton
          CO, TN, d: 05 Feb 1887 in Overton CO, TN; Y
...............8 John S. Cannon b: 1839 in Overton CO, TN, d: 11 Aug 1860 in Overton CO, TN; Y
...............8 Jasper Newton Cannon b: 26 May 1841 in Overton CO, TN, d: 06 Jul 1924 in Overton
          CO, TN; Y
...............8 Celia J. Cannon b: 1843 in Overton CO, TN, d: 22 Aug 1860 in Overton CO, TN; Y
...............8 Mary P. Cannon b: 1845 in Overton CO, TN, d: 1845 in Overton CO, TN; Y
...............8 Sarah Elizabeth Cannon b: 06 Apr 1848 in Overton CO, TN, d: 11 Jun 1931 in Trenton,
          Gibson CO, TN; Y
...............8 James T. Cannon b: 1850 in Overton CO, TN, d: 1854 in Overton CO, TN; Y
...............8 Martha E. Cannon b: 03 Sep 1854 in Overton CO, TN, d: 07 May 1928 in Overton CO.
          TN; Y
...............7 Alexander Cannon b: Bet. 1820–1825 in Overton CO, TN
...............7 Mary Jane Cannon b: 05 Jan 1822 in Livingstonl, Overton CO, TN, d: 19 Mar 1891 in
          Green Forest, Carroll CO, AR; Y
          + Jonathan Riley Norris b: 21 Oct 1818 in Wilkes CO, NC, m: 07 Apr 1843 in Oak Hill,
          Overton CO, TN, d: 15 Nov 1896 in Green Forest, Carroll CO, AR; Y
...............8 Francis Marion Norris b: 04 Feb 1844 in Oak Hill, Overton CO, TN, d: 30 Oct 1897 in
          Carroll CO, AR; Y
...............8 Riley Norris b: 1845 in Oak Hill, Overton CO, TN
...............8 Granville Newton Norris b: 16 Mar 1845 in Oak Hill, Overton CO, TN, d: 16 Nov 1925 ; Y
...............8 George Washington Norris b: 23 Jun 1846 in Oak Hill, Overton CO, TN, d: 1883 in Carroll
          CO, AR; Y
...............8 James Ephraim Norris b: 28 Sep 1848 in Oak Hill, Overton CO, TN, d: 26 Jul 1918 ; Y
...............8 Martha Elizabeth Norris b: 22 Jul 1850 in Oak Hill, Overton CO, TN
...............8 Andrew Jackson Norris b: 23 Mar 1852 in Carrollton, Carroll CO, AR, d: 1940 ; Y
...............8 Mary Jane Norris b: 1854 in Carrollton, Carroll CO, AR, d: 03 Mar 1899 ; Y
...............8 Thomas Gilbert "Tom" Norris b: 28 Nov 1856 in Carrollton, Carroll CO, AR, d: 23 May
          1932 ; Y
...............8 Martin Columbus Norris b: 15 Jul 1858 in Green Forest, Carroll CO, AR, d: 17 Sep 1880 ;
          Y
...............8 John Cannon Norris b: 14 Oct 1860 in Green Forest, Carroll CO, AR, d: 1939 ; Y
...............8 Benjamin Franklin Norris b: 20 Oct 1862 in Green Forest, Carroll CO. AR, d: 18 Aug 1898
          ; Y
...............8 Sarah Lavernia Norris b: 1865 in Green Forest, Carroll CO, AR, d: 1899 ; Y
...............8 Erasmus Lee Norris b: 14 Aug 1868 in Green Forest, Carroll CO, AR, d: 09 May 1897 ; Y
...............7 Delila Cannon b: Abt. 1826 in Overton CO, TN
          + Jesse Norris b: 1810 in Wilkes CO. NC, d: Bef. Dec 1849 in Oak Hill, Overton CO, TN; Y
...............8 Catherine Norris b: 1848 in Overton CO, TN
...............8 Thomas Jesse Norris b: Dec 1849 in Overton CO, TN
...............7 Patsy Cannon b: Abt. 1832 in Overton CO, TN
          + Hollers
...............7 Joel Cannon b: Abt. 1833 in Overton CO, TN
          + Celia Livesay
...............6 Jesse Lee b: 12 Jan 1790 in Washington Co., Va. d: 20 Sep 1866 in Waynesboro, TN; Y
          + Margaret Nelson b: 03 Sep 1805 in North Carolina, m: 15 Jun 1828
...............7 Nancy C. Lee b: 20 Sep 1832
...............7 Christian Chesley Lee b: 08 Dec 1833
          + [unknown spouse]
...............8 George William Lee b: Abt. 1858
          + [unknown spouse]
...............9 Claude Dean Lee b: Abt. 1884

+ [unknown spouse]
.........................10 Norma Monette Lee b: Abt. 191 AD
+ mr RIDDLE
.........................11 Susan (Susie) Monette RIDDLE
+ Mr POLLOCK
.........................12 Christopher POLLOCK
.........................12 Stephanie POLLOCK
.........................12 Sarah POLLOCK
...............7 Jesse Lee b: Abt. 1835
...............7 Diadema Lee b: Abt. 1836
...............7 Martha Lee b: Abt. 1841
...............7 Elizabeth Lee b: Abt. 1848
............6 John L. Lee b: 1791 in Saltville, Washington Co., Va, d: Bef. Jan 1870 in Overton Co., Tn; Y
+ Molly Rebecca Matthews b: 1796 in GA, m: 1813 in Overton Co. TN, d: 1870 in Overton
Co., Tn; Y
.................7 Mahalia Lee b: 18 Aug 1813, d: 20 Jan 1893 in Hiram Poston cemetery, Overton County,
Tennessee; Y
+ Hiram Poston b: 15 Jul 1811, m: Bet. 1829–1859, d: 25 Sep 1902 in Hiram Poston
cemetery, Overton County, Tennessee; Y
....................8 Zadock Poston b: 20 May 1835, d: 25 Mar 1916 ; Y
+ Mary Jane Langford b: 06 Dec 1840, m: 1855, d: 14 Mar 1928 ; Y
....................8 Alzora Poston b: 01 Sep 1837, d: 22 Apr 1923 in Hiram Poston cemetery, Overton
County, Tennessee; Y
....................8 Matilda Poston b: 1839, d: Bet. 1853–1933 ; Y
+ Wilbourn Stewart b: Bet. 1822–1842, m: Bet. 1853–1886, d: Bet. 1856–1928 ; Y
+ Amos Carmack b: 15 Oct 1849, d: 28 Jul 1911 ; Y
+ Wilburn Stewart
....................8 Mary (Polly) Poston b: 09 Sep 1840, d: Bet. 1892–1935 in Roaring River Cemetery,
Overton County, TN; Y
+ William Jackson Stewart b: 22 Jan 1834, m: Bet. 1853–1884, d: 01 Aug 1919 in
Roaring River Cemetery, Overton County, TN; Y
.........................9 Maggie Mahalia Stewart b: Bet. 1856–1882, d: Bet. 1872–1965 ; Y
.........................9 James Jefferson Stewart b: Bet. 1856–1882, d: Bet. 1876–1963 ; Y
.........................9 John Henry Stewart b: Bet. 1856–1882, d: Bet. 1876–1963 ; Y
.........................9 Ida May Stewart b: Bet. 1856–1882, d: Bet. 1872–1965 ; Y
.........................9 Sallie Stewart b: Bet. 1856–1882, d: Bet. 1872–1965 ; Y
.........................9 Jesse Davis Stewart b: Bet. 1856–1882, d: Bet. 1862–1963 ; Y
.........................9 Jenny Lind Stewart b: Bet. 1856–1882, d: Bet. 1872–1965 ; Y
.........................9 Lee Johnson Stewart b: Bet. 1856–1882, d: Bet. 1876–1963 ; Y
.........................9 Sanford Alford Stewart b: 01 Jan 1879, d: Bet. 1896–1969 ; Y
.........................9 Charles Lee Stewart b: 21 Aug 1879, d: Jun 1898 ; Y
.........................9 Hiram Stewart b: 1890, d: 1898 ; Y
....................8 Louis H. Poston b: 28 Jun 1842, d: 02 May 1916 in Copeland Cemetery, Overton County,
TN; Y
+ Sarah Copeland b: Bet. 1833–1854, m: 14 Dec 1871, d: Bet. 1876–1943 ; Y
....................8 Richard Jackson Poston b: 02 May 1844, d: 27 Mar 1919 in Collins, TX; Y
+ Nancy May Stewart b: Bet. 1840–1860, m: Bet. 1861–1894, d: Bet. 1861–1944 in
Collins, TX; Y
....................8 Huntsman Poston b: 1846, d: 1875 ; Y
+ Emmaline Warden b: Bet. 1829–1854, m: Bet. 1859–1874, d: Bet. 1872–1942 ; Y
.........................9 Erasmus Poston b: 17 Jul 1869 in Overton County, TN, d: 20 Feb 1943 in Oklahona
Cemetery, Overton County, TN; Y
+ Peek b: 1848, m: Bet. 1864–1874, d: Bet. 1864–1942 ; Y
+ Emeline Warden
....................8 Anna Poston b: 1848, d: Bet. 1862–1942 ; Y

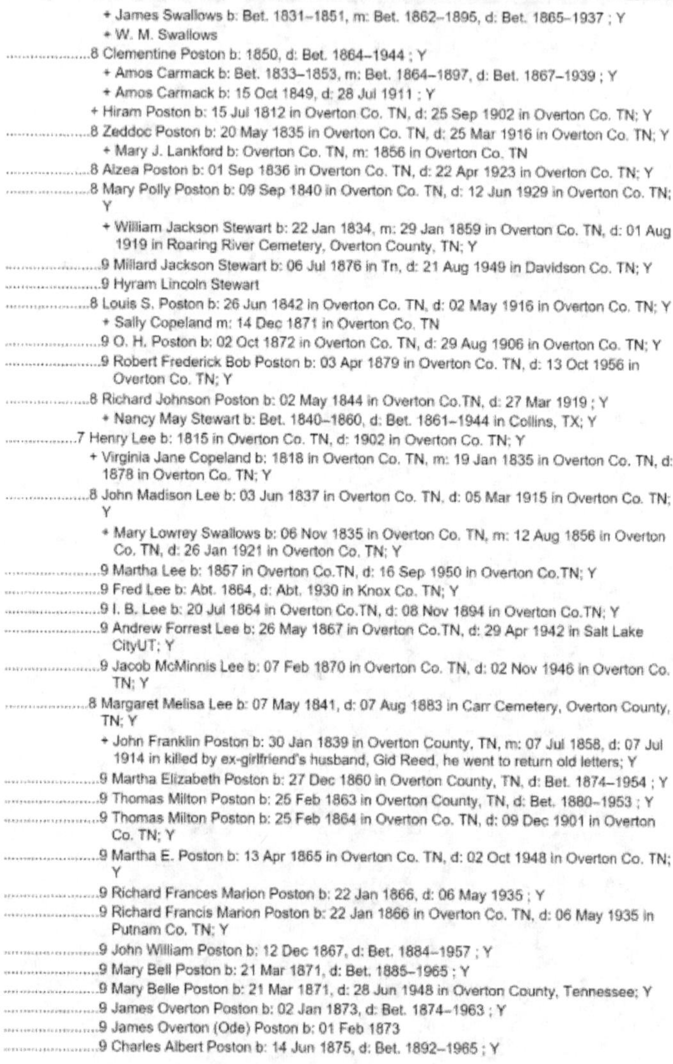

      + James Swallows b: Bet. 1831–1851, m: Bet. 1862–1895, d: Bet. 1865–1937 ; Y

      + W. M. Swallows

.................8 Clementine Poston b: 1850, d: Bet. 1864–1944 ; Y

      + Amos Carmack b: Bet. 1833–1853, m: Bet. 1864–1897, d: Bet. 1867–1939 ; Y

      + Amos Carmack b: 15 Oct 1849, d: 28 Jul 1911 : Y

    + Hiram Poston b: 15 Jul 1812 in Overton Co. TN, d: 25 Sep 1902 in Overton Co. TN; Y

.................8 Zeddoc Poston b: 20 May 1835 in Overton Co. TN, d: 25 Mar 1916 in Overton Co. TN; Y

      + Mary J. Lankford b: Overton Co. TN, m: 1856 in Overton Co. TN

.................8 Alzea Poston b: 01 Sep 1836 in Overton Co. TN, d: 22 Apr 1923 in Overton Co. TN; Y

.................8 Mary Polly Poston b: 09 Sep 1840 in Overton Co. TN, d: 12 Jun 1929 in Overton Co. TN; Y

      + William Jackson Stewart b: 22 Jan 1834, m: 29 Jan 1859 in Overton Co. TN, d: 01 Aug 1919 in Roaring River Cemetery, Overton County, TN; Y

.................9 Millard Jackson Stewart b: 06 Jul 1876 in Tn, d: 21 Aug 1949 in Davidson Co. TN; Y

.................9 Hyram Lincoln Stewart

.................8 Louis S. Poston b: 26 Jun 1842 in Overton Co. TN, d: 02 May 1916 in Overton Co. TN; Y

      + Sally Copeland m: 14 Dec 1871 in Overton Co. TN

.................9 O. H. Poston b: 02 Oct 1872 in Overton Co. TN, d: 29 Aug 1906 in Overton Co. TN; Y

.................9 Robert Frederick Bob Poston b: 03 Apr 1879 in Overton Co. TN, d: 13 Oct 1956 in Overton Co. TN; Y

.................8 Richard Johnson Poston b: 02 May 1844 in Overton Co.TN, d: 27 Mar 1919 ; Y

      + Nancy May Stewart b: Bet. 1840–1860, d: Bet. 1861–1944 in Collins, TX; Y

.................7 Henry Lee b: 1815 in Overton Co. TN, d: 1902 in Overton Co. TN; Y

      + Virginia Jane Copeland b: 1818 in Overton Co. TN, m: 19 Jan 1835 in Overton Co. TN, d: 1878 in Overton Co. TN; Y

.................8 John Madison Lee b: 03 Jun 1837 in Overton Co. TN, d: 05 Mar 1915 in Overton Co. TN; Y

      + Mary Lowrey Swallows b: 06 Nov 1835 in Overton Co. TN, m: 12 Aug 1856 in Overton Co. TN, d: 26 Jan 1921 in Overton Co. TN; Y

.................9 Martha Lee b: 1857 in Overton Co.TN, d: 16 Sep 1950 in Overton Co.TN; Y

.................9 Fred Lee b: Abt. 1864, d: Abt. 1930 in Knox Co. TN; Y

.................9 I. B. Lee b: 20 Jul 1864 in Overton Co.TN, d: 08 Nov 1894 in Overton Co.TN; Y

.................9 Andrew Forrest Lee b: 26 May 1867 in Overton Co.TN, d: 29 Apr 1942 in Salt Lake CityUT; Y

.................9 Jacob McMinnis Lee b: 07 Feb 1870 in Overton Co. TN, d: 02 Nov 1946 in Overton Co. TN; Y

.................8 Margaret Melisa Lee b: 07 May 1841, d: 07 Aug 1883 in Carr Cemetery, Overton County, TN; Y

      + John Franklin Poston b: 30 Jan 1839 in Overton County, TN, m: 07 Jul 1858, d: 07 Jul 1914 in killed by ex-girlfriend's husband, Gid Reed, he went to return old letters; Y

.................9 Martha Elizabeth Poston b: 27 Dec 1860 in Overton County, TN, d: Bet. 1874–1954 ; Y

.................9 Thomas Milton Poston b: 25 Feb 1863 in Overton County, TN, d: Bet. 1880–1953 ; Y

.................9 Thomas Milton Poston b: 25 Feb 1864 in Overton Co. TN, d: 09 Dec 1901 in Overton Co. TN; Y

.................9 Martha E. Poston b: 13 Apr 1865 in Overton Co. TN, d: 02 Oct 1948 in Overton Co. TN; Y

.................9 Richard Frances Marion Poston b: 22 Jan 1866, d: 06 May 1935 ; Y

.................9 Richard Francis Marion Poston b: 22 Jan 1866 in Overton Co. TN, d: 06 May 1935 in Putnam Co. TN; Y

.................9 John William Poston b: 12 Dec 1867, d: Bet. 1884–1957 ; Y

.................9 Mary Bell Poston b: 21 Mar 1871, d: Bet. 1885–1965 ; Y

.................9 Mary Belle Poston b: 21 Mar 1871, d: 28 Jun 1948 in Overton County, Tennessee; Y

.................9 James Overton Poston b: 02 Jan 1873, d: Bet. 1874–1963 ; Y

.................9 James Overton (Ode) Poston b: 01 Feb 1873

.................9 Charles Albert Poston b: 14 Jun 1875, d: Bet. 1892–1965 ; Y

.................9 Sallie Poston b: 05 Sep 1880 in Overton Co. TN, d: 19 Aug 1962 in Overton Co. TN; Y
.................9 Sally Ann Poston b: 05 Sep 1880 in Overton County, TN, d: Bet. 1894–1974 ; Y
.............8 Fred Lee b: 1843 in Overton Co. TN, d: Mo; Y
.............8 Hannah Elizabeth Lee b: 27 Dec 1845 in Overton County, Tennessee, d: 12 Jun 1880 in
             Overton County, Tennessee; Y
                 + Richard T. "Dick" Poston b: 08 Aug 1843 in Overton County, Tennessee-Oak and
                   Windle Communities, m: Bet. 1861–1877, d: 27 Jan 1924 in Overton County,
                   Tennessee-Copeland Cemetery; Y
.................9 Alonzo Lon Poston b: 22 Sep 1865, d: Bet. 1886–1955 ; Y
.................9 Sarah Elizabeth Poston b: 08 Jan 1867, d: 25 Dec 1941 ; Y
.................9 William Edward Poston b: 05 Nov 1870, d: 07 Dec 1952 ; Y
.................9 Mary Ellen Poston b: 14 Jan 1872, d: Bet. 1890–1966 ; Y
.................9 Frederic Poston b: 10 Sep 1876, d: 16 Dec 1958 ; Y
.................9 Johnnie Bell Poston b: 02 Sep 1877 in Overton County, Tennessee, d: 11 Jan 1954 in
                   Okalona Cemetery, Overton County; Y
.................9 Joe Abner Poston b: 12 Nov 1879, d: 07 Feb 1949 in Copeland Cemetery, Overton
                   County, TN; Y
.............8 Rebecca Ellen Lee b: 08 Nov 1848 in Overton Co. TN, d: 04 Jun 1918 in Overton Co.
             TN; Y
                 + Elias Hedrick b: Overton Co. TN
.............8 Bethiar Lee b: 05 Apr 1851 in Overton Co. TN, d: 03 Nov 1905 in Overton Co.TN; Y
                 + Marion H. Deck b: 08 Jul 1832 in Overton Co. TN, d: 13 Mar 1906 in Overton Co. TN; Y
.................9 Oliver G. Deck b: 27 Apr 1883 in Overton Co. TN, d: 24 Mar 1968 in Overton Co. TN; Y
.................9 Edna Deck
                 + Jane Victory b: Abt. 1829 in Tn, m: Abt. 1851, d: 1885 in Overton Co. TN; Y
.............8 Almeda Lee b: 1851 in Tn, d: 06 Jul 1931 in Overton Co. TN; Y
.............8 Mahaley Lee b: 23 Oct 1859 in Overton Co. TN, d: 23 Dec 1922 in Overton Co. TN; Y
                 + E. J. Stout
.............8 Mac M. Lee b: 01 Nov 1859 in Overton Co. TN, d: 10 Mar 1925 in Overton Co. TN; Y
                 + Almeda b: Abt. 1852
.............8 Altly D. Lee b: 1863 in Overton Co. TN
.............8 William Lee b: Dec 1869 in Overton Co. TN
.............8 James Virgil Lee b: 13 Jun 1871 in Overton Co. TN, d: 28 Jul 1942 in Overton Co. TN; Y
                 + Delia Wallace
.........7 Malachi Lee b: 15 Apr 1816 in Overton Co. TN, d: 14 Mar 1870 in Overton Co. TN; Y
             + Annie Cox b: 22 Feb 1822 in Overton Co. TN, m: Bef. 1839 in Overton Co. TN, d: Aft. 10
               Jul 1915 in Overton Co. TN; Y
.............8 Nancy Lee b: Abt. 1839 in Overton Co. TN
.............8 Rebecca Lee b: Abt. 1840 in Overton Co. TN
.............8 Obedience Biddie Lee b: 16 Sep 1842 in Overton Co. TN, d: 10 Jul 1915 in Overton Co.
             TN; Y
                 + Alvin Cull Boswell b: 10 Dec 1842 in Overton Co. TN, d: 01 Dec 1900 in Overton Co.
                   TN; Y
.............8 John Henry Lee b: 29 Apr 1846 in Overton Co. TN, d: 08 Apr 1923 in Overton Co. TN; Y
.............8 Matilda Lee b: Abt. 1848 in Overton Co. TN
.............8 Margaret Lee b: Abt. 1850 in Overton Co. TN
.............8 Canada Lee b: Abt. 1851 in Overton Co. TN
.............8 Anna Lee b: Abt. 1853 in Overton Co. TN
.............8 George Washington Lee b: Abt. 1857 in Overton Co. TN
                 + Belle Walker
.................9 Conway Lee b: 17 Sep 1883 in Overton Co. TN, d: 17 Jul 1967 in Overton Co. TN; Y
.............8 Overton Lee b: Abt. 1858 in Overton Co. TN
.............8 Margaret Epsy Lee b: 1860 in Overton Co. TN, d: 1896 in Overton Co. TN; Y
                 + James W. Seahorn b: 1852 in Overton Co. TN, d: 1938 in Overton Co. TN; Y
.............8 Larkin Lee

...............7 Canada Kennedy Lee b: 1818 in Overton Co. TN, d: 1890 in Overton Co.TN; Y
        + Marthy Maxwell b: 1823 in Overton Co. TN, m: Abt. 1840 in Overton Co. TN
...............8 Tennesse Lee b: Abt. 1841 in Overton Co. TN
...............8 Amela Lee b: Abt. 1842 in Overton Co. TN
...............8 Josiah Lee b: Abt. 1844 in Overton Co. TN
...............8 Martha Lee b: Abt. 1846 in Overton Co. TN
...............8 John Lee b: Abt. 1847 in Overton Co. TN
...............8 Sarah Lee b: Abt. 1855 in Overton Co. TN
...............8 Malissa Lee b: Abt. 1863 in Overton Co. TN
...............8 Emma Lee b: Abt. 1865 in Overton Co. TN
...............8 Thomas Lee b: Abt. 1867 in Overton Co. TN
...............8 George Lee b: Abt. 1871 in Overton Co. TN
...............7 Mary Lee b: 22 Dec 1820 in Overton Co. TN, d: 01 Nov 1897 ; Y
        + John Pool Yelton
...............7 Melinda Lee b: Abt. 1822 in Overton Co., Tn, d: 1876 in Tn; Y
        + Isaac Copper b: Abt. 1818 in Overton Co., Tn, m: 1841 in Overton Co., Tn
...............7 Washington Lee b: 1824 in Overton Co.TN, d: Wayne Co. TN; Y
...............7 Adam Lee b: Bet. 1825–1830 in Overton Co. TN, d: 1853 in Overton Co.TN; Y
...............7 James Lee b: Bet. 1825–1830 in Overton Co. TN, d: 1847 in Mexico; Y
...............7 Lucinda Lee b: Abt. 1825 in Overton Co.TN, d: Overton Co.TN; Y
        + Stephen H. Gardenhire
...............7 Huntsman Lee b: Overton Co. TN
...........6 Sarah Lee b: 14 Oct 1792 in Washington Co., Va, d: 12 Oct 1877 in Overton Co., Tn; Y
        + David STEWART b: Abt. 1784 in Overton Co., Tn, m: 1807 in Overton Co., Tn
        + John GREER b: Overton Co., Tn, m: 1853 in Overton Co., Tn
...........6 Stephan Lee b: Abt. 1794 in Washington Co., Va
...........6 Thomas Lee b: Abt. 1795 in Washington Co., Va
...........6 Isaac Lee b: Abt. 1796 in Washington Co., Va
...........6 Ambrose Lee b: Abt. 1798 in Washington Co., Va
...........6 Mary Lee b: Abt. 1799 in Washington Co., Va
.......4 Dorothy Dolly LEE b: Abt. 1740 in Va, d: Tn; Y
    + Thornton b: lived in TN
.......4 George LEE b: Abt. 1743 in Va, d: 1803 in National Rd between Vandalia & Urebar RIver in ILL;
Y
    + Nancy Pinkston b: Abt. 1753, m: ?
.........5 Matilda Lee b: Abt. 1789 in Madison County, Kentucky, d: 10 Mar 1844 in Missouri; Y
    + George Woolery b: Abt. 1787 in Madison County, Kentucky, m: 1810 in Madison County,
    Kentucky, d: 28 Feb 1844 in ?; Y
.........5 Stephen Lee b: Abt. 1791 in Madison County, Kentucky, d: Abt. 1854 in ?; Y
    + Leanna Roley m: 1834 in Clark County, Illinois
.........6 Harvey Lee b: 1854 in ?, d: 1932 in Oklahoma; Y
        + Eliza Hass b: Abt. 1856, m: ?
.........7 Thomas Everett Lee b: 1878 in ?, d: 1963 in Oklahoma; Y
        + Elizabeth Flood b: Abt. 1782 in Madison County, Kentucky, m: 1823 in Edgar County, Illinois,
        d: Bef. 1831 ; Y
        + Amanda Roley b: Abt. 1612, m: 1832 in Edgar County, Illinois
.........5 Nancy Lee b: Abt. 1795 in Madison County, Kentucky, d: 1869 in Illinois; Y
    + Abraham Walters b: ?, m: ?, d: ?; Y
.........5 Enoch Lee b: Abt. 1798 in Madison County, Kentucky, d: 1861 in Illinois; Y
    + Catherine Kidwell b: ?, m: 1822 in Crawford County, Illinois, d: ?; Y
.........5 Rachel Lee b: Abt. 1800 in Madison County, Kentucky, d: Aft. 1890 in Texas; Y
    + James Kidwell b: ?, m: ?, d: ?; Y
.........5 George Lee b: 31 Mar 1804 in Madison County, Kentucky, d: 1857 in ?; Y
    + Louvicy Kidwell b: ?, m: 13 Dec 1826 in Clark County, Illinois, d: ?; Y

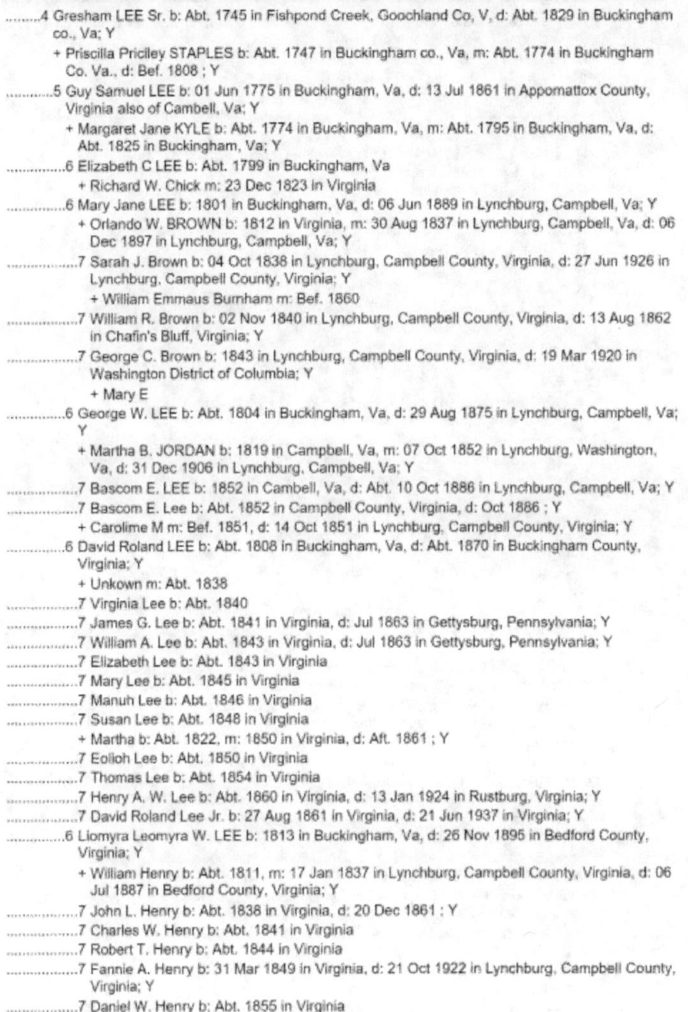

```
..........4 Gresham LEE Sr. b: Abt. 1745 in Fishpond Creek, Goochland Co, V, d: Abt. 1829 in Buckingham
          co., Va; Y
            + Priscilla Priciley STAPLES b: Abt. 1747 in Buckingham co., Va, m: Abt. 1774 in Buckingham
              Co. Va., d: Bef. 1808 ; Y
............5 Guy Samuel LEE b: 01 Jun 1775 in Buckingham, Va, d: 13 Jul 1861 in Appomattox County,
          Virginia also of Cambell, Va; Y
            + Margaret Jane KYLE b: Abt. 1774 in Buckingham, Va, m: Abt. 1795 in Buckingham, Va, d:
              Abt. 1825 in Buckingham, Va; Y
...............6 Elizabeth C LEE b: Abt. 1799 in Buckingham, Va
            + Richard W. Chick m: 23 Dec 1823 in Virginia
...............6 Mary Jane LEE b: 1801 in Buckingham, Va, d: 06 Jun 1889 in Lynchburg, Campbell, Va; Y
            + Orlando W. BROWN b: 1812 in Virginia, m: 30 Aug 1837 in Lynchburg, Campbell, Va, d: 06
              Dec 1897 in Lynchburg, Campbell, Va; Y
..................7 Sarah J. Brown b: 04 Oct 1838 in Lynchburg, Campbell County, Virginia, d: 27 Jun 1926 in
              Lynchburg, Campbell County, Virginia; Y
            + William Emmaus Burnham m: Bef. 1860
..................7 William R. Brown b: 02 Nov 1840 in Lynchburg, Campbell County, Virginia, d: 13 Aug 1862
              in Chafin's Bluff, Virginia; Y
..................7 George C. Brown b: 1843 in Lynchburg, Campbell County, Virginia, d: 19 Mar 1920 in
              Washington District of Columbia; Y
            + Mary E
...............6 George W. LEE b: Abt. 1804 in Buckingham, Va, d: 29 Aug 1875 in Lynchburg, Campbell, Va;
          Y
            + Martha B. JORDAN b: 1819 in Campbell, Va, m: 07 Oct 1852 in Lynchburg, Washington,
              Va, d: 31 Dec 1906 in Lynchburg, Campbell, Va; Y
..................7 Bascom E. LEE b: 1852 in Cambell, Va, d: Abt. 10 Oct 1886 in Lynchburg, Campbell, Va; Y
..................7 Bascom E. Lee b: Abt. 1852 in Campbell County, Virginia, d: Oct 1886 ; Y
            + Carolime M m: Bef. 1851, d: 14 Oct 1851 in Lynchburg, Campbell County, Virginia; Y
...............6 David Roland LEE b: Abt. 1808 in Buckingham, Va, d: Abt. 1870 in Buckingham County,
          Virginia; Y
            + Unkown m: Abt. 1838
..................7 Virginia Lee b: Abt. 1840
..................7 James G. Lee b: Abt. 1841 in Virginia, d: Jul 1863 in Gettysburg, Pennsylvania; Y
..................7 William A. Lee b: Abt. 1843 in Virginia, d: Jul 1863 in Gettysburg, Pennsylvania; Y
..................7 Elizabeth Lee b: Abt. 1843 in Virginia
..................7 Mary Lee b: Abt. 1845 in Virginia
..................7 Manuh Lee b: Abt. 1846 in Virginia
..................7 Susan Lee b: Abt. 1848 in Virginia
            + Martha b: Abt. 1822, m: 1850 in Virginia, d: Aft. 1861 ; Y
..................7 Eolioh Lee b: Abt. 1850 in Virginia
..................7 Thomas Lee b: Abt. 1854 in Virginia
..................7 Henry A. W. Lee b: Abt. 1860 in Virginia, d: 13 Jan 1924 in Rustburg, Virginia; Y
..................7 David Roland Lee Jr. b: 27 Aug 1861 in Virginia, d: 21 Jun 1937 in Virginia; Y
...............6 Liomyra Leomyra W. LEE b: 1813 in Buckingham, Va, d: 26 Nov 1895 in Bedford County,
          Virginia; Y
            + William Henry b: Abt. 1811, m: 17 Jan 1837 in Lynchburg, Campbell County, Virginia, d: 06
              Jul 1887 in Bedford County, Virginia; Y
..................7 John L. Henry b: Abt. 1838 in Virginia, d: 20 Dec 1861 ; Y
..................7 Charles W. Henry b: Abt. 1841 in Virginia
..................7 Robert T. Henry b: Abt. 1844 in Virginia
..................7 Fannie A. Henry b: 31 Mar 1849 in Virginia, d: 21 Oct 1922 in Lynchburg, Campbell County,
              Virginia; Y
..................7 Daniel W. Henry b: Abt. 1855 in Virginia
...............6 William F. LEE b: Abt. 1817 in Buckingham, Va, d: Bef. 1880 in Missouri; Y
```

+ Mary S. Schoolfield b: Abt. 1817 in Lynchburg, Campbell County, Virginia, m: 11 Dec 1838 in Lynchburg, Campbell County, Virginia

...............7 M. F. Lee b: Abt. 1844 in Howard County, Missouri

...............7 Elizabeth Lee b: Abt. 1847 in Howard County, Missouri

...............7 W. C. Lee b: Abt. 1854 in Howard County, Missouri

.............6 Robert Nelson LEE b: 19 Jun 1820 in Buckingham, Va, d: 16 Sep 1875 in Smith County, Tennessee; Y

+ Mary Jane Talbot m: 13 Oct 1841 in Lynchburg, Campbell County, Virginia, d: 30 Sep 1863 in Chesterfield County, Virginia; Y

...............7 Henry M. Lee b: Abt. 1843 in Lynchburg, Campbell County, Virginia, d: Pittsylvania County, Virginia; Y

...............7 Nancy L. Lee b: Abt. 1846 in Lynchburg, Campbell County, Virginia, d: 1940 ; Y

...............7 George W. Lee b: 21 Dec 1851 in Pittsylvania County, Virginia

...............7 Robert E. Lee b: Abt. 1854 in Virginia

...............7 Richard Jones Lee b: Abt. 1859 in Virginia

+ Margaret E. Eudailey b: Abt. 1840, m: 28 Aug 1864 in Charlotte County, Virginia

...............7 Peachie Lee b: Abt. 1867 in Virginia, d: 01 Feb 1871 in Virginia; Y

...............7 Ludwell Lee b: Abt. 1874 in Virginia

.............6 Ludwell Gresham LEE b: Bent Creek, Buckingham, Va, d: 29 Sep 1892 in Lynchburg, Campbell, Va; Y

+ Martha Susan HALL b: May 1821 in New York, m: 06 Dec 1843 in Lynchburg, Cambell, Va, d: 15 Aug 1874 in Campbell County, Virginia; Y

...............7 Katie Mary Lee b: Abt. 1846 in Lynchburg, Campbell County, Virginia, d: 1942 ; Y

+ James William Fulks m: 18 Jan 1876 in Lynchburg, Campbell County, Virginia

...............7 Henry Guy LEE b: 1848 in Lynchburg, Campbell, Va, d: 19 Mar 1861 in Lynchburg, Campbell, Va; Y

...............7 Adalade Addie LEE b: Abt. 1850 in Lynchburg, Campbell, Va

+ John Oliver Reams b: Abt. 1848, m: 22 Dec 1870 in Lynchburg, Campbell County, Virginia

...............7 Walter S. LEE b: Abt. 1852 in Lynchburg, Campbell, Va, d: Abt. 05 Feb 1908 in Campbell, Va; Y

...............7 Susan Blanche LEE b: 20 Jun 1854 in Lynchburg, Campbell, Va, d: Aft. 1900 ; Y

+ Frank Wilson Chase m: 03 Jan 1876 in Lynchburg, Campbell County, Virginia, d: Bef. 1900 ; Y

...............7 Francis Frank LEE b: 15 Mar 1857 in Lynchburg, Campbell, Va, d: 16 Aug 1943 in Lynchburg, Campbell County, Virginia; Y

+ Kate Johnson Peters m: 08 Oct 1891 in Lynchburg, Campbell County, Virginia, d: 07 May 1920 in Lynchburg, Campbell County, Virginia; Y

...............7 Lucy Kyle LEE b: Feb 1860 in Lynchburg, Campbell, Va

+ James Wilbur Shearer m: 06 Oct 1887 in Lynchburg, Campbell County, Virginia

+ Delilah Martin b: 12 Nov 1796 in Campbell County, Virginia, m: 09 Oct 1828 in Lynchburg, Campbell County, Virginia, d: 21 Jun 1888 in Appomattox County, Virginia; Y

.............6 Samuel Martin LEE b: Aug 1829 in Appomattox County, Virginia, d: 13 Sep 1909 in Appomattox County, Virginia; Y

+ Sarah E. Whitehead b: Abt. 1831, d: Jan 1895 in Appomattox County, Virginia; Y

+ Virginia Towns Wright b: Abt. 1831, d: Dec 1879 in Campbell County, Virginia; Y

...............7 George Daniel Lee b: 18 Oct 1850 in Campbell County, Virginia, d: 1917 in Lynchburg, Campbell County, Virginia; Y

...............7 James Henry Lee b: 02 Dec 1851 in Campbell County, Virginia, d: 12 Mar 1941 in Virginia; Y

...............7 William Sterling Lee b: 12 Aug 1853 in Campbell County, Virginia, d: 20 Aug 1943 in Lynchburg, Campbell County, Virginia; Y

...............7 Elzabeth Esther Lee b: 02 Oct 1855 in Campbell County, Virginia, d: 14 Dec 1946 in Lynchburg, Campbell County, Virginia; Y

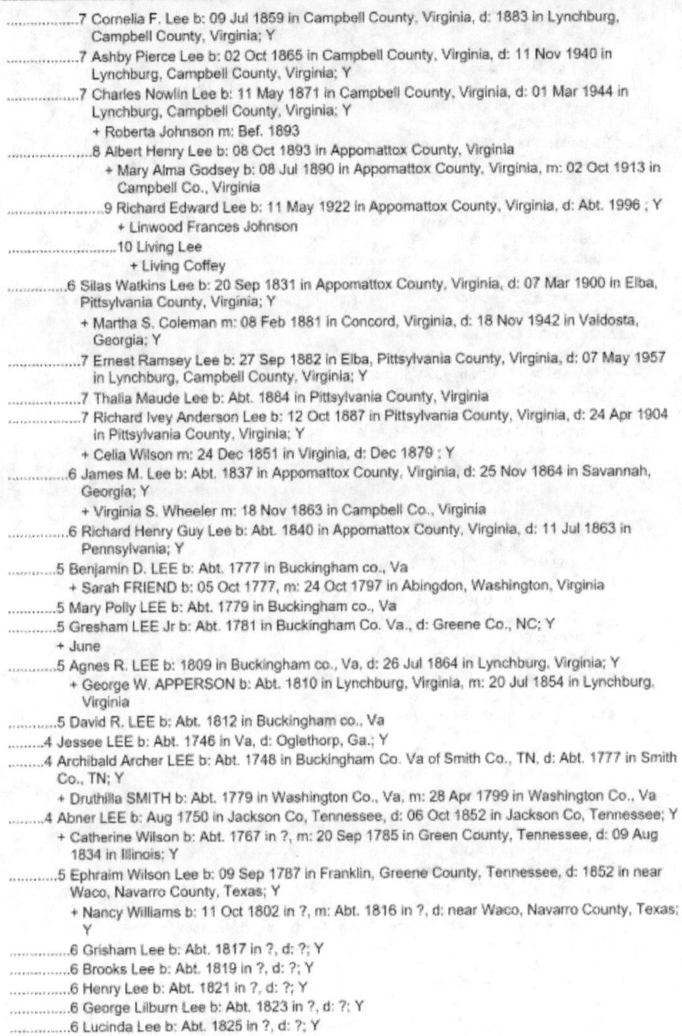

...............7 Cornelia F. Lee b: 09 Jul 1859 in Campbell County, Virginia, d: 1883 in Lynchburg, Campbell County, Virginia; Y

...............7 Ashby Pierce Lee b: 02 Oct 1865 in Campbell County, Virginia, d: 11 Nov 1940 in Lynchburg, Campbell County, Virginia; Y

...............7 Charles Nowlin Lee b: 11 May 1871 in Campbell County, Virginia, d: 01 Mar 1944 in Lynchburg, Campbell County, Virginia; Y

     + Roberta Johnson m: Bef. 1893

...............8 Albert Henry Lee b: 08 Oct 1893 in Appomattox County, Virginia

     + Mary Alma Godsey b: 08 Jul 1890 in Appomattox County, Virginia, m: 02 Oct 1913 in Campbell Co., Virginia

...............9 Richard Edward Lee b: 11 May 1922 in Appomattox County, Virginia, d: Abt. 1996 ; Y

     + Linwood Frances Johnson

...............10 Living Lee

     + Living Coffey

...............6 Silas Watkins Lee b: 20 Sep 1831 in Appomattox County, Virginia, d: 07 Mar 1900 in Elba, Pittsylvania County, Virginia; Y

     + Martha S. Coleman m: 08 Feb 1881 in Concord, Virginia, d: 18 Nov 1942 in Valdosta, Georgia; Y

...............7 Ernest Ramsey Lee b: 27 Sep 1882 in Elba, Pittsylvania County, Virginia, d: 07 May 1957 in Lynchburg, Campbell County, Virginia; Y

...............7 Thalia Maude Lee b: Abt. 1884 in Pittsylvania County, Virginia

...............7 Richard Ivey Anderson Lee b: 12 Oct 1887 in Pittsylvania County, Virginia, d: 24 Apr 1904 in Pittsylvania County, Virginia; Y

     + Celia Wilson m: 24 Dec 1851 in Virginia, d: Dec 1879 ; Y

...............6 James M. Lee b: Abt. 1837 in Appomattox County, Virginia, d: 25 Nov 1864 in Savannah, Georgia; Y

     + Virginia S. Wheeler m: 18 Nov 1863 in Campbell Co., Virginia

...............6 Richard Henry Guy Lee b: Abt. 1840 in Appomattox County, Virginia, d: 11 Jul 1863 in Pennsylvania; Y

...........5 Benjamin D. LEE b: Abt. 1777 in Buckingham co., Va

     + Sarah FRIEND b: 05 Oct 1777, m: 24 Oct 1797 in Abingdon, Washington, Virginia

...........5 Mary Polly LEE b: Abt. 1779 in Buckingham co., Va

...........5 Gresham LEE Jr b: Abt. 1781 in Buckingham Co. Va., d: Greene Co., NC; Y

     + June

...........5 Agnes R. LEE b: 1809 in Buckingham co., Va, d: 26 Jul 1864 in Lynchburg, Virginia; Y

     + George W. APPERSON b: Abt. 1810 in Lynchburg, Virginia, m: 20 Jul 1854 in Lynchburg, Virginia

...........5 David R. LEE b: Abt. 1812 in Buckingham co., Va

.........4 Jessee LEE b: Abt. 1746 in Va, d: Oglethorp, Ga.; Y

.........4 Archibald Archer LEE b: Abt. 1748 in Buckingham Co. Va of Smith Co., TN, d: Abt. 1777 in Smith Co., TN; Y

     + Druthilla SMITH b: Abt. 1779 in Washington Co., Va, m: 28 Apr 1799 in Washington Co., Va

.........4 Abner LEE b: Aug 1750 in Jackson Co, Tennessee, d: 06 Oct 1852 in Jackson Co, Tennessee; Y

     + Catherine Wilson b: Abt. 1767 in ?, m: 20 Sep 1785 in Green County, Tennessee, d: 09 Aug 1834 in Illinois; Y

...........5 Ephraim Wilson Lee b: 09 Sep 1787 in Franklin, Greene County, Tennessee, d: 1852 in near Waco, Navarro County, Texas; Y

     + Nancy Williams b: 11 Oct 1802 in ?, m: Abt. 1816 in ?, d: near Waco, Navarro County, Texas; Y

...............6 Grisham Lee b: Abt. 1817 in ?, d: ?; Y

...............6 Brooks Lee b: Abt. 1819 in ?, d: ?; Y

...............6 Henry Lee b: Abt. 1821 in ?, d: ?; Y

...............6 George Lilburn Lee b: Abt. 1823 in ?, d: ?; Y

...............6 Lucinda Lee b: Abt. 1825 in ?, d: ?; Y

...............6 Naomi Lee b: Abt. 1827 in ?, d: ?; Y

...........5 Richard Lee b: 18 Jan 1791 in Washington County, Virginia
...........5 Levi Lee b: 18 Jan 1791 in Washington County, Virginia, d: 26 Feb 1864 in Elgin, Bastrop
          County, Texas; Y
              + Mary Virginia Marcure b: 05 Dec 1798 in Burk County, North Carolina, m: 23 Jun 1815 in
              Jackson County, Tennessee, d: 1891 in Comanche County, Texas; Y
..............6 Lucinda Lee b: 14 Mar 1818 in Wayne County, Missouri, d: ?; Y
              + Meshack Skaggs b: ?, m: ?, d: ?; Y
..............6 Susanah Lee b: 1820 in Wayne County, Missouri, d: ?; Y
..............6 Catherine Lee b: 25 Dec 1821 in Wayne County, Missouri, d: 19 Nov 1856 in Georgetown,
          Texas; Y
..............6 William Lee b: 14 Jun 1824 in Wayne County, Missouri, d: ?; Y
..............6 Leroy Lee b: 13 Oct 1826 in TENNESSEE, d: 31 Mar 1897 in ?; Y
..............6 Sallie Lee b: 1830 in ?, d: ?; Y
..............6 George W. Lee b: 1831 in Arkansas, d: 1906 in Medina, Bandera County, Texas; Y
              + Artamice Moore b: ?, m: ?, d: ?; Y
.................7 Robert Elgin Lee b: 21 Jul 1872 in Elgin, Gastrop County, Texas, d: 06 Sep 1944 in Imola,
              Napa County, California; Y
..............6 Andrew A. Lee b: 1834 in ?, d: ?; Y
..............6 Ezekiel Lee b: 1836 in ?, d: ?; Y
..............6 Sarah Elizabeth Lee b: 1838 in ?, d: ?; Y
..............6 Mary Jane Lee b: 1841 in ?, d: ?; Y
..............6 Iziller Edna Lee b: 1843 in ?, d: ?; Y
              + James A. Graham b: ?, m: ?, d: ?; Y
...........5 George Washington Lee b: 15 Feb 1797 in Washington County, Virginia, d: 27 Dec 1870 in
          Sutter County, California; Y
              + Mahala Elvira Griffith b: 12 May 1802 in Jackson County, Tennessee, m: 16 Apr 1820 in ?, d:
              04 Jul 1852 ; Y
..............6 James Tilford Lee b: 05 Mar 1821 in Jackson County, Tennessee, d: 05 May 1903 in Trinidad
          County, California; Y
              + Jane McCook b: ?, m: 27 Sep 1841 in Washington County, Illinois, d: ?; Y
..............6 Abner Grisham Lee b: 23 Feb 1823 in Jackson County, Tennessee, d: 03 Sep 1903 in
          Trinidad County, California; Y
..............6 Ephraim Wilson Lee b: 24 Jul 1826 in Jackson County, Tennessee, d: 02 Jan 1879 in
          California; Y
              + Rachael E. McCook b: ?, m: Abt. 1849 in Washington County, Illinois, d: ?; Y
..............6 Polly Catherine Lee b: 25 Mar 1829 in Jackson County, Tennessee, d: 19 Jul 1831 in Illinois;
          Y
..............6 Milroy Griffith Lee b: 23 Aug 1831 in Nashville, Washington County, Illinois, d: 29 Jul 1877 in
          Yolo County, California; Y
              + Abigail Stoddard b: ?, m: 05 Jul 1855 in ?, d: ?; Y
.................7 Abner Grisham Lee b: 16 Apr 1856 in ?, d: ?; Y
..............6 Walter Campbell LEE b: Abt. 1834
..............6 Levi Woodbury Lee b: 03 Jan 1841
              + [unknown spouse]
.................7 George Frederick Lee
..............6 George Chisholm LEE b: Abt. 1843
...........5 Abner Lee Jr. b: Abt. 1799 in Jackson County, Tennessee, d: Aft. 1880 in Broan County, Texas;
          Y
...........5 William Lee b: Abt. 1801 in Jackson County, Tennessee, d: Aft. 1850 in ?; Y
...........5 Ailcy Lee b: Abt. 1805 in Jackson County, Tennessee, d: Aft. 1869 in ?; Y
              + Isiah Van Zandt m: ?
..............6 Parrizeda G. Vanzandt b: 1826 in Jackson County, Tennessee, d: ?; Y
..............6 John G. Vanzandt b: 1828 in Jackson County, Tennessee, d: ?; Y
              + Elizabeth Brown b: ?, m: Abt. 1853 in Jackson County, Tennessee, d: ?; Y
...........5 Malinda Lee b: Abt. 1807 in Jackson County, Tennessee, d: ?; Y

+ Exekiel Van Zandt m: Abt. 1830
.........5 Young Lee b: Abt. 1810 in Jackson County, Tennessee, d: ?; Y
+ Sally Johnson b: Abt. 1815, m: 12 Sep 1835 in Jackson County, Tennessee
.........5 Granville Lee b: Abt. 1837
.........5 Greenwood Lee b: Abt. 1840
.......4 Young LEE b: Abt. 1752 in Albemarle Co., Va of Buckingham Co., Va, d: 22 Sep 1840 in Smyth
Co., Va; Y
+ Jamima Mathews b: Abt. 1759 in Tilitson Parish, Buckingham, Virginia, m: 01 Dec 1775 in
Buckingham County, Virginia, d: 1830 ; Y
.........5 Susannah Lee b: Abt. 1776 in Buckingham Co., Virginia
.........5 Drusilla Lee b: Abt. 1778 in Washington Co., Va, d: 31 Oct 1862 in Smyth County, Virginia; Y
.........5 Mary Lee b: 16 Jul 1786 in Buckingham Co., Virginia, d: 18 Jan 1864 in Centerville, Ohio; Y
+ William Love McNeil b: ?, m: ?, d: ?; Y
.........6 Jesse McNeil b: ?, d: ?; Y
.........6 Gresham McNeil b: ?, d: ?; Y
.........5 Rhoda Lee b: Abt. 1788 in Buckingham Co., Virginia, d: Bef. 1833 ; Y
+ Epperson
.........5 Guy Lee b: Abt. 1790 in Washington Co., Va, d: Bef. 10 Jul 1833 in New Orleans, Louisiana; Y
.........5 Samuel Lee b: Abt. 1795 in Washington Co., Va
.........5 Melinda Malinda Lee b: 02 Apr 1800 in Washington Co., Va, d: 10 Dec 1882 in Ohio; Y
.........5 Thomas M. Lee b: Abt. 1803 in Washington Co., Va, d: 1871 in Smythe County, Virginia; Y
.........5 Jesse Lee b: Washington Co., Va, d: 1866 in Covington, Louisiana; Y
.......4 William C. LEE b: 24 Jan 1754 in Fishpond Creek, Goochland Co, V, d: 02 Dec 1835 in Green,
Ky; Y
+ Drusilla STAPLES b: Dec 1764 in Buckingham, Va, m: 13 Jan 1783 in Buckingham, Va, d: 04
Apr 1852 in Green, Ky; Y
.........5 Mary Ann LEE b: 10 Jan 1784 in Buckingham co., Va, d: 10 Oct 1813 ; Y
+ Phillip W. VAUGHAN b: Abt. 1782 in Buckingham co., Va
.........5 Samuel Yerwell LEE b: 12 May 1786 in Buckingham co., Va
.........5 William C. LEE b: 17 Feb 1789 in Mercer, Ky
+ Rhody PETTUS b: Abt. 1797 in Green Co., Ky, m: 23 Oct 1818 in Green Co., Ky
.........5 Nancy LEE b: 25 Oct 1791 in Mercer, Ky, d: 20 Oct 1855 ; Y
+ Nathan BRIDGEWATER b: 03 Dec 1792, m: 30 Jan 1826
.........5 Jackin LEE b: 03 Feb 1794 in Green, Ky, d: 11 Jan 1882 ; Y
+ Elizabeth COOK b: 06 Feb 1800, m: 18 Dec 1821 in Green Co., Ky
.........5 Robert Patterson LEE b: 06 Apr 1797 in Green, Ky, d: 28 Jul 1856 ; Y
+ Permella ATKINSON b: Abt. 1700 in Green Co., Ky, m: 15 Nov 1819 in Green Co., Ky
.........5 Betsey LEE b: 23 Sep 1799 in Green, Ky
+ GRAHAM m: 16 May 1812 in Green Co., Ky
.........5 Gresham H. LEE b: 30 Jul 1802 in Of, Adair, Kentucky, d: Bef. 1880 ; Y
+ Salina A. RICHARDSON b: Abt. 1803 in Charlotte Co., Virginia, m: 05 Mar 1833 in Green
Co., Ky
.........5 Phoebe Watkins LEE b: 22 Feb 1805 in Green, Ky
+ Foushee TIBBS b: Abt. 1801 in Green Co., Ky, m: 23 Oct 1832 in Green Co., Ky
.........5 Sally LEE b: 07 Jun 1807 in Green, Ky
+ Thomas W. GAINS b: Abt. 1805 in Green Co., Ky
.......4 Elizabeth LEE b: Abt. 1755 in Buckingham, Va, d: 19 Mar 1838 in Howard Co., MO; Y
+ Richard Bland Lee b: 31 Jul 1753 in of, Warrenton, Fauquier, Va, m: 1777 in Silver Creek,
Madison Co., KY, d: 1819 in Pointlick Creek, Madison, Co, Ky; Y
.........5 William Lee b: May 1778 in Fauquier Co., VA, d: May 1824 in near, Armstrong, Howard Co.,
Mo; Y
+ Elizabeth Ann Newell b: Abt. 1782 in of, Madison, Co, Ky, m: 1795 in Madison, Co, Ky
.........6 William Lee b: Abt. 1800 in <, Howard, MO>
.........6 Mary Lee b: Abt. 1802 in <, Howard, MO>
.........6 John Lee b: Abt. 1804 in <, Howard, MO>

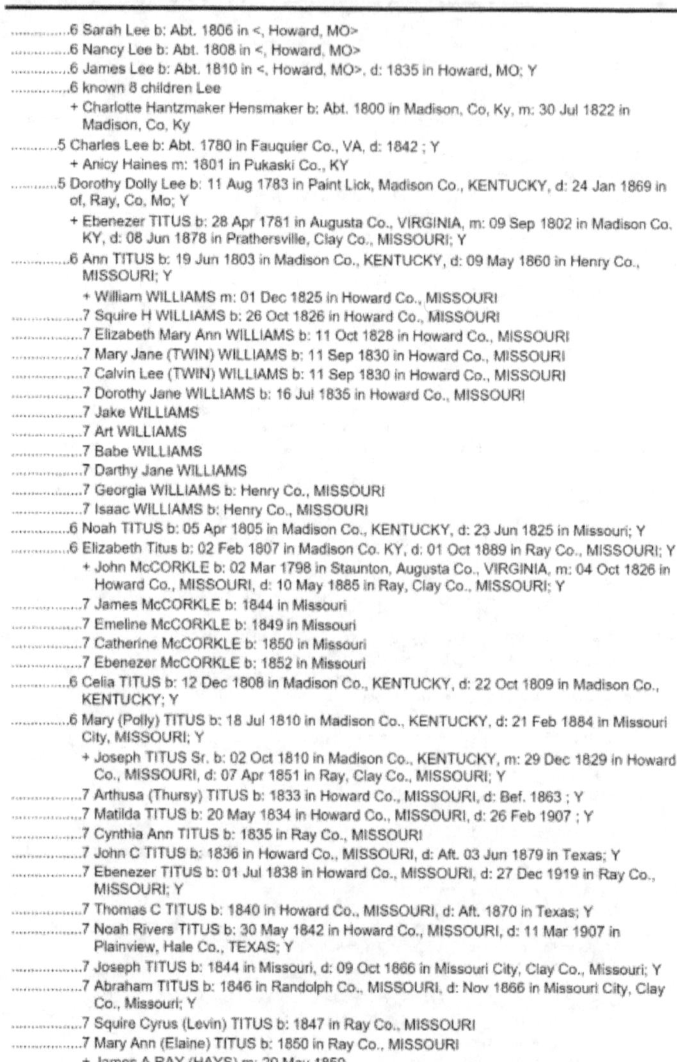

............6 Sarah Lee b: Abt. 1806 in <, Howard, MO>
............6 Nancy Lee b: Abt. 1808 in <, Howard, MO>
............6 James Lee b: Abt. 1810 in <, Howard, MO>, d: 1835 in Howard, MO; Y
............6 known 8 children Lee
        + Charlotte Hantzmaker Hensmaker b: Abt. 1800 in Madison, Co, Ky, m: 30 Jul 1822 in
          Madison, Co, Ky
..........5 Charles Lee b: Abt. 1780 in Fauquier Co., VA, d: 1842 ; Y
        + Anicy Haines m: 1801 in Pukaski Co., KY
..........5 Dorothy Dolly Lee b: 11 Aug 1783 in Paint Lick, Madison Co., KENTUCKY, d: 24 Jan 1869 in
          of, Ray, Co, Mo; Y
        + Ebenezer TITUS b: 28 Apr 1781 in Augusta Co., VIRGINIA, m: 09 Sep 1802 in Madison Co.
          KY, d: 08 Jun 1878 in Prathersville, Clay Co., MISSOURI; Y
............6 Ann TITUS b: 19 Jun 1803 in Madison Co., KENTUCKY, d: 09 May 1860 in Henry Co.,
          MISSOURI; Y
        + William WILLIAMS m: 01 Dec 1825 in Howard Co., MISSOURI
..............7 Squire H WILLIAMS b: 26 Oct 1826 in Howard Co., MISSOURI
..............7 Elizabeth Mary Ann WILLIAMS b: 11 Oct 1828 in Howard Co., MISSOURI
..............7 Mary Jane (TWIN) WILLIAMS b: 11 Sep 1830 in Howard Co., MISSOURI
..............7 Calvin Lee (TWIN) WILLIAMS b: 11 Sep 1830 in Howard Co., MISSOURI
..............7 Dorothy Jane WILLIAMS b: 16 Jul 1835 in Howard Co., MISSOURI
..............7 Jake WILLIAMS
..............7 Art WILLIAMS
..............7 Babe WILLIAMS
..............7 Darthy Jane WILLIAMS
..............7 Georgia WILLIAMS b: Henry Co., MISSOURI
..............7 Isaac WILLIAMS b: Henry Co., MISSOURI
............6 Noah TITUS b: 05 Apr 1805 in Madison Co., KENTUCKY, d: 23 Jun 1825 in Missouri; Y
............6 Elizabeth Titus b: 02 Feb 1807 in Madison Co. KY, d: 01 Oct 1889 in Ray Co., MISSOURI; Y
        + John McCORKLE b: 02 Mar 1798 in Staunton, Augusta Co., VIRGINIA, m: 04 Oct 1826 in
          Howard Co., MISSOURI, d: 10 May 1885 in Ray, Clay Co., MISSOURI; Y
..............7 James McCORKLE b: 1844 in Missouri
..............7 Emeline McCORKLE b: 1849 in Missouri
..............7 Catherine McCORKLE b: 1850 in Missouri
..............7 Ebenezer McCORKLE b: 1852 in Missouri
............6 Celia TITUS b: 12 Dec 1808 in Madison Co., KENTUCKY, d: 22 Oct 1809 in Madison Co.,
          KENTUCKY; Y
............6 Mary (Polly) TITUS b: 18 Jul 1810 in Madison Co., KENTUCKY, d: 21 Feb 1884 in Missouri
          City, MISSOURI; Y
        + Joseph TITUS Sr. b: 02 Oct 1810 in Madison Co., KENTUCKY, m: 29 Dec 1829 in Howard
          Co., MISSOURI, d: 07 Apr 1851 in Ray, Clay Co., MISSOURI; Y
..............7 Arthusa (Thursy) TITUS b: 1833 in Howard Co., MISSOURI, d: Bef. 1863 ; Y
..............7 Matilda TITUS b: 20 May 1834 in Howard Co., MISSOURI, d: 26 Feb 1907 ; Y
..............7 Cynthia Ann TITUS b: 1835 in Ray Co., MISSOURI
..............7 John C TITUS b: 1836 in Howard Co., MISSOURI, d: Aft. 03 Jun 1879 in Texas; Y
..............7 Ebenezer TITUS b: 01 Jul 1838 in Howard Co., MISSOURI, d: 27 Dec 1919 in Ray Co.,
          MISSOURI; Y
..............7 Thomas C TITUS b: 1840 in Howard Co., MISSOURI, d: Aft. 1870 in Texas; Y
..............7 Noah Rivers TITUS b: 30 May 1842 in Howard Co., MISSOURI, d: 11 Mar 1907 in
          Plainview, Hale Co., TEXAS; Y
..............7 Joseph TITUS b: 1844 in Missouri, d: 09 Oct 1866 in Missouri City, Clay Co., Missouri; Y
..............7 Abraham TITUS b: 1846 in Randolph Co., MISSOURI, d: Nov 1866 in Missouri City, Clay
          Co., Missouri; Y
..............7 Squire Cyrus (Levin) TITUS b: 1847 in Ray Co., MISSOURI
..............7 Mary Ann (Elaine) TITUS b: 1850 in Ray Co., MISSOURI
        + James A RAY (HAYS) m: 20 May 1859

...........6 Calvin Lee TITUS b: 20 May 1812 in Madison Co., KENTUCKY, d: 03 Oct 1830 in Madison Co., KENTUCKY; Y

...........6 Squire Cyrus (Caleb) TITUS b: 07 Jan 1816 in Madison Co., KENTUCKY, d: 08 Jan 1860 in Clay Co., MISSOURI; Y

    + Sarah Ashby LEEPER m: 16 Jan 1856, d: Aft. 1878 ; Y

...........7 Laura Ann TITUS b: 16 Jan 1857 in Missouri, d: 09 Feb 1880 in Missouri; Y

...........7 Cy Alice TITUS b: 04 Dec 1859 in Clay Co., MISSOURI, d: 1892 ; Y

    + Katherine J (Catherine) DENNY b: 23 Nov 1820 in Randolph Co., MISSOURI, m: 20 Oct 1842 in Armstrong, Howard Co., MISSOURI, d: 03 Feb 1854 in Clay Co., MISSOURI; Y

...........7 James Denny TITUS b: 28 Jul 1843 in Randolph Co., MISSOURI, d: 18 Apr 1902 in Richmond, Ray Co., MISSOURI; Y

...........7 Dorothy E TITUS b: 16 Jan 1845 in Missouri, d: 05 Apr 1862 in Missouri; Y

...........7 Artimissa (Minnie) TITUS b: 27 Nov 1846 in Howard Co., MISSOURI, d: 12 Jul 1920 in Clay Co., MISSOURI; Y

...........7 Elmyra Evaline (Elvira Amelia) TITUS b: 26 Jan 1849 in Missouri, d: Aft. 1930 in Missouri; Y

...........7 Alsy Catherine TITUS b: 26 Aug 1850 in Clay Co., MISSOURI, d: 10 Sep 1922 in Liberty, Clay Co., MISSOURI; Y

...........7 "Young" Ebenezer TITUS b: 18 Sep 1852, d: 04 Mar 1872 in Missouri; Y

...........7 Humphrey Putnam TITUS b: 27 Jan 1854 in Missouri, d: 20 Oct 1854 in Clay Co., MISSOURI; Y

...........6 Arthusa TITUS b: 08 Mar 1823 in Madison Co., KENTUCKY, d: 29 Jan 1888 in Ray Co., MISSOURI; Y

    + Murdock MARTIN b: 1815 in Moore Co., NORTH CAROLINA, m: 25 Oct 1840 in Howard Co., MISSOURI, d: Bef. 1848 in Missouri; Y

...........7 Mary Jane MARTIN b: 13 Jul 1842 in Henry Co., MISSOURI, d: 13 Mar 1923 in Pryor, OKLAHOMA; Y

...........7 Calvin Cyrus MARTIN b: 13 Apr 1844 in Ray Co., MISSOURI, d: 1934 in Clay Co., MISSOURI; Y

    + Jeremiah R (Josiah) FERGUSON b: 1819 in Virginia, m: 17 Aug 1848 in Ray Co., MISSOURI

...........7 William Franklin FERGUSON b: Jul 1849 in Ray Co., MISSOURI, d: 17 Mar 1924 in Boatman, Pryor, OKLAHOMA; Y

...........7 Dorothy S FERGUSON b: Sep 1850 in Missouri

...........7 Ebenezer FERGUSON b: 1851 in Ray Co., MISSOURI

...........7 Susan FERGUSON b: 1854 in Missouri, d: 1943 in Missouri; Y

...........7 John Calvin FERGUSON b: 1857 in Ray Co., MISSOURI

...........7 Roseanna FERGUSON b: 1858 in Ray Co., MISSOURI

...........7 Calvin FERGUSON b: 1860 in Missouri

...........7 Nevada FERGUSON b: Feb 1860 in Missouri, d: Aft. 1920 ; Y

...........7 Sterling FERGUSON b: 1862 in Ray Co., MISSOURI, d: Aft. 1920 in Ray, NORTH DAKOTA; Y

    + Titus TABENEZEC

...........5 Ann Talitha Lee b: 1785 in of, W.Va., Fauquier, Va, d: 22 Jul 1872 in Charleston, Hopkins County, TX; Y

    + Thomas McGuire b: 01 Aug 1781 in Montreal, Quebec, Canada, m: 07 Oct 1806, d: 23 Jul 1861 in Charleston, Hopkins County, TX; Y

...........6 Mary Ann "Polly" McGuire b: 03 Jul 1807, d: 09 Jul 1881 ; Y

    + Nathaniel G. Bryan b: 30 Aug 1806, d: Bet. 1860–1870 ; Y

...........6 Elizabeth McGuire b: 03 Jun 1809, d: Bet. Aug 1860–Jul 1880 ; Y

    + Clairborne Wilson Coats b: 1807

...........6 Temperance McGuire b: 27 May 1810 in Bedford County, TN, d: Aft. 18 Jun 1880 ; Y

    + John Wesley Carpenter b: Abt. 1806, d: 1841 in Jefferson County, IL; Y

...........7 Melia Ann Carpenter b: Sep 1830 in Nashville, Davidson Co., TN, d: 13 Nov 1909 ; Y

    + Thomas W. Bryan b: 22 Aug 1828, d: 08 Mar 1899 ; Y

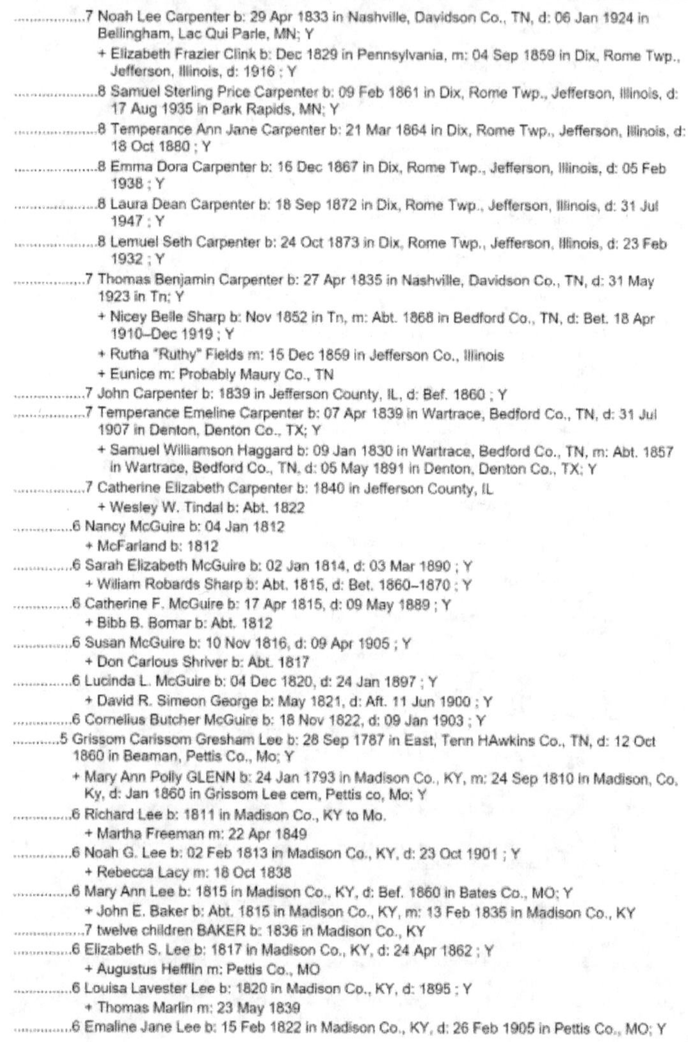

..................7 Noah Lee Carpenter b: 29 Apr 1833 in Nashville, Davidson Co., TN, d: 06 Jan 1924 in Bellingham, Lac Qui Parle, MN; Y

+ Elizabeth Frazier Clink b: Dec 1829 in Pennsylvania, m: 04 Sep 1859 in Dix, Rome Twp., Jefferson, Illinois, d: 1916 ; Y

..................8 Samuel Sterling Price Carpenter b: 09 Feb 1861 in Dix, Rome Twp., Jefferson, Illinois, d: 17 Aug 1935 in Park Rapids, MN; Y

..................8 Temperance Ann Jane Carpenter b: 21 Mar 1864 in Dix, Rome Twp., Jefferson, Illinois, d: 18 Oct 1880 ; Y

..................8 Emma Dora Carpenter b: 16 Dec 1867 in Dix, Rome Twp., Jefferson, Illinois, d: 05 Feb 1938 ; Y

..................8 Laura Dean Carpenter b: 18 Sep 1872 in Dix, Rome Twp., Jefferson, Illinois, d: 31 Jul 1947 ; Y

..................8 Lemuel Seth Carpenter b: 24 Oct 1873 in Dix, Rome Twp., Jefferson, Illinois, d: 23 Feb 1932 ; Y

..................7 Thomas Benjamin Carpenter b: 27 Apr 1835 in Nashville, Davidson Co., TN, d: 31 May 1923 in Tn; Y

+ Nicey Belle Sharp b: Nov 1852 in Tn, m: Abt. 1868 in Bedford Co., TN, d: Bet. 18 Apr 1910–Dec 1919 ; Y

+ Rutha "Ruthy" Fields m: 15 Dec 1859 in Jefferson Co., Illinois

+ Eunice m: Probably Maury Co., TN

..................7 John Carpenter b: 1839 in Jefferson County, IL, d: Bef. 1860 ; Y

..................7 Temperance Emeline Carpenter b: 07 Apr 1839 in Wartrace, Bedford Co., TN, d: 31 Jul 1907 in Denton, Denton Co., TX; Y

+ Samuel Williamson Haggard b: 09 Jan 1830 in Wartrace, Bedford Co., TN, m: Abt. 1857 in Wartrace, Bedford Co., TN, d: 05 May 1891 in Denton, Denton Co., TX; Y

..................7 Catherine Elizabeth Carpenter b: 1840 in Jefferson County, IL

+ Wesley W. Tindal b: Abt. 1822

..............6 Nancy McGuire b: 04 Jan 1812

+ McFarland b: 1812

..............6 Sarah Elizabeth McGuire b: 02 Jan 1814, d: 03 Mar 1890 ; Y

+ Wiliam Robards Sharp b: Abt. 1815, d: Bet. 1860–1870 ; Y

..............6 Catherine F. McGuire b: 17 Apr 1815, d: 09 May 1889 ; Y

+ Bibb B. Bomar b: Abt. 1812

..............6 Susan McGuire b: 10 Nov 1816, d: 09 Apr 1905 ; Y

+ Don Carlous Shriver b: Abt. 1817

..............6 Lucinda L. McGuire b: 04 Dec 1820, d: 24 Jan 1897 ; Y

+ David R. Simeon George b: May 1821, d: Aft. 11 Jun 1900 ; Y

..............6 Cornelius Butcher McGuire b: 18 Nov 1822, d: 09 Jan 1903 ; Y

..........5 Grissom Carissom Gresham Lee b: 28 Sep 1787 in East, Tenn HAwkins Co., TN, d: 12 Oct 1860 in Beaman, Pettis Co., Mo; Y

+ Mary Ann Polly GLENN b: 24 Jan 1793 in Madison Co., KY, m: 24 Sep 1810 in Madison, Co. Ky, d: Jan 1860 in Grissom Lee cem, Pettis co, Mo; Y

..............6 Richard Lee b: 1811 in Madison Co., KY to Mo.

+ Martha Freeman m: 22 Apr 1849

..............6 Noah G. Lee b: 02 Feb 1813 in Madison Co., KY, d: 23 Oct 1901 ; Y

+ Rebecca Lacy m: 18 Oct 1838

..............6 Mary Ann Lee b: 1815 in Madison Co., KY, d: Bef. 1860 in Bates Co., MO; Y

+ John E. Baker b: Abt. 1815 in Madison Co., KY, m: 13 Feb 1835 in Madison Co., KY

..................7 twelve children BAKER b: 1836 in Madison Co., KY

..............6 Elizabeth S. Lee b: 1817 in Madison Co., KY, d: 24 Apr 1862 ; Y

+ Augustus Hefflin m: Pettis Co., MO

..............6 Louisa Lavester Lee b: 1820 in Madison Co., KY, d: 1895 ; Y

+ Thomas Marlin m: 23 May 1839

..............6 Emaline Jane Lee b: 15 Feb 1822 in Madison Co., KY, d: 26 Feb 1905 in Pettis Co., MO; Y

+ Robert Luden FOWLER b: 18 Nov 1802 in Ky, m: 23 Sep 1841 in Pettis Co., MO, d: 22 Jun 1867 in Pettis Co., MO; Y

...............7 Robert Morrison Fowler b: 08 Jul 1840 in Pettis Co. Missouri, d: 22 Mar 1926 in Saline Co., Missouri; Y

+ Nancy Jane Felch b: 01 May 1848 in Pettis Co. Missouri, m: 1868 in Pettis Co. Missouri, d: 18 Jul 1924 in Saline Co., Missouri; Y

...............7 Mary A. Fowler b: 1843 in Pettis Co. Missouri

+ LAFAYETTE SHACKELFORD m: Abt. 1863 in Saline Co. Missouri

...............7 Luden Fowler b: 1845 in Pettis Co. Missouri, d: 1929 in Pettis Co. Missouri; Y

...............7 Lorinda Fowler b: 18 Dec 1848 in Pettis Co. Missouri, d: 1921 in Pettis Co. Missouri; Y

...............7 Emaline Fowler b: 29 Jul 1851 in Pettis Co. Missouri, d: 1946 in Pettis Co. Missouri; Y

...............7 Elizabeth Fowler b: Abt. 1852 in Pettis Co. Missouri

...............7 Lodoskey Fowler b: 22 Sep 1852 in Pettis Co. Missouri, d: 15 Jan 1875 in Pettis Co. Missouri; Y

...............7 Lavitha Fowler b: 22 Dec 1854 in Pettis Co. Missouri, d: 02 Sep 1942 ; Y

+ John Washington Rains b: Abt. 1852 in Pettis Co. Missouri, m: 01 Aug 1873 in Pettis Co. Missouri

...............7 Hannah Fowler b: 1855 in Pettis Co. Missouri

+ Frank L. Keeney m: 25 May 1885 in Pettis Co. Missouri

...............7 Loduska Fowler b: 22 Sep 1857 in Pettis Co. Missouri, d: 15 Jan 1875 in Pettis Co. Missouri; Y

...............7 Grissom Reed Fowler b: 21 Jun 1859 in Pettis Co. Missouri, d: 27 Jan 1888 in Pettis Co. Missouri; Y

...............7 James S. Fowler b: 10 Apr 1862 in Pettis Co. Missouri, d: 22 Jun 1872 in Pettis Co. Missouri; Y

...............7 Thomas Marshall Fowler b: 24 May 1864 in Pettis Co. Missouri, d: 22 Oct 1948 in Pettis Co. Missouri; Y

...........6 William Martin Lee b: 28 Dec 1825 in Madison Co., KY, d: 29 Sep 1911 in Pettis Co., MISSOURI; Y

+ Elizabeth Jane Jenkins b: 25 Feb 1830 in Missouri, m: 25 Jan 1848 in Sedalia, Pettis Co., MISSOURI, d: 06 Jan 1909 in Sedalia, Pettis Co., MISSOURI; Y

...............7 Mary Francis LEE b: 07 Jan 1850, d: 10 Feb 1850 in Beaman, Bowling Green Township, Pettis Co., MISSOURI; Y

...............7 Elizabeth Jane (Eliza Jane) LEE b: 1851 in Kentucky, d: 1923 in Pettis Co., MISSOURI; Y

+ Jeremiah WALKER b: Jan 1848 in Ohio, m: 11 Nov 1869 in Pettis Co., MISSOURI

...............8 Luther M WALKER b: 01 Feb 1876 in Missouri, d: 17 Dec 1946 ; Y

+ Letty THOMAS

...............8 Robert A WALKER b: May 1878 in Missouri

...............8 Norman WALKER b: 1880 in Missouri

+ Maude McCORMICK

...............8 Hattie W WALKER b: 1884 in Missouri

...............8 James A WALKER b: Jun 1886 in Missouri

+ Laura THOMAS

...............8 Child WALKER

...............8 Child WALKER

...............8 Child WALKER

...............8 Child WALKER

...............8 Child WALKER

...............8 Child WALKER

...............7 Sarah Louise LEE b: 01 Apr 1853 in Kentucky

+ Louis HAYNES b: 1852 in Kentucky, m: 03 Mar 1870 in Pettis Co., MISSOURI

...............8 William HAYNES

+ Emma HOWARD

...............8 Christopher HAYNES

+ Edna REYNOLD

...............7 Ruben Grissom LEE b: 02 Feb 1855 in Missouri, d: 05 Mar 1917 in Beaman, Bowling Green Township, Pettis Co., MISSOURI; Y

...............7 Katheryn Ann (Kate) LEE b: 26 Feb 1857 in Missouri, d: 17 Mar 1930 in Beaman, Bowling Green Township, Pettis Co., MISSOURI; Y

+ John L CRANFIELD m: 20 Mar 1873 in Pettis Co., MISSOURI

...............8 Clarence CRANFIELD b: 20 Mar 1885, d: 05 Aug 1885 ; Y

...............8 Charles Lewis CRANFIELD

...............8 Katie Lee CRANFIELD

...............8 Malicia Ann CRANFIELD

...............8 Margaret Elizabeth (Maggie) CRANFIELD

...............8 James CRANFIELD

...............8 William Edward CRANFIELD

...............8 Pearl CRANFIELD

...............8 Reuben N CRANFIELD

...............7 William Thomas LEE b: 05 Apr 1859 in Missouri, d: 27 Jul 1929 in Beaman, Bowling Green Township, Pettis Co., MISSOURI; Y

...............7 Nancy Elizabeth (Betty) LEE b: 15 Apr 1861 in Missouri, d: Beaman, Bowling Green Township, Pettis Co., MISSOURI; Y

+ A Jackson FARLEY m: 18 Oct 1883 in Pettis Co., MISSOURI

...............8 Charles FARLEY

...............8 Reuben Lou FARLEY

...............8 Earl FARLEY

...............8 Susie FARLEY

...............8 Clarence FARLEY

...............8 Lee FARLEY

...............8 Elizabeth FARLEY

...............7 Lucinda Ellison LEE b: 27 Mar 1863 in Missouri, d: 29 Mar 1929 in Sedalia, Pettis Co., MISSOURI; Y

+ Thomas Henry RECTOR b: 01 Mar 1860 in Missouri, m: 05 Jun 1879 in Pettis Co., MISSOURI, d: 24 Dec 1942 in Sedalia, Pettis Co., MISSOURI; Y

...............8 William Thomas RECTOR b: 28 Apr 1880, d: 1946 ; Y

...............8 LaLa Lee (Sarah) RECTOR b: 23 Oct 1892 in Pettis Co. Missouri, d: 07 Jun 1925 in Greeley, Weld Co., COLORADO; Y

+ George Allie BEAMAN b: 12 Apr 1888 in Beaman, Pettis Co., MISSOURI, m: 07 Jul 1909 in Pettis Co. Missouri

...............8 Carrie Louvica RECTOR b: 22 Jan 1901 in Missouri, d: 07 May 1993 in Sedalia, Pettis Co., MISSOURI; Y

+ Robert Floyd PARKER b: 06 Dec 1897 in Edwards, Benton Co., MISSOURI, m: 24 Sep 1916 in Sedalia, Pettis Co., MISSOURI, d: 10 Mar 1972 in Broken Arrow, Tulsa Co., MISSOURI; Y

...............9 Ralph Edmond PARKER b: 1918, d: 1995 ; Y

...............9 Charles Eugene PARKER b: 11 Apr 1920 in Kansas City, Jackson Co., MISSOURI

+ Alberta McNiece WHITE

+ Dorothy Marie WATSON b: 03 Nov 1922 in Sedalia, Pettis Co., MISSOURI, m: 12 Aug 1939 in Sedalia, Pettis Co., MISSOURI, d: 04 Dec 1970 in Kansas City, Jackson Co., MISSOURI; Y

...............10 Living PARKER

...............10 Living PARKER

...............10 Living PARKER

...............10 Living PARKER

...............10 Living PARKER

...............10 Living PARKER

...............9 Hubert Lee PARKER b: 1922

...............9 Mary Elizabeth PARKER b: 1924

...............9 Living PARKER

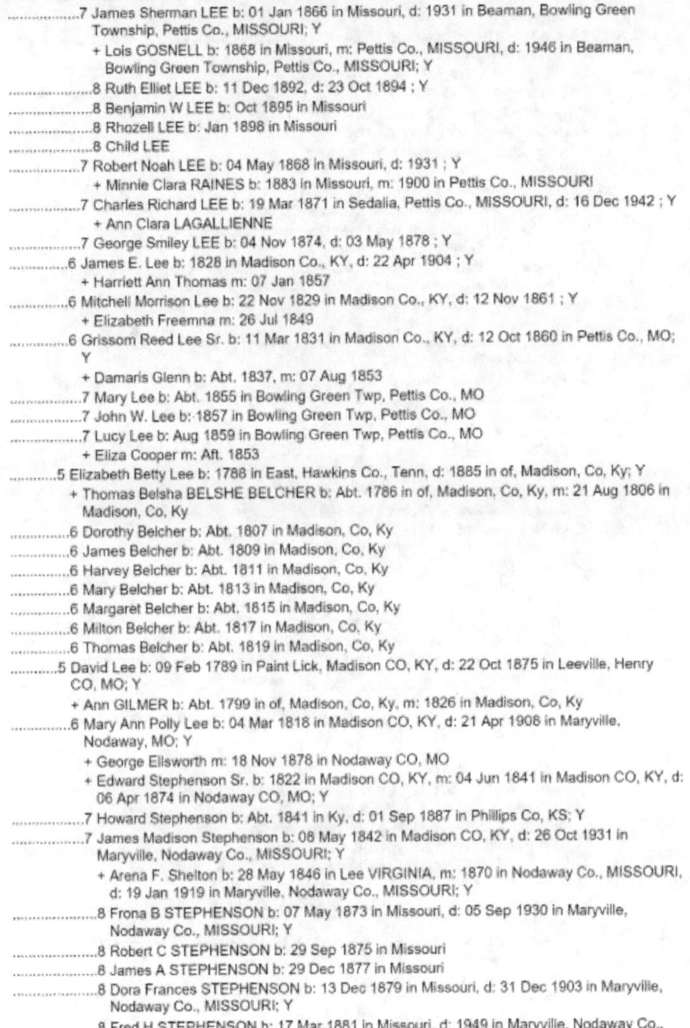

..............7 James Sherman LEE b: 01 Jan 1866 in Missouri, d: 1931 in Beaman, Bowling Green
              Township, Pettis Co., MISSOURI; Y
                + Lois GOSNELL b: 1868 in Missouri, m: Pettis Co., MISSOURI, d: 1946 in Beaman,
                  Bowling Green Township, Pettis Co., MISSOURI; Y
..............8 Ruth Elliet LEE b: 11 Dec 1892, d: 23 Oct 1894 ; Y
..............8 Benjamin W LEE b: Oct 1895 in Missouri
..............8 Rhozell LEE b: Jan 1898 in Missouri
..............8 Child LEE
..............7 Robert Noah LEE b: 04 May 1868 in Missouri, d: 1931 ; Y
                + Minnie Clara RAINES b: 1883 in Missouri, m: 1900 in Pettis Co., MISSOURI
..............7 Charles Richard LEE b: 19 Mar 1871 in Sedalia, Pettis Co., MISSOURI, d: 16 Dec 1942 ; Y
                + Ann Clara LAGALLIENNE
..............7 George Smiley LEE b: 04 Nov 1874, d: 03 May 1878 ; Y
..........6 James E. Lee b: 1828 in Madison Co., KY, d: 22 Apr 1904 ; Y
                + Harriett Ann Thomas m: 07 Jan 1857
..........6 Mitchell Morrison Lee b: 22 Nov 1829 in Madison Co., KY, d: 12 Nov 1861 ; Y
                + Elizabeth Freemna m: 26 Jul 1849
..........6 Grissom Reed Lee Sr. b: 11 Mar 1831 in Madison Co., KY, d: 12 Oct 1860 in Pettis Co., MO;
              Y
                + Damaris Glenn b: Abt. 1837, m: 07 Aug 1853
..............7 Mary Lee b: Abt. 1855 in Bowling Green Twp, Pettis Co., MO
..............7 John W. Lee b: 1857 in Bowling Green Twp, Pettis Co., MO
..............7 Lucy Lee b: Aug 1859 in Bowling Green Twp, Pettis Co., MO
                + Eliza Cooper m: Aft. 1853
..........5 Elizabeth Betty Lee b: 1788 in East, Hawkins Co., Tenn, d: 1885 in of, Madison, Co, Ky; Y
                + Thomas Belsha BELSHE BELCHER b: Abt. 1786 in of, Madison, Co, Ky, m: 21 Aug 1806 in
                  Madison, Co, Ky
..........6 Dorothy Belcher b: Abt. 1807 in Madison, Co, Ky
..........6 James Belcher b: Abt. 1809 in Madison, Co, Ky
..........6 Harvey Belcher b: Abt. 1811 in Madison, Co, Ky
..........6 Mary Belcher b: Abt. 1813 in Madison, Co, Ky
..........6 Margaret Belcher b: Abt. 1815 in Madison, Co, Ky
..........6 Milton Belcher b: Abt. 1817 in Madison, Co, Ky
..........6 Thomas Belcher b: Abt. 1819 in Madison, Co, Ky
..........5 David Lee b: 09 Feb 1789 in Paint Lick, Madison CO, KY, d: 22 Oct 1875 in Leeville, Henry
              CO, MO; Y
                + Ann GILMER b: Abt. 1799 in of, Madison, Co, Ky, m: 1826 in Madison, Co, Ky
..........6 Mary Ann Polly Lee b: 04 Mar 1818 in Madison CO, KY, d: 21 Apr 1908 in Maryville,
              Nodaway, MO; Y
                + George Ellsworth m: 18 Nov 1878 in Nodaway CO, MO
                + Edward Stephenson Sr. b: 1822 in Madison CO, KY, m: 04 Jun 1841 in Madison CO, KY, d:
                  06 Apr 1874 in Nodaway CO, MO; Y
..............7 Howard Stephenson b: Abt. 1841 in Ky, d: 01 Sep 1887 in Phillips Co, KS; Y
..............7 James Madison Stephenson b: 08 May 1842 in Madison CO, KY, d: 26 Oct 1931 in
              Maryville, Nodaway Co., MISSOURI; Y
                + Arena F. Shelton b: 28 May 1846 in Lee VIRGINIA, m: 1870 in Nodaway Co., MISSOURI,
                  d: 19 Jan 1919 in Maryville, Nodaway Co., MISSOURI; Y
..............8 Frona B STEPHENSON b: 07 May 1873 in Missouri, d: 05 Sep 1930 in Maryville,
              Nodaway Co., MISSOURI; Y
..............8 Robert C STEPHENSON b: 29 Sep 1875 in Missouri
..............8 James A STEPHENSON b: 29 Dec 1877 in Missouri
..............8 Dora Frances STEPHENSON b: 13 Dec 1879 in Missouri, d: 31 Dec 1903 in Maryville,
              Nodaway Co., MISSOURI; Y
..............8 Fred H STEPHENSON b: 17 Mar 1881 in Missouri, d: 1949 in Maryville, Nodaway Co.,
              MISSOURI; Y

+ Etho O
........8 Amanda E STEPHENSON b: 17 Jul 1953 in Maryville, Nodaway Co., MISSOURI, d: 22 Nov 1871 in Missouri; Y
    + Living OBERLENDER
........9 Living OBERLENDER
........8 Elijah W STEPHENSON
........8 Child STEPHENSON
......7 Rose Ann Stephenson b: 1844
    + J. Allen
......7 Elizabeth D. Stephenson b: Abt. 1847 in Ky
    + John G. Allen m: 12 Mar 1863 in Nodaway CO, MO
......7 Mary Jane Stephenson b: 06 Apr 1847 in Unknown, Madison, KY, d: 12 Jun 1887 in Barnard, Nodaway, MO; Y
    + Benjamin Franklin Frank Cook b: 26 Dec 1843 in Andrew, MO, m: 28 Aug 1862 in Barnard, Nodaway, MO, d: 30 May 1906 in Barnard, Nodaway, MO; Y
........8 James William Cook b: 02 Nov 1864 in Nodaway, MO, d: 17 Mar 1882 in Maryville, Nodaway, MO; Y
........8 Thomas Edward Cook b: 09 Apr 1866 in Maryville, Nodaway, MO, d: 18 Nov 1932 in Pomona, CA; Y
    + Ella Catherine ADKINS b: Jun 1868 in Logan Co., ILLINOIS, m: 15 Aug 1886 in Barnard, Nodaway Co., MISSOURI, d: Aft. 04 Feb 1958 in Pomona City, Los Angeles Co., California; Y
........9 Roy Edward COOK b: 28 Apr 1887 in Oklahoma, d: 21 Jun 1973 in Barnard, Nodaway Co., MISSOURI; Y
........9 Mary Lavona COOK b: Apr 1891 in Missouri
........9 Edith May COOK b: 22 Oct 1893
........9 George Harrison COOK b: 04 Nov 1895 in Oklahoma, d: Aft. 1918 ; Y
........9 Mable Gertrude COOK b: 07 Mar 1898 in Cushing, Oklahoma, d: 13 Oct 1996 in Barnard, Nodaway Co., MISSOURI; Y
........9 Living COOK
........8 Anna Roberta Cook b: 15 Nov 1867 in Missouri, d: 02 May 1934 in Maryville, Nodaway, MO; Y
    + William George Winterton BICKETT b: 23 Feb 1860, m: 21 Apr 1887 in Barnard, Nodaway CO, MO, d: 20 Mar 1932 in Maryville, Nodaway Co., MISSOURI; Y
........8 George Delano Cook b: 23 Dec 1869 in Lucas, Collin, TX, d: 13 Oct 1924 in Denver, Denver, Co; Y
    + Nancy Albertina JOHNSON b: 06 Aug 1871 in Phelps, Atchison Co., MISSOURI, m: 12 Jul 1890 in Barnard, Nodaway Co., MISSOURI, d: 31 Mar 1939 in Denver, Denver Co., Colorado; Y
........9 Edna Frances COOK b: 13 Mar 1892 in Missouri, d: 14 Apr 1968 in Lomita, Los Angeles Co., CALIFORNIA; Y
........9 George Walter COOK b: 14 May 1894 in Missouri, d: May 1982 ; Y
........9 Clarence Harland (TWIN) COOK Sr. b: 30 Dec 1896 in Barnard, Nodaway Co., MISSOURI, d: 02 Jan 1949 in Denver, Denver Co., Colorado; Y
........9 Lawrence Franklin (TWIN) COOK b: 30 Dec 1896 in Barnard, Nodaway Co., MISSOURI, d: 19 May 1972 in Denver, Denver Co., Colorado; Y
........9 Helen L COOK b: 10 Apr 1915 in Colorado, d: Feb 1971 ; Y
........8 Walter Scott Cook b: 18 Mar 1872 in Nodaway CO, MO, d: 25 May 1873 in Maryville, Nodaway, MO; Y
........8 Myrtle May (Mertie) COOK b: 24 Dec 1873 in Maryville, Nodaway Co., MISSOURI, d: 26 Jul 1939 in LaJunta, Otero, CO; Y
    + Daniel Raymond Sr BICKETT b: 26 Jun 1867 in St. Columbian, Conception Co., MISSOURI, m: 01 Dec 1891 in St. Columbian, Conception Co., MISSOURI, d: 04 Dec 1938 in La Junta, Otero Co., COLORADO; Y
........9 Alma Blanche BICKETT b: 11 Sep 1892 in Missouri, d: Jan 1926 in LaJunta, Otero Co., COLORADO; Y

.......................9 Daniel Raymond II BICKETT b: 20 Oct 1894 in Missouri, d: 02 Nov 1960 in LaJunta, Otero Co., COLORADO; Y

.......................9 Mary A BICKETT b: 29 Jun 1896 in Missouri, d: 1967 in LaJunta, Otero Co., COLORADO; Y

.......................9 Thaddeus Franklin BICKETT b: 28 Aug 1897 in Missouri, d: 16 Apr 1988 in LaJunta, Otero Co., COLORADO; Y

.......................9 Leona Constance BICKETT b: 22 Aug 1900 in Missouri

.......................9 Helen Gertrude BICKETT b: 24 Apr 1911 in La Junta, Otero Co., COLORADO, d: Mar 1974 in Twin Falls, IDAHO; Y

.......................9 Living BICKETT

.......................9 Living BICKETT

.......................9 Living BICKETT

.......................9 Living BICKETT

.......................9 Living BICKETT

.......................9 Living BICKETT

.......................8 John Franklin Cook b: 24 Oct 1875 in Missouri, d: 21 Mar 1953 in Los Angeles, CA; Y

     + Carrie P b: Abt. 1874 in Georgia

.......................8 Asa Bogard Cook b: 21 Nov 1877 in Missouri, d: 08 May 1926 in Loveland, Larimer, Co; Y

     + Beulah BUSHNELL b: 27 Nov 1879 in Wyoming, m: 19 Oct 1905 in Loveland, Larimer Co., COLORADO, d: 29 Jan 1955 in Loveland, Larimer Co., COLORADO; Y

.......................9 Living COOK

.......................9 Living COOK

.......................9 Living COOK

.......................9 Living COOK

.......................8 Charles Dean Cook b: 02 Apr 1879 in Barnard, Nodaway, MO, d: 13 Jan 1934 in carpenter; Y

     + Ruth Mae HILL b: 01 Dec 1881 in Ohio, m: 28 Nov 1901 in Larimer Co., COLORADO

.......................9 Ruth Vielda COOK b: 01 Feb 1910 in Montana, d: 01 Jun 1985 in San Diego, CALIFORNIA; Y

.......................9 Living COOK

.......................9 Living COOK

.......................9 Living COOK

.......................9 Living COOK

.......................8 William Harrison Cook b: 12 Jan 1882 in Missouri, d: 04 Aug 1900 in Payne Co., OK; Y

.......................8 Oteus Edgar Cook b: 11 Dec 1883, d: 23 Feb 1885 in Maryville, Nodaway, MO; Y

.......................8 Mary Gertrude Cook b: 14 Feb 1886 in Missouri, d: 25 Jun 1969 in Kern Co., CALIFORNIA; Y

     + William Alexander CAMPBELL b: 26 Jul 1865 in Alabama, m: Abt. 1904, d: 11 Jan 1947 in Kern Co., CALIFORNIA; Y

.......................9 Orian F CAMPBELL b: 15 Aug 1905 in Missouri, d: 09 Dec 1976 in Onyx, Kern Co., CALIFORNIA; Y

.......................7 William D. Stephenson b: Abt. 1849 in Ky, d: Nodaway County, MO; Y

.......................7 Edward "Bud" Stephenson b: Abt. 1849

     + Polly Webb

.......................7 Celia M. Stephenson b: Abt. 1850

     + James Jameson m: 17 Jan 1872 in Nodaway CO, MO

.......................7 Stephen D Lane STEPHENSON

     + Mary E PURCELL m: 06 Dec 1874 in Nodaway Co., MISSOURI

...............6 John Lee b: Abt. 1830

     + Ann Stephenson

    + Hetty Ann Hall b: Abt. 1810 in of, Madison, Co, Ky, m: 1843 in Madison, Co, Ky

...............6 Elizabeth Lee b: Abt. 1844 in Henry Co., IA

............5 Noah Green Lee b: 16 Jan 1790 in Paint Lick, Madison Co., Ky, d: 17 Feb 1853 in Boonville, COOPER, Co, Mo; Y

+ Sarah Sally Harvey b: 17 Feb 1795 in Madison, Co, Ky, m: 07 Apr 1814 in Madison, Co, Ky, d: 03 Aug 1859 in Booneville, Cooper Co., MISSOURI; Y

...........6 Nancy Alice LEE b: 03 Aug 1815 in Madison Co., KENTUCKY, d: 1860 ; Y

+ Abram ENYART b: 1814 in Madison Co., KENTUCKY, m: 01 Apr 1832 in Fayette, Howard Co., Missouri

...........7 Sarah Margaret ENYART b: 1832

...........7 Celia ENYART b: 1834

...........7 Mary ENYART b: 1836

...........7 Martha A ENYART b: 1838

...........7 Humphrey ENYART b: 1841

...........7 William ENYART b: 1843

...........7 Louisa ENYART b: 1845

...........7 Noah S ENYART b: 1847

...........7 Brunella ENYART b: 1849

...........6 Eliza J. (TWIN) LEE b: 27 Jul 1819 in Madison Co., KENTUCKY, d: Madison Co., KENTUCKY; Y

...........6 William Perry (TWIN) LEE b: 27 Jul 1819 in Madison Co., KENTUCKY, d: 17 Sep 1845 in Missouri; Y

...........6 Lucinda J LEE b: 21 Dec 1821 in Madison Co., KENTUCKY, d: 1892 ; Y

+ Bird Daniel PARKS b: 1819 in Madison Co., KENTUCKY, m: 19 Mar 1840 in Cooper Co., MISSOURI

...........7 Ann PARKS b: 1841 in Missouri

+ MILLER

...........7 Louisa PARKS b: 1843 in Missouri

...........7 Nancy E PARKS b: 1846 in Missouri

...........7 Jackson PARKS b: 1848 in Missouri

...........7 Mary B PARKS b: 1852 in Missouri

...........7 James T PARKS b: 1856 in Missouri

...........7 Susan PARKS b: 1858 in Missouri

...........7 Thomas PARKS b: 1860 in Missouri

...........6 Maria Louisa LEE b: 20 Aug 1824 in Madison Co., KENTUCKY, d: 06 Mar 1872 in Valley View, Cook Co., TEXAS; Y

...........6 Martha T LEE b: 25 Oct 1826 in Madison Co., KENTUCKY, d: 07 Jun 1863 ; Y

+ Jonathan M HUNT b: 1823 in Madison Co., KENTUCKY, m: 12 Dec 1844 in Cooper Co., MISSOURI, d: 1878 ; Y

...........7 William P HUNT b: 08 Jan 1847

+ Stella Carrington YANKEE m: 1903

+ Mary Medora Mc FARLAND m: 1868

...........7 Elizabeth J HUNT b: 1850

...........7 Nannie HUNT b: 1852

...........7 Lawrence L HUNT b: 1854

...........7 James R HUNT b: 1857

...........7 Hamilton HUNT b: 1859

...........6 Andrew Jackson LEE b: 06 Feb 1828 in Missouri, d: 22 Nov 1863 in Demopolis, ALABAMA; Y

...........6 Lawrence W. (Larry) LEE b: 27 Oct 1831 in Howard Co., MISSOURI, d: 16 Feb 1916 in Gainesville, Cook Co., TEXAS; Y

+ Mary A FEYER (FRYER) b: 1833 in Cooper Co., MISSOURI, m: 01 Nov 1859 in Cooper Co., MISSOURI

...........7 William Perry LEE b: 1862 in Missouri

...........7 Zoe LEE b: 1865 in Missouri

+ MANN

...........7 Porter LEE d: 1973 in Valley View, Cooke Co., TEXAS; Y

...........7 Ellen LEE

+ James M POTTER m: Cooke Co., Texas

...............8 Hugh POTTER
...............8 Child POTTER
    + Marrinda FRY
..........6 Sarah Elizabeth LEE b: 16 Feb 1834 in Cooper Co., MISSOURI, d: 23 Sep 1887 in Walla
    Walla, Walla Walla Co., WASHINTGON; Y
    + David Barton REAVIS b: 1832 in Cooper Co., MISSOURI, m: 21 Oct 1851 in Cooper Co.,
    MISSOURI, d: 1915 in Silver Lake, Union Co., OREGON; Y
...........7 Martha Alice REAVIS b: 1852 in Johnson Co., MISSOURI, d: Seattle, King Co.,
    WASHINGTON; Y
    + Charles WHEELER m: 16 Sep 1874 in Johnson Co., MISSOURI
...............8 Roy WHEELER
...............8 Guy WHEELER
...............8 Emerson WHEELER
...............8 Amy WHEELER
...........7 Thomas Albert (Tom) REAVIS b: 13 Sep 1853 in Blytheville, MISSOURI, d: 27 Mar 1938 in
    Hood River, Hood River Co., OREGON; Y
    + Ida DANIELS m: 05 Apr 1893 in Enterprise, Wallowa Co., OREGON
...............8 Gladys Lee REAVIS
...........7 William Perry REAVIS b: 1857 in Johnson Co., MISSOURI, d: 1903 in Wallowa, OREGON;
    Y
    + Mary SMITH m: Enterprise, Wallowa Co., OREGON
...........7 Gilbert Shores (Gil) REAVIS b: 14 Jan 1859 in Kingsville, Johnson Co., MISSOURI, d: 25
    Oct 1927 in Enterprise, Wallowa Co., OREGON; Y
    + Mattie Elizabeth JOHNSON m: 1891 in Enterprise, Wallowa Co., OREGON
...............8 David REAVIS b: 20 Nov 1894, d: Feb 1969 in Oregon; Y
    + Bertha Mary JOHNSON
...............8 Marie REAVIS
...............8 Maurice REAVIS
...............8 Claude REAVIS
...............8 Alice Lee REAVIS b: Enterprise, Wallowa Co., OREGON, d: Oakland, Alameda Co.,
    CALIFORNIA; Y
...........7 Mary Louise (Molly) REAVIS b: 10 Oct 1862 in Johnson Co., MISSOURI, d: 30 Oct 1949 in
    Silver Lake, Union Co., OREGON; Y
    + Aaron WADE b: 02 Dec 1849, m: 12 Sep 1883 in Wallowa, Wallowa Co., OREGON, d:
    27 Jul 1936 ; Y
...............8 Louise Lee (Louie) WADE b: 03 Aug 1884 in Wallowa, OREGON, d: Portland, Multnomah
    Co., Oregon; Y
...............8 Frederick Reavis WADE b: 1886 in Enterprise, Wallowa Co., OREGON, d: 1888 in
    Enterprise, Wallowa Co., OREGON; Y
...............8 James Clifford WADE b: 31 May 1889 in Wallowa, OREGON, d: Apr 1986 in Enterprise,
    Wallowa Co., OREGON; Y
...............8 Emma Fay WADE b: 10 Jun 1891 in Enterprise, Wallowa Co., OREGON, d: 24 Jul 1986
    in Richardson, Dallas Co., TEXAS; Y
...............8 Annis WADE b: 10 Apr 1893 in Enterprise, Wallowa Co., OREGON
...............8 Harold Aaron WADE b: 14 Sep 1896 in Enterprise, Wallowa Co., OREGON, d: Sep 1982
    in Oregon; Y
...............8 George Barton WADE b: 10 Mar 1898 in Wallowa, OREGON, d: Dec 1976 in Oregon; Y
...........7 James L REAVIS b: 11 Apr 1864 in Kingsville, Johnson Co., MISSOURI, d: Walla Walla,
    Walla Walla Co., WASHINGON; Y
    + Jenny WADE m: 06 Jul 1892 in Lostine, Wallowa Co., OREGON
...............8 Lois REAVIS
...............8 Doris REAVIS b: Walla Walla, Walla Walla Co., WASHINGON
...........7 Lawrence Joseph (Joe) REAVIS b: 10 Jan 1866 in Kingsville, Johnson Co., MISSOURI, d:
    16 Mar 1948 in Walla Walla, Walla Walla Co., WASHINGON; Y
    + Lucy OWENBY m: Jan 1890 in Enterprise, Wallowa Co., OREGON

..............7 Lewis David REAVIS b: 1867 in Kingsville, Johnson Co., MISSOURI, d: 1906 in Silver Lake, Union Co., OREGON; Y
    + Emma Mary PORTER m: Houstonia, Pettis Co., MISSOURI
..............8 Mildred Lee REAVIS
..............8 Lewis David II REAVIS
..........6 Thomas Burton LEE b: 16 Feb 1836 in Cooper Co., MISSOURI, d: 1867 ; Y
    + Mattie T FRIER b: 1838 in Cooper Co., MISSOURI, m: 17 Nov 1864 in Cooper Co., MISSOURI
..........6 Mary L LEE b: 1838 in Missouri, d: 1842 ; Y
..........6 Lewis A LEE b: 1838 in Howard Co., MISSOURI
........5 Matilda (Malinda) Lee b: 1792 in Madison, Co, Ky, d: 1827 in of, Madison, Co, Ky; Y
    + George Woolsey WOOLERY b: 1785 in Madison, Co, Ky, m: 09 Oct 1809 in Madison, Co, Ky, d: Apr 1840 in Cooper Co., MO; Y
..........6 Lawrence C. Woolery b: 20 Oct 1810 in <, Madison Co., KY>, d: 16 Jan 1862 ; Y
..........6 Izella Woolery b: 03 May 1812 in Of, Madison Co, KY, d: 27 Oct 1879 ; Y
..........6 Abraham Woolery b: 06 Jan 1814 in <, KY>, d: 25 Oct 1819 ; Y
..........6 Stephen C. Woolery b: 06 Aug 1815 in KY, d: 15 Jan 1892 ; Y
..........6 Nancy Woolery b: 01 Feb 1817 in <, KY>, d: 01 Jun 1865 ; Y
..........6 Cathy Woolery b: 21 Dec 1818 in <, MO>, d: 11 Sep 1879 ; Y
..........6 Enoch Francis Woolery b: 23 Mar 1821 in Mo, d: 09 Mar 1888 ; Y
..........6 Elizabeth Woolery b: 12 Jan 1823 in <, MO>
..........6 Jane Woolery b: 17 Sep 1824 in <, Madison Co., KY>
..........6 John Brisco Woolery b: 17 Aug 1827 in <, Madison Co., KY>, d: 1858 ; Y
..........6 George Woolery b: 14 Feb 1830 in <, Madison Co., KY>, d: 28 Feb 1844 ; Y
..........6 Matilda Lee Woolery b: 14 Feb 1830 in <, Madison Co., KY>, d: 10 Mar 1914 ; Y
........5 Thomas H. Lee b: 31 Dec 1795 in Madison, Co, Ky, d: 22 Dec 1871 in Howard, Co, Mo, 12 ch; Y
    + Gabriella HERNDON b: 23 Jan 1804 in Madison, Co, Ky, m: 17 Oct 1822 in Madison, Co, Ky, d: 18 Sep 1848 in 12, children; Y
..........6 Edmond Richard (Riley) LEE b: 1824 in Madison, Co, Ky, d: of Linn County, Missouri; Y
    + Nancy Catherine (Katie) ANDERSON b: 25 Sep 1828 in Howard Co., MISSOURI, m: 02 Mar 1843 in Chariton Township, Howard Co., MISSOURI
..............7 Amanda LEE b: 1844 in Missouri
..............7 Derenda LEE b: 1846 in Missouri
..............7 Thomas LEE b: 1849 in Missouri
..............7 Eliza LEE b: 1850 in Missouri
..............7 Nancy C LEE b: 1852 in Linn Co., Missouri
..............7 Elizabeth LEE b: 1855 in Linn County, Missouri
..............7 Gabriella LEE b: 1858 in Linn County, Missouri
..........6 J. H. Lee b: 21 Feb 1825, d: Chariton Co., MO; Y
    + Martha Forrest b: Abt. 1826 in Chariton Co., MO, m: 21 Dec 1846 in Chariton Co., MO
..............7 Claiborne Jackson Lee
..............7 W. D. Lee
..............7 Thomas J. Lee
..............7 Sterling Price Lee
..............7 J. H. Lee
..............7 Mary Lee
..............7 Sarah Lee
..............7 California Lee
..............7 Gabriella Lee
..........6 Lucy C. Lee b: 03 Dec 1846 in Missouri
    + Beverly A. Maddox b: 22 Oct 1843 in Mo
..............7 Joseph T. Maddox b: 31 Jan 1864, d: 10 Nov 1889 in Forest Green, Chariton Co., MO; Y
..............7 Alma L. Maddox b: 25 Apr 1865, d: 11 May 1943 in Chariton Co., MO; Y

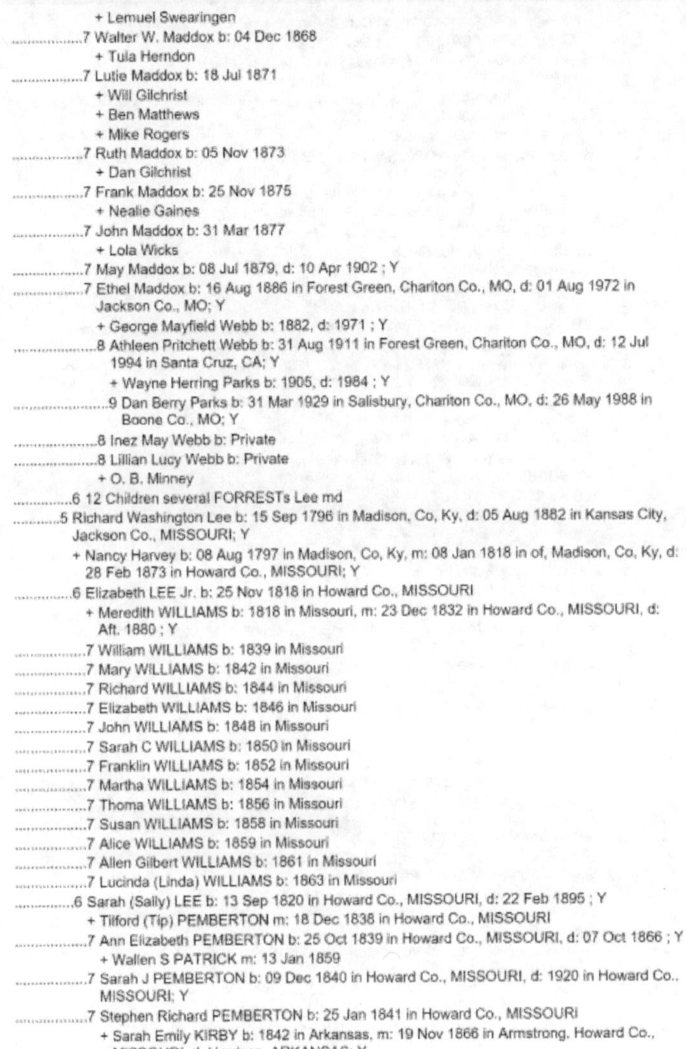

```
                        + Lemuel Swearingen
...............7 Walter W. Maddox b: 04 Dec 1868
                        + Tula Herndon
...............7 Lutie Maddox b: 18 Jul 1871
                        + Will Gilchrist
                        + Ben Matthews
                        + Mike Rogers
...............7 Ruth Maddox b: 05 Nov 1873
                        + Dan Gilchrist
...............7 Frank Maddox b: 25 Nov 1875
                        + Nealie Gaines
...............7 John Maddox b: 31 Mar 1877
                        + Lola Wicks
...............7 May Maddox b: 08 Jul 1879, d: 10 Apr 1902 ; Y
...............7 Ethel Maddox b: 16 Aug 1886 in Forest Green, Chariton Co., MO, d: 01 Aug 1972 in
                    Jackson Co., MO; Y
                        + George Mayfield Webb b: 1882, d: 1971 ; Y
...............8 Athleen Pritchett Webb b: 31 Aug 1911 in Forest Green, Chariton Co., MO, d: 12 Jul
                    1994 in Santa Cruz, CA; Y
                        + Wayne Herring Parks b: 1905, d: 1984 ; Y
...............9 Dan Berry Parks b: 31 Mar 1929 in Salisbury, Chariton Co., MO, d: 26 May 1988 in
                    Boone Co., MO; Y
...............8 Inez May Webb b: Private
...............8 Lillian Lucy Webb b: Private
                        + O. B. Minney
...........6 12 Children several FORRESTs Lee md
.........5 Richard Washington Lee b: 15 Sep 1796 in Madison, Co, Ky, d: 05 Aug 1882 in Kansas City,
                    Jackson Co., MISSOURI; Y
                        + Nancy Harvey b: 08 Aug 1797 in Madison, Co, Ky, m: 08 Jan 1818 in of, Madison, Co, Ky, d:
                    28 Feb 1873 in Howard Co., MISSOURI; Y
...............6 Elizabeth LEE Jr. b: 25 Nov 1818 in Howard Co., MISSOURI
                        + Meredith WILLIAMS b: 1818 in Missouri, m: 23 Dec 1832 in Howard Co., MISSOURI, d:
                    Aft. 1880 ; Y
...............7 William WILLIAMS b: 1839 in Missouri
...............7 Mary WILLIAMS b: 1842 in Missouri
...............7 Richard WILLIAMS b: 1844 in Missouri
...............7 Elizabeth WILLIAMS b: 1846 in Missouri
...............7 John WILLIAMS b: 1848 in Missouri
...............7 Sarah C WILLIAMS b: 1850 in Missouri
...............7 Franklin WILLIAMS b: 1852 in Missouri
...............7 Martha WILLIAMS b: 1854 in Missouri
...............7 Thoma WILLIAMS b: 1856 in Missouri
...............7 Susan WILLIAMS b: 1858 in Missouri
...............7 Alice WILLIAMS b: 1859 in Missouri
...............7 Allen Gilbert WILLIAMS b: 1861 in Missouri
...............7 Lucinda (Linda) WILLIAMS b: 1863 in Missouri
...............6 Sarah (Sally) LEE b: 13 Sep 1820 in Howard Co., MISSOURI, d: 22 Feb 1895 ; Y
                        + Tilford (Tip) PEMBERTON m: 18 Dec 1838 in Howard Co., MISSOURI
...............7 Ann Elizabeth PEMBERTON b: 25 Oct 1839 in Howard Co., MISSOURI, d: 07 Oct 1866 ; Y
                        + Wallen S PATRICK m: 13 Jan 1859
...............7 Sarah J PEMBERTON b: 09 Dec 1840 in Howard Co., MISSOURI, d: 1920 in Howard Co.,
                    MISSOURI; Y
...............7 Stephen Richard PEMBERTON b: 25 Jan 1841 in Howard Co., MISSOURI
                        + Sarah Emily KIRBY b: 1842 in Arkansas, m: 19 Nov 1866 in Armstrong, Howard Co.,
                    MISSOURI, d: Harrison, ARKANSAS; Y
```

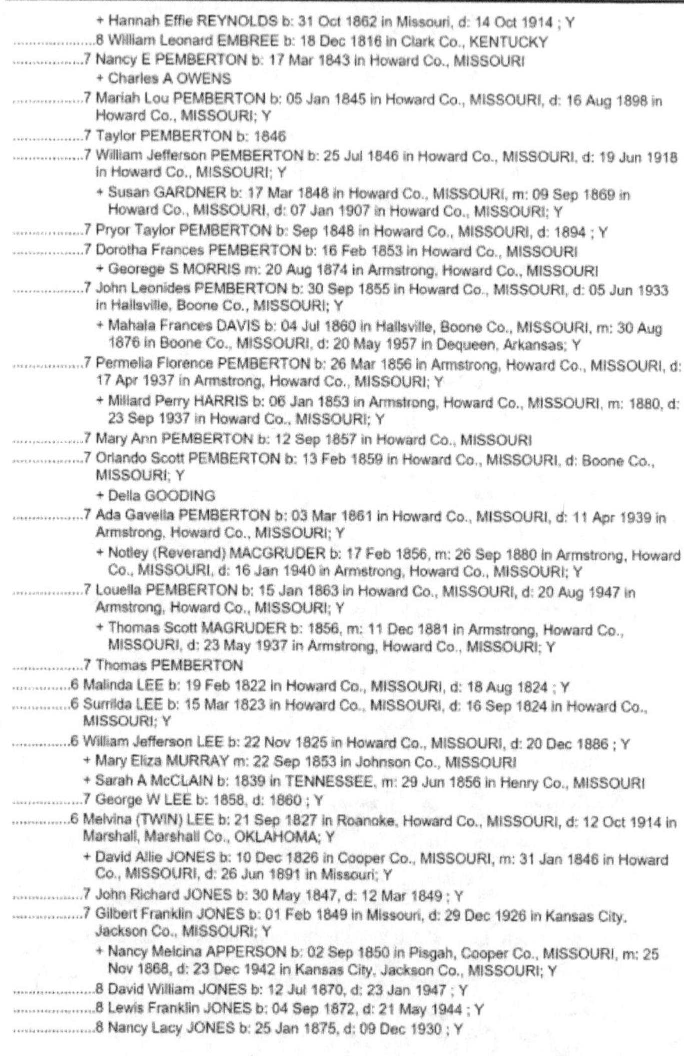

+ Hannah Effie REYNOLDS b: 31 Oct 1862 in Missouri, d: 14 Oct 1914 ; Y

.............8 William Leonard EMBREE b: 18 Dec 1816 in Clark Co., KENTUCKY

.............7 Nancy E PEMBERTON b: 17 Mar 1843 in Howard Co., MISSOURI

    + Charles A OWENS

.............7 Mariah Lou PEMBERTON b: 05 Jan 1845 in Howard Co., MISSOURI, d: 16 Aug 1898 in Howard Co., MISSOURI; Y

.............7 Taylor PEMBERTON b: 1846

.............7 William Jefferson PEMBERTON b: 25 Jul 1846 in Howard Co., MISSOURI, d: 19 Jun 1918 in Howard Co., MISSOURI; Y

    + Susan GARDNER b: 17 Mar 1848 in Howard Co., MISSOURI, m: 09 Sep 1869 in Howard Co., MISSOURI, d: 07 Jan 1907 in Howard Co., MISSOURI; Y

.............7 Pryor Taylor PEMBERTON b: Sep 1848 in Howard Co., MISSOURI, d: 1894 ; Y

.............7 Dorotha Frances PEMBERTON b: 16 Feb 1853 in Howard Co., MISSOURI

    + Georege S MORRIS m: 20 Aug 1874 in Armstrong, Howard Co., MISSOURI

.............7 John Leonides PEMBERTON b: 30 Sep 1855 in Howard Co., MISSOURI, d: 05 Jun 1933 in Hallsville, Boone Co., MISSOURI; Y

    + Mahala Frances DAVIS b: 04 Jul 1860 in Hallsville, Boone Co., MISSOURI, m: 30 Aug 1876 in Boone Co., MISSOURI, d: 20 May 1957 in Dequeen, Arkansas; Y

.............7 Permelia Florence PEMBERTON b: 26 Mar 1856 in Armstrong, Howard Co., MISSOURI, d: 17 Apr 1937 in Armstrong, Howard Co., MISSOURI; Y

    + Millard Perry HARRIS b: 06 Jan 1853 in Armstrong, Howard Co., MISSOURI, m: 1880, d: 23 Sep 1937 in Howard Co., MISSOURI; Y

.............7 Mary Ann PEMBERTON b: 12 Sep 1857 in Howard Co., MISSOURI

.............7 Orlando Scott PEMBERTON b: 13 Feb 1859 in Howard Co., MISSOURI, d: Boone Co., MISSOURI; Y

    + Della GOODING

.............7 Ada Gavella PEMBERTON b: 03 Mar 1861 in Howard Co., MISSOURI, d: 11 Apr 1939 in Armstrong, Howard Co., MISSOURI; Y

    + Notley (Reverand) MACGRUDER b: 17 Feb 1856, m: 26 Sep 1880 in Armstrong, Howard Co., MISSOURI, d: 16 Jan 1940 in Armstrong, Howard Co., MISSOURI; Y

.............7 Louella PEMBERTON b: 15 Jan 1863 in Howard Co., MISSOURI, d: 20 Aug 1947 in Armstrong, Howard Co., MISSOURI; Y

    + Thomas Scott MAGRUDER b: 1856, m: 11 Dec 1881 in Armstrong, Howard Co., MISSOURI, d: 23 May 1937 in Armstrong, Howard Co., MISSOURI; Y

.............7 Thomas PEMBERTON

.............6 Malinda LEE b: 19 Feb 1822 in Howard Co., MISSOURI, d: 18 Aug 1824 ; Y

.............6 Surrilda LEE b: 15 Mar 1823 in Howard Co., MISSOURI, d: 16 Sep 1824 in Howard Co., MISSOURI; Y

.............6 William Jefferson LEE b: 22 Nov 1825 in Howard Co., MISSOURI, d: 20 Dec 1886 ; Y

    + Mary Eliza MURRAY m: 22 Sep 1853 in Johnson Co., MISSOURI

    + Sarah A McCLAIN b: 1839 in TENNESSEE, m: 29 Jun 1856 in Henry Co., MISSOURI

.............7 George W LEE b: 1858, d: 1860 ; Y

.............6 Melvina (TWIN) LEE b: 21 Sep 1827 in Roanoke, Howard Co., MISSOURI, d: 12 Oct 1914 in Marshall, Marshall Co., OKLAHOMA; Y

    + David Allie JONES b: 10 Dec 1826 in Cooper Co., MISSOURI, m: 31 Jan 1846 in Howard Co., MISSOURI, d: 26 Jun 1891 in Missouri; Y

.............7 John Richard JONES b: 30 May 1847, d: 12 Mar 1849 ; Y

.............7 Gilbert Franklin JONES b: 01 Feb 1849 in Missouri, d: 29 Dec 1926 in Kansas City, Jackson Co., MISSOURI; Y

    + Nancy Melcina APPERSON b: 02 Sep 1850 in Pisgah, Cooper Co., MISSOURI, m: 25 Nov 1868, d: 23 Dec 1942 in Kansas City, Jackson Co., MISSOURI; Y

.............8 David William JONES b: 12 Jul 1870, d: 23 Jan 1947 ; Y

.............8 Lewis Franklin JONES b: 04 Sep 1872, d: 21 May 1944 ; Y

.............8 Nancy Lacy JONES b: 25 Jan 1875, d: 09 Dec 1930 ; Y

...............8 Richard Lee JONES b: 01 Nov 1876 in Pisgah, Cooper Co., MISSOURI, d: 22 May 1947
                ; Y
...............8 Minnie Peery (Perry) JONES b: 11 Aug 1879, d: 08 Feb 1969 ; Y
...............8 Mary Melcina JONES b: 04 Oct 1883, d: 1884 ; Y
...............8 Gertrude Apperson JONES b: 04 Jun 1887 in Pisgah, Cooper Co., MISSOURI, d: 08 Nov
                1952 in Kansas City, Jackson Co., MISSOURI; Y
...............8 Augusta Melvina JONES b: 27 Mar 1889, d: 27 Feb 1947 ; Y
...............7 William Alexander JONES b: 15 Dec 1851, d: 17 Apr 1871 ; Y
...............7 Louisa Annis JONES b: 01 Sep 1853, d: 16 Dec 1854 ; Y
...............7 David Louis JONES b: 14 Jul 1856, d: 26 Aug 1942 ; Y
                + Pernelia Frances BURRUS b: 05 Jun 1860, m: 30 Dec 1879
...............8 John Thomas JONES b: 14 Nov 1879, d: 27 Apr 1948 in Pisgah, Cooper Co.,
                MISSOURI; Y
...............8 Ollie Myrtle (Myrt) JONES b: 10 Nov 1882
...............8 Louis Thatcher JONES b: 21 Mar 1887
...............8 Elizabeth Melvina JONES b: 23 Feb 1889
...............8 Amanda (Mandy) Frances JONES b: 03 May 1891
...............8 Hettie Eunice (Tunie) JONES b: 27 Dec 1893
...............8 William David JONES b: 21 Feb 1897
...............7 Charles (Charley) Lee JONES b: 21 Dec 1857, d: 1941 ; Y
                + Louella MAXWELL b: 08 Feb 1868 in Dexter, TEXAS, m: 20 Dec 1885
...............8 Frederick Bismark JONES b: 20 Nov 1886
...............8 Charles Maxwell JONES b: 01 Mar 1888
...............8 David (Dave) Allie JONES b: 24 Jul 1889
...............8 Ella Mabel JONES b: 05 Nov 1891
...............8 William Potter JONES b: 25 Oct 1893
                + Carrie Elizabeth Woody b: 05 Nov 1893
...............8 Margaret JONES b: 31 Aug 1895
...............8 Leonard Gage JONES b: 12 Apr 1897
...............8 Dixie Bell JONES b: 22 Jan 1899
...............8 Living JONES
...............8 Living JONES
...............8 Living JONES
...............8 Living JONES
...............7 Minnie Avery JONES b: 06 May 1860
                + Sam PEERY
...............8 May PEERY
...............8 Sam PEERY
...............8 Essie PEERY
...............8 David PEERY
...............8 Nellie PEERY
...............8 W T PEERY
...............8 George PEERY
...............8 Roy PEERY
...............8 Eula PEERY
...............8 Nan PEERY
...............7 Thomas Beauregard JONES b: 22 Dec 1861
                + Alice DUNCAN
...............8 Mattie JONES
...............8 Sam J JONES
...............8 Guy JONES
...............8 Grace JONES
...............7 Nannie Wilmoth JONES b: 20 Nov 1865, d: 07 May 1951 ; Y
                + Sam F MILNER b: 24 Oct 1859

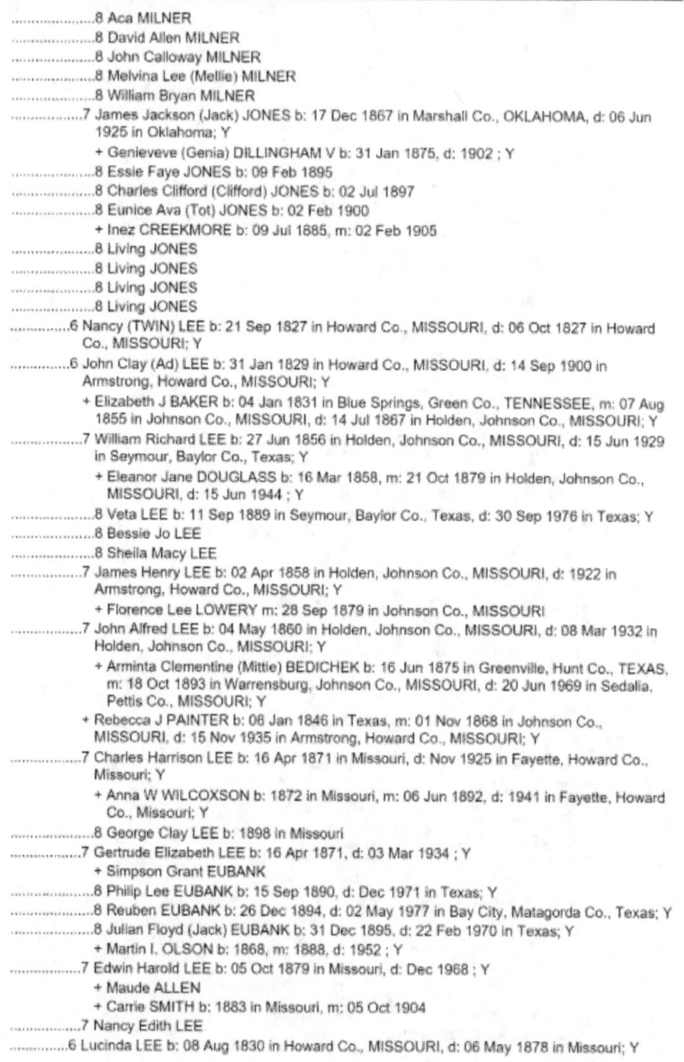

................8 Aca MILNER
................8 David Allen MILNER
................8 John Calloway MILNER
................8 Melvina Lee (Mellie) MILNER
................8 William Bryan MILNER
................7 James Jackson (Jack) JONES b: 17 Dec 1867 in Marshall Co., OKLAHOMA, d: 06 Jun
            1925 in Oklahoma; Y
            + Genieveve (Genia) DILLINGHAM V b: 31 Jan 1875, d: 1902 ; Y
................8 Essie Faye JONES b: 09 Feb 1895
................8 Charles Clifford (Clifford) JONES b: 02 Jul 1897
................8 Eunice Ava (Tot) JONES b: 02 Feb 1900
            + Inez CREEKMORE b: 09 Jul 1885, m: 02 Feb 1905
................8 Living JONES
................8 Living JONES
................8 Living JONES
................8 Living JONES
............6 Nancy (TWIN) LEE b: 21 Sep 1827 in Howard Co., MISSOURI, d: 06 Oct 1827 in Howard
            Co., MISSOURI; Y
............6 John Clay (Ad) LEE b: 31 Jan 1829 in Howard Co., MISSOURI, d: 14 Sep 1900 in
            Armstrong, Howard Co., MISSOURI; Y
            + Elizabeth J BAKER b: 04 Jan 1831 in Blue Springs, Green Co., TENNESSEE, m: 07 Aug
            1855 in Johnson Co., MISSOURI, d: 14 Jul 1867 in Holden, Johnson Co., MISSOURI; Y
................7 William Richard LEE b: 27 Jun 1856 in Holden, Johnson Co., MISSOURI, d: 15 Jun 1929
            in Seymour, Baylor Co., Texas; Y
            + Eleanor Jane DOUGLASS b: 16 Mar 1858, m: 21 Oct 1879 in Holden, Johnson Co.,
            MISSOURI, d: 15 Jun 1944 ; Y
................8 Veta LEE b: 11 Sep 1889 in Seymour, Baylor Co., Texas, d: 30 Sep 1976 in Texas; Y
................8 Bessie Jo LEE
................8 Sheila Macy LEE
................7 James Henry LEE b: 02 Apr 1858 in Holden, Johnson Co., MISSOURI, d: 1922 in
            Armstrong, Howard Co., MISSOURI; Y
            + Florence Lee LOWERY m: 28 Sep 1879 in Johnson Co., MISSOURI
................7 John Alfred LEE b: 04 May 1860 in Holden, Johnson Co., MISSOURI, d: 08 Mar 1932 in
            Holden, Johnson Co., MISSOURI; Y
            + Arminta Clementine (Mittie) BEDICHEK b: 16 Jun 1875 in Greenville, Hunt Co., TEXAS,
            m: 18 Oct 1893 in Warrensburg, Johnson Co., MISSOURI, d: 20 Jun 1969 in Sedalia,
            Pettis Co., MISSOURI; Y
            + Rebecca J PAINTER b: 06 Jan 1846 in Texas, m: 01 Nov 1868 in Johnson Co.,
            MISSOURI, d: 15 Nov 1935 in Armstrong, Howard Co., MISSOURI; Y
................7 Charles Harrison LEE b: 16 Apr 1871 in Missouri, d: Nov 1925 in Fayette, Howard Co.,
            Missouri; Y
            + Anna W WILCOXSON b: 1872 in Missouri, m: 06 Jun 1892, d: 1941 in Fayette, Howard
            Co., Missouri; Y
................8 George Clay LEE b: 1898 in Missouri
................7 Gertrude Elizabeth LEE b: 16 Apr 1871, d: 03 Mar 1934 ; Y
            + Simpson Grant EUBANK
................8 Philip Lee EUBANK b: 15 Sep 1890, d: Dec 1971 in Texas; Y
................8 Reuben EUBANK b: 26 Dec 1894, d: 02 May 1977 in Bay City, Matagorda Co., Texas; Y
................8 Julian Floyd (Jack) EUBANK b: 31 Dec 1895, d: 22 Feb 1970 in Texas; Y
            + Martin I. OLSON b: 1868, m: 1888, d: 1952 ; Y
................7 Edwin Harold LEE b: 05 Oct 1879 in Missouri, d: Dec 1968 ; Y
            + Maude ALLEN
            + Carrie SMITH b: 1883 in Missouri, m: 05 Oct 1904
................7 Nancy Edith LEE
............6 Lucinda LEE b: 08 Aug 1830 in Howard Co., MISSOURI, d: 06 May 1878 in Missouri; Y

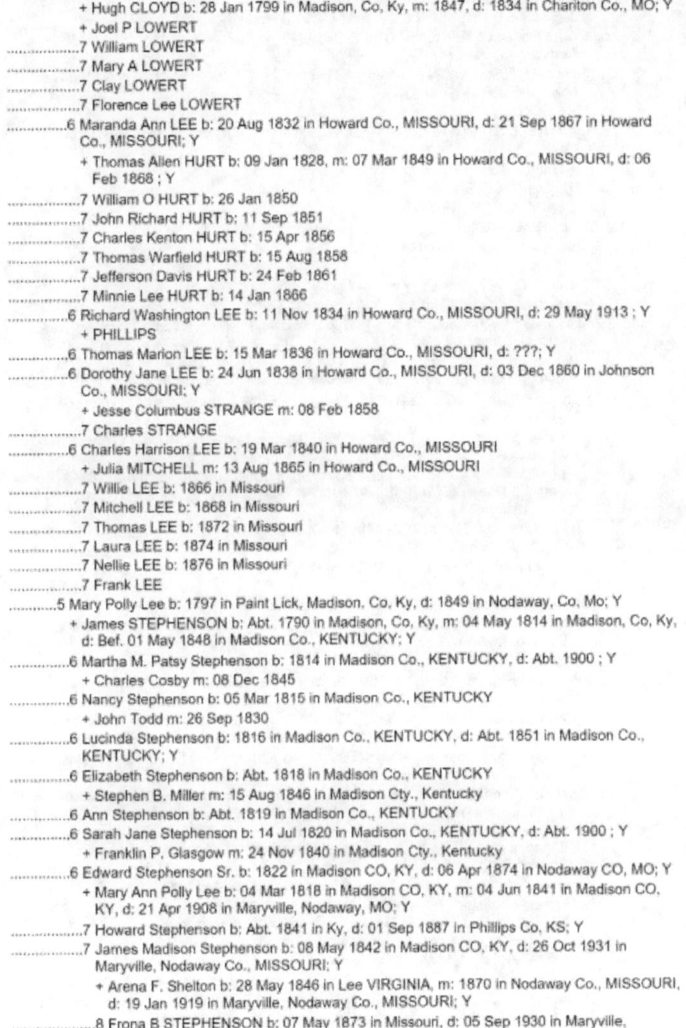

```
            + Hugh CLOYD b: 28 Jan 1799 in Madison, Co, Ky, m: 1847, d: 1834 in Chariton Co., MO; Y
            + Joel P LOWERT
..............7 William LOWERT
..............7 Mary A LOWERT
..............7 Clay LOWERT
..............7 Florence Lee LOWERT
..........6 Maranda Ann LEE b: 20 Aug 1832 in Howard Co., MISSOURI, d: 21 Sep 1867 in Howard
            Co., MISSOURI; Y
            + Thomas Allen HURT b: 09 Jan 1828, m: 07 Mar 1849 in Howard Co., MISSOURI, d: 06
            Feb 1868 ; Y
..............7 William O HURT b: 26 Jan 1850
..............7 John Richard HURT b: 11 Sep 1851
..............7 Charles Kenton HURT b: 15 Apr 1856
..............7 Thomas Warfield HURT b: 15 Aug 1858
..............7 Jefferson Davis HURT b: 24 Feb 1861
..............7 Minnie Lee HURT b: 14 Jan 1866
..........6 Richard Washington LEE b: 11 Nov 1834 in Howard Co., MISSOURI, d: 29 May 1913 ; Y
            + PHILLIPS
..........6 Thomas Marion LEE b: 15 Mar 1836 in Howard Co., MISSOURI, d: ???; Y
..........6 Dorothy Jane LEE b: 24 Jun 1838 in Howard Co., MISSOURI, d: 03 Dec 1860 in Johnson
            Co., MISSOURI; Y
            + Jesse Columbus STRANGE m: 08 Feb 1858
..............7 Charles STRANGE
..........6 Charles Harrison LEE b: 19 Mar 1840 in Howard Co., MISSOURI
            + Julia MITCHELL m: 13 Aug 1865 in Howard Co., MISSOURI
..............7 Willie LEE b: 1866 in Missouri
..............7 Mitchell LEE b: 1868 in Missouri
..............7 Thomas LEE b: 1872 in Missouri
..............7 Laura LEE b: 1874 in Missouri
..............7 Nellie LEE b: 1876 in Missouri
..............7 Frank LEE
..........5 Mary Polly Lee b: 1797 in Paint Lick, Madison, Co, Ky, d: 1849 in Nodaway, Co, Mo; Y
            + James STEPHENSON b: Abt. 1790 in Madison, Co, Ky, m: 04 May 1814 in Madison, Co, Ky,
            d: Bef. 01 May 1848 in Madison Co., KENTUCKY; Y
..........6 Martha M. Patsy Stephenson b: 1814 in Madison Co., KENTUCKY, d: Abt. 1900 ; Y
            + Charles Cosby m: 08 Dec 1845
..........6 Nancy Stephenson b: 05 Mar 1815 in Madison Co., KENTUCKY
            + John Todd m: 26 Sep 1830
..........6 Lucinda Stephenson b: 1816 in Madison Co., KENTUCKY, d: Abt. 1851 in Madison Co.,
            KENTUCKY; Y
..........6 Elizabeth Stephenson b: Abt. 1818 in Madison Co., KENTUCKY
            + Stephen B. Miller m: 15 Aug 1846 in Madison Cty., Kentucky
..........6 Ann Stephenson b: Abt. 1819 in Madison Co., KENTUCKY
..........6 Sarah Jane Stephenson b: 14 Jul 1820 in Madison Co., KENTUCKY, d: Abt. 1900 ; Y
            + Franklin P. Glasgow m: 24 Nov 1840 in Madison Cty., Kentucky
..........6 Edward Stephenson Sr. b: 1822 in Madison CO, KY, d: 06 Apr 1874 in Nodaway CO, MO; Y
            + Mary Ann Polly Lee b: 04 Mar 1818 in Madison CO, KY, m: 04 Jun 1841 in Madison CO,
            KY, d: 21 Apr 1908 in Maryville, Nodaway, MO; Y
..............7 Howard Stephenson b: Abt. 1841 in Ky, d: 01 Sep 1887 in Phillips Co, KS; Y
..............7 James Madison Stephenson b: 08 May 1842 in Madison CO, KY, d: 26 Oct 1931 in
            Maryville, Nodaway Co., MISSOURI; Y
            + Arena F. Shelton b: 28 May 1846 in Lee VIRGINIA, m: 1870 in Nodaway Co., MISSOURI,
            d: 19 Jan 1919 in Maryville, Nodaway Co., MISSOURI; Y
..............8 Frona B STEPHENSON b: 07 May 1873 in Missouri, d: 05 Sep 1930 in Maryville,
            Nodaway Co., MISSOURI; Y
```

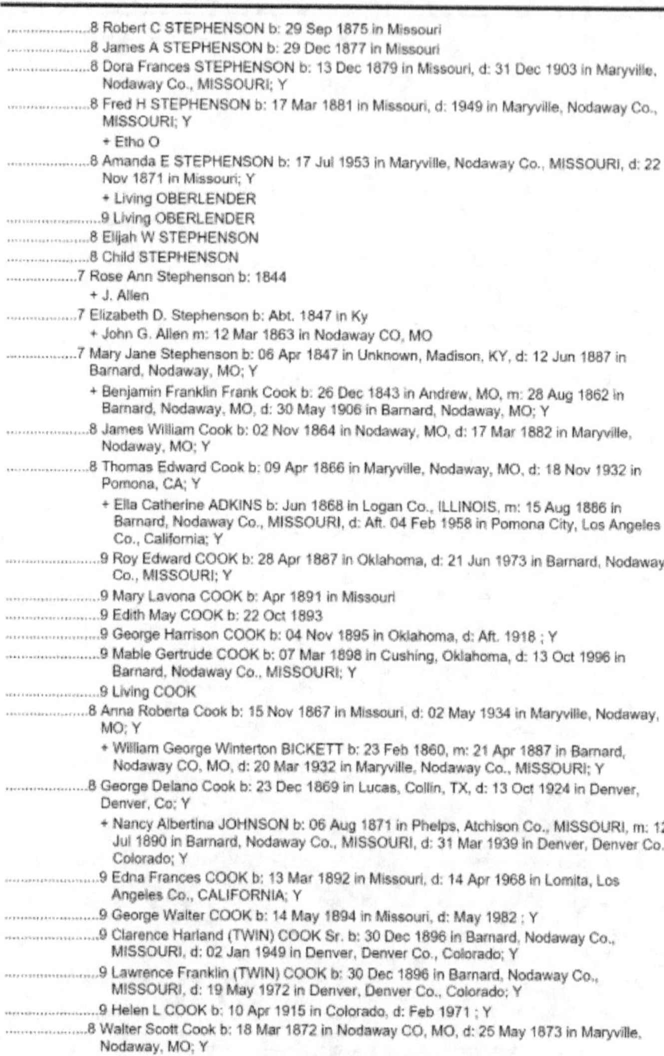

...............8 Robert C STEPHENSON b: 29 Sep 1875 in Missouri
...............8 James A STEPHENSON b: 29 Dec 1877 in Missouri
...............8 Dora Frances STEPHENSON b: 13 Dec 1879 in Missouri, d: 31 Dec 1903 in Maryville,
            Nodaway Co., MISSOURI; Y
...............8 Fred H STEPHENSON b: 17 Mar 1881 in Missouri, d: 1949 in Maryville, Nodaway Co.,
            MISSOURI; Y
            + Etho O
...............8 Amanda E STEPHENSON b: 17 Jul 1953 in Maryville, Nodaway Co., MISSOURI, d: 22
            Nov 1871 in Missouri; Y
            + Living OBERLENDER
...............9 Living OBERLENDER
...............8 Elijah W STEPHENSON
...............8 Child STEPHENSON
...............7 Rose Ann Stephenson b: 1844
            + J. Allen
...............7 Elizabeth D. Stephenson b: Abt. 1847 in Ky
            + John G. Allen m: 12 Mar 1863 in Nodaway CO, MO
...............7 Mary Jane Stephenson b: 06 Apr 1847 in Unknown, Madison, KY, d: 12 Jun 1887 in
            Barnard, Nodaway, MO; Y
            + Benjamin Franklin Frank Cook b: 26 Dec 1843 in Andrew, MO, m: 28 Aug 1862 in
              Barnard, Nodaway, MO, d: 30 May 1906 in Barnard, Nodaway, MO; Y
...............8 James William Cook b: 02 Nov 1864 in Nodaway, MO, d: 17 Mar 1882 in Maryville,
            Nodaway, MO; Y
...............8 Thomas Edward Cook b: 09 Apr 1866 in Maryville, Nodaway, MO, d: 18 Nov 1932 in
            Pomona, CA; Y
            + Ella Catherine ADKINS b: Jun 1868 in Logan Co., ILLINOIS, m: 15 Aug 1886 in
              Barnard, Nodaway Co., MISSOURI, d: Aft. 04 Feb 1958 in Pomona City, Los Angeles
              Co., California; Y
...............9 Roy Edward COOK b: 28 Apr 1887 in Oklahoma, d: 21 Jun 1973 in Barnard, Nodaway
            Co., MISSOURI; Y
...............9 Mary Lavona COOK b: Apr 1891 in Missouri
...............9 Edith May COOK b: 22 Oct 1893
...............9 George Harrison COOK b: 04 Nov 1895 in Oklahoma, d: Aft. 1918 ; Y
...............9 Mable Gertrude COOK b: 07 Mar 1898 in Cushing, Oklahoma, d: 13 Oct 1996 in
            Barnard, Nodaway Co., MISSOURI; Y
...............9 Living COOK
...............8 Anna Roberta Cook b: 15 Nov 1867 in Missouri, d: 02 May 1934 in Maryville, Nodaway,
            MO; Y
            + William George Winterton BICKETT b: 23 Feb 1860, m: 21 Apr 1887 in Barnard,
              Nodaway CO, MO, d: 20 Mar 1932 in Maryville, Nodaway Co., MISSOURI; Y
...............8 George Delano Cook b: 23 Dec 1869 in Lucas, Collin, TX, d: 13 Oct 1924 in Denver,
            Denver, Co; Y
            + Nancy Albertina JOHNSON b: 06 Aug 1871 in Phelps, Atchison Co., MISSOURI, m: 12
              Jul 1890 in Barnard, Nodaway Co., MISSOURI, d: 31 Mar 1939 in Denver, Denver Co.,
              Colorado; Y
...............9 Edna Frances COOK b: 13 Mar 1892 in Missouri, d: 14 Apr 1968 in Lomita, Los
            Angeles Co., CALIFORNIA; Y
...............9 George Walter COOK b: 14 May 1894 in Missouri, d: May 1982 ; Y
...............9 Clarence Harland (TWIN) COOK Sr. b: 30 Dec 1896 in Barnard, Nodaway Co.,
            MISSOURI, d: 02 Jan 1949 in Denver, Denver Co., Colorado; Y
...............9 Lawrence Franklin (TWIN) COOK b: 30 Dec 1896 in Barnard, Nodaway Co.,
            MISSOURI, d: 19 May 1972 in Denver, Denver Co., Colorado; Y
...............9 Helen L COOK b: 10 Apr 1915 in Colorado, d: Feb 1971 ; Y
...............8 Walter Scott Cook b: 18 Mar 1872 in Nodaway CO, MO, d: 25 May 1873 in Maryville,
            Nodaway, MO; Y

...............8 Myrtle May (Mertie) COOK b: 24 Dec 1873 in Maryville, Nodaway Co., MISSOURI, d: 26 Jul 1939 in LaJunta, Otero, CO; Y

    + Daniel Raymond Sr BICKETT b: 26 Jun 1867 in St. Columbian, Conception Co., MISSOURI, m: 01 Dec 1891 in St. Columbian, Conception Co., MISSOURI, d: 04 Dec 1938 in La Junta, Otero Co., COLORADO; Y

...............9 Alma Blanche BICKETT b: 11 Sep 1892 in Missouri, d: Jan 1926 in LaJunta, Otero Co., COLORADO; Y

...............9 Daniel Raymond II BICKETT b: 20 Oct 1894 in Missouri, d: 02 Nov 1960 in LaJunta, Otero Co., COLORADO; Y

...............9 Mary A BICKETT b: 29 Jun 1896 in Missouri, d: 1967 in LaJunta, Otero Co., COLORADO; Y

...............9 Thaddeus Franklin BICKETT b: 28 Aug 1897 in Missouri, d: 16 Apr 1988 in LaJunta, Otero Co., COLORADO; Y

...............9 Leona Constance BICKETT b: 22 Aug 1900 in Missouri

...............9 Helen Gertrude BICKETT b: 24 Apr 1911 in La Junta, Otero Co., COLORADO, d: Mar 1974 in Twin Falls, IDAHO; Y

...............9 Living BICKETT

...............9 Living BICKETT

...............9 Living BICKETT

...............9 Living BICKETT

...............9 Living BICKETT

...............9 Living BICKETT

...............8 John Franklin Cook b: 24 Oct 1875 in Missouri, d: 21 Mar 1953 in Los Angeles, CA; Y

    + Carrie P b: Abt. 1874 in Georgia

...............8 Asa Bogard Cook b: 21 Nov 1877 in Missouri, d: 08 May 1926 in Loveland, Larimer, Co; Y

    + Beulah BUSHNELL b: 27 Nov 1879 in Wyoming, m: 19 Oct 1905 in Loveland, Larimer Co., COLORADO, d: 29 Jan 1955 in Loveland, Larimer Co., COLORADO; Y

...............9 Living COOK

...............9 Living COOK

...............9 Living COOK

...............9 Living COOK

...............8 Charles Dean Cook b: 02 Apr 1879 in Barnard, Nodaway, MO, d: 13 Jan 1934 in carpenter; Y

    + Ruth Mae HILL b: 01 Dec 1881 in Ohio, m: 28 Nov 1901 in Larimer Co., COLORADO

...............9 Ruth Vielda COOK b: 01 Feb 1910 in Montana, d: 01 Jun 1985 in San Diego, CALIFORNIA; Y

...............9 Living COOK

...............9 Living COOK

...............9 Living COOK

...............9 Living COOK

...............8 William Harrison Cook b: 12 Jan 1882 in Missouri, d: 04 Aug 1900 in Payne Co., OK; Y

...............8 Oteus Edgar Cook b: 11 Dec 1883, d: 23 Feb 1885 in Maryville, Nodaway, MO; Y

...............8 Mary Gertrude Cook b: 14 Feb 1886 in Missouri, d: 25 Jun 1969 in Kern Co., CALIFORNIA; Y

    + William Alexander CAMPBELL b: 26 Jul 1865 in Alabama, m: Abt. 1904, d: 11 Jan 1947 in Kern Co., CALIFORNIA; Y

...............9 Orian F CAMPBELL b: 15 Aug 1905 in Missouri, d: 09 Dec 1976 in Onyx, Kern Co., CALIFORNIA; Y

...............7 William D. Stephenson b: Abt. 1849 in Ky, d: Nodaway County, MO; Y

...............7 Edward "Bud" Stephenson b: Abt. 1849

    + Polly Webb

...............7 Celia M. Stephenson b: Abt. 1850

    + James Jameson m: 17 Jan 1872 in Nodaway CO, MO

...............7 Stephen D Lane STEPHENSON

    + Mary E PURCELL m: 06 Dec 1874 in Nodaway Co., MISSOURI
    + Eliza SWEARENGEN m: 20 Sep 1855 in NC
............6 Andrew Stephenson b: Abt. 1824 in Madison Co., KENTUCKY
............6 David Stephenson b: 25 Dec 1825 in Louisville, Kentucky, d: 17 May 1916 ; Y
    + Louise Temple Griffith b: Abt. 1836 in Kentucky, m: 21 Sep 1856
............7 America (Addie) Stephenson b: Abt. 1859, d: 1944 in California; Y
    + Charles Brown
............8 Maggie Brown
............8 Minnie Brown
    + Frank Mozingo
............7 Carrie Stephenson b: Abt. 1863, d: Kansas City, Missouri; Y
    + John Hautzenradar
............7 Lucinda Stephenson b: Abt. 1867
    + Talbot
............7 James Stephenson b: Abt. 1871, d: 1935 in Sabetha, Kansas; Y
    + Rebecca Jennie Jones m: Carollton, Missouri
............7 Mary Stephenson
    + Herbert Davis
............7 Nellie Stephenson
    + Louis Rullman
............7 Martha Stephenson
    + Holcomb
............6 Richard Stephenson b: 14 Aug 1826 in Madison Co., KENTUCKY, d: 18 Apr 1881 in Stanberry, Missouri; Y
    + Nancy P. Walkup b: 04 Sep 1827 in Kentucky, m: 31 Jul 1848, d: 14 Oct 1906 in Stanberry, Missouri; Y
............7 Andrew Stephenson b: 08 Jul 1850 in Madison Cty., Kentucky, d: 07 Dec 1928 in Grant, Nebraska; Y
    + Martha Ann Swearington m: 20 Sep 1871 in Henry Co. Iowa
............7 James Stephenson b: 08 Mar 1854 in Stanberry, Missouri, d: 28 Sep 1928 in Stanberry, Mossouri; Y
............7 Martha Stephenson b: 24 Oct 1856 in Stanberry, Missouri, d: 21 Nov 1933 in Stanberry, Missouri; Y
    + William Alvin Stockton m: 21 Feb 1872 in Stanberry, MO
............7 Samuel Stephenson b: 07 Jun 1858 in Stanberry, Missouri, d: 27 Nov 1920 in Stroud, Oklahoma; Y
    + Emma Jane Beach m: 21 Dec 1880 in Missouri
............8 Cleota Stephenson
............8 Vira Ellen Stephenson
............8 Leota Stephenson
............8 Lela Ann Stephenson
............8 Frankie Stephenson
............8 Lottie Mae Stephenson
............8 Pearl Stephenson
............7 Mary Stephenson b: 24 Jan 1861 in Stanberry, Missouri, d: 1949 in Stanberry, Missouri; Y
    + Charles Smith
............7 Nancy Stephenson b: 18 Mar 1863, d: 16 Apr 1884 ; Y
............7 Elizabeth Stephenson b: 06 Mar 1865 in Stanberry, Missouri, d: 17 Jan 1938 ; Y
............7 Richard Irwin Stephenson b: 30 Mar 1867 in Gentry Cty. Missouri, d: 07 Jun 1924 in Stanberry, Missouri; Y
    + Mary Lee Swearingen b: 08 Jun 1864 in Near Plattsburg, Missouri, m: 30 Jan 1889, d: 13 Jan 1929 in Near Stanberry, Missouri; Y
............8 William Glen Stephenson b: 03 Mar 1890 in Imperial, Nebraska, d: 03 Oct 1969 in Springfield, Oregon; Y
............8 Ora Myrtle Stephenson b: 25 Apr 1891, d: 30 Apr 1981 ; Y

....................8 Wesley Stephenson b: 17 Nov 1892 in Imperial, Nebraska, d: 26 Oct 1947 in Mitchell, South Dakota; Y

....................8 Nina Ellen Stephenson b: 12 Jun 1895 in Stanberry, Missouri, d: 13 Aug 1898 in Stanberry, Missouri; Y

....................8 Dewey Fern Stephenson b: 15 Jun 1898 in Stanberry, Missouri, d: 01 Jan 1979 in Hastings, Nebraska; Y

    + Dollie Mae Butt b: 24 Aug 1898 in Stanberry, Missouri, m: 28 Nov 1917, d: 06 May 1941 in Hastings, Nebraska; Y

....................9 John Richard Stephenson b: 26 Sep 1918 in Stanberry, Missouri, d: 20 Oct 1978 in Lincoln, Nebraska; Y

    + Lucille Vollweiler b: 05 Jun 1910, m: 22 Mar 1942

....................10 Living Stephenson

    + Living Wall

....................11 Living Stephenson

    + Living Spry

....................12 Living Stephenson

....................12 Living Stephenson

....................11 Living Stephenson

    + Living Godsey (Nee Bolles)

....................12 Living Stephenson

....................12 Living Godsey

....................10 Living Stephenson

    + Living Schmidt

....................11 Living Schmidt

    + Living Farley

....................12 Living Farley

....................9 Dorothy May Stephenson b: 26 Jan 1922 in Stanberry, Missouri, d: 15 Sep 2003 in Lincoln, NE; Y

    + Rodney Duane Eldred (Bill) Jr. b: 29 Nov 1918 in Antioch, Nebraska, m: 14 Dec 1940, d: 06 Jan 2004 in Lincoln, NE; Y

....................10 Living Eldred

    + Living Jelinek

....................11 Living Jelinek

    + Living Nabower

....................10 Living Eldred

    + Living Kissler

....................11 Living Kissler

    + Living Young

....................12 Living Kissler

....................11 Living Kissler(DJ)

    + [unknown spouse]

....................12 Living Kissler

....................10 Living Eldred

    + Living Hazelwood

....................10 Living Eldred

    + Living Wingbermuehle

....................11 Living Eldred

....................11 Living Eldred

....................9 Norma Lucille Stephenson b: 27 Nov 1923 in Chadron, Nebraska, d: 08 Apr 2000 in Folsom, California; Y

    + William Penn Dier b: 23 Dec 1923, m: 07 Jun 1942 in Yuma, Arizona

....................10 Living Dier

    + Living Christian

....................11 Living Tucker

....................10 Living Dier

+ Living
+ Living Slonecker
..............................11 Living Slonecker
...................9 Robert Fern Stephenson b: 24 Feb 1927 in Hastings, Nebraska
+ Living Lukow
..........................10 Living Stephenson
+ Living Nathan
..............................11 Living Stephenson
..............................11 Living Stephenson
..........................10 Living Stephenson
+ Living
..............................11 Living Swaim
+ Living Wagner
..............................12 Living Wagner
..............................12 Living Wagner
..............................12 Living Wagner
..............................11 Living Swaim
..........................10 Living Stephenson
+ Living Busby
..............................11 Living Busby
..............................11 Living Busby
..............................11 Living Busby
...................9 William Thomas Stephenson b: 20 Mar 1931 in Hastings, Nebraska, d: 04 May 1987 in
Carmichael, Cal.; Y
+ Living Schlachter
..........................10 Living Stephenson
+ Living Friberg
..............................11 Living Friberg
..............................11 Living Friberg
+ Living Clowers
+ Living Cutter
..............................11 Living Cutter
..............................11 Living Cutter
..........................10 Living Stephenson
+ Living Pyle
..............................11 Living Stephenson
..............................11 Living Stephenson
..............................11 Living Stephenson
..........................10 Living Stephenson
+ Living Streeter
..............................11 Living Stephenson
+ Living Lopez
..............................12 Living Lopez
..............................12 Living Lopez
..............................12 Living Lopez
..............................11 Living Streeter
+ Living McGee
..............................12 Living Streeter
..............................12 Living Streeter
..........................10 Living Stephenson
+ Living Pyle
..............................11 Living Stephenson
..............................11 Living Stephenson
+ Living McGee

.................9 Living Stephenson
+ Annette Weidenkeller b: 01 May 1909 in Russia, d: 09 Sep 1970 ; Y
.................9 Norma Jean Weidenkeller b: 09 Feb 1931 in Hastings, Nebraska, d: San Diego,
CALIFORNIA; Y
+ Victor Reiners
.................10 Living Reiners
.................9 Jeanette Eileen Weidenkeller b: 20 Jan 1933 in Hastings, Nebraska, d: 01 Jan 1998 in
Western, Nebraska; Y
+ Robert Wright Meyers b: 10 Dec 1932 in Rockport, Mo., m: 31 May 1952 in Hastings,
Nebraska, d: 29 Jun 2004 in Western, NE.; Y
.................10 Living Meyers
+ Living Drake
.................11 Living Meyers
.................11 Living Meyers
.................11 Living Meyers
.................10 Living Meyers
+ Living Johnson
.................11 Living Meyers
.................11 Living Meyers
+ Living Davis
.................9 Living Stephenson
+ Living Radcliff
.................10 Living Stephenson
.................10 Living Stephenson
+ Living Warren
.................10 Living Stephenson
+ Living Brownlee
.................10 Living Stephenson
.................9 Living Weidenkeller
+ Forrest Sailors b: 26 Sep
.................10 Living Sailors
+ Living Dolezal
.................11 Living Dolezal
.................11 Living Dolezal
.................10 Living Sailors
+ Living Radcliff
+ Living Mahachek
.................11 Living Sailors
.................10 Living Sailors
+ Living Hanson
.................11 Living Sailors
.................11 Living Sailors
.................8 Mary Wanda Stephenson b: 02 Feb 1900 in Stanberry, Missouri, d: 06 Feb 1937 in
Hastings, Nebraska; Y
+ Albert Ray BUTT b: Abt. 1898, m: 29 Oct 1919
.................7 William Stephenson b: 26 Jun 1870 in Gentry Cty. Missouri, d: 17 Jan 1954 in Gentry Cty.
Missouri; Y
+ Sarah Frances Smith m: 03 Nov 1898
.................6 Grissum Stephenson b: Abt. 1828 in Madison Co., KENTUCKY
.................6 Sarah Jane Stephenson b: Abt. 1839 in Madison Co., KENTUCKY
+ Elijah W. Mercer m: 12 Mar 1863, d: 13 Mar 1872 ; Y
+ Noah G. Lee m: 19 Oct 1876
.................6 twelve see notes STEPHENSON
+ George Elsworth m: Abt. 1848 in Madison Co., Kentucky moved to Nodaway Co., MO

..........5 Delila Dilly Lee b: Abt. 1799 in Madison, Co, Ky, d: Henry Co., MO; Y
        + Hezekiah WRIGHT b: Abt. 1800 in Madison, Co, Ky, m: 12 Oct 1820 in Madison, Co, Ky
.............6 Serilda WRIGHT b: Abt. 1821 in Howard Co., MO
.............6 Gideon WRIGHT b: 1823 in Howard Co., MO
..........5 Nancy Ruth Lee b: 1800 in Madison, Co, Ky, d: of, Madison, Co, Ky; Y
        + Joel Perry TODD b: 08 Mar 1801 in of, Madison, Co, Ky, m: 31 Mar 1822 in Madison, Co, Ky,
          d: 18 Sep 1886 in 10, CH; Y
.............6 MArtha Ann TODD b: 16 Feb 1823 in Madison Co., KY
.............6 Richard TODD b: Abt. 1824 in Madison Co., KY
.............6 Elizabeth Betty TODD b: Abt. 1825 in Madison Co., KY
.............6 John TODD b: 01 Jan 1826 in Madison Co., KY
.............6 Irvine TODD b: 1828 in Madison Co., KY
.............6 Newton TODD b: 1830 in Madison Co., KY
.............6 Amanda TODD b: 02 Apr 1832 in Madison Co., KY
.............6 Lucinda TODD b: Apr 1834 in Madison Co., KY
.............6 Mary Jane TODD b: 26 Sep 1837 in Madison Co., KY
.............6 Joel Elias TODD b: 15 Nov 1839 in Kingston, Madison Co., KY
..........5 James B. Lee b: 26 Dec 1801 in Paint Lick Creek, Madison Co., KENTUCKY, d: 10 May 1864
          in Leesville, Henry, Co, Mo; Y
        + Naomi Nedonia CLOYD b: 18 Aug 1802 in Paint Lick, Madison Co., Ky., m: 28 Jul 1825 in
          Madison, Co, Ky, d: 22 Sep 1873 in Leesville, Henry Co., MO; Y
.............6 John C LEE b: 24 May 1826 in Missouri, d: Bef. Apr 1871 ; Y
        + Permelia Mc FALL b: 1837 in Kentucky, m: 07 Apr 1853 in Henry Co., MISSOURI
.............7 Lawrence W LEE b: 1855
.............7 Nancy J LEE b: 1860
.............7 John LEE b: 1862
.............7 William LEE b: 1866
.............7 George LEE b: 1868
.............6 Nancy LEE b: 1828 in Howard Co., MISSOURI, d: Howard Co., MISSOURI; Y
        + Alfred REED b: 25 Dec 1821 in Howard Co., MISSOURI, m: 21 Dec 1848, d: Henry Co.,
          MISSOURI; Y
.............7 James A REED b: 1852 in Henry Co., MISSOURI, d: Henry Co., MISSOURI; Y
.............7 John W REED b: 1853 in Henry Co., MISSOURI
.............7 Sarah M REED b: 1854 in Henry Co., MISSOURI
.............7 Mary Elizabeth (Bette) (May) REED b: 05 Apr 1856 in Henry Co., MISSOURI, d: 19 Jun
          1935 in Boatman, Mayes Co., OKLAHOMA; Y
        + William Franklin FERGUSON b: 03 Jul 1849 in Raywick, Marion Co., KENTUCKY, m: 18
          Jun 1873 in Henry Co., MISSOURI, d: 17 Mar 1924 in Boatman, Mayes Co.,
          OKLAHOMA; Y
.............8 Cyrus Alfred FERGUSON b: 09 Jan 1875 in Clay Co., MISSOURI, d: 23 Feb 1957 in
          Park, WYOMING; Y
        + Francis Fannie MOORE b: 1875 in Henry Co., MISSOURI, d: 19 Sep 1955 in
          Wyoming; Y
.............8 John FERGUSON b: 09 Sep 1876 in Henry Co., MISSOURI, d: 19 Sep 1955 in Park,
          WYOMING; Y
        + Anna MOORE b: 1876 in Missouri
.............9 Mary Elizabeth FERGUSON
.............9 Ruby FERGUSON
.............9 John Walter FERGUSON
.............8 Rosa FERGUSON b: 15 Sep 1878 in Henry Co., MISSOURI, d: 23 Oct 1936 ; Y
.............8 Roxy Lee FERGUSON b: 17 Mar 1881 in Ray Co., MISSOURI, d: 16 Oct 1967 in
          California; Y
        + John SMITH m: 07 Mar 1917
.............9 Beulah SMITH
.............9 Russell SMITH

................9 Dorothy SMITH
................9 Thelma SMITH
................8 Chelsley FERGUSON b: 11 Jun 1883 in Ray Co., MISSOURI, d: 16 Oct 1967 in
Chetopa, Kansas; Y
          + Maude M DAVOIT m: 07 Mar 1917
................9 Clifford Farris FERGUSON b: 22 Dec 1917, d: 22 Jul 1984 ; Y
................9 Freda FERGUSON b: 16 Jun 1921
................9 Ralph Russell FERGUSON b: 03 Mar 1927
................9 Letha FERGUSON b: 30 Dec 1929
................9 Ellis Victor FERGUSON
................9 Carl William FERGUSON
................9 Chesley Ray FERGUSON
................9 Living FERGUSON
................8 August (n) (Gus) FERGUSON b: 15 Mar 1886 in Ray Co., MISSOURI, d: 15 Mar 1943 in
Fort Scott, Bourbon Co., KANSAS; Y
          + Elese Gertrude MOORE b: 14 Jul 1904 in Garland, Bourbon Co., KANSAS, m: 22 Aug
             1921 in Fort Scott, Bourbon Co., KANSAS
................9 Lucille Marie FERGUSON b: 27 Oct 1924 in Swart, Vernon Co., MISSOURI
................9 Chester Eugene FERGUSON
................9 Living FERGUSON
          + Mae m: 1907
          + Mildred MOORE b: 08 Jun 1900 in Pettis Co., MISSOURI, m: 12 Nov 1917 in Nevada,
             Vernon Co., MISSOURI, d: 03 Dec 1919 in Harrison Township, Vernon Co, MISSOURI;
             Y
................9 Arthur Gus FERGUSON b: 06 Sep 1917 in Swart, Vernon Co., MISSOURI
................9 Francis FERGUSON d: 30 Nov 1919 in Vernon, Missouri; Y
................8 Olive Loretta FERGUSON b: 14 Sep 1891 in Ray Co., MISSOURI, d: 14 Jul 1960 in
Park, WYOMING; Y
          + James Harry (Mack) STANWAITY m: 11 Jan 1908
................9 Chester Clyde STANWAITY b: 01 Dec 1901 in Deerfield, Vernon Co., MISSOURI
................9 Ruby Arlene STANWAITY b: 19 Jan 1914 in Bourbon Co., KANSAS, d: 17 Jan 1915 ; Y
................9 Paul William STANWAITY b: 22 Dec 1916 in Deerfield, Vernon Co., MISSOURI
................9 Elmer Franklin STANWAITY b: 23 Aug 1919 in Deerfield, Vernon Co., MISSOURI
................9 Loretta Irene STANWAITY b: 25 May 1920 in Powell Park, WYOMING
................9 Gordon Harry STANWAITY b: 20 Nov 1924 in Powell Park, WYOMING
................8 Norah FERGUSON b: 14 Nov 1893 in Ray Co., MISSOURI, d: 17 Jan 1919 ; Y
          + WOODWARD OR Mc WATERS
................9 Raymond Mc Waters
................9 Joe Woodward
................8 Bertha FERGUSON b: 21 Feb 1896 in Ray Co., MISSOURI, d: 04 Sep 1985 in Boatman,
Mayes Co., OKLAHOMA; Y
          + Mose Flecher SHARP b: 25 Jan 1886, m: Bef. 1954, d: 14 Sep 1954 in Boatman,
             Mayes Co., OKLAHOMA; Y
................9 Owen SHARP b: 07 Jan 1920
................9 Patricia (Patty) SHARP
          + Al MAC WATERS m: Aft. 1954
................8 William Dewie FERGUSON b: 21 Feb 1898 in Ray Co., MISSOURI, d: Garland, Bourbon
Co., KANSAS; Y
          + Leona
................9 Joann FERGUSON
................9 Marilyn FERGUSON
................7 Marcy A REED b: 1858 in Henry Co., MISSOURI
................7 Amanda Fitzerland REED b: 17 Feb 1858 in Henry Co., MISSOURI, d: 26 Oct 1859 in
Henry Co., MISSOURI; Y

.................7 Richard Lee REED b: 28 Nov 1860 in Henry Co., MISSOURI, d: 20 Sep 1866 in Henry Co., MISSOURI; Y
.................7 Joseph A REED b: 29 Jan 1869, d: 27 Sep 1896 in Henry Co., MISSOURI; Y
.............6 William Dudley LEE b: 10 Mar 1829, d: 19 Mar 1900 ; Y
        + Malinda HARRISON b: 16 Feb 1842 in Illinois, m: 11 Jan 1860 in Henry Co., MISSOURI
.................7 David Albert LEE b: 13 Oct 1860
.................7 Carrie Ella LEE b: Nov 1866
.................7 Harrison B LEE b: 1869
.................7 Marion H LEE b: 12 Aug 1877 in Clinton. Henry Co., MISSOURI
.................7 William C LEE b: Feb 1880
.................7 Frank H LEE b: 01 Nov 1881
.................7 Paul H LEE b: 18 Mar 1883
.............6 Richard E LEE b: 1832 in Missouri, d: 1862 in Little Rock, ARKANSAS; Y
        + Elizabeth Jane JAMES b: 16 May 1842 in Muhlenberg Co., KENTUCKY, m: 17 Feb 1859 in Clinton. Henry Co., MISSOURI, d: 27 May 1929 in Clinton. Henry Co., MISSOURI; Y
.................7 Mary W LEE b: 26 May 1862 in Bethlehem Township, Henry Co., MISSOURI, d: 1945 ; Y
        + Robert Wilber HUEY b: 1857 in Montgomery Co., Ohio, d: 26 Feb 1912 in Henry Co., MISSOURI; Y
.....................8 Robert HUEY
.....................8 Blanche HUEY
.....................8 Albert HUEY
.....................8 Ernest HUEY
.............6 Mary (Polly) LEE b: 15 Sep 1832 in Howard Co., MISSOURI, d: 1922 in Henry Co., MISSOURI; Y
        + Solomon DAVIS b: 27 Apr 1825 in Richland Co., OHIO, m: 05 Dec 1854 in Henry Co., MISSOURI, d: 21 Oct 1901 ; Y
.................7 Richard H DAVIS b: 07 Oct 1856 in Missouri, d: 12 Apr 1893 ; Y
.................7 Naomi DAVIS b: 1857, d: 1941 ; Y
        + Joe VERMILLION
.................7 James I DAVIS b: 1860 in Missouri, d: 1914 ; Y
.................7 John William DAVIS b: 1860, d: 1914 in Bethlehem Township. Henry Co., MISSOURI; Y
        + Luiza
.................7 Mary Jane DAVIS b: 13 Jul 1863
.................7 Jefferson S DAVIS b: 1864, d: 1951 ; Y
.................7 George H DAVIS b: 1865, d: 1914 ; Y
.................7 Orlena DAVIS b: 1867
.................7 Henderson F DAVIS b: 1867, d: 1933 ; Y
        + Clara
.................7 Henderson F DAVIS b: 25 May 1867, d: 1933 ; Y
        + Clara
.................7 Arlena (Lena) DAVIS b: 28 Nov 1871
.................7 Sarah L (Sallie) DAVIS b: 16 Jan 1873
.............6 Margaret J LEE b: 17 Nov 1834 in Missouri, d: 10 Jun 1915 in Bethlehem Township. Henry Co., MISSOURI; Y
        + Horatio J (Herb) WILLIAMS b: 1832 in Missouri, m: Bef. 1860, d: Bef. 1871 ; Y
.................7 Dolphine E WILLIAMS b: 1858 in Missouri
.................7 Irvin C WILLIAMS b: 11 Jul 1859 in Missouri, d: 22 Jul 1891 in Henry Co., MISSOURI; Y
        + Caroline C GROFF b: 28 May 1855, m: Bef. 29 Jul 1880, d: 17 Apr 1939 ; Y
.....................8 Ida Elvire (Elva) WILLIAMS b: 29 Jul 1880
        + John F THRUSH m: 01 Jul 1900
.................7 G.L. WILLIAMS b: 21 Mar 1876
.............6 Irvin LEE b: 1836 in Missouri, d: Bef. 1871 ; Y
        + Karen M HURST b: 1835 in Kentucky, m: 23 Dec 1859 in Henry Co., MISSOURI
.................7 Job I LEE b: Aft. 1859

.............6 Pacifica A (TWIN) LEE b: 15 Nov 1838, d: 15 Nov 1838 ; Y
.............6 Narcissa A (TWIN) LEE b: 15 Nov 1838 in Howard Co., MISSOURI, d: 05 Jul 1920 ; Y
    + John J HERST b: 31 Aug 1838 in Kentucky, m: 1861
.................7 Edna Margaret HERST
.................7 James HERST
.................7 Naomi Lee HERST
.................7 Sallie Ann HERST
.................7 Mary Lucinda HERST
.............6 Sarah LEE b: 22 Aug 1842 in Henry Co., MISSOURI, d: 08 Sep 1927 in Gainesville, Cooke
    Co., TEXAS; Y
    + Bryant McGrath WRIGHT b: 01 Jan 1838 in Howard Co., MISSOURI, m: 04 Mar 1862 in
    Clinton, Henry Co., MISSOURI, d: 08 Apr 1924 in Gainesville, Cooke Co., TEXAS; Y
.................7 Ida Isabell WRIGHT b: 04 Mar 1863, d: 08 May 1900 ; Y
.................7 James Washington WRIGHT b: 12 Feb 1864 in Clinton, Henry Co., MISSOURI
.................7 Annie Mary WRIGHT b: 16 Jun 1865
.................7 Alfred McGrath WRIGHT b: 11 Jan 1867 in Clinton, Henry Co., MISSOURI, d: 18 May 1947
    in Mc Comb, Pike Co., MISSISSIPPI; Y
    + Ella Beatrice ARGO
.................8 Paul Lee WRIGHT b: 13 Nov 1897 in Gainesville, Cooke Co., TEXAS, d: 06 Nov 1973 in
    Gulfport, Harrison Co., MISSISSIPPI; Y
    + Lillie SAENZ m: 14 May 1919 in Long Beach, Harrison Co., MISSISSIPPI
.................8 William Bryant WRIGHT
.................7 Margaret Jane WRIGHT b: 04 Jul 1868 in Clinton, Henry Co., MISSOURI, d: 08 Dec 1932
    in Aubrey, Denton Co., TEXAS; Y
.................7 William Lee WRIGHT b: 21 Oct 1871, d: Clinton, Henry Co., MISSOURI; Y
.................7 Elmer Graves WRIGHT b: 02 Feb 1875
.................7 Calvin (TWIN) WRIGHT b: 20 Sep 1877, d: 20 Sep 1877 ; Y
.................7 Alvin (TWIN) WRIGHT b: 20 Sep 1877 in Loves Valley, OKLAHOMA, d: 20 Sep 1877 in
    Loves Valley, OKLAHOMA; Y
.................7 Oscar Wallace WRIGHT b: 01 Dec 1879, d: Ardmore, Carter, OKLAHOMA; Y
    + Fannie WILSON m: 04 Dec 1902 in Sherman, Grayson Co., Texas
.................7 Bessie Lee WRIGHT b: 03 Jun 1882, d: 14 Sep 1883 ; Y
.................7 Cora Alice WRIGHT b: 20 Sep 1884
    + Ralph E BRADLEY m: 19 May 1907 in Gainesville, Cooke Co., TEXAS
.................7 Gladys Wilhelmina WRIGHT b: 11 Nov 1886, d: 14 Oct 1887 ; Y
.................7 Child WRIGHT
.........5 Margaret Peggy Lee b: 1802 in Paint Lick, Madison Co., Ky of Chariton Co., MO, d: Linn Co.,
    MO of, Madison, Co, Ky; Y
    + Hugh CLOYD b: 28 Jan 1799 in Madison, Co, Ky, m: 19 Sep 1822 in Madison, Co, Ky, d:
    1834 in Chariton Co., MO; Y
.............6 Naomi CLOYD b: 1823 in Madison, Co, Ky
.............6 James CLOYD b: 1825 in Madison, Co, Ky
.............6 Mary Margaret CLOYD b: 1828 in Madison, Co, Ky
.............6 John CLOYD b: 1830 in Madison, Co, Ky
.............6 child CLOYD b: 1833 in Madison, Co, Ky, d: 1833 ; Y
    + David W. Dalton m: 1827 in Chariton Co., MO
.........5 Irvine Lee b: 1803 in Paint Lick, Madison Co., Ky, d: 1844 in of, Madison, Co, Ky; Y
    + Sarah HERNDON b: Abt. 1805 in of, Madison, Co, Ky, m: 27 Jul 1825 in Madison, Co, Ky, d:
    01 May 1843 in Madison, Co, Ky; Y
.............6 Zarred Zarilda (Larelda) Lee b: 12 Sep 1829 in of, Madison, Co, Ky, d: 27 Apr 1902 in Henry
    Co., MO; Y
    + Benjamin F CREWS b: Abt. 1827 in Henry Co., MO, m: Abt. 1850 in Henry Co., MO
.................7 Andrew Lee b: 1859 in Henry Co., MO
.................7 Elica Lee b: 1865 in Henry Co., MO
.............6 Ann Lee b: 1834 in of, Madison, Co, Ky, d: Bef. 1840 in Henry Co., MO; Y

...........6 William D. Lee b: 1839 in Henry Co., MO
    + Elizabeth Williams MERRITT b: 1801 in Madison, Co, Ky, m: 24 Jul 1843 in Howard Co., MO
...........6 Ann E. Lee b: 1845 in Henry, Co, Mo
    + Nancy GREEN
.........5 Lucinda Lee b: 1805 in Madison, Co, Ky, d: Bucklin, Linn, Co, Mo; Y
    + Francis Preston Forrest b: Abt. 1808 in of, Howard, Co, Mo, m: 31 Jul 1827 in Howard, Co, Mo, d: Yellow Creek Twp, Linn Co., Missouri; Y
...........6 Mary Ann Forrest b: Abt. 1829 in Howard Co., Missouri, d: 1879 in Baker Twp., Linn Co., Missouri; Y
    + John G. Bailey b: 01 Dec 1818 in Barren Co., Kentucky, m: 25 Dec 1846 in Linn Co., Missouri, d: 01 Feb 1897 in Linn Co., Missouri; Y
...........7 Andrew Jackson "Jack" Bailey b: 28 Dec 1846 in New Boston, Linn Co., Missouri, d: 06 Aug 1914 in Linn Co., Missouri; Y
    + Mary J. Phillips b: 15 Mar 1848 in Mo, m: 24 Oct 1869 in Linn Co., MO
...........8 James Walter Bailey b: 18 Jul 1870 in New Boston, Linn Co., MO, d: 20 Aug 1959 in Linn Co., MO; Y
...........8 Minnie Belle Bailey b: 1871, d: 1959 ; Y
...........8 Joseph Bailey b: 1874
...........8 George H. Bailey b: 1876, d: Jul 1954 ; Y
...........8 John Bailey b: 10 Apr 1878, d: 20 Jul 1879 ; Y
...........8 Wesley A. Bailey b: Feb 1880
...........8 Mella "Millie" Bailey b: Sep 1885
...........8 Julia E. Bailey b: Sep 1892, d: 1968 ; Y
...........8 Henry Bailey
...........7 Francis Marion Bailey b: 28 Jan 1848 in New Boston, Linn Co., Missouri, d: 29 Jul 1850 ; Y
...........7 Grandvill Bailey b: 07 May 1850 in New Boston, Linn Co., Missouri, d: Jan 1851 ; Y
...........7 Albert Hamilton Bailey b: 12 May 1852 in Bucklin, Linn Co., Missouri, d: 13 Feb 1913 in Wheeling, Livingston Co., Missouri; Y
    + Hannah Ellen Gross b: 18 Oct 1847 in Marion Twp., Hendricks Co., Indiana, m: 03 Sep 1874 in Brookfield, Linn Co., Missouri, d: 20 Jun 1928 in Chillicothe, Livingston Co., Missouri; Y
...........8 Theodonia Ella Bailey b: 12 Jun 1875 in Linn Co., Missouri, d: Bef. 1913 in Woodward Co., Oklahoma; Y
...........8 Emma Bailey b: 10 Aug 1879 in Linn Co., Missouri, d: 1932 in Brookfield, Linn Co., Missouri; Y
...........8 Samuel Martin "Mont" Bailey b: 22 Nov 1881 in New Boston, Linn Co., Missouri, d: 04 Dec 1964 in Bucklin, Linn Co., Missouri; Y
...........8 James Jessie Bailey b: 17 Feb 1883 in Linn Co., Missouri, d: Wheeling, Livingston Co., Missouri; Y
...........8 Ida Denver Bailey b: 06 Dec 1887 in Linn Co., Missouri, d: Bef. 1909 in Linn Co., MO; Y
...........8 Bertha Benton Bailey b: 25 Apr 1890 in New Boston, Linn Co., Missouri, d: 07 Sep 1966 in Woodward, Woodward Co., Oklahoma; Y
...........8 Lenora Maude Bailey b: 19 Feb 1892 in Baker Twp., Linn Co., Missouri, d: Mar 1969 in Modesto, Stanislaus Co., California; Y
...........7 Samuel Preston Bailey b: 29 Dec 1853 in New Boston, Linn Co., Missouri, d: 24 Nov 1923 in Linn Co., Missouri; Y
    + Nancy Ann Wyatt b: 1857 in Mo, m: 30 Dec 1873 in Linn Co., MO, d: 1932 in Linn Co., MO; Y
...........8 John M. Bailey b: 04 Jan 1875, d: 11 Jul 1876 in Linn Co., MO; Y
...........8 Preston A. Bailey b: 1877 in Linn Co., MO, d: 1962 in Linn Co., MO; Y
...........8 Mary Bailey b: 1880, d: 1959 in Linn Co., MO; Y
...........8 Roy Bailey b: 1881, d: 1959 in Linn Co., MO; Y
...........8 Rosa B. Bailey b: 11 May 1883 in Linn Co., MO, d: 01 Feb 1905 in Linn Co., MO; Y
...........8 James E. Bailey b: 10 Apr 1885 in Linn Co., MO, d: 04 Mar 1907 in Linn Co., MO; Y
...........8 Florence Bailey b: 1888, d: 1961 in Linn Co., MO; Y

...............8 Myrtle Bailey b: 1892, d: 1921 in Linn Co., MO; Y
...............8 Willie W. Bailey b: 10 Jan 1896, d: 1970 in Linn Co., MO; Y
...............8 Russell Bailey b: 1899, d: 1972 in Linn Co., MO; Y
...............8 Elmer Bailey
...............7 George Washington Bailey b: 09 May 1855 in New Boston, Linn Co., Missouri, d: 15 Apr
            1939 ; Y
            + Marian Melville b: Apr 1863 in Albany, NY, m: 16 Jul 1885 in Linn Co., MO
...............8 Lois M. Bailey b: Mar 1899 in Brookfield, Linn Co., MO
...............7 Beverly Joseph Bailey b: 12 Apr 1859 in New Boston, Linn Co., Missouri, d: 05 Dec 1872 ;
            Y
...............7 Richard Randolph Bailey b: 08 Oct 1861 in New Boston, Linn Co., Missouri
            + Nettie White m: 24 Mar 1884 in Linn Co., MO
...............7 Lucinda C. Bailey b: 20 Aug 1863 in New Boston, Linn Co., Missouri
            + William P. Moyer m: 31 Dec 1880
            + Pitt
...............7 Sarah O. Bailey b: 22 Aug 1865 in New Boston, Linn Co., Missouri, d: Linn Co., MO; Y
            + W. M. Davis m: 06 Jun 1889 in Moberly, MO
...............8 Jess Davis
...............7 Julia Ann Bailey b: 20 Jun 1867 in New Boston, Linn Co., Missouri
            + Robert H. Hall m: 20 Mar 1887 in CA
...............7 Margaret "Maggie" Bailey b: 27 Sep 1869 in New Boston, Linn Co., Missouri
...............7 Alonzo Lee "Lon" Bailey b: 04 Mar 1870 in New Boston, Linn Co., Missouri, d: 15 Oct 1942
            in Linn Co., Missouri; Y
            + "Willie" A. Mott b: 08 May 1880, m: 15 Dec 1898, d: 26 May 1960 in Linn Co., MO; Y
...............8 Everett Mott Bailey b: 21 Feb 1900, d: 03 Jan 1983 ; Y
...............8 Mattie Neal Bailey b: 21 Mar 1907, d: 1990 ; Y
...............8 Anna Pearl Bailey b: Private
...............6 Francis Marion Forrest b: 23 Oct 1829 in Missouri, d: 27 Jun 1894 in Pleasant Plains,
            Independence Co., Arkansas; Y
            + Rebecca R. Watkins b: 01 Dec 1839 in Brookfield, Linn Co., MO, m: 11 Jul 1855 in Linn
            Co., MO, d: 04 Aug 1910 in Dallas, Dallas Co., Tx; Y
...............7 Suffronia "Belle" Forrest b: 11 Nov 1856 in Linn Co., MO, d: 23 Feb 1925 in Hillsboro, Hill
            Co., TX; Y
...............7 Edwin Forrest b: 11 Oct 1858 in Linn Co., MO, d: 24 Jul 1924 in Blum, Hill Co., TX; Y
            + Martha Gage b: 23 Nov 1864 in Alexandria, Rapides Co., LA, m: 30 Nov 1880, d: 17 Mar
            1957 in Itasca, Hill Co., TX; Y
...............8 Harold Gage Forrest b: 11 Apr 1895 in Blum, Hill Co., TX, d: 27 Mar 1935 in Brownfield,
            Terry Co., TX; Y
...............7 Victoria Virginia Forrest b: Abt. 1861
...............7 Mattie Forrest b: Abt. 1863
...............7 Addie Forrest b: Abt. 1866
...............7 Marion Augustus Forrest b: Abt. 1869
...............7 Alice Forrest b: 05 May 1870 in Brookfield, Linn Co., MO, d: 20 Nov 1935 in Hillsboro, Hill
            Co., TX; Y
            + Edward Arastus Long b: 29 Oct 1864 in Port Gibson, Claiborne Co., MS, m: 05 Dec 1886
            in Hill Co., TX, d: 10 Jan 1936 in Hillsboro, Hill Co., TX; Y
...............7 Annie Forrest b: 05 May 1870, d: 1870 ; Y
...............7 Mary Forrest b: Abt. 1873
...............7 Cora Lee Forrest b: Bet. 1875–1877 in Hillsboro, Hill Co., TX
...............7 Cora Lee Forrest b: 03 Jul 1877 in Woodbury, Hill Co., TX, d: 28 Jun 1943 in Brownwood,
            Brown Co., TX; Y
            + James Bernard Moore Sr. b: 17 Apr 1873 in Brick Church, Giles Co., TN, m: 10 Jan 1896
            in Hill Co., TX, d: 08 Sep 1948 in Henderson, Rusk Co., TX; Y
...............8 James Bernard Moore Jr. b: 01 Mar 1897 in Waxahachie, Ellis Co., TX

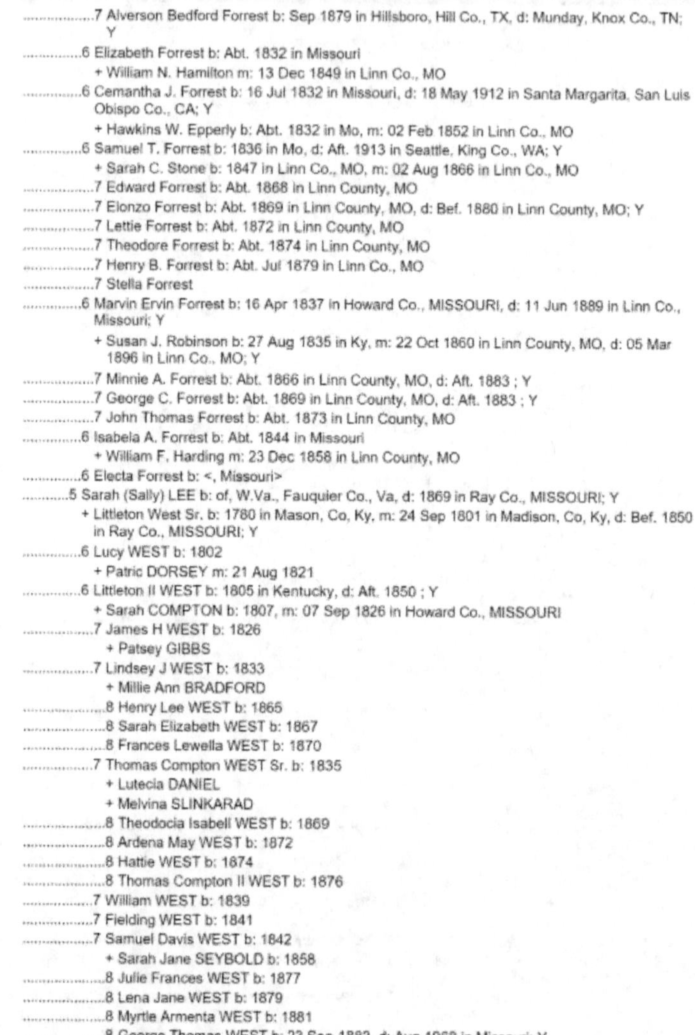

...............7 Alverson Bedford Forrest b: Sep 1879 in Hillsboro, Hill Co., TX, d: Munday, Knox Co., TN;
Y

.............6 Elizabeth Forrest b: Abt. 1832 in Missouri
+ William N. Hamilton m: 13 Dec 1849 in Linn Co., MO

.............6 Cemantha J. Forrest b: 16 Jul 1832 in Missouri, d: 18 May 1912 in Santa Margarita, San Luis Obispo Co., CA; Y
+ Hawkins W. Epperly b: Abt. 1832 in Mo, m: 02 Feb 1852 in Linn Co., MO

.............6 Samuel T. Forrest b: 1836 in Mo, d: Aft. 1913 in Seattle, King Co., WA; Y
+ Sarah C. Stone b: 1847 in Linn Co., MO, m: 02 Aug 1866 in Linn Co., MO

...............7 Edward Forrest b: Abt. 1868 in Linn County, MO

...............7 Elonzo Forrest b: Abt. 1869 in Linn County, MO, d: Bef. 1880 in Linn County, MO; Y

...............7 Lettie Forrest b: Abt. 1872 in Linn County, MO

...............7 Theodore Forrest b: Abt. 1874 in Linn County, MO

...............7 Henry B. Forrest b: Abt. Jul 1879 in Linn Co., MO

...............7 Stella Forrest

.............6 Marvin Ervin Forrest b: 16 Apr 1837 in Howard Co., MISSOURI, d: 11 Jun 1889 in Linn Co., Missouri; Y
+ Susan J. Robinson b: 27 Aug 1835 in Ky, m: 22 Oct 1860 in Linn County, MO, d: 05 Mar 1896 in Linn Co., MO; Y

...............7 Minnie A. Forrest b: Abt. 1866 in Linn County, MO, d: Aft. 1883 ; Y

...............7 George C. Forrest b: Abt. 1869 in Linn County, MO, d: Aft. 1883 ; Y

...............7 John Thomas Forrest b: Abt. 1873 in Linn County, MO

.............6 Isabela A. Forrest b: Abt. 1844 in Missouri
+ William F. Harding m: 23 Dec 1858 in Linn County, MO

.............6 Electa Forrest b: <, Missouri>

..........5 Sarah (Sally) LEE b: of, W.Va., Fauquier Co., Va, d: 1869 in Ray Co., MISSOURI; Y
+ Littleton West Sr. b: 1780 in Mason, Co, Ky, m: 24 Sep 1801 in Madison, Co, Ky, d: Bef. 1850 in Ray Co., MISSOURI; Y

.............6 Lucy WEST b: 1802
+ Patric DORSEY m: 21 Aug 1821

.............6 Littleton II WEST b: 1805 in Kentucky, d: Aft. 1850 ; Y
+ Sarah COMPTON b: 1807, m: 07 Sep 1826 in Howard Co., MISSOURI

...............7 James H WEST b: 1826
+ Patsey GIBBS

...............7 Lindsey J WEST b: 1833
+ Millie Ann BRADFORD

...................8 Henry Lee WEST b: 1865

...................8 Sarah Elizabeth WEST b: 1867

...................8 Frances Lewella WEST b: 1870

...............7 Thomas Compton WEST Sr. b: 1835
+ Lutecia DANIEL
+ Melvina SLINKARAD

...................8 Theodocia Isabell WEST b: 1869

...................8 Ardena May WEST b: 1872

...................8 Hattie WEST b: 1874

...................8 Thomas Compton II WEST b: 1876

...............7 William WEST b: 1839

...............7 Fielding WEST b: 1841

...............7 Samuel Davis WEST b: 1842
+ Sarah Jane SEYBOLD b: 1858

...................8 Julie Frances WEST b: 1877

...................8 Lena Jane WEST b: 1879

...................8 Myrtle Armenta WEST b: 1881

...................8 George Thomas WEST b: 23 Sep 1883, d: Aug 1968 in Missouri; Y

................8 Jesse Le Roy WEST b: 1885
................8 Charles WEST b: 02 Nov 1889, d: Nov 1986 in Indiana; Y
................8 Bertha Davis WEST b: 1893
................7 Elizabeth WEST b: 1845
................7 Sarah WEST b: 1849
............6 David WEST b: 1805 in Kentucky
            + Bernetta BREWER b: 1820 in Missouri, m: 07 Jan 1837 in Ray Co., MISSOURI
................7 Julia A WEST b: 1843 in Missouri
................7 John WEST b: 1846 in Missouri
................7 William Jasper WEST b: 1848 in Missouri
................7 Newton WEST b: 1855
................7 Henry WEST b: 1859
............6 Wilson Franklin WEST b: 1817 in TENNESSEE, d: Bef. 1860 ; Y
            + Julia Ann LILE b: 1824 in Missouri, m: 27 Apr 1843 in Ray Co., MISSOURI, d: Aft. 1870 ; Y
................7 James Franklin WEST b: 09 Sep 1845 in Richmond, Ray Co., MISSOURI, d: 27 Mar 1917
                in Boulder, Boulder Co., COLORADO; Y
                    + Isabel Frances RENFRO b: 1844 in Missouri, d: 1921 in Boulder, Boulder Co.,
                    COLORADO; Y
................8 Fannie WEST b: 1870 in Coffey, Daviess Co., MISSOURI
................8 Julia WEST b: 1873 in Coffey, Daviess Co., MISSOURI
................8 William Ernest (Will) WEST b: 20 Jan 1876 in Coffey, Daviess Co., MISSOURI, d: 15 Aug
                1963 ; Y
................8 Mary Catherine (Mollie) WEST b: 1878 in Coffey, Daviess Co., MISSOURI
................8 Ona WEST b: 08 Apr 1890 in Coffey, Daviess Co., MISSOURI, d: Mar 1977 ; Y
................7 Mary Jane WEST b: 25 Sep 1850 in Ray Co., MISSOURI, d: 21 Sep 1900 ; Y
                    + James McNEELEY b: 10 Mar 1852, m: 05 Dec 1880 in Daviess Co., Missouri, d: 25 Feb
                    1908 ; Y
............6 James M WEST b: 1818 in TENNESSEE
            + Mary VANDERPOOL m: 01 Jan 1842
................7 Peter WEST b: 1841 in Missouri
................7 Sarah WEST b: 1842 in Missouri
................7 Catherine WEST b: 1845 in Missouri
................7 Clementine WEST b: 1847 in Missouri
................7 Jane WEST b: 1849 in Missouri
............6 Clementine WEST b: 1824 in TENNESSEE
............6 Catherine WEST b: 1826 in TENNESSEE
............6 Caroline WEST b: 1828 in TENNESSEE
............6 Eliza WEST b: 1831 in TENNESSEE
............6 Thomas Jefferson WEST b: 1833 in TENNESSEE
            + Susan Jane MYERS b: Abt. 1844, m: 21 Oct 1858
................7 Alexandree Elizabeth WEST b: 1860
................7 James H WEST b: 10 Feb 1862, d: 27 Sep 1921 in Ray Co., MISSOURI; Y
                + Sallie
................7 John William WEST b: 1864
................7 Mary H WEST b: 1866, d: 1941 ; Y
................7 Serepetia Clementine (Rip) WEST b: 23 Nov 1867, d: 17 Feb 1946 ; Y
                + Horace C (Homer) RISLEY b: 17 Jun 1861, m: 1888, d: 29 Mar 1935 ; Y
................7 Rector F WEST b: 1868
................7 Thomas WEST b: May 1870, d: Bef. 1880 ; Y
................7 George C WEST b: 02 Jan 1872, d: Ray Co., MISSOURI; Y
                + Eva
................7 Alfred WEST b: 1874, d: 1942 in Ray Co., MISSOURI; Y
                + Mary H
............6 Susan Jane WEST

   + William RISLEY m: 05 Jan 1841 in Ray Co., MISSOURI
..............6 Jane WEST
..............6 Child WEST
..............6 Elizabeth WEST
..............6 John (Jonathan) C WEST d: 26 Oct 1894 in Ray Co., MISSOURI; Y
   + Nancy J
..............6 Child WEST
.........4 Mary Lee b: Abt. 1757 in Virginia, d: Abt. 1779 in Virginia; Y
  + Thomas Lee b: Abt. 1757 in Va of Bedford Co., TN, m: Abt. 1779, d: Abt. 1837 in Coffee
  County, Tennessee; Y
..........5 Peter Lee b: Abt. 1779 in Coffee Co., TN
   + Catherine (Katy) Caty McGUIRE b: 1789 in Lincoln Co., VA later Madison Co., Ky, m: 16 Mar
   1806 in Madison Co., KENTUCKY
..............6 William LEE b: Abt. 1807 in Madison Co., KY
..............6 James LEE b: Abt. 1809 in Madison Co., KY
..............6 Green LEE b: Abt. 1811 in Madison Co., KY
..............6 Peter LEE b: Abt. 1813 in Madison Co., KY
..............6 John LEE b: Abt. 1815 in Madison Co., KY
..............6 Melinda LEE b: Abt. 1817 in Madison Co., KY
   + Caleb BOWLS
..............6 Mary LEE b: Abt. 1819 in Madison Co., KY
   + Caleb BOWLS
..............6 Elizabeth (Betsey) LEE b: Abt. 1821 in Madison Co., KY
   + Galloway WALKER
  + Mary Elizabeth Betsy Miller b: Abt. 1746 in Delaware, m: 1769 in Buckingham Co., Va, d:
  Ballston, Va; Y
.........4 William MILLER LEE b: 01 Jul 1769 in Buckingham co., Va, d: Abt. 1870 in Rusk County, Texas;
 Y
  + Margaret Carson b: Abt. 1781 in Prince Edward County, Virginia, m: 06 Jan 1798 in Campbell
  County, Virginia, d: ?; Y
...........5 Mary Lee b: 10 Nov 1798 in Virginia, d: 24 Sep 1873 in Washington County, Texas; Y
  + Andrew Woods b: 11 Dec 1797 in York County, South Carolina, m: 14 Jan 1819 in Dallas
  County, Alabama, d: 25 Jul 1876 in Washington County, Texas; Y
...........5 William Carson Lee b: 24 Jan 1800 in Campbell County, Virginia of Logan Butler Co Ky, d: 30
  Jun 1876 in Terrell, Kaufman County, Texas; Y
  + Cynthia Woods b: 19 Apr 1802 in York County, South Carolina, m: 18 Nov 1825 in Dallas
  County, Alabama, d: 26 Jul 1876 in Wesley, Washington County, Texas; Y
..............6 Thadeus C. Lee b: Abt. 1828
..............6 Thomas William Lee b: 17 Nov 1829 in Dallas County, Alabama, d: ?; Y
  + Susan Jane Harris b: 12 Nov 1829 in Franklin County, Tennessee, m: ?, d: 09 Jan 1886 in
  ?; Y
................7 Carson H. Lee b: 26 May 1857 in Van Zandt Co. TX, d: 30 May 1857 in Van Zandt Co. TX;
  Y
................7 Thomas Edward Lee b: 17 Jul 1858 in Van Zandt County, Texas, d: 18 May 1933 in Motley
  Co. TX; Y
   + Mary Ellen Osborn b: 14 Dec 1869 in Coryell County, Texas, m: 08 Jan 1891 in Callahan
   County, TX, d: 12 Jun 1944 in ?; Y
..................8 Charles Emmitt Lee b: 30 Sep 1891, d: Oct 1951 ; Y
..................8 Harvey Carroll Lee b: 12 Aug 1893 in Cottonwood, TX, d: 19 Mar 1965 in Muleshoe, TX;
  Y
..................8 Eula Maude Lee b: 09 Jan 1895, d: 03 Oct 1968 in Durant, OK; Y
..................8 Russell Pendleton Lee b: 27 Aug 1896 in Abilene, Taylor County, Texas, d: Feb 1974 in
  Artesia, New Mexico; Y
   + Della Louise Bynum b: 14 Dec 1893 in ?, m: ?, d: Jan 1977 in ?; Y
.....................9 Living Lee

```
                    + Living Rowan
..........................10 Living Lee
.....................8 William Truett Lee b: 09 Jan 1898 in Dudley, TX, d: 15 Dec 1966 ; Y
.....................8 Ethel Lee b: 24 Mar 1900, d: 24 Aug 1900 in Beard, TX; Y
.....................8 Henry Oliver Lee b: 15 Aug 1901
.....................8 Robert Lee b: 08 Dec 1904, d: 16 Aug 1906 in Rochester, TX; Y
.....................8 Zelma Lee b: 23 Sep 1907
.....................8 Zena Mae Lee b: 19 Sep 1909, d: Nov 1997 ; Y
                    + Eliza Walker b: 11 Jul 1855 in Palo Pinto Co, TX, m: 20 Jan 1880 in Callahan County, TX,
                       d: 12 Jan 1889 in Lincoln Co, NM; Y
...................8 Etta Ella Lee b: 20 May 1882
...................8 Kesiah Susan Lee b: 15 Jul 1884
..................7 John Henry Lee b: 04 Mar 1860 in Van Zandt Co. TX, d: 30 Oct 1862 in Van Zandt Co. TX;
                       Y
.................7 Lee b: 13 Nov 1862 in Van Zandt Co. TX, d: 13 Nov 1862 in Van Zandt Co. TX; Y
.................7 Samuella Lee b: 22 Mar 1864 in Van Zandt Co. TX, d: 22 Oct 1865 in Van Zandt Co. TX; Y
.................7 James Emmitt Lee b: 11 Mar 1866 in Henderson County, TX, d: 11 Jul 1929 in Spur, TX; Y
                    + [unknown spouse]
...................8 Berts Lee b: Abt. 1890 in Tx
...................8 Elva Lee b: Abt. 1891 in Tx
...................8 Ernest Lee b: Abt. 1894 in Tx
...................8 Jesse Lee b: Abt. 1896 in Tx
...................8 Lawis Lee b: 1898 in Baird Co, TX, d: 11 Feb 1977 in Friona, TX; Y
...................8 Harvey Lee b: Abt. 1900 in Tx
...................8 Joe Lee b: Abt. 1902 in Tx
...................8 Frank Lee b: Abt. 1904 in Tx
...................8 John Lee b: Abt. 1906 in Tx
...............6 William Carson Lee Jr. b: Abt. 1832 in AL
                    + Eliza A. McSpadden m: 14 Aug 1856 in Van Zandt Co., TX
...............6 Sarah B. (aka Lorana or L B) Lee b: Abt. 1834 in Benton Co, AL
                    + James Taylor McSpadden b: 1826 in GA, m: 30 Nov 1856 in Van Zandt Co. TX
...................7 William Alfred McSpaddin b: Abt. 1858 in Tx, d: 1877 ; Y
...................7 Thaddus S (aka Thaddeus) McSpaddin b: 1860 in Tx
                    + Josie Blewitt
...................7 James J McSpaddin b: 1862
                    + Ollie Hicks
.............6 Margaret E. Lee b: Abt. 1836
                    + [unknown spouse]
...................7 Demplsey C Neill b: 1859
.............6 Joseph E. M. Lee b: Abt. 1838 in Benton Co. Al.
.............6 Cynthia P. Lee b: Abt. 1841 in Benton Co. AL, d: Aft. 1880 ; Y
                    + James Taylor McSpadden b: 1826 in GA, m: 05 Mar 1868 in Van Zandt Co. TX
...................7 Frena U (probably aka Eudora and Endora) McSpadden b: 1866 in Tx
...................7 George T. McSpaddin b: 1869 in Van Zandt Co. TX
                    + Johnnie Miller
...................7 Thomas Stonewall Jackson McSpaddin b: 1875, d: 1883 ; Y
...................7 Aurelius Milton McSpaddin b: 1879
............5 Elizabeth Lee b: 03 Mar 1803 in ?, d: ?; Y
............5 Thomas Helm Lee b: 12 Mar 1805 in ?, d: ?; Y
............5 Sarah Lee b: 17 Apr 1808 in ?, d: ?; Y
............5 Moses A. Lee b: 04 Dec 1811 in ?, d: ?; Y
............5 James Lee b: 11 May 1813 in ?, d: ?; Y
............5 Degrafton Lee b: 09 Oct 1815 in ?, d: Sep 1816 in ?; Y
............5 Wade Lee b: 19 Jan 1817 in ?, d: ?; Y
```

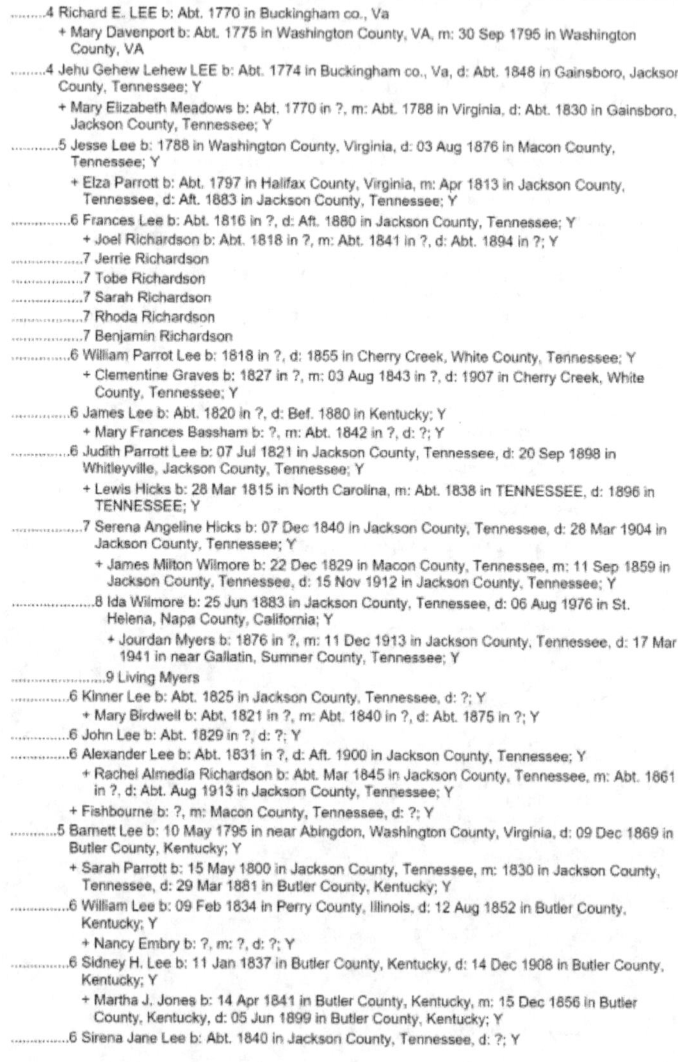

.........4 Richard E. LEE b: Abt. 1770 in Buckingham co., Va
+ Mary Davenport b: Abt. 1775 in Washington County, VA, m: 30 Sep 1795 in Washington County, VA

.........4 Jehu Gehew Lehew LEE b: Abt. 1774 in Buckingham co., Va, d: Abt. 1848 in Gainsboro, Jackson County, Tennessee; Y
+ Mary Elizabeth Meadows b: Abt. 1770 in ?, m: Abt. 1788 in Virginia, d: Abt. 1830 in Gainsboro, Jackson County, Tennessee; Y

............5 Jesse Lee b: 1788 in Washington County, Virginia, d: 03 Aug 1876 in Macon County, Tennessee; Y
+ Elza Parrott b: Abt. 1797 in Halifax County, Virginia, m: Apr 1813 in Jackson County, Tennessee, d: Aft. 1883 in Jackson County, Tennessee; Y

...............6 Frances Lee b: Abt. 1816 in ?, d: Aft. 1880 in Jackson County, Tennessee; Y
+ Joel Richardson b: Abt. 1818 in ?, m: Abt. 1841 in ?, d: Abt. 1894 in ?; Y

...................7 Jerrie Richardson

...................7 Tobe Richardson

...................7 Sarah Richardson

...................7 Rhoda Richardson

...................7 Benjamin Richardson

...............6 William Parrot Lee b: 1818 in ?, d: 1855 in Cherry Creek, White County, Tennessee; Y
+ Clementine Graves b: 1827 in ?, m: 03 Aug 1843 in ?, d: 1907 in Cherry Creek, White County, Tennessee; Y

...............6 James Lee b: Abt. 1820 in ?, d: Bef. 1880 in Kentucky; Y
+ Mary Frances Bassham b: ?, m: Abt. 1842 in ?, d: ?; Y

...............6 Judith Parrott Lee b: 07 Jul 1821 in Jackson County, Tennessee, d: 20 Sep 1898 in Whitleyville, Jackson County, Tennessee; Y
+ Lewis Hicks b: 28 Mar 1815 in North Carolina, m: Abt. 1838 in TENNESSEE, d: 1896 in TENNESSEE; Y

...................7 Serena Angeline Hicks b: 07 Dec 1840 in Jackson County, Tennessee, d: 28 Mar 1904 in Jackson County, Tennessee; Y
+ James Milton Wilmore b: 22 Dec 1829 in Macon County, Tennessee, m: 11 Sep 1859 in Jackson County, Tennessee, d: 15 Nov 1912 in Jackson County, Tennessee; Y

.......................8 Ida Wilmore b: 25 Jun 1883 in Jackson County, Tennessee, d: 06 Aug 1976 in St. Helena, Napa County, California; Y
+ Jourdan Myers b: 1876 in ?, m: 11 Dec 1913 in Jackson County, Tennessee, d: 17 Mar 1941 in near Gallatin, Sumner County, Tennessee; Y

.......................9 Living Myers

...............6 Kinner Lee b: Abt. 1825 in Jackson County, Tennessee, d: ?; Y
+ Mary Birdwell b: Abt. 1821 in ?, m: Abt. 1840 in ?, d: Abt. 1875 in ?; Y

...............6 John Lee b: Abt. 1829 in ?, d: ?; Y

...............6 Alexander Lee b: Abt. 1831 in ?, d: Aft. 1900 in Jackson County, Tennessee; Y
+ Rachel Almedia Richardson b: Abt. Mar 1845 in Jackson County, Tennessee, m: Abt. 1861 in ?, d: Abt. Aug 1913 in Jackson County, Tennessee; Y
+ Fishbourne b: ?, m: Macon County, Tennessee, d: ?; Y

............5 Barnett Lee b: 10 May 1795 in near Abingdon, Washington County, Virginia, d: 09 Dec 1869 in Butler County, Kentucky; Y
+ Sarah Parrott b: 15 May 1800 in Jackson County, Tennessee, m: 1830 in Jackson County, Tennessee, d: 29 Mar 1881 in Butler County, Kentucky; Y

...............6 William Lee b: 09 Feb 1834 in Perry County, Illinois, d: 12 Aug 1852 in Butler County, Kentucky; Y
+ Nancy Embry b: ?, m: ?, d: ?; Y

...............6 Sidney H. Lee b: 11 Jan 1837 in Butler County, Kentucky, d: 14 Dec 1908 in Butler County, Kentucky; Y
+ Martha J. Jones b: 14 Apr 1841 in Butler County, Kentucky, m: 15 Dec 1856 in Butler County, Kentucky, d: 05 Jun 1899 in Butler County, Kentucky; Y

...............6 Sirena Jane Lee b: Abt. 1840 in Jackson County, Tennessee, d: ?; Y

+ James S. Dunn b: ?, m: Aft. 1855 in ?, d: ?; Y
......6 Thomas Jefferson Lee b: 11 Feb 1843 in Jackson County, Tennessee, d: 25 Jul 1929 in Butler County, Kentucky; Y
+ Angeline Simpson b: 15 Dec 1849 in Kentucky, m: 10 Dec 1866 in Butler County, Kentucky, d: 26 Dec 1936 in Butler County, Kentucky; Y
......6 John Francis Marion Lee b: 27 May 1846 in Jackson County, Tennessee, d: 26 Dec 1907 in Grayson County, Kentucky; Y
+ Sarah Coppage Pennington b: ?, d: ?; Y
+ Nancy Jane Brooks b: ?, m: Sep 1863 in ?, d: ?; Y
......5 Daniel Lee b: Abt. 1796 in Washington County, Virginia, d: Abt. 1847 in Gainsboro, Jackson County, Tennessee; Y
+ Priscilla Teel b: Abt. 1799 in Elliots Creek, Franklin County, Virginia, m: Abt. 1819 in Jackson County, Tennessee, d: Aft. 1871 in Jackson County, Tennessee; Y
......6 Melvina Jane Lee b: 19 Nov 1824 in Jackson County, Tennessee, d: 19 May 1907 in ?; Y
+ David H. Draper b: 05 May 1821 in Jackson County, Tennessee, m: Abt. 1842 in ?, d: 19 May 1907 in Jackson County, Tennessee; Y
......6 James Haywood Lee b: Abt. 1827 in Bullards and Cub Creek, Jackson County, Tennessee, d: Abt. 1860 in Texas; Y
+ Angeline Brooks b: 13 Jan 1837 in Jackson County, Tennessee, m: Abt. 1853 in Jackson County, Tennessee, d: 26 Jul 1909 in Bell County, Texas; Y
......7 Mary Albertine Lee b: 15 Jan 1854 in Jackson County, Tennessee, d: 20 Feb 1935 in Temple, Bell County, Texas; Y
+ Thomas Dick Herring b: 06 Oct 1854 in TENNESSEE, m: 25 Oct 1874 in Gainsborough, Jackson County, Tennessee, d: 10 Dec 1934 in Temple, Bell County, Texas; Y
......8 Virgil Lee Herring b: 19 Jul 1875 in Jackson County, Tennessee, d: 30 Dec 1961 in Belton, Bell County, Texas; Y
+ Mary Garner b: 24 Dec 1880 in Belton, Bell County, Texas, m: 26 Sep 1897 in Belton, Bell County, Texas, d: 09 Mar 1957 in Belton, Bell County, Texas; Y
......9 Harold Donald Herring b: 26 Dec 1921 in Belton, Bell County, Texas, d: 12 Jun 1998 in Pueblo, Pueblo County, Colorado; Y
+ Living Ickes
......10 Living Herring
......6 Addaville Lee b: Abt. 1830 in Jackson County, Tennessee, d: Aft. 1890 in ?; Y
+ John H. Pyron b: Abt. 1820 in Macon County, Tennessee, m: ?, d: ?; Y
......6 Sarah Lee b: 13 Nov 1833 in Jackson County, Tennessee, d: 27 Apr 1900 in ?; Y
+ Silas Marion McCawley b: ?, m: ?, d: ?; Y
......6 Lafayette Lee b: 04 Jul 1835 in Jackson County, Tennessee, d: 27 Apr 1867 in ?; Y
+ Salley Darty b: 17 Apr 1842 in ?, m: Abt. 1859 in ?, d: Abt. Jul 1899 in ?; Y
......5 Elizabeth Lee b: Abt. 1798 in Washington County, Virginia, d: ?; Y
......5 Isaac Lee b: 1800 in Washington County, Virginia, d: 1882 in Tamaroa, Perry County, Illinois; Y
+ Sarah Rachel Pyron b: Abt. 1800 in North Carolina, m: Abt. 1819 in Jackson County, Tennessee, d: Abt. 1831 in Perry County, Illinois; Y
......6 Peter Lee b: 20 Feb 1820 in Jackson County, Tennessee, d: 17 Mar 1898 in Tamaroa, Perry County, Illinois; Y
......6 Lovuena Lee b: Abt. 1826 in Jackson County, Tennessee, d: Aft. 1870 in Jackson County, Tennessee; Y
+ Ralston Hampton Carver b: Abt. 1824 in Jackson County, Tennessee, m: Abt. 1845 in Jackson County, Tennessee, d: Abt. 1870 in ?; Y
......6 Sarelda Addaville Lee b: Apr 1829 in Jackson County, Tennessee, d: 04 Mar 1912 in Jackson County, Tennessee; Y
+ Thomas William Richardson b: Mar 1822 in Jackson County, Tennessee, m: 1844 in ?, d: 06 Oct 1862 in KNOXVILLE, TENNESSEE; Y
......7 Rachel Almedia Richardson b: Abt. Mar 1845 in Jackson County, Tennessee, d: Abt. Aug 1913 in Jackson County, Tennessee; Y

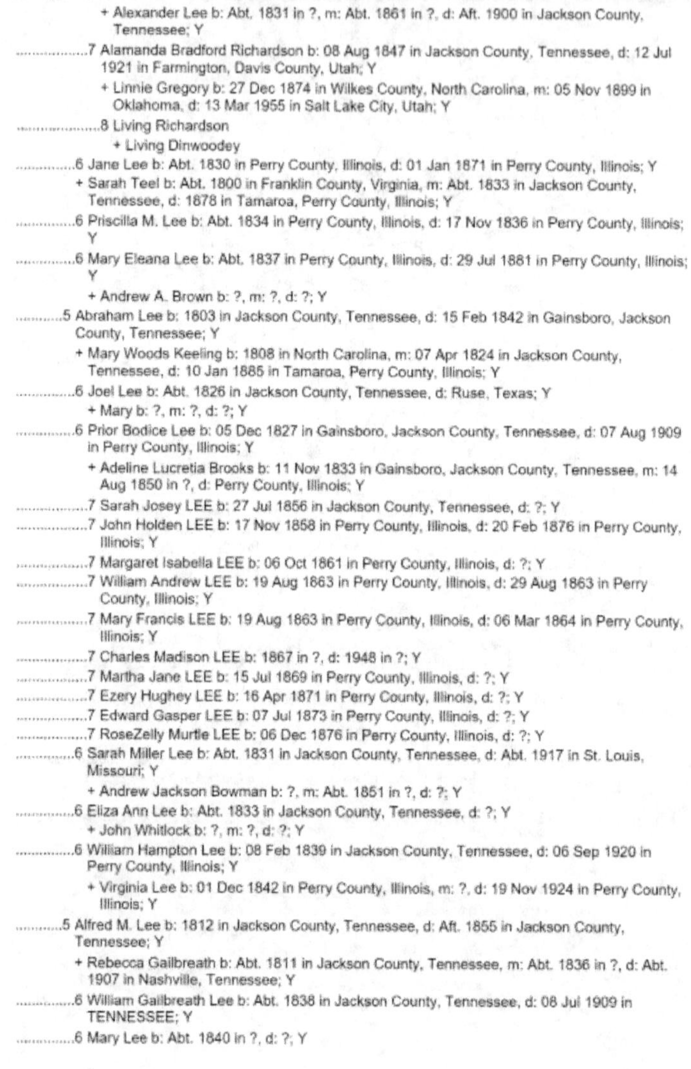

+ Alexander Lee b: Abt. 1831 in ?, m: Abt. 1861 in ?, d: Aft. 1900 in Jackson County, Tennessee; Y

.......7 Alamanda Bradford Richardson b: 08 Aug 1847 in Jackson County, Tennessee, d: 12 Jul 1921 in Farmington, Davis County, Utah; Y

+ Linnie Gregory b: 27 Dec 1874 in Wilkes County, North Carolina, m: 05 Nov 1899 in Oklahoma, d: 13 Mar 1955 in Salt Lake City, Utah; Y

.......8 Living Richardson

+ Living Dinwoodey

.......6 Jane Lee b: Abt. 1830 in Perry County, Illinois, d: 01 Jan 1871 in Perry County, Illinois; Y

+ Sarah Teel b: Abt. 1800 in Franklin County, Virginia, m: Abt. 1833 in Jackson County, Tennessee, d: 1878 in Tamaroa, Perry County, Illinois; Y

.......6 Priscilla M. Lee b: Abt. 1834 in Perry County, Illinois, d: 17 Nov 1836 in Perry County, Illinois; Y

.......6 Mary Eleana Lee b: Abt. 1837 in Perry County, Illinois, d: 29 Jul 1881 in Perry County, Illinois; Y

+ Andrew A. Brown b: ?, m: ?, d: ?; Y

.......5 Abraham Lee b: 1803 in Jackson County, Tennessee, d: 15 Feb 1842 in Gainsboro, Jackson County, Tennessee; Y

+ Mary Woods Keeling b: 1808 in North Carolina, m: 07 Apr 1824 in Jackson County, Tennessee, d: 10 Jan 1885 in Tamaroa, Perry County, Illinois; Y

.......6 Joel Lee b: Abt. 1826 in Jackson County, Tennessee, d: Ruse, Texas; Y

+ Mary b: ?, m: ?, d: ?; Y

.......6 Prior Bodice Lee b: 05 Dec 1827 in Gainsboro, Jackson County, Tennessee, d: 07 Aug 1909 in Perry County, Illinois; Y

+ Adeline Lucretia Brooks b: 11 Nov 1833 in Gainsboro, Jackson County, Tennessee, m: 14 Aug 1850 in ?, d: Perry County, Illinois; Y

.......7 Sarah Josey LEE b: 27 Jul 1856 in Jackson County, Tennessee, d: ?; Y

.......7 John Holden LEE b: 17 Nov 1858 in Perry County, Illinois, d: 20 Feb 1876 in Perry County, Illinois; Y

.......7 Margaret Isabella LEE b: 06 Oct 1861 in Perry County, Illinois, d: ?; Y

.......7 William Andrew LEE b: 19 Aug 1863 in Perry County, Illinois, d: 29 Aug 1863 in Perry County, Illinois; Y

.......7 Mary Francis LEE b: 19 Aug 1863 in Perry County, Illinois, d: 06 Mar 1864 in Perry County, Illinois; Y

.......7 Charles Madison LEE b: 1867 in ?, d: 1948 in ?; Y

.......7 Martha Jane LEE b: 15 Jul 1869 in Perry County, Illinois, d: ?; Y

.......7 Ezery Hughey LEE b: 16 Apr 1871 in Perry County, Illinois, d: ?; Y

.......7 Edward Gasper LEE b: 07 Jul 1873 in Perry County, Illinois, d: ?; Y

.......7 RoseZelly Murtle LEE b: 06 Dec 1876 in Perry County, Illinois, d: ?; Y

.......6 Sarah Miller Lee b: Abt. 1831 in Jackson County, Tennessee, d: Abt. 1917 in St. Louis, Missouri; Y

+ Andrew Jackson Bowman b: ?, m: Abt. 1851 in ?, d: ?; Y

.......6 Eliza Ann Lee b: Abt. 1833 in Jackson County, Tennessee, d: ?; Y

+ John Whitlock b: ?, m: ?, d: ?; Y

.......6 William Hampton Lee b: 08 Feb 1839 in Jackson County, Tennessee, d: 06 Sep 1920 in Perry County, Illinois; Y

+ Virginia Lee b: 01 Dec 1842 in Perry County, Illinois, m: ?, d: 19 Nov 1924 in Perry County, Illinois; Y

.......5 Alfred M. Lee b: 1812 in Jackson County, Tennessee, d: Aft. 1855 in Jackson County, Tennessee; Y

+ Rebecca Gailbreath b: Abt. 1811 in Jackson County, Tennessee, m: Abt. 1836 in ?, d: Abt. 1907 in Nashville, Tennessee; Y

.......6 William Gailbreath Lee b: Abt. 1838 in Jackson County, Tennessee, d: 08 Jul 1909 in TENNESSEE; Y

.......6 Mary Lee b: Abt. 1840 in ?, d: ?; Y

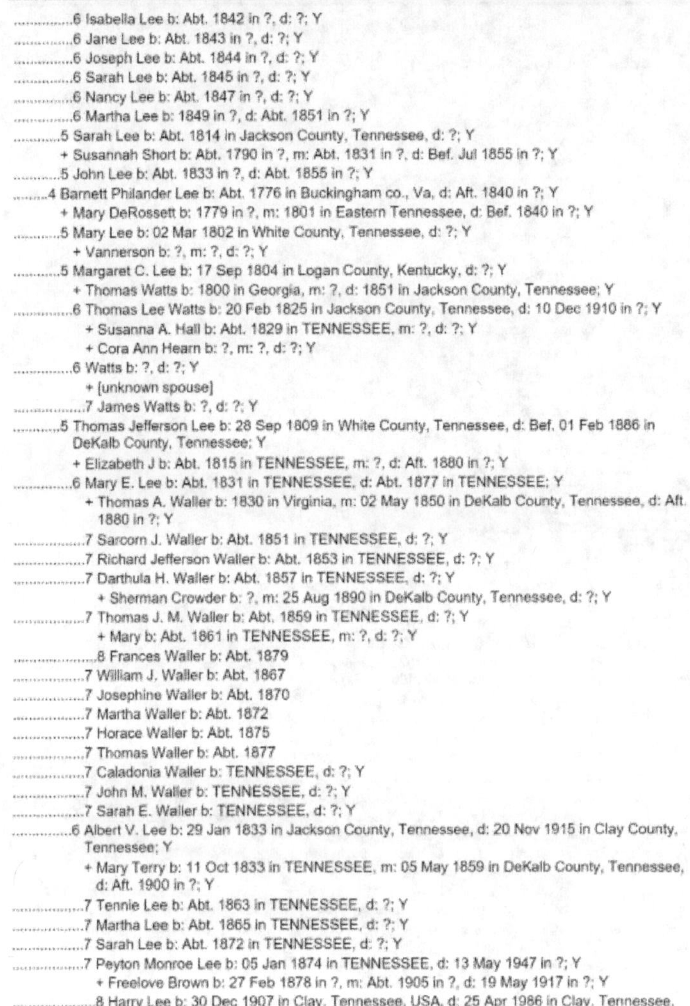

```
.............6 Isabella Lee b: Abt. 1842 in ?, d: ?; Y
.............6 Jane Lee b: Abt. 1843 in ?, d: ?; Y
.............6 Joseph Lee b: Abt. 1844 in ?, d: ?; Y
.............6 Sarah Lee b: Abt. 1845 in ?, d: ?; Y
.............6 Nancy Lee b: Abt. 1847 in ?, d: ?; Y
.............6 Martha Lee b: 1849 in ?, d: Abt. 1851 in ?; Y
..........5 Sarah Lee b: Abt. 1814 in Jackson County, Tennessee, d: ?; Y
      + Susannah Short b: Abt. 1790 in ?, m: Abt. 1831 in ?, d: Bef. Jul 1855 in ?; Y
..........5 John Lee b: Abt. 1833 in ?, d: Abt. 1855 in ?; Y
........4 Barnett Philander Lee b: Abt. 1776 in Buckingham co., Va, d: Aft. 1840 in ?; Y
      + Mary DeRossett b: 1779 in ?, m: 1801 in Eastern Tennessee, d: Bef. 1840 in ?; Y
..........5 Mary Lee b: 02 Mar 1802 in White County, Tennessee, d: ?; Y
         + Vannerson b: ?, m: ?, d: ?; Y
..........5 Margaret C. Lee b: 17 Sep 1804 in Logan County, Kentucky, d: ?; Y
         + Thomas Watts b: 1800 in Georgia, m: ?, d: 1851 in Jackson County, Tennessee; Y
............6 Thomas Lee Watts b: 20 Feb 1825 in Jackson County, Tennessee, d: 10 Dec 1910 in ?; Y
            + Susanna A. Hall b: Abt. 1829 in TENNESSEE, m: ?, d: ?; Y
            + Cora Ann Hearn b: ?, m: ?, d: ?; Y
............6 Watts b: ?, d: ?; Y
            + [unknown spouse]
............7 James Watts b: ?, d: ?; Y
..........5 Thomas Jefferson Lee b: 28 Sep 1809 in White County, Tennessee, d: Bef. 01 Feb 1886 in
DeKalb County, Tennessee; Y
         + Elizabeth J b: Abt. 1815 in TENNESSEE, m: ?, d: Aft. 1880 in ?; Y
............6 Mary E. Lee b: Abt. 1831 in TENNESSEE, d: Abt. 1877 in TENNESSEE; Y
            + Thomas A. Waller b: 1830 in Virginia, m: 02 May 1850 in DeKalb County, Tennessee, d: Aft.
            1880 in ?; Y
............7 Sarcorn J. Waller b: Abt. 1851 in TENNESSEE, d: ?; Y
............7 Richard Jefferson Waller b: Abt. 1853 in TENNESSEE, d: ?; Y
............7 Darthula H. Waller b: Abt. 1857 in TENNESSEE, d: ?; Y
            + Sherman Crowder b: ?, m: 25 Aug 1890 in DeKalb County, Tennessee, d: ?; Y
............7 Thomas J. M. Waller b: Abt. 1859 in TENNESSEE, d: ?; Y
            + Mary b: Abt. 1861 in TENNESSEE, m: ?, d: ?; Y
............8 Frances Waller b: Abt. 1879
............7 William J. Waller b: Abt. 1867
............7 Josephine Waller b: Abt. 1870
............7 Martha Waller b: Abt. 1872
............7 Horace Waller b: Abt. 1875
............7 Thomas Waller b: Abt. 1877
............7 Caladonia Waller b: TENNESSEE, d: ?; Y
............7 John M. Waller b: TENNESSEE, d: ?; Y
............7 Sarah E. Waller b: TENNESSEE, d: ?; Y
............6 Albert V. Lee b: 29 Jan 1833 in Jackson County, Tennessee, d: 20 Nov 1915 in Clay County,
            Tennessee; Y
            + Mary Terry b: 11 Oct 1833 in TENNESSEE, m: 05 May 1859 in DeKalb County, Tennessee,
            d: Aft. 1900 in ?; Y
............7 Tennie Lee b: Abt. 1863 in TENNESSEE, d: ?; Y
............7 Martha Lee b: Abt. 1865 in TENNESSEE, d: ?; Y
............7 Sarah Lee b: Abt. 1872 in TENNESSEE, d: ?; Y
............7 Peyton Monroe Lee b: 05 Jan 1874 in TENNESSEE, d: 13 May 1947 in ?; Y
            + Freelove Brown b: 27 Feb 1878 in ?, m: Abt. 1905 in ?, d: 19 May 1917 in ?; Y
............8 Harry Lee b: 30 Dec 1907 in Clay, Tennessee, USA, d: 25 Apr 1966 in Clay, Tennessee,
            USA; Y
```

+ Bonnie Lee Short b: 27 Jul 1908 in Clay, Tennessee, USA, m: 05 Apr 1930 in ?, d: 23 Aug 1989 in ?; Y

...............9 Living Lee

...............9 Living Lee

+ Living Pugh

...............10 Living Pugh

...............10 Living Pugh

...............9 Living Lee

+ Living Phillips

...............10 Living Lee

...............10 Living Lee

+ Living Davis

...............10 Living Lee

...............10 Living Lee

...............9 Living Lee

...............9 Living Lee

+ Living Fleming

...............10 Living Fleming

...............10 Living Fleming

...............9 Living Lee

+ Living Head

...............10 Living Head

...............10 Living Head

...............10 Living Head

...............9 Living Lee

+ Living Tackett

...............10 Living Lee

...............10 Living Lee

...............10 Living Lee

...............8 Hayden Lee b: 05 Jul 1909 in ?, d: 25 Sep 1947 in ?; Y

+ Settie Belle Sims b: 26 Jul 1876 in ?, m: Abt. 1927 in ?, d: 16 Aug 1960 in ?; Y

...............7 William Lee b: Abt. 1877 in TENNESSEE, d: ?; Y

...............6 Louisa J. Lee b: Abt. 1835 in TENNESSEE, d: Bef. 1880 in TENNESSEE; Y

+ Isaac R. Conger b: 18 Jan 1832 in Smith County, Tennessee, m: 06 Apr 1854 in DeKalb County, Tennessee, d: Abt. 1904 in Texas; Y

...............7 Mary J. Conger b: 18 Mar 1855 in TENNESSEE, d: ?; Y

+ John Exum b: ?, m: 13 May 1874 in DeKalb County, Tennessee, d: ?; Y

...............8 Dillard Exum b: TENNESSEE, d: ?; Y

...............7 William G. Conger b: Abt. 1859 in TENNESSEE, d: ?; Y

...............7 Nancy E. Conger b: Abt. 1865 in TENNESSEE, d: ?; Y

...............6 Sarah C. Lee b: Nov 1837 in Smith County, Tennessee, d: Aft. 1900 in ?; Y

+ James Peyton Terry b: 1835 in Putnam County, Tennessee, m: 18 Dec 1858 in DeKalb County, Tennessee, d: 1888 in ?; Y

...............6 Margaret Ann Lee b: 08 Mar 1839 in Smith County (?), Tennessee, d: 19 Jun 1885 in Blue Ridge, Collin County, Texas; Y

+ Felix Nelson Patterson b: 14 Feb 1817 in Wilson County, Tennessee, m: 10 May 1866 in DeKalb County, Tennessee, d: 19 Jul 1884 in Smithville, Dekalb County, Tennessee; Y

...............7 James Lee Patterson b: 01 Sep 1867 in Putnam County, Tennessee, d: 05 May 1940 in Tulsa, Oklahoma; Y

+ Livena Alice Mitchell b: 17 May 1873 in Exeter, Barry County, Missouri, m: 28 Aug 1889 in Balm, Cooke County, Texas, d: 10 Feb 1952 in Tulsa, Oklahoma; Y

...............8 Myrtle Jennette Patterson b: 17 Jun 1890 in Callisburg, Cooke County, Texas, d: 07 Aug 1964 in Los Angeles County, California; Y

+ Horace Edgar McMillien b: 25 Mar 1888 in Farmer, Young County, Texas, m: 09 Aug 1911 in Whitesboro, Cooke County, Texas, d: 08 May 1956 in Los Angeles County, California; Y
......................9 Wanda Ruth McMillien b: 12 Mar 1913 in Roger Mills County, Oklahoma, d: 11 Aug 1993 in Sebastopol, Sonoma County, California; Y
+ Evan Brice Arnold b: 28 Nov 1912 in Tulsa, Oklahoma, m: 07 Oct 1939 in Tulsa, Oklahoma, d: 04 Sep 1978 in South Gate, Los Angeles County, California; Y
......................10 Timothy Lee Arnold b: 11 Jun 1948 in Tulsa, Oklahoma, d: 11 Jun 1948 in Tulsa, Oklahoma; Y
......................10 Living Arnold
......................10 Living Arnold
......................9 Ada Onieta McMillien b: 25 Jun 1914 in Roger Mills County, Oklahoma, d: 02 May 1970 in West Covina, Los Angeles County, California; Y
+ Living Crysler
+ James W. Evans b: 08 Nov 1915 in Little Rock, ARKANSAS, m: ?, d: 22 Oct 1994 in Riverside County, California; Y
......................10 Living Evans
......................10 Living Evans
+ Lawrence Samuel Boisseau b: 14 Aug 1907 in Louisiana, m: Abt. 1934 in Tulsa, Oklahoma, d: 08 Oct 1987 in Nowata, Oklahoma; Y
......................10 Living Boisseau
......................10 Living Boisseau
......................9 Bernice Olive McMillien b: 09 Jul 1916 in Roger Mills County, Oklahoma, d: 21 Feb 1984 in Los Angeles County, California; Y
+ Charles Eugene Campbell b: 11 Nov 1904 in Arkansas, m: Abt. 1938 in Los Angeles, California, d: 30 May 1978 in Los Angeles County, California; Y
+ Living Layman
......................10 Living Layman
+ Living Lotte
......................9 Robert Marvin McMillien b: 19 Nov 1918 in Roger Mills County, Oklahoma, d: 26 Jun 1966 in California; Y
+ Living Oden
......................10 Living McMillien
......................10 Living McMillien
......................10 Living McMillien
......................10 Living McMillien
......................10 Living McMillien
+ Living
......................9 Living McMillien
+ Bettye Brock b: 24 Feb 1926 in Amarillo, Texas, d: 28 Dec 1993 in Susanville, California; Y
......................10 Living McMillien
......................10 Living McMillien
+ Living Coltart
+ Living
......................8 Minnie Alva Patterson b: 26 Nov 1891 in Tioga, Texas, d: 06 Sep 1990 in Cherry Valley, California; Y
+ Esper Earl Ray b: 18 Jan 1892 in Decatur, Texas, m: 15 Jul 1916 in Weatherford, Oklahoma, d: 06 Jan 1942 in Selma, California; Y
......................9 Living Ray
+ Tony Ragusa b: 20 Aug 1917 in ?, d: 04 Feb 1996 in ?; Y
+ Roland Erberich b: Pennsylvania, d: ?; Y
......................10 Living Erberich
......................9 Living Ray
+ Living Cagle

..........................10 Living Ray
..........................10 Living Ray
..........................10 Living Ray
..........................10 Living Ray
       + Living
..........................9 Living Ray
       + James Henry Stagner Jr. b: 24 Dec 1916 in Pecos, Texas, d: 12 Aug 1981 in Apple
         Valley, California; Y
..........................10 Living Stagner
..........................9 Living Ray
       + Living Rambaud
..........................10 Living Ray
..........................10 Living Ray
..........................9 Opal Jean Ray b: ?, d: ?; Y
..........................8 Olive Elizabeth Patterson b: 12 Dec 1896 in Weatherford, Texas, d: 22 Apr 1984 in
       Weslaco, Texas; Y
       + John Francis Gordon b: 19 Dec 1863 in Canada, m: Abt. 1915 in Boulder, Colorado, d:
         29 Jan 1936 in Edinburg, Hidalgo County, Texas; Y
..........................9 Living Gordon
       + Living Campbell
..........................10 Living Campbell
..........................10 Living Campbell
..........................10 Living Campbell
..........................9 Living Gordon
       + Living
..........................10 Living Gordon
       + Ernest G. McMahan b: 30 Nov 1892 in ?, m: Abt. 1974 in Boulder, Colorado, d: 08 Dec
         1978 in ?; Y
..........................8 Earl Anderson Patterson b: 15 Feb 1897 in Ardmore, Indian Territory, Oklahoma, d: 24
       Jan 1968 in Long Beach, California; Y
       + Thelma Rose Ray b: 24 Jan 1901 in Decatur, Wise County, Texas, m: Aug 1920 in
         Witchata Falls, Clay County, Texas, d: 22 Feb 1986 in Cherry Valley, Riverside County,
         California; Y
..........................9 Earl Anderson Patterson Jr. b: 1921 in Chicago, Illinois, d: Abt. 1942 in Europe or North
       Atlantic; Y
..........................9 Norman Ray Patterson b: 13 Aug 1923 in ?, d: 23 Nov 1981 in Bakersfield, California; Y
       + Living Turner
..........................10 Living Patterson
..........................9 Living Patterson
       + Living Bartlett
..........................10 Living Patterson
..........................10 Living Patterson
..........................10 Living Patterson
..........................10 Living Patterson
..........................10 Living Patterson
..........................10 Living Patterson
..........................8 Eunice Lillian Patterson b: 01 Jul 1900 in Bonham, Texas, d: 20 Sep 1983 in Peoria,
       Illinois; Y
       + Norman Williams b: 11 Nov 1901 in Chicago, Illinois, m: ?, d: 02 Nov 1976 in Peoria,
         Illinois; Y
..........................9 Living Williams
       + Living Colburn
..........................10 Living Williams
..........................10 Living Williams

...............8 Margaret Helenn Patterson b: 26 May 1902 in ?, d: 25 Jan 1987 in Little Rock, ARKANSAS; Y

    + Marion Monroe Brizendine b: 05 Apr 1901 in Salisbury, Missouri, m: ?, d: 29 Jan 1956 in Tulsa, Oklahoma; Y

...............9 James Monroe Brizendine b: 26 Oct 1923 in Tulsa, Oklahoma, d: ?; Y

    + Virginia Weaver b: 11 Jul 1925 in Winona, Texas, m: 21 Jul 1946 in Starrville, Smith County, Texas, d: 02 Sep 1991 in Tyler, Texas; Y

...............10 Living Brizendine

...............10 Living Brizendine

    + Living Sims

    + Bert Petty b: ?, m: ?, d: Abt. 1982 in Little Rock, Arkansas (?); Y

...............8 Verna Lucille Patterson b: 04 May 1906 in ?, d: 29 Jun 1993 in Temple, Texas; Y

    + Harold Henry Cox b: 07 Jul 1903 in ?, m: Topeka, Kansas, d: 11 Apr 1995 in Temple, Texas; Y

...............8 Edna May Patterson b: 19 Oct 1913 in Leedey, Oklahoma, d: Kerrville, Texas; Y

    + George Washington Cox b: 19 Feb 1905 in King City, Missouri, m: 20 Sep 1936 in Tulsa, Oklahoma, d: Kerrville, Texas; Y

...............9 David George Cox b: 06 Aug 1944 in Topeka, Kansas, d: 19 Jun 1996 in ?; Y

    + Living Steinert

...............10 Living Cox

...............9 Living Cox

    + Living Wright

...............10 Living Wright

...............10 Living Wright

...............9 Living Cox

    + Living Tristani

...............10 Living Cox

...............7 Thomas Nelson Patterson b: 02 Apr 1870 in Putnam County, Tennessee, d: 15 Feb 1945 in ?; Y

    + Lora Westbrook b: Aug 1876 in TENNESSEE, m: ?, d: ?; Y

...............8 Roy H. Patterson b: Mar 1896 in Texas

...............8 Edith Patterson b: Aug 1899 in Texas

...............8 Beuna Lee Patterson b: Aft. 1899 in ?

...............7 Victoria Tennessee Patterson b: 11 Jun 1876 in Putnam County, Tennessee, d: ?; Y

    + John Smyers b: ?, m: 04 Dec 1907 in ?, d: ?; Y

...............8 Living Smyers

    + Living Worsham

...............8 Living Smyers

...............8 Living Smyers

    + Living Cardin

...............9 Living Cardin

    + Living Ogilvie

...............10 Living Ogilvie

...............6 Thomas James Mathew Lee b: Abt. 1844 in TENNESSEE, d: Aft. 1880 in ?; Y

    + Sarah E. Garner b: ?, m: 06 Dec 1868 in DeKalb County, Tennessee, d: Abt. 1870 in ?; Y

    + Brunetta Ferrell b: Abt. 1850 in TENNESSEE, m: 23 Sep 1871 in DeKalb County, Tennessee, d: Aft. 1880 in ?; Y

...............7 James H. Lee b: Abt. 1876 in TENNESSEE, d: ?; Y

...............7 Ira H. Lee b: Abt. 1878 in TENNESSEE, d: ?; Y

...............6 Altemira D. Lee b: Sep 1845 in TENNESSEE, d: Bef. 1910 in TENNESSEE; Y

    + John B. Conger b: 27 Sep 1848 in DeKalb County, Tennessee, m: 19 Aug 1868 in DeKalb County, Tennessee, d: 12 Mar 1924 in DeKalb County, Tennessee; Y

...............7 Sarah Elizabeth Conger b: Abt. Sep 1869 in TENNESSEE, d: ?; Y

    + J. L. Foster b: ?, m: 09 Sep 1888 in DeKalb County, Tennessee, d: ?; Y

...............7 Mattie Conger b: Abt. 1871 in TENNESSEE, d: ?; Y

+ Sammie Carter b: ?, m: ?, d: ?; Y
...............8 Mollie Carter b: 10 Oct 1908 in DeKalb County, Tennessee, d: 22 Mar 1925 in DeKalb County, Tennessee; Y
...............7 Ednie Conger b: Abt. 1875 in TENNESSEE, d: ?; Y
...............7 Mollie Conger b: Jan 1878 in TENNESSEE, d: Aft. 1900 in ?; Y
...............7 Wilber Conger b: Abt. 1879 in TENNESSEE, d: ?; Y
...............7 Ned Conger b: Jan 1883 in TENNESSEE, d: ?; Y
...............7 Albert Conger b: Mar 1887 in TENNESSEE, d: ?; Y
+ Cora b: Abt. 1884 in TENNESSEE, m: ?, d: ?; Y
...............6 Joseph David Lawson Lee b: Abt. 1851 in TENNESSEE, d: ?; Y
+ Rutha L. Florida b: Abt. 1860 in TENNESSEE, m: 06 Dec 1874 in DeKalb County, Tennessee, d: ?; Y
...............7 Elizabeth Lee b: Abt. 1876 in TENNESSEE, d: ?; Y
...............7 Napoleon Lee b: Abt. 1879 in TENNESSEE, d: ?; Y
...............6 Anderson W. Pierson Lee b: Jan 1853 in TENNESSEE, d: Aft. 1900 in ?; Y
+ Mary Melvery Perry b: Abt. 1862 in TENNESSEE, m: 09 Mar 1876 in DeKalb County, Tennessee, d: ?; Y
...............7 Robert L. Lee b: Jun 1878 in TENNESSEE, d: ?; Y
...............7 Viola M. Lee b: May 1881 in TENNESSEE, d: ?; Y
...............7 John S. Lee b: Jan 1883 in TENNESSEE, d: ?; Y
...............7 Hettie L. Lee b: May 1889 in TENNESSEE, d: ?; Y
...............7 Oliver V. Lee b: Feb 1891 in TENNESSEE, d: ?; Y
...............7 Thomas L. Lee b: Mar 1893 in TENNESSEE, d: ?; Y
...............7 America L. Lee b: Sep 1898 in TENNESSEE
...............6 Theodocia M. Lee b: Abt. 1857 in TENNESSEE, d: ?; Y
...............6 Ada A. Lee b: Abt. 1859 in TENNESSEE, d: Bef. 1870 in ?; Y
...............6 Carrie I. Lee b: Abt. 1862 in TENNESSEE, d: ?; Y
+ Joseph P. Stephens b: Abt. 1855 in TENNESSEE, m: 11 May 1879 in DeKalb County, Tennessee, d: ?; Y
...............7 Maud Stephens b: 1880 in TENNESSEE, d: ?; Y
...............5 James Madison Lee b: 12 Jan 1812 in White County, Tennessee, d: Bef. 16 Dec 1878 in DeKalb County, Tennessee; Y
+ Elizabeth H b: Abt. 1816 in Virginia, m: ?, d: ?; Y
...............6 Lawson W. Lee b: Abt. 1838 in TENNESSEE, d: Jun 1864 in ?; Y
...............6 Philander Jackson Lee b: Abt. 1839 in TENNESSEE, d: ?; Y
+ Josephine Bethena Tyree b: ?, m: 19 Oct 1870 in DeKalb County, Tennessee, d: ?; Y
...............7 James Watkins Lee b: 1874 in DeKalb County, Tennessee, d: ?; Y
+ Nancy Strother Smith b: 1874 in Smithville, Dekalb County, Tennessee
...............8 Richard Henry Lee b: 09 Oct 1911 in ?, d: 08 Sep 1997 in Dallas, Texas; Y
...............6 Amanda M. Lee b: Abt. 1841 in TENNESSEE, d: ?; Y
...............6 Zebulon P. Lee b: Abt. 1843 in TENNESSEE, d: ?; Y
+ Virginia F. Atwell b: Abt. 1847 in TENNESSEE, m: 21 Mar 1869 in DeKalb County, Tennessee, d: ?; Y
...............7 Willie M. Lee b: Abt. 1870 in TENNESSEE, d: ?; Y
+ R. L. Jennings b: 15 Nov 1894 in ?, m: 15 Nov 1894 in DeKalb County, Tennessee, d: ?; Y
...............7 Josie E. Lee b: Abt. 1872 in TENNESSEE, d: ?; Y
...............7 Norah H. Lee b: Abt. 1873 in TENNESSEE, d: ?; Y
...............7 Harry H. Lee b: Abt. 1875 in TENNESSEE, d: ?; Y
...............7 Callie Lee b: Abt. 1877 in TENNESSEE, d: ?; Y
+ Bob Potter b: ?, m: 17 Sep 1894 in DeKalb County, Tennessee, d: ?; Y
...............7 Robert E. Lee b: Abt. 1879 in TENNESSEE, d: ?; Y
...............6 Mary J. Lee b: Abt. 1845 in TENNESSEE, d: ?; Y
...............6 James T. Lee b: Abt. 1847 in TENNESSEE, d: ?; Y
...............6 Richard Henry Lee b: Abt. 1849 in TENNESSEE, d: ?; Y

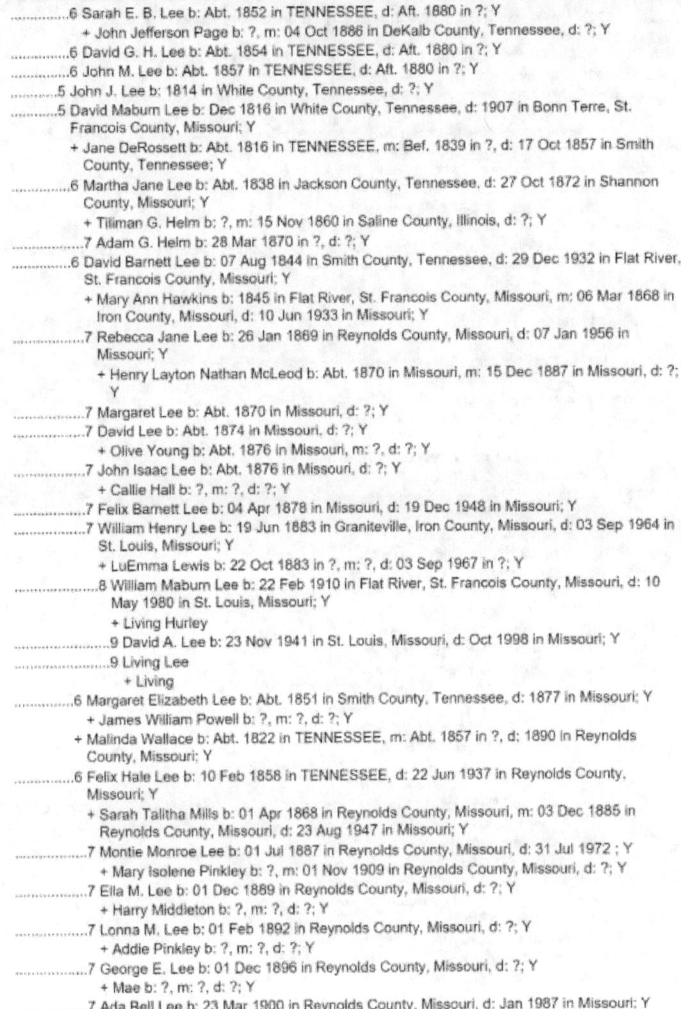

..........6 Sarah E. B. Lee b: Abt. 1852 in TENNESSEE, d: Aft. 1880 in ?; Y
.... + John Jefferson Page b: ?, m: 04 Oct 1886 in DeKalb County, Tennessee, d: ?; Y
..........6 David G. H. Lee b: Abt. 1854 in TENNESSEE, d: Aft. 1880 in ?; Y
..........6 John M. Lee b: Abt. 1857 in TENNESSEE, d: Aft. 1880 in ?; Y
..........5 John J. Lee b: 1814 in White County, Tennessee, d: ?; Y
..........5 David Maburn Lee b: Dec 1816 in White County, Tennessee, d: 1907 in Bonn Terre, St. Francois County, Missouri; Y
.... + Jane DeRossett b: Abt. 1816 in TENNESSEE, m: Bef. 1839 in ?, d: 17 Oct 1857 in Smith County, Tennessee; Y
..........6 Martha Jane Lee b: Abt. 1838 in Jackson County, Tennessee, d: 27 Oct 1872 in Shannon County, Missouri; Y
.... + Tiliman G. Helm b: ?, m: 15 Nov 1860 in Saline County, Illinois, d: ?; Y
...........7 Adam G. Helm b: 28 Mar 1870 in ?, d: ?; Y
..........6 David Barnett Lee b: 07 Aug 1844 in Smith County, Tennessee, d: 29 Dec 1932 in Flat River, St. Francois County, Missouri; Y
.... + Mary Ann Hawkins b: 1845 in Flat River, St. Francois County, Missouri, m: 06 Mar 1868 in Iron County, Missouri, d: 10 Jun 1933 in Missouri; Y
...........7 Rebecca Jane Lee b: 26 Jan 1869 in Reynolds County, Missouri, d: 07 Jan 1956 in Missouri; Y
.... + Henry Layton Nathan McLeod b: Abt. 1870 in Missouri, m: 15 Dec 1887 in Missouri, d: ?; Y
...........7 Margaret Lee b: Abt. 1870 in Missouri, d: ?; Y
...........7 David Lee b: Abt. 1874 in Missouri, d: ?; Y
.... + Olive Young b: Abt. 1876 in Missouri, m: ?, d: ?; Y
...........7 John Isaac Lee b: Abt. 1876 in Missouri, d: ?; Y
.... + Callie Hall b: ?, m: ?, d: ?; Y
...........7 Felix Barnett Lee b: 04 Apr 1878 in Missouri, d: 19 Dec 1948 in Missouri; Y
...........7 William Henry Lee b: 19 Jun 1883 in Graniteville, Iron County, Missouri, d: 03 Sep 1964 in St. Louis, Missouri; Y
.... + LuEmma Lewis b: 22 Oct 1883 in ?, m: ?, d: 03 Sep 1967 in ?; Y
...........8 William Maburn Lee b: 22 Feb 1910 in Flat River, St. Francois County, Missouri, d: 10 May 1980 in St. Louis, Missouri; Y
.... + Living Hurley
...........9 David A. Lee b: 23 Nov 1941 in St. Louis, Missouri, d: Oct 1998 in Missouri; Y
...........9 Living Lee
.... + Living
..........6 Margaret Elizabeth Lee b: Abt. 1851 in Smith County, Tennessee, d: 1877 in Missouri; Y
.... + James William Powell b: ?, m: ?, d: ?; Y
.... + Malinda Wallace b: Abt. 1822 in TENNESSEE, m: Abt. 1857 in ?, d: 1890 in Reynolds County, Missouri; Y
..........6 Felix Hale Lee b: 10 Feb 1858 in TENNESSEE, d: 22 Jun 1937 in Reynolds County, Missouri; Y
.... + Sarah Talitha Mills b: 01 Apr 1868 in Reynolds County, Missouri, m: 03 Dec 1885 in Reynolds County, Missouri, d: 23 Aug 1947 in Missouri; Y
...........7 Montie Monroe Lee b: 01 Jul 1887 in Reynolds County, Missouri, d: 31 Jul 1972 ; Y
.... + Mary Isolene Pinkley b: ?, m: 01 Nov 1909 in Reynolds County, Missouri, d: ?; Y
...........7 Ella M. Lee b: 01 Dec 1889 in Reynolds County, Missouri, d: ?; Y
.... + Harry Middleton b: ?, m: ?, d: ?; Y
...........7 Lonna M. Lee b: 01 Feb 1892 in Reynolds County, Missouri, d: ?; Y
.... + Addie Pinkley b: ?, m: ?, d: ?; Y
...........7 George E. Lee b: 01 Dec 1896 in Reynolds County, Missouri, d: ?; Y
.... + Mae b: ?, m: ?, d: ?; Y
...........7 Ada Bell Lee b: 23 Mar 1900 in Reynolds County, Missouri, d: Jan 1987 in Missouri; Y
.... + George Gibbons b: ?, m: ?, d: ?; Y

...............7 Ernest Raymond Lee b: 06 Feb 1903 in Reynolds County, Missouri, d: 15 May 1952 in Missouri; Y

+ Hattie Viola Williams b: ?, m: 13 Sep 1924 in Reynolds County, Missouri, d: ?; Y

...............6 Armenita Lee b: Abt. 1860 in Saline County, Illinois, d: ?; Y

...............6 Henry Wiseman Lee b: 25 Jan 1863 in Saline County, Illinois, d: 20 Oct 1934 in Reynolds County, Missouri; Y

+ Mary Armenda Mills b: 10 Mar 1873 in Reynolds County, Missouri, m: 01 May 1890 in Reynolds County, Missouri, d: 28 Mar 1944 in St. Louis County, Missouri; Y

...............7 Emma Leona Lee b: 11 Feb 1891

...............7 Robert Emit Lee b: 01 Feb 1894

...............7 Sherman Maborn Lee b: 05 Sep 1896

...............7 Lucy Jane Lee b: 29 Jan 1899

...............7 Mayme Viola Lee b: 15 Jul 1915 in Reynolds County, Missouri, d: 28 May 1999 in Boone County, Missouri; Y

...............7 Living Lee

...............7 Living Lee

...............7 Living Lee

...............7 Living Lee

+ Louisa Almore b: Jan 1880 in Lesterville, Reynolds County, Missouri, m: 18 May 1899 in Reynolds County, Missouri, d: ?; Y

+ Margaret Brooks b: 12 Feb 1855 in ?, m: 20 Apr 1891 in Reynolds County, Missouri, d: ?; Y

...........5 Lawson Lee b: 10 Oct 1818 in White County, Tennessee, d: ?; Y

...........5 Lindsey Lee b: ?, d: ?; Y

...........5 Polly Lee b: White County, Tennessee, d: ?; Y

+ Foster b: ?, m: ?, d: ?; Y

...........5 Roland Lee b: White County, Tennessee, d: ?; Y

.........4 Agnes LEE b: Abt. 1778

+ Cleborne DAVENPORT m: Abt. 1773

.........4 Arthur LEE b: Abt. 1779 in Buckingham co., Va, d: child; Y

.........4 Stephen LEE b: Abt. 1780 in Buckingham co., Va

+ Sarah ROACH see = 5819 b: Abt. 1782 in Washington County, VA, m: 01 Sep 1804 in Washington County, VA

......3 Mary LEE b: 1710 in Northumberland, Va, d: Aft. 1746 in Virginia; Y

......3 Charles LEE b: Abt. 1712 in Northumberland, Va

......3 William LEE b: Abt. 1714 in Northumberland, Va

......3 Young LEE b: Abt. 1718 in Buckingham co., Va, d: 1774 ; Y

......3 Peter LEE b: Abt. 1724 in Washington Co., Va of Madison Co., KY

+ Sarah Green b: Abt. 1738 in Northumbreland Co., Va, m: Abt. 1758

.........4 Thomas Lee b: Abt. 1757 in Va of Bedford Co., TN, d: Abt. 1837 in Coffee County, Tennessee; Y

+ Mary Lee b: Abt. 1757 in Virginia, m: Abt. 1779, d: Abt. 1779 in Virginia; Y

...........5 Peter Lee b: Abt. 1779 in Coffee Co., TN

+ Catherine (Katy) Caty McGUIRE b: 1789 in Lincoln Co., VA later Madison Co., Ky, m: 16 Mar 1806 in Madison Co., KENTUCKY

...............6 William LEE b: Abt. 1807 in Madison Co., KY

...............6 James LEE b: Abt. 1809 in Madison Co., KY

...............6 Green LEE b: Abt. 1811 in Madison Co., KY

...............6 Peter LEE b: Abt. 1813 in Madison Co., KY

...............6 John LEE b: Abt. 1815 in Madison Co., KY

...............6 Melinda LEE b: Abt. 1817 in Madison Co., KY

+ Caleb BOWLS

...............6 Mary LEE b: Abt. 1819 in Madison Co., KY

+ Caleb BOWLS

...............6 Elizabeth (Betsey) LEE b: Abt. 1821 in Madison Co., KY

+ Galloway WALKER

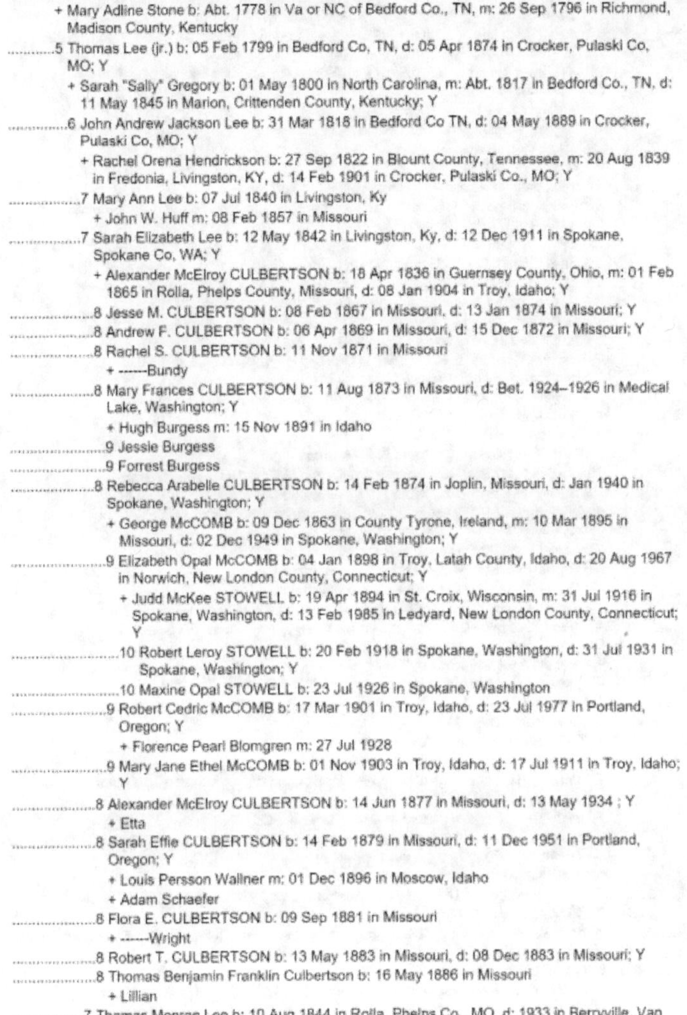

+ Mary Adline Stone b: Abt. 1778 in Va or NC of Bedford Co., TN, m: 26 Sep 1796 in Richmond, Madison County, Kentucky

............5 Thomas Lee (jr.) b: 05 Feb 1799 in Bedford Co, TN, d: 05 Apr 1874 in Crocker, Pulaski Co, MO; Y

　　+ Sarah "Sally" Gregory b: 01 May 1800 in North Carolina, m: Abt. 1817 in Bedford Co., TN, d: 11 May 1845 in Marion, Crittenden County, Kentucky; Y

............6 John Andrew Jackson Lee b: 31 Mar 1818 in Bedford Co TN, d: 04 May 1889 in Crocker, Pulaski Co, MO; Y

　　+ Rachel Orena Hendrickson b: 27 Sep 1822 in Blount County, Tennessee, m: 20 Aug 1839 in Fredonia, Livingston, KY, d: 14 Feb 1901 in Crocker, Pulaski Co., MO; Y

............7 Mary Ann Lee b: 07 Jul 1840 in Livingston, Ky

　　+ John W. Huff m: 08 Feb 1857 in Missouri

............7 Sarah Elizabeth Lee b: 12 May 1842 in Livingston, Ky, d: 12 Dec 1911 in Spokane, Spokane Co, WA; Y

　　+ Alexander McElroy CULBERTSON b: 18 Apr 1836 in Guernsey County, Ohio, m: 01 Feb 1865 in Rolla, Phelps County, Missouri, d: 08 Jan 1904 in Troy, Idaho; Y

............8 Jesse M. CULBERTSON b: 08 Feb 1867 in Missouri, d: 13 Jan 1874 in Missouri; Y

............8 Andrew F. CULBERTSON b: 06 Apr 1869 in Missouri, d: 15 Dec 1872 in Missouri; Y

............8 Rachel S. CULBERTSON b: 11 Nov 1871 in Missouri

　　+ ------Bundy

............8 Mary Frances CULBERTSON b: 11 Aug 1873 in Missouri, d: Bet. 1924–1926 in Medical Lake, Washington; Y

　　+ Hugh Burgess m: 15 Nov 1891 in Idaho

............9 Jessie Burgess

............9 Forrest Burgess

............8 Rebecca Arabelle CULBERTSON b: 14 Feb 1874 in Joplin, Missouri, d: Jan 1940 in Spokane, Washington; Y

　　+ George McCOMB b: 09 Dec 1863 in County Tyrone, Ireland, m: 10 Mar 1895 in Missouri, d: 02 Dec 1949 in Spokane, Washington; Y

............9 Elizabeth Opal McCOMB b: 04 Jan 1898 in Troy, Latah County, Idaho, d: 20 Aug 1967 in Norwich, New London County, Connecticut; Y

　　+ Judd McKee STOWELL b: 19 Apr 1894 in St. Croix, Wisconsin, m: 31 Jul 1916 in Spokane, Washington, d: 13 Feb 1985 in Ledyard, New London County, Connecticut; Y

............10 Robert Leroy STOWELL b: 20 Feb 1918 in Spokane, Washington, d: 31 Jul 1931 in Spokane, Washington; Y

............10 Maxine Opal STOWELL b: 23 Jul 1926 in Spokane, Washington

............9 Robert Cedric McCOMB b: 17 Mar 1901 in Troy, Idaho, d: 23 Jul 1977 in Portland, Oregon; Y

　　+ Florence Pearl Blomgren m: 27 Jul 1928

............9 Mary Jane Ethel McCOMB b: 01 Nov 1903 in Troy, Idaho, d: 17 Jul 1911 in Troy, Idaho; Y

............8 Alexander McElroy CULBERTSON b: 14 Jun 1877 in Missouri, d: 13 May 1934 ; Y

　　+ Etta

............8 Sarah Effie CULBERTSON b: 14 Feb 1879 in Missouri, d: 11 Dec 1951 in Portland, Oregon; Y

　　+ Louis Persson Wallner m: 01 Dec 1896 in Moscow, Idaho

　　+ Adam Schaefer

............8 Flora E. CULBERTSON b: 09 Sep 1881 in Missouri

　　+ ------Wright

............8 Robert T. CULBERTSON b: 13 May 1883 in Missouri, d: 08 Dec 1883 in Missouri; Y

............8 Thomas Benjamin Franklin Culbertson b: 16 May 1886 in Missouri

　　+ Lillian

............7 Thomas Monroe Lee b: 10 Aug 1844 in Rolla, Phelps Co., MO, d: 1933 in Berryville, Van Buren County, Arkansas; Y

+ Elizabeth Bible m: 06 Jul 1863 in Phelps County, Missouri
...............8 Sarah Ellen Lee b: 09 Jun 1873 in Pulaski County, Missouri, d: 1935 in Alba, Jasper County, Missouri; Y
+ Edward Yocam b: 05 Jan 1871 in Andrew County, Missouri, d: 1953 in Alba, Jasper County, Missouri; Y
.....................9 Mary Yocam b: 1909 in Missouri
+ Roy Morgan b: 17 Oct 1896 in Missouri, m: 1932
........................10 Living Morgan
+ Martha White
...............7 David Lee b: 06 Mar 1847 in Mo, d: 1907 in Mo; Y
+ Sarah Johnson b: Feb 1845 in Rolla, Phelps Co., MO, m: 28 Apr 1864 in Pulaski Co MO, d: 1904 in Cornwell, Latah, ID; Y
...............8 Sylvan Napolean Lee b: 28 Aug 1873 in Crocker, Pulask Co.i, MO, d: 15 Jun 1940 ; Y
...............8 Shell Edward Lee b: 08 Nov 1883 in Crocker, Pulask Co.i, MO, d: 14 Jun 1951 ; Y
...............8 Thomas Henry Lee b: 14 Nov 1885 in ID, d: 11 Jun 1911 in Lexington, OR; Y
...............8 Charles Alfred Lee b: 05 Jul 1887 in ID, d: 1932 ; Y
...............8 George Harrison Lee b: 01 Oct 1889 in ID
...............8 Earl Russell Lee b: 06 Jan 1891 in ID
...............7 Rebecca Jane Lee b: 16 Jul 1849 in Crocker, Pulask Co.i, MO, d: 18 Dec 1922 in New Swedesborg, Pulaski County, Missouri; Y
+ James Patton Caldwell m: 01 Mar 1868 in Missouri
...............7 Susan Sophronia Lee b: 24 Jan 1852 in Rolla, Phelps Co., MO, d: 08 Feb 1932 in Waynesville, Pulaski, MO; Y
+ Isiah X. Phillips m: 13 Oct 1870 in Missouri
...............7 Luke Lee b: 29 Sep 1854 in Rolla, Phelps Co., MO, d: Bef. 1900 in Mo; Y
+ Susan Henderson m: 21 Feb 1874 in Missouri
...............7 Mary Frances Marthy Lee b: 30 Oct 1856 in Rolla, Phelps Co., MO, d: 22 Apr 1861 in Crocker, Pulaski Co., Missouri; Y
...............7 Jessee Lee b: 22 May 1859 in Rolla, Phelps Co., MO, d: Pulaski, MO; Y
+ Rasell Anderson m: 23 Sep 1883 in Missouri
+ Belle Baker m: 02 Sep 1890 in Joplin, Missouri
...............7 Baby girl Lee b: 11 Aug 1861 in Pulaski, MO, d: 16 Aug 1861 in Pulaski, MO; Y
...........,..6 Asa Stone Lee b: 02 Dec 1819 in Bedford County, Tennessee, d: 09 Feb 1868 in Rutherford County, Tennessee; Y
+ Elizabeth Adeline Jacobs b: 25 Feb 1819 in Kentucky, m: 02 Aug 1838 in Golconda, Pope, Illinois, d: 05 May 1874 in Rutherford County, Tennessee; Y
...............7 Sarah Jane Lee b: 18 Apr 1839 in Livingston County, Kentucky
+ William Alexander Nesbitt
...............7 Thomas Jefferson Lee b: 25 Sep 1840 in Livingston County, Kentucky
+ Sarah Emmaline Brandon m: 12 Sep 1865
...............7 James Richard Lee b: 05 May 1842 in Livingston County, Kentucky, d: 06 Apr 1862 ; Y
...............7 Peter Lee b: Abt. 1843
...............7 Mandy Melviny Lee b: 01 Sep 1843 in Rutherford Co., TN
...............7 John Jacobs Lee b: 01 May 1845 in Rutherford County, Tennessee, d: 08 Aug 1926 in Rutherford County, Tennessee; Y
+ Amanda Melvina Jernigan m: 09 Sep 1866 in Coffee County, Tennessee
...............7 William Basil Lee b: 17 Dec 1846 in Rutherford Co., TN, d: 23 Aug 1864 ; Y
...............7 Evan Lee b: Abt. 1847
...............7 Jesse Marion Lee b: Jun 1848 in Rutherford Co., TN, d: 05 Sep 1849 in Rutherford County, Tennessee; Y
...............7 Richard Lee b: Abt. 1849
...............7 Mary Ann Lee b: 10 Apr 1850 in Rutherford Co., TN, d: 05 Sep 1931 in Nashville, Tennessee; Y
+ Cornelius Gordon

...............7 George Wesley Lee b: 10 Dec 1851 in Rutherford Co., TN, d: 19 Oct 1929 in Gotebo, Kiowa County, Oklahoma; Y
　　　　+ Emily Tennessee Shelton b: 12 Feb 1860 in Rutherford County, Tennessee, m: 30 Mar 1875 in Rutherford County, Tennessee, d: 08 Feb 1930 in Gotebo, Kiowa County, Oklahoma; Y
...............7 Nancy Elizabeth or Elizabeth Nancy Lee b: 01 Nov 1853 in Rutherford Co., TN, d: 23 Jan 1941 in Tullahoma, Tenn; Y
　　　　+ George Robertson Armstrong b: 31 Aug 1854 in Rutherford Co, Tenn, m: 21 Sep in Rutherford Co, Tennessee, d: 31 Jul 1934 in Shelbyville, Bedford co Tenn; Y
...............8 Willie Armstrong b: Abt. 1875
...............8 James R Armstrong b: Jul 1876
...............8 Susan Armstrong b: Abt. 1878
...............8 Tommie Armstrong b: Abt. 1880
...............8 Oscar Armstrong b: Oct 1881
...............8 Thomas J Armstrong b: 03 Dec 1882
...............8 George Wesley Armstrong b: 16 Apr 1884 in Bedford Co, Tenn, d: 29 Nov 1957 in Shelbyville, Bedford co Tenn; Y
　　　　+ Katie Virginia Gregory
...............8 Lee M Armstrong b: Nov 1892
...............8 Alice Armstrong b: Apr 1895
...............7 Debora Cely Lee b: 26 Apr 1855 in Rutherford Co., TN, d: 19 May 1855 in Rutherford County, Tennessee; Y
...............7 Miranda Hall Armindy M. Lee b: 05 Aug 1856 in Rutherford Co., TN
　　　　+ James H. Armstrong
...............7 Henry Miller Lee b: 03 Mar 1858 in Rutherford Co., TN, d: 13 Dec 1858 in Rutherford County, Tennessee; Y
...............7 Martha Frances Lee b: 25 Jul 1859 in Rutherford Co., TN, d: 04 Mar 1868 in Rutherford County, Tennessee; Y
...............7 Charles Lee b: 1861 in Rutherford County, Tennessee
...............6 Martha Lee b: Abt. 1823 in Coffee TN
...............6 Mary Ann Lee b: Abt. 1825 in Coffee TN, d: Bef. Dec 1859 in Crittenden County, Kentucky; Y
　　　　+ John W. MOORE b: 22 Apr 1825 in Livingston County, Kentucky, m: 03 May 1846 in Crittenden County, Kentucky, d: 06 Mar 1907 in Crittenden County, Kentucky; Y
...............7 John Thomas Moore b: 1850 in Crittenden County, Kentucky
　　　　+ Josephine Brookshire m: 31 Dec 1868 in Crittenden County, Kentucky
...............7 Elizabeth Jane Moore b: Apr 1854 in Crittenden County, Kentucky
　　　　+ Francis Marion Conger m: 07 Mar 1872 in Crittenden County, Kentucky
...............7 Margaret M. Moore b: 01 Feb 1857 in Crittenden County, Kentucky, d: 10 Dec 1880 ; Y
　　　　+ Paul W. Conger m: 22 Nov 1876 in Crittenden County, Kentucky
...............6 Thomas Jefferson Lee b: 1827 in Coffee TN, d: 21 Oct 1838 in Coffee County, Tennessee; Y
　　　　+ Sarah E. Garner b: Abt. 1829 in Tn
　　　　+ Cynthia Bigham
...............5 Alexander Lee b: 01 Aug 1800 in Kentucky, d: 07 Nov 1862 in Coffee County, Tennessee; Y
　　　　+ Mary Dennison b: 28 Apr 1805 in TENNESSEE, m: Abt. 1833 in TENNESSEE, d: 10 Mar 1870 in TENNESSEE; Y
...............6 Virginia Lee b: 1835
...............6 Ann Lee b: 1838
...............6 William Dennison Lee b: 1840 in TENNESSEE
　　　　+ Rebecca McKee b: Abt. 1851 in TENNESSEE
...............7 Alexander Lee b: 1869 in TENNESSEE
...............6 Mary Lee b: 1843
...............5 Grissom Lee b: 1805 in Kentucky, d: Bef. 1860 in Coffee County, Tennessee; Y
　　　　+ Lucinda Arnold b: 1806 in TENNESSEE, m: Abt. 1826, d: Bef. 1870 in TENNESSEE; Y
...............6 Elizabeth Lee b: 1828 in TENNESSEE, d: Aft. 1850 in TENNESSEE; Y
　　　　+ Robert Patton b: Abt. 1828 in TENNESSEE, d: Bef. 1900 in Coffee County, Tennessee; Y

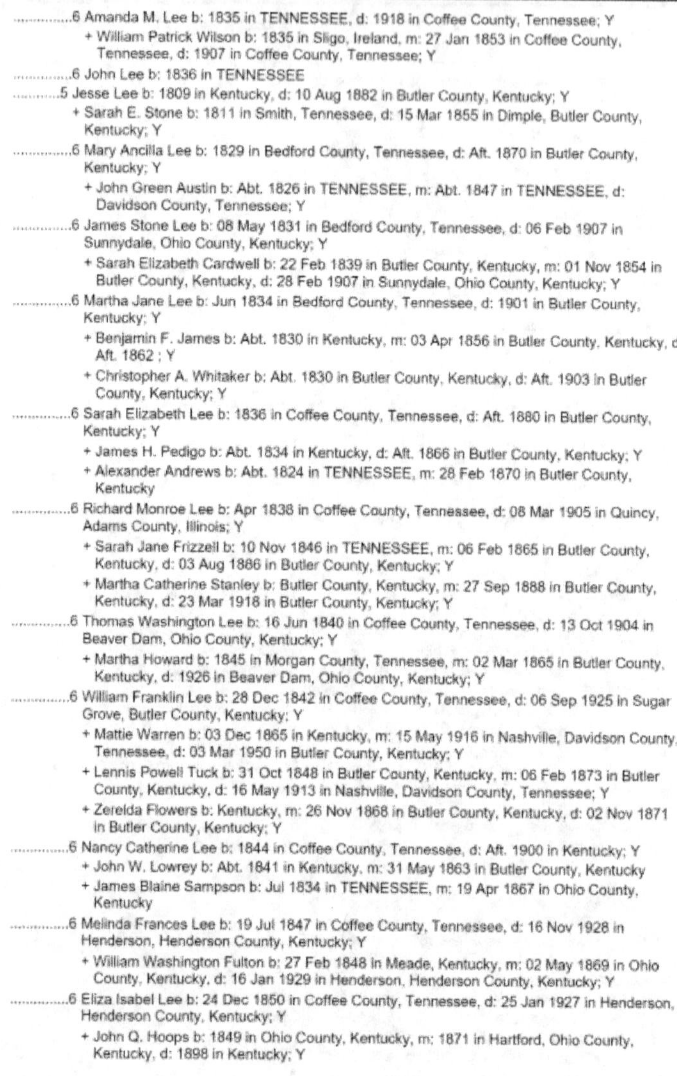

...............6 Amanda M. Lee b: 1835 in TENNESSEE, d: 1918 in Coffee County, Tennessee; Y
+ William Patrick Wilson b: 1835 in Sligo, Ireland, m: 27 Jan 1853 in Coffee County, Tennessee, d: 1907 in Coffee County, Tennessee; Y
...............6 John Lee b: 1836 in TENNESSEE
...........5 Jesse Lee b: 1809 in Kentucky, d: 10 Aug 1882 in Butler County, Kentucky; Y
+ Sarah E. Stone b: 1811 in Smith, Tennessee, d: 15 Mar 1855 in Dimple, Butler County, Kentucky; Y
...............6 Mary Ancilla Lee b: 1829 in Bedford County, Tennessee, d: Aft. 1870 in Butler County, Kentucky; Y
+ John Green Austin b: Abt. 1826 in TENNESSEE, m: Abt. 1847 in TENNESSEE, d: Davidson County, Tennessee; Y
...............6 James Stone Lee b: 08 May 1831 in Bedford County, Tennessee, d: 06 Feb 1907 in Sunnydale, Ohio County, Kentucky; Y
+ Sarah Elizabeth Cardwell b: 22 Feb 1839 in Butler County, Kentucky, m: 01 Nov 1854 in Butler County, Kentucky, d: 28 Feb 1907 in Sunnydale, Ohio County, Kentucky; Y
...............6 Martha Jane Lee b: Jun 1834 in Bedford County, Tennessee, d: 1901 in Butler County, Kentucky; Y
+ Benjamin F. James b: Abt. 1830 in Kentucky, m: 03 Apr 1856 in Butler County, Kentucky, d: Aft. 1862 ; Y
+ Christopher A. Whitaker b: Abt. 1830 in Butler County, Kentucky, d: Aft. 1903 in Butler County, Kentucky; Y
...............6 Sarah Elizabeth Lee b: 1836 in Coffee County, Tennessee, d: Aft. 1880 in Butler County, Kentucky; Y
+ James H. Pedigo b: Abt. 1834 in Kentucky, d: Aft. 1866 in Butler County, Kentucky; Y
+ Alexander Andrews b: Abt. 1824 in TENNESSEE, m: 28 Feb 1870 in Butler County, Kentucky
...............6 Richard Monroe Lee b: Apr 1838 in Coffee County, Tennessee, d: 08 Mar 1905 in Quincy, Adams County, Illinois; Y
+ Sarah Jane Frizzell b: 10 Nov 1846 in TENNESSEE, m: 06 Feb 1865 in Butler County, Kentucky, d: 03 Aug 1886 in Butler County, Kentucky; Y
+ Martha Catherine Stanley b: Butler County, Kentucky, m: 27 Sep 1888 in Butler County, Kentucky, d: 23 Mar 1918 in Butler County, Kentucky; Y
...............6 Thomas Washington Lee b: 16 Jun 1840 in Coffee County, Tennessee, d: 13 Oct 1904 in Beaver Dam, Ohio County, Kentucky; Y
+ Martha Howard b: 1845 in Morgan County, Tennessee, m: 02 Mar 1865 in Butler County, Kentucky, d: 1926 in Beaver Dam, Ohio County, Kentucky; Y
...............6 William Franklin Lee b: 28 Dec 1842 in Coffee County, Tennessee, d: 06 Sep 1925 in Sugar Grove, Butler County, Kentucky; Y
+ Mattie Warren b: 03 Dec 1865 in Kentucky, m: 15 May 1916 in Nashville, Davidson County, Tennessee, d: 03 Mar 1950 in Butler County, Kentucky; Y
+ Lennis Powell Tuck b: 31 Oct 1848 in Butler County, Kentucky, m: 06 Feb 1873 in Butler County, Kentucky, d: 16 May 1913 in Nashville, Davidson County, Tennessee; Y
+ Zerelda Flowers b: Kentucky, m: 26 Nov 1868 in Butler County, Kentucky, d: 02 Nov 1871 in Butler County, Kentucky; Y
...............6 Nancy Catherine Lee b: 1844 in Coffee County, Tennessee, d: Aft. 1900 in Kentucky; Y
+ John W. Lowrey b: Abt. 1841 in Kentucky, m: 31 May 1863 in Butler County, Kentucky
+ James Blaine Sampson b: Jul 1834 in TENNESSEE, m: 19 Apr 1867 in Ohio County, Kentucky
...............6 Melinda Frances Lee b: 19 Jul 1847 in Coffee County, Tennessee, d: 16 Nov 1928 in Henderson, Henderson County, Kentucky; Y
+ William Washington Fulton b: 27 Feb 1848 in Meade, Kentucky, m: 02 May 1869 in Ohio County, Kentucky, d: 16 Jan 1929 in Henderson, Henderson County, Kentucky; Y
...............6 Eliza Isabel Lee b: 24 Dec 1850 in Coffee County, Tennessee, d: 25 Jan 1927 in Henderson, Henderson County, Kentucky; Y
+ John Q. Hoops b: 1849 in Ohio County, Kentucky, m: 1871 in Hartford, Ohio County, Kentucky, d: 1898 in Kentucky; Y

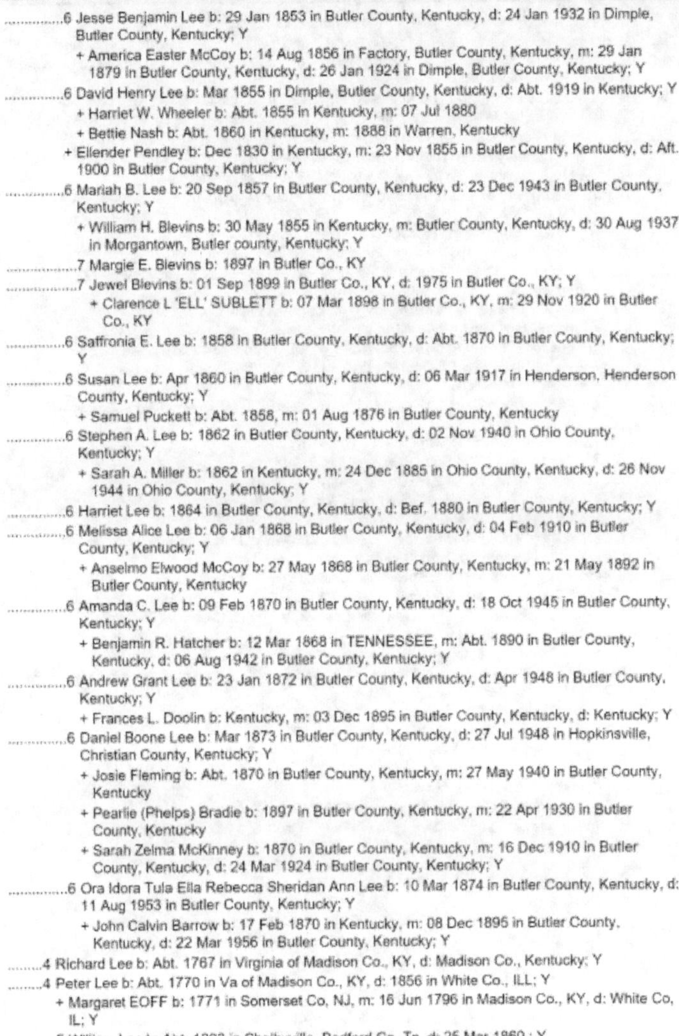

............6 Jesse Benjamin Lee b: 29 Jan 1853 in Butler County, Kentucky, d: 24 Jan 1932 in Dimple,
Butler County, Kentucky; Y
+ America Easter McCoy b: 14 Aug 1856 in Factory, Butler County, Kentucky, m: 29 Jan
1879 in Butler County, Kentucky, d: 26 Jan 1924 in Dimple, Butler County, Kentucky; Y
............6 David Henry Lee b: Mar 1855 in Dimple, Butler County, Kentucky, d: Abt. 1919 in Kentucky; Y
+ Harriet W. Wheeler b: Abt. 1855 in Kentucky, m: 07 Jul 1880
+ Bettie Nash b: Abt. 1860 in Kentucky, m: 1888 in Warren, Kentucky
+ Ellender Pendley b: Dec 1830 in Kentucky, m: 23 Nov 1855 in Butler County, Kentucky, d: Aft.
1900 in Butler County, Kentucky; Y
............6 Mariah B. Lee b: 20 Sep 1857 in Butler County, Kentucky, d: 23 Dec 1943 in Butler County,
Kentucky; Y
+ William H. Blevins b: 30 May 1855 in Kentucky, m: Butler County, Kentucky, d: 30 Aug 1937
in Morgantown, Butler county, Kentucky; Y
............7 Margie E. Blevins b: 1897 in Butler Co., KY
............7 Jewel Blevins b: 01 Sep 1899 in Butler Co., KY, d: 1975 in Butler Co., KY; Y
+ Clarence L 'ELL' SUBLETT b: 07 Mar 1898 in Butler Co., KY, m: 29 Nov 1920 in Butler
Co., KY
............6 Saffronia E. Lee b: 1858 in Butler County, Kentucky, d: Abt. 1870 in Butler County, Kentucky;
Y
............6 Susan Lee b: Apr 1860 in Butler County, Kentucky, d: 06 Mar 1917 in Henderson, Henderson
County, Kentucky; Y
+ Samuel Puckett b: Abt. 1858, m: 01 Aug 1876 in Butler County, Kentucky
............6 Stephen A. Lee b: 1862 in Butler County, Kentucky, d: 02 Nov 1940 in Ohio County,
Kentucky; Y
+ Sarah A. Miller b: 1862 in Kentucky, m: 24 Dec 1885 in Ohio County, Kentucky, d: 26 Nov
1944 in Ohio County, Kentucky; Y
............6 Harriet Lee b: 1864 in Butler County, Kentucky, d: Bef. 1880 in Butler County, Kentucky; Y
............6 Melissa Alice Lee b: 06 Jan 1868 in Butler County, Kentucky, d: 04 Feb 1910 in Butler
County, Kentucky; Y
+ Anselmo Elwood McCoy b: 27 May 1868 in Butler County, Kentucky, m: 21 May 1892 in
Butler County, Kentucky
............6 Amanda C. Lee b: 09 Feb 1870 in Butler County, Kentucky, d: 18 Oct 1945 in Butler County,
Kentucky; Y
+ Benjamin R. Hatcher b: 12 Mar 1868 in TENNESSEE, m: Abt. 1890 in Butler County,
Kentucky, d: 06 Aug 1942 in Butler County, Kentucky; Y
............6 Andrew Grant Lee b: 23 Jan 1872 in Butler County, Kentucky, d: Apr 1948 in Butler County,
Kentucky; Y
+ Frances L. Doolin b: Kentucky, m: 03 Dec 1895 in Butler County, Kentucky, d: Kentucky; Y
............6 Daniel Boone Lee b: Mar 1873 in Butler County, Kentucky, d: 27 Jul 1948 in Hopkinsville,
Christian County, Kentucky; Y
+ Josie Fleming b: Abt. 1870 in Butler County, Kentucky, m: 27 May 1940 in Butler County,
Kentucky
+ Pearlie (Phelps) Bradie b: 1897 in Butler County, Kentucky, m: 22 Apr 1930 in Butler
County, Kentucky
+ Sarah Zelma McKinney b: 1870 in Butler County, Kentucky, m: 16 Dec 1910 in Butler
County, Kentucky, d: 24 Mar 1924 in Butler County, Kentucky; Y
............6 Ora Idora Tula Ella Rebecca Sheridan Ann Lee b: 10 Mar 1874 in Butler County, Kentucky, d:
11 Aug 1953 in Butler County, Kentucky; Y
+ John Calvin Barrow b: 17 Feb 1870 in Kentucky, m: 08 Dec 1895 in Butler County,
Kentucky, d: 22 Mar 1956 in Butler County, Kentucky; Y
.........4 Richard Lee b: Abt. 1767 in Virginia of Madison Co., KY, d: Madison Co., Kentucky; Y
.........4 Peter Lee b: Abt. 1770 in Va of Madison Co., KY, d: 1856 in White Co., ILL; Y
+ Margaret EOFF b: 1771 in Somerset Co, NJ, m: 16 Jun 1796 in Madison Co., KY, d: White Co,
IL; Y
............5 William Lee b: Abt. 1803 in Shelbyville, Bedford Co, Tn, d: 25 Mar 1860 ; Y

+ Elizabeth Daniel m: Abt. 1827 in Prob. Bradford Co. TN
.........6 James Henry Lee b: 17 Aug 1829 in Poss. Bedford CO. TN, d: 16 Jul 1895 in Maunee, IL; Y
     + Susannah Matthews b: Abt. 1834 in ILL, m: 03 Feb 1850 in White Co., ILL, d: 03 Sep 1887 in Burnt Prairie, White Co., IL; Y
...........7 Mary E. Lee b: 1852 in Burnt Prairie, White Co., IL, d: White Co., ILL; Y
     + William J. "Will" Edwards b: White Co., ILL, m: 14 Mar 1872 in Carmi, White Co. IL
...........7 Peter L. Lee b: 1853 in Burnt Prairie, White Co., IL
...........7 William Henry Lee b: 1854 in Burnt Prairie, White Co., IL, d: Bef. 1877 ; Y
     + Melvina Caroline Edwards m: 11 May 1873 in Carmi, White Co. IL
...........7 Edith Katherine Lee b: 20 Oct 1855 in Burnt Prairie, White Co., IL, d: 26 Jul 1934 in Oliver, IN; Y
     + Newton Edwards m: 15 Mar 1874 in Carmi, White Co. IL
...........7 George F. Lee b: 1858 in Burnt Prairie, White Co., IL, d: Aft. 1880 ; Y
...........7 James Albert Lee b: 09 Feb 1861 in Burnt Prairie, White Co., IL, d: 06 Aug 1921 in West Frankfort, IL; Y
     + Larren Lane Edwards m: 07 Nov 1882 in Carmi, White Co. IL
...........7 Susan Mandy Lee b: 1863 in Burnt Prairie, White Co., IL
     + Shelton Morris b: Abt. 1860 in White Co., ILL, m: 30 Dec 1882 in White Co., ILL
...........7 Priscilla Alice Lee b: 28 Oct 1864 in Burnt Prairie, White Co., IL, d: 24 Dec 1936 in Burnt Prairie, White Co., IL; Y
     + William Henry Barbre b: Abt. 1862 in White Co., ILL, m: 17 Nov 1881 in Carmi, White Co. IL
...........7 Rease Lee b: 1867 in Burnt Prairie, White Co., IL
...........7 Annie Lee b: 1869 in Burnt Prairie, White Co., IL
...........7 Zacheus A. Lee b: 1872 in Burnt Prairie, White Co., IL
...........7 Samantha Lee b: 1875 in Burnt Prairie, White Co., IL
     + Sarah J. Minton b: Abt. 1831 in Tn, m: Abt. 1849
.......5 Reese Lee b: Abt. 1805 in Shelbyville, Bedford Co, Tn, d: Dec 1849 in Moultrie Co, Il; Y
     + Margaret Fisher m: 21 Jun 1848
.......5 Rebecca Lee b: Abt. 1807 in Shelbyville, Bedford Co, Tn, d: Bef. 1854 ; Y
     + Isaac DANIEL m: Abt. 1827 in Prob. Bradford Co. TN
.......5 James A Lee b: Abt. 1811 in Shelbyville, Bedford Co, Tn, d: 13 Jan 1860 in White Co, IL; Y
     + Nancy Bryant m: 20 May 1834
     + Sarah Daniel m: 05 Aug 1837
.......5 George Hanes Lee b: 16 Jul 1812 in Shelbyville, Bedford Co, Tn, d: 08 Sep 1888 in Moultrie Co, Il; Y
     + Lounica Ward b: 1812, m: 22 Aug 1832, d: 1886 ; Y
.........6 Elizabeth Lee b: 21 Sep 1833 in IL, d: 25 Oct 1833 ; Y
.........6 William Hanes Lee b: 30 Apr 1835 in IL, d: 22 Oct 1836 ; Y
.........6 James Llewellyn Lee b: 24 Apr 1837
.........6 Robert E Lee b: 13 Apr 1840
     + Elizabeth Ann Debruler m: 23 Nov 1865 in Moultrie Co, Il
...........7 John Wesley Lee b: 16 Sep 1874 in Moultrie Co, Il, d: 11 Nov 1961 ; Y
...........7 Ella Lee
...........7 Mabel Lee
     + Portner Cowell
...........7 Walter Lee
...........7 Bobby Lee
...........7 Rosa Lee
     + Wilson Fox
...........7 Goldie Lee
...........7 Lydia Lee
     + Adam B Reynolds
.........6 Peter Colbert Lee b: 04 May 1842 in White Co, IL, d: 24 Jan 1924 in Moultrie Co, Il; Y

+ Harriett Byrum Majors Allen m: 18 Nov 1909
+ Barbara Hill
...............7 Della Lee b: Moultrie Co, Il
+ Clint Smith
+ Sarah Hill
...............7 Mary Viola Lee b: 06 Feb 1866 in Bethany, Moultrie Co, Il, d: 01 Feb 1923 in Kirksville, Adair Co, Mo; Y
+ James Findley Reedy
...............7 Margaret Jane Lee b: 23 Nov 1867 in Bethany, Moultrie Co, Il, d: 18 Dec 1955 in LaPlatta, Mo; Y
+ Jacob Wilkinson
...............7 Charles Wesley Lee b: 24 Oct 1869 in Bethany, Moultrie Co, Il, d: 20 Feb 1940 in Atlanta, Mo; Y
+ Abigail Elizabeth Kratz m: 29 Jan 1896 in Shelby Co, Il
...............7 Willie Reed Lee b: Moultrie Co, Il
...............6 Margaret Millicent Lee b: 06 Jul 1844 in Moultrie Co, Il, d: 07 Nov 1903 in Stonington, Christian Co, Il; Y
+ Pleasant Fortner
...............7 George W Fortner b: 1872
+ Katie Schlecht
...............7 James W Fortner b: 1873, d: 1962 ; Y
...............7 Sarah L Fortner b: 1875
...............7 Maggie L Fortner b: 1877
...............7 Myrtle Ida Fortner b: 1883
...............7 Albert L Fortner b: 1886
...............7 Stafford Fortner b: 1889
...............6 Louisa Jane Lee b: 28 May 1847, d: 06 Mar 1922 in Sullivan, Moultrie Co, Il; Y
+ Josiah Collins Wright m: 05 Nov 1867 in Moultrie Co, Il
...............7 Dora Lounica Wright b: 05 Sep 1869
...............7 Elizabeth Wright b: 17 Jun 1871, d: 04 Feb 1961 ; Y
...............7 James Arthur Wright b: 16 Jun 1873, d: 29 Apr 1904 ; Y
...............7 Nancy Effie Wright b: 21 Jan 1877, d: 26 Sep 1964 ; Y
...............7 Levi Ansel Wright b: 21 Jul 1883, d: 02 Feb 1969 ; Y
...............6 George Nelson Lee b: 05 Feb 1850, d: 25 Feb 1851 ; Y
...............6 Nancy Caroline Lee b: 09 Feb 1852, d: 13 Aug 1852 ; Y
...............6 Benjamin Franklin Lee b: 26 Aug 1853, d: 07 Dec 1923 in Findley, Shelbyville Co, Il; Y
+ Louise G Bryson b: 1853, d: 1944 ; Y
...............7 William Lee b: 18 Nov 1873
...............7 Charles Bectel Lee b: 05 Feb 1875, d: Jan 1956 ; Y
...............7 Frances Marion Lee b: 16 Feb 1877, d: 10 Oct 1964 ; Y
...............7 Viola May Lee b: 22 May 1879, d: 21 Dec 1944 ; Y
...............7 Minnie Ethel Lee b: 29 Nov 1880, d: 31 Aug 1906 ; Y
...............7 Bessie Lerrica Lee b: 08 Mar 1883, d: 23 Jan 1964 in Shelby Co, Il; Y
...............7 Grace Pearl Lee b: 22 Feb 1885, d: 08 Oct 1962 in Moultrie Co, Il; Y
...............7 Manervie Agness Lee b: 02 Dec 1887
...............7 Maude Ellen Lee b: 02 Feb 1889 in Shelbyville, Shelby Co, Il, d: 15 Apr 1987 in Bethany, Moultrie Co, Il; Y
...............7 Lenord Elzy Lee b: 11 Sep 1892, d: Abt. 1918 in Bethany, Moultrie Co, Il; Y
...............7 James Edward Lee b: 13 Jan 1894, d: 02 Jul 1948 ; Y
...............7 Dora Edna Lee b: 25 Feb 1896, d: 01 Jan 1975 ; Y
...............7 John Buckneers Lee
...............6 John Buckneer Lee b: 14 Dec 1856, d: 09 Oct 1930 in Moultrie Co, Il; Y
...............6 Twin 1 Lee
...............6 Twin 2 Lee

...........5 John Lee b: Abt. 1814 in Shelbyville, Bedford Co, Tn, d: Bef. 1854 ; Y
...........5 Peter Lee Jr. b: Abt. 1816 in Shelbyville, Bedford Co, Tn, d: 05 Jun 1866 in White Co, IL; Y
　　　+ Mary Ann Polly Braddy b: Abt. 1820, m: 10 May 1841 in White Co, Il
..............6 Andrew Jackson Lee b: 20 Jul 1842, d: Abt. 1926 ; Y
　　　　+ Mary Funkhouser m: 24 Apr 1867 in White Co, Il
..............6 George W Lee b: 20 Jul 1842, d: 20 Aug 1874 in White Co, IL; Y
..............6 Reese Lee b: Abt. 1845
...........5 Jesse Franklin Lee b: Abt. 1818 in Shelbyville, Bedford Co, Tn, d: 22 Jul 1874 in White Co, IL;
　　Y
　　　　+ Elizabeth Daniel m: 20 Aug 1846 in White Co, Il
..............6 Matthew Lee b: Abt. 1847
..............6 Margaret Lee b: Abt. 1849 in White Co, IL
..............6 Elihu Lee b: Abt. 1850
..............6 Peter Collins Lee b: 15 Dec 1851 in White Co, IL, d: 18 Apr 1925 in White Co, IL; Y
..............6 Phebe Lee b: Abt. 1852, d: Abt. 1855 ; Y
..............6 Oliver C Lee b: Abt. 1854
　　　　+ Minerva Hughes m: Abt. 1854
.........4 William LEE b: Abt. 1773 in of Madison CO., KY
　　　　+ Mary Eoff b: Abt. 1775 in Richburg, Chester Co., SC, m: 05 Jan 1795 in Madison CO, KY
...2 William Lee II b: Abt. 1679/80 in b Northampton, Co, Va later Surry Co., Va, d: 04 Dec 1717 in will
　　probate, Richmond, Co, Virginia; Y
　　　+ Dorothy TAYLOR b: Abt. 1681 in of, Surry, King and Queen, Va, m: Abt. 1702 in of, Richmond, Co,
　　　Va, d: 25 Feb 1754 in will probate, Amelia, County, Virginia; Y
......3 William Lee iii or Jr. b: 14 May 1704 in N. Farnham, parish, Richmond Co. Va., d: 02 Jul 1764 in will
　　probate, Richmond, Co, Va Will Book 6, p. 361; Y
　　　+ Anne b: Abt. 1706 in Richmond, Co, Va, m: of, Richmond, Co, Va, d: Richmond, Co, Va; Y
.........4 Elizabeth Lee b: 1723/24 in Richmond, Co, Va
　　　+ Thomas HANKS b: 26 Jul 1728 in Richmond, Co, Va
...........5 Joseph HANKS b: 21 Feb 1764 in or, Richmond, Co, Va
...........5 Nancy HANKS b: 13 Sep 1766 in N. Farnham, parish, Richmond Co. Va., Va
.........4 Richard Lee b: Abt. 1726 in Richmond, Co, Va, d: 1764 in St Mary's, parish, MD; Y
　　　+ Mary Rose b: Abt. 1725 in of, Stafford, Co, Va, m: 29 Jun 1744 in Stafford, Co, Va
...........5 John Lee b: Abt. 1746 in of, St Mary, Co, MD, d: 12 Aug 1788 in probate Nelson, Co, Ky; Y
　　　　+ Elizabeth THOMPSON b: 09 Apr 1752 in Leonardtown, St.Mary's Co., MD, m: 16 Jan 1769 in
　　　　St. Mary's Co. Maryland, d: 1824 in Nelson, Co, Ky; Y
..............6 Eleanor Lee b: 1770 in St Mary's Co., MD of, Nelson, Co, Ky
　　　　+ Bennett HAYDEN b: Abt. 1767 in VA. of Nelson Co., KY, m: 19 Jan 1787 in Nelson CO., Ky,
　　　　d: 03 Jul 1794 in Nelson CO., Ky; Y
.................7 John HAYDEN b: Abt. 1789 in Nelson, Co, Ky
.................7 Elizabeth HAYDEN b: Abt. 1791 in Nelson, Co, Ky
..............6 Sarah Lee b: 1772 in of, Nelson, Co, Ky, d: 1825 ; Y
　　　　+ George CLARK b: 1760 in Va of Nelson Co., KY, m: 03 Oct 1793 in Nelson CO., Ky, d: Nov
　　　　1807 in Nelson Co, KY; Y
.................7 James Lee Clark b: 14 Feb 1794 in Nelson Co, KY, d: 21 May 1878 ; Y
　　　　+ Teresa 'Tracy' Beaven b: 1793, m: 05 Jan 1814 in Nelson Co, KY, d: Bef. 1878 ; Y
.................7 Elizabeth Clarke b: 01 Nov 1797, d: 11 Mar 1878 in Ky; Y
　　　　+ Elias Russell b: 22 Nov 1792, m: 19 Apr 1817 in Ky, d: 27 Jan 1872 in Ky; Y
....................8 Elias Russell b: Bet. 1817–1840
....................8 Mary Ann Russell b: 18 Mar 1818 in Washington Co, KY, d: 07 Jun 1899 in Marion Co,
　　　　KY; Y
....................8 John C Russell b: 09 Jan 1822 in 13/12/1885, d: 13 Dec 1885 in Ky; Y
....................8 Mary Ellen Russell b: 1830, d: 17 Mar 1855 in Marion Co, KY; Y
....................8 Elizabeth Russell b: 1832, d: 1915 in Raywick, KY; Y
....................8 Charles Ignatius Russell b: 06 Jun 1836, d: 28 Jan 1875 in Ky; Y
.................7 Mary Clark b: Abt. 1801

+ Benedict Joseph Beaven m: 08 Mar 1819 in Ky
.........7 Eleanor Clark b: Abt. 1802 in Nelson Co, KY, d: Bef. 1840 ; Y
+ John Winfield m: 22 Sep 1821 in Ky
.........7 Joseph Leander Clark b: Abt. 1806 in Nelson Co, KY, d: Aft. 1880 ; Y
+ Ann Henrietta Miles b: 22 Jul 1808 in Nelson Co, KY, m: 02 Jun 1829 in Ky, d: Sep 1880
in Hardin Co, KY; Y
.........8 Richard Miles Clark b: 11 Apr 1830 in Washington Co, KY, d: 23 Sep 1901 in Hardin Co,
KY; Y
+ Cornelius BROTHERS b: 03 Mar 1768 in Newtonwn, SMC, MD, m: 28 Feb 1791 in Nelson
CO., Ky, d: Abt. 1792 in Washington Co, KY; Y
.........7 John Lee Brothers b: 15 Jan 1792 in Nelson Co, KY, d: 1864 in SMC, MD: Y
+ Ann Riney m: 20 Nov 1830 in Marion Co, KY
+ Joseph John Beaven b: Abt. 1776 in Va of Nelson Co., KY, m: 21 Nov 1813 in Nelson CO.,
Ky, d: Bef. Feb 1819 in Nelson Co, KY; Y
.........6 Wilford Lee b: 29 Jul 1774 in of, Nelson, Co, Ky, d: 1849 in Bullin Co., Ky; Y
+ Rebecca Hill b: 1780 in of, Nelson, Co, Ky, m: 08 Aug 1796 in Nelson, Co, Ky, d: Abt. 1821
in Nelson CO., Ky; Y
.........7 John Lee b: 03 Oct 1798 in of, Nelson, Co, Ky, d: 17 Nov 1842 in Bardsrown, Nelson CO.,
Ky; Y
+ Elizabeth TROUTMAN b: Abt. 1809 in Boston, Nelson, KY, m: 14 Nov 1829 in Nelson
CO., Ky
.........8 Wilford Lee b: Abt. 1830 in Nelson CO., Ky
.........8 Catherine Lee b: Abt. 1832 in Nelson CO., Ky
.........8 Margaret Lee b: 02 May 1835 in Hardin Co., KY, d: 25 Jun 1891 in Charleston,
Mississippi Co., Mo.; Y
+ William Penn SWANK judge b: Abt. 1830 in Bullitt Co., Ky, of Charleston, Mississippi
Co. Mo., m: 01 Feb 1853 in Hardin Co., KY
.........8 Leonard Lee b: Abt. 1837 in Nelson CO., Ky
.........8 Aranella Lee b: Abt. 1839 in Nelson CO., Ky
.........8 Ora Lee b: Abt. 1841 in Nelson CO., Ky
.........7 Eleanor Lee b: 15 Jun 1800 in of, Nelson, Co, Ky, d: 1872 ; Y
+ Ben HARNETT b: Abt. 180 AD in Bardsrown, Nelson CO., Ky
.........7 Elizabeth Betsy Lee b: Abt. 1801 in of, Nelson, Co, Ky, d: 1824 ; Y
.........7 Sarah Lee b: 15 Jun 1803 in Bullit Co., Ky., d: 29 Jul 1892 in Charleston, Mississippi Co.
Mo.; Y
+ John SWANK b: Abt. 1800 in of Hardin Co., Ky., m: 11 Jun 1827 in Bullit Co., Ky.
.........8 William Penn SWANK judge b: Abt. 1830 in Bullitt Co., Ky, of Charleston, Mississippi Co.
Mo.
+ Margaret Lee b: 02 May 1835 in Hardin Co., KY, m: 01 Feb 1853 in Hardin Co., KY, d:
25 Jun 1891 in Charleston, Mississippi Co., Mo.; Y
.........8 Elizabeth SWANK b: Abt. 1831 in Bullitt Co., Ky, of Charleston, Mississippi Co. Mo., d:
Bef. 1892 in of Charleston, Mississippi Co. Mo.; Y
+ Mr Johnson b: Abt. 1833 in of Charleston, Mississippi Co. Mo.
.........8 Eliza E SWANK b: Abt. 1832 in Bullitt Co., Ky, of Charleston, Mississippi Co. Mo.
+ Mr GOODIN b: Abt. 1830 in of Charleston, Mississippi Co. Mo., m: 22 Sep 1857 in of
Charleston, Mississippi Co. Mo.
.........8 Margaret SWANK b: Abt. 1833 in Bullitt Co., Ky, of Charleston, Mississippi Co. Mo., d:
Bef. 1892 in of Charleston, Mississippi Co. Mo.; Y
+ Mr LANE b: Abt. 1833 in of Charleston, Mississippi Co. Mo.
.........8 Laura SWANK b: Abt. 1834 in Bullitt Co., Ky, of Charleston, Mississippi Co. Mo.
+ Thomas BECKWITH b: Abt. 1830 in of Charleston, Mississippi Co. Mo., m: 11 Mar
1863 in of Charleston, Mississippi Co. Mo.
.........8 Rebecca SWANK b: Abt. 1836 in Bullitt Co., Ky, of Charleston, Mississippi Co. Mo.
+ Mr SIMPSON b: Abt. 1830 in of Charleston, Mississippi Co. Mo.
.........7 ATKINSON H Lee b: 1807 in of, Nelson, Co, Ky

```
                    + WICOXEN
...........7 Mary Polly Lee b: 1809 in of, Nelson, Co, Ky
                + George FRENCH b: Abt. 1805 in Bardsrown, Nelson CO., Ky
...........7 Matilda Ann Lee b: 1813 in of, Nelson, Co, Ky, d: 20 May 1888 ; Y
...........7 Charles Lee b: 12 Jan 1815 in of, Nelson, Co, Ky, d: 26 Jul 1871 in Bullitt Co, Kentucky; Y
                + Lelilia SIMMONS b: Abt. 1805 in Bardsrown, Nelson CO., Ky, m: 07 Feb 1839 in Bullitt
                  Co, Kentucky
...........8 John A. Lee b: 1845 in Bullitt Co, Kentucky
...........8 Charles Lee b: 1848 in Bullitt Co, Kentucky
...........8 Rebecca Malvina (Mallie) Lee b: 1849 in Bullitt Co, Kentucky
...........8 Sophronia E. (Sophia) Lee b: 1853 in Bullitt Co, Kentucky
...........8 Henry L. Lee b: 1861 in Bullitt Co, Kentucky
...........7 Eliza Lee b: 24 Nov 1816 in of, Nelson, Co, Ky, d: 21 Jul 1853 in Louisville, Jefferson Co.,
                  KY; Y
                + Henry J.L. Craycraft b: 1816 in Washington, D.C., m: 18 Dec 1833 in Bullitt Co., KY
...........8 Walter Wilfred Lee Craycraft b: 24 Nov 1834
...........8 Thomas J. Craycraft b: 29 Aug 1836
...........8 William Edwin Craycraft b: 24 Aug 1838, d: 30 Mar 1904 in Confederate Home In Pewee
                  Valley; Y
...........8 Harry C. Craycraft b: 1845
                    + Kate Edelen m: 16 May 1870
...........7 Henry C Lee b: 24 Apr 1821 in of, Nelson, Co, Ky, d: child; Y
                + Margaret HILL b: 05 Jul 1795 in Ky, m: 14 Jul 1821 in Nelson CO., Ky
...........7 son Lee b: Abt. 1823 in Bullitt Co, Kentucky
...........7 William Lee b: 16 Feb 1825 in of, Nelson, Co, Ky
...........7 son also Lee b: Abt. 1828 in Bullitt Co, Kentucky
...........7 Phillip Lightfoot Lee b: 22 Oct 1832 in Bullitt Co, Kentucky, d: 03 Jul 1875 in Louisville,
                  Jefferson Co, Ky; Y
                + Belle Bland Bridgeford b: 1844 in Louisville, Jefferson Co, Ky, m: 23 Jun 1866 in
                  Louisville, Jefferson Co, Ky, d: 1903 in Louisville, Jefferson Co, Ky; Y
...........8 Maggie Lee b: 1868 in Louisville, Jefferson Co, Ky
...........8 Willie Lee b: 1870 in Louisville, Jefferson Co, Ky
...........8 Belle Lee b: 1874 in Louisville, Jefferson Co, Ky
.........6 Charles Lee b: 1776 in St Mary's Co., MD of, Nelson, Co, Ky, d: 1819 in Bullitt Co., Ky; Y
                + Margaret Marchon Maraman b: 1780 in Bardstown, Nelson CO., Ky, m: 05 Jun 1799 in
                  Nelson CO., Ky, d: 1851 in Hardin Co, KY; Y
...........7 Nancy Lee
                + James Morgan
...........7 John M. Lee
                + Martha Bane
...........8 Margaret Lee
                    + Andrew Middleton m: 09 Apr 1948 in Hardin Co, KY
...........7 Richard Lee
                + Ida Cundiff
...........7 Elizabeth Lee
                + John Shelton
...........7 Henry Lee
                + Margaret Elizabeth Pearman
...........7 Wilford Lee
                + Matilda Cundiff
                + Serilda Cundiff
...........7 William Buckman Lee
...........7 William F Lee
.........6 Mary Lee b: 1778 in of, Nelson, Co, Ky, d: 1839 ; Y
```

+ Francis MARRIMAN m: 08 Mar 1797 in Nelson CO., Ky
.........6 John "Jacky" Lee b: 1785 in St. Mary Co., Md of, Nelson, Co, Ky, d: 1835 ; Y
        + Elizabeth Hill b: Abt. 1788 in of, Nelson, Co, Ky, m: 30 Mar 1803 in Nelson, Co. Ky
............7 Sarah Sallie Lee b: 1804 in Bullitt Co, Kentucky, d: 1837 in Nelson Co.., Ky; Y
            + James M. Lee b: 14 Jul 1806 in Nelson Co.., Ky, m: Sep 1828 in Bullitt Co, Kentucky
...............8 Hooper C. Lee b: 1831 in Bullitt Co, Kentucky
...............8 Miles Thomas Lee b: 28 May 1833 in Bullitt Co, Kentucky, d: 08 Sep 1915 in Louisville,
            Jefferson Co, Ky; Y
                + Elizabeth (Bettie) Ann Greenwell b: Abt. 1848 in Mississippi Co, Missouri, m: Sep 1866
                in Mississippi Co, Missouri, d: Abt. 1871 in Bullitt Co, Kentucky; Y
..................9 Robert Lee b: 02 Nov 1868 in Mississippi Co, Missouri
..................9 Doss G. Lee b: 13 Mar 1870 in Bullitt Co, Kentucky
                + Ada Phligenia "Genie" HENDERSON b: Abt. 1867 in Mississippi Co, Missouri, m: 10
                Mar 1889 in Mississippi Co, Missouri
..................9 Miles Thomas Lee Jr. b: 19 Feb 1890 in Mississippi Co, Missouri
..................9 Genia A. Lee b: Feb 1900 in Mississippi Co, Missouri
...............8 John Thompson Lee b: 1836 in Bullitt Co, Kentucky, d: 18 Oct 1871 in Wolf Island,
            Mississippi Co, Missouri; Y
                + Mary Easley b: Abt. 1853 in Wolf Island, Mississippi Co, Missouri, m: 24 Feb 1861 in
                Wolf Island, Mississippi Co, Missouri
..................9 Joseph L. Lee b: 1862 in Wolf Island, Mississippi Co, Missouri
............7 Wilford Lee b: 1805 in Bullitt Co, Kentucky
............7 Rebecca Lee b: 1806 in Nelson Co.., Ky
............7 William Thompson LEE b: 05 Mar 1808 in Nelson Co.., Ky, d: 02 Jan 1862 in Wolf Island,
            Mississippi Co, Missouri; Y
                + Dorothy Gent Lee b: 29 Dec 1812 in Nelson Co.., Ky, m: 28 Jul 1829 in Nelson Co.., Ky,
                d: 26 Oct 1877 in Mississippi Co, Missouri; Y
...............8 Margaret Ann LEE b: 1830 in Bullitt Co, Kentucky
...............8 John Henry LEE b: 1832 in Bullitt Co, Kentucky
...............8 Elizabeth J. LEE b: 04 Jun 1835 in Bullitt Co, Kentucky
...............8 Nancy E. LEE b: 1837 in Bullitt Co, Kentucky
...............8 James A. LEE b: 31 Mar 1839 in Bullitt Co, Kentucky
...............8 William Riley LEE b: 1842 in Bullitt Co, Kentucky
...............8 Rebecca J. LEE b: 14 Sep 1844 in Bullitt Co, Kentucky
...............8 Elmina M. LEE b: 1846 in Bullitt Co, Kentucky
...............8 Susan R. W. LEE b: 1848 in Bullitt Co, Kentucky
...............8 Phillip Mack LEE b: 1851 in Mississippi Co, Missouri
............7 James B Lee b: 1809 in Nelson Co.., Ky, d: Bef. 1850 ; Y
                + Ellen Lee b: 1814 in Nelson Co.., Ky, m: 25 Jan 1836 in Nelson Co.., Ky, d: Abt. 1845 in
                Nelson Co.., Ky; Y
...............8 William Henry Lee b: 1837 in Nelson Co.., Ky
...............8 Malvina Lee b: 1839 in Nelson Co.., Ky
...............8 John Henry Lee b: 1841 in Nelson Co.., Ky
...............8 Mary J Lee b: 1843 in Nelson Co.., Ky
                + Jane Lee b: 1818 in Nelson Co.., Ky, m: Abt. 1847 in Nelson Co.., Ky
...............8 Stephen F. Lee b: 17 Apr 1849 in Nelson Co.., Ky, d: 17 Apr 1849 in Mississippi Co,
            Missouri; Y
............7 Miles Lee b: 1810 in Nelson Co.., Ky, d: 21 Jun 1878 in Bullitt Co., KY; Y
                + Sarah Cundiff b: Abt. 1819 in Bullitt Co., KY, m: 02 Jul 1840 in Bullitt Co., KY
...............8 Silas Lee b: Abt. 1855 in Bullitt Co., KY
                + Almeda Lee b: 1858 in Bullitt Co., KY
..................9 Miles Everett Lee b: 1880 in Hardin Co., KY
                    + Ethel Purcell
.....................10 Almeda Catherine Lee
.....................10 Carl Purcell Lee

...............9 Lizzie Lee b: 1883 in Hardin Co., KY
...............8 James H. Lee b: 29 Apr 1865 in Bullitt Co., KY, d: 18 Oct 1912 ; Y
     + Malvina Morgan b: 1816, m: 08 Dec 1834, d: Bef. 1840 in Bullitt Co., KY; Y
...............8 William Lee b: 1836 in Hardin Co., KY
       + Rebecca J Watson b: Abt. 1833 in Bullitt Co., KY, m: 1858 in Bullitt Co., KY
...............9 Sarah Lee b: 1859 in Hardin Co., KY
...............9 Miles A. Lee b: 17 Oct 1861 in Hardin Co., KY, d: 22 Apr 1875 ; Y
...............9 ELiza Lee b: 1863 in Hardin Co., KY
...............9 James Lee b: 1864 in Pine Tavern, Bullitt Co., Kentucky
...............9 P. Lee b: 1868 in Pine Tavern, Bullitt Co., Kentucky
...............9 Lillian "Lilly" Lee b: 08 Apr 1871 in Pine Tavern, Bullitt Co., Kentucky, d: 02 Apr 1955 in
      Louisville, Jefferson Co., KY; Y
      + John SHOPTAW b: 24 Mar 1860 in Bullitt Co., KY, d: 20 Apr 1955 in Louisville,
      Jefferson Co., KY; Y
...............10 GOLDIE ELIZABETH SHOPTAW b: 17 Dec 1894 in Louisville, Jefferson Co., KY, d:
      02 Apr 1988 in Meritt Island, FL; Y
...............10 Florine SHOPTAW b: 07 Aug 1902 in Louisville, Jefferson Co., KY, d: 14 Mar 1965
      in Lawton OK; Y
...............10 John Allen SHOPTAW b: 28 Aug 1907 in Louisville, Jefferson Co., KY, d: 27 Oct
      1934 in Louisville, Jefferson Co., KY; Y
...............10 Cora SHOPTAW b: Louisville, Jefferson Co., KY, d: 28 Dec 1990 in Louisville,
      Jefferson Co., KY; Y
...............9 H. Lee b: 1876 in of Pine Tavern, Bullitt Co., Kentucky
...............7 ELiza J. Lee b: 02 Sep 1811 in Nelson Co., Ky, d: 01 May 1890 in Bullitt Co, Kentucky; Y
...............7 Atkinson Hill Lee b: 27 Mar 1819 in Bullitt Co, Kentucky, d: 16 Jul 1885 in Hardin County
     KY; Y
     + Laura Susan Morgan b: 29 Jun 1821 in Hardin County KY, m: 02 Mar 1840 in Hardin, KY,
     d: 21 Apr 1891 in Hardin County KY; Y
...............8 Elizabeth Jane Lee b: 20 Mar 1843 in Hardin County, KY, d: 06 Jan 1892 in
     Elizabethtown, Hardin County, KY; Y
     + James Chenoweth Percefull b: 23 Jun 1838 in Hardin County KY, m: 07 Oct 1862 in
     Hardin County KY, d: 10 Jan 1926 in Elizabethtown, Hardin County, KY; Y
...............9 Laura H Percefull b: 25 Sep 1863 in Hardin County KY, d: 01 Jan 1892 in Hardin
     County KY; Y
...............9 Raleigh Jane Percefull b: 04 May 1865 in Hardin County KY, d: 16 Nov 1900 in Hardin
     County KY; Y
...............9 Susan 'Sudie' Percefull b: 12 May 1867 in Hardin County KY, d: 22 May 1933 ; Y
...............9 James Atkinson Perceful b: 29 May 1869 in Hardin County KY, d: 21 Jan 1962 in
     Hardin County KY; Y
...............9 Isa Belle Percefull b: 10 Feb 1871 in Elizabethtown, Hardin County KY, d: 20 Dec 1946
     in Elizabethtown, Hardin County KY; Y
...............9 Mary Elizabeth Percefull b: 15 Jun 1873 in Hardin County KY, d: 17 Jun 1950 in
     Hodgenville, Laure County KY (lived at Boston KY); Y
...............9 Cora Lee Percefull b: 25 Jul 1875 in Hardin County KY, d: (lived at Hodgensville KY); Y
...............9 Almeda Percefull b: 15 Aug 1877 in Hardin County KY, d: 08 Jan 1893 in Hardin County
     KY; Y
...............9 John William Percefull b: 01 Sep 1879
...............9 Wesley Morris Percefull b: 23 Dec 1881 in Hardin County KY, d: (lived in Louisville KY);
     Y
...............9 Clarence Percefull b: 15 Mar 1884 in Hardin County KY
...............9 Isaac Cleveland Percefull b: 11 Apr 1886 in Hardin County KY
...............9 Anne Arra Percefull b: 19 Nov 1888 in Hardin County KY, d: (lived in Louisville KY); Y
...............8 Sarah E Lee b: 1847 in Hardin Co., KY, d: Bef. 1860 ; Y
...............8 John William Lee b: 01 Sep 1851 in Hardin Co., KY, d: 23 Jan 1885 in Hardin Co., KY; Y

...............8 Miles Lee b: 20 Sep 1853 in Hardin Co., KY, d: 13 Feb 1936 in Boston, Nelson County, Kentucky; Y

+ Ellen PERRY b: 21 Jan 1860 in Hardin Co., KY, m: 21 Oct 1880 in Hardin Co., KY

...............9 Helen Lee b: Abt. 1882 in Hardin Co., KY

...............8 Wesley Lee b: 1855 in Hardin Co., KY

...............8 Almeda Lee b: 1858 in Bullitt Co., KY

+ Silas Lee b: Abt. 1855 in Bullitt Co., KY

...............9 Miles Everett Lee b: 1880 in Hardin Co., KY

+ Ethel Purcell

...............10 Almeda Catherine Lee

...............10 Carl Purcell Lee

...............9 Lizzie Lee b: 1883 in Hardin Co., KY

...............8 Mary Eliza Lee b: 1858 in Hardin Co., KY

+ William CISSELL b: Abt. 1856 in Hardin Co., KY, m: 25 Sep 1879 in Hardin Co., KY

...............8 Thomas Atkinson Lee b: 1861 in Hardin Co., KY, d: 18 Jan 1929 in Tonieville, LaRue County, Kentucky; Y

+ Lula CISSELL b: Abt. 1863 in Ky

...............8 Robert E Lee b: 10 Jul 1864 in Hardin Co., KY, d: 13 Jun 1944 in Hardin Co., KY; Y

+ Blanche MUNFORD b: 04 Jan 1867 in Hardin Co., KY, m: 20 Dec 1883 in Hardin Co., KY, d: 10 Jan 1890 in Hardin Co., KY; Y

...............9 Ernest Morgan Lee b: 23 Aug 1885 in Hardin Co., KY, d: 11 Jul 1953 ; Y

+ Jean COOK b: Abt. 1888 in Hardin Co., KY, m: 05 Jan 1910 in Hardin Co., KY

...............9 Thomas M. Lee b: 1887 in Hardin Co., KY

...............9 Miles Lee b: Jan 1890 in Hardin Co., KY

+ Martha L. "Mattie" BUSH b: 13 Mar 1866 in Elizabethtown, Hardin, Kentucky, USA, m: 30 Sep 1891 in Hardin Co., KY, d: 22 May 1947 in Elizabethtown, Hardin County, Kentucky; Y

...............9 female Lee b: Abt. 1893 in Hardin Co., KY

+ William Harper EDLIN b: 17 Aug 1885 in Hardin Co., KY, m: Abt. 1909 in Hardin Co., KY, d: Jan 1968 ; Y

...............10 Gilbert EDLIN b: 02 Oct 1910 in Hardin Co., KY, d: 12 Aug 1980 ; Y

...............9 Dennis D. LEE b: 19 Apr 1901 in Hardin Co., KY, d: 22 May 1978 ; Y

...............9 girl Lee b: Abt. 1903 in Hardin Co., KY

...............8 Albert M Lee b: 1869 in Hardin Co., KY, d: Aft. 1944 ; Y

...............6 William Henry Lee b: 1786 in Nelson, Co, Ky, d: 13 Jul 1852 in Bullitt Co., Ky; Y

+ Sarah Sallie YOUNGER b: 26 Feb 1794 in Bullitt, of Nelson Co., Ky, m: 12 Dec 1811 in Bullitt Co. Ky (License 11 Dec)

...............7 Henry T. Lee b: 1812 in Nelson Co.., Ky, d: 10 Dec 1863 in Bullitt Co, Kentucky; Y

+ Rebecca Lee b: 1820 in Nelson Co.., Ky, m: 12 Apr 1834 in Nelson Co.., Ky

...............8 Elinore Lee b: 1835 in Nelson Co.., Ky

...............8 Nancy Jane Lee b: 1837 in Nelson Co.., Ky

+ Thomas Jefferson Weekly b: Abt. 1832 in Ky, m: 28 Jun 1853 in Mississippi Co, Missouri

...............9 John Weekly b: 1858 in Washington Co., KY

...............9 Mary E. Weekly b: 1861 in Washington Co., KY

...............9 Anna D. Weekly b: 1863 in Washington Co., KY

...............9 William Weekly b: 1865 in Washington Co., KY

...............9 Maria J. Weekly b: 1872 in Washington Co., KY

...............9 Emma F. Weekly b: 1874 in Washington Co., KY

...............9 Margaret M. Weekly b: 1877 in Washington Co., KY

...............8 Sarah Ann Lee b: 1839 in Nelson Co.., Ky

+ William Greenwell b: Abt. 1832 in Bullitt Co., Ky, m: 20 Nov 1853 in Bullitt Co., Ky

...............8 William Henry Lee b: 11 Mar 1841 in Nelson Co.., Ky, d: 17 Feb 1917 in Bullitt Co., Ky; Y

+ Rebecca Cundiff b: 15 Oct 1840 in Bullitt Co., Ky, m: 05 Sep 1861 in Bullitt Co., Ky, d: 08 Feb 1911 in Bullitt Co., Ky; Y

...........9 Charles Lee b: 1862 in Bullitt Co., Ky
...........9 Ardelia Lee b: 1865 in Bullitt Co., Ky
...........9 Joseph Lee b: 1867 in Bullitt Co., Ky
...........9 Amanda Lee b: 12 Mar 1869 in Bullitt Co., Ky
...........9 Roberson E. Lee b: 1871 in Bullitt Co., Ky
...........9 Harry Lee b: 1877 in Bullitt Co., Ky
...........9 Samuel Lee b: Mar 1880 in Bullitt Co., Ky
...........9 Grover Lee b: 1887 in Bullitt Co., Ky
...........9 Orleans Lee b: Bullitt Co., Ky
...........8 Albert Lee b: 1843 in Nelson Co.., Ky
...........8 Ardelia Lee b: 1848 in Nelson Co.., Ky
...........8 John T. Lee b: Nelson Co.., Ky
...........7 Elizabeth LEE b: 10 Apr 1815 in Bullitt Co., Ky, d: 01 May 1892 in Bullitt Co., Ky; Y
+ Nicholas SIMMONS b: 30 Sep 1799 in Bullitt Co., Ky, m: 28 Jun 1832 in Bullitt Co., Ky
...........8 Sarah Ann SIMMONS b: 1834 in Bullitt Co., Ky
...........8 Mary Jane SIMMONS b: 1838 in Bullitt Co., Ky
...........8 George W. SIMMONS b: Dec 1842 in Bullitt Co., Ky
...........8 William H. SIMMONS b: 1844 in Bullitt Co., Ky
...........8 Samuel McKay SIMMONS b: Bullitt Co., Ky
...........7 Holbdert J. Lee b: 1818 in Nelson Co., Ky, d: Abt. 1840 in Bullitt Co., Ky; Y
...........7 Eliza Lee b: 25 Mar 1825 in Bullitt Co., Ky, d: 03 Mar 1887 in Bullitt Co., Ky; Y
+ James CROAN Jr. b: 09 Oct 1818 in Sheperdsville, Bullitt Co., Ky, m: 10 Jun 1847 in Sheperdsville, Bullitt Co., Ky
...........8 Malissa Adalate CROAN b: 01 May 1848 in Bullitt Co., Ky, d: 18 Dec 1873 in Bullitt Co., Ky; Y
+ William Harrison Shepherd b: 15 Jan 1841 in Bullitt Co., Ky, m: 09 Mar 1865 in Bullitt Co., Ky
...........8 Edward F CROAN b: 04 Apr 1850 in Sheperdsville, Bullitt Co., Ky, d: 01 Jul 1851 in Sheperdsville, Bullitt Co., Ky; Y
...........8 Roxanna CROAN b: 28 Apr 1852 in Sheperdsville, Bullitt Co., Ky, d: 20 Jan 1873 in Sheperdsville, Bullitt Co., Ky; Y
+ J. H. MILLER b: Abt. 1850 in Bullit Co. Ky
...........8 Josephine CROAN b: 26 Jan 1855 in Sheperdsville, Bullitt Co., Ky, d: 13 Dec 1873 in Sheperdsville, Bullitt Co., Ky; Y
+ R. H. MILLER b: Abt. 1850 in Bullit Co. Ky
...........8 Edward CROAN II b: Abt. 1856 in Sheperdsville, Bullitt Co., Ky, d: Bef. 1910 in Sheperdsville, Bullitt Co., Ky; Y
+ Nannie McDaniel b: Abt. 1858 in Bullit Co. Ky
...........8 Oscar CROAN b: Abt. 1859 in Sheperdsville, Bullitt Co., Ky
+ Mandy b: Abt. 1860 in Bullit Co. Ky
...........8 Robert Bruce CROAN b: Jun 1861 in Sheperdsville, Bullitt Co., Ky, d: 1952 in Sheperdsville, Bullitt Co., Ky; Y
+ Christia Ann STANFIELD b: 22 Mar 1876 in Washington Co. Ak
...........9 Edith CROAN b: 17 Mar 1893 in Nowata, Oklahoma, d: 18 Mar 1951 in Seattle, King, WA; Y
+ Charles Clark (GOFF) ROE b: 25 Apr 1887 in Grand Rapids, MI, d: of West Seattle, King, Wa; Y
...........10 Edward G. ROE b: Abt. 1920 in of Tacoma, Wa
+ [unknown spouse]
...........11 Katie ROE b: Abt. 1960 in Tacoma, Wa, d: in 2000 living in Houston; Y
+ Tony KRATOCHVIL m: of Houston TX
...........12 boy 1 KRATOCHVIL b: 1994 in age 6 in 2000, Houston, TX
...........12 boy 2 KRATOCHVIL b: age 3 1/2 Aug 2000, Houston, TX
...........9 James Edward CROAN b: Jan 1895 in Nowata, Oklahoma, d: 14 Jan 1924 ; Y
...........9 Stella CROAN b: 1897 in Nowata, Oklahoma

...................8 James W CROAN b: Abt. 1864 in Sheperdsville, Bullitt Co., Ky, d: 1944 in Sheperdsville,
      Bullitt Co., Ky; Y
      + Fannie b: Abt. 1865 in Bullit Co. Ky
...................8 Clarence L. CROAN b: May 1866 in Sheperdsville, Bullitt Co., Ky
...................7 Orleans LEE b: 19 Apr 1826 in of Bullitt, Nelson Co., Ky
      + Mary (Dolly) Cundiff b: 23 Jan 1828 in Bullitt Co., Ky, m: 29 Jan 1846 in Bullitt Co., Ky, d:
      12 Feb 1879 in Bullitt Co., Ky; Y
...................8 Amanda J. LEE b: 1847 in Bullitt Co., Ky
...................8 John Henry LEE b: 10 Mar 1851 in Bullitt Co., Ky
...................8 Mary Allis LEE b: 03 Oct 1853 in Bullitt Co., Ky
...................8 Charles Douglas LEE b: 1856 in Bullitt Co., Ky
...................8 Sarah. E. LEE b: 09 Feb 1859 in Bullitt Co., Ky
...................8 Orleans LEE b: 1861 in Bullitt Co., Ky
...................8 Emma LEE b: 1864 in Bullitt Co., Ky
...................8 Mary Moly LEE b: 1870 in Bullitt Co., Ky
...................8 William Thomas LEE b: Bullitt Co., Ky
...................8 W. LEE b: Bullitt Co., Ky
      + Laura Shelby Williams b: Abt. 1848 in Bullitt Co., Ky, m: 1881 in Bullitt Co., Ky
...................8 Nora LEE b: 1883 in Bullitt Co., Ky
...................7 Sarah A Lee b: Abt. 1827 in Bullitt Co., Ky, d: 1872 in Bullitt Co., Ky; Y
      + Thomas Snodder Snawder b: 1827 in Sheperdsville, Bullitt Co., Ky, m: 30 Apr 1848 in
      Jefferson Co., KY
...................8 John Monterville Snawder b: 09 May 1848 in Bullitt Co., Ky, d: 11 Nov 1941 ; Y
...................8 Alvarado) Snawder b: 16 Dec 1849 in Bullitt Co., Ky, d: 24 Dec 1908 ; Y
...................8 Edward Snawder b: 1851 in Bullitt Co., Ky
...................8 William Thomas Snawder b: 25 Jul 1853 in Bullitt Co., Ky
...................8 Mary Snawder b: 1855 in Bullitt Co., Ky, d: 1855 ; Y
...................8 Alice Victoria Snawder b: 25 Dec 1856 in Bullitt Co., Ky, d: 28 Feb 1914 ; Y
...................8 George Washington Snawder b: 22 Jun 1857 in Bullitt Co., Ky, d: 28 Feb 1941 ; Y
...................8 Joseph C.) Snawder b: 20 Jun 1860 in Bullitt Co., Ky, d: 09 Mar 1916 ; Y
...................8 Sarah Elizabeth Snawder b: 1862 in Bullitt Co., Ky
...................8 James Henry Snawder b: 12 Mar 1865 in Bullitt Co., Ky, d: 10 Dec 1942 ; Y
...................8 Henry Lee Snawder b: 25 Sep 1868 in Bullitt Co., Ky, d: 18 Dec 1937 ; Y
...................8 Vereda Adeline) Snawder b: Jan 1870 in Bullitt Co., Ky, d: 1888 in Bullitt Co., Ky; Y
      + Joseph E. Turner b: 1827 in Bullitt Co., Ky, m: 1844 in Bullitt Co., Ky
...................7 Amanda Ruth Lee b: 11 May 1831 in Nelson Co., Kentucky, d: 30 Jul 1890 in Bullitt Co.,
      Ky; Y
      + John J. GREENWELL b: 25 Jul 1814 in Nelson, Co, Ky, m: 02 May 1848 in Bullitt Co., Ky,
      d: 22 Apr 1890 in Bullitt Co., Ky; Y
...................8 Mary Jane Greenwell b: 29 Jun 1849 in Bullitt Co., Kentucky
...................8 Henrietta Greenwell b: 28 Jun 1850 in Bullitt Co., Kentucky
...................8 Eugnia Heade Greenwell b: 20 Mar 1852 in Bullitt Co., Kentucky
...................8 Phillip Augustus Greenwell b: 20 Mar 1854 in Bullitt Co., Kentucky
...................8 Benjamin Frank Greenwell b: 04 Apr 1856 in Bullitt Co., Kentucky
...................8 Sarah Ann Greenwell b: 04 Jul 1858 in Bullitt Co., Kentucky
...................8 Lillian Meyer Greenwell b: 04 Dec 1861 in Bullitt Co., Kentucky
...................8 Lenora Greenwell b: 06 Apr 1864 in Bullitt Co., Kentucky
...................8 Minnie Lee Greenwell b: 06 Jul 1866 in Bullitt Co., Kentucky
...................8 Robert Lee Greenwell b: Abt. 1868 in Bullitt Co., Kentucky
...................8 St. Elmo Greenwell b: 06 May 1869 in Bullitt Co., Kentucky
...................8 Cordelia J. Greenwell b: Abt. 1870 in Bullitt Co., Kentucky
...................7 Dorothy Dolly Lee b: 1833 in Bullitt Co., Ky, d: 1891 in Bullitt Co., Ky; Y
      + John W. "V.V." GLENN b: 14 Aug 1814 in Va of Sheperdsville, Bullitt Co., Ky, m: 16 Mar
      1852 in Sheperdsville, Bullitt Co., Ky, d: 25 Feb 1875 in Bullitt Co., Ky; Y

.................8 Samuel P. GLENN b: 1853 in Bullitt Co., Ky
.................8 Angue GLENN b: 1855 in Bullitt Co., Ky
.................8 Ethelbert GLENN b: 1857 in Bullitt Co., Ky
.................8 John William GLENN b: 24 Sep 1859 in Bullitt Co., Ky
.................8 Mary Millie GLENN b: 1863 in Bullitt Co., Ky
.................8 Leila GLENN b: 1868 in Bullitt Co., Ky
.................8 Betty GLENN b: 1870 in Bullitt Co., Ky
.................8 Herbert GLENN b: 1874 in Bullitt Co., Ky
.................7 Cynthia Lee b: Abt. 1836 in of Bullitt, Nelson Co., Ky
       + John W CAMMPBELL b: Abt. 1834 in Sheperdsville, Bullitt Co., Ky
.............6 Henry Harry "Lightfoot" Lee b: 1786 in of, Nelson, Co, Ky, d: 30 Mar 1864 in Mississippi Co, Missouri; Y
       + Ann NORRIS b: 1783 in St. Mary's Co, Maryland, m: 12 Sep 1805 in Bardstown, Nelson Co.., Ky, d: Sep 1854 in Mississippi Co, Missouri; Y
.................7 James M. Lee b: 14 Jul 1806 in Nelson Co.., Ky
       + Sarah Sallie Lee b: 1804 in Bullitt Co, Kentucky, m: Sep 1828 in Bullitt Co, Kentucky, d: 1837 in Nelson Co.., Ky; Y
.................8 Hooper C. Lee b: 1831 in Bullitt Co, Kentucky
.................8 Miles Thomas Lee b: 28 May 1833 in Bullitt Co, Kentucky, d: 08 Sep 1915 in Louisville, Jefferson Co, Ky; Y
       + Elizabeth (Bettie) Ann Greenwell b: Abt. 1848 in Mississippi Co, Missouri, m: Sep 1866 in Mississippi Co, Missouri, d: Abt. 1871 in Bullitt Co, Kentucky; Y
.................9 Robert Lee b: 02 Nov 1868 in Mississippi Co, Missouri
.................9 Doss G. Lee b: 13 Mar 1870 in Bullitt Co, Kentucky
       + Ada Phligenia "Genie" HENDERSON b: Abt. 1867 in Mississippi Co, Missouri, m: 10 Mar 1889 in Mississippi Co, Missouri
.................9 Miles Thomas Lee Jr. b: 19 Feb 1890 in Mississippi Co, Missouri
.................9 Genia A. Lee b: Feb 1900 in Mississippi Co, Missouri
.................8 John Thompson Lee b: 1836 in Bullitt Co, Kentucky, d: 18 Oct 1871 in Wolf Island, Mississippi Co, Missouri; Y
       + Mary Easley b: Abt. 1853 in Wolf Island, Mississippi Co, Missouri, m: 24 Feb 1861 in Wolf Island, Mississippi Co, Missouri
.................9 Joseph L. Lee b: 1862 in Wolf Island, Mississippi Co, Missouri
       + Margaret Atcher b: 31 Jul 1807 in Leesville, VA, m: Sep 1838 in Hardin Co., KY, d: 07 Jan 1867 in Wolf Island, Mississippi Co, Missouri; Y
.................8 Rachel Lee b: Oct 1839 in Bullitt Co, Kentucky
.................8 ELizabeth Bettie A. Lee b: 1841 in Bullitt Co, Kentucky
.................8 Christopher Henry Lee b: 24 Jul 1842 in Bullitt Co, Kentucky
.................7 Rhodolphus Norris Lee b: 1807 in Nelson Co.., Ky, d: Dec 1865 in Little Rock, ARKANSAS; Y
       + Nancy VIELLIERS b: 1808 in Nelson Co.., Ky, m: 27 Jul 1829 in Nelson Co.., Ky
.................8 Sylvester Lee b: 1835 in Bullitt Co, Kentucky
.................8 M. Emiline "Emily" Lee b: 1837 in Bullitt Co, Kentucky
.................8 Isabella Lee b: Abt. 1839 in Bullitt Co, Kentucky
.................8 Palmye Lee b: 1841 in Bullitt Co, Kentucky
.................8 M.A. Lee b: 1843 in Bullitt Co, Kentucky
.................8 Christopher Lee b: 1845 in Bullitt Co, Kentucky
.................8 Thomas Loy Lee b: 1846 in Bullitt Co, Kentucky
.................8 William Lee b: 1848 in Bullitt Co, Kentucky
.................8 Kate Lee b: 1850 in Mississippi Co, Missouri
.................8 Mary Lee b: 1852 in Mississippi Co, Missouri
.................7 Robert M. Lee b: 09 Aug 1809 in Nelson Co.., Ky, d: 15 Nov 1878 in Bullitt Co, Kentucky; Y
       + Elizabeth Caswell b: 10 Sep 1809 in Bullitt Co, Kentucky, m: 11 Apr 1831 in Bullitt Co, Kentucky
.................8 Ellen Elizabeth Lee b: 07 Jan 1832 in Bullitt Co, Kentucky

..................8 Malinda A. Lee b: 16 Feb 1833 in Bullitt Co, Kentucky
..................8 Daid L. Lee b: 22 Jul 1834 in Bullitt Co, Kentucky
..................8 James M. Lee b: 1836 in Bullitt Co, Kentucky
..................8 John S. "Lar" Lee b: 1838 in Bullitt Co, Kentucky
..................8 William Jefferson Lee b: 11 Mar 1840 in Bullitt Co, Kentucky
..................8 Rhodolphus Doss Lee b: 08 Jul 1841 in Bullitt Co, Kentucky
          + Laura Pearl b: Abt. 1851 in Bullitt Co, Kentucky, m: 09 Aug 1871 in Bullitt Co, Kentucky
..................8 Vinda C. Lee b: 1875 in Bullitt Co, Kentucky
..................8 Sidney P. Lee b: Abt. 1877 in Bullitt Co, Kentucky
..................8 Sada M. Lee b: Abt. 1879 in Bullitt Co, Kentucky
..................8 Lewis R. Lee b: Abt. 1881 in Bullitt Co, Kentucky
..................7 Elizabeth Lee b: 1811 in Nelson Co.., Ky
          + John R. HILL b: Abt. 1805 in Ky, m: 23 Jan 1827 in Hardin Co., KY
..................8 Joseph HILL b: Abt. 1830 in Larue Co., Ky
..................8 Nancy A. HILL b: 02 Dec 1832 in Larue Co., Ky
..................8 Mary E. HILL b: 1834 in Larue Co., Ky
..................8 Stephen HILL b: 1836 in Larue Co., Ky
..................8 John H. HILL b: Abt. 1838 in Larue Co., Ky
..................8 Susan J. HILL b: Abt. 1841 in Larue Co., Ky
..................8 Elizabeth H. HILL b: 1844 in Larue Co., Ky
..................8 Rebecca Jane HILL b: 1850 in Larue Co., Ky
..................7 Dorothy Gent Lee b: 29 Dec 1812 in Nelson Co.., Ky, d: 26 Oct 1877 in Mississippi Co,
          Missouri; Y
          + William Thompson LEE b: 05 Mar 1808 in Nelson Co.., Ky, m: 28 Jul 1829 in Nelson
          Co.., Ky, d: 02 Jan 1862 in Wolf Island, Mississippi Co, Missouri; Y
..................8 Margaret Ann LEE b: 1830 in Bullitt Co, Kentucky
..................8 John Henry LEE b: 1832 in Bullitt Co, Kentucky
..................8 Elizabeth J. LEE b: 04 Jun 1835 in Bullitt Co, Kentucky
..................8 Nancy E. LEE b: 1837 in Bullitt Co, Kentucky
..................8 James A. LEE b: 31 Mar 1839 in Bullitt Co, Kentucky
..................8 William Riley LEE b: 1842 in Bullitt Co, Kentucky
..................8 Rebecca J. LEE b: 14 Sep 1844 in Bullitt Co, Kentucky
..................8 Elmina M. LEE b: 1846 in Bullitt Co, Kentucky
..................8 Susan R. W. LEE b: 1848 in Bullitt Co, Kentucky
..................8 Phillip Mack LEE b: 1851 in Mississippi Co, Missouri
..................7 Ellen Lee b: 1814 in Nelson Co.., Ky, d: Abt. 1845 in Nelson Co.., Ky; Y
          + James B Lee b: 1809 in Nelson Co.., Ky, m: 25 Jan 1836 in Nelson Co.., Ky, d: Bef. 1850
          ; Y
..................8 William Henry Lee b: 1837 in Nelson Co.., Ky
..................8 Malvina Lee b: 1839 in Nelson Co.., Ky
..................8 John Henry Lee b: 1841 in Nelson Co.., Ky
..................8 Mary J Lee b: 1843 in Nelson Co.., Ky
..................7 Jane Lee b: 1818 in Nelson Co.., Ky
          + James B Lee b: 1809 in Nelson Co.., Ky, m: Abt. 1847 in Nelson Co.., Ky, d: Bef. 1850 ; Y
..................8 Stephen F. Lee b: 17 Apr 1849 in Nelson Co.., Ky, d: 17 Apr 1849 in Mississippi Co,
          Missouri; Y
..................7 Rebecca Lee b: 1820 in Nelson Co.., Ky
          + Henry T. Lee b: 1812 in Nelson Co.., Ky, m: 12 Apr 1834 in Nelson Co.., Ky, d: 10 Dec
          1863 in Bullitt Co, Kentucky; Y
..................8 Elinore Lee b: 1835 in Nelson Co.., Ky
..................8 Nancy Jane Lee b: 1837 in Nelson Co.., Ky
          + Thomas Jefferson Weekly b: Abt. 1832 in Ky, m: 28 Jun 1853 in Mississippi Co,
          Missouri
..................9 John Weekly b: 1858 in Washington Co., KY

.....................9 Mary E. Weekly b: 1861 in Washington Co., KY
.....................9 Anna D. Weekly b: 1863 in Washington Co., KY
.....................9 William Weekly b: 1865 in Washington Co., KY
.....................9 Maria J. Weekly b: 1872 in Washington Co., KY
.....................9 Emma F. Weekly b: 1874 in Washington Co., KY
.....................9 Margaret M. Weekly b: 1877 in Washington Co., KY
.....................8 Sarah Ann Lee b: 1839 in Nelson Co.., Ky
          + William Greenwell b: Abt. 1832 in Bullitt Co., Ky, m: 20 Nov 1853 in Bullitt Co., Ky
.....................8 William Henry Lee b: 11 Mar 1841 in Nelson Co.., Ky, d: 17 Feb 1917 in Bullitt Co., Ky; Y
          + Rebecca Cundiff b: 15 Oct 1840 in Bullitt Co., Ky, m: 05 Sep 1861 in Bullitt Co., Ky, d:
            08 Feb 1911 in Bullitt Co., Ky; Y
.....................9 Charles Lee b: 1862 in Bullitt Co., Ky
.....................9 Ardelia Lee b: 1865 in Bullitt Co., Ky
.....................9 Joseph Lee b: 1867 in Bullitt Co., Ky
.....................9 Amanda Lee b: 12 Mar 1869 in Bullitt Co., Ky
.....................9 Roberson E. Lee b: 1871 in Bullitt Co., Ky
.....................9 Harry Lee b: 1877 in Bullitt Co., Ky
.....................9 Samuel Lee b: Mar 1880 in Bullitt Co., Ky
.....................9 Grover Lee b: 1887 in Bullitt Co., Ky
.....................9 Orleans Lee b: Bullitt Co., Ky
.....................8 Albert Lee b: 1843 in Nelson Co.., Ky
.....................8 Ardelia Lee b: 1848 in Nelson Co.., Ky
.....................8 John T. Lee b: Nelson Co.., Ky
.....................7 Margaret Ann Lee b: 17 Aug 1822 in Nelson Co.., Ky, d: 25 Oct 1895 in Bullitt Co,
            Kentucky; Y
          + William Dawson b: 04 Feb 1818 in Nelson Co.., Ky, m: 16 Aug 1838 in Nelson Co.., Ky
.....................8 Kitty Jane Dawson b: 30 Jul 1840 in Bullitt Co, Kentucky
.....................8 Elizabeth E. Dawson b: 14 Feb 1842 in Bullitt Co, Kentucky
.....................8 Rachel L. Dawson b: 1847 in Bullitt Co, Kentucky
.....................8 William J. (W.) Dawson b: 1848 in Bullitt Co, Kentucky
.....................8 John R. Dawson b: 07 Sep 1850 in Bullitt Co, Kentucky
.....................8 Nancy A. Dawson b: 1854 in Bullitt Co, Kentucky
.....................8 James Dawson b: 1856 in Bullitt Co, Kentucky
.....................8 Charles "Charley" J. Dawson b: 1859 in Bullitt Co, Kentucky
.....................8 Lee Dawson b: 22 Jun 1866 in Bullitt Co, Kentucky
.....................7 Ignatius Lee b: 1824 in Nelson Co.., Ky, d: Bef. 04 Dec 1862 in Mississippi Co, Missouri; Y
          + Gilly CARR b: Abt. 1824 in Hardin Co.., KY, m: 17 Jan 1843 in Hardin Co., KY
.....................8 Eliza Ellen Lee b: 1844 in Bullitt Co, Kentucky
.....................8 John Jesse Lee b: 1846 in Bullitt Co, Kentucky
.....................8 Malissa "Matilda" S. Lee b: 1848 in Bullitt Co, Kentucky
.....................8 Sarah Ann "Bid" Lee b: Nov 1849 in Bullitt Co, Kentucky
.....................7 Thomas T. Lee b: 01 Mar 1827 in Nelson Co.., Ky, d: 10 Nov 1874 in Bullitt Co, Kentucky; Y
          + Elizabeth HOWLETT b: 02 Jun 1828 in Bullitt Co, Kentucky, m: 07 Feb 1847 in Bullitt Co,
            Kentucky
.....................8 William H. "Billy" Lee b: 1848 in Bullitt Co, Kentucky
.....................8 James Robert Lee b: 1851 in Bullitt Co, Kentucky
.....................8 Kate "Kitty" A. Lee b: 1853 in Bullitt Co, Kentucky
.....................8 Sanford or Samuel Lee b: 1856 in Bullitt Co, Kentucky
.....................8 Charles S. Lee b: 12 Jan 1858 in Bullitt Co, Kentucky
.....................8 Sarilda "Rilda" E. Lee b: 1860 in Bullitt Co, Kentucky
.....................8 Nat D. Lee b: 1867 in Bullitt Co, Kentucky
.....................8 Clay H Lee b: 02 Aug 1969 in Bullitt Co, Kentucky
.....................7 Jesse Lee b: 1828 in Nelson Co.., Ky

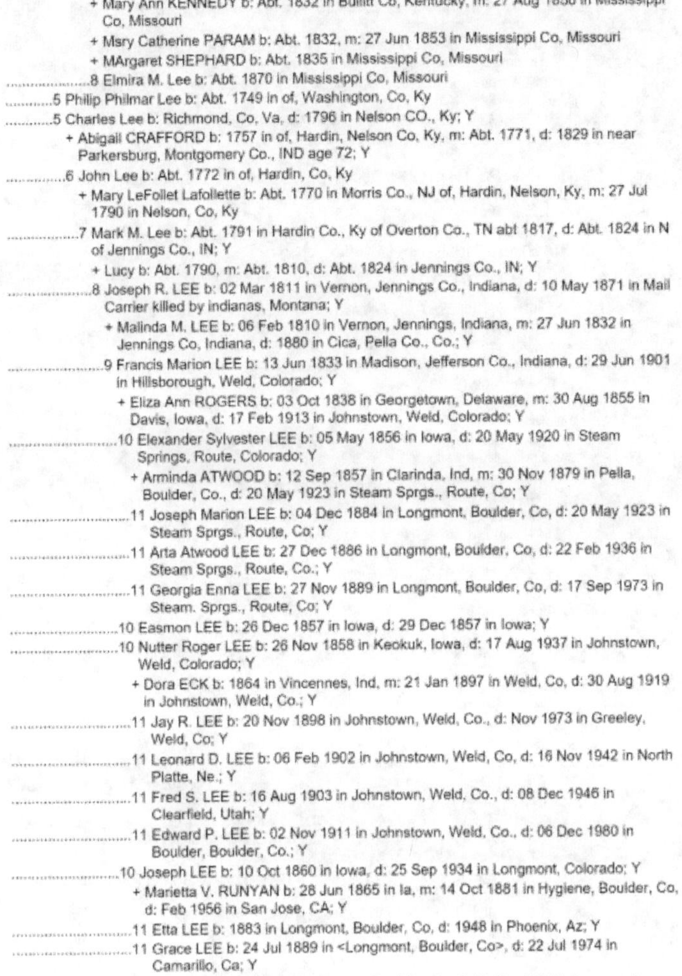

+ Mary Ann KENNEDY b: Abt. 1832 in Bullitt Co, Kentucky, m: 27 Aug 1850 in Mississippi Co, Missouri

+ Msry Catherine PARAM b: Abt. 1832, m: 27 Jun 1853 in Mississippi Co, Missouri

+ MArgaret SHEPHARD b: Abt. 1835 in Mississippi Co, Missouri

........8 Elmira M. Lee b: Abt. 1870 in Mississippi Co, Missouri

........5 Philip Philmar Lee b: Abt. 1749 in of, Washington, Co, Ky

........5 Charles Lee b: Richmond, Co, Va, d: 1796 in Nelson CO., Ky; Y

+ Abigail CRAFFORD b: 1757 in of, Hardin, Nelson Co, Ky, m: Abt. 1771, d: 1829 in near Parkersburg, Montgomery Co., IND age 72; Y

........6 John Lee b: Abt. 1772 in of, Hardin, Co, Ky

+ Mary LeFollet Lafollette b: Abt. 1770 in Morris Co., NJ of, Hardin, Nelson, Ky, m: 27 Jul 1790 in Nelson, Co, Ky

........7 Mark M. Lee b: Abt. 1791 in Hardin Co., Ky of Overton Co., TN abt 1817, d: Abt. 1824 in N of Jennings Co., IN; Y

+ Lucy b: Abt. 1790, m: Abt. 1810, d: Abt. 1824 in Jennings Co., IN; Y

........8 Joseph R. LEE b: 02 Mar 1811 in Vernon, Jennings Co., Indiana, d: 10 May 1871 in Mail Carrier killed by indianas, Montana; Y

+ Malinda M. LEE b: 06 Feb 1810 in Vernon, Jennings, Indiana, m: 27 Jun 1832 in Jennings Co, Indiana, d: 1880 in Cica, Pella Co., Co.; Y

........9 Francis Marion LEE b: 13 Jun 1833 in Madison, Jefferson Co., Indiana, d: 29 Jun 1901 in Hillsborough, Weld, Colorado; Y

+ Eliza Ann ROGERS b: 03 Oct 1838 in Georgetown, Delaware, m: 30 Aug 1855 in Davis, Iowa, d: 17 Feb 1913 in Johnstown, Weld, Colorado; Y

........10 Elexander Sylvester LEE b: 05 May 1856 in Iowa, d: 20 May 1920 in Steam Springs, Route, Colorado; Y

+ Arminda ATWOOD b: 12 Sep 1857 in Clarinda, Ind, m: 30 Nov 1879 in Pella, Boulder, Co., d: 20 May 1923 in Steam Sprgs., Route, Co; Y

........11 Joseph Marion LEE b: 04 Dec 1884 in Longmont, Boulder, Co, d: 20 May 1923 in Steam Sprgs., Route, Co; Y

........11 Arta Atwood LEE b: 27 Dec 1886 in Longmont, Boulder, Co, d: 22 Feb 1936 in Steam Sprgs., Route, Co.; Y

........11 Georgia Enna LEE b: 27 Nov 1889 in Longmont, Boulder, Co, d: 17 Sep 1973 in Steam. Sprgs., Route, Co; Y

........10 Easmon LEE b: 26 Dec 1857 in Iowa, d: 29 Dec 1857 in Iowa; Y

........10 Nutter Roger LEE b: 26 Nov 1858 in Keokuk, Iowa, d: 17 Aug 1937 in Johnstown, Weld, Colorado; Y

+ Dora ECK b: 1864 in Vincennes, Ind, m: 21 Jan 1897 in Weld, Co, d: 30 Aug 1919 in Johnstown, Weld, Co.; Y

........11 Jay R. LEE b: 20 Nov 1898 in Johnstown, Weld, Co., d: Nov 1973 in Greeley, Weld, Co; Y

........11 Leonard D. LEE b: 06 Feb 1902 in Johnstown, Weld, Co, d: 16 Nov 1942 in North Platte, Ne.; Y

........11 Fred S. LEE b: 16 Aug 1903 in Johnstown, Weld, Co., d: 08 Dec 1946 in Clearfield, Utah; Y

........11 Edward P. LEE b: 02 Nov 1911 in Johnstown, Weld, Co., d: 06 Dec 1980 in Boulder, Boulder, Co.; Y

........10 Joseph LEE b: 10 Oct 1860 in Iowa, d: 25 Sep 1934 in Longmont, Colorado; Y

+ Marietta V. RUNYAN b: 28 Jun 1865 in Ia, m: 14 Oct 1881 in Hygiene, Boulder, Co, d: Feb 1956 in San Jose, CA; Y

........11 Etta LEE b: 1883 in Longmont, Boulder, Co, d: 1948 in Phoenix, Az; Y

........11 Grace LEE b: 24 Jul 1889 in <Longmont, Boulder, Co>, d: 22 Jul 1974 in Camarillo, Ca; Y

........11 Ray R. LEE b: 1893 in Longmont, Boulder, Co, d: 19 Mar 1931 in Longmont, Boulder, Co; Y

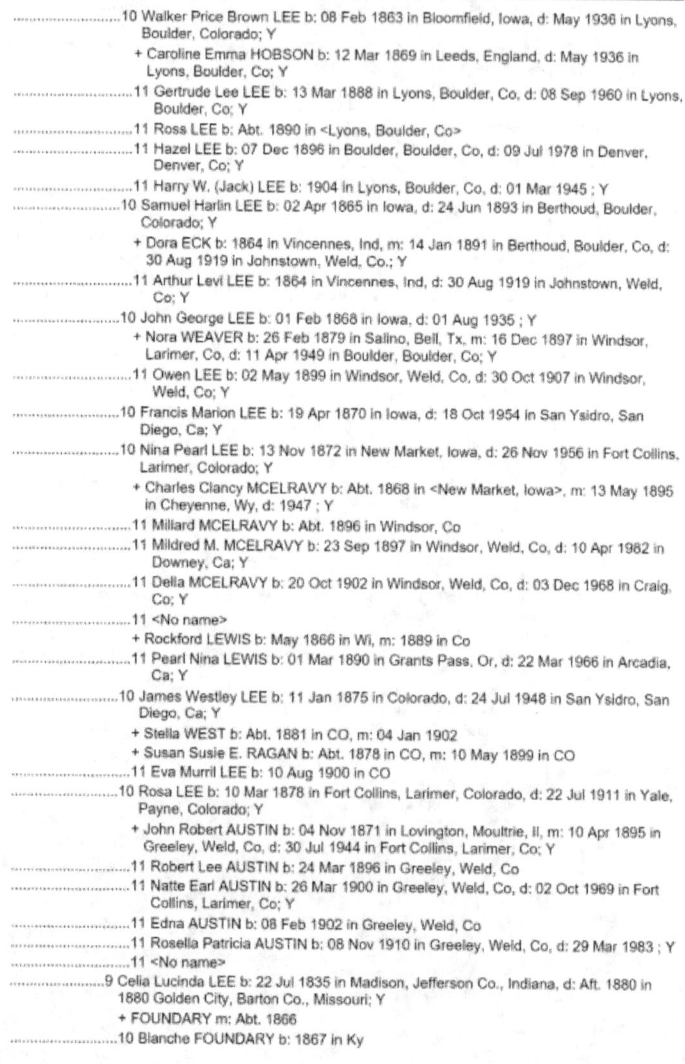

...................10 Walker Price Brown LEE b: 08 Feb 1863 in Bloomfield, Iowa, d: May 1936 in Lyons, Boulder, Colorado; Y

     + Caroline Emma HOBSON b: 12 Mar 1869 in Leeds, England, d: May 1936 in Lyons, Boulder, Co; Y

...................11 Gertrude Lee LEE b: 13 Mar 1888 in Lyons, Boulder, Co, d: 08 Sep 1960 in Lyons, Boulder, Co; Y

...................11 Ross LEE b: Abt. 1890 in <Lyons, Boulder, Co>

...................11 Hazel LEE b: 07 Dec 1896 in Boulder, Boulder, Co, d: 09 Jul 1978 in Denver, Denver, Co; Y

...................11 Harry W. (Jack) LEE b: 1904 in Lyons, Boulder, Co, d: 01 Mar 1945 ; Y

...................10 Samuel Harlin LEE b: 02 Apr 1865 in Iowa, d: 24 Jun 1893 in Berthoud, Boulder, Colorado; Y

     + Dora ECK b: 1864 in Vincennes, Ind, m: 14 Jan 1891 in Berthoud, Boulder, Co, d: 30 Aug 1919 in Johnstown, Weld, Co.; Y

...................11 Arthur Levi LEE b: 1864 in Vincennes, Ind, d: 30 Aug 1919 in Johnstown, Weld, Co; Y

...................10 John George LEE b: 01 Feb 1868 in Iowa, d: 01 Aug 1935 ; Y

     + Nora WEAVER b: 26 Feb 1879 in Salino, Bell, Tx, m: 16 Dec 1897 in Windsor, Larimer, Co, d: 11 Apr 1949 in Boulder, Boulder, Co; Y

...................11 Owen LEE b: 02 May 1899 in Windsor, Weld, Co, d: 30 Oct 1907 in Windsor, Weld, Co; Y

...................10 Francis Marion LEE b: 19 Apr 1870 in Iowa, d: 18 Oct 1954 in San Ysidro, San Diego, Ca; Y

...................10 Nina Pearl LEE b: 13 Nov 1872 in New Market, Iowa, d: 26 Nov 1956 in Fort Collins, Larimer, Colorado; Y

     + Charles Clancy MCELRAVY b: Abt. 1868 in <New Market, Iowa>, m: 13 May 1895 in Cheyenne, Wy, d: 1947 ; Y

...................11 Millard MCELRAVY b: Abt. 1896 in Windsor, Co

...................11 Mildred M. MCELRAVY b: 23 Sep 1897 in Windsor, Weld, Co, d: 10 Apr 1982 in Downey, Ca; Y

...................11 Della MCELRAVY b: 20 Oct 1902 in Windsor, Weld, Co, d: 03 Dec 1968 in Craig, Co; Y

...................11 <No name>

     + Rockford LEWIS b: May 1866 in Wi, m: 1889 in Co

...................11 Pearl Nina LEWIS b: 01 Mar 1890 in Grants Pass, Or, d: 22 Mar 1966 in Arcadia, Ca; Y

...................10 James Westley LEE b: 11 Jan 1875 in Colorado, d: 24 Jul 1948 in San Ysidro, San Diego, Ca; Y

     + Stella WEST b: Abt. 1881 in CO, m: 04 Jan 1902

     + Susan Susie E. RAGAN b: Abt. 1878 in CO, m: 10 May 1899 in CO

...................11 Eva Murril LEE b: 10 Aug 1900 in CO

...................10 Rosa LEE b: 10 Mar 1878 in Fort Collins, Larimer, Colorado, d: 22 Jul 1911 in Yale, Payne, Colorado; Y

     + John Robert AUSTIN b: 04 Nov 1871 in Lovington, Moultrie, Il, m: 10 Apr 1895 in Greeley, Weld, Co, d: 30 Jul 1944 in Fort Collins, Larimer, Co; Y

...................11 Robert Lee AUSTIN b: 24 Mar 1896 in Greeley, Weld, Co

...................11 Natte Earl AUSTIN b: 26 Mar 1900 in Greeley, Weld, Co, d: 02 Oct 1969 in Fort Collins, Larimer, Co; Y

...................11 Edna AUSTIN b: 08 Feb 1902 in Greeley, Weld, Co

...................11 Rosella Patricia AUSTIN b: 08 Nov 1910 in Greeley, Weld, Co, d: 29 Mar 1983 ; Y

...................11 <No name>

...................9 Celia Lucinda LEE b: 22 Jul 1835 in Madison, Jefferson Co., Indiana, d: Aft. 1880 in 1880 Golden City, Barton Co., Missouri; Y

     + FOUNDARY m: Abt. 1866

...................10 Blanche FOUNDARY b: 1867 in Ky

.........................10 Ezekial FOUNDARY b: 1870 in Ky
.........................10 Maud FOUNDARY b: 1872 in Ky
.........................10 Selle FOUNDARY b: 1876 in Mo
.................9 Richard Mark LEE b: 25 Jan 1837 in Grove Twp., Davis Co., Iowa, d: 18 Apr 1906 in
                  Boulder, Colorado; Y
                  + Mary Jane DAUGHTRY b: 30 Aug 1841 in Bloomington, OH, m: 16 Mar 1864 in
                    Stiles, Ia, d: 22 Apr 1917 in Parkman, Wyo; Y
.........................10 Hattie LEE b: 14 Feb 1869 in Denver, Co, d: 18 Dec 1934 in Cortez, Montezuma,
                     Co; Y
                     + Elmer Joseph OWEN b: 23 Jul 1868 in Springfield, In, m: 24 Apr 1891 in Longmont,
                       Boulder, Co, d: 16 May 1917 in Parkman, Wy; Y
.........................11 Lottie OWEN b: 13 Mar 1893 in Ohlman, Wy, d: 05 Jun 1944 ; Y
.........................11 Ollie OWEN b: 31 Oct 1897 in Parkman, Wy, d: 29 Nov 1976 ; Y
.........................11 Ira OWEN b: 06 Nov 1899 in Parkman, Wy, d: 30 Apr 1919 ; Y
.................9 John Braxton LEE b: 11 Dec 1839 in Grove Twp., Davis Co., Ia., d: 24 Feb 1919 in
                  Pueblo, Pueblo Co., Co.; Y
                  + Margaret MILLER b: 09 Feb 1869 in Plum Creek, Arap. Co., Co., m: 09 Feb 1869 in
                    Plum Creek, Arap, Co., d: 17 Jun 1908 in Cortez, Montezuma, Co.; Y
.........................10 Emma LEE b: 16 Feb 1870 in Longmont, Colorado, d: 18 Jan 1949 in Cortez,
                     Cortez, Colorado; Y
                     + William H. ELLERMEYER b: 25 Aug 1866 in Quasqenton, Behnn, Iowa, m: 07 Nov
                       1889, d: 16 Jan 1945 in El Paso, El Paso, Tx; Y
.........................11 Minnie Margaret ELLERMEYER b: 23 Oct 1892 in Berthoud, Co
.........................11 Carrie Isabel ELLERMEYER b: 02 Jan 1894 in Berthoud, Larimer, Co.
.........................11 ELLERMEYER b: 1895 in Berthoud, Larimer, Co, d: 1895 in Berthoud, Larimer,
                     Co; Y
.........................11 Jessie May ELLERMEYER b: 12 Jan 1896 in Berthoud, Larimer, Co
.........................11 Anna Pearl ELLERMEYER b: 14 Oct 1897 in Berthoud, Larimer, Co
.........................11 William Augustus ELLERMEYER b: 20 Jan 1899 in Cortez, Montezuma, Co, d: 01
                     Feb 1899 in Cortez, Montezuma, Co; Y
.........................11 Emma Lee ELLERMEYER b: 30 Mar 1901 in Loveland, Larimer, Co
.........................11 Wilma Olga ELLERMEYER b: 07 Mar 1912 in Cortez, Montezuma, Co, d: 05 Oct
                     1955 in Mesa, Maricopa, Az; Y
.........................11 <No name>
.........................10 George R. LEE b: 29 May 1872 in Lyons, Boulder, Co, d: 17 May 1950 in Cortez,
                     Montezuma, Co; Y
                     + Maggie June WHITE b: Abt. 1874 in <Lyons, Boulder, Co>, m: 05 Dec 1895 in
                       Lyons, Boulder, Co
.........................11 Melvina Margaret LEE b: 03 Apr 1897 in Loveland, Weld, Co, d: 03 Aug 1974 in
                     Cortez, Montezuma, Co.; Y
.........................11 Elmer LEE b: Abt. 1899 in <Loveland, Weld, Co>
.........................11 Emma LEE b: 1900 in <Loveland, Weld, Co>
.........................10 Richard L. LEE b: 1879 in <Lyons, Boulder, Co>
                     + Grace RILEY b: Abt. 1880 in <Loveland, Weld, Co>, m: 03 Jan 1901 in Loveland,
                       Weld, Co
.........................11 Maude Fern LEE b: Feb 1902 in Loveland, Weld, Co, d: May 1905 in Loveland,
                     Weld, Co; Y
.........................11 Clifford LEE b: Abt. 1904 in Loveland, Weld, Co, d: Jan 1905 in Loveland, Weld,
                     Co; Y
.................9 Amanda Jane LEE b: 06 May 1841 in Grove Twp., Davis, Iowa, d: 28 Oct 1913 in
                  Longmont, Boulder Co., Co; Y
                  + William S. NOBLE b: 08 Jun 1823 in New York City, N.y. Co., Ny, m: 04 Dec 1859 in
                    Stylesville, Davis County, Ia, d: 22 Nov 1871 in Littleton, Arapaho, Co; Y
.........................10 William Guest NOBLE b: 05 Sep 1860 in Davis, Ia, d: 14 Apr 1918 in Denver,
                     Denver, Co; Y

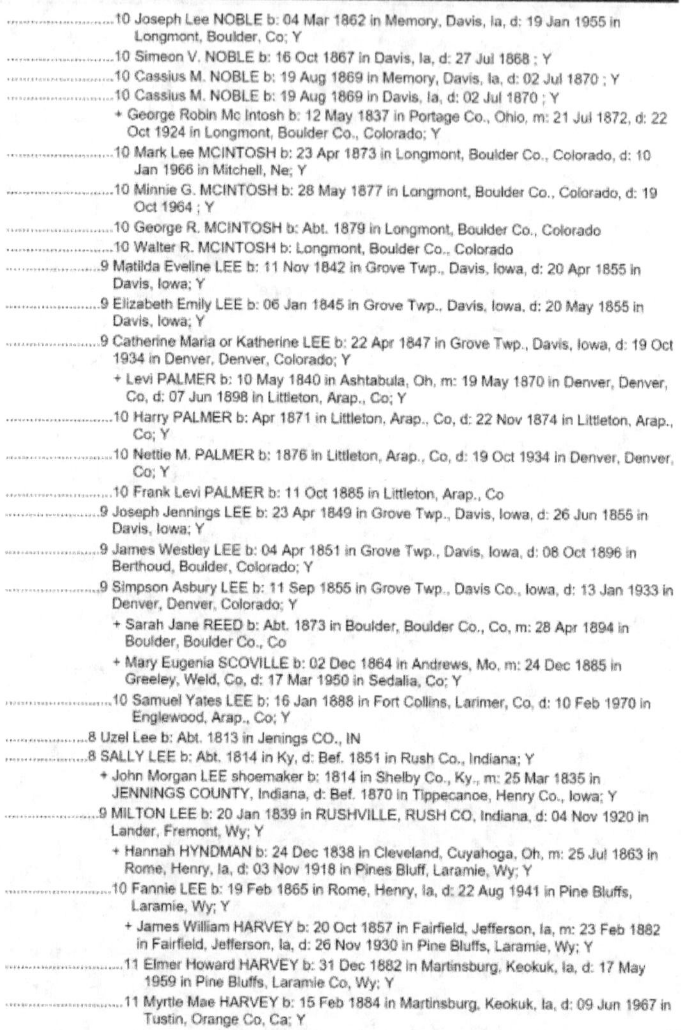

............10 Joseph Lee NOBLE b: 04 Mar 1862 in Memory, Davis, Ia, d: 19 Jan 1955 in Longmont, Boulder, Co; Y

............10 Simeon V. NOBLE b: 16 Oct 1867 in Davis, Ia, d: 27 Jul 1868 ; Y

............10 Cassius M. NOBLE b: 19 Aug 1869 in Memory, Davis, Ia, d: 02 Jul 1870 ; Y

............10 Cassius M. NOBLE b: 19 Aug 1869 in Davis, Ia, d: 02 Jul 1870 ; Y

+ George Robin Mc Intosh b: 12 May 1837 in Portage Co., Ohio, m: 21 Jul 1872, d: 22 Oct 1924 in Longmont, Boulder Co., Colorado; Y

............10 Mark Lee MCINTOSH b: 23 Apr 1873 in Longmont, Boulder Co., Colorado, d: 10 Jan 1966 in Mitchell, Ne; Y

............10 Minnie G. MCINTOSH b: 28 May 1877 in Longmont, Boulder Co., Colorado, d: 19 Oct 1964 ; Y

............10 George R. MCINTOSH b: Abt. 1879 in Longmont, Boulder Co., Colorado

............10 Walter R. MCINTOSH b: Longmont, Boulder Co., Colorado

............9 Matilda Eveline LEE b: 11 Nov 1842 in Grove Twp., Davis, Iowa, d: 20 Apr 1855 in Davis, Iowa; Y

............9 Elizabeth Emily LEE b: 06 Jan 1845 in Grove Twp., Davis, Iowa, d: 20 May 1855 in Davis, Iowa; Y

............9 Catherine Maria or Katherine LEE b: 22 Apr 1847 in Grove Twp., Davis, Iowa, d: 19 Oct 1934 in Denver, Denver, Colorado; Y

+ Levi PALMER b: 10 May 1840 in Ashtabula, Oh, m: 19 May 1870 in Denver, Denver, Co, d: 07 Jun 1898 in Littleton, Arap., Co; Y

............10 Harry PALMER b: Apr 1871 in Littleton, Arap., Co, d: 22 Nov 1874 in Littleton, Arap., Co; Y

............10 Nettie M. PALMER b: 1876 in Littleton, Arap., Co, d: 19 Oct 1934 in Denver, Denver, Co; Y

............10 Frank Levi PALMER b: 11 Oct 1885 in Littleton, Arap., Co

............9 Joseph Jennings LEE b: 23 Apr 1849 in Grove Twp., Davis, Iowa, d: 26 Jun 1855 in Davis, Iowa; Y

............9 James Westley LEE b: 04 Apr 1851 in Grove Twp., Davis, Iowa, d: 08 Oct 1896 in Berthoud, Boulder, Colorado; Y

............9 Simpson Asbury LEE b: 11 Sep 1855 in Grove Twp., Davis Co., Iowa, d: 13 Jan 1933 in Denver, Denver, Colorado; Y

+ Sarah Jane REED b: Abt. 1873 in Boulder, Boulder Co., Co, m: 28 Apr 1894 in Boulder, Boulder Co., Co

+ Mary Eugenia SCOVILLE b: 02 Dec 1864 in Andrews, Mo, m: 24 Dec 1885 in Greeley, Weld, Co, d: 17 Mar 1950 in Sedalia, Co; Y

............10 Samuel Yates LEE b: 16 Jan 1888 in Fort Collins, Larimer, Co, d: 10 Feb 1970 in Englewood, Arap., Co; Y

............8 Uzel Lee b: Abt. 1813 in Jenings CO., IN

............8 SALLY LEE b: Abt. 1814 in Ky, d: Bef. 1851 in Rush Co., Indiana; Y

+ John Morgan LEE shoemaker b: 1814 in Shelby Co., Ky., m: 25 Mar 1835 in JENNINGS COUNTY, Indiana, d: Bef. 1870 in Tippecanoe, Henry Co., Iowa; Y

............9 MILTON LEE b: 20 Jan 1839 in RUSHVILLE, RUSH CO, Indiana, d: 04 Nov 1920 in Lander, Fremont, Wy; Y

+ Hannah HYNDMAN b: 24 Dec 1838 in Cleveland, Cuyahoga, Oh, m: 25 Jul 1863 in Rome, Henry, Ia, d: 03 Nov 1918 in Pines Bluff, Laramie, Wy; Y

............10 Fannie LEE b: 19 Feb 1865 in Rome, Henry, Ia, d: 22 Aug 1941 in Pine Bluffs, Laramie, Wy; Y

+ James William HARVEY b: 20 Oct 1857 in Fairfield, Jefferson, Ia, m: 23 Feb 1882 in Fairfield, Jefferson, Ia, d: 26 Nov 1930 in Pine Bluffs, Laramie, Wy; Y

............11 Elmer Howard HARVEY b: 31 Dec 1882 in Martinsburg, Keokuk, Ia, d: 17 May 1959 in Pine Bluffs, Laramie Co, Wy; Y

............11 Myrtle Mae HARVEY b: 15 Feb 1884 in Martinsburg, Keokuk, Ia, d: 09 Jun 1967 in Tustin, Orange Co, Ca; Y

.................................11 James Edward HARVEY b: 19 Mar 1885 in Martinsburg, Keokuk, Ia, d: 26 Nov 1953 in Ontario, Malbeur Co, Or; Y
.................................11 Robert Earl HARVEY b: 03 Jan 1889 in Albia, Monroe Co., Ia, d: 24 Apr 1974 in Wheatland, Platte Co., Wy; Y
   + [unknown spouse]
.................................12 Kathleen HARVEY b: Abt. 1930
   + Mr Hopkins
.................................12 Hazel HARVEY
.................................11 Mary Leona Hazel HARVEY b: 15 Apr 1892 in Albia, Monroe, Ia, d: 05 Sep 1961 in Overton, Clark, Nv; Y
.................................11 Lelia Ruth HARVEY b: 29 Sep 1894 in Albia, Monroe, Ia, d: 26 Jun 1973 in Seattle, Kitsap Co, Wa; Y
.................................11 Clara Eldora HARVEY b: 14 Jun 1896 in Albia, Monroe, Ia, d: 07 Nov 1898 in Albia, Monroe Co, Iowa; Y
.........................10 Rosa Mae LEE b: 12 Apr 1867 in Rome, Henry, Ia, d: 01 May 1868 ; Y
.........................10 Peter Smith LEE b: 28 Aug 1868 in Rome, Henry, Ia, d: 11 Jan 1941 in Brigham City, Box Elder, Ut; Y
   + Annie CLARK b: 07 Apr 1885 in Bicknell, Wayne, Ut, m: 28 Mar 1911 in Wilson, Teton, Wy, d: 09 Aug 1953 in Ogden, Weber, Ut; Y
.........................11 Clinton Smith LEE b: 04 Dec 1911 in Wilson, Teton, Wy, d: 24 Dec 1969 ; Y
.........................11 Theo Bell LEE b: 21 Oct 1913 in Albin, Laramie, Wy, d: 11 Nov 1918 ; Y
.........................11 Oral Clark LEE b: 25 Sep 1919 in Brigham City, Box Elder, Ut, d: 03 Mar 1992 in Ogden, Weber, Utah; Y
.........................11 living 2000
.........................11 livinf 2000
.........................10 Lena Rivers LEE b: 27 Jul 1871 in Rome, Henry, Ia, d: 14 May 1873 ; Y
.........................10 Mary Ellen Shay LEE b: 14 Nov 1875 in Rome, Henry, Ia, d: 05 May 1943 ; Y
   + John Henry JACKSON b: Abt. 1873, m: 05 Sep 1894
.....................9 Peter Smith LEE b: 1842 in Rush Co., Indiana
.................8 Peter Lee b: 19 Mar 1815 in Jenings CO., IN, d: 11 Jun 1894 in Carlton, Hamilton Co., Tx; Y
   + Salina TOBEY b: 17 Feb 1822 in Jenings CO., IN, m: 01 Apr 1841 in Vernon, Jennings, Indiana, d: 1846 in Camden Co., Mo.; Y
.....................9 Sarah Lee b: 1842 in Camden Co., Mo.
.....................9 Wheeler Lee b: 09 Oct 1846 in Camden Co., Mo.
   + Nancy (Barnett) Janes b: 1824 in of Benton or Camden Co., Mo., m: 19 Jan 1851 in Benton Co., Mo, d: 1865 in Camden Co., Mo.; Y
.....................9 Mary Janes "Mollie" Lee b: 29 Dec 1851 in Camden Co., Mo.
.....................9 Samule Urbane Lee b: 01 Dec 1853 in Camden Co., Mo.
.....................9 Thomas Jefferson "Jeff" Lee b: 12 Mar 1856 in Camden Co., Mo.
.....................9 Alexander Campbell Lee b: Abt. 1857 in Camden Co., Mo.
.....................9 Virginia Jennifer Lee b: 1860 in Camden Co., Mo.
.....................9 William Calvin Lee b: 1864 in Camden Co., Mo.
   + Mary Caroline "Polly" STIDHAM b: 28 Apr 1833 in Tn, m: Abt. 1866 in Vernon Co., Mo.
.....................9 Abigail "Abby" Lee b: 02 Oct 1867 in Hamilton Co., Tx
.....................9 Grant "Billy" Lee b: 1870 in Camden Co., Mo.
.....................9 Tony Lee b: 1873 in Hamilton Co., Tx
.....................9 Roas Belle Lee b: 03 Jul 1876 in Hamilton Co., Tx
.................8 Richard Lee b: Abt. 1819 in Jenings CO., IN
.................8 Selah Lee b: Abt. 1820 in Jenings CO., IN
.................8 Rebecca Lee b: 06 Oct 1821 in Jenings CO., IN
   + Daniel T. DAVIS b: Abt. 1820 in IA, m: 1853
.....................9 Mary Louise DAVIS b: 18 Oct 1856 in Salem, Henry, Iowa, d: 07 Sep 1942 in Long Beach, Los Angeles, California; Y

+ Napoleon Bonaparte SPURRIER b: 14 Jan 1860 in Henry Co., IA, m: 29 Mar 1881 in Lamoni, Decatur, Iowa

...............7 Joseph L. Lee b: Abt. 1793 in Overton Co., Tn, d: 1851 in Round Prairie Twp, Jefferson Co., Iowa; Y

     + Mary MAYBERRY OR MABERY b: 21 May 1797 in Near Mammoth Cave, Kentucky, m: 1818 in Jennings Co., IN, d: 13 Oct 1860 in Henry Co., IA; Y

...............8 William Lee b: 1819 in Delaware (later Decatur) Co IN of Henry Co., Iowa, d: Aft. 1870 in Tippecanoe, Henry Co., Iowa; Y

     + Mary Martha Bennet b: 1818 in Ohio, m: Abt. 1855 in Henry Co., Iowa, d: Aft. 1870 in Tippecanoe, Henry Co., Iowa; Y

...............9 M. Mary Lee b: 1856 in Scott, Henry Co., Iowa

...............9 F. Emma Lee b: 1859 in Scott, Henry Co., Iowa

...............8 Harrison Lee b: Abt. 1822 in Henry Co., Indiana, d: Tippecanoe, Henry Co., Iowa; Y

     + Marthena b: NC, m: Abt. 1843 in Indiana

...............9 Martin Lee b: 1844 in Indiana

...............9 Sarah Lee b: 1848 in Indiana

...............9 Winifred S. Lee b: 1853 in Tippecanoe, Henry Co., Iowa

...............9 Mary J. Lee b: 1856 in Tippecanoe, Henry Co., Iowa

...............9 William S. L. Lee b: 1863 in Tippecanoe, Henry Co., Iowa

...............9 Pleasant Lee b: Indiana

...............8 Abigail Lee b: 1826 in Henry Co., Indiana, d: Henry Co., Iowa; Y

...............8 Pleasant Lee b: 1828 in Henry Co., IN, d: 1865 in Henry Co., Iowa; Y

     + Mary Lee b: 1840 in Iowa, m: 1858 in Henry Co., Iowa

...............9 Jonathan Lee b: 1859 in Tippecanoe, Henry Co., Iowa

...............8 Joseph Lee b: Nov 1830 in Indiana, d: 1911 in Dixon County or Freemont Dodge County Nebraska; Y

     + Mary Polly Lee b: Mar 1841 in Vernon, Jenings Co., IN of Tippecanoe, Henry Co., Iowa, m: 1858 in Henry Co., IA, d: 1903 in Arkansas; Y

...............9 Nancy Alice Lee b: 02 Feb 1868 in Washington County, Iowa, d: 31 Jan 1957 in Loveland, Colorado USA 435 West 4th Street; Y

     + Asakiah Stypes Mills b: 12 Sep 1869 in Hardin County, Iowa, m: Abt. 1899, d: 06 Dec 1959 in Springdale Washington County, Arkansas; Y

...............10 Bessie Belle Mills b: 1899, d: 1984 ; Y

...............10 Sherman Mills b: 29 Jul 1900 in Henry County, Iowa, USA, d: 07 Jul 1977 in Loveland, Colorado USA 435 West 4th Street; Y

     + Mary Elizabeth Mitts b: 13 May 1909 in Harper County, Oklahoma, m: 27 May 1928 in New London, Henry County, Iowa USA

...............11 Living Mills

...............11 Living Mills

...............11 Living Mills

...............11 Living Mills

...............11 Living Mills

...............11 Living Mills

...............11 Mills d: 1946 ; Y

...............10 Daisy Mae Mills b: 1902, d: 1920 ; Y

...............10 Violet Mary Mills b: 1905, d: 1991 ; Y

...............10 Viola Mills b: 1905, d: 1997 ; Y

...............10 Iliff Sylvester Mills b: 1907, d: 1999 in Mt Pleasant, Iowa, USA; Y

...............9 Martin E. Lee b: Nov 1874 in Tippecanoe, Henry Co., IA

...............9 Anna B. Lee b: Jul 1877 in Tippecanoe, Henry Co., IA, d: Canada; Y

...............9 Edward Benton Lee b: 03 Dec 1881 in Tippecanoe, Henry Co., IA, d: 13 Jan 1952 in Provo Utah; Y

     + Hester Lydia Rowe b: 23 Aug 1878 in Willow Springs, Hutton Valley, Howell Co., MO, m: 01 Aug 1912 in Sioux City, Woodbury, IA., d: 15 Apr 1974 in South Elmonte, Los Angeles Co., CA 91733; Y

.................10 Ellis Edward Lee b: 05 May 1913 in Allen, NE, d: 17 Jul 1995 in South El Monte, Los
    Angeles Co., CA; Y
    + Wilma Jean Rahn b: Private
.................10 Saint Elmo Green Lee b: 31 Jan 1915 in Meadowbrook, Alberta, Canada, d: 06 Jan
    2000 in Rogers, Benton Co., Arkansas; Y
    + Madeline b: Private
    + Arlene June Ainge b: 29 Nov 1918 in Utah, m: 20 Mar 1937 in Payson, Utah, d: 04
    Jul 1984 in Whittier California; Y
.................11 Living Lee
    + Living
.................12 Living Lee
.................12 Living Lee
.................12 Living Lee
.................12 Living Lee
.................9 Jonathan W. Lee b: Tippecanoe, Henry Co., IA
.................9 Perry D. Lee b: Tippecanoe, Henry Co., IA
.................9 Melissa Rebecca Lee b: Tippecanoe, Henry Co., IA
.................8 Mary Lee b: 1833 in Henry Co., Indiana
.................8 Eastman Lee b: Abt. 1840 in Indiana, d: Aug 1860 in Tippecanoe, Henry Co., Iowa; Y
.................8 Mark T. Lee b: IN of Henry Co., Indiana
    + Esther F b: 1846 in IN, m: Abt. 1862
.................9 Nathaniel M. Lee b: 1863 in Tippecanoe, Henry Co., Iowa
.................9 Franklin A Lee b: 1865 in Tippecanoe, Henry Co., Iowa
.................9 Jenette M. Lee b: 1867 in Tippecanoe, Henry Co., Iowa
.................8 John Lee b: KY of Delawar (later Decatur) Co IN Co., IN a
    + Charity b: Abt. 1824 in Kentucky, m: Abt. 1845
.................9 Margaret Lee b: 1846 in Ky
.................9 Mahlon T. Lee b: Mar 1848 in Ky
.................9 John Thomas Lee b: Oct 1854 in Scott, Henry Co., Iowa, d: Clay County, Nebraska; Y
    + Lavina E. Kepper b: Aug 1851 in Ohio, m: Abt. 1880 in Iowa, d: Clay County,
    Nebraska; Y
.................10 Hollis M Lee b: Dec 1886
.................10 Charity L. Lee b: 16 Nov 1888 in Nebraska, d: Oct 1985 in Nebraska; Y
    + David B. Massie b: 23 May 1881 in Nebraska, m: Nebraska, d: Dec 1969 in
    Nebraska; Y
.................11 Leila E. Massie b: Abt. 1917
.................11 Jerry M. Massie b: Abt. 1926
.................10 Lurlie B. Lee b: 24 May 1891 in Nebraska, d: Nov 1981 in Nebraska; Y
.................10 Olive Leona Lee b: 24 Mar 1895 in Fairfied Nebraska (possibly March 25), d:
    Gillette, Wyoming; Y
    + Glen Van Osborn b: 08 May 1892 in Rooks County, Kansas, d: Feb 1978 in Gillette,
    Wyoming; Y
.................11 Harvey Clinton Osborn b: 18 Jan 1921 in Gillette, Wyoming, USA, d: 09 Jun 1994
    in Wright, Wyoming, USA; Y
    + Dorothy Sanders
.................12 Living Osborn
    + Living Leino
.................13 Daniel Zebediah Deleon b: 05 Jun 1978, d: 13 Dec 2000 ; Y
.................13 Living Deleon
    + Living Wilcox
    + Living DeLeon
.................12 Living Osborn
    + Living
.................13 Living Osborn
.................13 Living Osborn

.........................12 Living Osborn
                   + Living Neff
.........................13 Living Neff
.........................13 Living Neff
.........................12 Living Osborn
                   + Living Taussig
.........................13 Living Taussig
.........................13 Living Taussig
.........................13 Living Taussig
.........................13 Living Taussig
.........................13 Living Taussig
.........................13 Living Taussig
                   + Linda Angle
                   + Ada Mintz
.........................11 Dorcas Ruth Osborn b: 15 Sep 1922
                   + Herb King
.........................12 Living King
                   + Living
.........................12 Living King
                   + Living Couch
                   + Living Radecki
.........................13 Living Radecki
                     + Living Wamsley
.........................14 Living Wamsley
                   + Living McGillvary
.........................14 Living McGillvary
.........................14 Living McGillvary
.........................13 Living Radecki
.........................12 Living King
                   + Living Grueb
.........................13 Living Grueb
                   + Living
.........................14 Living Grueb
.........................13 Living Grueb
                   + Living Timmers
.........................14 Living Timmers
.........................14 Living Timmers
.........................12 Living King
                   + Living
.........................13 Living King
.........................13 Living King
                   + Living
.........................14 Living King
.........................14 Living King
.........................13 Living King
.........................11 Living Osborn
                   + Ruth Marylin Unruh b: 22 Jul 1938 in Dundee, Illinois, USA, d: 04 Jul 2002 in
                     Buffalo, Johnson County, Wyoming, USA (burried in Dundee, IL); Y
.........................12 Living Osborn
                   + Living Gerritsen Ir.
.........................12 Living Osborn
.........................10 Ellis Lee
.........................10 Guy Lee
.........................9 Mary Lee b: 1857 in Scott, Henry Co., Iowa

...................9 Peter Lee b: Jan 1860 in Scott, Henry Co., Iowa
...................9 Elizabeth E. Ella Lee b: 1863 in Scott, Henry Co., Iowa
...................9 Henry Lee b: 1867 in Scott, Henry Co., Iowa
...............7 John Lee Jr. b: Abt. 1799 in Hardin Co., Ky of Clinton Co., Ky
          + Margaret FLEMING b: Abt. 1801 in Clinton Co., Ky, m: Abt. 1821
...............8 John Vance Lee b: Abt. 1823 in IN of Clinton CO., KY
          + [unknown spouse]
...............9 Uzel Lee b: Abt. 1850 in Henry, Iowa
...............8 Mary Jane LEE b: 21 Oct 1837 in Clinton, Ky, d: 07 Apr 1915 in Pickett, Tn; Y
          + Benjamin Jackson MEANS b: 01 Apr 1837 in Clinton, Ky, m: 27 Oct 1859 in Clinton, Ky,
          d: 26 Aug 1921 in Pickett, Tn; Y
...............9 Alvis S. MEANS b: 19 Aug 1861 in Clinton, Ky, d: 06 Feb 1921 in Clinton, Ky; Y
...............9 Susan Olive MEANS b: 1863 in <, Clinton, Ky>
...............9 Lazrus W. MEANS b: 01 Nov 1865 in Clinton, Ky, d: 08 Oct 1955 in Star Point, Pickett,
          Tn; Y
...............9 Joseph Richard MEANS b: 08 Sep 1868 in <, Clinton, Ky>, d: 17 Apr 1952 ; Y
...............9 Rosetta MEANS b: 08 Dec 1870 in Clinton, Ky, d: 15 Jun 1957 in Livingston, Overton,
          Tn; Y
...............9 Ahijah Adrine MEANS b: 08 Sep 1873 in Clinton, Ky, d: 12 Mar 1928 in Pickett, Tn; Y
...............9 George Azel MEANS b: Dec 1879 in <, Clinton, Ky>
...............7 William Isaac Lee b: 1800 in Cumberland Co., KY, d: 1834 in Cumberland Co., KY; Y
          + Oney P. Bow b: 06 Oct 1804 in Louisa Co., Virginia, m: 08 Jul 1828 in Cumberland Co.,
          KY, d: 24 May 1848 in Burkesville, Cumberland Co., Kentucky; Y
...............8 John Nathaniel Lee b: 28 Jun 1829 in Burksfield, Cumberland Co., d: 05 Nov 1852 in
          Burksfield, Cumberland Co. Ky; Y
          + Margaret E. BRAKE b: 1835 in Cumberland Co., KY, m: Abt. 1850 in Cumberland Co.,
          KY
...............9 William Malone Lee b: 19 Jun 1851 in Cumberland Co., KY, d: 12 Sep 1935 in
          Burkesville, Cumberland, Kentucky; Y
          + Elzania Narcis Marcum b: 1856 in Cumberland Co. Kentucky, m: 1875 in Cumberland
          Co., KY, d: Y
...............10 Nannie Lee b: 1876 in Cumberland Co., KY, d: Y
          + Thomas Marcum m: Abt. 1896, d: Y
...............11 Dora Marcum d: Y
          + Eddie Strover d: Y
...............11 Maggie Marcum d: Y
          + Riley Stockton d: Y
...............10 Betty M. Lee b: 1879 in Cumberland Co., KY, d: Y
          + Ben Groce d: Y
...............11 Roy Groce d: Y
          + Richard Arlin Gamer d: Y
...............11 Odell Groce d: Y
...............11 Stanley Pleas Groce d: Y
          + Alma Hoots d: Y
...............11 Paul Groce d: Y
          + Lovie Abston d: Y
...............10 James Alvis Garfield Lee b: 1880 in Cumberland Co., KY, d: Burkesville,
          Cumberland, Kentucky; Y
          + Emily Alta L. Wright b: 23 Nov 1882, m: 07 Feb 1904, d: Burkesville, Cumberland,
          Kentucky; Y
...............11 Willie Edith Lee b: 20 Feb 1905, d: Y
          + Stanley Ewing d: Y
...............11 Homer Harrison Lee b: 02 Sep 1906, d: Y
          + Ruby Duff d: Y
...............11 Charles Hubert Lee b: 20 Feb 1916, d: 13 Feb 1918 ; Y

...................10 Lou Critten Lee b: 1883 in Cumberland Co., KY, d: Y
          + Charlie Wright m: 1902 in Cumberland Co., KY, d: Y
...................10 Myrtle Lee b: Abt. 1885 in Cumberland Co., KY, d: Y
          + J.A. Thomas d: Y
...................10 Fannie Lee b: Abt. 1888 in Cumberland Co., KY, d: Y
          + Tim Hicks d: Y
...................10 John A. Lee b: 1891 in Cumberland Co., KY area, d: Y
          + Iva Anderson d: Y
...................11 Hollis Garland Lee b: 20 Nov 1917 in Cumberland County, Kentucky, d: 06 Jul
          1989 in Cumberland County, Kentucky; Y
...................10 Lillie Lee b: 1893 in Cumberland Co., KY, d: Y
          + Glenn Hicks d: Y
...............9 Oney C. Lee b: 10 Sep 1852 in Cumberland Co., KY
...............8 Isaac T. Lee b: 29 May 1831 in Burksfield, Cumberland Co. Ky, d: 11 Nov 1859 in
          Burksfield, Cumberland Co. Ky; Y
............7 Uzel Lee b: 14 Oct 1806 in Hardin Co., Ky of Jennings Co., IN, d: 15 Oct 1842 in Henry
          Co., Iowa; Y
          + Elizabeth Settles Betsy Lee b: 1809 in Jennings Co., IN, m: 07 Feb 1827 in Jennings Co.,
          IN
...............8 John Graves Lee b: Abt. 1828 in Jenings CO., IN
...............8 Louisa Lee b: Abt. 1832 in Jenings CO., IN
...............8 Mary Lee b: Abt. 1835 in Jenings CO., IN
...............8 Celia Lee b: Abt. 1838 in Jenings CO., IN
...............8 Elizabeth Settles Lee II b: Abt. 1841 in Jenings CO., IN or Henry Co., IA
............7 Charles LEE b: Hardin Co., Ky of Overton Co., TN abt 1817, d: Aft. 1865 in Christian
          County, Illinois; Y
          + Jane FLEMING b: North Carolina, m: Abt. 1815 in NC, d: 1873 in Christian County,
          Illinois; Y
...............8 Mary (Polly) LEE b: 1818 in Illinois, d: Texas; Y
...............8 John LEE b: 1820 in Tennessee, d: Texas; Y
          + Lucinda ASKINS b: Abt. 1823 in Ohio, m: 10 Feb 1842 in Fayette Co., Illinois
...............9 Ann LEE b: 1845 in Fayette Co., Illinois
...............9 David LEE b: 1847 in Fayette Co., Illinois
...............9 William LEE b: 1850 in Fayette Co., Illinois
...............8 Sarah (Sally) LEE b: 1823 in Tennessee, d: Texas; Y
...............8 William LEE b: 1827 in Tennessee
...............8 Rosanna LEE b: 1830 in Tennessee
...............8 Richard LEE b: 26 Nov 1835 in Fayette County, Illinois, d: 02 Nov 1912 in Chiristian Co.,
          ILL; Y
          + Lucinda CROCKER b: Christian Co., IL, m: Abt. 1857 in Christian Co., IL, d: Abt. 1866
          in Christian Co., IL; Y
...............9 Charles H. LEE b: 1857 in Christian Co., IL
          + Jane Fleming b: Christian Co., IL
...................10 Millie Rozetta Lee b: 07 May 1875 in Christian Co., IL, d: 31 Aug 1947 ; Y
          + James Weeden Hallford b: 30 Jul 1867 in Fayette City, Fayette Co., IL, m: 31 Mar
          1896 in Christian Co., IL, d: 30 Jun 1959 in Springfield, Sangamon Co., IL; Y
...................11 Glenn Edwin Hallford b: 09 May 1900 in Edinburg, Christian Co., IL, d: 24 Dec
          1987 in Springfield, Sangamon Co., IL; Y
...................11 Ernest Lee Hallford b: 07 Jul 1901 in Edinburg, Christian Co., IL, d: 12 Oct 1968 in
          Springfield, Sangamon Co., IL; Y
...................11 Russell Herman Hallford b: 12 Aug 1906 in Edinburg, Christian Co., IL, d: May
          1995 ; Y
...................11 Virgil James Hallford b: 13 Jun 1908 in Edinburg, Christian Co., IL, d: Nov 1981 in
          Springfield, Sangamon Co., IL; Y

.....................11 Ralph Paul Hallford b: 31 May 1913 in Edinburg, Christian Co., IL, d: 28 Jun 1988
          in Springfield, Sangamon Co., IL; Y
.....................11 Neva Irene Hallford
.....................11 Matella May Hallford
...........9 Ausley LEE b: 1862 in Christian Co., IL
...........9 Elizabeth LEE b: Nov 1879 in Christian Co., IL
...........9 Jesse LEE b: Christian Co., IL
          + Sarah Ann Holland b: 16 Jul 1847 in Youngstown, OHIO, m: 19 May 1867 in Chiristian
          Co., ILL, d: 29 Aug 1932 in Chiristian Co., ILL; Y
...........9 Lemuel LEE b: 1868 in Christian Co., IL
...........9 Willis LEE b: 1869 in Christian Co., IL
...........9 Emner LEE b: 1871 in Christian Co., IL
...........9 Millia LEE b: 1873 in Christian Co., IL
...........9 Wesley LEE b: 1876 in Christian Co., IL
...........9 Laura LEE b: 1878 in Christian Co., IL
...........9 Franklin LEE b: Jun 1880 in Christian Co., IL
...........9 Bessie Leola LEE b: 17 Jan 1890 in Fayette Co., ILL, d: 19 Mar 1972 in Christian Co.,
          ILL; Y
             + Herman Baker b: 15 Oct 1891 in Washington CO., IN, m: 17 Dec 1918 in Chiristian
             Co., ILL, d: 18 Feb 1965 in Chiristian Co., ILL; Y
.........8 Willis LEE b: 07 May 1837 in Illinois, d: 10 Jun 1913 ; Y
          + Laura A b: 1844 in Ohio, m: Abt. 1865 in Christian Co., IL
...........9 John E. LEE b: 1866 in Christian Co., IL
...........9 E. .J. LEE b: 1875 in Christian Co., IL
...........9 David H. LEE b: 1879 in Christian Co., IL
...........9 M. A. LEE b: 1879 in Illinois Twp, Rush Co., Kansas
.........8 Armsby LEE b: 1839 in Fayette County, Illinois, d: Abt. 26 Jul 1871 in Christian Co., IL; Y
          + Effa MATHEWS b: Abt. 1843 in Christian Co., IL, m: 01 Jun 1871 in Christian Co., IL
.........8 William LEE b: 1845 in Christian Co., IL
.........8 David C. LEE b: 1847 in Christian Co., IL
.........8 Lana Y. LEE b: 1849 in Christian Co., IL
......6 Thomas Lee b: Abt. 1774 in of, Hardin, Co, Ky
......6 Elizabeth Lee b: Abt. 1777 in of, Hardin, Co, Ky
......6 Rebekah Lee b: Abt. 1783 in of, Hardin, Co, Ky
          + Nathan BARTLETT b: Abt. 1780 in of, Hardin, Co, Ky, m: 10 Oct 1803 in Hardin, Co, Ky
.......7 John BARTLETT b: Abt. 1814 in Hardin Co., KY
.......7 Solomon BARTLETT b: Abt. 1815 in Hardin Co., KY
.......7 Jesse BARTLETT b: Abt. 1817 in Hardin Co., KY
......6 Nancy Lee b: 01 Apr 1784 in Hardy Co., (W) Va. To Hardin Co., Ky 1790, d: 21 Oct 1865 in
          Parkersburg, Montgomery, Co, Ind; Y
          + Uzal Usual LaFollatte LeFollet LaFollette b: 07 Jun 1772 in of, Hardin, Nelson, Ky, m: 28
          Jul 1798 in Nelson, Co, Ky, d: 14 Aug 1844 in Putnam CO., IN; Y
.......7 Joseph LaFollette b: 24 Apr 1801 in Hardin County, Kentucky, d: 30 Apr 1877 in Putnam
          County, Indiana; Y
          + Hester Hinton b: 06 Jan 1799 in Hardin Co., KY, m: 22 Oct 1821 in Hardin Co., KY, d: 27
          Oct 1873 in Putnham CO., IN; Y
.........8 Letitia LaFollette b: 27 May 1823 in New Albany, Floyd, in, d: 07 Apr 1863 in Montgomery
          Cemetery, Denton's Valley; Y
          + John Howard b: 03 Jun 1822 in Putnam, IN, m: 25 Dec 1844 in Putnam CO., IN, d: 10
          Apr 1895 ; Y
...........9 Tilman Howard b: 03 Feb 1847 in Putnam CO., IN, d: 05 Apr 1863 in Putnam CO., IN;
          Y
...........9 George W. Howard b: 19 Aug 1848 in Montgomery Co., Ind, d: 14 Jun 1881 ; Y
          + Mary M. Wren b: 31 Jan 1852 in Putnam Co., Indiana, m: 12 Dec 1872
.............10 Franklin Howard b: 23 Jan 1874 in Montgomery Co., Ind, d: 13 Aug 1875 ; Y

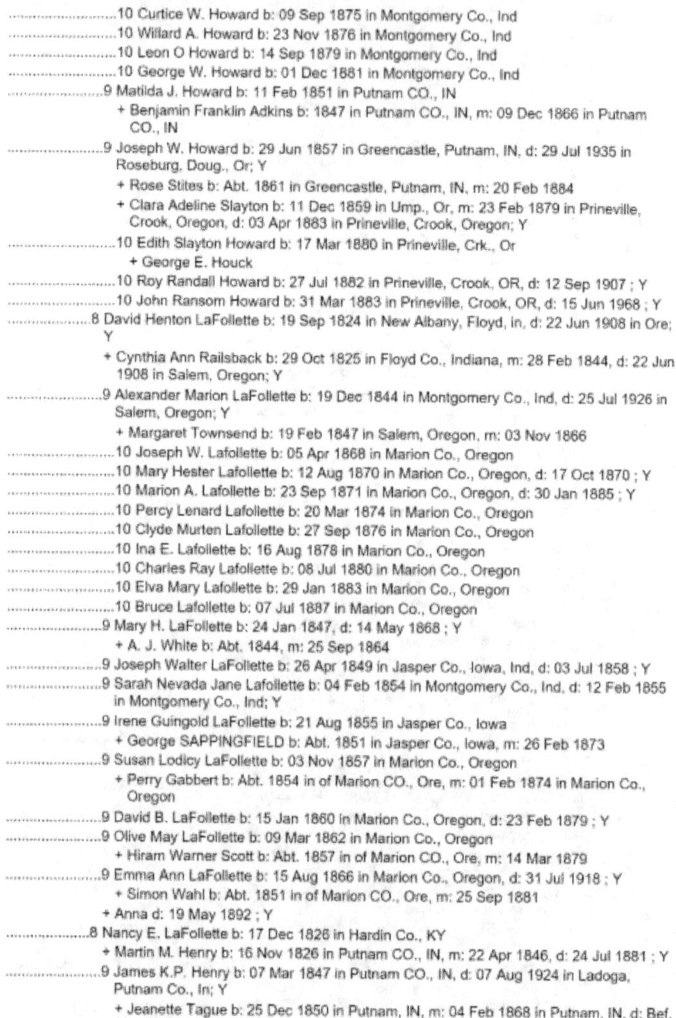

```
.....................10 Curtice W. Howard b: 09 Sep 1875 in Montgomery Co., Ind
.....................10 Willard A. Howard b: 23 Nov 1876 in Montgomery Co., Ind
.....................10 Leon O Howard b: 14 Sep 1879 in Montgomery Co., Ind
.....................10 George W. Howard b: 01 Dec 1881 in Montgomery Co., Ind
...................9 Matilda J. Howard b: 11 Feb 1851 in Putnam CO., IN
                    + Benjamin Franklin Adkins b: 1847 in Putnam CO., IN, m: 09 Dec 1866 in Putnam
                      CO., IN
...................9 Joseph W. Howard b: 29 Jun 1857 in Greencastle, Putnam, IN, d: 29 Jul 1935 in
                    Roseburg, Doug., Or; Y
                    + Rose Stites b: Abt. 1861 in Greencastle, Putnam, IN, m: 20 Feb 1884
                    + Clara Adeline Slayton b: 11 Dec 1859 in Ump., Or, m: 23 Feb 1879 in Prineville,
                      Crook, Oregon, d: 03 Apr 1883 in Prineville, Crook, Oregon; Y
...................10 Edith Slayton Howard b: 17 Mar 1880 in Prineville, Crk., Or
                    + George E. Houck
...................10 Roy Randall Howard b: 27 Jul 1882 in Prineville, Crook, OR, d: 12 Sep 1907 ; Y
...................10 John Ransom Howard b: 31 Mar 1883 in Prineville, Crook, OR, d: 15 Jun 1968 ; Y
.................8 David Henton LaFollette b: 19 Sep 1824 in New Albany, Floyd, in, d: 22 Jun 1908 in Ore;
                  Y
                    + Cynthia Ann Railsback b: 29 Oct 1825 in Floyd Co., Indiana, m: 28 Feb 1844, d: 22 Jun
                      1908 in Salem, Oregon; Y
...................9 Alexander Marion LaFollette b: 19 Dec 1844 in Montgomery Co., Ind, d: 25 Jul 1926 in
                    Salem, Oregon; Y
                    + Margaret Townsend b: 19 Feb 1847 in Salem, Oregon, m: 03 Nov 1866
...................10 Joseph W. Lafollette b: 05 Apr 1868 in Marion Co., Oregon
...................10 Mary Hester Lafollette b: 12 Aug 1870 in Marion Co., Oregon, d: 17 Oct 1870 ; Y
...................10 Marion A. Lafollette b: 23 Sep 1871 in Marion Co., Oregon, d: 30 Jan 1885 ; Y
...................10 Percy Lenard Lafollette b: 20 Mar 1874 in Marion Co., Oregon
...................10 Clyde Murten Lafollette b: 27 Sep 1876 in Marion Co., Oregon
...................10 Ina E. Lafollette b: 16 Aug 1878 in Marion Co., Oregon
...................10 Charles Ray Lafollette b: 08 Jul 1880 in Marion Co., Oregon
...................10 Elva Mary Lafollette b: 29 Jan 1883 in Marion Co., Oregon
...................10 Bruce Lafollette b: 07 Jul 1887 in Marion Co., Oregon
...................9 Mary H. LaFollette b: 24 Jan 1847, d: 14 May 1868 ; Y
                    + A. J. White b: Abt. 1844, m: 25 Sep 1864
...................9 Joseph Walter LaFollette b: 26 Apr 1849 in Jasper Co., Iowa, Ind, d: 03 Jul 1858 ; Y
...................9 Sarah Nevada Jane Lafollette b: 04 Feb 1854 in Montgomery Co., Ind, d: 12 Feb 1855
                    in Montgomery Co., Ind; Y
...................9 Irene Guingold LaFollette b: 21 Aug 1855 in Jasper Co., Iowa
                    + George SAPPINGFIELD b: Abt. 1851 in Jasper Co., Iowa, m: 26 Feb 1873
...................9 Susan Lodicy LaFollette b: 03 Nov 1857 in Marion Co., Oregon
                    + Perry Gabbert b: Abt. 1854 in of Marion CO., Ore, m: 01 Feb 1874 in Marion Co.,
                      Oregon
...................9 David B. LaFollette b: 15 Jan 1860 in Marion Co., Oregon, d: 23 Feb 1879 ; Y
...................9 Olive May LaFollette b: 09 Mar 1862 in Marion Co., Oregon
                    + Hiram Warner Scott b: Abt. 1857 in of Marion CO., Ore, m: 14 Mar 1879
...................9 Emma Ann LaFollette b: 15 Aug 1866 in Marion Co., Oregon, d: 31 Jul 1918 ; Y
                    + Simon Wahl b: Abt. 1851 in of Marion CO., Ore, m: 25 Sep 1881
                    + Anna d: 19 May 1892 ; Y
.................8 Nancy E. LaFollette b: 17 Dec 1826 in Hardin Co., KY
                    + Martin M. Henry b: 16 Nov 1826 in Putnam CO., IN, m: 22 Apr 1846, d: 24 Jul 1881 ; Y
...................9 James K.P. Henry b: 07 Mar 1847 in Putnam CO., IN, d: 07 Aug 1924 in Ladoga,
                    Putnam Co., In; Y
                    + Jeanette Tague b: 25 Dec 1850 in Putnam, IN, m: 04 Feb 1868 in Putnam, IN, d: Bef.
                      1935 in Ladoga, Montgomery, In.; Y
```

..............10 Minnie Henry b: 21 Dec 1868 in Ladoga, Putnam Co., In, d: 06 Jan 1892 in Ladoga, Putnam Co., In; Y

..............10 A. Edna Henry b: 22 Dec 1868 in Ladoga, Indiana, d: Jan 1893 ; Y

..............10 Mary Louise Henry b: 08 Nov 1870 in Ladoga, Indiana

..............10 Mollie Jane Henry b: 08 Nov 1870 in Boone Co., In

..............10 Charles Henry b: 05 May 1873 in Boone Co., In, d: 28 Nov 1936 in Hammond, Lake, In; Y

..............10 Myrtle Henry b: 18 Nov 1876 in Boone Co., In

..............10 Floyd Henry b: 09 Feb 1881 in Boone Co., In

..............10 Otto Henry b: 07 Mar 1883 in Boone Co., In

..............9 Lewis C. Henry b: 04 Jun 1848

..............9 Louisa C. Henry b: 18 Mar 1853

..............9 Andrew L. Henry b: 20 Oct 1856

..............9 Mary C. Henry b: 07 Jan 1860

..............9 John M. Henry b: 26 Jan 1864

..............9 M. Alice Henry b: 02 Mar 1866

..............9 Martin M. Henry b: 12 Aug 1867

..............8 John H. LaFollette b: 05 Jun 1828 in Putnam CO., IN, d: 15 Nov 1905 in Blakesburg, Wapello Co., Iowa; Y

        + Angeline Easley b: 09 Jul 1837 in Montgomery County, Indiana, m: 08 May 1851, d: 27 Oct 1905 in Blakesburg, Wapello Co., Iowa; Y

..............9 Joseph LaFollette b: 29 Apr 1852 in Putnam CO., IN

        + Mary B. Morgan b: Abt. 1855 in Blakesburg, Wapello, Iowa, m: 08 Apr 1883

..............10 Edgar Grover Lafollette b: 12 Jun 1884 in Glenn Ellen, Ca, d: Jul 1963 in Ore; Y

..............9 Parry LaFollette b: 08 Apr 1853 in Blakesburg, Wapello Co., Iowa, d: 03 Feb 1893 in Afton, Union, Iowa; Y

        + Henry T Jones b: 03 Feb 1847 in Crawfordsville, Montgomery, Indiana, m: 24 Feb 1874 in Iowa, d: 23 Jan 1935 in Entiat, Chelan, Wa; Y

..............10 Thomas Erwin Jones b: 24 Nov 1874 in Blakesburg, Wapello, Iowa, d: 11 Apr 1958 in Entiat, Chelan, Wa; Y

..............10 Joshua Henton Jones b: 18 Apr 1878 in Blakesburg, Wapello, Iowa, d: 10 Feb 1975 in Seattle, King, WA; Y

..............10 Mildred Magdalene Jones b: 12 Jan 1880 in Blakesburg, Wapello, Iowa, d: 30 Jun 1964 in Newburg, Oregon; Y

..............10 Winnifred Rachel Jones b: 31 Dec 1881 in Afton, Union, Iowa, d: 02 Feb 1923 in Entiat, Chelan, Wa; Y

..............10 Joseph Henry Jones b: 29 Feb 1884 in Afton, Union, Iowa, d: 18 Mar 1884 in Afton, Union, Iowa; Y

..............10 Jesse Truman Jones b: 29 Feb 1884 in Afton, Union, Iowa, d: 18 Mar 1884 in Seattle, King, WA; Y

..............10 William Early Jones b: 16 Nov 1885 in Afton, Union, Iowa, d: Jul 1967 in Briggsdale, Franklin, Ohio; Y

..............10 Albert Anderson Jones b: 04 Nov 1888 in Afton, Union, Iowa, d: 15 Apr 1980 in Entiat, Chelan, Wa; Y

..............10 Merrill Wilson Jones b: 16 Jun 1890 in Afton, Union, Iowa, d: 02 Dec 1974 in Wenatchee, Chelan, WA; Y

..............10 Frances Elizabeth Jones b: 02 Jan 1892 in Afton, Union, Iowa, d: Jul 1967 in Seabeck, Kitsap, Wa; Y

..............9 Nancy LaFollette b: 19 Jun 1854 in Blakesburg, Wapello Co., Iowa, d: 25 Dec 1854 ; Y

..............9 Hester LaFollette b: 24 Jan 1856 in Blakesburg, Wapello Co., Iowa

..............9 Daniel LaFollette b: 22 Dec 1857 in Wapello Co. Iowa, d: 13 Jun 1913 in Automwa, Iowa; Y

        + Margaret J. Butt b: 18 Jan 1846 in Wapello Co. Iowa, m: 29 Feb 1880, d: 17 Sep 1910 ; Y

..............10 Nora Lafollette b: 06 Oct 1886 in Iowa, d: 26 Sep 1887 ; Y

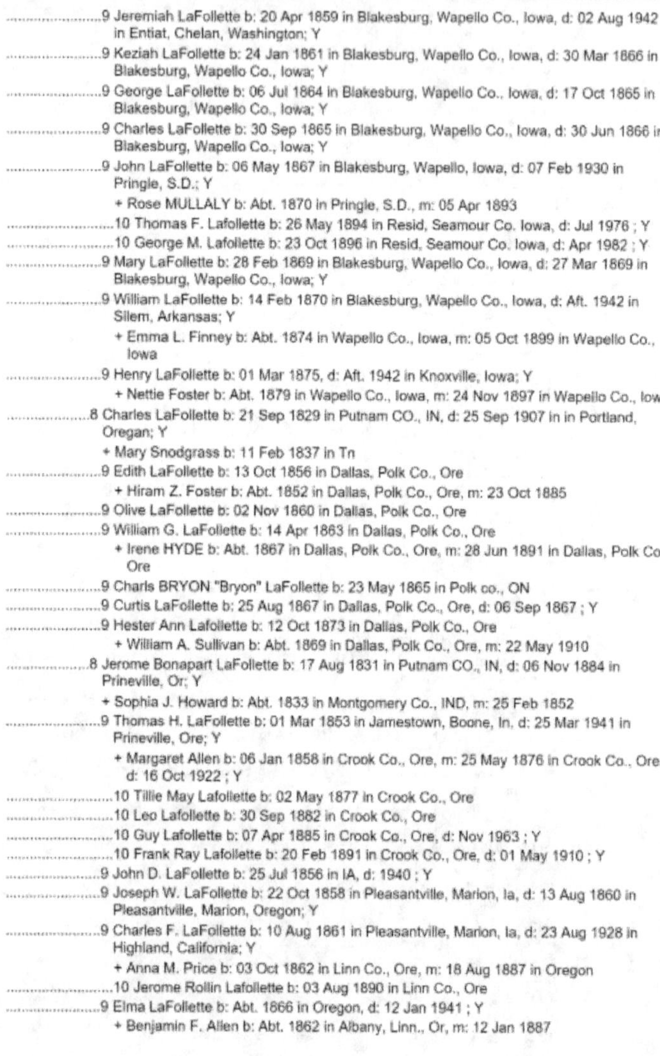

............9 Jeremiah LaFollette b: 20 Apr 1859 in Blakesburg, Wapello Co., Iowa, d: 02 Aug 1942 in Entiat, Chelan, Washington; Y

............9 Keziah LaFollette b: 24 Jan 1861 in Blakesburg, Wapello Co., Iowa, d: 30 Mar 1866 in Blakesburg, Wapello Co., Iowa; Y

............9 George LaFollette b: 06 Jul 1864 in Blakesburg, Wapello Co., Iowa, d: 17 Oct 1865 in Blakesburg, Wapello Co., Iowa; Y

............9 Charles LaFollette b: 30 Sep 1865 in Blakesburg, Wapello Co., Iowa, d: 30 Jun 1866 in Blakesburg, Wapello Co., Iowa; Y

............9 John LaFollette b: 06 May 1867 in Blakesburg, Wapello, Iowa, d: 07 Feb 1930 in Pringle, S.D.; Y

+ Rose MULLALY b: Abt. 1870 in Pringle, S.D., m: 05 Apr 1893

............10 Thomas F. Lafollette b: 26 May 1894 in Resid, Seamour Co. Iowa, d: Jul 1976 ; Y

............10 George M. Lafollette b: 23 Oct 1896 in Resid, Seamour Co. Iowa, d: Apr 1982 ; Y

............9 Mary LaFollette b: 28 Feb 1869 in Blakesburg, Wapello Co., Iowa, d: 27 Mar 1869 in Blakesburg, Wapello Co., Iowa; Y

............9 William LaFollette b: 14 Feb 1870 in Blakesburg, Wapello Co., Iowa, d: Aft. 1942 in Silem, Arkansas; Y

+ Emma L. Finney b: Abt. 1874 in Wapello Co., Iowa, m: 05 Oct 1899 in Wapello Co., Iowa

............9 Henry LaFollette b: 01 Mar 1875, d: Aft. 1942 in Knoxville, Iowa; Y

+ Nettie Foster b: Abt. 1879 in Wapello Co., Iowa, m: 24 Nov 1897 in Wapello Co., Iowa

............8 Charles LaFollette b: 21 Sep 1829 in Putnam CO., IN, d: 25 Sep 1907 in in Portland, Oregan; Y

+ Mary Snodgrass b: 11 Feb 1837 in Tn

............9 Edith LaFollette b: 13 Oct 1856 in Dallas, Polk Co., Ore

+ Hiram Z. Foster b: Abt. 1852 in Dallas, Polk Co., Ore, m: 23 Oct 1885

............9 Olive LaFollette b: 02 Nov 1860 in Dallas, Polk Co., Ore

............9 William G. LaFollette b: 14 Apr 1863 in Dallas, Polk Co., Ore

+ Irene HYDE b: Abt. 1867 in Dallas, Polk Co., Ore, m: 28 Jun 1891 in Dallas, Polk Co., Ore

............9 Charls BRYON "Bryon" LaFollette b: 23 May 1865 in Polk co., ON

............9 Curtis LaFollette b: 25 Aug 1867 in Dallas, Polk Co., Ore, d: 06 Sep 1867 ; Y

............9 Hester Ann Lafollette b: 12 Oct 1873 in Dallas, Polk Co., Ore

+ William A. Sullivan b: Abt. 1869 in Dallas, Polk Co., Ore, m: 22 May 1910

............8 Jerome Bonapart LaFollette b: 17 Aug 1831 in Putnam CO., IN, d: 06 Nov 1884 in Prineville, Or; Y

+ Sophia J. Howard b: Abt. 1833 in Montgomery Co., IND, m: 25 Feb 1852

............9 Thomas H. LaFollette b: 01 Mar 1853 in Jamestown, Boone, In. d: 25 Mar 1941 in Prineville, Ore; Y

+ Margaret Allen b: 06 Jan 1858 in Crook Co., Ore, m: 25 May 1876 in Crook Co., Ore, d: 16 Oct 1922 ; Y

............10 Tillie May Lafollette b: 02 May 1877 in Crook Co., Ore

............10 Leo Lafollette b: 30 Sep 1882 in Crook Co., Ore

............10 Guy Lafollette b: 07 Apr 1885 in Crook Co., Ore, d: Nov 1963 ; Y

............10 Frank Ray Lafollette b: 20 Feb 1891 in Crook Co., Ore, d: 01 May 1910 ; Y

............9 John D. LaFollette b: 25 Jul 1856 in IA, d: 1940 ; Y

............9 Joseph W. LaFollette b: 22 Oct 1858 in Pleasantville, Marion, Ia, d: 13 Aug 1860 in Pleasantville, Marion, Oregon; Y

............9 Charles F. LaFollette b: 10 Aug 1861 in Pleasantville, Marion, Ia, d: 23 Aug 1928 in Highland, California; Y

+ Anna M. Price b: 03 Oct 1862 in Linn Co., Ore, m: 18 Aug 1887 in Oregon

............10 Jerome Rollin Lafollette b: 03 Aug 1890 in Linn Co., Ore

............9 Elma LaFollette b: Abt. 1866 in Oregon, d: 12 Jan 1941 ; Y

+ Benjamin F. Allen b: Abt. 1862 in Albany, Linn., Or, m: 12 Jan 1887

.................9 Edgar Alen Poe LaFollette b: 01 May 1869 in Albany, Linn, Oregon, d: 13 Mar 1956 in
Hillsboro, Or; Y
+ Annie Elizabeth Gulliford b: 22 Mar 1872 in Prineville, Or, m: 31 May 1891 in
Prineville, Crook, Oregon, d: 03 Jun 1935 in Hubbard, Or; Y
...............10 Fay Lafollette b: 07 Aug 1892 in Halsey, Linn., Or, d: 09 May 1965 ; Y
...............10 Dewey Lafollette b: 01 May 1898 in Prineville, Or, d: 10 Feb 1978 in Stvincent
Hospital, Hillsboro, Or; Y
...............10 Frieda Lorene Lafollette b: 17 Jun 1905 in Prineville, Oregon, Crook, Or, d: 10 Aug
1917 ; Y
.................9 James L. LaFollette b: 24 Feb 1874 in Prineville, Crook, OR, d: 26 Mar 1890 in
Prineville, Crook, OR; Y
...............8 Jeremiah LaFollette b: 21 Apr 1833 in Putnam CO., IN, d: 10 Jul 1907 in Buchanan Co.
Mo; Y
+ Sarah E. Parrish b: Abt. 1842 in Adams Co., Iowa, m: 23 Oct 1862 in Adams County,
Iowa
.................9 Hester Ann. LaFollette b: 22 Nov 1863 in Knoxville, Iowa
.................9 Olive Gertrude LaFollette b: 19 Aug 1866 in Knoxville, Iowa
.................9 Sarah L. LaFollette b: 24 Dec 1869 in Knoxville, Iowa, d: 30 Dec 1871 in Knoxville,
Iowa; Y
.................9 Minnie Lenora LaFollette b: 04 Dec 1871 in Knoxville, Iowa
.................9 Charles Henry LaFollette b: 18 Apr 1874 in Knoxville, Iowa
.................9 Jessie Summer LaFollette b: 02 Nov 1876 in Knoxville, Iowa
.................9 Dora Maud LaFollette b: 16 Apr 1880 in Knoxville, Iowa
.................9 Grover Cleveland LaFollette b: 23 Nov 1883 in Knoxville, Iowa
.................9 Edward Elsworth LaFollette b: 25 Mar 1886 in Knoxville, Iowa
+ Sarah E. BURNETT b: Abt. 1835 in Montgomery Co., IND, m: 24 May 1857 in
Montgomery Co., IND, d: Bef. 1861 in Montgomery Co., IND; Y
...............8 Walter Briscoe LaFollette b: 30 Mar 1834 in Putnam CO., IN, d: 30 Sep 1882 ; Y
+ Julia A. Dodd b: Abt. 1834 in Montgomery Co., IND, m: 19 Oct 1854 in Putnam County,
Indiana, d: 16 Jul 1922 in Carthage, Mo; Y
.................9 Joseph LaFollette b: 05 Oct 1855 in Putnam CO., IN, d: 01 Jul 1910 ; Y
+ Anna HILL b: Abt. 1858 in Dade Co., MO, m: 13 Dec 1891
...............10 Walter Briscoe LaFollette b: 23 Jan 1901 in Putnam CO., IN, d: Feb 1976 in Kansas;
Y
+ Jennie TERMIN b: Abt. 1860 in Putnam CO., IN, m: 06 Sep 1895 in Putnam CO., IN
.................9 Woodson Frank LaFollette b: 13 May 1857 in Marion Co., Iowa, d: 08 Aug 1938 ; Y
+ Sarah Elizabeth WHITE b: 26 Jan 1859 in Bates Co., MO, m: 24 Nov 1875, d: 28 Apr
1899 ; Y
...............10 Albert Anderson LaFollette b: 07 Aug 1877 in Butler Co., Mo.
...............10 Charles Griffeth LaFollette b: 14 Oct 1879 in Butler Co., Mo.
...............10 John Dodd LaFollette b: 27 Nov 1881 in Butler Co., Mo.
+ Nora Mabel VANDERPOOL b: Abt. 1865 in Marion Co., Iowa, m: 25 Nov 1920 in
Marion Co., Iowa
+ Ruby Edna Irwin b: Abt. 1861 in Marion Co., Iowa, m: 10 Mar 1901
.................9 Charles LaFollette b: 26 Jul 1859 in Putnam CO., IN, d: 15 Mar 1922 in Bates Co., MO;
Y
+ Jennie May KEGARREIS b: 27 Feb 1874 in Bates Co., Mo., m: 01 Dec 1897, d: 12
Feb 1942 in Butler, Bates Co., Mo.; Y
...............10 Minnie Davis LAFOLLETTE b: 27 Feb 1899 in Bates Co., Mo.
...............10 Sarah Lee LAFOLLETTE b: 15 Nov 1900 in Bates Co., Mo., d: 25 Jun 1903 ; Y
...............10 Dixie Ann LAFOLLETTE b: 29 Oct 1901 in Bates Co., Mo., d: 16 Jul 1903 ; Y
...............10 Lawrence Ray LAFOLLETTE b: 20 Feb 1905 in Bates Co., Mo., d: May 1971 in Mo.;
Y
...............10 James Everett LAFOLLETTE b: 29 May 1915 in Bates Co., Mo., d: Dec 1982 in Mo.;
Y

....................9 Amanda A. LaFollette b: 23 Mar 1861 in Putnam CO., IN, d: 08 Apr 1864 in Putnam CO., IN; Y
....................9 Daniel V. LaFollette b: 26 Dec 1862 in Montgomery Co., IND
    + Minnie E. CALLAHAN b: Abt. 1867 in Montgomery Co., IND, m: 29 Feb 1888 in Jay County, Indiana
....................9 James A. LaFollette b: 24 Nov 1865 in Boone Co., IND, d: 20 Oct 1866 ; Y
....................9 William Alonzo LaFollette b: 20 Jun 1867 in Putnam CO., IN
    + Emma "Luna" E. DAVIS b: Abt. 1870 in Putnam CO., IN, m: 24 Apr 1889 in Lewis County, Missouri
....................9 Olive May. LaFollette b: 03 May 1869 in Putnam CO., IN
    + John T. GREEN b: Abt. 1865 in Putnam CO., IN, m: 23 Nov 1887
....................9 Walter Tazewell LaFollette b: 19 Jun 1872 in Cass Co., MO
    + Nannie WILLIAMS b: Abt. 1876 in Cass Co., MO, m: 27 Oct 1906 in Cass Co., MO
    + Lucy M. HEDRICK b: 13 Aug 1872 in Cass Co., Mo., m: 07 Dec 1893, d: 09 Mar 1906 ; Y
....................10 Ruth LA FOLLETTE b: 23 Apr 1899 in Butler Co., Mo., d: 02 Oct 1911 ; Y
....................9 Sarah Hester LaFollette b: 16 Sep 1874 in Cass Co., MO
    + Walter August DECKER b: Abt. 1870 in Cass Co., MO, m: 19 Feb 1896 in Cass Co., MO
....................9 Christa A. LaFollette b: 27 Apr 1877 in Bates Co., MO
    + Edwin Lincoln CLARK b: Abt. 1873 in Bates Co., MO, m: 14 Jun 1911
....................8 Christiana LaFollette b: 07 Oct 1836 in Putnam CO., IN, d: 1890 in Putnam CO., IN; Y
    + Thomas Hamilton b: 29 Sep 1827 in Putnam, Floyd Co., IN, m: 10 Oct 1852, d: 05 Jan 1892 ; Y
....................8 Alexander H. LaFollette b: 27 Aug 1838 in Putnam CO., IN, d: Putnam CO., IN; Y
....................8 Isaac LaFollette b: 28 Feb 1840 in Putnam CO., IN, d: 1840 in Putnam CO., IN; Y
....................8 baby girl LaFollette b: 30 Apr 1843 in Putnam CO., IN, d: 1843 in Putnam CO., IN; Y
....................8 Mary C. LaFollette b: 17 Sep 1844 in Putnam CO., IN
    + Samuel N. Harshbarger b: Abt. 1841 in Montgomery Co., IND, m: 10 Dec 1862 in Putnham CO., IN
....................9 Hester A. Harshbarger b: 29 May 1865 in Montgomery Co., IND
    + David B HOSTELLER m: 17 Oct 1888
....................9 David H. Harshbarger b: 08 Jul 1867 in Montgomery Co., IND
    + Flora E. Turner m: 15 Dec 1887
....................9 Charles O. Harshbarger b: 12 Oct 1870 in Montgomery Co., IND
    + Stella M BOLING m: 01 Sep 1892
....................7 Robert G. LaFollette b: 16 Aug 1804 in Hardin County, Kentucky, d: 03 Nov 1876 in Montgomery Co., IND; Y
    + Mary Swank b: 01 Oct 1807 in Kentucky, m: 01 Jun 1826 in Hardin County, Kentucky, d: 08 Aug 1881 in Jefferson district, Boone Co., Indiana; Y
....................8 Mary Jane LaFollette b: 16 Mar 1827 in Montgomery Co., IND, d: 25 Mar 1844 in Montgomery Co., IND; Y
....................8 Elizabeth Betsy A. LaFollette b: 03 Nov 1828 in Montgomery Co., IND, d: 1881 in Montgomery Co., IND; Y
    + George W. Frame b: Abt. 1826 in Montgomery Co., IND, m: 18 Apr 1849 in Montgomery Co., IND
....................9 Mary E. Frame b: 23 Feb 1850
    + James Harvey Srader b: Abt. 1848 in Montgomery Co., IND, m: 18 Jan 1869
....................10 Dory Srader
....................10 Omer Srader
....................10 Eva Srader
....................10 James Srader
....................9 William R. Frame b: 10 Oct 1852 in Montgomery Co., IND
    + Mary Doyle b: Abt. 1854 in Montgomery Co., IND, m: 1871
....................10 Minnie Frame b: Abt. 1876 in Montgomery Co., IND

....................10 Charles W. Frame b: Abt. 1878 in Montgomery Co., IND
          + Emma L. YOUNG
          + Howard CLOSE
..............8 Nancy Angeline LaFollette b: 02 Nov 1830 in Montgomery Co., IND, d: 04 Feb 1847 in Montgomery Co., IND; Y
..............8 Jacob Swank. LaFollette b: 17 Feb 1832 in Montgomery Co., IND, d: 12 Feb 1917 in Jefferson district, Boone Co., Indiana; Y
          + Sarah Elizabeth Young b: Abt. 1834 in Montgomery Co., IND, m: 19 Sep 1856 in Putnam CO., IN, d: Jefferson district, Boone Co., Indiana; Y
..............9 Sarah J. LaFollette b: 17 Jul 1858 in Jefferson district, Boone Co., Indiana
..............9 Mary F. LaFollette b: 03 Sep 1861 in Jefferson district, Boone Co., Indiana
..............9 William R. LaFollette b: 24 Nov 1863 in Jefferson district, Boone Co., Indiana
..............9 Charles C. LaFollette b: 19 Sep 1867 in Jefferson district, Boone Co., Indiana
..............8 Milton LaFollette b: 06 Jul 1834 in Montgomery Co., IND, d: Jefferson district, Boone Co., Indiana; Y
          + Elizabeth J. Grider b: Abt. 1838 in Montgomery Co., IND, m: 26 Aug 1858 in Putnam CO., IN
..............9 Eliza LaFollette b: Abt. 1859 in Jefferson district, Boone Co., Indiana
..............9 Martha LaFollette b: Abt. 1864 in Jefferson district, Boone Co., Indiana
..............9 George LaFollette b: Abt. 1869 in Jefferson district, Boone Co., Indiana
..............9 Caroline A. LaFollette b: Abt. 1871 in Jefferson district, Boone Co., Indiana
..............9 William H. LaFollette b: Abt. 1873 in Jefferson district, Boone Co., Indiana
..............9 Emma L. LaFollette b: Abt. 1875 in Jefferson district, Boone Co., Indiana
..............9 Mary E. LaFollette b: Abt. 1877 in Jefferson district, Boone Co., Indiana
..............8 Sarah E. LaFollette b: 21 Oct 1836
          + Joshua H. Bruce b: Abt. 1834 in Montgomery Co., IND, m: 18 Nov 1855 in Montgomery Co., IND, d: 26 Apr 1891 in Sterns Co, MN; Y
..............9 Mary P. Bruce b: 22 Nov 1856
..............9 Sarah M. Bruce b: 28 Aug 1859
..............9 Angeline Bruce b: 10 Nov 1861, d: 12 Sep 1862 ; Y
..............9 Eliza E. Bruce b: 16 Jun 1863
..............9 Charles R. Bruce b: 13 Nov 1865
..............9 William Bruce b: 03 Dec 1867
..............9 Joshua Bruce b: 22 Jan 1870, d: 06 Oct 1888 ; Y
..............9 James M. Bruce b: 18 Jan 1873
..............9 Mable O. Bruce b: 29 Jun 1879
..............8 Melvina LaFollette b: 19 Jan 1839
..............8 James U. LaFollette b: 24 Jul 1841
          + America Gott b: Abt. 1845, m: 10 May 1865 in Montgomery Co., IND
..............9 Stella A. LaFollette b: Abt. 1869
..............9 William R. LaFollette b: Abt. 1871
..............9 Lulu M. LaFollette b: Abt. 1875
..............9 Bertie C. LaFollette b: Abt. 1879
..............8 Lucinda LaFollette b: 30 Jan 1844 in Montgomery Co., IND, d: 25 Jul 1844 in Montgomery Co., IND; Y
..............7 Isaac LaFollette b: 22 Sep 1806 in Hardin County, Kentucky, d: 08 Dec 1873 in Putnam CO., IN; Y
          + Nancy H. Hinton Duvall b: 24 Oct 1801 in Hardin Co., KY, m: 15 Jul 1830 in Hardin County, Kentucky, d: 11 Sep 1864 in Putnam CO., IN; Y
..............8 Brisco LaFollette b: 17 Apr 1831 in Putnam CO., IN, d: Abt. 1835 in Small child; Y
..............8 Mary J. LaFollette b: 09 Feb 1833 in New Albany, Floyd Co., IN, d: Abt. 1853 ; Y
          + Samuel "Newton" Young b: Abt. 1831 in New Albany, Floyd Co., IN, m: 01 Feb 1849 in New Albany, Floyd Co., IN
..............9 Lucretia Young b: 11 Aug 1850 in Parkersburg, Putnam Co., In, d: 22 Sep 1929 in Jamestown, Boone, In; Y

+ Charles THOMAS Coshow b: 01 Jan 1844 in near Racoon, Putnham CO., IN, m: 18 Nov 1868 in Miss., d: 27 Sep 1924 in Indianapolis, Marion Co., IN; Y

.............10 Bertha Coshow b: 23 Nov 1869, d: 10 Sep 1951 ; Y

+ Ord COOK m: 23 Mar 1892

.............10 Francis Eli Coshow b: 23 Jul 1871, d: 06 Apr 1960 ; Y

+ Sophronia E. "Froncia" WILLIAMS b: 11 Dec 1872, m: 02 Nov 1890

.............10 Thomas A. Coshow b: 12 Mar 1873, d: 02 Feb 1952 ; Y

+ Hessie YOUNG m: 16 Aug 1897

.............10 Newton Coshow b: 12 Mar 1875, d: 07 Jan 1977 in child; Y

.............10 Kate V. Coshow b: 10 Sep 1877

+ Henry Hancock b: Abt. 185 AD, m: 28 Mar 1894

.............10 Lilia Coshow b: 12 Oct 1880

.............10 Grover Fletcher Coshow b: 02 Sep 1888 in Jamestown, Boone Co., IN, d: 07 Nov 1980 in Holladay, Salt Lake, UT; Y

+ Alice Vilate Brinton b: 03 Feb 1898 in South Cottonwood, Salt Lake Co., UT, m: 17 Mar 1926

.............11 Berylene Coshow

.............11 Grover Fletcher Coshow

.............11 Mary Coshow

.............11 Audrey Coshow

.............9 Francis M. Young b: 10 Apr 1852

.............8 Nancy E. LaFollette b: 02 Mar 1835 in Putnam CO., IN

+ Thomas S. Wright b: Abt. 1831 in Putnam CO., IN, m: 12 Mar 1852 in Putnam County, Indiana

.............9 Mary L. Wright b: 10 Jun 1853

.............9 Isaac L. Wright b: 25 Apr 1856

.............9 Alice Wright b: 01 Jun 1858

.............9 Alexander M. Wright b: 24 Nov 1860

.............9 Nancy E. Wright b: 21 Apr 1863

.............9 George Wright b: 09 Dec 1866

.............9 Clara Wright b: 21 Feb 1869

.............9 Thomas H. Wright b: 25 Apr 1871

.............9 Erastus Wright b: 27 May 1874

.............9 Susan Wright b: 18 Jun 1876

.............9 Daisy Wright b: 30 Apr 1879

.............8 John Henry LaFollette b: 05 Feb 1837 in Floyd Co., IN

+ Julia HARRISON m: Sep 1859

+ Henrietta Henry m: 1863

+ Ella Stewart m: 1872 in Champaign Co., IL

.............8 Alexander M. LaFollette b: 16 Jan 1839 in Floyd Co., IN

.............8 Hester A. LaFollette b: 10 Mar 1841 in Floyd Co., IN

+ Benjamin FLETCHER b: Abt. 1839 in Montgomery Co., IND, m: 18 Mar 1862 in Montgomery Co., IND

.............8 Sarah Lucetta "Settie" LAFOLLETTE b: 07 Feb 1844 in Floyd Co., IN, d: 29 Sep 1881 in Putnam Co., Ind; Y

+ Samuel HYMER b: 21 Feb 1841 in Putnam Co., Ind, m: 08 Nov 1864 in Putnam CO., IN, d: 19 Sep 1881 ; Y

.............9 Lillie Lee HYMER b: 11 Sep 1867 in Putnam Co., Ind

.............9 James Isaac HYMER b: 16 Oct 1869 in Putnam Co., Ind

.............9 Jesse Otis HYMER b: 03 Nov 1871 in Putnam Co., Ind

.............9 Warren Franklin HYMER b: 19 Dec 1879 in Putnam Co., Ind

+ Mary C. HINTON b: 30 Jul 1815 in Hardin Co., KY

.............7 John LaFollette b: 12 Mar 1808 in Hardin Co., KY, d: 29 Aug 1882 in Putnam CO., IN; Y

+ Elizabeth Bruce b: 13 Nov 1807 in Knox Co., Indiana, m: 27 Sep 1827 in Putnam CO., IN, d: 08 Sep 1883 in Putnam CO., IN; Y

................8 Sarah P. LaFollette b: 19 Sep 1828 in Hardin Co., KY
      + David P MEYERS b: Abt. 1828 in Putnam CO., IN, m: 08 Apr 1849 in Putnam CO., IN
................8 William B. LaFollette b: 25 Oct 1829 in Putnam CO., IN, d: 03 Oct 1904 in Franklin Co.
    Kans; Y
      + Mary A. Kyle b: Abt. 1833 in Montgomery Co., IND, m: 26 Dec 1851 in Montgomery
      Co., IND
................9 George E. LaFollette b: 12 Nov 1852
................9 John W. LaFollette b: 03 Apr 1854
................9 Martha E. LaFollette b: 18 Dec 1855 in Montgomery Co., IND
      + John M BYRD b: Abt. 1863 in Montgomery Co., IND, m: 26 Feb 1874 in Montgomery
      Co., IND
................9 Sarah E. LaFollette b: 22 Oct 1857 in Montgomery Co., IND
      + Joseph S. HOWARD b: Abt. 1855 in Montgomery Co., IND, m: 23 Sep 1875
................9 James F. LaFollette b: 18 Dec 1859 in Montgomery Co., IND
      + Tedency A. SMITH b: Abt. 1850 in Montgomery Co., IND, m: 11 Sep 1883
................9 Myrtle E. LaFollette b: 19 Mar 1862
................9 Charles A. LaFollette b: 18 Jul 1864
................9 Lettie LaFollette b: 08 Nov 1866
................9 Anna G. LaFollette b: 17 Mar 1869 in Montgomery Co., IND
................9 Robert E.L. LaFollette b: 05 Jun 1871 in Montgomery Co., IND
................9 Erastus LaFollette b: 15 Jun 1873 in Montgomery Co., IND
................8 Nancy A. LaFollette b: 21 Mar 1831 in Putnam CO., IN, d: 1888 in Roachdale, Indiana; Y
      + Elijah Grantham b: 1820 in Putnam CO., IN, m: 27 Nov 1851 in Putnam CO., IN
................9 John H. Grantham b: 28 Oct 1852
................9 Jesse B. Grantham b: 29 Nov 1853
................9 Mary E. Grantham b: 27 Nov 1855
................8 James U. LaFollette b: 14 Mar 1833 in Putnam CO., IN, d: 27 Oct 1833 in child; Y
................8 John H. LaFollette b: 27 Jul 1834 in Putnam CO., IN
      + Mary C Brookshire b: Abt. 1836 in Montgomery Co., IND, m: 05 Jan 1860 in
      Montgomery Co., IND
................8 Mary L. LaFollette b: 01 May 1836 in Putnam CO., IN
      + John T. Harris b: Putnam County, Indiana, m: 22 Sep 1872 in Putnam County, Indiana
................8 Elizabeth "Betty" Hall. LaFollette b: 11 Apr 1838 in Putnam CO., IN, d: 12 Sep 1838 in
    Putnam CO., IN; Y
................8 Anna ELIZABETH LaFollette b: 29 Sep 1840 in Putnam CO., IN
      + John F. Britton b: Abt. 1837 in Putnam CO., IN, m: 29 Sep 1868 in Putnam County,
      Indiana
      + Smalley
................8 Deliah J. "Eliza" LaFollette b: 1845 in Putnam CO., IN
      + William P. Young b: Abt. 1843 in Putnam CO., IN, m: 23 Sep 1865
................9 Elmer B. Young b: 30 May 1866 in Putnam CO., IN
................8 Charles H. LaFollette b: 1849 in Montgomery Co., IND, d: Bef. 1890 in Putnam CO., IN;
    Y
      + Margaret C. Wright b: Abt. 1851, m: 01 Oct 1871 in Putnam CO., IN
................9 Living LaFollette
............7 William LaFollette b: 28 Jun 1810 in Hardin, Co, Ky, d: 09 Feb 1881 in Clark Co, IA; Y
      + Letitia "Letty" Harrison b: 08 Jun 1812 in Harrison Co. Ind, m: 04 Oct 1831 in
      Montgomery County, Indiana, d: 06 Feb 1868 in Clarke Co., Iowa; Y
................8 John T. LaFollette b: Abt. 1837 in Putnham CO., IN
      + Miss C. Mossbarger
................8 Joshua LaFollette b: Abt. 1840 in Putnham CO., IN
      + Susannah
................8 William LaFollette b: Abt. 1845 in Putnham CO., IN
................8 James LaFollette b: Abt. 1847 in Putnham CO., IN

.................8 Nancy Kelly LaFollette b: 21 Sep 1849 in Boone Co, IN, d: 17 May 1909 in Osceola, Clarke Co., Iowa; Y

+ Christopher Columbus "Lum" Perdue b: 07 Oct 1841 in Cabell Co., VA, m: 29 Aug 1866 in Osceola, Clarke, Ia, d: 17 Feb 1914 in Dallas Co., Ia; Y

.................9 James William Perdue b: 18 May 1867 in IA, d: 1947 ; Y

.................9 Francis Marion Perdue b: 12 Apr 1869 in IA

.................9 Clarence Edward Perdue b: 05 Mar 1873 in IA

.................9 Hattie Vitella Perdue b: 25 Dec 1875 in IA

.................9 Giles Christopher Perdue b: 07 Sep 1878 in IA

.................9 Susan A. Perdue b: 01 Mar 1882 in IA

.................9 Ella Mae Perdue b: 1884 in Clarke Co., Ia, d: 23 Sep 1886 ; Y

.................9 Martha Josphine Perdue b: 25 Aug 1886, d: Aug 1976 ; Y

.................9 Mary E. Perdue b: 25 Aug 1886

.................9 Jessie Florence Perdue b: 12 Aug 1890

.................9 Daniel Deloss Perdue b: Sep 1893

.................7 Mary Harris LaFollette b: 10 Apr 1812 in Hardin Co., KY, d: Boone Co. IN; Y

+ Solomon Beck b: 1806, m: 12 Sep 1829 in Putnam CO., IN, d: Boone Co. IN; Y

.................8 Mary Elizabeth. Mollie Beck b: Abt. 1851 in Boone Co. IN

+ John Dudley Lawler b: 1849 in Indianapolis Marion Co Indianna, m: 30 Aug 1871 in Edgar Co., ILL, d: Edgar Co., ILL; Y

.................9 George M. H Lawler b: 1872 in Edgar Co., ILL

.................9 Mary Ella Lawler b: 23 Dec 1872 in Edgar Co., ILL

.................9 John Solomon Lawler b: 12 Apr 1876 in Edgar Co., ILL

.................9 Lyida Izaora Lawler b: 15 Mar 1878 in Edgar Co., ILL

.................9 Edna M. Lawler b: 1880 in Edgar Co., ILL

.................9 Lucy Oliver Lawler b: 1882 in Edgar Co., ILL

.................9 Nancy Rose Lawler b: 18 Apr 1885 in Near Hume, Edgar Co., Ill

.................9 Cecil Lawler b: 02 Sep 1888 in Shiloh, Edgar Co., Ill

.................9 Charles Dudley Lawler b: 06 Sep 1890 in Edgar Co., ILL

.................9 John W. Lawler b: 06 Sep 1890 in Edgar Co., ILL

.................9 Horace J. Lawler b: 29 Jul 1892 in Douglas Co Ill, d: Aug 1962 in Edgar Co., ILL; Y

+ Bessie E Mopps b: 09 Aug 1894 in Paris Edgar Co Illinois, m: Abt. 1916 in Paris Edgar Co Illinois

.................10 John Dudley Lawler b: 02 Jun 1917 in Paris Edgar Co Illinois

.................10 Horace Allen Lawler b: 01 Jun 1919 in Paris Edgar Co Illinois

.................9 Hazel Gertrude Lawler b: 19 Jun 1894 in Edgar Co., ILL

.................9 Zona B. Lawler b: 06 Aug 1896 in Edgar Co., ILL

.................8 George Beck b: Boone Co. IN

.................8 James L. Beck b: Boone Co. IN

.................8 Nancy Beck b: Boone Co. IN

.................8 John Beck b: Boone Co. IN

.................8 William Beck b: Boone Co. IN

.................8 Josiah Beck b: Boone Co. IN

.................7 Nancy LaFollette b: 29 Sep 1814 in Hardin Co., KY

+ James Glogow Edwards b: Abt. 1812 in Nelson CO., Ky, m: 03 Apr 1834 in Nelson CO., Ky, d: 09 Dec 1879 in Putnam CO., IN; Y

.................8 Mary Edwards b: 28 Aug 1835 in Putnam CO., IN

.................8 James U. Edwards b: 28 Apr 1837 in Putnam CO., IN

.................8 Howard M. Edwards b: 16 Jul 1839 in Putnam CO., IN

.................8 Melvina Edwards b: 21 Dec 1840 in Putnam CO., IN

.................8 John F. Edwards b: 09 Jun 1843 in Putnam CO., IN

.................8 Issac C. Edwards b: 07 Jun 1845 in Putnam CO., IN

.................8 Rachel E. Edwards b: 03 Sep 1847 in Putnam CO., IN

.................8 Nancy J. Edwards b: 08 Dec 1849 in Putnam CO., IN

..................8 Charles P. Edwards b: 04 Dec 1851 in Putnam CO., IN, d: 03 Apr 1854 ; Y
..................8 Robert F. Edwards b: 17 Jan 1853 in Putnam CO., IN
..................8 Joseph W. Edwards b: 13 May 1855 in Putnam CO., IN
..................7 Rebecca J. LaFollette b: 30 May 1817 in Hardin Co., KY, d: 18 Jan 1894 in near Racoon, Putnham CO., IN; Y
          + Thomas A. Coshow b: 1815 in Nelson CO., Ky, m: 09 Oct 1835 in Nelson CO., Ky, d: 25 Jun 1858 in near Racoon, Putnham CO., IN; Y
..................8 John H. Coshow b: 02 Aug 1837 in near Racoon, Putnham CO., IN, d: 31 Aug 1862 in Volunteer Union Army; Y
..................8 David Coshow b: 15 Feb 1839 in near Racoon, Putnham CO., IN
          + Mary F ADAMS b: Abt. 1840 in Montgomery Co., IND, m: 15 Nov 1861 in Montgomery Co., IND
..................9 Thomas Coshow b: 04 Jul 1862 in Montgomery Co., IND
          + Cyntha H BAKER b: Abt. 1865 in Montgomery Co., IND, m: 12 Oct 1885
..................9 Robert Coshow b: 31 Mar 1871 in Montgomery Co., IND
          + Ella STONE b: Abt. 1872 in Montgomery Co., IND, m: 1892 in Montgomery Co., IND
..................9 Anna Coshow b: 19 Jul 1873 in Montgomery Co., IND
          + James T Fugate b: Abt. 1869 in Montgomery Co., IND, m: 17 Jan 1889 in Montgomery Co., IND
..................8 Nancy Coshow b: 18 Sep 1840 in near Racoon, Putnham CO., IN, d: 01 Jan 1862 in near Racoon, Putnham CO., IN; Y
          + George RIGGLE b: Abt. 1839 in Ind, m: Abt. 1861 in Montgomery Co., IND, d: 1861 in near Racoon, Putnham CO., IN; Y
..................9 Lottie (Riggles) Coshow b: 07 Dec 1861 in near Parkersburg, Montgomery Co., IND, d: 1913 in near Parkersburg, Montgomery Co., IND; Y
          + Henry FALL b: 1861 in Ind, m: 07 Dec 1881 in Putnham CO., IN, d: 1927 in near Parkersburg, Montgomery Co., IND; Y
..................10 Buford L. FALL b: 04 Sep 1882 in Montgomery Co., IND, d: 30 Dec 1944 in Racooon, Indiana; Y
          + [unknown spouse]
..................11 Donald FALL
..................10 Benjamin L. FALL b: 28 Aug 1888 in Montgomery Co., IND
..................8 Jacob Coshow b: 19 Apr 1842 in near Racoon, Putnham CO., IN, d: 12 Aug 1861 ; Y
..................8 Charles THOMAS Coshow b: 01 Jan 1844 in near Racoon, Putnham CO., IN, d: 27 Sep 1924 in Indianapolis, Marion Co., IN; Y
          + Lucretia Young b: 11 Aug 1850 in Parkersburg, Putnam Co., In, m: 18 Nov 1868 in Miss., d: 22 Sep 1929 in Jamestown, Boone, In; Y
..................9 Bertha Coshow b: 23 Nov 1869, d: 10 Sep 1951 ; Y
          + Ord COOK m: 23 Mar 1892
..................9 Francis Eli Coshow b: 23 Jul 1871, d: 06 Apr 1960 ; Y
          + Sophronia E. "Froncia" WILLIAMS b: 11 Dec 1872, m: 02 Nov 1890
..................9 Thomas A. Coshow b: 12 Mar 1873, d: 02 Feb 1952 ; Y
          + Hessie YOUNG m: 16 Aug 1897
..................9 Newton Coshow b: 12 Mar 1875, d: 07 Jan 1977 in child; Y
..................9 Kate V. Coshow b: 10 Sep 1877
          + Henry Hancock b: Abt. 185 AD, m: 28 Mar 1894
..................9 Lilia Coshow b: 12 Oct 1680
..................9 Grover Fletcher Coshow b: 02 Sep 1888 in Jamestown, Boone Co., IN, d: 07 Nov 1980 in Holladay, Salt Lake, UT; Y
          + Alice Vilate Brinton b: 03 Feb 1898 in South Cottonwood, Salt Lake Co., UT, m: 17 Mar 1926
..................10 Berylene Coshow
..................10 Grover Fletcher Coshow
..................10 Mary Coshow
..................10 Audrey Coshow

...............8 Richard H. Coshow b: 01 Jan 1846 in near Racoon, Putnham CO., IN
...............8 Sarah E. Coshow b: 02 Jan 1848 in near Racoon, Putnham CO., IN
+ Charles Wilson m: 05 Mar 1874, d: no children; Y
...............8 Mary J Coshow b: 29 Dec 1849 in near Racoon, Putnham CO., IN
...............8 Eli Coshow b: 11 Mar 1852 in near Racoon, Putnham CO., IN
+ Lucy H. McMurtrey b: Abt. 1850, m: 05 Jan 1873
...............9 Luella Coshow b: 07 Oct 1873
...............9 Alberta Coshow b: 22 Mar 1875, d: 25 Oct 1875 in child; Y
...............9 Acy Coshow b: 21 Aug 1878
...............9 Wallace Coshow b: 08 Jul 1880
...............8 Martha E. Coshow b: 27 Feb 1854 in near Racoon, Putnham CO., IN
...............8 Rebecca C Coshow b: 03 Mar 1856 in near Racoon, Putnham CO., IN, d: 03 Jul 1861 in near Racoon, Putnham CO., IN; Y
...........7 James LaFollette b: 11 Feb 1819 in Hardin Co., KY, d: 15 Sep 1890 in near Parkersburg, Putnam Co., IND; Y
+ Catherine Easley b: 1827 in Indiana, m: 02 Sep 1847, d: 1909 in near Parkersburg, Putnam Co., IND; Y
...............8 Nancy J. LaFollette b: 28 Jun 1848, d: 1924 in near Parkersburg, Montgomery Co., IND; Y
+ Talbott Sutherlin b: 1845, m: 12 Jan 1868, d: 1912 in near Parkersburg, Montgomery Co., IND; Y
...............9 James S. Sutherlin b: 20 Oct 1868
...............9 Joseph A. Sutherlin b: 25 Sep 1869
...............9 Elonzo Sutherlin b: 07 Aug 1871
...............9 Mary Alice Sutherlin b: 13 Jan 1873
...............9 infant dau Sutherlin b: 1874, d: 1874 ; Y
...............9 Oliver F. Sutherlin b: 19 Dec 1875
...............9 Catherine Sutherlin b: 03 Sep 1877
...............9 George T. Sutherlin b: 31 Mar 1880
...............9 John T. Sutherlin b: 21 Feb 1884 in near Parkersburg, Montgomery Co., IND
...............9 Ethel Sutherlin b: 05 Feb 1888
...............8 Mary F. LaFollette b: 09 Mar 1850
+ William H. Hicks b: Abt. 1847 in Montgomery Co., IND, m: 07 Dec 1878
...............8 Elizabeth A. LaFollette b: 10 May 1851 in Montgomery Co., IND
+ Samuel F. Fischer b: Abt. 1849 in Montgomery Co., IND, m: 16 Nov 1873 in Montgomery Co., IND
...............9 Sallis C. Fischer b: 12 Oct 1874 in Montgomery Co., IND
...............9 Mary E. Fischer b: 06 Mar 1880 in Montgomery Co., IND
...............9 James S. Fischer b: 05 Jul 1881 in Montgomery Co., IND
...............9 Fannie B. Fischer b: 01 Aug 1883 in Montgomery Co., IND
...............9 William R. Fischer b: 13 Jun 1886 in Montgomery Co., IND
...............9 Mellie C. Fischer b: 16 Sep 1888 in Montgomery Co., IND
...............8 Sarah C. LaFollette b: 20 Sep 1853, d: 14 Feb 1860 ; Y
...............8 Daniel E. LaFollette b: 01 Oct 1855
...............8 Joseph F. LaFollette b: 05 Oct 1856 in Indiana
+ Sylvania M. Ruffner b: Abt. 1857 in Indiana, m: 12 Apr 1877
...............9 Lillie M. LaFollette b: Abt. 1877
...............9 William F. LaFollette b: Abt. 1879
...............8 Robert E. LaFollette b: 28 Oct 1859
+ Sarah J. Payton m: 24 Dec 1882
...............9 Anna B. LaFollette b: 15 Dec 1883
...............9 Hallie C. LaFollette b: 16 May 1888 in Montgomery Co., IND
+ Warren J. SPENCE R b: Abt. 1886 in Montgomery Co., IND, m: 22 Jun 1915 in Montgomery Co., IND
...............8 James Uzal. LaFollette b: 23 Jul 1862

+ Nannie Rogers m: 13 Jan 1886
.........................9 Ancil S. LaFollette b: Aft. 1866
.........................9 Nora B. LaFollette b: 18 Oct 1886
.........................9 James E. LaFollette b: 23 May 1888
.........................9 Ruth L. LaFollette b: 16 Apr 1893
.........................8 Rebecca A. LaFollette b: 22 Jul 1864, d: 01 Dec 1867 ; Y
.........................8 George W. LaFollette b: 09 Feb 1867
+ Hattie J. Parsons m: 05 Sep 1889
.........................9 Ida M. LaFollette b: 13 Nov 1890
.........................9 Lida C. LaFollette b: 28 Dec 1891
.........................9 Elmer U. LaFollette b: 13 Nov 1893
.........................7 Thomas LaFollette b: 14 Sep 1821 in Hardin Co., KY, d: Montgomery Co., IND; Y
+ Melinda Margaret. Kennedy b: Abt. 1827 in Kentucky, m: 08 Sep 1842 in Putnam CO.,
IN, d: 1893 in Montgomery Co., IND; Y
.........................8 Joseph U. LaFollette b: 17 Jun 1844 in Russell, Putnam Co., IN
+ Silva J. Coatney b: Abt. 1845 in Montgomery Co., IND, m: 16 Feb 1872 in Montgomery
Co., IND
.........................9 Maud M. LaFollette b: Dec 1874
.........................9 Angeline N. LaFollette b: 28 Oct 1876
.........................9 William K. LaFollette b: 26 Dec 1878
.........................9 Charles F. LaFollette b: 30 Mar 1886
.........................9 Lee B. LaFollette b: 23 Jun 1888
.........................8 John W. LaFollette b: 13 Sep 1846 in Russell, Putnam Co., IN
+ Louisa F. b: Abt. 1852 in Kentucky
.........................9 Effie M. LaFollette b: Abt. 1871
.........................9 Musa P. LaFollette b: Abt. 1873
.........................9 Carlie F. LaFollette b: Abt. 1876
.........................9 Malinda M. LaFollette b: Abt. 1879
.........................8 James T. LaFollette b: 16 Jul 1848 in Russell, Putnam Co., IN, d: Feb 1893 in
Montgomery Co., IND; Y
.........................8 Nancy Angeline LaFollette b: 15 Oct 1850 in Montgomery Co., IND
+ James Rutledge b: Abt. 1848 in Montgomery Co., IND
.........................8 Delilah J. LaFollette b: 07 Aug 1852 in Montgomery Co., IND
.........................8 Sarah J. LaFollette b: 22 Sep 1854 in Montgomery Co., IND
.........................8 Mary P. LaFollette b: 06 Oct 1856 in Montgomery Co., IND
+ John RUTLEDGE b: Abt. 1854 in Montgomery Co., IND, m: Abt. 1876
.........................8 Georgia A. LaFollette b: 17 Dec 1859 in Montgomery Co., IND
.........................8 Robert F. LaFollette b: 07 Dec 1862 in Montgomery Co., IND
+ Emma C. Rutledge b: Abt. 13 AD in Montgomery Co., IND, m: 20 Dec 1883
.........................9 Warren L. LaFollette b: 23 Sep 1884 in Montgomery Co., IND
.........................9 Thomas LaFollette b: 23 Jan 1887 in Montgomery Co., IND
.........................8 Effie May LaFollette b: 13 Jun 1867 in Montgomery Co., IND
.........................7 George W. LaFollette b: 05 Oct 1824 in Hardin Co., KY, d: Aug 1897 in Montgomery Co.,
IND; Y
+ Susannah B."Susan" Nofsinger b: 1827 in Botetourt Co., Va, m: 31 Dec 1846 in
Kentucky, d: 1902 in Montgomery Co., IND; Y
.........................8 Francis M. LaFollette b: 07 Aug 1848 in Montgomery Co., IND
+ Cornelia E. Shannon b: Abt. 1850 in Montgomery Co., IND, m: 28 Nov 1878
.........................9 Earl LaFollette b: 09 Dec 1879
.........................9 Ethel LaFollette b: 08 Oct 1881, d: 09 Sep 1882 ; Y
.........................9 Carrie LaFollette b: 08 Dec 1882
.........................9 Rushton LaFollette b: 22 Dec 1885
.........................9 Foster LaFollette b: 19 Nov 1888, d: 09 Jan 1889 ; Y
.........................9 Harold LaFollette b: 18 Mar 1890

.................9 Paul LaFollette b: 18 Nov 1893, d: Aug 1896 ; Y
                + Molly P Stamper b: Abt. 1850 in Montgomery Co., IND, m: 16 Nov 1870 in Montgomery
                  Co., IND
.................9 Clarence A LaFollette b: 27 Mar 1871 in Floyd Co, IN, d: 11 Sep 1871 in Floyd Co, IN;
                  Y
.................8 Joseph W. LaFollette b: 21 Aug 1851 in Montgomery Co., IND
                + Alice Buchanan b: Abt. Mar 185 AD in Montgomery Co., IND, m: 16 Sep 1875
.................9 William C. LaFollette b: 26 Nov 1876, d: 22 Aug 1877 ; Y
.................9 Bessie F. LaFollette b: 06 Aug 1885
.................9 George L LaFollette b: 26 Jul 1888
.................9 Lou S. LaFollette b: 22 Dec 1892
.................8 Mary E. LaFollette b: 07 Jul 1853 in Montgomery Co., IND
.................8 Robert W. LaFollette b: 17 Feb 1855 in Montgomery Co., IND
.................8 Nancy A. LaFollette b: 13 Apr 1857 in Montgomery Co., IND
.................8 Carrie H. LaFollette b: 27 Feb 1859 in Montgomery Co., IND
.................8 Thomas or Wallace W. LaFollette b: 05 Mar 1861 in Montgomery Co., IND
                + Minnie Elmore m: 24 Dec 1884
.................9 Edith LaFollette b: 02 Aug 1885
.................9 Edna LaFollette b: 02 Aug 1885
.................9 Mary H. LaFollette b: 08 Jan 1887
.................9 Susan M. LaFollette b: 19 Aug 1892
.................8 James Oliver. LaFollette b: 15 Aug 1865 in Montgomery Co., IND
                + Effie Burroughs
.................7 Phoebe Ann LaFollette twin b: 05 Aug 1827 in Hardin Co., KY, d: Montgomery Co., IND; Y
                + Peter W. Nofsinger b: 1823 in Botetourt Co., Va, m: 04 Oct 1847 in Montgomery Co.,
                  IND, d: 07 Jan 1871 in Montgomery Co., IND; Y
.................8 Thomas H. Nofsinger b: 1848 in Montgomery Co., IND
                + Sarah J. HESS b: Abt. 1852 in Montgomery Co., IND, m: 1872 in Montgomery Co., IND
.................8 George W. Nofsinger b: 1850 in Montgomery Co., IND
                + Mary J. HESS b: Abt. 1852 in Montgomery Co., IND, m: 1875 in Montgomery Co., IND
.................8 Nancy C. Nofsinger b: 1852 in Montgomery Co., IND
                + James S. Forgey b: Abt. 1750 in Montgomery Co., IND, m: 1879 in Montgomery Co.,
                  IND
.................8 Mary H. Nofsinger b: 1854 in Montgomery Co., IND, d: 1858 in Montgomery Co., IND; Y
.................8 Susan B. Nofsinger b: 1858 in Montgomery Co., IND
                + H. F. Hurst b: Abt. 1856 in Montgomery Co., IND, m: 1875 in Montgomery Co., IND
.................7 Elizabeth A. LaFollette twin b: 05 Aug 1827 in Hardin, Co, Ky, d: 02 Jan 1864 in Putnam
                  CO., IN; Y
                + John B. Henry b: Abt. 1825 in Putnam CO., IN, m: 15 Feb 1846 in Putnam CO., IN, d: 14
                  Oct 1886 in Putnam CO., IN; Y
.................8 David R. Henry b: 07 Dec 1846 in Montgomery Co., IND
                + Emily F ROBBINS. b: Abt. 1848 in Montgomery Co., IND, m: 05 Nov 1871 in
                  Montgomery Co., IND
.................8 Nancy J. Henry b: 17 Feb 1848 in Montgomery Co., IND, d: 04 Nov 1865 in Montgomery
                  Co., IND; Y
.................8 Lydia M. Henry b: 03 Dec 1857 in Montgomery Co., IND
                + William J Gill b: Abt. 1855 in Montgomery Co., IND, m: 1877 in Montgomery Co., IND
.................8 Martin T. Henry b: 18 Dec 1858 in Montgomery Co., IND
                + Sarah L EGGERS b: Abt. 1860 in Montgomery Co., IND, m: 03 Jun 1893 in
                  Montgomery Co., IND
.............6 Charles Lee jr b: Abt. 1785 in of, Hardin, Co. Ky
.............6 Mary Polly Lee b: 08 Feb 1787 in of, Hardin, Co, Ky, d: 1855 in Montgomery County, In; Y
                + Jessie LaFollette b: 23 Aug 1781 in Va. of, Hardin, Co, Ky, m: 25 Jul 1808 in Hardin, Co,
                  Ky, d: 01 Dec 1845 in Franklin Township, Jay, Indiana; Y
.................7 Rebecca LaFollette b: 16 Apr 1809

```
                + Isac Nicely m: 1830
...............7 William LaFollette b: Jun 1810
...............7 Phoebe LaFollette b: 12 Feb 1812
                + Jeptha Beck
...............8 Robert F. Beck b: 27 Dec 1831
                  + Angeline Lee
...............9 Walter Beck
...............9 Anna Beck
...............9 Lucy Beck
...............9 Susan Beck
...............9 Gertrude Beck
...............8 William Beck
...............7 Abigail LaFollette b: Nov 1813
                + David Fergeson m: 05 Jul 1838 in Nelson CO., Ky
...............8 Female Fergeson
...............8 Female Fergeson
...............7 Warren C. LaFollette b: 15 Aug 1815
...............7 Josiah L. LaFollette b: 04 Jul 1817, d: Abt. 1862 in Primrose Wisconsin; Y
                + Mary Buchanan
...............8 Robert Marion LaFollette b: 14 Jun 1855 in Primrose Wisconsin, d: 18 Jun 1925 ; Y
                  + Belle Case m: 31 Dec 1881 in Baraboo Wisconsin, d: 18 Aug 1931 ; Y
...............9 Fola LaFollette b: Abt. 1882
...............9 Robert M Jr LaFollette b: 06 Feb 1895 in Wisconsin?
...............9 Philip Fox LaFollette b: 08 May 1897 in Wisconsin?
...............9 Mary LaFollette b: 16 Aug 1899 in Wisconsin?
...............8 Joseph LaFollette
...............8 William LaFollette
                + Mary FERGUSON d: 21 Apr 1894 ; Y
...............8 Josephine LaFollette b: Abt. 1853 in IN
...............8 Robert Marion LaFollette b: 14 Jun 1855 in Primrose Wisconsin, d: 18 Jun 1925 ; Y
                  + Belle CASE b: Abt. 1859, m: 31 Dec 1881 in Baraboo Wisconsin
...............9 Mary LaFollette b: Abt. 1880 in WI
...............9 Fola LaFollette
...............9 Phillip Fox LaFollette
...............9 Robert Marion LaFollette Jr.
...............7 Nancy Ann LaFollette b: May 1819 in Nelson CO., Ky
                + Zachariah Fergeson b: Abt. 1817 in Nelson CO., Ky, m: 26 Oct 1843 in Nelson CO., Ky
...............7 Jane LaFollette b: Oct 1822
...............7 Elhanan LaFollette b: Jul 1824
...............7 Robert W. LaFollette b: Nov 1826 in Indiana
                + Eliza J. Young m: Abt. 1851 in Kentucky
...............7 Harvey Marion LaFollette b: 16 Apr 1832 in Putnam Co, IN, d: 04 Sep 1865 in Boone Co,
                IN; Y
                + Susan F. Fullemvider b: 10 Dec 1835, m: 22 Dec 1853, d: 01 Oct 1918 ; Y
...............8 Clara LaFollette b: 20 Dec 1854 in Dane Co, WI
...............8 Charles Smner LaFollette b: 14 Mar 1856 in Dane Co, WI
...............8 Warren Jasper "Jasper" LaFollette b: 22 Apr 1857 in Dane Co, WI
...............8 Harvey Marion. LaFollette Jr. b: 09 Sep 1858 in Dane Co, WI
...............8 Robert Winchester LaFollette b: 10 Dec 1859 in Boone Co, IN, d: Dec 1859 in baby
                Boone Co, IN; Y
...............8 William Leroy. LaFollette b: 30 Nov 1860 in Thornton, Boone Co IND, d: 20 Dec 1934 in
                Colfax WA; Y
                + Mary TABOR b: Abt. 1863 in Ore, m: 1886 in Pulman. WA
...............9 Suzanne LaFollette b: 24 Jun 1893, d: 23 Apr 1983 in Stanford CA; Y
```

...............9 Warren Jasper LaFollette b: 07 Feb 1895 in Albion WA, d: 17 Feb 1939 in Colfax WA; Y
...............9 Robert Chester LaFollette b: 03 Mar 1897
...............9 Eva LaFollette b: 21 Aug 1900, d: 29 Jun 1986 in Colfax, WA; Y
...............9 Tabor LaFollette d: 1960 in Colfax WA; Y
...............9 Melcena LaFollette
...............9 Roy LaFollette d: 1950 in Wa; Y
...............8 Grant LaFollette b: 19 Nov 1862 in Boone Co, IN
...........6 Edmund or Edward Lee b: Abt. 1789 in Hardin Co., KY of Nelson Co., Ky
              + Abigail CRAWFORD b: Abt. 1788 in of Hardin Co., KY, m: 21 Dec 1808 in Hardin Co., KY
...........6 Abigail Lee b: Abt. 1792 in of, Hardin, Co, Ky
              + Green Lee b: Abt. 1790 in of, Hardin, Co, Ky, m: 17 Dec 1812 in Hardin, Co, Ky
...........7 child Lee
.........4 Nancy Anna Lee b: Abt. 1728 in Richmond, Co, Va, d: 08 Oct 1808 in Rockingham Co., Va; Y
           + Joseph HANKS b: 29 Dec 1725 in N.Farnham Parish, Richmond, Co, Va, m: 26 May 1756 in
           Richmond, Co, Va, d: 1793 in Nelson, Co, Ky; Y
...........5 Thomas HANKS b: 1757 in Richmond, Co, Va, d: 1834 in Logan Co., Ohio; Y
           + Elizabeth Ryan m: 1793 in Hampshire Co., Va (now W Va.)
...........6 Joseph HANKS b: Abt. 1794
              + Margaret ALEXANDER b: Abt. 1795, m: 30 Mar 1814
...........6 Peter HANKS b: 01 Mar 1796 in Hampshire Co., Va (now W Va.), d: 19 Jul 1883 in Jackson
           Twp, Logan Co., Ohio; Y
              + Rachel HAZEN b: Abt. 1800 in Ohio, m: Abt. 1818, d: 1869 in Jackson Twp, Logan Co.,
              Ohio; Y
...........7 Thomas HANKS b: Abt. 1819 in Jackson Twp, Logan Co., Ohio
...........7 Smith HANKS b: Abt. 1821 in Jackson Twp, Logan Co., Ohio
...........7 William HANKS b: Abt. 1823 in Jackson Twp, Logan Co., Ohio
...........7 Rachel HANKS b: Abt. 1825 in Jackson Twp, Logan Co., Ohio
...........7 Mariah HANKS b: Abt. 1827 in Jackson Twp, Logan Co., Ohio
...........7 Simon HANKS b: Abt. 1829 in Jackson Twp, Logan Co., Ohio
...........7 Elizabeth HANKS b: Abt. 1831 in Jackson Twp, Logan Co., Ohio
...........7 John P. HANKS b: Abt. 1833 in Jackson Twp, Logan Co., Ohio
...........6 Absalom HANKS b: 1800 in Hampshire Co. Va (WVa) or Ross Co., Ohio, d: 13 Mar 1872 in
           Harmon Twp., Clark Co., Ohio; Y
              + Harriet Clymer b: Abt. 1805 in Ohio, m: 01 Nov 1824
...........7 Elizabeth HANKS b: Abt. 1825 in Harmon Twp., Clark Co., Ohio
...........7 Absalom HANKS Jr. b: Abt. 1827 in Harmon Twp., Clark Co., Ohio
...........7 Mary HANKS b: Abt. 1829 in Harmon Twp., Clark Co., Ohio
...........7 Susanna HANKS b: Abt. 1831 in Harmon Twp., Clark Co., Ohio
...........7 George Washington HANKS b: Abt. 1833 in Harmon Twp., Clark Co., Ohio
...........7 Rebecca Harriet HANKS b: Abt. 1835 in Harmon Twp., Clark Co., Ohio
...........7 Jospeh Clymer HANKS b: Abt. 1837 in Harmon Twp., Clark Co., Ohio
...........7 Thomas Jefferson HANKS b: Abt. 1839 in Harmon Twp., Clark Co., Ohio
...........7 William Henry HANKS b: Abt. 1841 in Harmon Twp., Clark Co., Ohio
...........7 Sarah Jane HANKS b: Abt. 1843 in Harmon Twp., Clark Co., Ohio
...........7 Isaac Turner HANKS b: Abt. 1845 in Harmon Twp., Clark Co., Ohio
...........7 Martha HANKS b: Abt. 1849 in Harmon Twp., Clark Co., Ohio
...........7 Austin Jerome HANKS b: Abt. 1851 in Harmon Twp., Clark Co., Ohio
...........7 Samida HANKS b: Abt. 1853 in Harmon Twp., Clark Co., Ohio
...........7 Emily HANKS b: Abt. 1855 in Harmon Twp., Clark Co., Ohio
...........6 Isaac HANKS b: Abt. 1803 in Ross Co., Ohio, d: Ross Co., Ohio; Y
              + Margaret Rapholse (Raypole) b: Abt. 1805, m: 20 Mar 1827
...........6 William HANKS b: 1805 in Ross Co., Ohio
              + Margaret Thompson b: Abt. 1806, m: 01 Jun 1826
...........6 Sarah HANKS b: Abt. 1807 in Ross Co., Ohio

+ Artemus Cunningham
.............6 Nancy HANKS b: 1813 in Ross Co., Ohio, d: 13 Oct 1842 in Scott Co., IN; Y
+ William Henry Ellinger b: 1810, m: 1836, d: 1894 ; Y
.................7 Joseph J. Ellinger b: 1837, d: 1922 ; Y
.................7 Sarah Jane (Christie) Ellinger b: 1839, d: 1925 ; Y
.................7 Mary Elizabeth (Foster) Ellinger b: 1841, d: 1883 ; Y
.................7 Nancy Ann (Kieth) Ellinger b: 1842, d: 1936 ; Y
..........5 Charles HANKS b: 1759 in WVa
+ Christina Hargraves Hargrave Hargrove b: Abt. 1778, m: 01 Feb 1798 in St. Martinville, LA
..............6 Joseph HANKS b: 12 Apr 1799 in Lafayette Parish, LA
..............6 Celeste HANKS b: 27 Feb 1801 in Lafayette Parish, LA
..............6 Jean HANKS b: 15 Feb 1803 in Lafayette Parish, LA
..............6 Charles HANKS b: 03 Jul 1805 in Lafayette Parish, LA
..............6 Thomas HANKS b: 25 Feb 1807 in Lafayette Parish, LA
..............6 Anne HANKS b: 15 Mar 1809 in Lafayette Parish, LA, d: 1872 in Landry Parish, LA; Y
..............6 Benjamin HANKS b: 04 Apr 1811 in Lafayette Parish, LA
..............6 Melanie HANKS b: 11 Apr 1814 in Lafayette Parish, LA
..............6 Joseph Aldred HANKS b: 03 Mar 1816 in Lafayette Parish, LA, d: 1872 in St Marinville, St
Martin Parish, LA; Y
..............6 Hilarie HANKS b: 07 Mar 1818 in Lafayette Parish, LA
..............6 Martin HANKS b: 02 Jun 1823 in Lafayette Parish, LA
..............6 Ralph HANKS b: 02 Jun 1826 in Lafayette Parish, LA
..............6 Meliacaire HANKS b: 17 May 1827 in Lafayette Parish, LA
..............6 Nathaniel HANKS b: 08 Nov 1828 in Lafayette Parish, LA
..........5 James HANKS b: 1761, d: 1785 in VA; Y
+ Lucy SHIPLEY b: Abt. 1762, m: Abt. 1781, d: 1825 in Mercer Co., KY; Y
..............6 Nancy HANKS b: 05 Feb 1784, d: 05 Oct 1818 ; Y
..........5 Joshua HANKS b: Abt. 1763 in Richmond, Co, Va
..........5 William HANKS b: Abt. 1766 in Rappahannock Country Virginia, d: Abt. 1852 in Macon Co, IL;
Y
+ Elizabeth HALL b: Abt. 1766 in Va- to Nelson Co., KY, m: 12 Sep 1793 in Nelson County,
Kentucky
..............6 Nancy HANKS b: 13 Jun 1794, d: 12 Feb 1873 ; Y
..............6 James HANKS b: 23 Jun 1795, d: 1852 ; Y
..............6 William HANKS b: Abt. 1799, d: 1846 ; Y
..............6 twelve children HANKS b: Abt. 1800 in Ky
..............6 John HANKS b: 09 Feb 1802, d: 11 Mar 1889 ; Y
+ Susan WILSON b: Abt. 1806 in Grayson Co., KY, m: 1826
..............6 Elizabeth HANKS b: Abt. 1804
..............6 Sarah HANKS b: Abt. 1806
..............6 Charles HANKS b: 07 Mar 1807
..............6 Joseph HANKS b: Abt. 1809
..............6 Celia HANKS b: Abt. 1811
..............6 Lucinda HANKS b: 1813, d: 1890 ; Y
..............6 Andrew Jackson HANKS b: 15 May 1816
..........5 Lucy HANKS b: 1770 in Richmond, Co, Va, d: 1833 in Mercer County, Kentucky; Y
+ Henry Sparrow b: Abt. 1765
+ Elisha Lingan Hall b: 1763, d: 1818 ; Y
..............6 Nancy HANKS b: 05 Feb 1784 in Campbell Co., KY, d: 05 Oct 1818 in Pigeon Creek,
Gentryville, IN; Y
+ Thomas Lincoln b: 06 Jan 1778 in Linville Creek, Augusta, Va, m: 1806, d: 07 Jan 1851 in
Goose Nest Prairie, Coles, Il; Y
.................7 Sarah Lincoln b: 10 Feb 1807 in Elizabethtown, Hardin Co., KY, d: 20 Jan 1828 in Spencer
Co, In; Y

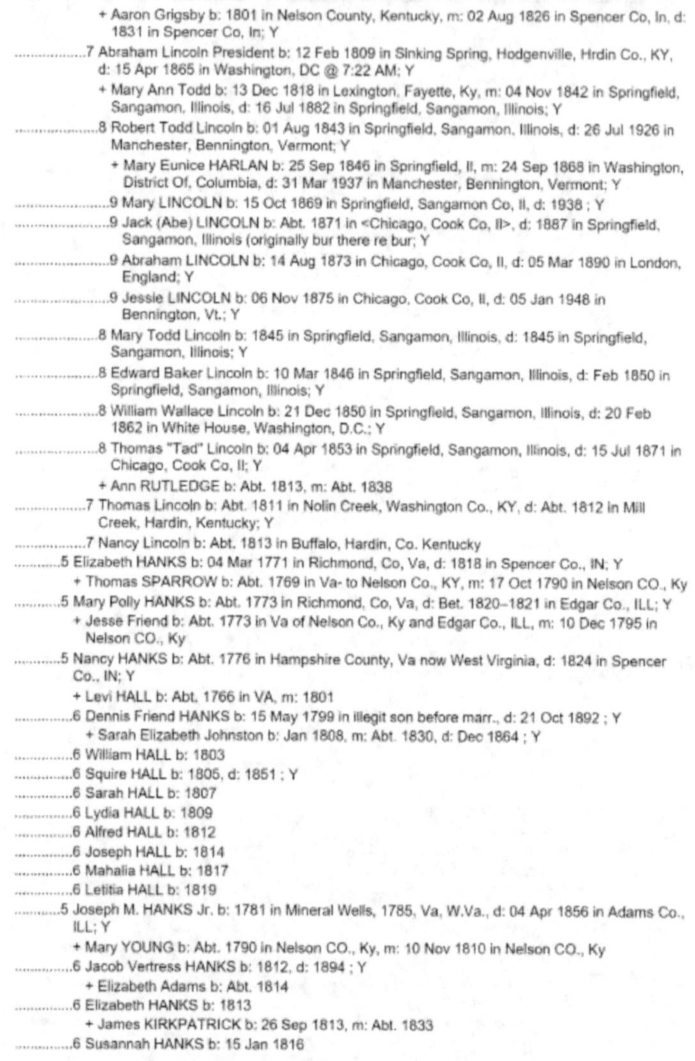

+ Aaron Grigsby b: 1801 in Nelson County, Kentucky, m: 02 Aug 1826 in Spencer Co, In, d: 1831 in Spencer Co, In; Y

...............7 Abraham Lincoln President b: 12 Feb 1809 in Sinking Spring, Hodgenville, Hrdin Co., KY, d: 15 Apr 1865 in Washington, DC @ 7:22 AM; Y

+ Mary Ann Todd b: 13 Dec 1818 in Lexington, Fayette, Ky, m: 04 Nov 1842 in Springfield, Sangamon, Illinois, d: 16 Jul 1882 in Springfield, Sangamon, Illinois; Y

...............8 Robert Todd Lincoln b: 01 Aug 1843 in Springfield, Sangamon, Illinois, d: 26 Jul 1926 in Manchester, Bennington, Vermont; Y

+ Mary Eunice HARLAN b: 25 Sep 1846 in Springfield, Il, m: 24 Sep 1868 in Washington, District Of, Columbia, d: 31 Mar 1937 in Manchester, Bennington, Vermont; Y

...............9 Mary LINCOLN b: 15 Oct 1869 in Springfield, Sangamon Co, Il, d: 1938 ; Y

...............9 Jack (Abe) LINCOLN b: Abt. 1871 in <Chicago, Cook Co, Il>, d: 1887 in Springfield, Sangamon, Illinois (originally bur there re bur; Y

...............9 Abraham LINCOLN b: 14 Aug 1873 in Chicago, Cook Co, Il, d: 05 Mar 1890 in London, England; Y

...............9 Jessie LINCOLN b: 06 Nov 1875 in Chicago, Cook Co, Il, d: 05 Jan 1948 in Bennington, Vt.; Y

...............8 Mary Todd Lincoln b: 1845 in Springfield, Sangamon, Illinois, d: 1845 in Springfield, Sangamon, Illinois; Y

...............8 Edward Baker Lincoln b: 10 Mar 1846 in Springfield, Sangamon, Illinois, d: Feb 1850 in Springfield, Sangamon, Illinois; Y

...............8 William Wallace Lincoln b: 21 Dec 1850 in Springfield, Sangamon, Illinois, d: 20 Feb 1862 in White House, Washington, D.C.; Y

...............8 Thomas "Tad" Lincoln b: 04 Apr 1853 in Springfield, Sangamon, Illinois, d: 15 Jul 1871 in Chicago, Cook Co, Il; Y

+ Ann RUTLEDGE b: Abt. 1813, m: Abt. 1838

...............7 Thomas Lincoln b: Abt. 1811 in Nolin Creek, Washington Co., KY, d: Abt. 1812 in Mill Creek, Hardin, Kentucky; Y

...............7 Nancy Lincoln b: Abt. 1813 in Buffalo, Hardin, Co. Kentucky

...........5 Elizabeth HANKS b: 04 Mar 1771 in Richmond, Co, Va, d: 1818 in Spencer Co., IN; Y

+ Thomas SPARROW b: Abt. 1769 in Va- to Nelson Co., KY, m: 17 Oct 1790 in Nelson CO., Ky

...........5 Mary Polly HANKS b: Abt. 1773 in Richmond, Co, Va, d: Bet. 1820–1821 in Edgar Co., ILL; Y

+ Jesse Friend b: Abt. 1773 in Va of Nelson Co., Ky and Edgar Co., ILL, m: 10 Dec 1795 in Nelson CO., Ky

...........5 Nancy HANKS b: Abt. 1776 in Hampshire County, Va now West Virginia, d: 1824 in Spencer Co., IN; Y

+ Levi HALL b: Abt. 1766 in VA, m: 1801

...........6 Dennis Friend HANKS b: 15 May 1799 in illegit son before marr., d: 21 Oct 1892 ; Y

+ Sarah Elizabeth Johnston b: Jan 1808, m: Abt. 1830, d: Dec 1864 ; Y

...........6 William HALL b: 1803

...........6 Squire HALL b: 1805, d: 1851 ; Y

...........6 Sarah HALL b: 1807

...........6 Lydia HALL b: 1809

...........6 Alfred HALL b: 1812

...........6 Joseph HALL b: 1814

...........6 Mahalia HALL b: 1817

...........6 Letitia HALL b: 1819

...........5 Joseph M. HANKS Jr. b: 1781 in Mineral Wells, 1785, Va, W.Va., d: 04 Apr 1856 in Adams Co., ILL; Y

+ Mary YOUNG b: Abt. 1790 in Nelson CO., Ky, m: 10 Nov 1810 in Nelson CO., Ky

...........6 Jacob Vertress HANKS b: 1812, d: 1894 ; Y

+ Elizabeth Adams b: Abt. 1814

...........6 Elizabeth HANKS b: 1813

+ James KIRKPATRICK b: 26 Sep 1813, m: Abt. 1833

...........6 Susannah HANKS b: 15 Jan 1816

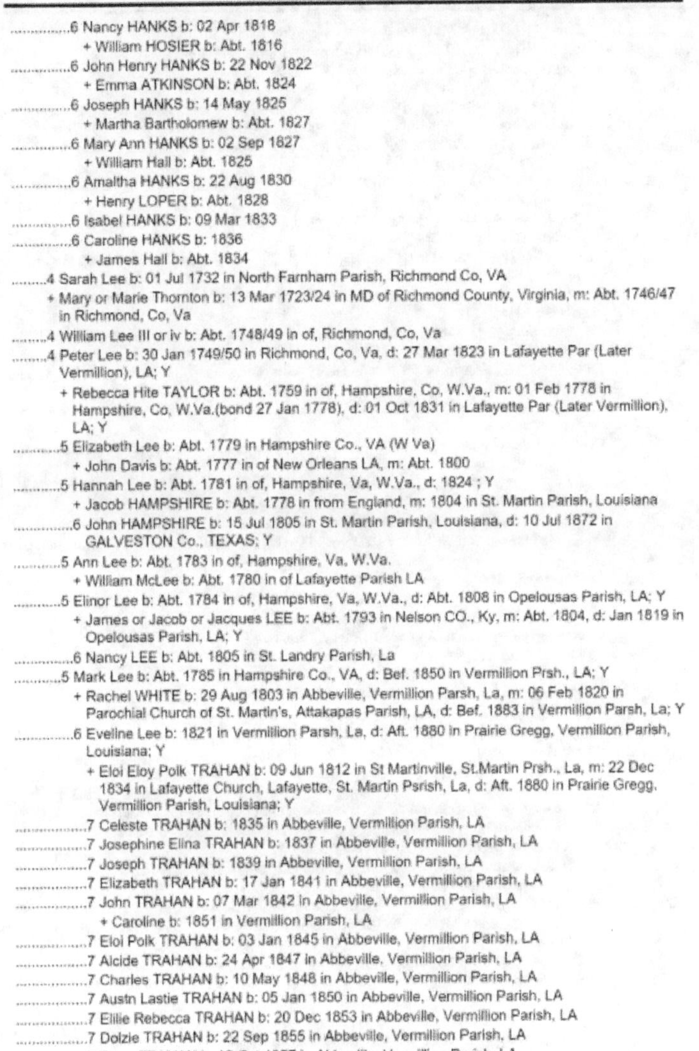

............6 Nancy HANKS b: 02 Apr 1818
            + William HOSIER b: Abt. 1816
............6 John Henry HANKS b: 22 Nov 1822
            + Emma ATKINSON b: Abt. 1824
............6 Joseph HANKS b: 14 May 1825
            + Martha Bartholomew b: Abt. 1827
............6 Mary Ann HANKS b: 02 Sep 1827
            + William Hall b: Abt. 1825
............6 Amaltha HANKS b: 22 Aug 1830
            + Henry LOPER b: Abt. 1828
............6 Isabel HANKS b: 09 Mar 1833
............6 Caroline HANKS b: 1836
            + James Hall b: Abt. 1834
.........4 Sarah Lee b: 01 Jul 1732 in North Farnham Parish, Richmond Co, VA
         + Mary or Marie Thornton b: 13 Mar 1723/24 in MD of Richmond County, Virginia, m: Abt. 1746/47
           in Richmond, Co, Va
.........4 William Lee III or iv b: Abt. 1748/49 in of, Richmond, Co, Va
.........4 Peter Lee b: 30 Jan 1749/50 in Richmond, Co, Va, d: 27 Mar 1823 in Lafayette Par (Later
           Vermillion), LA; Y
         + Rebecca Hite TAYLOR b: Abt. 1759 in of, Hampshire, Co, W.Va., m: 01 Feb 1778 in
           Hampshire, Co, W.Va.(bond 27 Jan 1778), d: 01 Oct 1831 in Lafayette Par (Later Vermillion),
           LA; Y
...........5 Elizabeth Lee b: Abt. 1779 in Hampshire Co., VA (W Va)
            + John Davis b: Abt. 1777 in of New Orleans LA, m: Abt. 1800
...........5 Hannah Lee b: Abt. 1781 in of, Hampshire, Va, W.Va., d: 1824 ; Y
            + Jacob HAMPSHIRE b: Abt. 1778 in from England, m: 1804 in St. Martin Parish, Louisiana
............6 John HAMPSHIRE b: 15 Jul 1805 in St. Martin Parish, Louisiana, d: 10 Jul 1872 in
            GALVESTON Co., TEXAS; Y
...........5 Ann Lee b: Abt. 1783 in of, Hampshire, Va, W.Va.
            + William McLee b: Abt. 1780 in of Lafayette Parish LA
...........5 Elinor Lee b: Abt. 1784 in of, Hampshire, Va, W.Va., d: Abt. 1808 in Opelousas Parish, LA; Y
            + James or Jacob or Jacques LEE b: Abt. 1793 in Nelson CO., Ky, m: Abt. 1804, d: Jan 1819 in
              Opelousas Parish, LA; Y
............6 Nancy LEE b: Abt. 1805 in St. Landry Parish, La
...........5 Mark Lee b: Abt. 1785 in Hampshire Co., VA, d: Bef. 1850 in Vermillion Prsh., LA; Y
            + Rachel WHITE b: 29 Aug 1803 in Abbeville, Vermillion Parsh, La, m: 06 Feb 1820 in
              Parochial Church of St. Martin's, Attakapas Parish, LA, d: Bef. 1883 in Vermillion Parsh, La; Y
............6 Eveline Lee b: 1821 in Vermillion Parsh, La, d: Aft. 1880 in Prairie Gregg, Vermillion Parish,
            Louisiana; Y
            + Eloi Eloy Polk TRAHAN b: 09 Jun 1812 in St Martinville, St.Martin Prsh., La, m: 22 Dec
              1834 in Lafayette Church, Lafayette, St. Martin Psrish, La, d: Aft. 1880 in Prairie Gregg,
              Vermillion Parish, Louisiana; Y
...............7 Celeste TRAHAN b: 1835 in Abbeville, Vermillion Parish, LA
...............7 Josephine Elina TRAHAN b: 1837 in Abbeville, Vermillion Parish, LA
...............7 Joseph TRAHAN b: 1839 in Abbeville, Vermillion Parish, LA
...............7 Elizabeth TRAHAN b: 17 Jan 1841 in Abbeville, Vermillion Parish, LA
...............7 John TRAHAN b: 07 Mar 1842 in Abbeville, Vermillion Parish, LA
            + Caroline b: 1851 in Vermillion Parish, LA
...............7 Eloi Polk TRAHAN b: 03 Jan 1845 in Abbeville, Vermillion Parish, LA
...............7 Alcide TRAHAN b: 24 Apr 1847 in Abbeville, Vermillion Parish, LA
...............7 Charles TRAHAN b: 10 May 1848 in Abbeville, Vermillion Parish, LA
...............7 Austn Lastie TRAHAN b: 05 Jan 1850 in Abbeville, Vermillion Parish, LA
...............7 Elilie Rebecca TRAHAN b: 20 Dec 1853 in Abbeville, Vermillion Parish, LA
...............7 Dolzie TRAHAN b: 22 Sep 1855 in Abbeville, Vermillion Parish, LA
...............7 Perry TRAHAN b: 12 Oct 1857 in Abbeville, Vermillion Parish, LA

.............7 Severin TRAHAN b: 27 Jul 1859 in Abbeville, Vermillion Parish, LA
.............7 Marc Eloi TRAHAN b: 08 Jul 1861 in Abbeville, Vermillion Parish, LA
.............7 Jesse Edwin TRAHAN b: 14 Jan 1863 in Abbeville, Vermillion Parish, LA, d: 27 Feb 1919 in
　　　　　Sulphur, Calcasieu Parish, Louisiana; Y
　　　　　+ Hortense LIBERSAT b: 14 Dec 1872 in Henry, Vermilion Parish, Louisiana, m: 19 Jan
　　　　　　1898 in Abbeville, Vermillion, La, d: 20 Apr 1953 in Port Arthur, Jefferson Co., Texas; Y
..................8 Alice Rose TRAHAN b: 25 Oct 1898 in Henry, Vermilion, La, d: 21 Feb 1976 in Port
　　　　　Arthur, Jefferson, Tx; Y
..................8 Jesse Owen TRAHAN b: 14 Jan 1900 in Henry, Vermilion, La, Tx, d: 29 Jan 1962 in Port
　　　　　Arthur, Jefferson, Tx; Y
..................8 Zoe Marie TRAHAN b: 28 Oct 1901 in Henry, Vermilion, La, Tx, d: 16 Apr 1982 in
　　　　　Nederland, Jefferson Co., Tx; Y
..................8 Claude Noah TRAHAN b: 08 Sep 1902 in Henry, Vermilion, La, d: 20 Apr 1952 in Port
　　　　　Arthur, Jefferson, Tx; Y
..................8 Charles Clifton TRAHAN b: 04 Apr 1905 in Henry, Vermilion, Tx, d: 17 May 1975 in
　　　　　Houston, Harris, Tx; Y
..................8 Minos Henry TRAHAN b: 21 Nov 1907 in Henry, Vermilion, La, d: 07 Jul 1968 in Port
　　　　　Arthur, Jefferson, Tx; Y
..................8 Eloi Polk TRAHAN b: 14 Jul 1910 in Henry, Vermilion Parish, Louisiana, d: 26 Dec 1986
　　　　　in Groves, Jefferson, Texas; Y
.............6 Elizabeth Lee b: 1823 in Vermillion Parsh, La, d: 16 May 1909 in Henry Protestant Cemetary
　　　　　Henry, Louisiana; Y
　　　　　+ William (Ludwig Wilhelm) HENRY (KATTENTIT) b: 08 Jul 1818 in Copenhagen, Denmark,
　　　　　m: Abt. 1848 in Louisiana, d: 08 Sep 1885 in Henry, LA; Y
.............7 Julie (Julia) HENRY b: 1848, d: 01 Sep 1926 ; Y
　　　　　+ Johnny PETRY
.............7 Dennis B HENRY b: 01 Jun 1851 in Henry, LA, d: 21 Nov 1924 in Pasadena, CA; Y
　　　　　+ Emma (Althea) SHERPARD b: 07 Jan 1853 in Louisiana, d: 09 Aug 1916 in Pomona, CA;
　　　　　Y
..................8 William HENRY b: 21 Jun 1877
..................8 Seth Marvin HENRY b: 06 Nov 1880
..................8 Elmer Wayne HENRY b: 15 Oct 1882, d: 1965 ; Y
..................8 Herman HENRY b: 20 Aug 1889, d: 26 Jul 1964 ; Y
..................8 Martha Pearl HENRY b: 1891, d: 1897 ; Y
..................8 Francis Winifred HENRY
..................8 Eubulus Owen HENRY
.............7 Robert S. HENRY b: 01 May 1852, d: 31 Mar 1913 ; Y
　　　　　+ Anna K. MOSS b: 17 Mar 1862, d: 21 Nov 1936 ; Y
.............7 Stephen M. HENRY b: 15 Apr 1856, d: 25 Jul 1892 ; Y
　　　　　+ Elizabeth Mary (Betty) MORGAN b: 25 Jul 1858 in Alabama, m: 03 Jan 1877, d: 26 Oct
　　　　　1942 in Lake Arthur, LA; Y
..................8 Walter Steve HENRY b: 04 Jul 1878 in Henry, LA, d: 05 Jun 1956 in Kansas City, MO; Y
　　　　　+ Elizabeth (Betty) HARRISON b: 05 Dec 1881 in Gibsland, LA, m: 24 Jan 1906 in
　　　　　　Gibsland, LA, d: 01 Nov 1955 in Rayne, LA; Y
.......................9 Violet Elizabeth HENRY b: 23 Oct 1917 in Iota, LA, d: 17 Dec 1984 ; Y
.......................9 Cecil Walter HENRY
..................8 Lela Mae HENRY b: 09 May 1881, d: 06 May 1967 in Jennings, LA; Y
　　　　　+ Adolph George BARTELS b: 15 Sep 1879 in Louisiana, m: 20 Sep 1905 in Henry,
　　　　　　Louisiana, d: 01 Jan 1935 ; Y
.......................9 Shelby BARTELS b: 04 Aug 1917 in Evangeline, Acadia, LA
.......................9 Callie Estelle BARTELS
.......................9 Howell BARTELS d: 28 Jan 1984 ; Y
.......................9 Claudia Mae BARTELS d: Sep 1968 ; Y
..................8 Pearl Elizabeth HENRY b: 14 Apr 1883 in Henry, Louisiana, d: 27 Dec 1958 in San
　　　　　Bernardino, California; Y

+ Horace (Orace) A. CHOATE b: 11 Sep 1894 in Chenieraux Tigre, Louisiana, m: 05 Mar 1914 in Henry, LA, d: 04 Apr 1964 in Yuma, Arizona; Y
.........9 Clint Horace CHOATE b: 09 Sep 1915 in Iota, Louisiana, d: 30 Oct 1997 in Flagstaff, Arizona; Y
.........9 Morgan Henry CHOATE b: 01 Nov 1917 in Nederland, Texas, d: 20 Mar 1936 in San Antonio, Texas; Y
.........9 Samuel Lloyd CHOATE b: 29 Nov 1919 in Iota, Louisiana
.........9 Lulu Pearl CHOATE b: 06 Jan 1924 in Abbeville, Louisiana, d: 17 Feb 1925 in Abbeville, Louisiana; Y
.........9 Brady Earl CHOATE b: 08 Sep 1925 in Jennings, Louisians, d: 08 Jan 1989 in Karnes, TX; Y
.........9 Joyce Gloria CHOATE b: 04 Feb 1928 in New Braunfels, Texas, d: Jun 1986 in Prescott, AZ; Y
.........8 William Milton HENRY b: 31 Jan 1886
+ Alma HAWKINS b: 1897, m: 21 Jan 1914 in Abeville, LA, d: 21 Apr 1983 ; Y
.........9 Marvin Milton HENRY b: 11 Jun 1915, d: 31 Mar 1962 in Liberty, TX; Y
.........9 Earl HENRY b: 05 Feb 1917
.........8 Alberdia Altha HENRY b: 19 Aug 1888, d: Dec 1983 ; Y
+ John Clive FISHER b: 24 Jun 1871, m: 05 Jan 1910 in Henry, Louisiana, d: 28 Dec 1965 ; Y
.........9 Altha FISHER b: 03 Dec 1913
.........8 Lloyd Thomas HENRY b: 30 Jun 1890, d: 27 Feb 1961 in Andrew, Vermilion Parish, La; Y
+ Fay Elizabeth PULLIN m: 01 Mar 1931 in Crowley, LA
.........9 Living HENRY
.........9 Living HENRY
.........9 Living HENRY
.........9 Living HENRY
.........7 Samuel Bascom HENRY b: 29 May 1858
+ Ardelle Elizabeth MACKIE
+ Lena LEE
.........7 William Harrison HENRY b: 05 May 1863, d: 11 Aug 1927 ; Y
+ Victoria HEBERT
.........7 Emma Mary Anne HENRY b: 1865
+ Sam GLAZER
+ Micheau Loyd BOLYARD
.........6 Harrison Taylor Lee b: 1825 in Vermillion Parsh, La, d: 19 Nov 1888 in Vermillion Parsh, La; Y
+ Delilah Singleton b: 1832 in Empire of Mexico, now Harris County, TX, m: 24 Sep 1854 in Harris County, TX, d: 16 Dec 1870 in Harris Co., TX; Y
.........7 James S. Lee b: 1856 in Vermillion Parish, LA
.........7 Emily C. Lee b: 1859 in Vermillion Parish, LA
.........7 Harrison Taylor Lee Jr. b: 02 Oct 1860 in Harris Co., TX
.........6 Austin Lee b: 22 Jun 1827 in Henry, Vermillion Prsh, La, d: 24 Apr 1900 in Henry, Vermillion Prsh, La; Y
+ Emelia TOUPS b: 24 Nov 1833 in <Henery, La>, m: Abt. 1850, d: 03 Oct 1905 ; Y
.........7 Mary LEE b: 1852 in Vermelion Parish. LA
.........7 William LEE b: 1854 in Vermelion Parish. LA
.........7 Amanda (Mandy) LEE b: 1856 in Vermelion Parish. LA
.........7 Joseph Austin LEE b: 05 Jul 1857 in Vermelion Parish. LA, d: 25 Nov 1927 in Port Arthur, Jefferson, Tx; Y
.........7 Thomas LEE b: 1859 in Vermelion Parish. LA
.........7 Oliver (Ollie) LEE b: Abt. 1861 in <Henery, La>
.........7 Edgar LEE b: Abt. 1863 in <Henery, La>
.........7 Elizabeth LEE b: Abt. 1865 in <Henery, La>
.........7 Amelia LEE b: Abt. 1867 in <Henery, La>

..............7 Ovelia (Veal) LEE b: <Henery, La>
.............6 Caroline Cordelia Lee b: 1833 in St. Martin Prsh, La
       + Robert Collins b: Vermillion Parish, LA, m: Abt. 1853 in Vermillion Parish, LA
..............7 Robert Alexandra Collins b: 10 Apr 1848 in Vermillion Parish, LA, d: 17 Mar 1917 in Henry
          Parish, LA; Y
          + Jeanna Hartley MOSS b: 1856 in Vermillion Parish, LA, m: 02 Jul 1872 in Vermillion
          Parish, LA
..............8 Clohe A. Collins b: 1875 in Vermillion Parish, LA
..............8 Thomas E. Collins b: 1875 in Vermillion Parish, LA
..............8 Margeret E. Collins b: 1877 in Vermillion Parish, LA
..............8 John C. Collins b: 1879 in Vermillion Parish, LA
..............7 Rebecca Collins b: 1851 in Vermillion Parish, LA
.............6 Mary Jane LEE b: 29 Dec 1836 in St. Martin Prsh, La, d: 16 Dec 1891 ; Y
          + Holston CHOATE b: 13 Jun 1828 in of Vermelion Parish. LA, m: 10 Jun 1855 in Vermelion
          Parish. LA, d: 03 Dec 1885 ; Y
..............7 Benjamin Franklin CHOATE b: 08 Feb 1857 in Vermillion Parish, Louisiana
          + Mary Elizabeth BUFORD
..............8 John Walter CHOATE
          + Julia CESSAC
..............9 Mary Nellie CHOATE
..............9 Beatrice Julia CHOATE
..............8 Benjamin Franklin CHOATE Jr.
          + Sylvia CESSAC
..............9 Mary Viola CHOATE
..............9 Joseph Earl CHOATE
..............9 Wanda Nell CHOATE
..............9 Delores June CHOATE
..............8 Warren CHOATE
          + Alice DEROCHE
..............8 Mary Leona CHOATE
          + Avery HEBERT
..............9 Ella Ruth HEBERT
..............9 Mary Maxine HEBERT
..............8 Mary Jane CHOATE
          + Noah BERWICK
..............9 Chester BERWICK
..............9 Mary Alice BERWICK
..............9 Prentice Leon BERWICK
..............9 Rayleon BERWICK
..............7 Francis E. CHOATE b: 11 Dec 1858
          + Ovey TRAHAN
..............7 Nancy Ann CHOATE b: 13 Feb 1862 in Vermillion Parish, Louisiana
          + Joe GUIDRY
..............8 Allen GUIDRY
..............8 Adam GUIDRY
..............8 Leona GUIDRY
..............8 Lee Anna GUIDRY
..............7 Rachel Sophia CHOATE b: 26 Dec 1867 in Vermillion Parish, Louisiana
          + Madison DUPLANTIS
..............8 Zebelon DUPLANTIS
..............8 Ella DUPLANTIS
..............8 John DUPLANTIS
..............8 Luke DUPLANTIS
..............8 Edna DUPLANTIS

...................8 Eno DUPLANTIS
...................7 Mary Leona CHOATE b: 09 May 1869 in Vermillion Parish, Louisiana
...................7 John Jefferson CHOATE b: 02 Mar 1871 in Vermillion Parish, Louisiana, d: 10 Mar 1911 ; Y
      + Lena GRAY
...................8 John William CHOATE b: 1901
...................8 Henry Edmond CHOATE b: 27 Sep 1904
...................8 George Washington CHOATE b: 13 Dec 1906
...................8 Harrison Ervin CHOATE
...................8 Maxcel CHOATE
...................7 James Bascum CHOATE b: 07 Feb 1875 in Vermillion Parish, Louisiana, d: 24 Jan 1939 ; Y
      + Leona CHOATE
...................8 Robert CHOATE
...................8 Ronald CHOATE
...................8 Henry D. CHOATE
      + Ada LEBOUEF
...................8 Edna CHOATE
      + Clyde JONES
...................8 Norwood CHOATE
...............6 Mark Lee b: 1839 in St. Martin Prsh, La, d: 1929 ; Y
...............6 Edgar Lee b: 1841 in St. Martin Prsh, La, d: Abt. 1878 in Vermillion Parish, LA; Y
      + Mary R. PETRY b: 1841 in Vermelion Parish. LA, m: Abt. 1861 in Vermelion Parish. LA, d: 1883 in Vermillion Parish, LA; Y
...................7 Cornelius L. Lee b: 1862 in Vermelion Parish. LA
...................7 Caroline E. Lee b: 1871 in Vermelion Parish. LA
...................7 Mary E. Lee b: 1874 in Vermelion Parish. LA
...................7 Anna A. Lee b: 1876 in Vermelion Parish. LA
...................7 Adelia V. Delia Lee b: Vermelion Parish. LA
...................7 Henry M. Lee b: Vermelion Parish. LA
............5 Emilie Lee b: Abt. 1789 in of, Hampshire, Va, W.Va.
............5 Nancy Lee b: Abt. 1794 in of, Hampshire, Va, W.Va.
      + Thomas J. Wellborn b: Abt. 1792 in VA, m: 08 Mar 1824 in St. Landry's Parish, Louisiana
............5 Mary Marie Lee b: Abt. 1798 in of, Hampshire, Va, W.Va.
............5 John Lee b: Abt. 1800 in Hampshire Co., V(WVa) ofSt. Landry's Parish, Louisiana, d: Bef. 1886 in Lafayette, LA; Y
      + Jane Susan BRYAN b: Abt. 1804 in Hampshire Co., V(WVa) ofSt. Landry's Parish, Louisiana, m: 03 Aug 1824 in Lafayette Par (Later Vermillion), LA
...............6 Octavia LEE b: 21 Mar 1821 in Hampshire Co., V(WVa) ofSt. Landry's Parish, Louisiana, d: Bet. 1857–1925 ; Y
      + Michael DURKS b: Abt. 1820 in Lafayette, Lafayette Parish, La, m: 31 Mar 1852 in Lafayette, Lafayette Parish, La
...............6 Sophia Taylor LEE b: Abt. 1823 in listed abt 1822 Hampshire Co., V(WVa), d: Bet. 1858–1926 ; Y
      + John CAMPBELL Jr. m: 24 Oct 1853 in Lafayette, Lafayette Parish, La
...............6 Joanna Lee b: Abt. 1825
      + Andrew DYER m: 19 Oct 1843 in Lafayette, Lafayette Parish, La
...............6 Althea LEE b: Abt. 1826, d: Bet. 1837–1926 ; Y
      + David RIGGS b: 03 Feb 1828 in Louisiana, d: 06 Jan 1899 in Iberia Parish, LA; Y
...............6 Elizabeth LEE b: Abt. 1828, d: 29 Dec 1908 in Lafayette, Lafayette Parish, La; Y
...............6 Emily Rebecca LEE b: Abt. 1830, d: Bet. 1871–1939 ; Y
      + William H. HAWKINS m: 12 Oct 1866 in Lafayette, Lafayette Parish, La
...............6 Elvira LEE b: Abt. 1832, d: Bet. 1837–1926 ; Y
      + Samuel T. JOINER b: Abt. 1830 in Lafayette, Lafayette Parish, La
...............6 Robert Bryan LEE b: Abt. 1834, d: Bet. 1850–1926 ; Y

..............6 Jane LEE b: Abt. 1840, d: Abt. 1843 ; Y
............5 Peter Pierre Lee Jr. b: 03 Mar 1807 in St Martin, parish, LA, d: Abbeville, Vermillion Parish, La.;
          Y
          + Clementine Rollin b: 1845 in Lafayette Parish, Louisiana, d: Aft. 1880 in Abbeville, Vermillion
            Parish, La.; Y
..............6 Aristide Rollan Lee b: 27 Feb 1862 in Abbeville, Vermillion Parish, La., d: 10 Oct 1922 in
          Henry, La.; Y
          + Euseide Dubois b: 21 Jan 1870 in Abbeville, La., m: 06 Feb 1888 in Abbeville, Vermillion
            Parish, La., d: 10 Aug 1964 in Henry, La.; Y
..............7 Justilia Lee b: 30 Sep 1892 in Henry, La., d: 07 Jul 1980 in Henry, La.; Y
          + Thomas Bradshaw Delino b: 13 Sep 1885 in Henry, LA, m: 14 Nov 1910 in Bancker, La.,
            d: 02 Dec 1963 in Henry, LA; Y
..............8 Kefer Thomas Delino b: 19 Nov 1912 in Henry, LA, d: 18 Nov 1958 in Henry, LA; Y
          + Mary Iris Nunez b: 19 Jul 1913, m: 29 Aug 1931 in Bancker, LA, d: 23 Dec 1997 ; Y
..............9 James Dale Delino b: 09 Aug 1936, d: 29 Jan 1990 ; Y
          + Living Hoffpauir
..............10 Living Delino II II
          + Living O'Bryan
..............11 Kyle Anthony Delino b: 23 Jul 1985, d: 23 Oct 1987 ; Y
..............11 Living Delino
..............11 Living Delino
..............11 Living Delino III III
..............10 Living Delino
..............9 Living Delino
..............8 Thomas Bradshaw Delino II II b: 23 Oct 1914 in Henry, La., d: 30 Nov 2005 in Abbeville,
          La.; Y
          + Lorena Marie Choate b: 16 Oct 1915 in Cheniere Au Tigre, LA, m: 23 Feb 1938 in
            Abbeville, LA - St. Mary Magdalen
..............9 Derryl Wayne Delino b: 05 Nov 1938, d: 15 Aug 2000 ; Y
          + Living Romero
..............10 Living Delino
          + Living Lacombe
..............11 Living Delino
..............11 Living Delino
          + Living Miller
..............10 Living Delino
..............10 Living Delino
          + Living Bourque
..............10 Living Delino
          + Living Vincent
..............11 Living Delino
..............11 Living Delino
..............11 Living Delino
..............11 Living Delino
..............10 Living Delino
          + Living Duplantis
..............11 Living Duplantis
..............11 Living Duplantis
          + Living Suire
..............9 Living Delino
          + Living Bienvenue
..............10 Living Delino
          + Living Jett IV IV
..............11 Living Jett
..............11 Living Jett

...........................10 Living Delino
...........................10 Living Delino
                    + Living Hebert
...........................11 Living Hebert
...........................11 Living Hebert
...........................9 Living Delino
                    + Living Bourque
...........................9 Living Delino
                    + Living Richard
...........................10 Living Delino
                    + Living Meaux
...........................11 Living Meaux
...........................11 Living Meaux
...........................10 Living Delino
                    + Living Thomas
...........................11 Living Delino
                    + Living Marceaux
...........................11 Living Delino
...........................10 Living Delino
...........................8 Cephus "Nat" Delino b: 08 May 1917, d: 06 Apr 1983 ; Y
                    + Mary Lou Bartee b: 03 Oct 1926, m: 06 Jun 1948
...........................8 Elta Mae Delino b: 18 Aug 1919 in Henry, LA
                    + Ambler (Fitzgerald) Branham b: 28 Jan 1908 in Virginia, m: 03 Jul 1938
...........................9 Living Branham
...........................9 Living Branham
                    + Living Twill
...........................10 Living Twill II II
...........................10 Living Twill
                    + Living Godsick
...........................11 Living Godsick
...........................11 Living Godsick
...........................10 Living Twill
                    + Living Meinhardt
...........................11 Living Twill
...........................9 Living Branham
                    + Jefferson Loyd Galbreath b: 12 Nov 1936 in Bude, Miss., d: 14 Mar 1999 in Pleasant
                      Hill, Ca.; Y
...........................10 Living Galbreath
...........................10 Living Galbreath
...........................10 Living Galbreath
                    + Living Loeb
...........................9 Living Branham
...........................7 Noah Lee b: 17 Nov 1904
                    + Eumea "Teet" Borque b: 01 Sep 1899, d: 10 Mar 1980 ; Y
...........................8 Living Lee
...........................8 Living Lee
...........................8 Living Lee
...........................7 Elisa "Pete" Lee
                    + Claude Nance
...........................7 Norma Lee
                    + Narcisse Robicheaux
...........................7 Willis Lee
                    + Ada Morvant
...........................8 Brenda Fay Lee

....................8 Dorothy Mae Lee
....................8 Purvis Lee
....................7 Nolia Lee
              + Nicholas Ross
....................8 Nicholas Ross
....................7 Nomie Lee
              + Martel Hebert b: 12 Feb 1894, d: 27 Mar 1973 ; Y
....................8 Aristide Lee Hebert
....................8 Alizia Hebert
....................7 Jenius Lee
              + Agnes Vaughn
....................8 Jenius Lee
....................7 Lydia Lee
              + Edwin Ramke
....................8 Lina Ramke
....................8 Edith Ramke
....................8 Iris Ramke
....................8 Grace Ramke
....................8 Zoie Ramke
....................8 O.V. Ramke d: WW II; Y
....................7 Marie Anna Lee
              + Martin Calvin Pickett
....................8 Living Pickett
....................8 Living Pickett
....................8 Living Pickett
....................8 Living Pickett
....................8 Presley Pickett
....................7 George Lee
              + Alice Dauphine
..............6 Erestile Lee b: Abt. 1864 in Abbeville, Vermillion Parish, La., d: Bef. 1870 in Abbeville,
              Vermillion Parish, La.; Y
..............6 Henry Lee b: Abt. 1866 in Abbeville, Vermillion Parish, La., d: Bef. 1870 in Abbeville,
              Vermillion Parish, La.; Y
..............6 Nancy Lee b: 17 Jul 1871 in Prairie Gregg, Vermillion Parish, Louisiana, d: 28 Apr 1951 ; Y
              + Ursin Primeaux b: 06 Jun 1861, d: 31 Jul 1937 ; Y
....................7 Aledia Joseph Primeaux b: Jan 1893
....................7 Alita Mary Primeaux b: Nov 1895
....................7 Myrtis Primeaux b: Jan 1897
....................7 Esmai Primeaux b: Oct 1899
....................7 Stella Roberta Primeaux
....................7 Gussie Primeaux
....................7 Robert Emos Primeaux
....................7 Amy Rebecca Primeaux
..............6 Peter Lee b: 1873 in Prairie Gregg, Vermillion Parish, Louisiana
              + Katherine Robert DeHart
              + Louise Foster
..............6 Polly Ann Lee b: 1873 in Prairie Gregg, Vermillion Parish, Louisiana
              + JT Thibodeaux
..............6 John Taylor Lee b: 1875 in Prairie Gregg, Vermillion Parish, Louisiana
              + Alzino Dyson
..............6 Rebecca Lee b: Vermillion Parish, LA
              + Andrew Moss b: Dec 1860
....................7 Laura Moss b: Oct 1886
....................7 Effie Moss b: May 1887

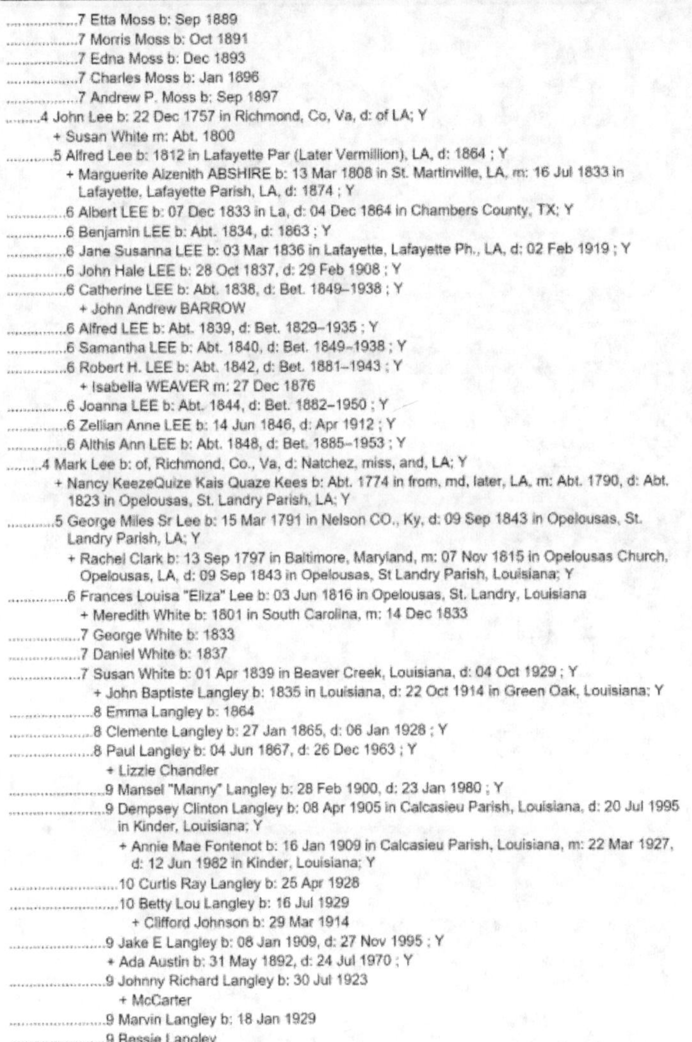

```
................7 Etta Moss b: Sep 1889
................7 Morris Moss b: Oct 1891
................7 Edna Moss b: Dec 1893
................7 Charles Moss b: Jan 1896
................7 Andrew P. Moss b: Sep 1897
.........4 John Lee b: 22 Dec 1757 in Richmond, Co, Va, d: of LA; Y
         + Susan White m: Abt. 1800
.........5 Alfred Lee b: 1812 in Lafayette Par (Later Vermillion), LA, d: 1864 ; Y
             + Marguerite Alzenith ABSHIRE b: 13 Mar 1808 in St. Martinville, LA, m: 16 Jul 1833 in
               Lafayette, Lafayette Parish, LA, d: 1874 ; Y
.............6 Albert LEE b: 07 Dec 1833 in La, d: 04 Dec 1864 in Chambers County, TX; Y
.............6 Benjamin LEE b: Abt. 1834, d: 1863 ; Y
.............6 Jane Susanna LEE b: 03 Mar 1836 in Lafayette, Lafayette Ph., LA, d: 02 Feb 1919 ; Y
.............6 John Hale LEE b: 28 Oct 1837, d: 29 Feb 1908 ; Y
.............6 Catherine LEE b: Abt. 1838, d: Bet. 1849–1938 ; Y
             + John Andrew BARROW
.............6 Alfred LEE b: Abt. 1839, d: Bet. 1829–1935 ; Y
.............6 Samantha LEE b: Abt. 1840, d: Bet. 1849–1938 ; Y
.............6 Robert H. LEE b: Abt. 1842, d: Bet. 1881–1943 ; Y
             + Isabella WEAVER m: 27 Dec 1876
.............6 Joanna LEE b: Abt. 1844, d: Bet. 1882–1950 ; Y
.............6 Zellian Anne LEE b: 14 Jun 1846, d: Apr 1912 ; Y
.............6 Althis Ann LEE b: Abt. 1848, d: Bet. 1885–1953 ; Y
.........4 Mark Lee b: of, Richmond, Co., Va, d: Natchez, miss, and, LA; Y
         + Nancy KeezeQuize Kais Quaze Kees b: Abt. 1774 in from, md, later, LA, m: Abt. 1790, d: Abt.
           1823 in Opelousas, St. Landry Parish, LA; Y
.............5 George Miles Sr Lee b: 15 Mar 1791 in Nelson CO., Ky, d: 09 Sep 1843 in Opelousas, St.
           Landry Parish, LA; Y
             + Rachel Clark b: 13 Sep 1797 in Baltimore, Maryland, m: 07 Nov 1815 in Opelousas Church,
               Opelousas, LA, d: 09 Sep 1843 in Opelousas, St Landry Parish, Louisiana; Y
.............6 Frances Louisa "Eliza" Lee b: 03 Jun 1816 in Opelousas, St. Landry, Louisiana
             + Meredith White b: 1801 in South Carolina, m: 14 Dec 1833
................7 George White b: 1833
................7 Daniel White b: 1837
................7 Susan White b: 01 Apr 1839 in Beaver Creek, Louisiana, d: 04 Oct 1929 ; Y
             + John Baptiste Langley b: 1835 in Louisiana, d: 22 Oct 1914 in Green Oak, Louisiana; Y
................8 Emma Langley b: 1864
................8 Clemente Langley b: 27 Jan 1865, d: 06 Jan 1928 ; Y
................8 Paul Langley b: 04 Jun 1867, d: 26 Dec 1963 ; Y
             + Lizzie Chandler
................9 Mansel "Manny" Langley b: 28 Feb 1900, d: 23 Jan 1980 ; Y
................9 Dempsey Clinton Langley b: 08 Apr 1905 in Calcasieu Parish, Louisiana, d: 20 Jul 1995
               in Kinder, Louisiana; Y
                 + Annie Mae Fontenot b: 16 Jan 1909 in Calcasieu Parish, Louisiana, m: 22 Mar 1927,
                   d: 12 Jun 1982 in Kinder, Louisiana; Y
................10 Curtis Ray Langley b: 25 Apr 1928
................10 Betty Lou Langley b: 16 Jul 1929
                 + Clifford Johnson b: 29 Mar 1914
................9 Jake E Langley b: 08 Jan 1909, d: 27 Nov 1995 ; Y
             + Ada Austin b: 31 May 1892, d: 24 Jul 1970 ; Y
................9 Johnny Richard Langley b: 30 Jul 1923
             + McCarter
................9 Marvin Langley b: 18 Jan 1929
................9 Bessie Langley
```

...............9 Jessie Langley
...............9 James Carroll Langley
...............9 Frank Langley
...............9 Barney Earl Langley
...............9 Lois Langley
...............8 Emily "Millie" Langley b: 11 Jul 1867 in Hickory Flat, Calcasieu Parish, Louisiana, d: 31 Jul 1918 in Kinder. Allen Parish, Louisiana; Y
   + Narcise Fruge' b: 1864 in Calcasieu Parish, Louisiana, d: 1899 in Calcasieu Parish, Louisiana; Y
...............9 Evaline Marie Fruge' b: 10 Mar 1899 in Calcasieu Parish, Louisiana, d: 12 Feb 1976 in DeRidder, Louisiana; Y
   + Desire "Red" Fontenot b: 04 Jul 1888 in Kinder, Louisiana, d: 21 Jun 1971 in DeRidder, Louisiana; Y
...............10 Lee Edward Fontenot b: 26 Sep 1927
...............10 Bessie Fontenot
   + Daniel F Cooley
...............10 Daisy Fontenot
   + Edwin A England b: 10 Feb 1906, d: 09 Feb 1981 in Kinder, Louisiana; Y
...............8 Andrew Langley b: 28 Dec 1869, d: 26 Apr 1915 in Kinder, Allen Parish, Louisiana - Green oaks Cemetery; Y
   + Vena Bell b: 22 Apr 1887 in Kinder, Allen Parish, Louisiana, m: Kinder, Allen Parish, Louisiana, d: 18 Mar 1979 in Kinder, Allen Parish, Louisiana - Green oaks Cemetery; Y
...............9 Austin J. Rev. Langley b: 19 Dec 1904, d: 18 Mar 1978 in Kinder, Allen Parish, Louisiana; Y
   + Jessie Mae McPherson b: 22 Jun 1909, m: Louisiana, d: 31 Dec 1988 in Kinder, Allen Parish, Louisiana; Y
...............10 William J "Billy" Langley b: 22 Jun 1928 in Kinder, Louisiana, d: 25 Apr 2005 in Kinder, Louisiana; Y
   + Living
   + Living Taylor
...............11 Living Langley
   + Living Castille
...............11 Living Langley
   + Living Marcantel
...............11 Living Langley
   + Living
...............11 Living Langley
   + Living Saloom
...............11 Living Langley
   + Living Fontenot
...............11 Living Langley
   + Living
...............10 Reginald D. Rev. Langley b: 14 Aug 1935 in Louisiana, d: 30 Apr 1990 in Kinder, Allen Parish, Louisiana; Y
   + Living Walker
...............10 Darlene Langley b: Louisiana
   + David Arnold
...............9 Daniel Langley b: 10 May 1908, d: 25 Dec 1944 ; Y
...............9 Louetta Langley b: 21 Nov 1911 in Kinder, Allen Parish, Louisiana
   + Sr. Stagg J. Preston d: Kinder, Allen Parish, Louisiana; Y
...............10 Living Stagg
...............10 Living Stagg
...............10 Living Preston
...............9 Lessie Mae Langley b: 19 Dec 1914 in Kinder, Allen Parish, Louisiana, d: 26 Jun 1960 in Kinder, Allen Parish, Louisiana; Y

......................+ Alphan Thibodeaux b: 19 Jun 1915, d: 25 Dec 1993 in Kinder, Allen Parish, Louisiana; Y
.....................10 Living Thibodeaux
.....................10 Living Thibodeaux
.....................8 Napoleon Langley b: 1872
.....................8 Austin Langley b: 1874
.....................7 Martin White b: 10 Feb 1840 in Opelousas, La, d: 25 May 1900 in Green Oak, La; Y
......................+ Marie Selina Pitre b: Abt. 1850, m: Abt. 1871, d: Aft. 1926 ; Y
.....................8 Louis White b: 03 Sep 1872 in Calcasieu Parish, Louisiana, d: 20 Oct 1907 in Calcasieu Parish, Louisiana; Y
......................+ Catherine Rigmaiden b: 16 Aug 1869
......................+ Mary Ann Rigmaiden b: 1868 in Calcasieu Parish, Louisiana, d: Calcasieu Parish, Louisiana; Y
......................+ Mary Ann Rigmaiden b: 1868 in Calcasieu Parish, Louisiana, d: Calcasieu Parish, Louisiana; Y
.....................8 Eliza Frances White b: 09 Jun 1875, d: 1941 ; Y
......................+ Ernest Marcantel b: 13 Jun 1861
.....................8 Mary Ann White b: 13 Nov 1876 in Calcasieu Parish, Louisiana, d: 11 Oct 1959 in Calcasieu Parish, Louisiana; Y
......................+ John Shoemake b: 1877 in Calcasieu Parish Louisiana
.....................9 Fred Shoemake b: 19 Oct 1917 in Big Woods, Louisiana, d: 30 Jan 2005 in Sulphur, Louisiana; Y
......................+ Edna St Germain
.....................10 Living Shoemake
.....................10 Living Shoemake
.....................10 Living Shoemake
.....................10 Living Shoemake
.....................10 Living Shoemake
......................+ Living Conner
.....................9 Lena Shoemake
......................+ St Germain
.....................8 Etta White b: 15 Sep 1881, d: 14 Jan 1918 ; Y
.....................8 Emma White b: 03 Jan 1884 in Calcasieu Parish, Louisiana, d: 23 Oct 1958 ; Y
......................+ Evander Jefferson Lyons b: 12 May 1869 in Calcasieu Parish, Louisiana, m: 01 Sep 1907, d: Bet. 1870–1972 ; Y
.....................8 Louisa White b: 11 Feb 1887 in Calcasieu Parish, Louisiana
......................+ William Irvin Marcantel
.....................8 Guidian White b: 18 Sep 1889 in Calcasieu Parish, Louisiana, d: 18 Dec 1894 ; Y
.....................8 Odelia White b: 25 May 1892 in Green Oak, Louisiana, d: 30 Mar 1974 in Sulphur, Louisiana; Y
......................+ Carrol Marcantel b: 28 Mar 1897 in Big Woods, Louisiana, m: 14 Mar 1916 in Calcasieu Parish, Louisiana, d: 04 Dec 1977 in Sulphur, Louisiana; Y
.....................9 Merle Marie Marcantel b: 05 Sep 1924 in DeQuincy, Louisiana
......................+ Olan Budde Bunch b: 19 Jan 1920 in Westlake, Louisiana, m: 09 Jan 1943
.....................10 Living Bunch
......................+ Living Koop
.....................9 Living Marcantel
......................+ Living Mullins
.....................8 Octavia White
.....................7 Lucinda White b: 16 Dec 1845 in Kinder, Louisiana, d: 21 Jan 1909 ; Y
......................+ William Jackson b: 08 Jul 1829 in Monmouth, England, d: 22 Dec 1907 in Elton, Louisiana; Y
.....................8 Mary Elizabeth Jackson b: 19 Nov 1871, d: Elton, Louisiana; Y
......................+ Dennis Bertrand b: 21 Aug 1849 in Elton, Louisiana, m: Abt. 1886, d: 1899 ; Y
.....................9 Amelia Bertrand b: 18 Oct 1886, d: 09 Mar 1976 in Elton, Louisiana; Y

+ Basile Marcantel b: 12 Jul 1883, m: 07 Jan 1904 in Welsh, La, d: 15 Aug 1952 in Jefferson Davis Parish, Louisiana; Y

..........................10 Kersay Leon Marcantel b: 11 Feb 1906 in Welsh, Louisiana

..........................9 Lezina Marie Bertrand b: 05 Jun 1892 in Elton, Louisiana, d: 20 Jan 1954 in Lafayette, Louisiana; Y

+ Bertrand E Garbarino b: 24 Jun 1891 in Elton, Louisiana, d: Abt. 1983 ; Y

..........................10 Medwyn D Garbarino b: 07 Nov 1922 in Elton, Louisiana

+ Lila Lee Shipp b: 22 Jul 1927 in Dallas, Texas

..........................9 Jacob William Bertrand b: 22 Jul 1897 in Elton, Louisiuana, d: Mar 1978 in Lake Charles, Louisiana; Y

+ Luda "Ludie" Treme b: 04 Sep 1900 in Jennings, Louisiana, d: 28 Apr 1970 ; Y

..........................10 Alvin Lee Bertrand b: 1919 in Elton, Louisiana, d: 26 Feb 2006 in Baton Rouge, Louisiana; Y

+ Mary Nickie Ellis m: 1942

..........................11 Living Bertrand

+ Living Trowbridge

..........................12 Living Bertrand

..........................12 Living Bertrand

..........................11 Living Bertrand

+ Living Thames

..........................12 Living Thames

..........................12 Living Thames

..........................10 Sherman V Bertrand b: 08 Sep 1920 in Elton, Louisiana, d: 05 Oct 2000 in Bernice, Louisiana; Y

+ Margaret Followell

..........................10 Jacob W Jr Bertrand b: 22 Jul 1925, d: 01 Aug 1990 ; Y

+ Pauline "Polly" Houston b: 07 Oct 1917 in Grant, Louisiana, d: 22 Jul 1998 in DeQuincy, Louisiana; Y

..........................11 Living Bertrand

+ Living Collet

..........................10 Huey "Tucker" Bertrand b: 10 Feb 1932 in Perkins Settlement, Louisiana, d: 21 Mar 2006 in DeQuincy, Louisiana; Y

+ Living Biven

..........................11 Living Bertrand

+ Living

..........................12 Living Bertrand

+ Living Klingonsmith

..........................12 Living Bertrand

..........................12 Living Bertrand

..........................11 Living Bertrand

+ Living Fflessner

..........................12 Living Fflessner

..........................12 Living Fflessner

..........................10 Gene Bertrand b: 20 Nov 1937 in Perkins, Louisiana, d: 03 Mar 2001 in Lake Charles, Louisiana; Y

+ Living Billedeaux

..........................11 Living Bertrand

+ Living Campbell

..........................11 Living Bertrand

..........................10 Living Bertrand

+ Living Materne

..........................10 Living Bertrand

..........................10 Living Bertrand

+ Living Walker

..........................10 Living Bertrand

................+ Living Fontenot
....................8 Anna Isabelle Jackson b: 01 Sep 1876 in Bayou Serpent, Louisiana
........................+ Valsin Bertrand b: 15 Jul 1869 in Elton, Louisiana, m: 12 May 1901 in Jennings, LA, d:
........................28 Aug 1932 in Elton, Louisiana; Y
....................9 Emas Bertrand b: 29 Jul 1894 in Elton, Louisiana
....................9 Emma Bertrand b: 03 Nov 1896 in Hickory Flat, Allen Parish, Louisiana
....................9 Odele Bertrand b: 16 Dec 1898 in Hickory Flat, Allen Parish, Louisiana
....................9 Dave Bertrand b: 25 Feb 1901, d: Dec 1974 in Kinder, Louisiana; Y
........................+ Pearl LaCaze b: 1911
....................9 William Bertrand b: 08 Jan 1903
....................9 Sosthene Bertrand b: 26 Feb 1905
....................9 Lucinda Bertrand b: 26 Apr 1907 in Elton, Louisiana
....................9 Thomas Bertrand b: 22 Feb 1909 in Elton, Louisiana
........................+ Laura Mae Fontenot
....................8 Christina Jackson b: 18 Mar 1883 in Jennings, Louisiana
........................+ Prevat Bertrand b: 31 May 1881 in Elton, Louisiana
................7 Emily White b: 1846
....................+ Howell Myers
................7 Elizabeth White
....................+ Francis Peet
....................+ Francois Pitre
................7 Louisa White
............6 George Miles Jr Lee b: 19 Sep 1818 in Opelousas, St Landry Parish, Louisiana, d: Abt. 1890
............in Opelousas, St Landry Parish, Louisiana; Y
................+ Phinette Newel Goff b: Abt. 1840 in Missouri, m: 10 Sep 1858 in Opelousas, St Landry
................Parish, Louisiana, d: 16 Aug 1863 in Opelousas, St Landry Parish, Louisiana; Y
................7 Robert Elisha Lee b: 12 Aug 1863 in Church Point, Acadia Parish, Louisiana, d: 24 Sep
................1934 in Opelousas, St Landry Parish, Louisiana; Y
....................+ Marie Auristillia Thibodeaux b: 26 Mar 1870 in Church Point, Acadia Parish, Louisiana, m:
....................30 Oct 1882 in Opelousas, St Landry Parish, Louisiana, d: Abt. 1955 in Opelousas, St
....................Landry Parish, Louisiana; Y
....................8 Angelina Lee b: 15 Oct 1886 in Opelousas, St Landry Parish, Louisiana, d: 06 Oct 1971
....................in Opelousas, St Landry Parish, Louisiana; Y
........................+ Felix Hidalgo b: 09 Jun 1885 in Opelousas, St Landry Parish, Louisiana, m: Abt. 1904
........................in Opelousas, St Landry Parish, Louisiana, d: 05 Jan 1959 in Opelousas, St Landry
........................Parish, Louisiana; Y
....................9 Albert Hidalgo b: 10 Oct 1907 in Opelousas, St Landry Parish, Louisiana, d: 02 Feb
....................1988 in Opelousas, St Landry Parish, Louisiana; Y
........................+ Eve Lagrange b: 20 Aug 1906 in Opelousas, St Landry Parish, Louisiana, m: Abt.
........................1926 in Opelousas, St Landry Parish, Louisiana, d: Abt. 1992 in Opelousas, St
........................Landry Parish, Louisiana; Y
....................10 Living Albert
....................10 Living Hidalgo
....................10 Living Hidalgo
....................10 Living Hidalgo
....................10 Living Hidalgo
....................10 Nelma Hidalgo b: Private
........................+ Pervis Fontenot b: Private, m: Private
....................11 Living Fontenot
....................11 Living Fontenot
....................11 Living Fontenot
....................10 Lorraine Hidalgo b: Private
....................9 Jr Hidalgo Felix b: 21 Jan 1909 in Opelousas, St Landry Parish, Louisiana, d: 22 Aug
....................1955 in Opelousas, St Landry Parish, Louisiana; Y

+ Million Lafleur b: Abt. 1909 in Opelousas, St Landry Parish, Louisiana, m: Bet. 1925–1948, d: Abt. 1993 in Opelousas, St Landry Parish, Louisiana; Y

......................9 Sidney Hidalgo b: 28 Apr 1910 in Opelousas, St Landry Parish, Louisiana, d: 23 Jan 1995 in Lafayette, Lafayette Parish, Louisiana; Y

+ Lillian Andrepont b: Private, m: Private

......................9 Angelina Hidalgo b: 07 Sep 1913 in Opelousas, St Landry Parish, Louisiana, d: Abt. 1973 in Opelousas, St Landry Parish, Louisiana; Y

+ Eldon Bertrand b: Abt. 1912 in Opelousas, St Landry Parish, Louisiana, m: Abt. 1934 in Opelousas, St Landry Parish, Louisiana, d: Abt. 1994 in Opelousas, St Landry Parish, Louisiana; Y

......................9 Andrew Hidalgo b: 25 Jan 1915 in Opelousas, St Landry Parish, Louisiana, d: 10 Oct 1974 in Opelousas, St Landry Parish, Louisiana; Y

+ Ora Bihm b: Abt. 1915 in Opelousas, St Landry Parish, Louisiana, m: Abt. 1935 in Opelousas, St Landry Parish, Louisiana, d: Abt. 1993 in Opelousas, St Landry Parish, Louisiana; Y

......................9 Elvin Hidalgo b: 15 Mar 1916 in Opelousas, St Landry Parish, Louisiana, d: 09 Mar 1984 in Opelousas, St Landry Parish, Louisiana; Y

+ Marie Ola Carroll b: Abt. 1919 in Opelousas, St Landry Parish, Louisiana, m: Abt. 1937 in Opelousas, St Landry Parish, Louisiana, d: Abt. 1994 in Opelousas, St Landry Parish, Louisiana; Y

......................9 Howard Hidalgo b: 16 Dec 1917 in Opelousas, St Landry Parish, Louisiana, d: 06 Jul 1992 in Opelousas, St Landry Parish, Louisiana; Y

+ Amy Boudreaux b: Abt. 1918 in Opelousas, St Landry Parish, Louisiana, m: Abt. 1938 in Opelousas, St Landry Parish, Louisiana, d: 02 Sep 1992 in Opelousas, St Landry Parish, Louisiana; Y

......................9 Lulu Hidalgo b: 28 Jul 1919 in Opelousas, St Landry Parish, Louisiana, d: Abt. 1985 in Opelousas, St Landry Parish, Louisiana; Y

+ Sidney Courville b: Abt. 1919 in Opelousas, St Landry Parish, Louisiana, m: Bet. 1935–1965, d: Abt. 1995 in Opelousas, St Landry Parish, Louisiana; Y

......................9 Agatha Hidalgo b: 12 Mar 1924 in Opelousas, St Landry Parish, Louisiana, d: Abt. 1991 in Lafayette, Lafayette Parish, Louisiana; Y

+ Gil Castille b: Abt. 1924 in Lafayette, Lafayette Parish, Louisiana, m: Abt. 1946 in Opelousas, St Landry Parish, Louisiana, d: 05 Feb 1990 in Lafayette, Lafayette Parish, Louisiana; Y

......................9 Annabell Hidalgo b: 08 Apr 1929 in Opelousas, St Landry Parish, Louisiana, d: 03 Jan 1930 in Opelousas, St Landry Parish, Louisiana; Y

......................9 Frank Hidalgo

+ Helen Miller

......................9 Living Hidalgo

+ Delma Reed b: Abt. 1927 in Opelousas, St Landry Parish, Louisiana, d: Abt. 1994 in Baton Rouge, E.Baton Rouge Parish, Louisiana; Y

......................9 Living Hidalgo

+ Roland Stanford b: Abt. 1922 in Opelousas, St Landry Parish, Louisiana, d: Abt. Oct 1995 in Opelousas, St Landry Parish, Louisiana; Y

......................9 Bessie Elizabeth Hidalgo b: Private

+ Leo Devillier b: 13 Jul 1913 in Opelousas, St Landry Parish, Louisiana, m: Private, d: 30 Oct 1990 in Opelousas, St Landry Parish, Louisiana; Y

......................10 Living Devillier

+ Living Valin

......................11 Living Valin

+ Living Duplechain

......................12 Living Valin

......................12 Living Valin

......................11 Living Valin

+ Living James

......................12 Living Comeaux

.........................11 Living Valin
                         + Living Bellow
.........................10 Living Devillier
                         + Living Roppolo
.........................11 Living Roppolo
                         + Living Barker
.........................12 Living Roppolo
.........................11 Living Roppolo
                         + Living O'Sullivan
.........................11 Living Roppolo
                         + Living Rock
.........................12 Living Rock
.........................12 Living Rock
.........................10 Living Devillier
                         + Living Carter
                         + Masayo Sakashita b: 02 Mar 1936 in Yokosuka, Kanagawa Ken, Japan, d: 14 Aug
                           1982 in San Diego, San Diego County, California; Y
.........................11 Living Devillier
                         + Living Herzog
.........................12 Living Devillier
.........................10 Living Devillier
                         + Living Ronald
.........................11 Living Sanchez
                         + Living Aucoin
.........................12 Living Sanchez
.........................11 Living Ronald
                         + Living Poche
.........................12 Living Sanchez
.........................12 Living Sanchez
.........................11 Living Sanchez
                         + Living Zeringue
.........................12 Living Zeringue
.........................9 Odile Hidalgo b: Private
                         + Numa Vidrine b: Abt. 1921 in Eunice, St.Landry Parish, Louisiana, m: Private, d: Abt.
                           1994 in Eunice, St.Landry Parish, Louisiana; Y
                       + Sophie Smith b: Abt. 1825 in Opelousas, St Landry Parish, Louisiana, m: 31 Oct 1844 in
                         Opelousas, St Landry Parish, Louisiana, d: Abt. 1857 in Opelousas, St Landry Parish,
                         Louisiana; Y
.........................7 Vaenez M. "Vienna" Lee b: 12 Nov 1845 in Opelousas, St Landry Parish, Louisiana, d: Abt.
                         1903 in Opelousas, St Landry Parish, Louisiana; Y
                         + Alphonse G. Fontenot b: Abt. 1843 in Opelousas, St Landry Parish, Louisiana, m: 05 Dec
                           1865 in Opelousas, St Landry Parish, Louisiana, d: Abt. 1904 in Opelousas, St Landry
                           Parish, Louisiana; Y
.........................8 Oscar Fontenot b: 02 Nov 1872 in Washington, St.Landry Parish, Louisiana, d: Abt. 1954
                         in Washington, St.Landry Parish, Louisiana; Y
                         + Ozayier Fontenot b: 28 Mar 1886 in Kinder, Louisiana, m: Bet. 1901–1930, d: 07 May
                           1957 in Kinder, Louisiana; Y
.........................9 Ignaise Fontenot b: 26 Feb 1908, d: 17 Jan 1994 in Kinder, Louisiana; Y
                         + Louis Sonnier b: 19 Sep 1904 in Soileau, Louisiana, m: 1923, d: 1967 in Kinder,
                           Louisiana; Y
.........................10 Verlin John Sonnier
.........................10 Joe C Sonnier
.........................10 Vidalee Sonnier
                         + Loyvee Whitaker
.........................11 Living Whitaker

...........................11 Living Valin
                        + Living Bellow
.........................10 Living Devillier
                        + Living Roppolo
.........................11 Living Roppolo
                        + Living Barker
.........................12 Living Roppolo
.........................11 Living Roppolo
                        + Living O'Sullivan
.........................11 Living Roppolo
                        + Living Rock
.........................12 Living Rock
.........................12 Living Rock
.........................10 Living Devillier
                        + Living Carter
                        + Masayo Sakashita b: 02 Mar 1936 in Yokosuka, Kanagawa Ken, Japan, d: 14 Aug
                           1982 in San Diego, San Diego County, California; Y
.........................11 Living Devillier
                        + Living Herzog
.........................12 Living Devillier
.........................10 Living Devillier
                        + Living Ronald
.........................11 Living Sanchez
                        + Living Aucoin
.........................12 Living Sanchez
.........................11 Living Ronald
                        + Living Poche
.........................12 Living Sanchez
.........................12 Living Sanchez
.........................11 Living Sanchez
                        + Living Zeringue
.........................12 Living Zeringue
.......................9 Odile Hidalgo b: Private
                        + Numa Vidrine b: Abt. 1921 in Eunice, St.Landry Parish, Louisiana, m: Private, d: Abt.
                           1994 in Eunice, St.Landry Parish, Louisiana; Y
                     + Sophie Smith b: Abt. 1825 in Opelousas, St Landry Parish, Louisiana, m: 31 Oct 1844 in
                        Opelousas, St Landry Parish, Louisiana, d: Abt. 1857 in Opelousas, St Landry Parish,
                        Louisiana; Y
.................7 Vaenez M. "Vienna" Lee b: 12 Nov 1845 in Opelousas, St Landry Parish, Louisiana, d: Abt.
                     1903 in Opelousas, St Landry Parish, Louisiana; Y
                     + Alphonse G. Fontenot b: Abt. 1843 in Opelousas, St Landry Parish, Louisiana, m: 05 Dec
                        1865 in Opelousas, St Landry Parish, Louisiana, d: Abt. 1904 in Opelousas, St Landry
                        Parish, Louisiana; Y
.................8 Oscar Fontenot b: 02 Nov 1872 in Washington, St.Landry Parish, Louisiana, d: Abt. 1954
                     in Washington, St.Landry Parish, Louisiana; Y
                     + Ozayier Fontenot b: 28 Mar 1886 in Kinder, Louisiana, m: Bet. 1901–1930, d: 07 May
                        1957 in Kinder, Louisiana; Y
.........................9 Ignaise Fontenot b: 26 Feb 1908, d: 17 Jan 1994 in Kinder, Louisiana; Y
                        + Louis Sonnier b: 19 Sep 1904 in Soileau, Louisiana, m: 1923, d: 1967 in Kinder,
                           Louisiana; Y
.........................10 Verlin John Sonnier
.........................10 Joe C Sonnier
.........................10 Vidalee Sonnier
                        + Loyvee Whitaker
.........................11 Living Whitaker

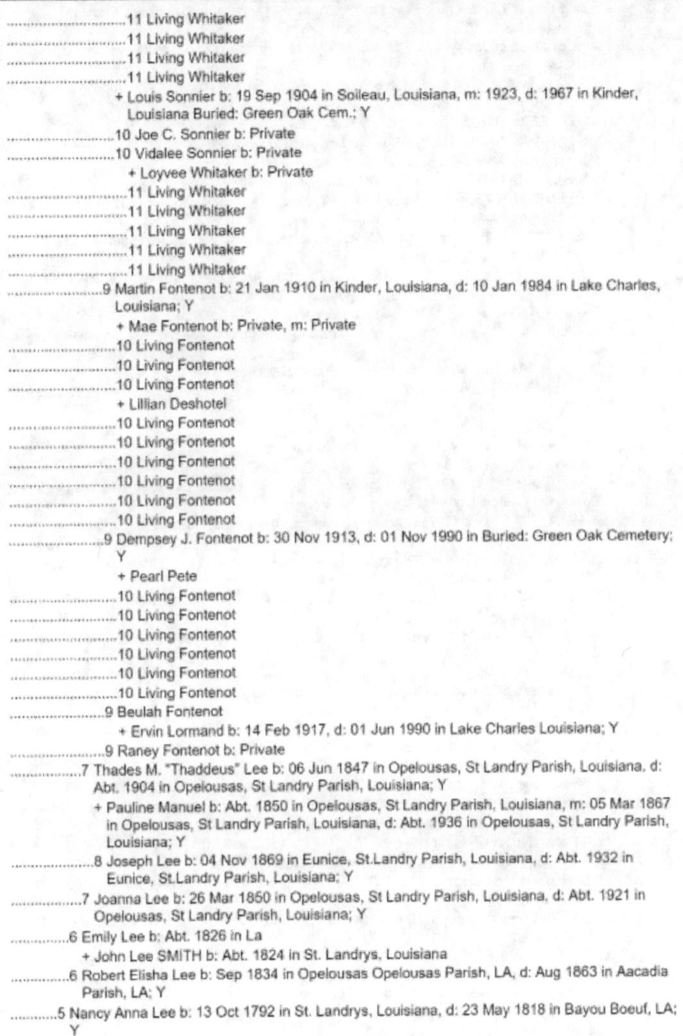

.................11 Living Whitaker
.................11 Living Whitaker
.................11 Living Whitaker
.................11 Living Whitaker
    + Louis Sonnier b: 19 Sep 1904 in Soileau, Louisiana, m: 1923, d: 1967 in Kinder,
      Louisiana Buried: Green Oak Cem.; Y
.................10 Joe C. Sonnier b: Private
.................10 Vidalee Sonnier b: Private
    + Loyvee Whitaker b: Private
.................11 Living Whitaker
.................11 Living Whitaker
.................11 Living Whitaker
.................11 Living Whitaker
.................11 Living Whitaker
.................9 Martin Fontenot b: 21 Jan 1910 in Kinder, Louisiana, d: 10 Jan 1984 in Lake Charles,
      Louisiana; Y
    + Mae Fontenot b: Private, m: Private
.................10 Living Fontenot
.................10 Living Fontenot
.................10 Living Fontenot
    + Lillian Deshotel
.................10 Living Fontenot
.................10 Living Fontenot
.................10 Living Fontenot
.................10 Living Fontenot
.................10 Living Fontenot
.................10 Living Fontenot
.................9 Dempsey J. Fontenot b: 30 Nov 1913, d: 01 Nov 1990 in Buried: Green Oak Cemetery;
      Y
    + Pearl Pete
.................10 Living Fontenot
.................10 Living Fontenot
.................10 Living Fontenot
.................10 Living Fontenot
.................10 Living Fontenot
.................10 Living Fontenot
.................9 Beulah Fontenot
    + Ervin Lormand b: 14 Feb 1917, d: 01 Jun 1990 in Lake Charles Louisiana; Y
.................9 Raney Fontenot b: Private
.................7 Thades M. "Thaddeus" Lee b: 06 Jun 1847 in Opelousas, St Landry Parish, Louisiana, d:
      Abt. 1904 in Opelousas, St Landry Parish, Louisiana; Y
    + Pauline Manuel b: Abt. 1850 in Opelousas, St Landry Parish, Louisiana, m: 05 Mar 1867
      in Opelousas, St Landry Parish, Louisiana, d: Abt. 1936 in Opelousas, St Landry Parish,
      Louisiana; Y
.................8 Joseph Lee b: 04 Nov 1869 in Eunice, St.Landry Parish, Louisiana, d: Abt. 1932 in
      Eunice, St.Landry Parish, Louisiana; Y
.................7 Joanna Lee b: 26 Mar 1850 in Opelousas, St Landry Parish, Louisiana, d: Abt. 1921 in
      Opelousas, St Landry Parish, Louisiana; Y
.................6 Emily Lee b: Abt. 1826 in La
    + John Lee SMITH b: Abt. 1824 in St. Landrys, Louisiana
.................6 Robert Elisha Lee b: Sep 1834 in Opelousas Opelousas Parish, LA, d: Aug 1863 in Aacadia
      Parish, LA; Y
.................5 Nancy Anna Lee b: 13 Oct 1792 in St. Landrys, Louisiana, d: 23 May 1818 in Bayou Boeuf, LA;
      Y

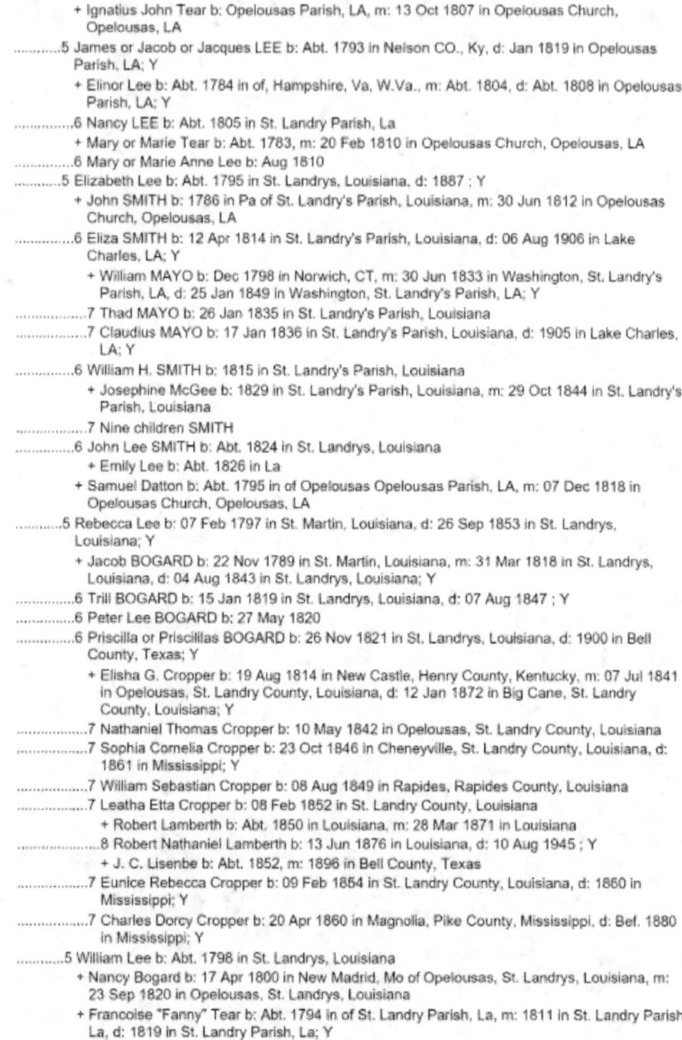

+ Ignatius John Tear b: Opelousas Parish, LA, m: 13 Oct 1807 in Opelousas Church, Opelousas, LA

..........5 James or Jacob or Jacques LEE b: Abt. 1793 in Nelson CO., Ky, d: Jan 1819 in Opelousas Parish, LA; Y

+ Elinor Lee b: Abt. 1784 in of, Hampshire, Va, W.Va., m: Abt. 1804, d: Abt. 1808 in Opelousas Parish, LA; Y

..............6 Nancy LEE b: Abt. 1805 in St. Landry Parish, La

+ Mary or Marie Tear b: Abt. 1783, m: 20 Feb 1810 in Opelousas Church, Opelousas, LA

..............6 Mary or Marie Anne Lee b: Aug 1810

..........5 Elizabeth Lee b: Abt. 1795 in St. Landrys, Louisiana, d: 1887 ; Y

+ John SMITH b: 1786 in Pa of St. Landry's Parish, Louisiana, m: 30 Jun 1812 in Opelousas Church, Opelousas, LA

..............6 Eliza SMITH b: 12 Apr 1814 in St. Landry's Parish, Louisiana, d: 06 Aug 1906 in Lake Charles, LA; Y

+ William MAYO b: Dec 1798 in Norwich, CT, m: 30 Jun 1833 in Washington, St. Landry's Parish, LA, d: 25 Jan 1849 in Washington, St. Landry's Parish, LA; Y

..............7 Thad MAYO b: 26 Jan 1835 in St. Landry's Parish, Louisiana

..............7 Claudius MAYO b: 17 Jan 1836 in St. Landry's Parish, Louisiana, d: 1905 in Lake Charles, LA; Y

..............6 William H. SMITH b: 1815 in St. Landry's Parish, Louisiana

+ Josephine McGee b: 1829 in St. Landry's Parish, Louisiana, m: 29 Oct 1844 in St. Landry's Parish, Louisiana

..............7 Nine children SMITH

..............6 John Lee SMITH b: Abt. 1824 in St. Landrys, Louisiana

+ Emily Lee b: Abt. 1826 in La

+ Samuel Datton b: Abt. 1795 in of Opelousas Opelousas Parish, LA, m: 07 Dec 1818 in Opelousas Church, Opelousas, LA

..........5 Rebecca Lee b: 07 Feb 1797 in St. Martin, Louisiana, d: 26 Sep 1853 in St. Landrys, Louisiana; Y

+ Jacob BOGARD b: 22 Nov 1789 in St. Martin, Louisiana, m: 31 Mar 1818 in St. Landrys, Louisiana, d: 04 Aug 1843 in St. Landrys, Louisiana; Y

..............6 Trill BOGARD b: 15 Jan 1819 in St. Landrys, Louisiana, d: 07 Aug 1847 ; Y

..............6 Peter Lee BOGARD b: 27 May 1820

..............6 Priscilla or Priscillas BOGARD b: 26 Nov 1821 in St. Landrys, Louisiana, d: 1900 in Bell County, Texas; Y

+ Elisha G. Cropper b: 19 Aug 1814 in New Castle, Henry County, Kentucky, m: 07 Jul 1841 in Opelousas, St. Landry County, Louisiana, d: 12 Jan 1872 in Big Cane, St. Landry County, Louisiana; Y

..............7 Nathaniel Thomas Cropper b: 10 May 1842 in Opelousas, St. Landry County, Louisiana

..............7 Sophia Cornelia Cropper b: 23 Oct 1846 in Cheneyville, St. Landry County, Louisiana, d: 1861 in Mississippi; Y

..............7 William Sebastian Cropper b: 08 Aug 1849 in Rapides, Rapides County, Louisiana

..............7 Leatha Etta Cropper b: 08 Feb 1852 in St. Landry County, Louisiana

+ Robert Lamberth b: Abt. 1850 in Louisiana, m: 28 Mar 1871 in Louisiana

..............8 Robert Nathaniel Lamberth b: 13 Jun 1876 in Louisiana, d: 10 Aug 1945 ; Y

+ J. C. Lisenbe b: Abt. 1852, m: 1896 in Bell County, Texas

..............7 Eunice Rebecca Cropper b: 09 Feb 1854 in St. Landry County, Louisiana, d: 1860 in Mississippi; Y

..............7 Charles Dorcy Cropper b: 20 Apr 1860 in Magnolia, Pike County, Mississippi, d: Bef. 1880 in Mississippi; Y

..........5 William Lee b: Abt. 1798 in St. Landrys, Louisiana

+ Nancy Bogard b: 17 Apr 1800 in New Madrid, Mo of Opelousas, St. Landrys, Louisiana, m: 23 Sep 1820 in Opelousas, St. Landrys, Louisiana

+ Francoise "Fanny" Tear b: Abt. 1794 in of St. Landry Parish, La, m: 1811 in St. Landry Parish, La, d: 1819 in St. Landry Parish, La; Y

...........6 William Lee Jr. b: 24 Nov 1813 in St Landry Parish, LA
         + Mary Bonnett b: 11 Feb 1814, m: 03 Jul 1832 in Opelousas Church, Opelousas, St. Landry
           Parish, LA
...........7 eleven children Lee
...........6 Jean John Lee b: 18 Feb 1815 in St. Landry Parish, La
         + Elisa Jane Rulong b: 01 Feb 1817 in Opelousas, St Landry Parish, Louisiana, m: 15 Jul
           1836 in Opelousas, St Landry Parish, Louisiana
...........7 John Theodore Lee b: 20 Aug 1837 in Opelousas, St Landry Parish, Louisiana
...........6 Ann Francoise Lee b: 17 Jul 1819 in St. Landry Parish, La
.........5 Peter Lee b: Abt. 1800 in St. Martin Parish, Louisiana
......3 Charles Lee Sr. b: 18 Sep 1706 in Richmond, Co, N Farnham Parish, Va, d: 1799 in will probate,
       Cumberland, Co, Va; Y
       + Ann Dabbs b: Abt. 1716 in of, Charlotte, Co, Va, m: Abt. 1736 in Charlotte, Co, Va, d: 1795 in will
         probate, Cumberland, Co, Va; Y
.........4 Charles Lee jr b: Abt. 1737 in of, Cumberland, Co, Va, d: 29 Dec 1820 in Winchester, Franklin,
         Co, Tenn; Y
         + Susannah PEARCE b: Abt. 1736 in of, Cumberland, Campbell, Va, m: 26 Jan 1786 in License,
           Cumberland, Co, rnd 8 feb, Va, d: 12 Mar 1815 in Winchester, Franklin, Co, Tenn; Y
...........5 Richard Henry LEE b: 14 Nov 1786 in Cumberland, Co Va, d: 25 Jun 1831 ; Y
...........5 Mildred Dabbs Lee b: 03 Mar 1788 in Cumberland, Co Va, d: 10 Sep 1838 in Cumberland, Co
         Va; Y
         + James Vance Acklin b: 02 Nov 1780 in Abingdon, Washington County, Virginia, m: 11 Oct
           1815 in Cumberland, Co, Va, d: Abt. 1844 ; Y
...........5 Edmond Pearce LEE b: 18 Apr 1789 in Cumberland, Co Va, d: 1879 in Franklin, Co TN; Y
         + Susan L ANDERSON b: Abt. 1791 in Cumberland, Co Va, m: 16 Feb 1813 in Campbell, Co,
           Va
...........6 Hugh W. Lee b: Abt. 1814
...........6 Martha H. Lee b: Abt. 1816
         + Mr. McNeil
...........6 Blair Lee b: Abt. 1818
...........6 Angela Rebecca Lee b: Abt. 1820
...........6 George M. Lee b: Abt. 1824
...........6 Susan Edmonia Lee b: Abt. 1826
...........6 Judith F. Lee b: Abt. 1830
...........5 Catherine Butcher LEE b: 12 Feb 1791 in Cumberland, Co Va, d: Y
         + John C. Turner b: 1795 in Patrick Co., Virginia, m: 1818 in Winchester, Franklin Co.,
           TENNESSEE, d: 1822 in Winchester, Franklin Co., TENNESSEE; Y
...........6 Charles Lee Turner b: 1820 in Franklin Co., Tennessee, d: 01 Feb 1928 in RED ROCK,
         BASTROP CO., TEXAS; Y
         + Mary Jane Spindle b: Abt. 1821 in Spotsylvania Co., Virginia, m: 12 Jan 1842 in
           Winchester, Franklin Co., TENNESSEE, d: Abt. 1875 in RED ROCK, BASTROP CO.,
           TEXAS; Y
...........7 Sophronia C. Turner b: 1842 in Franklin Co., Tennessee, d: 1899 in WATTERSON,
         BASTROP CO., TEXAS; Y
...........7 William P. Turner b: 04 Dec 1844 in Franklin Co., Tennessee, d: 04 Aug 1845 in Franklin
         Co., Tennessee; Y
...........7 Lemuel Amaziah C. Turner b: 1846 in Winchester, Franklin Co., TENNESSEE, d: 01 Feb
         1928 in RED ROCK, BASTROP CO., TEXAS; Y
...........7 Robert P. Turner b: 30 Aug 1852 in Franklin Co., Tennessee, d: 30 Jun 1854 in Franklin
         Co., Tennessee; Y
...........7 Agnes "Annas" Turner b: 1853 in Franklin Co., Tennessee, d: Bet. 1867–1947 ; Y
...........7 Elizabeth "Elisole" Turner b: 1854 in Franklin Co., Tennessee, d: Bet. 1855–1948 ; Y
...........7 Joseph A. Turner b: 13 Feb 1856 in Franklin Co., Tennessee, d: 22 Feb 1856 in Franklin
         Co., Tennessee; Y
...........6 John Baldwin Turner b: Abt. 1823 in Franklin Co., Tennessee, d: Aft. 1856 in TENNESSEE; Y

+ Mary b: Abt. 1825 in TENNESSEE, m: Abt. 1842 in Franklin Co., Tennessee, d: Bet. 1850–1919 ; Y

...............7 John Turner b: Abt. 1844 in Franklin Co., Tennessee, d: Bet. 1845–1934 ; Y

...............7 Mildred Turner b: Abt. 1846 in Franklin Co., Tennessee, d: Bet. 1847–1940 ; Y

.............6 Callaway Turner b: 1825 in Franklin Co., Tennessee, d: Bet. 1854–1916 ; Y

+ Adeline b: 1825 in Franklin Co., Tennessee, m: Abt. 1844 in Franklin Co., Tennessee, d: Bet. 1854–1919 ; Y

...............7 Mary C. Turner b: 1845 in Franklin Co., Tennessee, d: Bet. 1846–1939 ; Y

...............7 Murray C. Turner b: 1848 in Franklin Co., Tennessee, d: Bet. 1849–1938 ; Y

...............7 Frances C. Turner b: Apr 1850 in Franklin Co., Tennessee, d: 1941 in Franklin Co., Tennessee; Y

...........5 Mary Ann LEE b: 17 Nov 1792 in Cumberland, Co Va, d: 1860 in Franklin Co., Va; Y

+ Alexander S. ACKLIN b: Jul 1785 in Cumberland, Co Va, m: 20 Nov 1817 in Cumberland Co., VA, d: Feb 1834 in Franklin Co., Tennessee; Y

.............6 Morris Newton ACKLIN b: Abt. 1818, d: 22 Jul 1890 in Clarke Co., MS; Y

...........5 Charles P LEE b: 18 May 1794 in Cumberland, Co Va, d: Franklin, Co TN; Y

+ Mary Langhorne BONDURANT b: Abt. 1800 in Cumberland, Co Va, m: 22 Dec 1817 in Cumberland, Co, Va

...........5 Baldwin Madison LEE b: 04 Jan 1798 in Cumberland, Co Va

...........5 John Hopkins LEE b: 12 Nov 1799 in Cumberland, Co Va, d: 12 Sep 1858 in Belton, TX; Y

+ Mary TURNER b: Abt. 1800 in of, Franklin, Co TN, m: 15 Apr 1819 in Franklin, Co TN, d: Belton, TX; Y

+ Sarah Turner b: 27 Aug 1803 in PATRICK CO., VA., m: 15 Apr 1819 in Franklin Co., Tn., d: 21 Feb 1879 in BELTON, TEXAS; Y

.............6 John Turner Lee b: 29 Jan 1820 in Franklin Co., TN, d: 27 Sep 1839 in Franklin Co., TN; Y

.............6 Edward Finch Lee b: 21 Mar 1821 in Winchester, Franklin, Tn, d: 09 May 1903 in San Angelo, Tom Green, Tx; Y

+ Rebecca Ann Taylor b: 21 Nov 1818 in Franklin County, Tx, m: 21 Jan 1845 in Franklin County, Tn, d: 30 Jul 1899 in Belton, Bell, Tx; Y

...............7 Harriet Rebecca LEE b: 26 Jun 1846 in Franklin, Tn, d: 06 Nov 1918 ; Y

...............7 Mary Melvina LEE b: 14 Sep 1847 in Franklin, Tn

...............7 William Taylor LEE b: 25 Mar 1849 in Franklin County, Tn, d: 11 Feb 1907 in Comanche, Comanche, Tx; Y

+ Virginia Octavene CHALK b: 28 Aug 1850 in Maury County, Tn, m: 03 Feb 1875 in Belton, Bell, Tx, d: 22 Aug 1923 in Blanket, Brown, Tx; Y

...................8 Frank Zeuxes LEE b: 02 Dec 1875 in Comanche, Com, Tx, d: 05 Jun 1940 ; Y

...................8 Jessa LEE b: 25 Apr 1877 in Comanche, Com, Tx, d: 13 Jul 1958 ; Y

...................8 Edward Finch LEE b: 11 Oct 1878 in Comanche, Comanche, Tx, d: 06 Oct 1929 in Waller, Waller, Tx; Y

+ Golda GUIRNEY b: Abt. 1882 in Comanche, Comanche Co., Tx, m: 1911 in Comanche, Comanche Co., Tx

+ Ada Ann POOL b: 04 Mar 1879 in Ogden, Weber, Ut, m: 05 Jun 1907 in Salt Lake City, Salt Lake, Ut, d: 16 Jun 1957 in Ogden, Weber, Ut; Y

.......................9 <No name>

.......................9 <No name>

.......................9 <No name>

.......................9 <No name>

...................8 Lois LEE b: 11 May 1880 in Belton, Bell, Tx, d: 23 May 1881 ; Y

...................8 William Taylor LEE b: 19 Sep 1882 in Belton, Bell, Tx, d: 02 Feb 1965 ; Y

...................8 Mary Octavene LEE b: 02 Feb 1885 in Comanche, Com., Tx, d: 08 Dec 1965 ; Y

...................8 Knox LEE b: 05 Feb 1887 in Comanche, Com., Tx, d: 09 Apr 1947 ; Y

...................8 Byrd LEE b: 02 Oct 1889 in Comanche, Com., Tx, d: 22 Sep 1976 in Brownwood, Brown, Tx; Y

...................8 Carl LEE b: 12 Mar 1891 in Comanche, Com., Tx, d: 09 Aug 1957 ; Y

...................8 Homer LEE b: 29 Sep 1893 in Comanche, Com., Tx, d: 10 Jul 1971 ; Y

..............7 Sarah Carline LEE b: 06 Dec 1850 in Franklin, Tn, d: 18 Jun 1864 ; Y
..............7 Elizabeth Ann LEE b: 29 Nov 1852 in Bell, Tn, d: 08 Jun 1864 ; Y
..............7 Susan Amanda LEE b: 19 Apr 1855 in Bell, Tn
　　　　+ Joshua A. MITCHELL b: Abt. 1849 in Bell Co., TN, m: Abt. 1872 in Bell Co., TN, d:
　　　　　Grainger Co., Tennessee; Y
..............8 Sarah L. MITCHELL b: 1873 in Grainger Co., Tennessee
..............8 Letha O. MITCHELL b: 1877 in Grainger Co., Tennessee
..............7 Lucy Belle LEE b: 01 Apr 1857 in Bell, Tn
..............7 Robert Edward LEE b: 23 Jan 1859 in Bell, Tn, d: 18 Aug 1859 ; Y
..............7 Brownlow Franklin LEE b: 22 Aug 1860 in Bell, Tn, d: 21 May 1934 ; Y
　　　　+ Mary Maddy FARR b: Abt. 1864 in Bell Co., TX
　　　　+ Ida May POTTS b: Abt. 1864 in Bell Co., TX
............6 Sarah Pearce Lee b: 19 Dec 1822 in Franklin Co., TN
　　　　+ Benjamin Ben J. Taylor b: Abt. 1820 in Franklin Co., TN, m: 13 Jul 1842 in Franklin Co., TN
............6 Judith Ann Lee b: 11 Sep 1824 in Franklin Co., TN, d: 08 Feb 1839 in Franklin Co., TN; Y
............6 Francis M. Lee b: 1826
............6 Charles Lee b: 12 Nov 1828 in Franklin Co., TN, d: 09 Aug 1851 in Franklin Co., TN; Y
............6 William Roberson Turner Lee b: 30 Nov 1830 in Franklin Co., TN, d: Nov 1901 in Tyler,
　　　　Texas; Y
　　　　+ Amanda C. Emaline MOrris b: 1835 in Franklin Co., TN, m: 01 Oct 1851 in MS
..............7 S. Lee b: 1860 in Precinct 3, Tyler, Texas
..............7 Amanda Lee b: 1865 in Precinct 3, Tyler, Texas
..............7 Robert Lee b: 1867 in Precinct 3, Tyler, Texas
..............7 John M Lee b: 1876 in Precinct 3, Tyler, Texas
............6 Baldwin Pierce Lee b: 31 Jul 1832 in Franklin, Tennessee, d: 22 Oct 1912 ; Y
　　　　+ Mary Ann Morris b: 15 Oct 1830 in Of, Bell, Texas, m: 07 Oct 1852, d: 20 Feb 1897 ; Y
..............7 John Edward Lee b: 22 Jun 1853 in Bell, Texas, d: 31 Jan 1938 ; Y
..............7 Susan June Lee b: 12 Nov 1855 in Bell, Texas, d: Feb 1922 ; Y
..............7 Eliza Alexander Lee b: 15 Sep 1857 in Bell, Texas, d: 10 Sep 1898 ; Y
..............7 Adeline Kinney Lee b: 12 Sep 1867 in Bell, Texas, d: 11 Jul 1948 ; Y
..............7 Unavailable
............6 Elizabeth Ann Lee b: 26 Jul 1834 in Franklin Co., TN, d: 15 Feb 1913 ; Y
　　　　+ Martin V. Wiseman b: Abt. 1832 in Franklin Co., TN, m: 17 Oct 1854 in Franklin Co., TN
............6 Adaline Anderson Lee b: 01 Oct 1836 in Franklin Co., TN, d: 28 Feb 1901 in Bell Co., TX; Y
　　　　+ Robert D. Kinney b: 01 Aug 1830 in New Jersey, m: 31 May 1858 in Bell Co., TX, d: Bell,
　　　　　Texas; Y
..............7 Sarah Ellen Kinney b: 04 Aug 1860 in Bell, Texas, d: 11 Nov 1861 ; Y
..............7 Andrew John Kinney b: 29 Dec 1861 in Bell, Texas, d: 27 Mar 1910 ; Y
..............7 Mary Ellen Kinney b: 16 Jul 1864 in Bell, Texas, d: 03 Oct 1864 ; Y
..............7 Bethany Ann Kinney b: 08 Jan 1867 in Bell, Texas, d: 08 Sep 1900 ; Y
..............7 Robert D. Kinney Jr. Jr. b: 01 Aug 1868 in Bell, Texas, d: 04 Mar 1937 ; Y
..............7 Bauldwin Lee Kinney b: 06 Oct 1869 in Bell, Texas, d: 06 Jul 1870 ; Y
..............7 Adaline Kinney b: 18 Oct 1870 in Bell, Texas, d: 06 Sep 1871 ; Y
............6 Mary Eveline Lee b: 04 Oct 1838
　　　　+ Andrew Mitchell Keller b: 09 Feb 1830 in Bedford Co., TN, m: 1856 in Bedford Co., TN, d:
　　　　　Abt. 1923 in Tx; Y
............6 Henry Harrison Lee b: 25 Mar 1841 in Franklin Co., TN, d: 05 Sep 1841 in Franklin Co., TN;
　　　　Y
............6 Musedore Caroline Lee b: 10 May 1845 in Franklin Co., TN, d: 27 Aug 1853 in Franklin Co.,
　　　　TN; Y
............6 Benjamin Deckerd Lee b: 31 Mar 1849 in Franklin Co., TN, d: 12 Dec 1912 ; Y
　　　　+ Susan Allie Grider b: Abt. 1849 in Bell Co., TX, m: 21 Nov 1865 in Bell Co., TX, d: Aft. 1880
　　　　　; Y
..............7 John Lee b: 1868 in Belton, Bell Co., TX
..............7 Cora Lee b: 1872 in Belton, Bell Co., TX

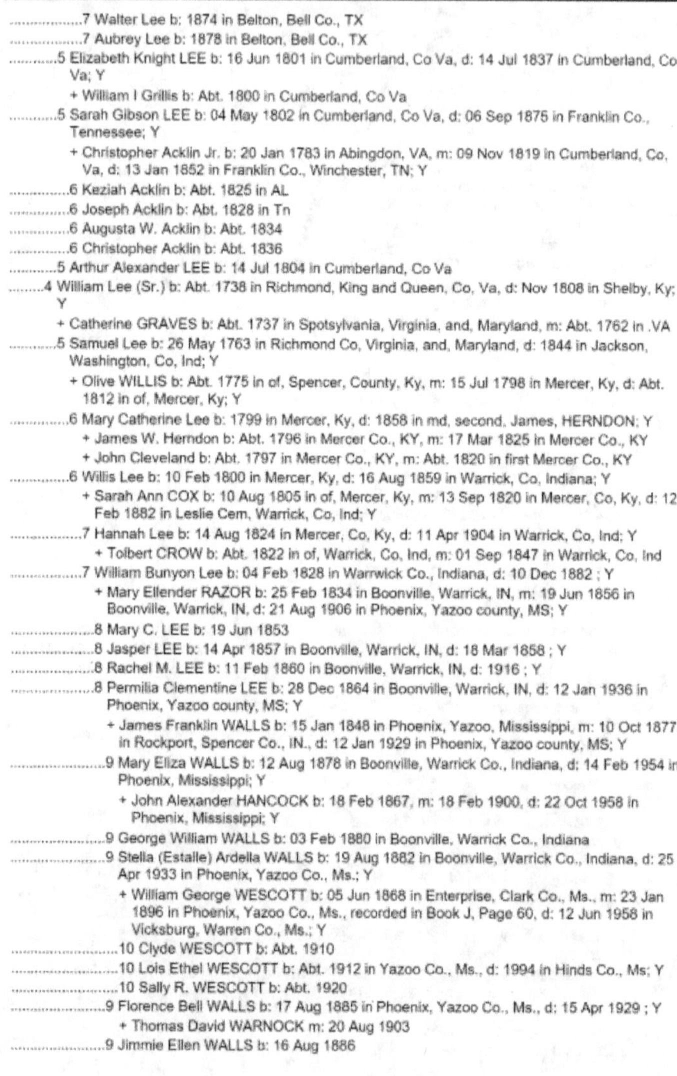

................7 Walter Lee b: 1874 in Belton, Bell Co., TX

................7 Aubrey Lee b: 1878 in Belton, Bell Co., TX

............5 Elizabeth Knight LEE b: 16 Jun 1801 in Cumberland, Co Va, d: 14 Jul 1837 in Cumberland, Co Va; Y

    + William I Grillis b: Abt. 1800 in Cumberland, Co Va

............5 Sarah Gibson LEE b: 04 May 1802 in Cumberland, Co Va, d: 06 Sep 1875 in Franklin Co., Tennessee; Y

    + Christopher Acklin Jr. b: 20 Jan 1783 in Abingdon, VA, m: 09 Nov 1819 in Cumberland, Co, Va, d: 13 Jan 1852 in Franklin Co., Winchester, TN; Y

................6 Keziah Acklin b: Abt. 1825 in AL

................6 Joseph Acklin b: Abt. 1828 in Tn

................6 Augusta W. Acklin b: Abt. 1834

................6 Christopher Acklin b: Abt. 1836

............5 Arthur Alexander LEE b: 14 Jul 1804 in Cumberland, Co Va

.........4 William Lee (Sr.) b: Abt. 1738 in Richmond, King and Queen, Co, Va, d: Nov 1808 in Shelby, Ky; Y

    + Catherine GRAVES b: Abt. 1737 in Spotsylvania, Virginia, and, Maryland, m: Abt. 1762 in .VA

............5 Samuel Lee b: 26 May 1763 in Richmond Co, Virginia, and, Maryland, d: 1844 in Jackson, Washington, Co, Ind; Y

    + Olive WILLIS b: Abt. 1775 in of, Spencer, County, Ky, m: 15 Jul 1798 in Mercer, Ky, d: Abt. 1812 in of, Mercer, Ky; Y

................6 Mary Catherine Lee b: 1799 in Mercer, Ky, d: 1858 in md, second, James, HERNDON; Y

    + James W. Herndon b: Abt. 1796 in Mercer Co., KY, m: 17 Mar 1825 in Mercer Co., KY

    + John Cleveland b: Abt. 1797 in Mercer Co., KY, m: Abt. 1820 in first Mercer Co., KY

................6 Willis Lee b: 10 Feb 1800 in Mercer, Ky, d: 16 Aug 1859 in Warrick, Co, Indiana; Y

    + Sarah Ann COX b: 10 Aug 1805 in of, Mercer, Ky, m: 13 Sep 1820 in Mercer, Co, Ky, d: 12 Feb 1882 in Leslie Cem, Warrick, Co, Ind; Y

................7 Hannah Lee b: 14 Aug 1824 in Mercer, Co, Ky, d: 11 Apr 1904 in Warrick, Co, Ind; Y

    + Tolbert CROW b: Abt. 1822 in of, Warrick, Co, Ind, m: 01 Sep 1847 in Warrick, Co, Ind

................7 William Bunyon Lee b: 04 Feb 1828 in Warrwick Co., Indiana, d: 10 Dec 1882 ; Y

    + Mary Ellender RAZOR b: 25 Feb 1834 in Boonville, Warrick, IN, m: 19 Jun 1856 in Boonville, Warrick, IN, d: 21 Aug 1906 in Phoenix, Yazoo county, MS; Y

................8 Mary C. LEE b: 19 Jun 1853

................8 Jasper LEE b: 14 Apr 1857 in Boonville, Warrick, IN, d: 18 Mar 1858 ; Y

................8 Rachel M. LEE b: 11 Feb 1860 in Boonville, Warrick, IN, d: 1916 ; Y

................8 Permilia Clementine LEE b: 28 Dec 1864 in Boonville, Warrick, IN, d: 12 Jan 1936 in Phoenix, Yazoo county, MS; Y

    + James Franklin WALLS b: 15 Jan 1848 in Phoenix, Yazoo, Mississippi, m: 10 Oct 1877 in Rockport, Spencer Co., IN., d: 12 Jan 1929 in Phoenix, Yazoo county, MS; Y

................9 Mary Eliza WALLS b: 12 Aug 1878 in Boonville, Warrick Co., Indiana, d: 14 Feb 1954 in Phoenix, Mississippi; Y

    + John Alexander HANCOCK b: 18 Feb 1867, m: 18 Feb 1900, d: 22 Oct 1958 in Phoenix, Mississippi; Y

................9 George William WALLS b: 03 Feb 1880 in Boonville, Warrick Co., Indiana

................9 Stella (Estalle) Ardella WALLS b: 19 Aug 1882 in Boonville, Warrick Co., Indiana, d: 25 Apr 1933 in Phoenix, Yazoo Co., Ms.; Y

    + William George WESCOTT b: 05 Jun 1868 in Enterprise, Clark Co., Ms., m: 23 Jan 1896 in Phoenix, Yazoo Co., Ms., recorded in Book J, Page 60, d: 12 Jun 1958 in Vicksburg, Warren Co., Ms.; Y

................10 Clyde WESCOTT b: Abt. 1910

................10 Lois Ethel WESCOTT b: Abt. 1912 in Yazoo Co., Ms., d: 1994 in Hinds Co., Ms; Y

................10 Sally R. WESCOTT b: Abt. 1920

................9 Florence Bell WALLS b: 17 Aug 1885 in Phoenix, Yazoo Co., Ms., d: 15 Apr 1929 ; Y

    + Thomas David WARNOCK m: 20 Aug 1903

................9 Jimmie Ellen WALLS b: 16 Aug 1886

...................9 Frank Napolin WALLS b: 13 Jun 1888 in Phoenix, Yazoo Co., Ms., d: 28 May 1927 in
MS; Y
+ M. Naomie HICKS b: Apr 1883 in Phoenix, Yazoo Co., Ms., m: 25 Oct 1916 in Ms??,
d: 31 Dec 1929 in Mississippi; Y
...................10 James WALLS b: 1918 in MS, d: 1929 in MS; Y
...................10 Bill (William Anderson) WALLS b: Abt. 1920
...................10 George Franklin WALLS b: 20 Nov 1922 in MS
...................10 Joe (Joseph Albert) WALLS d: 1927 in MS; Y
...................9 Addie Trudie WALLS b: 25 Oct 1890 in Phoenix, Yazoo Co., Ms., d: 29 Jun 1969 in
Phoenix, Mississippi; Y
+ Joseph Thomas PARKER b: 28 Nov 1882, m: 25 Oct 1906, d: 09 Jul 1966 in
Phoenix, Mississippi; Y
...................10 Sadie PARKER b: 18 May 1912 in Yazoo Co., Ms., d: 13 Jun 1998 ; Y
...................9 Janie (Nancy Jane) WALLS b: 11 Nov 1892 in Phoenix, Yazoo Co., Ms., d: 26 Mar
1981 in Canton, Madison Co, Mississippi; Y
+ Tom (Thomas Carter) HICKS Jr b: 22 Aug 1885 in Warren County, Mississippi, m: 16
Oct 1906, d: 19 Mar 1950 ; Y
...................10 Annie Mae HICKS b: 06 Jun 1908 in Phoenix, Mississippi, d: 09 Jan 1974 in
Canton, Madison Co, Mississippi; Y
...................10 Jim (James Thomas) HICKS b: 30 Sep 1911 in Mississippi, d: 24 Mar 1981 in
Phoenix, Mississippi; Y
...................9 Pearl Lee WALLS b: 06 Feb 1895 in Phoenix, Yazoo Co., Ms., d: 09 Dec 1963 ; Y
+ Albert Jackson GALLOWAY b: 22 Jul 1887, m: 02 Mar 1909, d: 04 Oct 1941 ; Y
...................9 Lillie Mae WALLS b: 21 Dec 1896 in Phoenix, Yazoo Co., Ms., d: 09 Aug 1963 in
Phoenix, Yazoo county, MS; Y
...................9 Nellie (Nell Maude) WALLS b: 14 Aug 1899 in Phoenix, Yazoo Co., Mississippi, d: 18
Oct 1952 in Mississippi (Wesley Chapel Cem. At Phoenix, Ms.); Y
+ Joe (Joseph Wilson) HICKS b: 25 Dec 1889 in Philidelphia, Mississippi, m: 27 Jan
1914 in Phoenix, Yazoo Co., MS- Recorded in Book I, Page 200, d: 09 Mar 1951 in
Mississippi (Wesley Chapel Cem. At Phoenix, Ms.); Y
...................10 Neil Busby ((Nellie Bee) HICKS b: 09 Dec 1914 in Mississippi, d: 06 Jun 1997 in
Canton, Madison Co, Mississippi 39046; Y
...................10 Joe Brooks HICKS b: 25 May 1920 in Mississippi, d: 18 Sep 1981 in Picayune,
Mississippi 39466; Y
...................10 Thomas Jackson HICKS b: 29 Jan 1925 in Phoenix, Mississippi, d: 30 Sep 2000 in
Haughton, Louisiana; Y
...................8 Hannah Lavina LEE b: 17 May 1867 in Boonville, Warrick, IN, d: 09 Sep 1937 ; Y
...................8 George Bunyon LEE b: 19 Aug 1869 in Boonville, Warrick, IN, d: 22 Jan 1945 ; Y
...................8 William Jacob LEE b: 08 Sep 1870 in Perry County, MS ??, d: 12 Aug 1919 in MS; Y
+ Eva Ardella WALLS b: 06 Nov 1878 in Phoenix, Yazoo Co., Mississippi, m: 04 Feb
1895 in Phoenix, Yazoo Co., Mississippi, d: 03 Oct 1900 in Phoenix, Yazoo Co.,
Mississippi; Y
...................9 Grace LEE b: 27 Jul 1896
+ Steve Greene
...................9 Nellie LEE d: 1933 ; Y
+ Isaac "Ike" FOSTER
...................9 Daughter LEE
+ Elizabeth "Bettie" SANDERS b: 16 Feb 1880, d: 23 Apr 1952 ; Y
...................9 Gertrude Cornetius LEE b: 23 Oct 1902, d: 02 Sep 1981 ; Y
+ Ollie BRYANT
+ Archie SUBER
+ Hubert ROUTH
...................9 Leonard Douglas LEE b: 13 Jul 1908, d: 20 Nov 1959 ; Y
+ Livivg SCHOLTS
...................9 Myrtle LEE b: 23 Feb 1914, d: 20 May 1987 in Jackson, Ms; Y

+ Ruzy Lester POWELL b: 20 Dec 1901 in Warren Co., MS, d: 06 Feb 1990 ; Y
...................10 Living POWELL
...................10 Living POWELL
...................10 Living POWELL
...................10 Living POWELL
+ CHAMBERS
...................9 Living LEE
...................9 Living LEE
+ COODY
...................9 Livivg LEE
+ Living CAMPBELL
...................9 Living LEE
+ PITCHFORD
...................8 Sarah A. LEE b: 10 Feb 1873 in Boonville, Warrick, IN
...................7 Washington HALE Lee b: 10 Dec 1829 in Mercer, Co, Ky, d: 02 Oct 1902 in Warrick, Co, Ind; Y
+ Louisa LESLIE b: Abt. 1830 in of, Warrick, Co, Ind, m: 12 Mar 1850 in Warrick, Co, Ind, d: Warwick Co., Ind; Y
...................8 William Lee b: 1856 in Warwick Co., Ind
...................8 John Lee b: 1859 in Warwick Co., Ind
...................8 Sarah C. Lee b: 1861 in Warwick Co., Ind
...................8 Hannah E Lee b: 1872 in Warwick Co., Ind
+ Sarah E b: 1846 in Warwick Co., Ind, m: Warwick Co., Ind
...................8 Margaret J. Lee b: Feb 1870 in Warwick Co., Ind
...................7 Nancy Jane Lee b: Abt. 1834 in Mercer, Co, Ky, d: 29 Dec 1859 in Warrick, Co, Ind; Y
+ Samuel CROW b: Abt. 1830 in of, Warrick, Co, Ind, m: 20 Mar 1851 in Warrick, Co, Ind, d: 02 Feb 1865 in Florence, SC; Y
...................8 Hannah Armatilda CROW b: 03 Jul 1852 in Owen TWP, Warrick, Co, Ind, d: 27 Jan 1902 in Ohio, twp, Warrick, Ind; Y
...................8 Sarah e CROW b: 15 Oct 1854 in Owen TWP, Warrick, Co, Ind
...................7 Rebecca Lee b: 03 Feb 1837 in Mercer, Co, Ky, d: 25 Mar 1900 in Boone TWP, Warrick, Co, Ind; Y
+ Samuel CROW b: Abt. 1830 in of, Warrick, Co, Ind, m: 01 May 1862 in Warrick, Co, Ind, d: 02 Feb 1865 in Florence, SC; Y
...................7 Celisia Malissa Lee b: 1838 in Mercer, Co, Ky
+ HARRISON CROW b: Abt. 1838 in of, Warrick, Co, Ind, m: 07 Feb 1861 in Warrick, Co, Ind
...................7 Greenup Goldsmith Lee b: 1841 in Mercer, Co, Ky, d: 1918 ; Y
+ Elizabeth Charlotte McNeely b: 09 Oct 1841 in of, Warrick, Co, Ind, m: 03 Aug 1865 in Warrick, Co, Ind
...................8 Edna Cora LEE b: Abt. 1867
+ Eugene CAMP b: Abt. 1865 in Gibson County, Indiana, m: 10 Apr 1890 in Gibson County, Indiana
...................9 ten see notes CAMP b: Abt. 1891 in Gibson County, Indiana
...................8 Effie Lee b: Abt. 1869 in Gibson County, Indiana
+ William SYMONDS b: Abt. 1867 in Gibson County, Indiana, m: 17 May 1903 in Gibson County, Indiana
...................9 ten children see notes SYMONDS b: Abt. 1904 in Gibson County, Indiana
...................8 James H. Lee b: 1872 in Gibson County, Indiana
+ Amanda LOWE b: Abt. 1874 in Gibson County, Indiana, m: 28 Jun 1903 in Gibson County, Indiana
...................8 Naomi Jane Lee b: 1876 in Gibson County, Indiana
+ James IGLEHEART b: Abt. 1874 in Gibson County, Indiana, m: Abt. 1905 in Gibson County, Indiana
...................9 Elizabeth IGLEHEART b: Abt. 1906 in Gibson County, Indiana

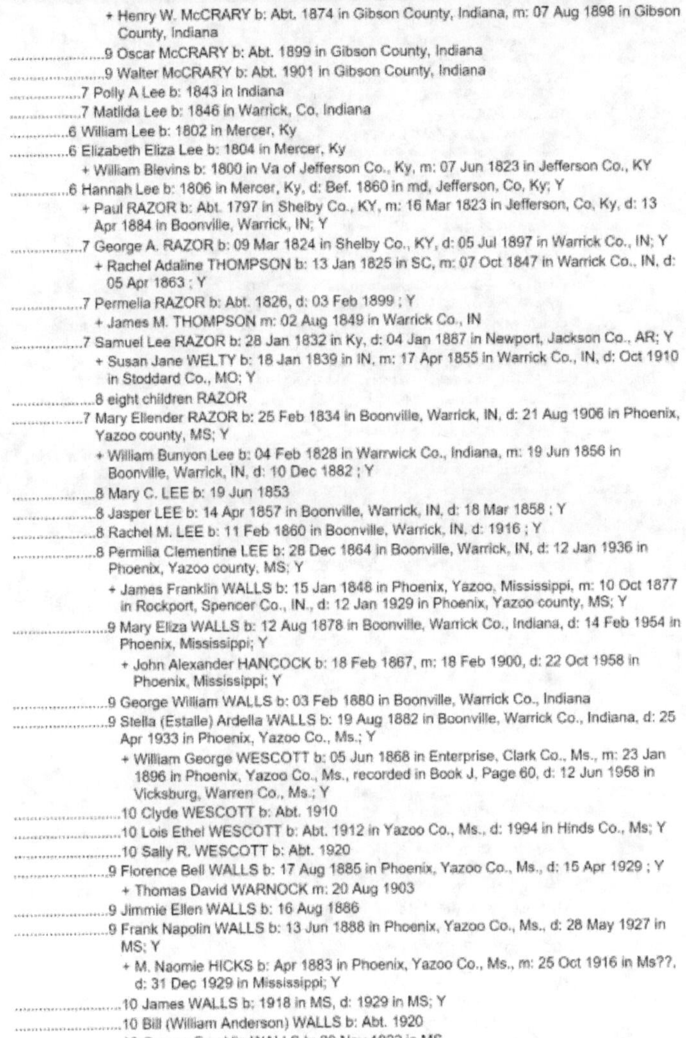

+ Henry W. McCRARY b: Abt. 1874 in Gibson County, Indiana, m: 07 Aug 1898 in Gibson County, Indiana
...............9 Oscar McCRARY b: Abt. 1899 in Gibson County, Indiana
...............9 Walter McCRARY b: Abt. 1901 in Gibson County, Indiana
...............7 Polly A Lee b: 1843 in Indiana
...............7 Matilda Lee b: 1846 in Warrick, Co, Indiana
............6 William Lee b: 1802 in Mercer, Ky
............6 Elizabeth Eliza Lee b: 1804 in Mercer, Ky
+ William Blevins b: 1800 in Va of Jefferson Co., Ky, m: 07 Jun 1823 in Jefferson Co., KY
............6 Hannah Lee b: 1806 in Mercer, Ky, d: Bef. 1860 in md, Jefferson, Co, Ky; Y
+ Paul RAZOR b: Abt. 1797 in Shelby Co., KY, m: 16 Mar 1823 in Jefferson, Co, Ky, d: 13 Apr 1884 in Boonville, Warrick, IN; Y
...............7 George A. RAZOR b: 09 Mar 1824 in Shelby Co., KY, d: 05 Jul 1897 in Warrick Co., IN; Y
+ Rachel Adaline THOMPSON b: 13 Jan 1825 in SC, m: 07 Oct 1847 in Warrick Co., IN, d: 05 Apr 1863 ; Y
...............7 Permelia RAZOR b: Abt. 1826, d: 03 Feb 1899 ; Y
+ James M. THOMPSON m: 02 Aug 1849 in Warrick Co., IN
...............7 Samuel Lee RAZOR b: 28 Jan 1832 in Ky, d: 04 Jan 1887 in Newport, Jackson Co., AR; Y
+ Susan Jane WELTY b: 18 Jan 1839 in IN, m: 17 Apr 1855 in Warrick Co., IN, d: Oct 1910 in Stoddard Co., MO; Y
...............8 eight children RAZOR
...............7 Mary Ellender RAZOR b: 25 Feb 1834 in Boonville, Warrick, IN, d: 21 Aug 1906 in Phoenix, Yazoo county, MS; Y
+ William Bunyon Lee b: 04 Feb 1828 in Warrwick Co., Indiana, m: 19 Jun 1856 in Boonville, Warrick, IN, d: 10 Dec 1882 ; Y
...............8 Mary C. LEE b: 19 Jun 1853
...............8 Jasper LEE b: 14 Apr 1857 in Boonville, Warrick, IN, d: 18 Mar 1858 ; Y
...............8 Rachel M. LEE b: 11 Feb 1860 in Boonville, Warrick, IN, d: 1916 ; Y
...............8 Permilia Clementine LEE b: 28 Dec 1864 in Boonville, Warrick, IN, d: 12 Jan 1936 in Phoenix, Yazoo county, MS; Y
+ James Franklin WALLS b: 15 Jan 1848 in Phoenix, Yazoo, Mississippi, m: 10 Oct 1877 in Rockport, Spencer Co., IN., d: 12 Jan 1929 in Phoenix, Yazoo county, MS; Y
...............9 Mary Eliza WALLS b: 12 Aug 1878 in Boonville, Warrick Co., Indiana, d: 14 Feb 1954 in Phoenix, Mississippi; Y
+ John Alexander HANCOCK b: 18 Feb 1867, m: 18 Feb 1900, d: 22 Oct 1958 in Phoenix, Mississippi; Y
...............9 George William WALLS b: 03 Feb 1880 in Boonville, Warrick Co., Indiana
...............9 Stella (Estalle) Ardella WALLS b: 19 Aug 1882 in Boonville, Warrick Co., Indiana, d: 25 Apr 1933 in Phoenix, Yazoo Co., Ms.; Y
+ William George WESCOTT b: 05 Jun 1868 in Enterprise, Clark Co., Ms., m: 23 Jan 1896 in Phoenix, Yazoo Co., Ms., recorded in Book J, Page 60, d: 12 Jun 1958 in Vicksburg, Warren Co., Ms.; Y
...............10 Clyde WESCOTT b: Abt. 1910
...............10 Lois Ethel WESCOTT b: Abt. 1912 in Yazoo Co., Ms., d: 1994 in Hinds Co., Ms; Y
...............10 Sally R. WESCOTT b: Abt. 1920
...............9 Florence Bell WALLS b: 17 Aug 1885 in Phoenix, Yazoo Co., Ms., d: 15 Apr 1929 ; Y
+ Thomas David WARNOCK m: 20 Aug 1903
...............9 Jimmie Ellen WALLS b: 16 Aug 1886
...............9 Frank Napolin WALLS b: 13 Jun 1888 in Phoenix, Yazoo Co., Ms., d: 28 May 1927 in MS; Y
+ M. Naomie HICKS b: Apr 1883 in Phoenix, Yazoo Co., Ms., m: 25 Oct 1916 in Ms??, d: 31 Dec 1929 in Mississippi; Y
...............10 James WALLS b: 1918 in MS, d: 1929 in MS; Y
...............10 Bill (William Anderson) WALLS b: Abt. 1920
...............10 George Franklin WALLS b: 20 Nov 1922 in MS

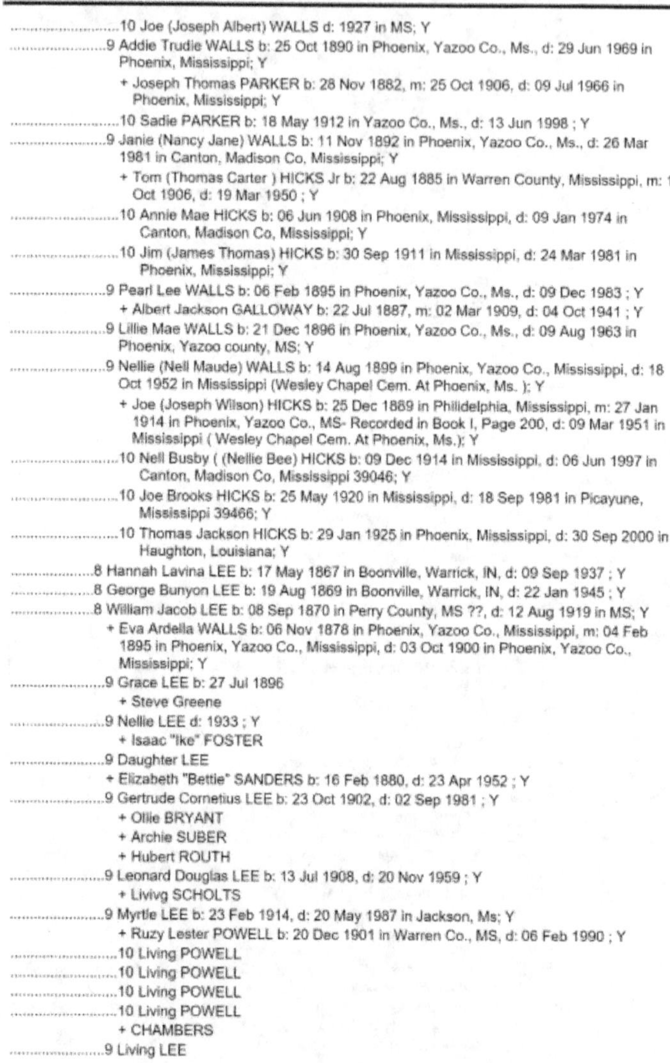

...............10 Joe (Joseph Albert) WALLS d: 1927 in MS; Y
...............9 Addie Trudie WALLS b: 25 Oct 1890 in Phoenix, Yazoo Co., Ms., d: 29 Jun 1969 in
      Phoenix, Mississippi; Y
      + Joseph Thomas PARKER b: 28 Nov 1882, m: 25 Oct 1906, d: 09 Jul 1966 in
        Phoenix, Mississippi; Y
...............10 Sadie PARKER b: 18 May 1912 in Yazoo Co., Ms., d: 13 Jun 1998 ; Y
...............9 Janie (Nancy Jane) WALLS b: 11 Nov 1892 in Phoenix, Yazoo Co., Ms., d: 26 Mar
      1981 in Canton, Madison Co, Mississippi; Y
      + Tom (Thomas Carter) HICKS Jr b: 22 Aug 1885 in Warren County, Mississippi, m: 16
        Oct 1906, d: 19 Mar 1950 ; Y
...............10 Annie Mae HICKS b: 06 Jun 1908 in Phoenix, Mississippi, d: 09 Jan 1974 in
        Canton, Madison Co, Mississippi; Y
...............10 Jim (James Thomas) HICKS b: 30 Sep 1911 in Mississippi, d: 24 Mar 1981 in
        Phoenix, Mississippi; Y
...............9 Pearl Lee WALLS b: 06 Feb 1895 in Phoenix, Yazoo Co., Ms., d: 09 Dec 1983 ; Y
      + Albert Jackson GALLOWAY b: 22 Jul 1887, m: 02 Mar 1909, d: 04 Oct 1941 ; Y
...............9 Lillie Mae WALLS b: 21 Dec 1896 in Phoenix, Yazoo Co., Ms., d: 09 Aug 1963 in
      Phoenix, Yazoo county, MS; Y
...............9 Nellie (Nell Maude) WALLS b: 14 Aug 1899 in Phoenix, Yazoo Co., Mississippi, d: 18
      Oct 1952 in Mississippi (Wesley Chapel Cem. At Phoenix, Ms.); Y
      + Joe (Joseph Wilson) HICKS b: 25 Dec 1889 in Phllidelphia, Mississippi, m: 27 Jan
        1914 in Phoenix, Yazoo Co., MS- Recorded in Book I, Page 200, d: 09 Mar 1951 in
        Mississippi (Wesley Chapel Cem. At Phoenix, Ms.); Y
...............10 Nell Busby ((Nellie Bee) HICKS b: 09 Dec 1914 in Mississippi, d: 06 Jun 1997 in
        Canton, Madison Co, Mississippi 39046; Y
...............10 Joe Brooks HICKS b: 25 May 1920 in Mississippi, d: 18 Sep 1981 in Picayune,
        Mississippi 39466; Y
...............10 Thomas Jackson HICKS b: 29 Jan 1925 in Phoenix, Mississippi, d: 30 Sep 2000 in
        Haughton, Louisiana; Y
...............8 Hannah Lavina LEE b: 17 May 1867 in Boonville, Warrick, IN, d: 09 Sep 1937 ; Y
...............8 George Bunyon LEE b: 19 Aug 1869 in Boonville, Warrick, IN, d: 22 Jan 1945 ; Y
...............8 William Jacob LEE b: 08 Sep 1870 in Perry County, MS ??, d: 12 Aug 1919 in MS; Y
      + Eva Ardella WALLS b: 06 Nov 1878 in Phoenix, Yazoo Co., Mississippi, m: 04 Feb
        1895 in Phoenix, Yazoo Co., Mississippi, d: 03 Oct 1900 in Phoenix, Yazoo Co.,
        Mississippi; Y
...............9 Grace LEE b: 27 Jul 1896
      + Steve Greene
...............9 Nellie LEE d: 1933 ; Y
      + Isaac "Ike" FOSTER
...............9 Daughter LEE
      + Elizabeth "Bettie" SANDERS b: 16 Feb 1880, d: 23 Apr 1952 ; Y
...............9 Gertrude Cornetius LEE b: 23 Oct 1902, d: 02 Sep 1981 ; Y
      + Ollie BRYANT
      + Archie SUBER
      + Hubert ROUTH
...............9 Leonard Douglas LEE b: 13 Jul 1908, d: 20 Nov 1959 ; Y
      + Livivg SCHOLTS
...............9 Myrtle LEE b: 23 Feb 1914, d: 20 May 1987 in Jackson, Ms; Y
      + Ruzy Lester POWELL b: 20 Dec 1901 in Warren Co., MS, d: 06 Feb 1990 ; Y
...............10 Living POWELL
...............10 Living POWELL
...............10 Living POWELL
...............10 Living POWELL
      + CHAMBERS
...............9 Living LEE

.................9 Living LEE
     + COODY
.................9 Livivg LEE
     + Living CAMPBELL
.................9 Living LEE
     + PITCHFORD
.................8 Sarah A. LEE b: 10 Feb 1873 in Boonville, Warrick, IN
.................7 Rebecca L. RAZOR b: 10 Feb 1836 in Boonville, Warrick, IN, d: 12 Dec 1895 in Boonville,
    Warrick, IN; Y
     + Thomas FISHER b: Abt. 1834 in IN, m: 13 Jun 1858 in Warrick Co., IN
.................7 Paul the 3rd RAZOR b: Abt. 1838 in IN, d: Augusta, AR; Y
     + Mariah TAYLOR b: Abt. 1840 in IN, m: 02 Dec 1869 in Warrick Co., IN
.................7 William H. RAZOR b: Abt. 1840 in IN
.................7 Hannah E. RAZOR b: Abt. 1842 in IN
     + Talbot CROW
.................7 Thomas J. RAZOR b: Abt. 1845 in IN
     + Surilda THOMPSON b: 18 Jul 1854, m: 25 Jul 1872 in Warrick Co., IN
.................6 John Lee b: 1807 in Mercer, Ky
.................6 Samuel Lee b: 30 Sep 1808 in Mercer, Ky, d: Warrwick Co., Indiana; Y
    + Nancy MORELAND b: 1814 in Warrwick Co., Indiana, m: Abt. 1832 in Warrwick Co.,
    Indiana, d: Warwick Co., Ind; Y
.................7 Olive Lee b: 1833 in Warrwick Co., Indiana
    + CLAYTON W. ARMSTRONG b: Abt. 1831 in Boonville, Warrick Co., Indiana, m: 17 May
    1853 in Boonville, Warrick Co., Indiana
.................7 Millie Lee b: 1835 in Warrwick Co., Indiana
.................7 William Carrol Lee b: 1836, d: 1879 ; Y
    + Hannah Langford b: Abt. 1838 in Indiana
.................8 William Frederick Lee b: 1859 in Warrwick Co., Indiana
.................8 Nancy M Lee b: 1863 in Warrwick Co., Ind
.................8 Olive Lee b: 1867 in Warrwick Co., Indiana
.................8 Florie Lee b: 1869 in Warrwick Co., Indiana
.................8 Early Marshall Lee b: 04 Dec 1875, d: Feb 1966 ; Y
    + Ethel Trafina Eilenberger b: 14 Dec 1884, m: Abt. 1902, d: Sep 1956 ; Y
.................9 Sharlett Vanona Lee b: 20 Jul 1903, d: 02 Aug 1978 in Bandera, Texas; Y
    + King Robert Buchanan d: 02 Aug 1978 in Bandera, Texas; Y
.................10 Vanona Ruth Buchanan b: 05 Aug 1926 in Pt. Arthur, Texas, d: 02 Aug 1978 in
    Bandera, Texas; Y
.................10 Living Buchanan
.................10 Living Buchanan
.................9 Donnel Curtis Lee b: Jan 1911, d: 17 Dec 1981 ; Y
.................9 Juanita Lee b: Feb 1914
.................9 girl Lee
.................9 girl two Lee
.................9 girl three Lee
.................9 total 7 ch Lee b: M, f, f, f
.................7 Nancy Ann Lee b: 1838 in Warrwick Co., Indiana, d: Bef. 1883 ; Y
    + Philetus Piletus Campbell b: 17 Feb 1836 in Cuyhogga Co., Ohio, m: Abt. 1858, d: 13
    May 1901 in Warrwick Co., Indiana; Y
.................8 Ermina A. Campbell b: 1860 in Warrwick Co., Ind
.................8 Julia M. Campbell b: 1862 in Warrwick Co., Indiana
.................8 William Oliver Campbell b: 1866 in Warrwick Co., Indiana, d: 31 Jul 1902 in oklahoma
    (just moved there); Y
    + Martha Jane Cottrell b: 16 Jul 1870 in Scott Township, Vanderburgh Co., Indi, m: 03
    Mar 1887 in Warrwick Co., Indiana

.................9 Lawrence Clifford Campbell b: 07 Sep 1889 in Boonville, Warrwick Co., Indiana, d: Dec 1990 in Centralia, Nemaha, Kansas; Y

+ Margaret Howell b: 1890 in Garnett, Andeson Co., KS, m: 1909 in Garnett, Andeson Co., KS, d: 1960 in Centralia, Nemaha, Kansas; Y

.................10 Charles Albert Campbell b: 30 Jul 1913 in Oskaloosa, Jefferson, Kansas

.................10 Dorothy Mae Campbell b: 16 Apr 1929 in Junction City, KS, d: 27 Dec 2002 in Very III Nov 2002; Y

+ Jack Michael Stemper b: 04 Apr 1919 in Bellwood, Butler Co., Kansas, m: Abt. 1930 in of Kansas

.................11 Linda Stemper b: 24 Apr 1949 in Omaha, Sarpy co., KS, d: lives in LIncoln, NEB; Y

+ BAtliner b: Abt. 1932

+ JENSEN m: Abt. 1971

.................12 Lia Michelle JENSEN b: 04 Sep 1973 in Neb

.................12 Brian Reed JENSEN b: 07 Feb 1976 in Neb

.................10 Helen Campbell d: DDerby KS; Y

.................10 Margaret Campbell d: living 2002 Federricksburg, VA; Y

.................9 Lawrence Campbell b: Abt. 1890 in Warrwick Co., Indiana

+ Mary Margaret HOWELL

.................10 Dorothy Campbell

+ Stemper

.................9 Ethel Campbell b: Abt. 1892 in Warrwick Co., Indiana, d: Booneville, Warrwick Co., IN, age 3 Idress caught fire; Y

.................8 Willa C. Campbell b: 1870 in Warrwick Co., Indiana

+ Nancy LUTZ b: Abt. 1868 in Warrwick Co., Indiana, m: Feb 1887

.................8 Grace Campbell b: Abt. 1871 in Warrwick Co., Indiana

.................8 Ethel Campbell b: Abt. 1873 in Warrwick Co., Indiana, d: Abt. 1874 in baby sister died as baby; Y

.................7 Samuel J. Lee b: 1841 in Warrwick Co., Indiana

.................7 Sarah J. Lee b: 1843 in Warrwick Co., Indiana

.................7 John W. Lee b: 1845 in Boon, Warrwick Co., Indiana

.................7 George S Lee b: 1848 in Warrwick Co., Indiana

.................7 Henry W Lee b: Feb 1850 in Boonville, Warrick Co., Indiana

.................7 Simon Lee b: 1852 in Warwick Co., Ind

+ Rachel Wood or Mrs Duttin b: 1824 in Ky, m: 28 Oct 1858 in of Warwick Co., Ind

.................7 Joseph Lee b: 1859 in Warwick Co., Ind

.................6 Thomas Lee b: Abt. 1810 in Mercer Co., KY

+ Mary Margaret Mitchell b: Abt. 1790 in of, Mercer, Co, Ky, m: 15 Jan 1813 in Mercer, Co, Ky, second wife

.................5 William Lee (Jr.) b: 28 Aug 1768 in Richmond Co, Va, Hardy, W.Va., d: 26 Dec 1844 in Washington, Co, Ind; Y

+ Jane Mitchell b: 18 May 1774 in NC, of, Spring Mill, Washington, Indiana, m: 11 Feb 1792 in Mercer, Co, Ky, d: 26 Dec 1844 in Spring Mill, Washington, Ind; Y

.................6 Elizabeth Lee b: 22 Nov 1792 in Mercer Co., Ky, d: 04 Jul 1833 in Salem, Washington Co., (Cholera), Ind; Y

.................6 Jonathan Lee b: 26 Jul 1795 in Mercer Co., Ky, d: 13 Jul 1862 in Jackson Co., Ind; Y

+ Deborah BRITTAIN b: 05 Dec 1793 in VA, m: 06 Feb 1817 in Shelby Co., KY, d: 31 Dec 1866 in Jackson Co., IN; Y

.................7 Samuel Lee b: 27 Mar 1818 in Washinton Co., Indiana, d: 09 Feb 1910 in Jackson Co., Indiana; Y

+ Mary Polly KILLEY b: 19 Jan 1819 in Carter Co., Tennessee, m: 30 Aug 1838 in Jonesboro, Washington Co., Tn, d: 30 Jul 1886 in Hempstead Co., Arkansas; Y

.................8 Joshua Kelly Lee b: 1839 in Jackson Co., Indiana, d: 1903 ; Y

.................8 Jonathan Lee b: 1841 in Jackson Co., Indiana, d: 1921 ; Y

.................8 Robert Lee b: 1849 in Jackson Co., Indiana

................8 Isabel Lee b: 1854 in Jackson Co., Indiana
................8 Mary Esther Lee b: 1859 in Jackson Co., Indiana
................7 Jane ELizabetth Lee b: Abt. 1819 in Jackson Co., Indiana, d: Abt. 1847 in Jackson Co.,
            Indiana; Y
            + Kinchen KILLEY b: Jonesboro, Washington Co., Tennessee, m: 14 Nov 1839 in Jackson
              Co., Indiana
................8 Levi KILLEY b: 09 Jul 1842 in Jackson Co., Indiana
................8 Deborah "Debby" KILLEY b: 17 Mar 1844 in Jackson Co., Indiana
................7 Mary Polly Lee b: Abt. 1822 in Jackson Co., Indiana
................7 William Lee b: Abt. 1827 in Jackson Co., Indiana
................7 Sarah Lee b: 28 Jun 1829 in Jackson Co., Indiana, d: 23 May 1857 ; Y
            + Kinchen KILLEY b: Jonesboro, Washington Co., Tennessee, m: 10 Feb 1848 in Jackson
              Co., Indiana
................8 Jonathan KILLEY b: 1849 in Jackson Co., Indiana
................8 Elizabeth KILLEY b: 1852 in Jackson Co., Indiana
................8 Mary J. KILLEY b: 1854 in Jackson Co., Indiana
................7 John Lee b: Abt. 1832 in Jackson Co., Indiana
            + Lydia b: 1826, m: Abt. 1850 in Jackson Co., IN
................8 Elizabeth Lee b: 1859 in Jackson Co., IN
................8 John Lee b: 1951 in Jackson Co., IN
................6 William Lee b: 28 Jul 1796 in Mercer, Ky
            + Rosannah HARRYMAN b: Abt. 1805 in of Washington Co., IN, m: 24 Jan 1826 in
              Washington CO., IN
................6 Mitchell Lee b: 24 Jul 1798 in Mercer Co., Ky, d: 15 Jul 1871 in Washington, County, Ind; Y
            + Sarah * WRIGHT b: 20 Jul 1800 in Kentucky, m: 24 Jan 1826 in Livonia, Washington Co.,
              Indiana
................7 Martha Jane LEE b: Mar 1827 in Washington, Indiana
................7 Joseph Green LEE b: 16 Dec 1828 in Livonia, Washington Co., Indiana
................7 Arretta LEE b: 10 Mar 1830 in Washington, Indiana
................6 Kate Lee b: 21 Sep 1800 in Washington, County, Ind
................6 Sarah Lee b: 10 Apr 1803 in Washington, County, Ind, d: 27 Nov 1855 in Monroe Co., Ind; Y
................6 Samuel Lee b: 06 May 1805 in Shelby, Co, Ky, d: 25 Sep 1848 in Washington Co., IN; Y
            + Rebecca COLGLAZER b: 1810 in of, Ohio, m: 28 Dec 1830 in Washington, Co, Ind, d:
              1905 ; Y
................7 Christina Jane Tina Lee b: 15 Sep 1832 in Washington, Co, Ind, d: Sep 1924 in Labette,
            Kansas; Y
            + Francis CLICK b: Abt. 1830 in of, Washington, Co, Ind, m: no children
................7 David William Lee b: 29 Mar 1838 in Washington, Co, Ind, d: 1908 in Mitchell, Lawrence,
            Indiana; Y
            + Harriet Newell Godfrey b: Abt. 1840 in Mitchell, Lawrence, Ind, m: Abt. 1865 in
              Washington, Co, Ind, d: Mitchell, Lawrence, Ind; Y
................8 Alonzo Ellsworth Lee b: 05 Apr 1867 in Campbellsburg, Washington, Co, Ind, d: 05 Feb
            1963 in Eugene, Ore; Y
            + Anna McMunn b: Abt. 1869 in of, Washington, Co, Ind
................9 Howard Lee b: Abt. 1892 in of, Washington, Co, Ind
................9 GLENN Lee b: Abt. 1894 in of, Washington, Co, Ind
................9 Lawrence Lee b: Abt. 1897 in of, Washington, Co, Ind
................9 Inez Lee b: Abt. 1900 in of, Washington, Co, Ind
................8 Emma Louise Lee b: 04 Sep 1868 in Mitchell, Lawrence, Ind, d: 08 Apr 1953 in Parsons,
            Labette, Kansas; Y
            + Anson Burlingame Carter b: 16 Oct 1854 in Washington, Co, Ind, m: 12 Nov 1894, d:
              Jul 1908 in Labette, Labette, Kansas; Y
................9 Clifford MURRAY Carter b: 09 Oct 1895 in of, Labette, Co, Kansas, d: Aug 1980 in
            Parsons, Labette, Kansas; Y

...................9 Francis Edward Carter b: 22 Aug 1897 in of, Labette, Co, Kansas, d: 27 Nov 1988 in Parsons, Labette, Kansas; Y

...................9 Delbert Fred Carter b: 02 Dec 1900 in of, Labette, Co, Kansas, d: 09 Feb 1990 in Parsons, Labette, Ks; Y

+ Beaula WILSON b: Abt. 1902 in of, Labette, Co, Kansas

...................10 Jack Carter b: Abt. 1925 in of, Labette, Co, Kansas

+ Rita HYATT b: Abt. 1928

...................11 Rodney Carter b: Abt. 1950

...................11 Stephen Carter b: Abt. 1955

...................11 Deb Deborah Carter b: Abt. 1958

...................10 Patricia Carter b: Abt. 1928 in of, Labette, Co, Kansas

...................9 Mabel Carter b: 18 Aug 1902 in of, Labette, Co, Kansas, d: Aft. 1992 ; Y

+ Roy Jones b: Abt. 1900 in of, Labette, Co, Kansas

...................10 Leroy Jones b: Abt. 1927 in of, Labette, Co, Kansas

...................10 Kenneth Jones b: Abt. 1929 in of, Labette, Co, Kansas

...................9 Burliegh Lee Carter b: 01 Jul 1906 in of, Labette, Co, Kansas, d: 20 Feb 1963 in Oswego, Labette, Kansas; Y

+ Zelma Elaine LANSDOWN b: 19 Apr 1917 in Parsons, Labette, Co, Kansas, m: 20 Feb 1936 in Oswego, Labette, Ks, d: Aft. 1992 ; Y

...................10 Ronald Keith Carter b: 29 Aug 1939 in Parsons, Labette, Co, Kansas

+ Margaret Karen KASTEN b: 07 Mar 1944 in Jackson, Cape Giraideau, Mo, m: 03 Aug 1968 in McClelland, AFB, Sacramento, CA

...................11 Christine Marie Carter b: 18 Dec 1969 in Mather, AFB, Sacramento, CA

...................11 Gabrellia Louise Carter b: 04 Sep 1973 in Homestead, AFB, Dade, FL

...................10 William Lee Carter b: 04 Nov 1944 in Parsons, Labette, Co, Kansas

+ Louita Burke b: Abt. 1946 in of, Labette, Ks, m: Abt. 1970 in of, Kansas

...................11 Ronald Shawn Carter b: 1966 in of, Labette, Ks

...................11 Donna Sue Ellis Carter b: Abt. 1969 in of, Labette, Ks

...................10 Joan Carol Carter b: Parsons, Labette, Co, Kansas

+ GORDON HARPER b: Abt. 1936 in of, Labette, Ks, m: 22 Sep 1957 in Parsons, Labette, Ks

...................11 Skyler Wayne HARPER b: 1958 in Parsons, Labette, Ks

...................11 SCOTT David HARPER b: 1960 in Parsons, Labette, Ks

...................11 Shari Dawn HARPER b: 1961 in Parsons, Labette, Ks

...................11 Suzzane Carol HARPER b: 1963 in Parsons, Labette, Ks

...................9 Pearl Newell Carter b: Aug 1908 in of, Labette, Co, Kansas

+ Dermit Loren RICH b: Abt. 1906 in of, Labette, Co, Kansas, m: Parsons, Labette, Kansas

...................10 Merle Dean RICH b: Abt. 1938 in of, Labette, Co, Kansas

...................10 DARRELL RICH b: Abt. 1940 in of, Labette, Co, Kansas

+ James Rose b: Abt. 1905

...................10 Betty Rose b: Abt. 1932 in of, Labette, Co, Kansas

+ James LANDIS

...................11 Ronald LANDIS

...................11 Caroline LANDIS

...................11 John LANDIS

...................11 Catherine LANDIS

...................10 Dorothy Rose b: Abt. 1936 in of, Labette, Co, Kansas

+ Wayne STRINGER

...................11 Vickie STRINGER

...................11 Tim STRINGER

...................11 Susan STRINGER

...................11 Lucy STRINGER

...................8 Orlo Mitchell Lee b: 14 Apr 1870 in Mitchell, Lawrence, Ind, d: Parsons, Labette, Kansas; Y

+ Jessica Shoemaker b: Abt. 1872 in of, Washington, Co, Ind, d: Labette, Kansas; Y
...............9 Ohma Lee b: Abt. 1895 in of, Labette, Kansas
...............9 Velma Lee b: Abt. 1897 in of, Labette, Kansas
...............9 Lois Lee b: Abt. 1899 in of, Labette, Kansas
...............9 Betty Lee b: Abt. 1902 in of, Labette, Kansas
...............9 Helen Lee b: Abt. 1904 in of, Labette, Kansas
...............8 Carrie Isabella Lee b: 22 Oct 1871 in Mitchell, Lawrence, Ind, d: Mitchell, Lawrence, Ind; Y
+ Thomas NEIDEFFER b: Abt. 1869 in of, Washington, Co, Ind
+ Cindy b: second wife, no children
...............7 Sarah Elizabeth Sallie Lee b: Apr 1848 in Washington, Co, Ind, d: 17 Apr 1946 in Glendale, Los Angeles, CA; Y
+ Sanford Carter b: Abt. 1846 in of, Washington, Co, Ind
...............8 Peter Carter b: Abt. 1880 in of, Washington, Co, Ind
...............8 Orin Carter b: Abt. 1882 in of, Washington, Co, Ind
...............8 Samuel Carter b: Abt. 1884 in of, Washington, Co, Ind
...............6 John Lee b: 28 Jan 1807 in Shelby, County, Ky, d: 1823 ; Y
...............6 Finley or Finlay Lee b: 28 Jan 1809 in Shelby, Co, Ky
...............6 Lucinda Lee b: 03 Dec 1811 in Shelby, Co, Ky
...............6 Benjamin Lee b: 15 Apr 1814 in Shelby, Co, Ky, d: child; Y
...............5 John Lee b: 1771 in Hardy, Co, Va, W.Va., d: 1844 in Mitchell, Washington, Co, Ind; Y
+ Elizabeth Mitchell b: 13 Dec 1777 in NC, m: 18 Oct 1798 in Mercer, County, Ky, d: 15 Sep 1822 in Washington, County, Ind; Y
...............6 Nancy Lee b: 1800 in Mercer, County, Ky, d: of Madison CO., KY; Y
...............6 William Lee b: 10 Dec 1801 in Mercer Co., Ky 1805 of Shelby Co., KY
...............6 Joseph Lee b: Abt. 1802 in Mercer, County, Ky
...............6 Eliza Lee b: Abt. 1804 in Mercer, County, Ky
...............6 Catherine Lee b: Abt. 1804 in Mercer, County, Ky
...............6 Robert Lee b: 07 Nov 1806 in Mercer, County, Ky, d: 01 Jul 1855 ; Y
+ Lucinda OWENS b: 14 Dec 1812 in of, Mitchell, Co, Indiana, m: 10 Mar 1832 in Mitchell, Co, Indiana, d: 19 Feb 1884 ; Y
...............7 William Lee b: 20 Jan 1833 in of, Mitchell, Co, Indiana, d: 15 Jan 1893 ; Y
+ Elizabeth Thomas b: Abt. 1835 in of, Mitchell, Co, Indiana
...............7 Greenup Lee b: 12 Jul 1835 in of, Mitchell, Co, Indiana, d: 04 Aug 1903 ; Y
...............7 Sarah Lee b: 26 Sep 1837 in of, Mitchell, Co, Indiana, d: 16 Apr 1895 ; Y
...............7 Robert Lee b: 07 Apr 1839 in of, Mitchell, Co, Indiana, d: 01 Jul 1863 ; Y
...............7 Elisha B Lee b: 22 Oct 1840 in of, Mitchell, Co, Indiana, d: 30 Jan 1904 ; Y
+ Anna TRINKLE b: 09 Oct 1843 in of, Mitchell, Co, Indiana, m: Abt. 1860, d: 07 Nov 1913 ; Y
...............8 Mary Lee b: 02 May 1861 in of, Mitchell, Co, Indiana, d: 01 Jan 1862 in Mitchell, Co, Ind; Y
...............8 John W. Lee b: 18 Mar 1863 in of, Mitchell, Co, Indiana, d: 17 Nov 1932 ; Y
+ Mary Medlock
...............9 Harry Lee b: 1888 in Mitchell, Indiana, USA
...............9 Ernest Lee b: Abt. 1890
...............8 Delila W. Delta Lee b: 29 Oct 1865 in of, Mitchell, Co, Indiana, d: 20 Mar 1926 ; Y
+ Frank WATTS
...............8 Alonzo Franklin Lee b: 13 Jan 1867 in Washington, Co, Ind, d: 17 Jan 1945 in Salem, Washington, County, Indiana; Y
+ Mellisa Ellen ADAMS b: 02 Oct 1866, m: 01 Dec 1888 in Salem, Ind, d: 26 Sep 1910 in Farm, Salem, Ore; Y
...............9 Lula Blanche Lee b: 03 Apr 1890 in Washington, Co, Ind, d: 04 Apr 1949 in Palmyra, Ind; Y
+ John VORGANG b: Abt. 1890 in of, Ore
...............10 John VORGANG b: Abt. 1915 in of, Palmyra, Ind, d: Abt. 1940 in age, 24; Y

...............10 Letah VORGANG b: Abt. 1916 in of, Palmyra, Ind
...............9 Elmer Lee b: 09 Nov 1892 in Washington, Co, Ind, d: 05 Feb 1897 in Washington, Co, Ind; Y
...............9 Roy Lee b: 01 Oct 1894 in Washington, Co, Ind, d: 17 Sep 1979 ; Y
    + [unknown spouse]
...............10 Gaylord Lee b: Abt. 1920 in Washington, Co, Palmyra, Ind
...............9 Ralph Lee b: 12 May 1897 in Washington, Co, Ind, d: 29 Jun 1955 in Manito, Ill; Y
    + Lydia Florence BOSTON b: 06 Dec 1895 in Farm, North, Palmyra, Ind, m: 1920 in Indianapolis, Indiana, d: 15 Dec 1979 in Milton Freewater, Ore; Y
...............10 Helen Virginia COFFEEN Lee b: 13 May 1921 in Indianapolis, Ind
    + WILLIS Alvin COFFEEN b: 13 May 1921 in Medford, Ore, m: 26 May 1946 in College Place, Wa
...............9 Ray Lee b: 05 Nov 1900 in Farm, near, Salem, Ind, d: 12 Feb 1978 in Milwaukee, Wis; Y
    + Gertrude PURLEE m: 28 Dec 1928
...............10 Paul Lee b: 18 Jun 1930 in Washington, Co, Palmyra, Ind
...............9 Anna Mae Lee b: 07 Apr 1903 in Washington, Co, Ind, d: 03 Jun 1976 in Corydon, Ind; Y
    + Shelby ADAMS b: Abt. 1901 in Washington, Co, Ind, m: 28 Feb 1934 in Ind
...............10 David ADAMS b: Abt. 1940 in of, Corydon, Ind, area
...............10 Mary Ellen ADAMS b: of, Corydon, Ind, area
...............10 Edward ADAMS b: of, Corydon, Ind, area
    + Voyles OTT b: Abt. 1903 in Washington, Co, Ind, m: 28 Feb 1934 in Corydon, Ind, may be first, marriage
...............9 Clyde Lee b: 02 Feb 1907 in Washington, Co, Ind, d: 14 Dec 1981 ; Y
...............9 Clara Belle Lee b: 08 Sep 1907 in Washington, Co, Ind, d: Aft. 1992 ; Y
    + Merle ZINK b: Abt. 1905 in of, Washington, Co, Ind, m: 30 Apr 1966 in Palmyra, Ind
...............8 Robert Lee b: 25 Oct 1869 in Mitchell Co., IN, d: 1954 ; Y
    + Minnie WIRES b: Abt. 1871 in Mitchell Co., IN
...............9 Elva Lee b: 30 Jan 1894 in Orange Co., IND
...............9 Elsie Lee b: 13 Nov 1895 in Orange Co., IND
...............9 Clyde Lee b: 17 Jun 1898 in Orange Co., IND
    + Fannie RIBBLE
...............9 Ralph Lee b: Abt. 1894
...............9 Ray Lee b: Abt. 1895 in Orange Co., IND
...............9 Hallie Lee b: Abt. 1897 in Orange Co., IND
...............9 Mary Ruth Lee b: Abt. 1899 in Orange Co., IND
...............9 Robert Lee b: Abt. 1901 in Orange Co., IND
...............9 Homer Lee
...............9 Faye Lee
...............9 Lois Lee
...............8 Louisa B. Lee b: 12 Mar 1871, d: 1947 ; Y
    + Oscar BIRITH
...............9 Charles BIRITH b: Abt. 1893 in Orange Co., IND
...............9 Clara BIRITH b: Abt. 1895 in Orange Co., IND
...............8 Minnie E. Lee b: 19 Dec 1873 in twin, d: 18 Dec 1943 ; Y
    + Sanford MEADOWS b: 1869
...............9 Eva MEADOWS
...............8 Mintie E. Mittie Lee b: 19 Dec 1873 in twin, d: 09 Feb 1961 ; Y
    + Dan RICHARDSON
...............8 Charles E. Lee b: 12 Apr 1874, d: 21 Jun 1960 ; Y
    + Lydia SWARMS
...............9 Edna Lee b: adopted
...............8 Bruce "H. Bruce" Lee b: 24 Jul 1876, d: 20 Jun 1949 ; Y

```
                    + Abby Voyles b: 1880
.....................9 Opal Lee b: 1902
.....................9 Noble Lee
.....................9 Lola Lee
                    + Lelia GASSWAY b: 1880 in second wife, m: second wife
.....................8 Lillian J. Lillie Lee b: Nov 1879, d: 25 Jul 1974 ; Y
                    + Otto SCHAEFER b: 1875
.....................9 Lee SCHAEFER b: 1901
.....................9 Hazel SCHAEFER b: Abt. 1903
.....................9 Edythe SCHAEFER b: Abt. 1905
.....................8 Jessie Lee b: 25 Jul 1882, d: 13 May 1907 ; Y
                    + Inez ROUT
.....................9 Jesse Lee b: Abt. 1905
.....................9 Clyde Lee
.....................8 infant girl b: 1883
.....................7 Mary Lee b: 08 Sep 1842 in of, Mitchell, Co, Indiana, d: 1912 ; Y
                    + WRIGHT
.....................7 Melissa Lee b: 30 May 1844 in of, Mitchell, Co, Indiana
                    + STARK
.....................7 John Lee b: Abt. 1846 in Ky, later, Mitchell, Ind
.....................7 Phoebe Lee b: Abt. 1848
.....................7 Lucinda Lee b: 07 Nov 1850 in of, Mitchell, Co, Indiana
                    + Henry McKinley
.....................7 Martha Lee b: 23 Dec 1851 in of, Mitchell, Co, Indiana, d: 18 Oct 1938 ; Y
                    + James THIXRON b: 04 Nov 1844, d: 18 Jan 1932 ; Y
.................6 Greenup Lee b: Abt. 1810 in of, Washington, Indiana, d: 1858 in Putnam County, Indiana; Y
                    + Virginia J. Walls b: Abt. 1823 in Putnam County, Indiana, m: 1843 in Putnam County,
                      Indiana, d: Aft. 1880 in Putnam County, Indiana; Y
.....................7 Sarah Ella Lee b: Abt. 1853 in Greencastle, Putnam, Indiana
                    + Charles W. Daggy b: Abt. 1844 in Putnam County, Indiana, m: 1873 in Putnam County,
                      Indiana
.....................8 Minnie Daggy b: 1875 in Greencastle, Putnam, Indiana
.................6 Lewis Lee b: Abt. 1812 in of, Washington, Indiana
.................6 Frances Lee b: Abt. 1814 in of, Washington, Indiana
.............5 Caty Lee b: 17 Mar 1772 in Richmond Co, Virginia, of Hardy, W.Va., d: Shelbyville, Shelby Co.,
             Kentucky; Y
                    + HUDSON HAMMOND b: 01 Feb 1769 in of, Woodford, Co, Ky, m: 12 Feb 1793 in Woodford,
                      Co, Ky, d: Shelbyville, Shelby Co., Kentucky; Y
.................6 George HAMMOND b: 15 Mar 1794 in Shelbyville, Shelby Co., Kentucky
.................6 Fieldin HAMMOND b: 21 Jul 1795 in Shelbyville, Shelby Co., Kentucky
.................6 Elizabeth HAMMOND b: 27 Dec 1796 in Shelbyville, Shelby Co., Kentucky
.................6 William HAMMOND b: 10 Nov 1798 in Shelbyville, Shelby, Ky
.................6 Hutson L. HAMMOND Jr. b: 20 Oct 1800 in Shelbyville, Shelby, Ky
                    + SARAH TAYLOR b: Abt. 1805 in Shelby Co., Ky, m: 03 Mar 1825
.....................7 Hudson N. HAMMOND b: 1823 in Shelby Co., Ky
.....................7 Elizabeth A. HAMMOND b: 1828 in Shelby Co., Ky
                    + Jackson J. Yount b: 1824 in Franklin, Georgia, d: 21 Sep 1865 ; Y
.....................8 Uberta Yount b: Abt. 1852 in Homer, Champaign, Illinois
.................6 Pressley HAMMOND b: 28 Oct 1802 in Shelbyville, Shelby Co., Kentucky
.................6 Lee HAMMOND b: 17 Oct 1804 in Shelbyville, Shelby Co., Kentucky
.................6 Caty HAMMOND b: 07 Jun 1807 in Shelbyville, Shelby Co., Kentucky
.................6 Julie Ann HAMMOND b: 07 Oct 1809 in Shelbyville, Shelby Co., Kentucky
.............5 Winney Lee b: Abt. 1774 in Richmond Co, Virginia, Hardy, W.Va., d: 1850 in Ohio, County, Ky;
             Y
```

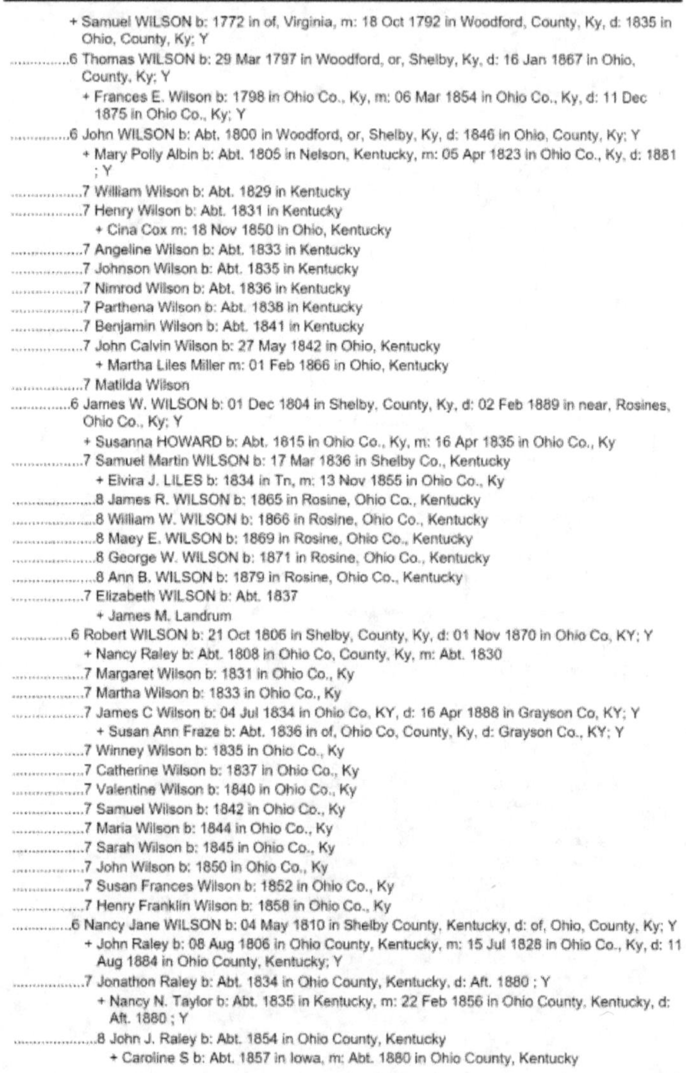

+ Samuel WILSON b: 1772 in of, Virginia, m: 18 Oct 1792 in Woodford, County, Ky, d: 1835 in Ohio, County, Ky; Y

...........6 Thomas WILSON b: 29 Mar 1797 in Woodford, or, Shelby, Ky, d: 16 Jan 1867 in Ohio, County, Ky; Y

    + Frances E. Wilson b: 1798 in Ohio Co., Ky, m: 06 Mar 1854 in Ohio Co., Ky, d: 11 Dec 1875 in Ohio Co., Ky; Y

...........6 John WILSON b: Abt. 1800 in Woodford, or, Shelby, Ky, d: 1846 in Ohio, County, Ky; Y

    + Mary Polly Albin b: Abt. 1805 in Nelson, Kentucky, m: 05 Apr 1823 in Ohio Co., Ky, d: 1881 ; Y

...........7 William Wilson b: Abt. 1829 in Kentucky

...........7 Henry Wilson b: Abt. 1831 in Kentucky

    + Cina Cox m: 18 Nov 1850 in Ohio, Kentucky

...........7 Angeline Wilson b: Abt. 1833 in Kentucky

...........7 Johnson Wilson b: Abt. 1835 in Kentucky

...........7 Nimrod Wilson b: Abt. 1836 in Kentucky

...........7 Parthena Wilson b: Abt. 1838 in Kentucky

...........7 Benjamin Wilson b: Abt. 1841 in Kentucky

...........7 John Calvin Wilson b: 27 May 1842 in Ohio, Kentucky

    + Martha Liles Miller m: 01 Feb 1866 in Ohio, Kentucky

...........7 Matilda Wilson

...........6 James W. WILSON b: 01 Dec 1804 in Shelby, County, Ky, d: 02 Feb 1889 in near, Rosines, Ohio Co., Ky; Y

    + Susanna HOWARD b: Abt. 1815 in Ohio Co., Ky, m: 16 Apr 1835 in Ohio Co., Ky

...........7 Samuel Martin WILSON b: 17 Mar 1836 in Shelby Co., Kentucky

    + Elvira J. LILES b: 1834 in Tn, m: 13 Nov 1855 in Ohio Co., Ky

...........8 James R. WILSON b: 1865 in Rosine, Ohio Co., Kentucky

...........8 William W. WILSON b: 1866 in Rosine, Ohio Co., Kentucky

...........8 Maey E. WILSON b: 1869 in Rosine, Ohio Co., Kentucky

...........8 George W. WILSON b: 1871 in Rosine, Ohio Co., Kentucky

...........8 Ann B. WILSON b: 1879 in Rosine, Ohio Co., Kentucky

...........7 Elizabeth WILSON b: Abt. 1837

    + James M. Landrum

...........6 Robert WILSON b: 21 Oct 1806 in Shelby, County, Ky, d: 01 Nov 1870 in Ohio Co, KY; Y

    + Nancy Raley b: Abt. 1808 in Ohio Co, County, Ky, m: Abt. 1830

...........7 Margaret Wilson b: 1831 in Ohio Co., Ky

...........7 Martha Wilson b: 1833 in Ohio Co., Ky

...........7 James C Wilson b: 04 Jul 1834 in Ohio Co, KY, d: 16 Apr 1888 in Grayson Co, KY; Y

    + Susan Ann Fraze b: Abt. 1836 in of, Ohio Co, County, Ky, d: Grayson Co., KY; Y

...........7 Winney Wilson b: 1835 in Ohio Co., Ky

...........7 Catherine Wilson b: 1837 in Ohio Co., Ky

...........7 Valentine Wilson b: 1840 in Ohio Co., Ky

...........7 Samuel Wilson b: 1842 in Ohio Co., Ky

...........7 Maria Wilson b: 1844 in Ohio Co., Ky

...........7 Sarah Wilson b: 1845 in Ohio Co., Ky

...........7 John Wilson b: 1850 in Ohio Co., Ky

...........7 Susan Frances Wilson b: 1852 in Ohio Co., Ky

...........7 Henry Franklin Wilson b: 1858 in Ohio Co., Ky

...........6 Nancy Jane WILSON b: 04 May 1810 in Shelby County, Kentucky, d: of, Ohio, County, Ky; Y

    + John Raley b: 08 Aug 1806 in Ohio County, Kentucky, m: 15 Jul 1828 in Ohio Co., Ky, d: 11 Aug 1884 in Ohio County, Kentucky; Y

...........7 Jonathon Raley b: Abt. 1834 in Ohio County, Kentucky, d: Aft. 1880 ; Y

    + Nancy N. Taylor b: Abt. 1835 in Kentucky, m: 22 Feb 1856 in Ohio County, Kentucky, d: Aft. 1880 ; Y

...........8 John J. Raley b: Abt. 1854 in Ohio County, Kentucky

    + Caroline S b: Abt. 1857 in Iowa, m: Abt. 1880 in Ohio County, Kentucky

..................8 Sorenzo P. Raley b: Abt. 1856 in Ohio County, Kentucky
..................8 Clarence A. Raley b: Abt. 1858 in Ohio County, Kentucky
..................8 Nancy E. Raley b: Abt. 1860 in Ohio County, Kentucky
..................8 Debbie A. Raley b: Abt. 1863 in Ohio County, Kentucky
  + Samuel K. Allen m: 27 Oct 1886 in Ohio County, Kentucky
..................8 Mary E. Raley b: Abt. 1865 in Ohio County, Kentucky
..................7 Mary E. Raley b: Abt. 1836 in Kentucky, d: 26 Nov 1892 in Ohio County, Kentucky; Y
  + David C. Black b: Abt. 1837, m: 24 Jan 1868 in Ohio County, Kentucky, d: 06 Nov 1908 in
  Ohio County, Kentucky; Y
..................8 Francis R. Black b: 21 Mar 1877 in Ohio County, Kentucky, d: 27 Oct 1880 in Ohio
  County, Kentucky; Y
..................7 Julia Ann Raley b: Abt. 1838 in Kentucky
  + Henry L. Taylor m: 14 Nov 1856 in Ohio County, Kentucky
..................7 James Wesley Raley b: Abt. 1840 in Ohio County, Kentucky, d: 1917 in Ohio County,
  Kentucky; Y
  + Lucy Ann Rice b: Abt. 1842 in Kentucky, m: 01 Feb 1859 in Ohio County, Kentucky, d:
  Bet. 1876–29 Nov 1880 in Ohio County, Kentucky; Y
..................8 John M. Raley b: Abt. 1862 in Ohio County, Kentucky
..................8 James W. Raley b: Abt. 1863 in Ohio County, Kentucky
..................8 Hannah A. Raley b: 04 May 1865 in Ohio County, Kentucky, d: 28 Aug 1896 in Kentucky;
  Y
  + William H. Allen b: May 1860 in Kentucky, m: 02 Feb 1885 in Ohio County, Kentucky
..................8 Thomas L. Raley b: Abt. 1869 in Ohio County, Kentucky
  + Susie Owen m: 29 Nov 1893 in Ohio County, Kentucky
..................8 George S. Raley b: Abt. 1870 in Kentucky
..................8 Robert H. Raley b: Abt. 1873 in Kentucky
..................8 Barbara A. Raley b: Abt. 1876 in Kentucky
  + Almeda Autry b: Mar 1848, m: 29 Nov 1880 in Ohio County, Kentucky
..................8 Estill Raley b: May 1883
  + Lucy Ann Boyd m: 17 Dec 1902 in Ohio County, Kentucky
..................8 Ollie Raley b: Apr 1885
..................8 Worth Raley b: Jul 1891
..................7 Nancy Raley b: Abt. 1842 in Kentucky
..................6 Benjamin P WILSON b: Abt. 1812 in Shelby, or, Jefferson, Ky
  + Susan Sarah LAYMAN b: Abt. 1806 in Grayson Co., KY, m: Abt. 1834 in Grayson Co., KY
..................7 Mahala WILSON b: Abt. 1840 in Grayson Co., KY
..................7 Marshall WILSON b: Abt. 1848 in Winfield, Kansas
..................7 Benjamin WILSON b: Abt. 1860 in Winfield, Kansas
..................6 Nimrod D WILSON b: 01 Nov 1816 in Jefferson, County, Ky, d: 08 Oct 1886 in Grayson Co.,
  KY; Y
  + Delphia Renfrow b: 01 Apr 1815 in Butler County, Kentucky, m: 16 Aug 1838 in Grayson
  County, Kentucky
..................7 Susanna Wilson b: 12 Sep 1839 in Grayson County, Kentucky
  + Willis Dockery b: Grayson Co., KY
..................8 William F. Dockery b: 1868 in Grayson Co., KY, d: 1930 in Leitchfield, Grayson Co.,
  Kentucky; Y
  + Nadine Hunter b: Abt. 1868, m: Bef. 1892
..................9 Ruby Lewis Dockery b: Abt. 1892
..................8 Bent Dockery b: Grayson Co., KY
..................7 William Henry Wilson b: 17 Mar 1842 in Grayson County, Kentucky, d: 01 Sep 1911 in
  Grayson Co., Kentucky; Y
  + Amanda Frances Bratcher b: 29 Mar 1855 in Grayson County, Kentucky, d: 04 Sep 1911
  in Ohio County, Kentucky; Y
..................8 Geneva Wilson b: Abt. 1876
..................8 Homer Wilson b: Abt. 1878

.................8 Martin Wilson b: Abt. 1880
.................8 Curtis Wilson b: Abt. 1882
.................8 Judson Wilson b: 22 Mar 1884
.................7 Minerva Jane Wilson b: 04 Oct 1843 in Grayson County, Kentucky
    + John Parks d: Bef. 1880 ; Y
.................8 William H. Parks b: 1870
    + Liza Bratcher
.................8 Alonzo E. Parks b: 27 Sep 1871, d: 21 Jan 1952 in Grayson Co., Kentucky; Y
    + Ora Dell Watson b: 12 Jul 1886 in Kentucky, m: 05 Nov 1905 in Grayson County, Kentucky, d: 03 Nov 1913 ; Y
.................9 Garland Parks b: 1907, d: 11 Sep 1996 in Grayson County, Kentucky; Y
    + Golda Mae Basham
.................9 Aud Parks b: 14 Jan 1913, d: 06 Jun 1986 ; Y
.................9 Bennie B. Parks b: 26 Feb 1916, d: 07 Jun 1972 ; Y
.................9 Shelton Parks b: 02 May 1917, d: 29 Jul 1980 ; Y
.................9 Gertha Mae Parks b: 23 Dec 1920, d: 16 Sep 1985 ; Y
.................9 Hayward Parks b: 21 Oct 1928, d: 13 May 1999 ; Y
    + [unknown spouse]
.................10 Hayward Parks Jr. b: 21 Feb 1947 in Kentucky, d: 15 Aug 1988 : Y
.................8 Robert P. Parks b: 1873
.................8 Cinderelia J. Parks b: 1875
.................8 Cortie Parks
.................8 Vessie Parks
.................7 John Harden Wilson b: 25 May 1845 in Grayson County, Kentucky
    + Hester Ann Dockery b: Nov 1855 in MO., m: Abt. 1867
.................8 Willie M. Wilson b: 1868
.................8 Estill E. Wilson b: 1869
.................8 Amanda V. Wilson b: 1873
    + Frank C. Hardy b: 1876, m: 05 Apr 1898 in Grayson County, Kentucky
.................9 Ava Myrtle HARDY b: 27 Mar 1900
    + Marion Morris Payton b: Apr 1883 in Kentucky, d: 25 May 1965 in Kentucky; Y
.................9 Earl Hardy
.................8 Sarah E. Wilson b: Nov 1874
.................8 Henry H. Wilson b: 19 Apr 1876, d: 22 Feb 1956 ; Y
    + Emma C. Hardy b: 21 Nov 1878, m: 25 May 1899, d: 09 Sep 1956 ; Y
.................9 Hena Wilson b: 17 Mar 1903, d: 09 Jul 1976 ; Y
.................8 Walter C. Wilson b: 30 Mar 1879, d: 03 Apr 1971 ; Y
    + Lillian E. Hardy b: 29 Dec 1883, m: 26 Apr 1903 in Grayson County, Kentucky
.................8 Cora Wilson b: 18 Mar 1881
.................8 Mary Letitia Wilson b: Apr 1883
.................8 Finis W. Wilson b: Mar 1886
.................8 Alonzo W. Wilson
    + Susanna Dockery
.................7 Presley P. Wilson b: 05 Oct 1846 in Grayson County, Kentucky, d: 10 Feb 1942 ; Y
    + Mary E. Hopper b: Abt. 1860 in Kentucky
.................8 Thomas D. Wilson b: Jul 1879 in Grayson County, Kentucky
.................7 Nimrod J. Wilson b: 06 Feb 1848 in Grayson County, Kentucky
    + Kitty Ashford
.................7 David L. Wilson b: 01 Oct 1849 in Grayson County, Kentucky
    + Luticia C. Mercer b: Abt. 1858
.................8 Luther D. Wilson b: 1876
.................8 Lemeul O. Wilson b: 1878
.................7 Owen T. Wilson b: 13 Sep 1851
    + Sudie Hopper

.............7 Eliza Allen Wilson b: 21 Aug 1853 in Grayson County, Kentucky
.............7 Aaron Van Wilson b: 11 Feb 1855 in Grayson County, Kentucky, d: 14 Apr 1939 ; Y
　　　+ Rhoda E. Carter b: 20 Dec 1857, d: 17 Aug 1919 ; Y
.............8 Laton Wilson b: 04 Dec 1882, d: 16 Jan 1883 ; Y
.............8 Emet Wilson b: 23 Jan 1884, d: 22 Mar 1884 ; Y
.............8 Ernest Wilson b: 23 Jan 1884, d: 31 May 1884 ; Y
.............8 Clyda D. Wilson b: 26 May 1886, d: 01 Jun 1971 ; Y
.............8 Edgar M. Wilson b: 08 Apr 1888, d: 03 Nov 1968 ; Y
.............8 Fadetta Wilson b: 07 Jul 1894, d: 25 Mar 1956 ; Y
.............8 Cora Wilson b: 29 Oct 1897
.............8 Ossie Wilson b: 17 Sep 1899
.............8 Jesse R. Wilson
.............7 Josephine Wilson b: 05 Nov 1856 in Grayson County, Kentucky, d: 10 Sep 1903 ; Y
　　　+ Sylverter V. Patterson b: 07 Sep 1856, m: Abt. 1879 in Grayson County, Kentucky, d: 29 Dec 1940 ; Y
.............8 Forrest Layton Patterson b: 01 Jun 1882, d: 08 Dec 1979 in Ohio County, Kentucky; Y
　　　+ Clara Payton
.............8 Versie Mae Patterson b: 30 Dec 1896, d: 23 Mar 1979 ; Y
　　　+ Mink Ferry
.............8 Florence Patterson
.............8 Pearlie Patterson
.............8 Earnest Patterson
.............8 Stella Patterson
.............7 Franklin L. Wilson b: 06 Mar 1858 in Grayson County, Kentucky, d: 26 May 1941 ; Y
　　　+ C. Lizzie Wilson b: 09 Mar 1864, d: 17 Apr 1921 ; Y
.............8 Sarah E. Wilson b: 23 Jun 1885, d: 07 May 1923 ; Y
.............8 Loy Wilson b: 08 Sep 1887
.............8 Jerome H. Wilson
.............8 Norman Wilson
.............8 Bent Wilson
.............8 Naomi Wilson
.............6 Sarah Sally WILSON b: 24 Nov 1818 in Bullitt, Ky, d: of, Ohio, County, Ky; Y
.............6 Melissa WILSON b: 1820 in Bullitt, Ky, d: Aft. 1880 in of, Ohio Co, County, Ky; Y
.............6 Daniel L. or T. WILSON b: 18 Jun 1821 in Bullitt, Ky, d: 24 Dec 1874 in Warren, Ill; Y
　　　+ Amelia Mariah ALLEN b: Abt. 1828 in Ohio Co., Ky, m: 18 Apr 1843 in Ohio Co., Ky
.............6 Samuel WILSON b: Abt. 1822 in Bullitt, Ky, d: 18 Jun 1901 in Grayson, County, Ky; Y
　　　+ Mary
.............6 Elizabeth Betsy WILSON b: Shelby, Ky, d: 1851 in age 42, Ohio, County, Ky; Y
　　　+ William Autry b: Abt. 1807 in Ohio Co., Ky
.............6 Henry H WILSON b: Jefferson, Ky, d: Bef. Jun 1880 in Ohio Co, KY; Y
　　　+ Temperance White b: Abt. 1814 in Ohio Co, KY, m: 30 Jan 1835 in Ohio Co, KY, d: Abt. 1880 in Ohio Co, KY; Y
.............7 Julia A. Wilson b: Abt. 1837
.............7 Thomas B. Wilson b: Abt. 1839
.............7 Daniel Thornberg Wilson b: 25 Feb 1841 in Ohio Co, KY, d: 02 Jun 1924 in Ohio Co, KY; Y
　　　+ Sarah Elizabeth Arnold b: 18 Jan 1851 in Ohio Co, KY, m: 03 Jul 1865 in Ohio Co, KY, d: 29 Oct 1923 in Ohio Co, KY; Y
.............8 John H. Wilson b: Abt. 1867
.............8 William Luther Wilson b: 22 Aug 1868 in Ohio Co, KY, d: 16 Aug 1947 in Ohio Co, KY; Y
　　　+ Sara Ford b: 29 Oct 1887 in Ohio Co, KY, m: Abt. 22 Aug 1900
.............9 William Daniel Wilson b: 25 Jul 1889
.............9 Allie Wilson b: 30 Aug 1890
.............9 Lesley Wilson b: 03 Mar 1891
.............9 Blanch Wilson b: 22 Apr 1892

....................9 Herbert Wilson b: 27 Oct 1893
....................9 Janie Wilson b: 14 Feb 1895
....................9 Byron Wilson b: 22 Aug 1897 in Ohio Co., Ky
....................9 Oral Wilson b: 02 May 1899 in Ohio Co., Ky
....................9 Grude Wilson b: 24 Feb 1900 in Ohio Co., Ky, d: Jan 1983 in Hartford, Ohio, KY; Y
....................9 Denver Wilson b: Abt. 1902 in Ohio Co., Ky, d: Bef. 2003 ; Y
....................9 Belmer Wilson b: Abt. 1904 in Ohio Co., Ky, d: Bef. 2003 ; Y
....................9 Arthur Wilson b: 06 May 1905, d: May 1985 in Ohio Co, KY; Y
        + Winnie Cook b: 14 May 1914 in Maystown, KY?, m: 13 Aug 1929 in Valparaiso, In, d: 22 Jun 2003 in Ohio County Hospital, Hartford, Okio, KY; Y
....................10 Gary Dean Wilson
....................10 William Ray Wilson
....................10 Michael Joe Wilson
....................10 Sara Mae Wilson
....................10 Betty Jean Wilson
....................9 Mattie Wilson b: Abt. 1907 in Ohio Co., Ky, d: Bef. 2003 ; Y
....................9 Tallie Wilson b: Abt. 1909 in Ohio Co., Ky, d: Bef. 2003 ; Y
....................9 Frankey Edith Wilson b: Abt. 1911 in Ohio Co., Ky, d: Bef. 2002 ; Y
....................8 Polly A. Wilson b: Abt. 1871
....................8 Job S. Wilson b: Abt. 1873
....................8 Elijah Ky. Wilson b: Abt. 1875
....................8 Cordelia E. Wilson b: Abt. 1877
....................8 Pricilla C. Wilson b: 1880
....................7 Nancy M. Wilson b: Abt. 1843
....................7 Mary Wilson b: Abt. 1845
....................7 Philena Wilson b: Abt. 1847
....................7 Quintus C. Wilson b: Abt. 1852 in Ohio Co, KY, d: Abt. 1884 in Enterprise, IN; Y
        + Mary Elizabeth Smith b: 06 Feb 1851 in Ohio Co, KY, d: 28 Dec 1906 in Ohio Co, KY; Y
....................8 Lou Wilson b: 14 Apr 1872 in Ohio Co, KY, d: 22 Apr 1952 ; Y
....................8 Dickie Wilson b: Abt. 1874, d: Abt. 1883 ; Y
....................8 Verner Day Wilson b: 01 Jan 1876 in Ohio Co, KY, d: 27 Jul 1961 in Linden, Cass Co, TX; Y
....................8 Johnny Wilson b: Abt. 1881, d: Abt. 1883 ; Y
....................8 Alice Eugene Wilson b: 10 Jan 1884, d: 27 Aug 1969 ; Y
....................8 Bettie Wilson
....................7 Samuel H. Wilson b: Abt. 1855
....................7 Susan Wilson b: Abt. 1858
....................7 Palmyra Wilson
        + Rebecca Dangel m: Bef. 1835
............6 William WILSON b: Woodford, or, Shelby, Ky, d: 1826 in Ohio, County, Ky; Y
..........5 Richard Lee b: Abt. 1776 in Richmond Co, Va, of Hardy, W.Va., d: Abt. 1840 in Henry Co., Iowa; Y
        + Selah Cela Celia SETTLES b: Abt. 1776 in Va of, Mercer, Co, Ky, m: 27 Sep 1798 in Mercer, Co, Ky, d: Henry Co., Iowa; Y
..........6 Richard Henry Lee b: 1800 in Mercer Co., Ky of Jennings Co., Indiana, d: 1875 in Jefferson Co., IA; Y
        + Elizabeth Sage b: Abt. 1815 in Jennings Co., Indiana, m: 07 Mar 1833 in Jennings Co., Indiana
....................7 Celia Jane Lee b: 1834 in Jennings Co., Indiana
....................7 Ann "Lonnda" Lee b: 1836 in Jennings Co., Indiana
....................7 Nancy Lee b: 1839 in Jennings Co., IN
....................7 Malissa Lee b: 1840 in Jennings Co., IN
....................7 Margaret Lee b: 1841 in Jennings Co., IN
....................7 Charles Lee b: 1843 in Jefferson Co., IA

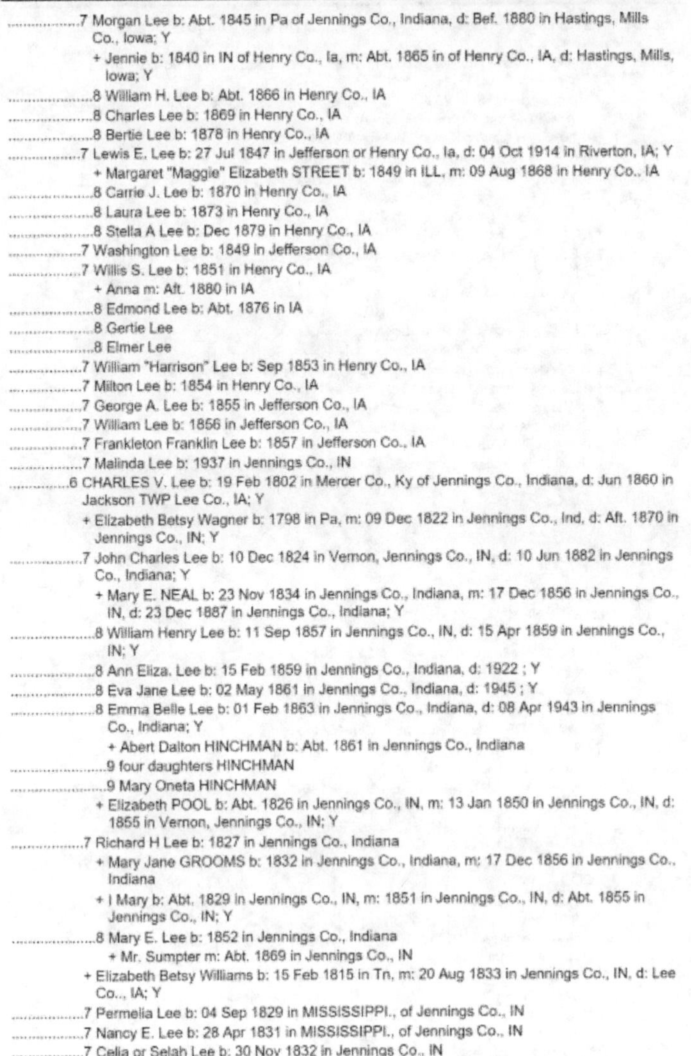

...........7 Morgan Lee b: Abt. 1845 in Pa of Jennings Co., Indiana, d: Bef. 1880 in Hastings, Mills Co., Iowa; Y

+ Jennie b: 1840 in IN of Henry Co., Ia, m: Abt. 1865 in of Henry Co., IA, d: Hastings, Mills, Iowa; Y

...........8 William H. Lee b: Abt. 1866 in Henry Co., IA

...........8 Charles Lee b: 1869 in Henry Co., IA

...........8 Bertie Lee b: 1878 in Henry Co., IA

...........7 Lewis E. Lee b: 27 Jul 1847 in Jefferson or Henry Co., Ia, d: 04 Oct 1914 in Riverton, IA; Y

+ Margaret "Maggie" Elizabeth STREET b: 1849 in ILL, m: 09 Aug 1868 in Henry Co., IA

...........8 Carrie J. Lee b: 1870 in Henry Co., IA

...........8 Laura Lee b: 1873 in Henry Co., IA

...........8 Stella A Lee b: Dec 1879 in Henry Co., IA

...........7 Washington Lee b: 1849 in Jefferson Co., IA

...........7 Willis S. Lee b: 1851 in Henry Co., IA

+ Anna m: Aft. 1880 in IA

...........8 Edmond Lee b: Abt. 1876 in IA

...........8 Gertie Lee

...........8 Elmer Lee

...........7 William "Harrison" Lee b: Sep 1853 in Henry Co., IA

...........7 Milton Lee b: 1854 in Henry Co., IA

...........7 George A. Lee b: 1855 in Jefferson Co., IA

...........7 William Lee b: 1856 in Jefferson Co., IA

...........7 Frankleton Franklin Lee b: 1857 in Jefferson Co., IA

...........7 Malinda Lee b: 1937 in Jennings Co., IN

...........6 CHARLES V. Lee b: 19 Feb 1802 in Mercer Co., Ky of Jennings Co., Indiana, d: Jun 1860 in Jackson TWP Lee Co., IA; Y

+ Elizabeth Betsy Wagner b: 1798 in Pa, m: 09 Dec 1822 in Jennings Co., Ind, d: Aft. 1870 in Jennings Co., IN; Y

...........7 John Charles Lee b: 10 Dec 1824 in Vernon, Jennings Co., IN, d: 10 Jun 1882 in Jennings Co., Indiana; Y

+ Mary E. NEAL b: 23 Nov 1834 in Jennings Co., Indiana, m: 17 Dec 1856 in Jennings Co., IN, d: 23 Dec 1887 in Jennings Co., Indiana; Y

...........8 William Henry Lee b: 11 Sep 1857 in Jennings Co., IN, d: 15 Apr 1859 in Jennings Co., IN; Y

...........8 Ann Eliza. Lee b: 15 Feb 1859 in Jennings Co., Indiana, d: 1922 ; Y

...........8 Eva Jane Lee b: 02 May 1861 in Jennings Co., Indiana, d: 1945 ; Y

...........8 Emma Belle Lee b: 01 Feb 1863 in Jennings Co., Indiana, d: 08 Apr 1943 in Jennings Co., Indiana; Y

+ Abert Dalton HINCHMAN b: Abt. 1861 in Jennings Co., Indiana

...........9 four daughters HINCHMAN

...........9 Mary Oneta HINCHMAN

+ Elizabeth POOL b: Abt. 1826 in Jennings Co., IN, m: 13 Jan 1850 in Jennings Co., IN, d: 1855 in Vernon, Jennings Co., IN; Y

...........7 Richard H Lee b: 1827 in Jennings Co., Indiana

+ Mary Jane GROOMS b: 1832 in Jennings Co., Indiana, m: 17 Dec 1856 in Jennings Co., Indiana

+ I Mary b: Abt. 1829 in Jennings Co., IN, m: 1851 in Jennings Co., IN, d: Abt. 1855 in Jennings Co., IN; Y

...........8 Mary E. Lee b: 1852 in Jennings Co., Indiana

+ Mr. Sumpter m: Abt. 1869 in Jennings Co., IN

+ Elizabeth Betsy Williams b: 15 Feb 1815 in Tn, m: 20 Aug 1833 in Jennings Co., IN, d: Lee Co., IA; Y

...........7 Permelia Lee b: 04 Sep 1829 in MISSISSIPPI., of Jennings Co., IN

...........7 Nancy E. Lee b: 28 Apr 1831 in MISSISSIPPI., of Jennings Co., IN

...........7 Celia or Selah Lee b: 30 Nov 1832 in Jennings Co., IN

.............7 Sarah J. Lee b: 04 Aug 1834 in Jennings Co., IN, d: 17 Feb 1839 in Jackson TWP Lee Co., IA; Y

.............7 George Washington Lee b: 04 Mar 1836 in Jennings Co., IN, d: 06 Mar 1896 in Jackson TWP Lee Co., IA; Y

    + Elizabeth Dwyer b: 27 Feb 1841 in Indiana, m: 25 Sep 1859 in Appanoose, IA, d: 28 Jun 1902 in Jackson TWP Lee Co., IA; Y

.............8 William H. Lee b: 1860 in Jackson TWP, Lee Co., IA

.............8 Charles ALBERT Lee b: 1862 in Jackson TWP, Lee Co., IA

.............8 James W. Lee b: 1864 in Jackson TWP, Lee Co., IA

.............8 Ida Lee b: 1866 in Jackson TWP, Lee Co., IA

.............8 John Lee b: 1868 in Jackson TWP, Lee Co., IA

.............8 Thomas Lee b: 1870 in Jackson TWP, Lee Co., IA

.............8 Edward R. Lee b: 1872 in Jackson TWP, Lee Co., IA, d: 19 Oct 1936 in Will Proate Lee CO., IA; Y

    + I Addie b: 1876 in Iowa

.............9 Elsie Lee b: 1917 in Jackson TWP Lee Co., IA

.............8 Frederick Lee b: 1876 in Jackson TWP, Lee Co., IA

.............8 Lewis Lee b: Abt. 1881 in Jackson TWP, Lee Co., IA

.............7 Mary A. Lee b: 12 Dec 1837 in Jennings Co., IN, d: 1839 in Jackson TWP Lee Co., IA; Y

.............7 Elizabeth Lee b: 31 Jan 1840 in Jackson TWP Lee Co., IA, d: 20 Feb 1873 ; Y

.............7 Rebesky Lee b: 13 Apr 1842 in Jackson TWP Lee Co., IA

.............7 Charles Henry "Harry" Lee b: 31 Jan 1845 in Jackson TWP Lee Co., IA, d: Jan 1862 in Jackson TWP Lee Co., IA; Y

.............7 Usual Uzel or Vzel Lee b: 11 Sep 1846 in Jackson TWP Lee Co., IA, d: 1902 ; Y

.............7 William L Lee b: 10 Apr 1848 in Jackson TWP Lee Co., IA, d: 16 Sep 1849 in Jackson TWP Lee Co., IA; Y

.............7 Matilda Lee b: 04 Nov 1852 in Jackson TWP Lee Co., IA, d: 24 Oct 1855 in Jackson TWP Lee Co., IA; Y

.............7 Martha E. Lee b: 30 Jun 1855 in Jackson TWP Lee Co., IA, d: 20 Sep 1855 in Jackson TWP Lee Co., IA; Y

.............7 James F. Lee b: Jackson TWP Lee Co., IA

.............6 MARY JANE (POLLY) LEE b: 22 Feb 1806 in Jennings County, Indiana, d: 03 Sep 1840 in HENRY CO., IA; Y

    + JABEZ VAN DOREN b: 09 Apr 1798 in Shippensburg, Cumberland County, Pennsylvania, m: 1819 in Jennings Co., IN, d: Aft. 1872 in Jefferson Co., IA; Y

.............7 Rachel VAN DOREN (twin) b: 28 Jun 1820 in Jennings County, Indiana

.............7 CALVIN L VAN DOREN (twin) b: 28 Jun 1820 in Jennings County, Indiana

.............7 JOHN WARF VAN DOREN b: 27 Sep 1821 in Jennings County, Indiana

.............7 SELIA CAROLINE VAN DOREN (twin) b: 19 Apr 1822 in Jennings County, Indiana

.............7 Isaac VAN DOREN (twin) b: 19 Apr 1822 in Jennings County, Indiana

.............7 RICHARD HENRY VAN DOREN b: 24 Jul 1823

.............7 Gardelia VAN DOREN b: 1824 in Jennings County, Indiana

.............7 Willis Washington VAN DOREN b: 03 Feb 1825 in Jennings County, Indiana, d: 15 Jul 1904 in Mount Pleasant, Henry County, Iowa; Y

.............7 William Riley VAN DOREN b: 02 Jul 1827 in Jennings County, Indiana, d: 1883 in Carrol CO., IA; Y

    + Rachel (Woodson) SMITH b: 12 Jul 1822 in Cherry Grove, Wayne County, Indiana, m: 08 Aug 1846 in Henry County, Iowa

.............7 James Alexander VAN DOREN b: 19 Feb 1829 in Jennings County, Indiana, d: 29 Jul 1908 in Moravia, Appanoose County, Iowa; Y

.............7 Betsey Ann VAN DOREN b: 30 Jun 1831 in Jennings County, Indiana

.............7 Malinda Evelyn VAN DOREN b: 16 Jun 1832 in Jennings County, Indiana

.............7 Nancy Angeline VAN DOREN b: 28 Oct 1833 in Jennings County, Indiana, d: 12 Feb 1908 in Mcdonalds, Missouri; Y

.............7 Jasper Lee VAN DOREN b: 13 Mar 1835 in Jennings County, Indiana, d: 23 May 1911 ; Y

.............7 EMILY JANE VAN DOREN b: 10 Jan 1836 in Jennings County, Indiana, d: 18 Sep 1877 in Moravia, Appanoose County, Iowa; Y

.............7 LEWIS LEANDER VAN DOREN b: 26 May 1838 in Jennings County, Indiana, d: 17 Apr 1911 ; Y

.............6 Lewis Runo or Rulan LEE b: Abt. 1807 in Mercer Co., Ky of Jennings Co., IN, d: Jun 1881 in Creed Huntly, McDonald County, Missouri; Y

+ Julia ANN EDDLEMAN b: 1809 in Kentucky, m: 25 Nov 1828 in Jefferson Co. IN

.............7 Cynthia ANN LEE b: 1830 in Jennings Co., IN, d: 29 Mar 1891 in Montgomery Co., KS; Y

+ Walker Price BROWN b: Abt. 1829 in Ky of Davis Co., IA, m: 30 Aug 1849 in Davis Co., Iowa, d: Miss; Y

.............8 Mary E. Lee BROWN b: 1855 in Davis Co., Iowa

.............8 Lewis F. BROWN b: 1857 in Davis Co., Iowa

.............7 JOHN H. LEE b: Abt. 1833 in Jennings Co., IN of Davis Co., IA

+ NANCY THOMPSON b: Abt. 1835 in <, KY>, m: 02 May 1863 in JEFFERSON CO., IA

.............8 ELA May LEE b: 1864 in Sac Co., IA

.............8 CLARA LEE b: 1866 in Sac Co., IA, d: 18 Oct 1871 in GRANT CITY, IA; Y

.............8 EMMA LEE b: 02 Jul 1869 in Sac Co., IA, d: 09 Sep 1870 in GRANT CITY, IA; Y

+ Elizabeth Eliza A. CONWAY b: Abt. 1835 in <, Davis Co., IA>, m: 25 Nov 1855 in Davis Co., IA, d: Bef. 1862 in Davis Co., Iowa; Y

.............8 Sarah A. LEE b: 1858 in Warren Co., IA

.............8 Wesley LEE b: 1860 in Warren Co., IA

.............7 DANIEL LEE b: Abt. 1835 in Jennings Co., IN, d: 09 Apr 1874 in Grant City, Sac Co., IA; Y

+ Susan Bennett b: Abt. 1840 in <, Davis Co., IA>, m: 12 Apr 1860 in Davis Co., Iowa

.............8 MARY JANE LEE b: 1861 in Davis Co., IA

.............8 Lewis Henry. LEE b: 23 Feb 1862 in Davis Co, IA, d: 02 Dec 1929 in Sac twsp, Sac Co., IA; Y

+ Elizabeth Marion STILTS b: 27 Sep 1865 in Whiteside Co., ILL, m: 12 Nov 1884, d: 04 Jul 1941 in Farnhamville, Calhoun, IA; Y

.............9 Hazel Olive Lee b: Aug 1869 in Sac Co IA

.............9 Henry Melvin Lee b: 14 Sep 1885 in Auburn, Sac, IA, d: 10 Sep 1942 in Sidney, Fremont, IA; Y

+ Sarah Rozella BENSON b: 08 Jun 1891 in Sac Twp Sac Co., IA, m: 29 Jul 1907 in Sac City, Sac, IA

.............10 Elizabeth Jeannette Lee b: 29 Jun 1908 in Sac City, Sac Co., IA

.............10 Golda Lee b: 20 Sep 1910 in Park River, Walsh Co., ND

.............10 Ada Lee b: 03 Sep 1912 in Park River, Walsh Co., ND

.............9 Maggie E. Lee b: Sep 1886 in Sac Co IA, d: 07 May 1887 in Sac Co IA; Y

.............9 Danny Lee b: Jul 1888 in Sac Co IA, d: 09 Dec 1889 in Sac Co IA; Y

.............9 Fay S. Lee b: May 1890 in Sac Co IA

.............9 Ray Lee b: 17 Oct 1891 in Sac Co IA, d: Jan 1974 in Sac Co IA; Y

.............9 Esther Lee b: Aug 1893 in Sac Co IA, d: 1967 in CA; Y

.............9 Loretta Lee b: Aug 1899 in Sac Co IA

.............9 Rachel Lee b: 1902 in Sac Co IA

.............9 Arnum Lee b: 16 Jan 1904 in Sac Co IA, d: Sep 1972 ; Y

.............9 Anna Mae Lee b: 05 Sep 1906 in Sac Co IA, d: Apr 1977 ; Y

.............8 John W. LEE b: 23 Nov 1865 in GRANT CITY, Sac Co., IA, d: 20 Dec 1866 in GRANT CITY, Sac Co., IA; Y

.............7 RICHARD H. LEE b: 25 Jan 1837 in Grove Twp., Davis, Iowa, d: 18 Apr 1906 in Boulder, Colorado; Y

+ Mary Jane DAUGHTY b: 30 Aug 1841 in Bloomington, OH, m: 16 Mar 1856 in Davis Co., IA, d: 22 Apr 1917 in Parkman, Wyo; Y

.............8 Mary E. LEE b: Abt. 1857 in Lawrence CO., MO

.............8 Lacey S. LEE b: 1858 in Lawrence CO., MO

.............8 Lewis F. LEE b: 1859 in Lawrence CO., MO

.............8 Sarah E. LEE b: 1863 in Lawrence CO., MO

....................8 James H. LEE b: 1865 in Lawrence CO., MO
....................8 Richard LEE b: 1866 in Lawrence CO., MO
....................8 Mary A. LEE b: 1867 in Lawrence CO., MO
....................8 William LEE b: 1868 in Lawrence CO., MO
....................8 Hattie LEE b: 14 Feb 1869 in Denver, Co, d: 18 Dec 1934 in Cortez, Montezuma, Co; Y
...................7 Celia (Ellen) E. LEE b: 11 Aug 1837 in Decatur Co., IN, d: 20 Dec 1887 in Kansas; Y
  + Lyman Wyatt ARCHER b: 02 Mar 1834 in Indiana, USA, m: 02 Jan 1859 in Davis Co., IA, d: 27 Feb 1916 in Inglewood Park, CA; Y
....................8 David Erastas Archer b: 08 Dec 1859 in Davis Co., Iowa, d: 1928 ; Y
....................8 twelve children ARCHER b: Abt. 1860
....................8 Sarah Jane Archer b: 08 Jul 1861 in Davis Co., Iowa, d: Kansas; Y
  + Clent Williams
  + John Robinson
....................8 Cynthia Ann Archer b: 27 Dec 1862 in Davis, Iowa, USA
  + Edward Bivins b: 24 Feb 1861 in Libertyville, Jefferson, Iowa, USA, m: 16 Apr 1882 in Davis, Iowa, USA
....................9 Jesse Lewis Bivins b: 04 Apr 1883 in Pittsburg, Crawford, Kansas, USA
  + Lelah Bingle b: Abt. 1885, m: 15 Feb 1904
....................9 Anna May Bivins b: 25 Jan 1885
  + James T Nett b: Abt. 1883, m: 25 Dec 1902
....................9 Thomas Edward Bivins b: 18 Oct 1886, d: 19 Nov 1923 ; Y
  + Mary Ellen Gaither b: Abt. 1888, m: 14 May 1923
....................9 Albert Ray Bivins b: 12 Sep 1888
  + Olive Rose Hoskins b: Abt. 1890, m: 17 Sep 1911
....................9 Samuel Erastus Bivins b: 17 Jul 1890, d: 10 Mar 1891 ; Y
....................9 Francis Abraham Bivins b: 26 Jan 1892
  + Bessie E Mahurin b: Abt. 1894, m: 20 Apr 1918
....................9 Iva Belle Bivins Twin b: 23 Jul 1896, d: 28 Oct 1897 ; Y
....................9 Ira Ellis Bivins Twin b: 23 Jul 1896, d: 01 Nov 1897 ; Y
....................9 Lyman Wyatt Bivins b: Aug 1898, d: 13 Nov 1900 ; Y
....................9 Hubert Ernest Bivins b: 10 Jan 1901
  + Frances Trivett b: Abt. 1903, m: 17 Jul 1924
....................9 Robert Theodore Bivins b: Feb 1904
  + Alice M Riley b: Abt. 1906, m: 11 Apr 1925
....................9 George Bivins b: Sep 1907, d: Sep 1907 ; Y
....................8 Earastus Archer b: 1863 in Davis, Iowa, USA
....................8 Mary Julia Archer b: 12 Feb 1864 in Davis Co., Iowa, d: 30 Jan 1952 ; Y
  + William Erastus Lemmon b: 29 Jul 1857 in Troy, Davis, Iowa, USA, m: 22 Oct 1884 in Of Troy, Davis, Iowa
....................9 Albert Lemmon b: Aft. 1885
....................9 Nellie Lemmon b: Aft. 1885
....................8 Francis Cleopatria Archer b: 01 Nov 1865 in Davis Co., Iowa, d: 08 Jul 1952 in Stockton, Ca; Y
  + Lewis Ellison m: 18 Mar 1916 in Stockton, Ca
....................8 John Walker Archer b: 16 Jul 1867 in Davis Co., Iowa, d: 23 Nov in Stockton, Ca; Y
....................8 Eva Elizabeth Archer b: 28 Jul 1869 in Davis Co., Iowa, d: 04 Aug 1870 in Davis Co., Iowa; Y
....................8 Charles Lewis Archer b: 23 Jul 1871 in Davis Co., Iowa, d: 1887 in Davis Co., Iowa; Y
....................8 William Edward Archer b: 12 Aug 1874 in Davis Co., Iowa, d: 1891 in Davis Co., Iowa; Y
....................8 Marcus Arthur Archer b: 16 Dec 1876 in Davis Co., Iowa, d: 03 Jul 1939 in Inglewood Park, CA; Y
....................8 Lydia Ellen ARCHER b: 10 May 1878 in Davis Co., Iowa, d: 06 May 1974 in Bakersfield, Kern Co., CA; Y
  + Joseph Samuel Davis b: Abt. 1885 in Co., m: 17 Feb 1895 in Pueblo Colorado, d: Bakersfield, Kern Co., CA; Y

...........7 SARAH L. (JANE) LEE b: Abt. 1840 in Davis Co., Iowa
　　+ DAVID (DANIEL) Bennett b: Abt. 1840 in <, IA>, m: 12 Jan 1860 in Davis Co., Iowa
...........7 Amos LEE b: 03 Jul 1841 in Fairfield, IA, d: 11 Aug 1909 in Boise, ID; Y
　　+ Alice Selina LELIA HAGER b: 10 Oct 1864 in Yreka CA, m: 03 Jul 1895, d: 22 Aug 1937 in Hoquiam, WA; Y
...........8 LELIA Selena LEE b: 26 Mar 1896 in Boise, ID, d: 05 Nov 1972 in Chula Vista, CA; Y
...........8 Eila LEE b: 23 May 1897 in Boise, ID, d: 15 May 1984 in Imperial Beach, CA; Y
　　+ Nancy E b: Abt. 1844, m: Abt. 1890, d: Abt. 1892 ; Y
...........7 LEWIS LEE b: 03 Jul 1844 in Buchanan, Jefferson, Iowa, d: 21 Sep 1911 in Elk City, Montgomery Co., KS; Y
　　+ Fransina ANN DOWNING b: Abt. 1845 in Buchanan, Jefferson, Iowa, m: 09 Jun 1863 in Buchanan, Jefferson, Iowa
...........7 WILLIAM Wesley LEE b: 1847 in Henry Co., IA, d: 16 Jun 1876 in hanged, OQUAWKA, HENDERSON CO., IL; Y
　　+ ANNA Marcia STALLUM b: Abt. 1850 in <, IA>, m: 05 Feb 1865 in Divorced 10 Aug 1867, d: 15 Apr 1912 in Baker City, OR; Y
...........8 WILLIAM SHERMAN LEE b: Dec 1866
　　+ Maggie E. Wilson b: <, IA>, m: 30 Dec 1869
...........7 MARY Iowa LEE b: 1849 in IA
　　+ Elias B MULKINS b: 01 Nov 1841 in Waukesha, WI, m: 14 Jul 1864, d: 24 Mar 1915 in BENTON, MN; Y
...........8 LEWIS HENRY MULKINS b: 1865 in Fairfield, JEFFERSON, IA, d: 1932 in Webb City, MO, MO; Y
...........8 Julia MULKINS b: 1867 in Fairfield, JEFFERSON, IA
...........8 ALBERT Elias MULKINS b: 16 Jan 1870 in Fairfield, JEFFERSON, IA, d: 29 Jan 1936 in Rich Hill, MO; Y
...........8 SAMUEL (Ed) EDWARD MULKINS b: 1872 in Fairfield, JEFFERSON CO., IA
　　+ F. L. SELF b: 1852 in IN, m: 04 Jun 1877 in Joplin, Jasper, MO
...........7 Louisa ADELINE LEE b: 1853 in DAVIS CO. IA, d: 12 Oct 1913 in SAN ANTONIO, TX; Y
　　+ WINFIELD Elias DILLON b: 04 Jul 1852 in MD, m: 04 May 1871 in Davis Co., IA
...........8 WILLIAM ARTHER DILLON b: 16 Feb 1872 in PARLEE, JEFFERSO, IA, d: 1958 ; Y
　　+ ELIZABETH d: 1947 in SUPERIOR, CO; Y
...........9 EVERETT DILLON d: 1905 ; Y
...........8 Minnie Isabell DILLON b: 1875 in Fairfield, JEFFERSO, IA
...........8 FRANCES May DILLON b: 1876 in Fairfield, JEFFERSO, IA, d: 1941 ; Y
　　+ FRED KEKES d: 1941 ; Y
...........8 DAVID Wesley DILLON b: 23 Aug 1878 in Fairfield, JEFFERSON. IA
...........8 ANNA C DILLON b: 1879 in LEAVENSWORTH, Kansas
...........8 ROSETTA LELA DILLON b: 09 Dec 1880 in LEAVENSWORTH, Kansas
　　+ ALFRED DIEU m: 1916 in CO
...........8 GEORGE ALLEN DILLON b: 29 Dec 1888 in Litchfield, KS, d: 21 Nov 1972 in LONGMONT, CO; Y
　　+ MARGARET JANE JONES b: 24 Nov 1889 in COAL CREAK, CO., m: 24 Nov 1909, d: 10 May 1961 in LAFAYETTE, CO.; Y
...........9 Herman Miller DILLON b: 25 Aug 1910 in MARSHALL, BOULDER, CO., d: 07 Jul 1985 ; Y
...........9 ELIZABETH May DILLON b: 11 Jun 1912 in LAFAYETTE, BOULDER, CO., d: 05 Feb 1990 in LAFAYETTE, BOULDER, CO.; Y
...........9 MARY ROSETTA DILLON b: 07 Nov 1915 in SUPERIOR, BOULDER, CO., d: 30 Nov 1986 in LAFAYETTE, BOULDER, CO.; Y
...........9 DAVID JOHN GEORGE DILLON b: 16 Jun 1917 in EVANSTON, WELD, CO., d: 02 Sep 1982 in Price, Ut.; Y
...........9 WILLIAM GEORGE DILLON b: 20 Jul 1919 in LOUISVILLE, BOULDER, CO.. d: May 1969 in DENVER, CO.; Y

...................9 HELEN IRENE DILLON b: 03 Jan 1922 in SUPERIOR, BOULDER, CO., d: 26 Nov 1983 ; Y

...................9 DONALD REED DILLON b: 23 Feb 1924 in SUPERIOR, BOULDER, CO., d: 14 Feb 1984 ; Y

...................9 RUTH ELAIN DILLON b: 20 Apr 1928 in LAFAYETTE, BOULDER, CO., d: 14 May 1947 ; Y

...................9 Ralph Raymond DILLON b: 28 Jan 1930 in LAFAYETTE, BOULDER, CO., d: Sep 1930 in LAFAYETTE, BOULDER, CO.; Y

...................9 SHIRLEY MARIE DILLON b: 14 Mar 1935 in LAFAYETTE, BOULDER, CO., d: 24 May 1993 ; Y

...................9 Living DILLON

...................9 Living DILLON

...................9 Living DILLON

...................9 Living DILLON

...................8 Herman DILLON b: Jun 1890 in Litchfield, Crawford, Kansas

...................8 Esther ALNURA JANETT DILLON b: 23 May 1892 in Litchfield, CRAFORD, Kansas

...................8 CHARLES DILLON d: 22 Aug 1887 in PITTSBURG, KAN; Y

...................8 JOHN Amos DILLON b: THURBER, TX ?

 + Frankie Spears m: 12 Jul 1880 in Creed Huntly, McDonald County, Missouri

.............6 Elizabeth Settles Betsy Lee b: 1809 in Jennings Co., IN

 + Uzel Lee b: 14 Oct 1806 in Hardin Co., Ky of Jennings Co., IN, m: 07 Feb 1827 in Jennings Co., IN, d: 15 Oct 1842 in Henry Co., Iowa; Y

...................7 John Graves Lee b: Abt. 1828 in Jenings CO., IN

...................7 Louisa Lee b: Abt. 1832 in Jenings CO., IN

...................7 Mary Lee b: Abt. 1835 in Jenings CO., IN

...................7 Celia Lee b: Abt. 1838 in Jenings CO., IN

...................7 Elizabeth Settles Lee II b: Abt. 1841 in Jenings CO., IN or Henry Co., IA

 + Michael LETTNER b: Abt. 1804 in of IA, m: Abt. 1843 in IA

.............6 Malinda M. LEE b: 06 Feb 1810 in Vernon, Jennings, Indiana, d: 1880 in Cica, Pella Co., Co.; Y

 + Joseph R. LEE b: 02 Mar 1811 in Vernon, Jennings Co., Indiana, m: 27 Jun 1832 in Jennings Co, Indiana, d: 10 May 1871 in Mail Carrier killed by indianas, Montana; Y

...................7 Francis Marion LEE b: 13 Jun 1833 in Madison, Jefferson Co., Indiana, d: 29 Jun 1901 in Hillsborough, Weld, Colorado; Y

 + Eliza Ann ROGERS b: 03 Oct 1838 in Georgetown, Delaware, m: 30 Aug 1855 in Davis, Iowa, d: 17 Feb 1913 in Johnstown, Weld, Colorado; Y

...................8 Elexander Sylvester LEE b: 05 May 1856 in Iowa, d: 20 May 1920 in Steam Springs, Route, Colorado; Y

 + Arminda ATWOOD b: 12 Sep 1857 in Clarinda, Ind, m: 30 Nov 1879 in Pella, Boulder, Co., d: 20 May 1923 in Steam Sprgs., Route, Co; Y

...................9 Joseph Marion LEE b: 04 Dec 1884 in Longmont, Boulder, Co, d: 20 May 1923 in Steam Sprgs., Route, Co; Y

...................9 Arta Atwood LEE b: 27 Dec 1886 in Longmont, Boulder, Co, d: 22 Feb 1936 in Steam Sprgs., Route, Co.; Y

...................9 Georgia Enna LEE b: 27 Nov 1889 in Longmont, Boulder, Co, d: 17 Sep 1973 in Steam. Sprgs., Route, Co; Y

...................8 Easmon LEE b: 26 Dec 1857 in Iowa, d: 29 Dec 1857 in Iowa; Y

...................8 Nutter Roger LEE b: 26 Nov 1858 in Keokuk, Iowa, d: 17 Aug 1937 in Johnstown, Weld, Colorado; Y

 + Dora ECK b: 1864 in Vincennes, Ind, m: 21 Jan 1897 in Weld, Co, d: 30 Aug 1919 in Johnstown, Weld, Co.; Y

...................9 Jay R. LEE b: 20 Nov 1898 in Johnstown, Weld, Co., d: Nov 1973 in Greeley, Weld, Co; Y

...................9 Leonard D. LEE b: 06 Feb 1902 in Johnstown, Weld, Co, d: 16 Nov 1942 in North Platte, Ne.; Y

................9 Fred S. LEE b: 16 Aug 1903 in Johnstown, Weld, Co., d: 08 Dec 1946 in Clearfield, Utah; Y

................9 Edward P. LEE b: 02 Nov 1911 in Johnstown, Weld, Co., d: 06 Dec 1980 in Boulder, Boulder, Co.; Y

............8 Joseph LEE b: 10 Oct 1860 in Iowa, d: 25 Sep 1934 in Longmont, Colorado; Y

    + Marietta V. RUNYAN b: 28 Jun 1865 in Ia, m: 14 Oct 1881 in Hygiene, Boulder, Co, d: Feb 1956 in San Jose, CA; Y

................9 Etta LEE b: 1883 in Longmont, Boulder, Co, d: 1948 in Phoenix, Az; Y

................9 Grace LEE b: 24 Jul 1889 in <Longmont, Boulder, Co>, d: 22 Jul 1974 in Camarillo, Ca; Y

................9 Ray R. LEE b: 1893 in Longmont, Boulder, Co, d: 19 Mar 1931 in Longmont, Boulder, Co; Y

............8 Walker Price Brown LEE b: 08 Feb 1863 in Bloomfield, Iowa, d: May 1936 in Lyons, Boulder, Colorado; Y

    + Caroline Emma HOBSON b: 12 Mar 1869 in Leeds, England, d: May 1936 in Lyons, Boulder, Co; Y

................9 Gertrude Lee LEE b: 13 Mar 1888 in Lyons, Boulder, Co, d: 08 Sep 1960 in Lyons, Boulder, Co; Y

................9 Ross LEE b: Abt. 1890 in <Lyons, Boulder, Co>

................9 Hazel LEE b: 07 Dec 1896 in Boulder, Boulder, Co, d: 09 Jul 1978 in Denver, Denver, Co; Y

................9 Harry W. (Jack) LEE b: 1904 in Lyons, Boulder, Co, d: 01 Mar 1945 ; Y

............8 Samuel Harlin LEE b: 02 Apr 1865 in Iowa, d: 24 Jun 1893 in Berthoud, Boulder, Colorado; Y

    + Dora ECK b: 1864 in Vincennes, Ind, m: 14 Jan 1891 in Berthoud, Boulder, Co, d: 30 Aug 1919 in Johnstown, Weld, Co.; Y

................9 Arthur Levi LEE b: 1864 in Vincennes, Ind, d: 30 Aug 1919 in Johnstown, Weld, Co; Y

............8 John George LEE b: 01 Feb 1868 in Iowa, d: 01 Aug 1935 ; Y

    + Nora WEAVER b: 26 Feb 1879 in Salino, Bell, Tx, m: 16 Dec 1897 in Windsor, Larimer, Co, d: 11 Apr 1949 in Boulder, Boulder, Co; Y

................9 Owen LEE b: 02 May 1899 in Windsor, Weld, Co, d: 30 Oct 1907 in Windsor, Weld, Co; Y

............8 Francis Marion LEE b: 19 Apr 1870 in Iowa, d: 18 Oct 1954 in San Ysidro, San Diego, Ca; Y

............8 Nina Pearl LEE b: 13 Nov 1872 in New Market, Iowa, d: 26 Nov 1956 in Fort Collins, Larimer, Colorado; Y

    + Charles Clancy MCELRAVY b: Abt. 1868 in <New Market, Iowa>, m: 13 May 1895 in Cheyenne, Wy, d: 1947 ; Y

................9 Millard MCELRAVY b: Abt. 1896 in Windsor, Co

................9 Mildred M. MCELRAVY b: 23 Sep 1897 in Windsor, Weld, Co, d: 10 Apr 1982 in Downey, Ca; Y

................9 Della MCELRAVY b: 20 Oct 1902 in Windsor, Weld, Co, d: 03 Dec 1968 in Craig, Co; Y

................9 <No name>

    + Rockford LEWIS b: May 1866 in Wi, m: 1889 in Co

................9 Pearl Nina LEWIS b: 01 Mar 1890 in Grants Pass, Or, d: 22 Mar 1966 in Arcadia, Ca; Y

............8 James Westley LEE b: 11 Jan 1875 in Colorado, d: 24 Jul 1948 in San Ysidro, San Diego, Ca; Y

    + Stella WEST b: Abt. 1881 in CO, m: 04 Jan 1902

    + Susan Susie E. RAGAN b: Abt. 1878 in CO, m: 10 May 1899 in CO

................9 Eva Murril LEE b: 10 Aug 1900 in CO

............8 Rosa LEE b: 10 Mar 1878 in Fort Collins, Larimer, Colorado, d: 22 Jul 1911 in Yale, Payne, Colorado; Y

    + John Robert AUSTIN b: 04 Nov 1871 in Lovington, Moultrie, Il, m: 10 Apr 1895 in Greeley, Weld, Co, d: 30 Jul 1944 in Fort Collins, Larimer, Co; Y

................9 Robert Lee AUSTIN b: 24 Mar 1896 in Greeley, Weld, Co

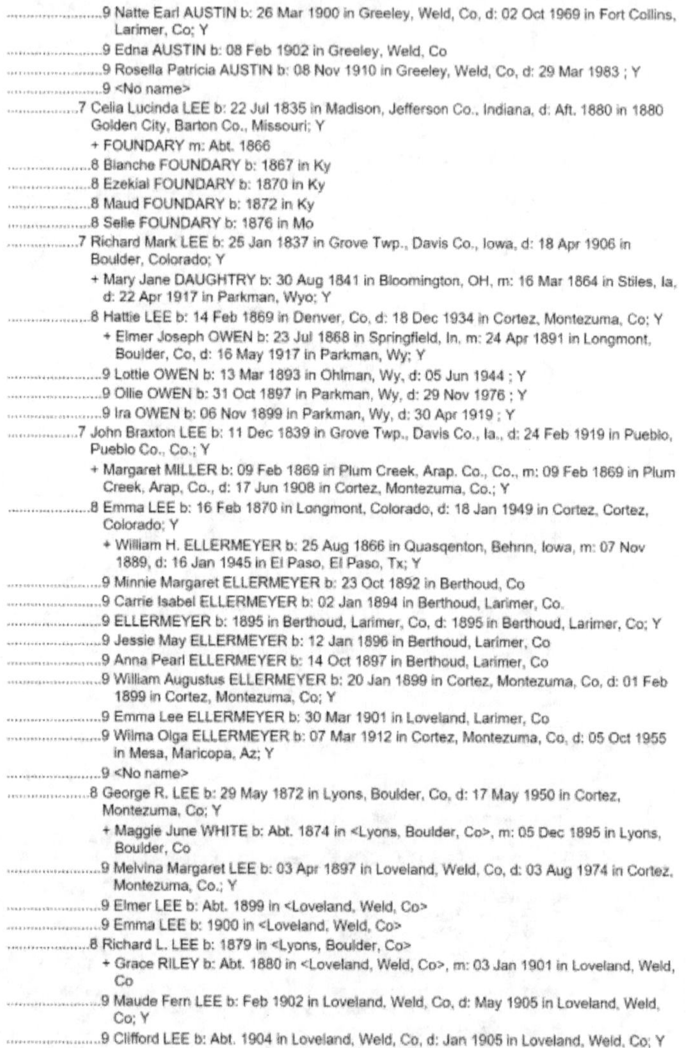

...................9 Natte Earl AUSTIN b: 26 Mar 1900 in Greeley, Weld, Co, d: 02 Oct 1969 in Fort Collins, Larimer, Co; Y

...................9 Edna AUSTIN b: 08 Feb 1902 in Greeley, Weld, Co

...................9 Rosella Patricia AUSTIN b: 08 Nov 1910 in Greeley, Weld, Co, d: 29 Mar 1983 ; Y

...................9 <No name>

...............7 Celia Lucinda LEE b: 22 Jul 1835 in Madison, Jefferson Co., Indiana, d: Aft. 1880 in 1880 Golden City, Barton Co., Missouri; Y

+ FOUNDARY m: Abt. 1866

...................8 Blanche FOUNDARY b: 1867 in Ky

...................8 Ezekial FOUNDARY b: 1870 in Ky

...................8 Maud FOUNDARY b: 1872 in Ky

...................8 Selie FOUNDARY b: 1876 in Mo

...............7 Richard Mark LEE b: 25 Jan 1837 in Grove Twp., Davis Co., Iowa, d: 18 Apr 1906 in Boulder, Colorado; Y

+ Mary Jane DAUGHTRY b: 30 Aug 1841 in Bloomington, OH, m: 16 Mar 1864 in Stiles, Ia, d: 22 Apr 1917 in Parkman, Wyo; Y

...................8 Hattie LEE b: 14 Feb 1869 in Denver, Co, d: 18 Dec 1934 in Cortez, Montezuma, Co; Y

+ Elmer Joseph OWEN b: 23 Jul 1868 in Springfield, In, m: 24 Apr 1891 in Longmont, Boulder, Co, d: 16 May 1917 in Parkman, Wy; Y

...................9 Lottie OWEN b: 13 Mar 1893 in Ohlman, Wy, d: 05 Jun 1944 ; Y

...................9 Ollie OWEN b: 31 Oct 1897 in Parkman, Wy, d: 29 Nov 1976 ; Y

...................9 Ira OWEN b: 06 Nov 1899 in Parkman, Wy, d: 30 Apr 1919 ; Y

...............7 John Braxton LEE b: 11 Dec 1839 in Grove Twp., Davis Co., Ia., d: 24 Feb 1919 in Pueblo, Pueblo Co., Co.; Y

+ Margaret MILLER b: 09 Feb 1869 in Plum Creek, Arap. Co., Co., m: 09 Feb 1869 in Plum Creek, Arap, Co., d: 17 Jun 1908 in Cortez, Montezuma, Co.; Y

...................8 Emma LEE b: 16 Feb 1870 in Longmont, Colorado, d: 18 Jan 1949 in Cortez, Cortez, Colorado; Y

+ William H. ELLERMEYER b: 25 Aug 1866 in Quasqenton, Behnn, Iowa, m: 07 Nov 1889, d: 16 Jan 1945 in El Paso, El Paso, Tx; Y

...................9 Minnie Margaret ELLERMEYER b: 23 Oct 1892 in Berthoud, Co

...................9 Carrie Isabel ELLERMEYER b: 02 Jan 1894 in Berthoud, Larimer, Co.

...................9 ELLERMEYER b: 1895 in Berthoud, Larimer, Co, d: 1895 in Berthoud, Larimer, Co; Y

...................9 Jessie May ELLERMEYER b: 12 Jan 1896 in Berthoud, Larimer, Co

...................9 Anna Pearl ELLERMEYER b: 14 Oct 1897 in Berthoud, Larimer, Co

...................9 William Augustus ELLERMEYER b: 20 Jan 1899 in Cortez, Montezuma, Co, d: 01 Feb 1899 in Cortez, Montezuma, Co; Y

...................9 Emma Lee ELLERMEYER b: 30 Mar 1901 in Loveland, Larimer, Co

...................9 Wilma Olga ELLERMEYER b: 07 Mar 1912 in Cortez, Montezuma, Co, d: 05 Oct 1955 in Mesa, Maricopa, Az; Y

...................9 <No name>

...................8 George R. LEE b: 29 May 1872 in Lyons, Boulder, Co, d: 17 May 1950 in Cortez, Montezuma, Co; Y

+ Maggie June WHITE b: Abt. 1874 in <Lyons, Boulder, Co>, m: 05 Dec 1895 in Lyons, Boulder, Co

...................9 Melvina Margaret LEE b: 03 Apr 1897 in Loveland, Weld, Co, d: 03 Aug 1974 in Cortez, Montezuma, Co.; Y

...................9 Elmer LEE b: Abt. 1899 in <Loveland, Weld, Co>

...................9 Emma LEE b: 1900 in <Loveland, Weld, Co>

...................8 Richard L. LEE b: 1879 in <Lyons, Boulder, Co>

+ Grace RILEY b: Abt. 1880 in <Loveland, Weld, Co>, m: 03 Jan 1901 in Loveland, Weld, Co

...................9 Maude Fern LEE b: Feb 1902 in Loveland, Weld, Co, d: May 1905 in Loveland, Weld, Co; Y

...................9 Clifford LEE b: Abt. 1904 in Loveland, Weld, Co, d: Jan 1905 in Loveland, Weld, Co; Y

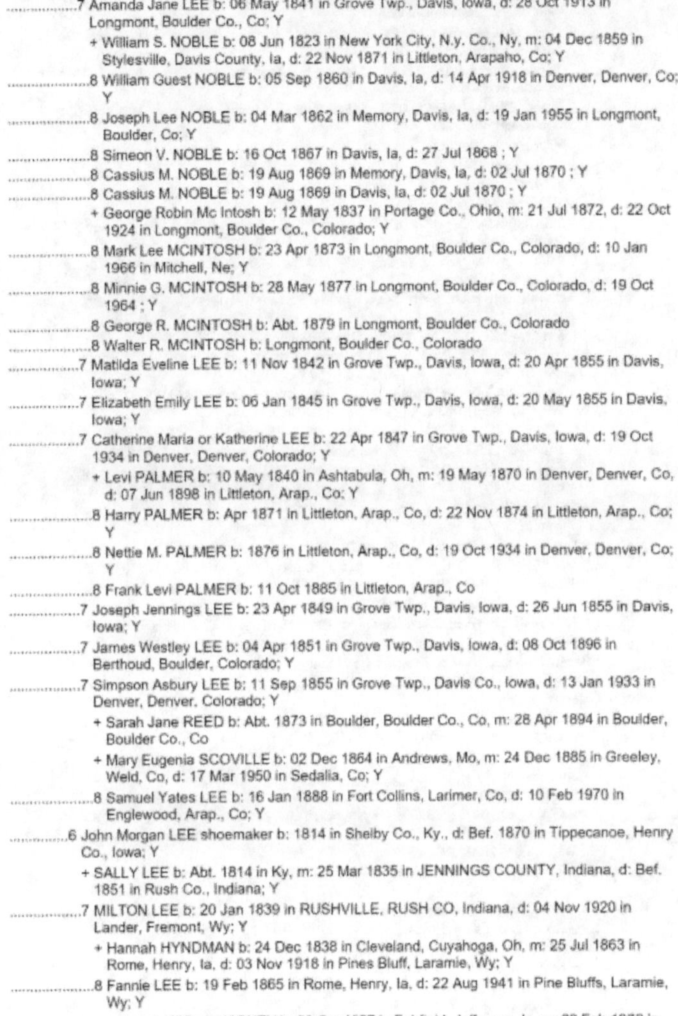

.........7 Amanda Jane LEE b: 06 May 1841 in Grove Twp., Davis, Iowa, d: 28 Oct 1913 in
          Longmont, Boulder Co., Co; Y
          + William S. NOBLE b: 08 Jun 1823 in New York City, N.y. Co., Ny, m: 04 Dec 1859 in
            Stylesville, Davis County, Ia, d: 22 Nov 1871 in Littleton, Arapaho, Co; Y
........8 William Guest NOBLE b: 05 Sep 1860 in Davis, Ia, d: 14 Apr 1918 in Denver, Denver, Co;
          Y
........8 Joseph Lee NOBLE b: 04 Mar 1862 in Memory, Davis, Ia, d: 19 Jan 1955 in Longmont,
          Boulder, Co; Y
........8 Simeon V. NOBLE b: 16 Oct 1867 in Davis, Ia, d: 27 Jul 1868 ; Y
........8 Cassius M. NOBLE b: 19 Aug 1869 in Memory, Davis, Ia, d: 02 Jul 1870 ; Y
........8 Cassius M. NOBLE b: 19 Aug 1869 in Davis, Ia, d: 02 Jul 1870 ; Y
          + George Robin Mc Intosh b: 12 May 1837 in Portage Co., Ohio, m: 21 Jul 1872, d: 22 Oct
            1924 in Longmont, Boulder Co., Colorado; Y
........8 Mark Lee MCINTOSH b: 23 Apr 1873 in Longmont, Boulder Co., Colorado, d: 10 Jan
          1966 in Mitchell, Ne; Y
........8 Minnie G. MCINTOSH b: 28 May 1877 in Longmont, Boulder Co., Colorado, d: 19 Oct
          1964 ; Y
........8 George R. MCINTOSH b: Abt. 1879 in Longmont, Boulder Co., Colorado
........8 Walter R. MCINTOSH b: Longmont, Boulder Co., Colorado
.........7 Matilda Eveline LEE b: 11 Nov 1842 in Grove Twp., Davis, Iowa, d: 20 Apr 1855 in Davis,
          Iowa; Y
.........7 Elizabeth Emily LEE b: 06 Jan 1845 in Grove Twp., Davis, Iowa, d: 20 May 1855 in Davis,
          Iowa; Y
.........7 Catherine Maria or Katherine LEE b: 22 Apr 1847 in Grove Twp., Davis, Iowa, d: 19 Oct
          1934 in Denver, Denver, Colorado; Y
          + Levi PALMER b: 10 May 1840 in Ashtabula, Oh, m: 19 May 1870 in Denver, Denver, Co,
            d: 07 Jun 1898 in Littleton, Arap., Co; Y
........8 Harry PALMER b: Apr 1871 in Littleton, Arap., Co, d: 22 Nov 1874 in Littleton, Arap., Co;
          Y
........8 Nettie M. PALMER b: 1876 in Littleton, Arap., Co, d: 19 Oct 1934 in Denver, Denver, Co;
          Y
........8 Frank Levi PALMER b: 11 Oct 1885 in Littleton, Arap., Co
.........7 Joseph Jennings LEE b: 23 Apr 1849 in Grove Twp., Davis, Iowa, d: 26 Jun 1855 in Davis,
          Iowa; Y
.........7 James Westley LEE b: 04 Apr 1851 in Grove Twp., Davis, Iowa, d: 08 Oct 1896 in
          Berthoud, Boulder, Colorado; Y
.........7 Simpson Asbury LEE b: 11 Sep 1855 in Grove Twp., Davis Co., Iowa, d: 13 Jan 1933 in
          Denver, Denver, Colorado; Y
          + Sarah Jane REED b: Abt. 1873 in Boulder, Boulder Co., Co, m: 28 Apr 1894 in Boulder,
            Boulder Co., Co
          + Mary Eugenia SCOVILLE b: 02 Dec 1864 in Andrews, Mo, m: 24 Dec 1885 in Greeley,
            Weld, Co, d: 17 Mar 1950 in Sedalia, Co; Y
........8 Samuel Yates LEE b: 16 Jan 1888 in Fort Collins, Larimer, Co, d: 10 Feb 1970 in
          Englewood, Arap., Co; Y
.....6 John Morgan LEE shoemaker b: 1814 in Shelby Co., Ky., d: Bef. 1870 in Tippecanoe, Henry
          Co., Iowa; Y
          + SALLY LEE b: Abt. 1814 in Ky, m: 25 Mar 1835 in JENNINGS COUNTY, Indiana, d: Bef.
            1851 in Rush Co., Indiana; Y
.........7 MILTON LEE b: 20 Jan 1839 in RUSHVILLE, RUSH CO, Indiana, d: 04 Nov 1920 in
          Lander, Fremont, Wy; Y
          + Hannah HYNDMAN b: 24 Dec 1838 in Cleveland, Cuyahoga, Oh, m: 25 Jul 1863 in
            Rome, Henry, Ia, d: 03 Nov 1918 in Pines Bluff, Laramie, Wy; Y
........8 Fannie LEE b: 19 Feb 1865 in Rome, Henry, Ia, d: 22 Aug 1941 in Pine Bluffs, Laramie,
          Wy; Y
          + James William HARVEY b: 20 Oct 1857 in Fairfield, Jefferson, Ia, m: 23 Feb 1882 in
            Fairfield, Jefferson, Ia, d: 26 Nov 1930 in Pine Bluffs, Laramie, Wy; Y

....................9 Elmer Howard HARVEY b: 31 Dec 1882 in Martinsburg, Keokuk, Ia, d: 17 May 1959 in Pine Bluffs, Laramie Co, Wy; Y
....................9 Myrtle Mae HARVEY b: 15 Feb 1884 in Martinsburg, Keokuk, Ia, d: 09 Jun 1967 in Tustin, Orange Co, Ca; Y
....................9 James Edward HARVEY b: 19 Mar 1885 in Martinsburg, Keokuk, Ia, d: 26 Nov 1953 in Ontario, Malbeur Co, Or; Y
....................9 Robert Earl HARVEY b: 03 Jan 1889 in Albia, Monroe Co., Ia, d: 24 Apr 1974 in Wheatland, Platte Co., Wy; Y
        + [unknown spouse]
....................10 Kathleen HARVEY b: Abt. 1930
        + Mr Hopkins
....................10 Hazel HARVEY
....................9 Mary Leona Hazel HARVEY b: 15 Apr 1892 in Albia, Monroe, Ia, d: 05 Sep 1961 in Overton, Clark, Nv; Y
....................9 Lelia Ruth HARVEY b: 29 Sep 1894 in Albia, Monroe, Ia, d: 26 Jun 1973 in Seattle, Kitsap Co, Wa; Y
....................9 Clara Eldora HARVEY b: 14 Jun 1896 in Albia, Monroe, Ia, d: 07 Nov 1898 in Albia, Monroe Co, Iowa; Y
....................8 Rosa Mae LEE b: 12 Apr 1867 in Rome, Henry, Ia, d: 01 May 1868 ; Y
....................8 Peter Smith LEE b: 28 Aug 1868 in Rome, Henry, Ia, d: 11 Jan 1941 in Brigham City, Box Elder, Ut; Y
        + Annie CLARK b: 07 Apr 1885 in Bicknell, Wayne, Ut, m: 28 Mar 1911 in Wilson, Teton, Wy, d: 09 Aug 1953 in Ogden, Weber, Ut; Y
....................9 Clinton Smith LEE b: 04 Dec 1911 in Wilson, Teton, Wy, d: 24 Dec 1969 ; Y
....................9 Theo Bell LEE b: 21 Oct 1913 in Albin, Laramie, Wy, d: 11 Nov 1918 ; Y
....................9 Oral Clark LEE b: 25 Sep 1919 in Brigham City, Box Elder, Ut, d: 03 Mar 1992 in Ogden, Weber, Utah; Y
....................9 living 2000
....................9 livinf 2000
....................8 Lena Rivers LEE b: 27 Jul 1871 in Rome, Henry, Ia, d: 14 May 1873 ; Y
....................8 Mary Ellen Shay LEE b: 14 Nov 1875 in Rome, Henry, Ia, d: 05 May 1943 ; Y
        + John Henry JACKSON b: Abt. 1873, m: 05 Sep 1894
................7 Peter Smith LEE b: 1842 in Rush Co., Indiana
        + MARY ANN SMITH b: Switzerland, Indiana, m: 27 May 1852 in HENRY CO., IA
................7 Ira LEE b: 1854 in Henry Co., Iowa
................7 Sarah Jane LEE b: 1856 in Henry Co., Iowa
................6 PETER LEE b: 19 Mar 1815 in Shelby Co., Ky., d: 11 Jun 1894 in Carlton, Hamilton Co., Texas; Y
        + Salina Tobey b: 17 Feb 1822 in Vernon, Jennings Co., Ind, m: 01 Apr 1841 in Vernon, Jennings, Indiana, d: 1850 in Camden Co., MO; Y
................7 Sarah Lee b: 1842 in Camden Co, MO
        + John EVANS
        + W. F. HALL d: Hamilton Co., Tx; Y
................7 Wheeler Lee b: 09 Oct 1846 in Camden Co., MO, d: 15 Apr 1924 in O'Brien, TX; Y
        + Emily Reed b: 05 Apr 1852 in Rusk Co., TX, m: 16 Mar 1876 in Hamilton Co., Tx, d: 27 May 1906 in Haskell Co., TX; Y
................8 Lycurgus Edgar Lee b: 08 Oct 1878 in Hamilton Co., Tx, d: 01 May 1919 in Rochester, Haskell Co., TX; Y
        + Ethel Garner m: Hamilton Co., Tx
................9 Lindell Dick Lee b: Private
................9 Naomi Lee b: Private
        + Ruth Williams m: Hamilton Co., Tx
................9 Bernice Lee b: Private
................9 Lois Lee b: Private

...............8 Walter Best Lee b: 27 May 1881 in Hamilton Co., Tx, d: 06 Oct 1936 in Spur, Dickens Co., TX; Y
+ Emma Loe b: 08 Apr 1900 in Hamilton Co., Tx, d: 17 Oct 1979 in Spur, Dickens Co., TX; Y
+ Mattie Hall b: 16 Dec 1883 in Comanche Co., TX, m: Hamilton Co., Tx, d: 06 Dec 1919 in Ralls, Crosby Co., TX; Y
...............8 Margaret Alma Lee b: 31 Dec 1884 in Hamilton Co., Tx, d: 06 Nov 1962 in Ralls, Crosby Co., TX; Y
+ Otho Mimms b: 10 Aug 1883 in Comanche Co., TX, m: 27 Dec 1906 in Haskell Co., TX, d: 06 Apr 1951 ; Y
...............9 Otho Leroy Mimms b: 1908
+ Eva Belle Steward b: Private, m: Private
...............9 Darrell Wyman Mimms b: Private
+ Bonnie Bess Burkett b: Private, m: Private
...............9 Glen Wheeler Pete Mimms b: Private
+ Bobbye Fern Bratton b: Private, m: Private
...............9 Jewell Mimms b: Private
+ William David Taylor b: 03 Feb 1912 in Haskell, TX, m: Private, d: 07 Jan 1988 in Lubbock, TX; Y
...............9 Dalton Dwayne Mimms b: Private
+ Beulah Faye Thomas b: Private, m: Private
...............9 Virgil Marvin Mimms b: Private
+ Living Webb
...............9 Gladys Emily Mimms b: Private
+ Clarence Conly Gilstrap b: Private, m: Private
...............9 Doris Larue Mimms b: Private
+ Arthur Jackson Moorman b: Private, m: Private
...............9 Leona Maebell Mimms b: Private
+ Lloyd M. Blanton b: 23 Nov 1915, m: Private, d: Jul 1987 in Erath Co., TX; Y
...............9 Ola Jerrine Mimms b: Private
+ James Hiram Parks b: Private, m: Private
...............9 Vera Merle Mimms b: Private
+ John Rodney McFarland b: Private, m: Private
...............9 Claudia Alma Mimms b: Private
+ Tom L. Porter b: Private, m: Private
...............8 Alfred Elmore Lee b: 26 Feb 1887 in Hamilton Co., Tx, d: 10 Jan 1923 in Dickens, TX; Y
+ Ozella Mimms b: 07 Dec 1887 in Comanche Co., TX, m: 10 May 1908 in Haskell Co., TX, d: 23 Mar 1956 in Stockton, Ca; Y
...............9 Arvil Wheeler Lee b: 15 Oct 1909 in O'Brien, TX, d: 10 Jan 1923 in Dickens, TX; Y
+ Josephine Elvira Wright b: Private, m: Private
+ Johnnie Elizabeth Mayo b: 20 Jun 1908 in Boswell, OK, m: 06 Dec 1928 in Boswell, OK, d: 15 Oct 1980 in Stockton, Ca; Y
...............10 Veda Elaine Lee b: Private
...............9 Wayland Alfred Lee b: 28 Feb 1912 in Hamilton Co., Tx, d: 02 Nov 1983 in Stockton, Ca; Y
+ Lucy Marie Blair b: Private, m: Private
...............9 Duward Edwin Lee b: 09 Aug 1919 in Colorado Springs, CO, d: 17 Mar 1999 ; Y
+ Helen Faye Hines b: Private, m: Private
...............9 Mildred Anna Lee b: Private
+ Jimmie Kenneth White m: Private, d: 21 Aug 2001 in Spur, Dickens Co., TX; Y
...............9 Bernard Ray Lee b: Private
+ M. Novelle Scott b: Private, m: Private
...............9 Ella Dorine Lee b: Private
+ Norman Warren b: Private, m: Private
...............8 Virgil Porter Lee b: 18 May 1891 in Hamilton Co., Tx, d: Houston, Harris Co., TX; Y

+ Thelma Lee Clark m: 10 Aug 1929 in Evansville, WI
.............9 Living Lee
+ Phil Randolph b: Private
.............9 Living Lee
+ Charles Nix b: Private
.............8 Edwin Stirman Lee b: 04 Aug 1893 in Hamilton Co., Tx, d: 27 Dec 1977 in Spur, Dickens Co., TX; Y
+ Lillie Gay Cooner b: 22 Oct 1899, m: 1921 in Haskell Co., TX, d: Oct 1977 in Dickens, TX; Y
.............9 Annette Lee b: Private
+ Bill Fox b: Private, m: Private
.............9 LaVorise Lee b: Private
+ Med McKnight b: Private, m: Private
+ Lydia Alice (Roberts) Nobel
+ Mary Caroline "Polly" [427f] Stidham b: 28 Apr 1833 in Tennessee, m: Abt. 1866 in Vernon co., Missouri, d: 17 Oct 1899 in Haskell, Hamilton Co., Texas; Y
.............7 Abigail Abbie Lee b: 02 Oct 1867 in Hamilton Co., Texas, d: 14 Jun 1928 in Haskel, Texas; Y
+ William Archibald "Will" Mcdougle b: 08 Oct 1858, m: 16 Nov 1890 in Hamilton Co., TX, d: 31 Mar 1929 ; Y
.............8 Walter Tant Mcdougle b: 30 Aug 1891 in Hamilton Co., TX, d: Oct 1954 in Haskel, TX; Y
+ Bertie Mustin m: 1921
.............8 George D. Mcdougle b: 20 Mar 1894 in Hamilton Co., TX, d: 18 Dec 1967 in Haskel, TX; Y
+ never Married
.............8 Alexander Lee Mcdougle b: 28 Jan 1896
+ Jane Legrand m: 12 Dec 1920
.............8 Rosa Nellie Mcdougle b: 24 Sep 1897
+ Claud Sexton m: 1914
.............8 Mary Gertrude "Gertie" Mcdougle b: 08 Sep 1899
+ William Grover Butler
.............9 Grover Chester Butler b: 13 Aug 1924, d: 10 Aug 1996 ; Y
.............9 Living Butler
.............9 Living Butler
.............9 Living Butler
.............9 Living Butler
.............9 Living Butler
.............9 Living Butler
.............8 John Calvin Mcdougle b: 17 Feb 1904
.............8 Jenny Neal Mcdougle b: 05 Mar 1906
+ Orvel Cole
.............7 Grant "Billy" Lee b: 1870
.............7 Tony Lee b: Abt. 1873
+ Mammie
.............8 Vallie Lee
.............8 Travis Lee
.............7 Rosa Belle Lee b: 03 Jul 1876 in Texas, d: 06 Aug 1968 in Alex, Oklahoma; Y
+ William Perry Palmer b: 04 Aug 1872 in Mississippi, m: 15 Jul 1899 in Hamilton Co., TX, d: 10 Oct 1938 ; Y
.............8 Wiley Perry Palmer b: 10 Jun 1900 in Texas, d: 26 May 1985 in Alex, Oklahoma; Y
.............8 Mary Virginia Palmer b: 26 Nov 1901 in Texas, d: 11 Dec 1991 in Chickasha, Oklahoma; Y
+ Joe Armstrong d: Alex, Oklahoma; Y
+ Edgar Morgan b: Tennessee
.............9 Lester Edgar Morgan b: 12 Sep 1921, d: Jul 1968 ; Y

...............9 Norma Zora Morgan b: 09 Feb 1925 in Lenoire City, Tennessee, d: 14 May 2002 in Chickosha, OK; Y

　　+ Willis Dean POLK b: Abt. 1923, m: 05 Feb 1942 in Chickasha, Oklahoma

...............9 Wanda Morgan b: 17 Mar 1933 in Alex, Oklahoma, d: 22 Oct 1996 in Prague, Oklahoma; Y

...............9 Living Morgan

...............8 Velma Palmer b: 24 Jan 1906

...............8 Luna Palmer b: 22 Dec 1907

　　+ George (Bill) Armstrong b: 22 Jul 1912 in Chickasha, Oklahoma, d: 20 May 1981 in Chickasha, Oklahoma; Y

...............9 Stephen Lee Armstrong b: 21 Mar 1950 in Chickasha, Oklahoma, d: 21 Mar 1950 in Chickasha, Oklahoma; Y

...............9 Living Armstrong

...............8 Hazel Palmer

　　+ Cox

...............8 Elwa Palmer

　　+ William (Alex?) Shaw

...............9 Living Shaw

...............9 Living Shaw

...............9 Living Shaw

　　+ Nancy (Barnett) JANES b: 1824 in Camden Co, MO, m: 19 Jan 1851 in Benton Co., Mo, d: 1870 in Camden County, MO; Y

...............7 Mary JANES (Mollie) Lee b: 29 Dec 1851 in Camden Co, MO, d: 1940 in Haskel, TX; Y

...............7 Samuel Urbane Lee b: 18 Dec 1853 in Camden Co, MO, d: 05 Mar 1881 in Haskel, TX; Y

...............7 Thomas Jefferson (Jeff) Lee b: 12 Mar 1856 in Camden Co, MO, d: 20 Feb 1937 in Haskel, TX; Y

...............7 Alexander Campbell Lee b: 1857

...............7 Virginia Jennifer (Jennie) Lee b: 1860

...............7 William Calvin Lee b: 1864 in Camden Co, MO

...............6 Martin Lee b: 15 Apr 1817 in Shelby Co., Ky., d: 30 Apr 1900 in Tippecanoe, Henry Co., Iowa; Y

　　+ Lydia Ann RILEY b: 25 Aug 1821 in CINCINATI, Hamilton Co., OH, m: 09 Aug 1838 in Vernon, Jenings Co., IN, d: 18 Nov 1903 in Henry Co., Iowa; Y

...............7 Jonathan LEE b: 09 Nov 1839 in Vernon, Jenings Co., IN, d: 1921 ; Y

　　+ Alice BOYD b: Abt. 1845, m: 03 Nov 1869

...............8 Oliver B. LEE b: 1872 in Tippecanoe, Henry Co., IA

...............8 Rolf LEE b: 1878 in Tippecanoe, Henry Co., IA

　　+ Mary HARTER m: 19 May 1858, d: Abt. 1868 in Tippecanoe, Henry Co., IA; Y

...............8 Curtis E. LEE b: 1862 in Tippecanoe, Henry Co., IA

...............8 Edwin H. LEE b: 1866 in Tippecanoe, Henry Co., IA

...............7 Mary Polly Lee b: Mar 1841 in Vernon, Jenings Co., IN of Tippecanoe, Henry Co., Iowa, d: 1903 in Arkansas; Y

　　+ Joseph Lee b: Nov 1830 in Indiana, m: 1858 in Henry Co., IA, d: 1911 in Dixon County or Freemont Dodge County Nebraska; Y

...............8 Nancy Alice Lee b: 02 Feb 1868 in Washington County, Iowa, d: 31 Jan 1957 in Loveland, Colorado USA 435 West 4th Street; Y

　　+ Asakiah Stypes Mills b: 12 Sep 1869 in Hardin County, Iowa, m: Abt. 1899, d: 06 Dec 1959 in Springdale Washington County, Arkansas; Y

...............9 Bessie Belle Mills b: 1899, d: 1984 ; Y

...............9 Sherman Mills b: 29 Jul 1900 in Henry County, Iowa, USA, d: 07 Jul 1977 in Loveland, Colorado USA 435 West 4th Street; Y

　　+ Mary Elizabeth Mitts b: 13 May 1909 in Harper County, Oklahoma, m: 27 May 1928 in New London, Henry County, Iowa USA

...............10 Living Mills

...............10 Living Mills

...........................10 Living Mills
...........................10 Living Mills
...........................10 Living Mills
...........................10 Living Mills
...........................10 Mills d: 1946 ; Y
...........................9 Daisy Mae Mills b: 1902, d: 1920 ; Y
...........................9 Violet Mary Mills b: 1905, d: 1991 ; Y
...........................9 Viola Mills b: 1905, d: 1997 ; Y
...........................9 Iliff Sylvester Mills b: 1907, d: 1999 in Mt Pleasant, Iowa, USA; Y
...........................8 Martin E. Lee b: Nov 1874 in Tippecanoe, Henry Co., IA
...........................8 Anna B. Lee b: Jul 1877 in Tippecanoe, Henry Co., IA, d: Canada; Y
...........................8 Edward Benton Lee b: 03 Dec 1881 in Tippecanoe, Henry Co., IA, d: 13 Jan 1952 in
      Provo Utah; Y
    + Hester Lydia Rowe b: 23 Aug 1878 in Willow Springs, Hutton Valley, Howell Co., MO,
      m: 01 Aug 1912 in Sioux City, Woodbury, IA., d: 15 Apr 1974 in South Elmonte, Los
      Angeles Co., CA 91733; Y
...........................9 Ellis Edward Lee b: 05 May 1913 in Allen, NE, d: 17 Jul 1995 in South El Monte, Los
      Angeles Co., CA; Y
    + Wilma Jean Rahn b: Private
...........................9 Saint Elmo Green Lee b: 31 Jan 1915 in Meadowbrook, Alberta, Canada, d: 06 Jan
      2000 in Rogers, Benton Co., Arkansas; Y
    + Madeline b: Private
    + Arlene June Ainge b: 29 Nov 1918 in Utah, m: 20 Mar 1937 in Payson, Utah, d: 04
      Jul 1984 in Whittier California; Y
...........................10 Living Lee
    + Living
...........................11 Living Lee
...........................11 Living Lee
...........................11 Living Lee
...........................11 Living Lee
...........................8 Jonathan W. Lee b: Tippecanoe, Henry Co., IA
...........................8 Perry D. Lee b: Tippecanoe, Henry Co., IA
...........................8 Melissa Rebecca Lee b: Tippecanoe, Henry Co., IA
...........................7 Rebecca LEE b: Abt. 1843 in Vernon, Jenings Co., IN of Tippecanoe, Henry Co., Iowa, d:
      03 May 1879 in Tippecanoe, Henry Co., Iowa; Y
    + William Bill LAMBERT b: 1839 in of Henry Co., IA, d: Aft. 1890 in Tippecanoe, Henry Co.,
      IA; Y
...........................7 Martin Lee Jr. b: 1845 in Vernon, Jenings Co., IN
    + Matlda b: 1835 in IN, m: Abt. 1879 in IN
...........................8 ALfred Lee b: Mar 1880 in Tippecanoe, Henry Co., Iowa
...........................7 Elizabeth LEE b: Abt. 1847 in Tippecanoe, Henry Co., Iowa
    + MARGARET HOCKET b: 13 Dec 1803 in NC
...........................6 Isaac F. LEE b: 25 Dec 1818 in State Line, KY&TN, d: 03 Jul 1902 in Tippecanoe Township,
      Henry County, Iowa; Y
    + Elizabeth G. Connell b: 05 Feb 1824 in NEAR VERNON, IN, m: 03 Dec 1841 in
      JEFFERSON CO., IA, d: 07 Jul 1902 in Jefferson County, Iowa; Y
...........................7 John LEE b: 1843 in IA, d: 1863 in Civil War; Y
...........................7 James Henry LEE b: 05 Jan 1845, d: Nov 1848 ; Y
...........................7 Rebecca Jane Lee b: 03 Aug 1848 in IA, d: Abt. 1861 ; Y
...........................7 Joseph Gray Lee b: 06 Aug 1851, d: Abt. Jul 1853 ; Y
...........................7 Sovilla Anna Lee b: 14 Jul 1853 in HENRY CO., IA, d: 16 Dec 1918 in ROUND PRAIRE
      TWP, JEFFERSON CO., IA; Y
...........................7 Roswell Spencer Lee b: 17 Dec 1854 in Jefferson County, Iowa, d: 08 Dec 1886 in ROUND
      PRAIRE, JEFFERSON CO. IA; Y

+ Nancy Lucinda Canady b: 15 Aug 1855 in Round Praire Township, Jefferson County, Iowa, m: 21 Nov 1875 in Jefferson County, Iowa, d: 04 Jan 1918 in Birmingham, Iowa; Y

............8 Sarah Elizabeth Lee b: 29 Aug 1876 in Henry County, Iowa, d: 14 Jun 1938 in Libertyville, Jefferson County, Iowa; Y

+ Hubert Elmer Young b: 11 Nov 1873 in Lane County, Kansas, m: 27 Aug 1893 in Henry County, Iowa, d: 17 Mar 1954 in Mt. Pleasant, Iowa; Y

............9 Anna Mae Young b: 13 Apr 1894 in Henry County, Iowa, d: Mt. Pleasant, Iowa; Y

+ Harold R. Young b: 24 Nov 1888, m: 01 Mar 1911 in Mt. Pleasant, Iowa, d: 30 Jan 1965 ; Y

............9 Myrtle Jane Young b: 28 Oct 1895 in near, Salem, Iowa, d: 01 Jun 1984 in Iowa Medical Center, Burlington, Iowa; Y

+ Alvin Omer Kinney m: 04 Nov 1914

............9 Mary Agnes Young b: 19 Aug 1897 in Henry County, Iowa, d: 28 May 1966 in Fairfield, Iowa; Y

+ Guy Litton b: 09 May 1893, m: 01 Mar 1919

............9 Emly Macil Lucinda Young b: 24 Jul 1900 in Henry County, Iowa, d: 19 Jun 1978 in Waterloo, Iowa; Y

+ John Albert Vandenburg b: 26 Jun 1899, m: 19 Jun 1922, d: 04 Aug 1972 ; Y

............9 Andrew Jackson Young b: 20 May 1902 in Salem, Iowa, d: Galesburg, Illinois; Y

+ [unknown spouse]

............10 Imogene Ruth Young b: 13 Nov 1926, d: Feb 1928 ; Y

............9 Elsie Lucinda Young b: 06 Dec 1903 in Henry County, Iowa, d: 30 Jun 1960 in Arizona; Y

+ Earl A. Kenyon b: 25 Jun 1900, m: 01 Dec 1921, d: 29 Jul 1952 ; Y

............9 Iva Edna Young b: 07 Jul 1905 in Henry Co., IA

+ Steve Edwin Coleman b: Abt. 1903 in Henry Co., IA

............9 Louva Elbertine Young b: 07 May 1907 in Henry Co., IA

+ Richard Eyestone b: Abt. 1905 in Henry Co., IA, m: 30 Jun 1928 in Henry Co., IA

+ William Deutsch m: 16 Apr 1977

............9 Walter Lee Young b: 06 May 1909 in Henry County, Iowa, d: 09 Oct 1981 in Ventura, California; Y

............9 John Arthur Young b: 28 Jun 1911 in Henry County, Iowa, d: 22 May 1927 in Libertyville, Iowa; Y

............9 Floyd William Young b: 26 Jan 1915 in Salem IA

+ Mildred Heckenburg

............8 John Emsley Lee b: 24 Mar 1879 in Jefferson County, Iowa, d: 31 Jan 1963 ; Y

+ Ida Pearl Schulz b: 13 Aug 1887 in Hillsboro (?), Iowa, m: 06 Sep 1906, d: 03 Jun 1970 ; Y

............9 Elmer Herman Lee b: 05 Jul 1907 in Van Buren County, Iowa, d: 15 Oct 1995 ; Y

+ C. Maxine Tucker m: 22 Dec 1927, d: 15 Jun 1990 ; Y

............9 Harry Albert Lee b: 27 Jul 1909 in Henry County, Iowa, d: 17 Jun 1993 ; Y

+ Mildred Tweedy b: 1909, m: 28 Feb 1930, d: 1996 ; Y

............9 Grace Irene Lee b: 04 Mar 1912 in Henry Co., IA

+ Clarence Bailey

............9 Dorothy Louise Lee b: 06 Aug 1914 in Henry Co., IA

+ Dallas Swan

............9 Opal Mae Lee b: 18 Apr 1917 in Henry Co., IA

+ Carl Johnson

............10 Ruth Ann Johnson

............9 Evelyn Ruth Lee b: 29 Dec 1919

............9 Wilma Francis Lee b: 23 Mar 1923, d: 27 Oct 1987 ; Y

+ Orville McDowell

............9 John Lee Jr. b: 29 Aug 1925 in or Aug. 30, d: 12 Feb 1978 ; Y

............9 Lloyd Eugene Lee b: 03 Jul 1929 in Henry Co., IA

+ Meralene Bailey m: 05 Mar 1955

...............8 Clarence Lee b: 18 Jul 1882 in Henry County, Iowa, d: 09 Jun 1959 in Jefferson County, Iowa; Y
+ Maude Gire m: 29 Mar 1905 in Birmingham, Iowa
...............9 Roy Lee b: 21 Dec 1905, d: 10 Jan 1959 ; Y
+ Jesse Thompson
...............9 Grace Lee b: 03 Mar 1907 in Van Buren County, Iowa, d: 16 May 1972 in Fairfield, Jefferson County, Iowa; Y
...............9 Arthur Lee b: 19 Aug 1908 in Van Buren County, Iowa, d: 13 Jan 1966 in Coralville, Iowa; Y
...............9 Helen Lee b: 15 Jun 1914 in Henry Co., IA
+ Clarence Van Ness
...............9 Harold Lee b: 22 Oct 1926 in Henry Co., IA
...............8 Effie Amelia Lee b: 21 Jul 1885, d: 19 Apr 1931 ; Y
+ Stephen Asa Jones m: 08 May 1901
...............9 Lucinda Jones b: 1903
+ [unknown spouse]
...............10 Donald Rinabarger d: Abt. 1976 ; Y
...............9 John Jones b: 1904 in Henry Co., IA
...............9 William Jones b: 1905 in Henry Co., IA
...............9 James Jones b: 1908 in Henry Co., IA
...............9 Minnie Jones b: 1910 in Henry Co., IA
...............9 Mary Jones b: 1912 in Henry Co., IA
...............9 Stanley Jones b: 1914 in Henry Co., IA
...............9 Edna Jones b: 1916 in Henry Co., IA
...............9 Sam Jones b: Abt. 1918 in Henry Co., IA
...............9 Earl George Jones b: Abt. 1920 in Henry Co., IA
...............7 Martha Lee b: 1857
+ John C. Harter
...............7 Joshua C. Lee b: 03 Apr 1858 in Van Buren Co., Iowa, d: 11 Oct 1911 in from asphyxiation, Burlington, Iowa; Y
+ Cerintha Evelyn Long b: 14 Jun 1857 in Jefferson County, Iowa, m: 02 Nov 1875, d: 27 May 1950 in possibly, Henry County, Iowa; Y
...............8 Luella Esther Ann Lee b: 11 Aug 1877 in Jefferson County, Iowa, d: 03 Dec 1944 ; Y
+ David Samuel Barton b: 01 Oct 1871 in Henry County, Iowa, m: 10 Apr 1895, d: 13 Mar 1940 ; Y
...............9 Thomas Earl Barton b: 21 Oct 1895, d: Dec 1982 in probably, Henry County, Iowa; Y
+ Lee McDowell m: 02 Mar 1921
...............9 Susie Barton b: 27 Feb 1897
...............9 Amy Ann Barton b: 28 Apr 1899 in Henry County, Iowa, d: 16 Jul 1974 in Henry County, Iowa; Y
...............9 Daisey Barton b: 25 Mar 1901
+ Ray Standley m: 06 Oct 1920
...............9 Jay F Barton b: 27 Mar 1903, d: Jul 1982 in probably, Mt Pleasant, Henry County, Iowa; Y
+ Marie McElwee m: 20 Sep 1922 in Henry County, Iowa
...............9 Mary J Barton b: 1906, d: Aft. 1925 ; Y
+ McElwee
...............9 Dale Barton b: 1914 in Henry Co., IA
...............8 Melvin C Lee b: 03 Oct 1879, d: 07 May 1944 in Mt Pleasant, Henry County, Iowa; Y
+ Doris Phiepot m: 24 Feb 1915 in Memphis, Missouri
...............8 Orin Isaac Lee b: 29 May 1881 in Henry County, Iowa, d: 23 Apr 1968 in Burlington, Iowa; Y
+ Jennie Anderson m: Sep 1906
...............9 Herman Lester Lee b: 04 Dec 1907, d: 07 Aug 1997 in probably, Mediapolis, Des Moines County, Iowa; Y

..................9 Viola Gustava Lee b: 13 Nov 1909, d: 07 Oct 1993 in probably, Phoenix, Maricopa
County, Arizona; Y
..................9 Minnie Caroline Lee b: 23 Feb 1913 in Yarmouth, Illinois, d: 02 Mar 1978 in Phoenix,
Arizona; Y
..................9 Gladys Lucille Lee b: 25 Oct 1915, d: 06 Nov 1917 ; Y
..................9 Raymond Carl Lee b: 30 Apr 1924, d: 1968 in Cedar Rapids, Iowa; Y
..................9 Carlyle Eugene Lee b: 14 Oct 1929, d: 1968 in Denver, Colorado; Y
+ Elsie Nelson m: 08 Apr 1955
..................8 Charles LeRoy Lee b: 29 Jul 1883 in Des Moines, Polk County, Iowa, d: 21 Feb 1947 in
Rockford, Illinois; Y
..................8 Francis Elizabeth Lee b: 14 Jul 1885, d: 28 Jan 1938 ; Y
+ Richard Holaday
..................9 Holaday
..................8 Chester J Lee b: 08 Jun 1887 in Henry County, Iowa, d: 12 Oct 1974 in Burlington, Iowa;
Y
+ Minnie Scott m: 16 Feb 1915 in West Burlington, Iowa
..................8 Ida May Lee b: 08 Mar 1890 in Jefferson County, Iowa, d: 16 Jun 1979 in Wayland, Iowa;
Y
+ John Hudson m: 04 Mar 1909, d: 1963 ; Y
..................9 Irene Velma Hudson d: 1979 in New Bloomfield, Missouri; Y
+ Thomas
..................9 Eva Hudson d: 1979 ; Y
+ Brown
..................8 Linnie Dell Lee b: 23 Jul 1891 in Jefferson County, Iowa, d: 25 Sep 1974 in New London,
Iowa; Y
+ Nyra Gill b: 1885 in Henry Co., IA, m: Abt. 1912
..................9 Glenn Gill b: 02 Dec 1913 in Henry Co., IA, d: Dec 1984 in Hoisington, Barton, KS; Y
..................9 Alice Gill b: Feb 1916 in Henry Co., IA, d: Bef. 1974 ; Y
..................9 Lester Gill b: 1922 in Henry Co., IA, d: Bef. 1974 ; Y
..................9 Richard Gill b: Henry Co., IA, d: Bef. 1974 ; Y
..................8 Clifford Isiah Lee b: 17 Dec 1894 in Jefferson County, Iowa, d: Nov 1985 in probably,
Burlington, Des Moines County, Iowa; Y
+ Maude M Piper m: 09 Jan 1918
..................9 Roy Kenneth Lee b: 24 Jan 1921, d: 15 Sep 1963 in Memphis, Missouri; Y
..................8 Bernice Lee b: 10 Mar 1897 in Jefferson County, Iowa, d: 10 Jul 1946 in Burlington, Iowa;
Y
+ Orvill Dean m: 13 Feb 1917 in Des Moines County, Iowa
..................8 Alpha Harold Lee b: 27 Aug 1900, d: Apr 1958 in Burlington, Iowa; Y
..................7 Nancy Arminda Lee b: 06 Jul 1862, d: Abt. 1864 ; Y
..................7 Ollie May Lee b: 05 Oct 1864, d: 08 Oct 1864 ; Y
..................6 James W. LEE b: 1820 in Mercer Co., KY of Jennings Co., IND, d: of Lee Co., IA; Y
+ ELIZABETH CREED b: Abt. 1822 in NC, m: 05 Nov 1840 in JEFFERSON CO., IA
..................7 MARY A LEE b: 1842 in LEE CO., IA
..................7 Isaac BARNUM LEE b: 22 Dec 1844 in LEE CO., IA, d: 17 Feb 1923 in Beaver Creek,
Clackamas Co., Oregon; Y
+ Mary b: 1842 in Mo, m: Abt. 1864 in Mo
..................8 James D. LEE b: 1865 in Mo
..................8 Sarah F. LEE b: 1867 in Mo
..................8 Ann E. LEE b: 1869 in Mo
..................8 Martha E. LEE b: 1871 in Mo
..................8 Mary I LEE b: 1872 in Mo
..................8 Nancy J. LEE b: 1875 in Beaver Creek, Clackamas Co., Oregon
..................8 Margaret LEE b: 1877 in Beaver Creek, Clackamas Co., Oregon
..................7 SARAH E LEE b: 1849 in LEE CO., IA
..................7 NANCY LEE b: 1853 in LEE CO., IA

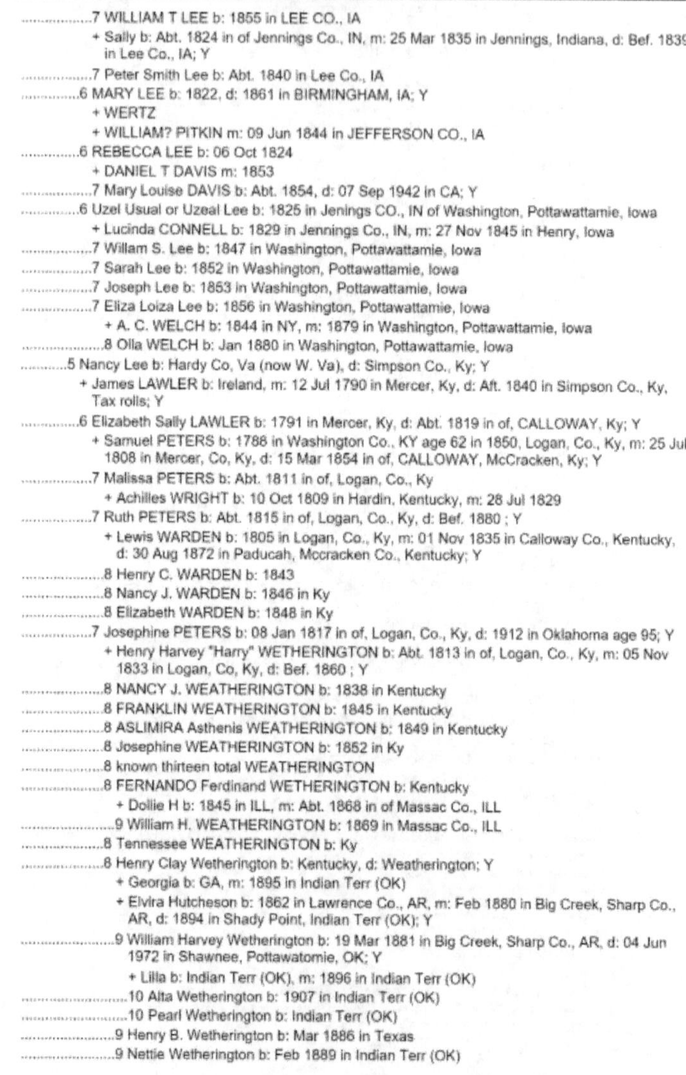

..............7 WILLIAM T LEE b: 1855 in LEE CO., IA
    + Sally b: Abt. 1824 in of Jennings Co., IN, m: 25 Mar 1835 in Jennings, Indiana, d: Bef. 1839 in Lee Co., IA; Y
..............7 Peter Smith Lee b: Abt. 1840 in Lee Co., IA
.............6 MARY LEE b: 1822, d: 1861 in BIRMINGHAM, IA; Y
    + WERTZ
    + WILLIAM? PITKIN m: 09 Jun 1844 in JEFFERSON CO., IA
.............6 REBECCA LEE b: 06 Oct 1824
    + DANIEL T DAVIS m: 1853
..............7 Mary Louise DAVIS b: Abt. 1854, d: 07 Sep 1942 in CA; Y
.............6 Uzel Usual or Uzeal Lee b: 1825 in Jenings CO., IN of Washington, Pottawattamie, Iowa
    + Lucinda CONNELL b: 1829 in Jennings Co., IN, m: 27 Nov 1845 in Henry, Iowa
..............7 Willam S. Lee b: 1847 in Washington, Pottawattamie, Iowa
..............7 Sarah Lee b: 1852 in Washington, Pottawattamie, Iowa
..............7 Joseph Lee b: 1853 in Washington, Pottawattamie, Iowa
..............7 Eliza Loiza Lee b: 1856 in Washington, Pottawattamie, Iowa
    + A. C. WELCH b: 1844 in NY, m: 1879 in Washington, Pottawattamie, Iowa
..................8 Olla WELCH b: Jan 1880 in Washington, Pottawattamie, Iowa
..........5 Nancy Lee b: Hardy Co, Va (now W. Va), d: Simpson Co., Ky; Y
    + James LAWLER b: Ireland, m: 12 Jul 1790 in Mercer, Ky, d: Aft. 1840 in Simpson Co., Ky, Tax rolls; Y
.............6 Elizabeth Sally LAWLER b: 1791 in Mercer, Ky, d: Abt. 1819 in of, CALLOWAY, Ky; Y
    + Samuel PETERS b: 1788 in Washington Co., KY age 62 in 1850, Logan, Co., Ky, m: 25 Jul 1808 in Mercer, Co, Ky, d: 15 Mar 1854 in of, CALLOWAY, McCracken, Ky; Y
..............7 Malissa PETERS b: Abt. 1811 in of, Logan, Co., Ky
    + Achilles WRIGHT b: 10 Oct 1809 in Hardin, Kentucky, m: 28 Jul 1829
..............7 Ruth PETERS b: Abt. 1815 in of, Logan, Co., Ky, d: Bef. 1880 ; Y
    + Lewis WARDEN b: 1805 in Logan, Co., Ky, m: 01 Nov 1835 in Calloway Co., Kentucky, d: 30 Aug 1872 in Paducah, Mccracken Co., Kentucky; Y
..............8 Henry C. WARDEN b: 1843
..............8 Nancy J. WARDEN b: 1846 in Ky
..............8 Elizabeth WARDEN b: 1848 in Ky
..............7 Josephine PETERS b: 08 Jan 1817 in of, Logan, Co., Ky, d: 1912 in Oklahoma age 95; Y
    + Henry Harvey "Harry" WETHERINGTON b: Abt. 1813 in of, Logan, Co., Ky, m: 05 Nov 1833 in Logan, Co, Ky, d: Bef. 1860 ; Y
..............8 NANCY J. WEATHERINGTON b: 1838 in Kentucky
..............8 FRANKLIN WEATHERINGTON b: 1845 in Kentucky
..............8 ASLIMIRA Asthenis WEATHERINGTON b: 1849 in Kentucky
..............8 Josephine WEATHERINGTON b: 1852 in Ky
..............8 known thirteen total WEATHERINGTON
..............8 FERNANDO Ferdinand WETHERINGTON b: Kentucky
    + Dollie H b: 1845 in ILL, m: Abt. 1868 in of Massac Co., ILL
..................9 William H. WEATHERINGTON b: 1869 in Massac Co., ILL
..............8 Tennessee WEATHERINGTON b: Ky
..............8 Henry Clay Wetherington b: Kentucky, d: Weatherington; Y
    + Georgia b: GA, m: 1895 in Indian Terr (OK)
    + Elvira Hutcheson b: 1862 in Lawrence Co., AR, m: Feb 1880 in Big Creek, Sharp Co., AR, d: 1894 in Shady Point, Indian Terr (OK); Y
..................9 William Harvey Wetherington b: 19 Mar 1881 in Big Creek, Sharp Co., AR, d: 04 Jun 1972 in Shawnee, Pottawatomie, OK; Y
    + Lilla b: Indian Terr (OK), m: 1896 in Indian Terr (OK)
......................10 Alta Wetherington b: 1907 in Indian Terr (OK)
......................10 Pearl Wetherington b: Indian Terr (OK)
..................9 Henry B. Wetherington b: Mar 1886 in Texas
..................9 Nettie Wetherington b: Feb 1889 in Indian Terr (OK)

...............9 Mattie Wetherington b: Mar 1891 in Indian Terr (OK)
...............9 Anna Mae Wetherington b: May 1893 in Indian Terr (OK), d: 1994 ; Y
...............7 Nancy PETERS b: Abt. 1816 in of, Logan, Co., Ky, d: 03 Sep 1853 in SIMPSON, Co. Ky; Y
          + Jonathan CALDWELL b: Abt. 1806 in of, Logan, Co., Ky
...............7 Mahala PETERS b: of, Logan, Co., Ky, d: Aft. 1881 in Bishops Mill, Marshall Co., Kentucky;
          Y
          + Lewis Henderson b: 1806 in Granville Co., NC of, Logan, Co., Ky, m: 04 Sep 1829 in
          Logan, Co, Ky, d: 1881 in Bishops Mill, Marshall Co., Kentucky; Y
...............8 James L. Henderson b: Abt. 1830 in Calloway Co., Ky of Bishops Mill, Marshall Co.,
          Kentucky
          + Mary Ann MOFIELD b: Abt. 1832 in Marshall Co., KY, m: 15 Apr 1852 in Marshall Co.,
          KY
...............8 Richard "Rich" W. Henderson b: 1836 in Calloway Co., Ky of Bishops Mill, Marshall Co.,
          Kentucky
          + Mary Ann b: Abt. 1845 in of Bishops Mill, Marshall Co., Kentucky, m: Abt. 1865 in of
          Calloway Co., Kentucky
...............9 William A. Henderson b: 1866 in ILL
...............9 Lewis F. Henderson b: 1868 in Bishops Mill, Marshall Co., Kentucky
...............9 Richard U. Henderson b: 1870 in Bishops Mill, Marshall Co., Kentucky
...............9 Charles D. Henderson b: 1874 in Bishops Mill, Marshall Co., Kentucky
...............9 Ella Henderson b: 1878 in Bishops Mill, Marshall Co., Kentucky
...............8 Samuel Henderson b: 1839 in Calloway Co., Ky of Bishops Mill, Marshall Co., Kentucky
          + Margaret Ann b: Abt. 1841 in Bishops Mill, Marshall Co., Kentucky, m: Abt. 1861 in
          Bishops Mill, Marshall Co., Kentucky
...............9 Mary Alice Henderson b: 1862 in Bishops Mill, Marshall Co., Kentucky, d: Abt. 1946 in
          Marshall Co., KY; Y
          + William Alexander INMAN b: 27 Aug 1855 in Marshall Co., KY, m: Abt. 1879 in
          Marshall Co., KY
...............10 Arthur Ray INMAN b: 13 Jan 1883 in Marshall Co., KY
...............10 Florence INMAN b: Abt. 1885 in Marshall Co., KY
...............10 Edna INMAN b: 1887 in Marshall Co., KY
...............10 Charles Maxie INMAN b: 1889 in Marshall Co., KY
...............10 William Oliver INMAN b: 18 Jan 1895 in Marshall Co., KY
...............10 Wilson Herbert INMAN b: 28 Feb 1901 in Marshall Co., KY
...............10 David Lewis INMAN b: 01 Feb 1903 in Marshall Co., KY
...............10 Rhoda U. INMAN b: Marshall Co., KY
...............9 Samuel L. Henderson b: 1865 in Bishops Mill, Marshall Co., Kentucky
...............9 Sarah A. Henderson b: 1867 in Bishops Mill, Marshall Co., Kentucky
...............9 Nancy E. Henderson b: 1869 in Bishops Mill, Marshall Co., Kentucky
...............9 Richard W Henderson b: 1871 in Bishops Mill, Marshall Co., Kentucky
...............9 John F. Henderson b: 1873 in Bishops Mill, Marshall Co., Kentucky
...............9 Naoma Henderson b: 1876 in Bishops Mill, Marshall Co., Kentucky
...............9 Ruth Henderson b: 1879 in Bishops Mill, Marshall Co., Kentucky
...............9 Orpha Henderson b: 1880 in Bishops Mill, Marshall Co., Kentucky
...............8 Victoria Catherine "Katie" Henderson b: Abt. 1844 in Calloway Co., Ky of Bishops Mill,
          Marshall Co., Kentucky
          + Robert Wesley b: Abt. 1842 in Bishops Mill, Marshall Co., Kentucky, m: Abt. 1864, d:
          Abt. 1867 in Marshall Co., KY; Y
...............9 Victoria Isabel "Belle" Wesley b: Abt. 1865 in Bishops Mill, Marshall Co., Kentucky
          + Robert W. NELSON b: Abt. 1842 in Marshall Co., KY, m: 10 Dec 1868 in Marshall Co.,
          KY
...............6 Samuel LAWLER b: 17 Jun 1793 in Mercer Co., Ky, d: 25 Feb 1870 in home of son Silas,
          Denton, Denton Co., Tx; Y
          + Mary NEELY b: 28 Jul 1800 in Ohio Co., Ky, m: 12 Feb 1818 in Galliton, Sumner, Tn, d: 12
          Aug 1868 in Franklin, SIMPSON, Ky; Y

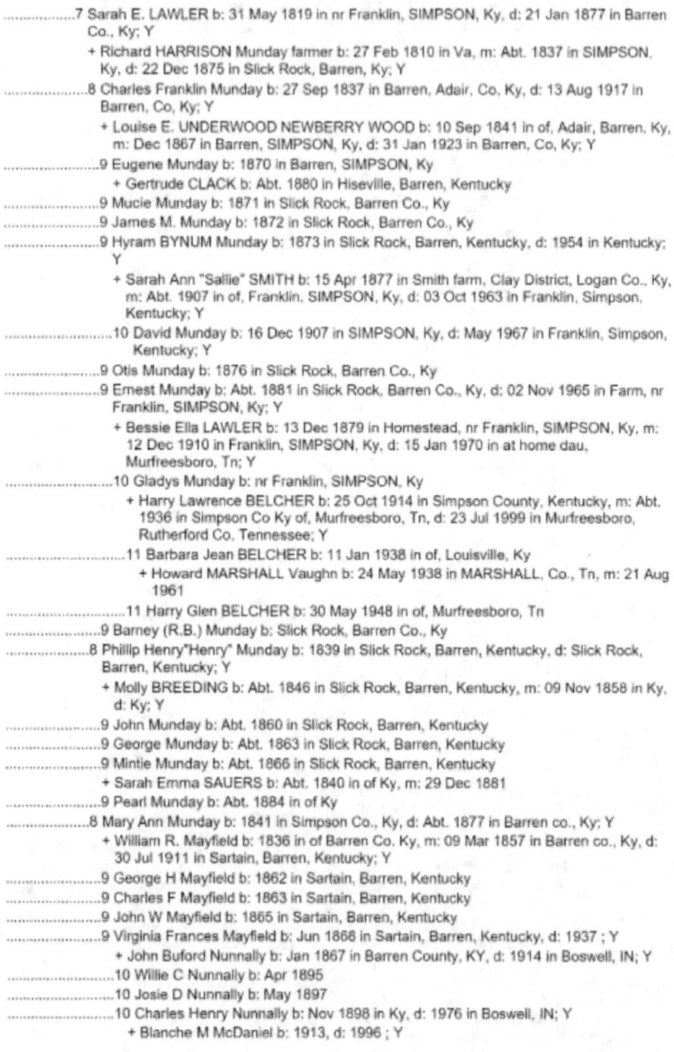

....................7 Sarah E. LAWLER b: 31 May 1819 in nr Franklin, SIMPSON, Ky, d: 21 Jan 1877 in Barren
Co., Ky; Y
   + Richard HARRISON Munday farmer b: 27 Feb 1810 in Va, m: Abt. 1837 in SIMPSON,
Ky, d: 22 Dec 1875 in Slick Rock, Barren, Ky; Y
....................8 Charles Franklin Munday b: 27 Sep 1837 in Barren, Adair, Co, Ky, d: 13 Aug 1917 in
Barren, Co, Ky; Y
   + Louise E. UNDERWOOD NEWBERRY WOOD b: 10 Sep 1841 in of, Adair, Barren, Ky,
m: Dec 1867 in Barren, SIMPSON, Ky, d: 31 Jan 1923 in Barren, Co, Ky; Y
....................9 Eugene Munday b: 1870 in Barren, SIMPSON, Ky
   + Gertrude CLACK b: Abt. 1880 in Hiseville, Barren, Kentucky
....................9 Mucie Munday b: 1871 in Slick Rock, Barren Co., Ky
....................9 James M. Munday b: 1872 in Slick Rock, Barren Co., Ky
....................9 Hyram BYNUM Munday b: 1873 in Slick Rock, Barren, Kentucky, d: 1954 in Kentucky;
Y
   + Sarah Ann "Sallie" SMITH b: 15 Apr 1877 in Smith farm, Clay District, Logan Co., Ky,
m: Abt. 1907 in of, Franklin, SIMPSON, Ky, d: 03 Oct 1963 in Franklin, Simpson,
Kentucky; Y
....................10 David Munday b: 16 Dec 1907 in SIMPSON, Ky, d: May 1967 in Franklin, Simpson,
Kentucky; Y
....................9 Otis Munday b: 1876 in Slick Rock, Barren Co., Ky
....................9 Ernest Munday b: Abt. 1881 in Slick Rock, Barren Co., Ky, d: 02 Nov 1965 in Farm, nr
Franklin, SIMPSON, Ky; Y
   + Bessie Ella LAWLER b: 13 Dec 1879 in Homestead, nr Franklin, SIMPSON, Ky, m:
12 Dec 1910 in Franklin, SIMPSON, Ky, d: 15 Jan 1970 in at home dau,
Murfreesboro, Tn; Y
....................10 Gladys Munday b: nr Franklin, SIMPSON, Ky
   + Harry Lawrence BELCHER b: 25 Oct 1914 in Simpson County, Kentucky, m: Abt.
1936 in Simpson Co Ky of, Murfreesboro, Tn, d: 23 Jul 1999 in Murfreesboro,
Rutherford Co, Tennessee; Y
....................11 Barbara Jean BELCHER b: 11 Jan 1938 in of, Louisville, Ky
   + Howard MARSHALL Vaughn b: 24 May 1938 in MARSHALL, Co., Tn, m: 21 Aug
1961
....................11 Harry Glen BELCHER b: 30 May 1948 in of, Murfreesboro, Tn
....................9 Barney (R.B.) Munday b: Slick Rock, Barren Co., Ky
....................8 Phillip Henry"Henry" Munday b: 1839 in Slick Rock, Barren, Kentucky, d: Slick Rock,
Barren, Kentucky; Y
   + Molly BREEDING b: Abt. 1846 in Slick Rock, Barren, Kentucky, m: 09 Nov 1858 in Ky,
d: Ky; Y
....................9 John Munday b: Abt. 1860 in Slick Rock, Barren, Kentucky
....................9 George Munday b: Abt. 1863 in Slick Rock, Barren, Kentucky
....................9 Mintie Munday b: Abt. 1866 in Slick Rock, Barren, Kentucky
   + Sarah Emma SAUERS b: Abt. 1840 in of Ky, m: 29 Dec 1881
....................9 Pearl Munday b: Abt. 1884 in of Ky
....................8 Mary Ann Munday b: 1841 in Simpson Co., Ky, d: Abt. 1877 in Barren co., Ky; Y
   + William R. Mayfield b: 1836 in of Barren Co. Ky, m: 09 Mar 1857 in Barren co., Ky, d:
30 Jul 1911 in Sartain, Barren, Kentucky; Y
....................9 George H Mayfield b: 1862 in Sartain, Barren, Kentucky
....................9 Charles F Mayfield b: 1863 in Sartain, Barren, Kentucky
....................9 John W Mayfield b: 1865 in Sartain, Barren, Kentucky
....................9 Virginia Frances Mayfield b: Jun 1868 in Sartain, Barren, Kentucky, d: 1937 ; Y
   + John Buford Nunnally b: Jan 1867 in Barren County, KY, d: 1914 in Boswell, IN; Y
....................10 Willie C Nunnally b: Apr 1895
....................10 Josie D Nunnally b: May 1897
....................10 Charles Henry Nunnally b: Nov 1898 in Ky, d: 1976 in Boswell, IN; Y
   + Blanche M McDaniel b: 1913, d: 1996 ; Y

................................11 Living Nunnally
................................11 Living Nunnally
......................9 Mary A Mayfield b: 1872 in Sartain, Barren, Kentucky
......................9 Wilks H Mayfield b: 1873 in Sartain, Barren, Kentucky
......................9 Ephraim B Mayfield b: 1875 in Sartain, Barren, Kentucky
......................8 Margaret Jane Munday Puss b: 13 Jul 1842 in Barren, Co, Ky, d: 06 Sep 1920 in Adair,
          Logan, Ky; Y
              + John Pickney Dickson b: 30 Oct 1844 in Leatherwood, Adair, Kentucky, m: Aug 1865 in
                 eloped, d: Adair, Co, Ky; Y
......................9 Sarah Elizabeth Dickson b: 12 Jan 1867 in Cumberland, Co, Ky, d: 22 Apr 1946 ; Y
......................9 James Henry Dickson b: 03 Oct 1868 in Cumberland, Co, Ky, d: 30 Mar 1944 ; Y
......................9 Mary Elizabeth Dickson b: 28 Oct 1869 in Cumberland, Co, Ky, d: 17 Aug 1884 ; Y
......................9 George Thomas Dickson b: 25 Dec 1870 in Cumberland, Co, Ky, d: 13 Jul 1939 ; Y
......................9 Frances Ermen Dickson b: 07 Mar 1872 in Metcalfe, Co, Ky, d: 28 May 1947 ; Y
......................9 Robert Franklin Dickson b: 23 Mar 1873 in Hart, Co, Ky, d: 14 Jun 1903 ; Y
......................9 Nancy J Nan Dickson b: 03 Mar 1875 in Metcalfe, Co, Ky, d: 12 Aug 1924 ; Y
......................9 Charles G Dickson b: 11 Oct 1876 in Metcalfe, Co, Ky, d: 24 Sep 1944 ; Y
......................9 Lena Virginia Dickson b: 09 Jul 1878 in Metcalfe, Co, Ky, d: 23 Dec 1957 ; Y
              + Henry PARSONS b: Abt. 1877 in of Adair Co. Ky
......................9 Arminta Ann Mint Dickson b: 09 Mar 1881 in Metcalfe, Co, Ky, d: 02 Jul 1930 ; Y
              + Amos Jackson COOMER b: 1879 in Adair Co., KY
......................10 Dallas Owen COOMER b: 1906 in Columbia Ky., d: 22 Jun 1993 ; Y
              + Mary Magdalena JANES b: 1911 in Ky, d: 23 Dec 1968 ; Y
......................11 Jerry COOMER b: Abt. 1934
......................11 Dan COOMER b: Abt. 1936
......................11 Dallas COOMER b: Abt. 1938
......................11 Janice COOMER b: Abt. 1940
......................11 James COOMER b: Abt. 1942
......................10 Signora COOMER b: Abt. 1908 in Columbia Ky.
......................10 Delphia COOMER b: Abt. 1910 in Columbia Ky.
......................10 John COOMER b: Abt. 1912 in Columbia Ky.
......................9 Ina Mae Dickson b: 30 May 1882 in Metcalfe, Co, Ky, d: 09 Jan 1897 ; Y
......................9 Sallie Bell Dickson b: 09 Jul 1884 in Metcalfe, Co, Ky, d: 16 Jun 1940 in Chicago, Cook
          Co., ILL; Y
              + Fount Evan Gabbert Gorman b: 23 Nov 1881 in Toria, Adair Co., Ky, m: 06 Dec 1899
                 in Red Lick, Metcalfe, Kentucky, d: 22 Apr 1945 in Chicago, Cook Co., ILL; Y
......................10 Ora Anna Gabbert b: 09 Jan 1901 in Toria, Adair Co., Ky, d: 31 May 1973 in Summit.
          Cook Co., ILL; Y
              + Mr. Roach
......................11 Lisie Roach
......................11 Lee Roach
              + Ira Rawson
......................10 Bessie Gabbert b: Abt. 1903 in Toria, Adair Co., Ky
              + Sherman Herring
......................11 Bruce
              + George Shafer
              + Everett Empy
......................10 Ella Pearl Gabbert b: 12 Sep 1905 in Toria, Adair Co., Ky, d: 27 Oct 1937 in Summit.
          Cook Co., ILL; Y
              + Sherman Herring
......................10 Emmison David Gabbert b: 26 Jan 1907 in Toria, Adair Co., Ky, d: 31 Jul 1954 in
          Chicago, Cook Co., ILL; Y
......................10 Cleo Belle Gabbert b: 06 Sep 1908 in Toria, Adair Co., Ky, d: 30 May 1960 in
          Chicago, Cook Co., ILL; Y

.....................10 John Alford Gabbert b: 30 Mar 1910 in Toria, Adair Co., Ky, d: 05 Apr 1966 in
  Hickory Hills, Oaklawn, Cook Co., ILL; Y

.....................10 Dora Jane (Theodora Jane) Gabbert b: 20 Nov 1911 in Toria, Adair Co., Ky, d: 12
  Sep 1982 in Phoenix, AZ; Y

 + Joseph

.....................11 Josephine Pearl Weidlich b: 06 Jan 1930 in Argo, Ill, d: 14 May 2004 in Mesa, AZ;
  Y

  + Williard Lee Harris b: 16 Oct 1927 in Red Bay ALA, m: 29 Sep 1945 in Alcorn
   Co., MS (div 1966), d: 01 Sep 2001 in Tempe AZ; Y

.....................12 Particia Ann Harris b: 22 Oct 1947 in Chicago, Cook Co., ILL

  + Philip Eugene HOWARD b: 12 Mar 1947 in Athens TN, m: 22 Jul 1966 in Oak
   Lawn, ILL

.....................13 Michelle Marie HOWARD b: 18 Feb 1969 in Oak Park, Cook Co, ILL

  + Pale' Antoine Cloud b: 15 Mar 1969 in ATLANTA GA, m: 31 Oct 1991 in Meza
   AZ

.....................14 Jazmyn Michelle Cloud b: 08 May 1993 in Samaritan Hospital, Mesa, AZ

.....................14 Jayden Shannon-Palae' Cloud b: 18 Dec 1997 in Samaritan Hospital, Mesa,
  AZ

  + Stephan Madison Thompson b: 23 Aug 1969 in Georgia, m: 20 Feb 1988 in
   div abt 1990

.....................13 Christopher Bradley HOWARD b: 29 May 1974 in Oak Park, Cook Co, ILL

  + Rebecca Lee Carter b: Abt. 1976 in California, m: 10 Oct 1990 in Tempe AZ
   (div ca 2000)

.....................14 Alyssa Lee Rena HOWARD b: 01 Jan 1991 in Phoeniz AZ

.....................14 Caitlia Marie HOWARD b: 10 Aug 1992 in Phoeniz AZ

.....................14 Rachel Christina HOWARD b: 27 Mar 1995 in Phoeniz AZ

.....................14 Ana Rae HOWARD b: 07 Oct 1998 in Phoeniz AZ

.....................12 Larry Wayne Harris b: 28 Feb 1949 in Oak Park, Cook Co, ILL, d: 14 Dec 1960
  in Berwin, ILL; Y

.....................12 Karen Lee Harris b: Chicago, Cook Co., ILL

  + Ernest Welby Forest II b: Abt. 1944

.....................13 Ernest Welby Forest III

.....................13 Patti Jo Forest

.....................13 Cynthia Lee Forest

  + Mark Love

.....................14 Matthew Love

  + Kieth Leno

.....................14 Shoshanna Rose Leno b: Oct 1997

.....................14 William Skye Leno

  + Michael Koch

.....................13 William Michael Koch

  + Daniel

  + Richard Vanderbeck b: 02 Feb 1934 in ILL, d: 14 Dec 1960 in Berwin, ILL; Y

 + Frank Weidlich b: 06 Aug 1905, m: 1936, d: 04 Jul 1983 ; Y

.....................11 Patricia Ann Weidlich b: Abt. 1936

  + Clifford Pavis

.....................12 Richard Pavis b: 31 Aug 1967

  + Roy Hicks

  + Raymond Boonstra b: 02 Aug 1933, m: Abt. 1956 in div 15 Aug 1962

.....................12 Linda Raeleen Boonstra b: 13 Apr 1957

.....................12 Laura Jane Boonstra b: 10 Dec 1958

  + Raloh Richard Redwinski b: 29 Nov 1939, m: Abt. 1963 in div Sep 1971

.....................12 Richelle Joyce Redwinski b: 30 May 1963

 + Sherman Herring

.....................11 William Weildlich b: 09 Dec 1932, d: 22 May 2002 ; Y

+ Carol b: 30 May 1932, m: 1956
.......................12 Sandra Weiidlich b: 1959
.......................12 William Richard Weiidlich b: 1963
.......................12 Jeffrey Weiidlich b: 1969
.......................10 Lucille Gabbert b: 17 Apr 1915 in Toria, Adair Co., Ky, d: 16 Sep 1916 in Toria, Adair
    Co., Ky; Y
.......................10 Quinton Gabbert b: 03 Mar 1919, d: 07 Dec 2000 in Los Angeles, Los Angeles Co,
    California; Y
.......................10 Dorothy Marie Gabbert b: 11 Aug 1923 in Chicago, Cook Co., ILL, d: 29 Sep 1923 in
    Chicago, Cook Co., ILL; Y
.......................10 Oscar Rufus (Ronald O.) Gabbert
.......................10 Raymond Gabbert
.......................9 John David Dickson b: 02 Jun 1886 in Metcalfe, Co, Ky, d: 01 May 1951 ; Y
    + Naomi COOMER b: 02 Aug 1885 in of, Adair, Co, Ky, d: 06 Jun 1975 in Danville,
      Vermilion, Co, Ill; Y
.......................10 Della Lee Dickson b: 13 Aug 1907 in of, Adair, Co, Ky
    + Fred WOODYARD b: 04 Jul 1881 in of, Edgar, Co, Ill, m: 15 Dec 1927 in Vermilion,
      Co, Ill, d: 26 Jun 1961 in Danville, Vermilion, Co, Ill; Y
.......................11 Elsie Corine WOODYARD b: 09 Aug 1930 in Vermilion, Co, Ill
.......................11 Doris Joan WOODYARD b: 11 Aug 1933 in Edgar, Co, Ill, d: 31 Mar 1949 ; Y
.......................10 Hallie May Dickson b: 18 Sep 1911 in Hart, Co, Ky, d: 05 Oct 1911 in Hart, Co, Ky; Y
.......................10 David Clifton Dickson b: 26 Jul 1913 in Hart, Co, Ky
    + Grace Enid MATHEWS b: 21 Nov 1917 in Rising City, Neb, m: 24 Dec 1943 in
      Chicago, Cook, Co, Ill
.......................10 Chester Ray Dickson b: 29 Apr 1918 in Hart, Co, Ky, d: 27 Jun 1927 in of, Ill; Y
.......................10 Ernest MORROW Dickson b: 26 Apr 1920 in Adair, Co, Ky
    + Jeanette Helen EDMISTON b: 25 Jul 1928 in Vermilion, Co, Ill, m: 18 Jan 1949 in
      Vermilion, Co, Ill
.......................11 Cynthia Ann Dickson b: 14 Oct 1949 in Vermilion, Co, Ill
.......................11 Catherine Sue Dickson b: 30 Jan 1951 in Vermilion, Co, Ill
.......................11 Charles ALLEN Dickson b: 29 Sep 1953 in Vermilion, Co, Ill
.......................11 Cheryl Lynn Dickson b: 18 Dec 1956 in Vermilion, Co, Ill
.......................10 Margaret Marie Dickson b: 19 Mar 1922 in Edgar, Ill
.......................10 Elsie Pauline Dickson b: 17 Mar 1924 in Edgar, Ill, d: 27 Jun 1927 in of, Ill; Y
.......................8 Samuel Finley LAWLER Munday b: 27 Feb 1844 in Barren, Ky, d: 01 Mar 1934 in White
    House, Tx; Y
    + Sarah E. Dickson b: 27 Jul 1850 in Leatherwood, Adair, Kentucky, m: 1865 in Metcalfe,
      Ky, d: 09 Mar 1883 in Leatherwood, Adair, Kentucky; Y
.......................9 James Richard Munday b: Jan 1866 in Leatherwood, Adair, Kentucky, d: Jun 1901 ; Y
    + Lena Rivers COOMER b: 15 Nov 1869 in Adair, Co, Ky, m: 19 Nov 1885 in Adair, Co,
      Ky, d: 03 Feb 1953 in of, Adair, Co, Ky; Y
.......................9 Elizabeth Frances Munday b: 14 Mar 1869 in Leatherwood, Adair, Kentucky, d: 23 Apr
    1957 in Adair, Co, Ky; Y
    + Montgomery Mack COOMER b: 24 Jul 1861 in Adair, Co, Ky, m: 19 Jul 1893 in Adair,
      Co, Ky, d: 13 Nov 1948 in of, Adair, Co, Ky; Y
.......................9 Mary Jane Munday b: 06 Jul 1871 in Leatherwood, Adair, Kentucky, d: 27 Jun 1931 ; Y
.......................9 John Munday b: Abt. 1873 in Leatherwood, Adair, Kentucky
    + Elizabeth Frazier BENETT b: Abt. 1860 in of Ky, m: 03 Feb 1884 in Adair Co., KY aft
      death, Sarah
.......................8 Nancy Catherine "Kate" Munday b: 26 Sep 1846 in of, Barren, Co, Ky, d: 14 Aug 1920 in
    of, Barren, Co, Ky; Y
    + George Marcum Dallas SHIPLEY b: 23 Jan 1847 in Hawkins Co., TN of, Adair, Co, Ky,
      m: 23 Jan 1896 in Barren Co., Ky. d: 25 Dec 1928 in Barren, Co, Ky; Y
.......................9 Barbara C. SHIPLEY b: 1872 in Barren Co., Ky
.......................9 Nathan SHIPLEY b: 1876 in Barren Co., Ky

....................9 Rachel Dora A. SHIPLEY b: 1878 in Barren Co., Ky
....................9 Laura SHIPLEY b: 1889 in Barren Co., Ky
....................8 Sarah ELiza Munday Sally b: 1848 in Slick Rock, Barren Co., Ky
+ William C. PICKETT b: Abt. 1850 in Slick Rock, Barren Co., Ky, m: 25 Mar 1874
....................9 Harry PICKETT b: Abt. 1876 in of Ky
....................9 Byrd PICKETT. b: Abt. 1878 in of Ky
....................9 George PICKETT b: Abt. 1880 in of Ky
....................9 John PICKETT b: Abt. 1883 in of Ky
....................8 James William Munday b: 27 Jun 1850 in Barren, Ky, d: Oklahoma City, Okla; Y
+ Mollie LANE b: Abt. 1854 in of Ky, m: 16 Jun 1890
....................8 Margery Frances Munday b: 1852 in Barren, Ky
+ W. P. Booker b: Abt. 1850 in of Ky, m: 16 Jun 1890
....................9 Finley Booker b: Abt. 1892 in of Ky
....................9 Frances Booker b: Abt. 1895 in of Ky
....................8 Robert HARRISON Munday b: 1854 in Slick Rock, Barren, Kentucky, d: 14 Jul 1905 in
Metcalfe, Ky; Y
+ Millisia Frances SPEAR Fannie b: Abt. 1856 in of Ky, m: 17 Jun 1890
....................9 Jewel Munday b: Abt. 1892 in of Ky
....................9 Alice Munday b: Abt. 1895 in of Ky
....................9 GORDON Munday b: Abt. 1897 in of Ky
....................8 Elizabeth WHITE Lizzie Munday b: 1856 in Barren, Ky
+ John A. Farrell FERRELL b: Abt. 1860 in of Ky, m: 20 Dec 1892
....................8 L. W. Munday b: 1858, d: child; Y
....................8 Thomas Finley Munday b: 1859 in Barren, Ky
+ Mollie SAUNDERS b: Abt. 1861 in of Ky, m: 02 Aug 1887
....................9 Earl Munday b: Abt. 1890 in of Ky
....................9 Morgan Munday b: Abt. 1894 in of Ky
....................8 John Richard Munday b: Abt. 1864 in Barren, Ky, d: Abt. Oct 1893 in of, Franklin,
SIMPSON, Ky; Y
+ Alice Gertrude LAWLER b: 04 Dec 1870 in Homestead, nr Franklin, SIMPSON, Ky, m:
19 Dec 1889 in Franklin, SIMPSON, Ky, d: 20 Oct 1893 ; Y
....................9 Etta Irene Munday b: Sep 1890 in Franklin, SIMPSON, Ky
+ Jepson Jessie J. Matthews b: Abt. 1890 in of, Simpson Co., Ky, m: Abt. 1911 in
Franklin, SIMPSON, Ky
....................10 Mary Lee Matthews b: 13 Oct 1913 in of, Franklin, SIMPSON, Ky
+ BYRON CONLEY b: 20 May 1903 in Lawrenceville, Lawrence Co., Ill of Franklin,
SIMPSON, Ky, d: Jul 1982 in Bartow, Polk Co., Florida; Y
....................11 Louette CONLEY b: 23 Jan 1936 in Fla
+ C.D. Moore b: Abt. 1934 in of FLA
....................11 Homer Lee CONLEY b: 03 Jan 1937 in Fla
+ Gayle W b: Abt. 1939 in FL, m: Abt. 1960
....................11 Norma Jean CONLEY b: 30 Jun 1938 in Fla
....................11 Warren CONLEY b: 30 Dec 1939 in Fla
....................11 Mary B. CONLEY b: 27 Dec 1940 in Fla
....................11 Paul CONLEY b: 13 Oct 1942 in Fla
....................11 Dale CONLEY b: 18 Nov 1943 in Fla
....................11 Jennie K. CONLEY b: 18 Dec 1944 in Fla
....................11 Barbara CONLEY b: 15 May 1946 in Fla
....................11 Ruth CONLEY b: 25 May 1949 in Fla
....................10 Jessie Matthews b: 11 Apr 1915 in of, Franklin, SIMPSON, Ky
+ Jessie GORDON b: 04 Mar 1914
....................11 Alyce F. GORDON b: 11 Jul 1940
+ Jack JESUP b: Abt. 1940
....................12 Alicia Lynette Jessup b: 21 Nov 1958

.......................11 Janyee I. GORDON b: 11 Jul 1940 in twins
　　　　+ Dean HARLOD b: Abt. 1940
.......................12 Albert Elden Dean b: 04 Oct 1958
.......................11 Patricia A. GORDON b: 22 Dec 1942
.......................11 Connie L. GORDON b: 15 Aug 1944
.......................10 Robert E. Matthews b: 05 Jan 1928 in of, Franklin, SIMPSON, Ky
　　　　+ Iris PRICE b: Abt. 1930
.......................11 Robert E. Matthews Jr. b: 10 Dec 1949
.......................11 Raymond Matthews b: 03 Dec 1953
.......................11 Bettie Gene Matthews b: 03 Jan 1954
.......................11 Peggie A. Matthews b: 15 Sep 1955
.......................11 Brenda Q. Matthews b: 15 Jun 1957
.......................9 Ira EARL MUNDAY b: 11 Sep 1892 in Franklin, SIMPSON, Ky, d: 30 May 1971 in
　　　　Barren Co., Ky; Y
　　　　+ Veda Allie PEDIGO b: 11 Feb 1897 in Barren Co., Ky, m: 1921 in Barren Co., Ky, d:
　　　　01 Mar 1963 in Barren Co., Ky; Y
.......................8 Ina Lee Munday b: Aug 1864 in Barren Co., Ky
　　　　+ Henry C. "Clay" Whitaker b: Sep 1858 in Jackson Co., TN of Barren Co., Ky, m: Dec
　　　　1886
.......................9 Jessie B. Whitaker b: Nov 1887 in Barren Co., Ky
.......................9 David Winton Whitaker b: Sep 1894 in Barren Co., Ky
.......................9 Robert C. Whitaker b: Abt. 1896 in Barren Co., Ky
.......................7 James W LAWLER b: 08 Mar 1821 in nr Franklin, SIMPSON, Ky, d: 10 Jan 1899 in St Jo,
　　　　Montague, Tx; Y
　　　　+ Sabrina A COX b: 09 Jun 1822 in of, SIMPSON, Ky, m: 14 Jun 1840 in Robertson Co.,
　　　　Tn, d: 1850 census, SIMPSON, Co, Ky; Y
.......................8 William Francis LAWLER b: 25 Nov 1841 in nr Franklin, SIMPSON, Ky, d: 24 Jun 1934 in
　　　　St Jo, Montague, Tx; Y
　　　　+ Mary T. REDWIN b: 1847 in Ark of, Denton Co., Tx, m: Abt. 1867 in of, Denton Co., Tx,
　　　　d: Abt. 1873 in Denton Co., Tx; Y
.......................9 William Henry LAWLER Blacksmith b: 01 Feb 1870 in of, Denton, Texas, d: 24 Feb
　　　　1941 in Longdale, Blaine, Oklahoma; Y
　　　　+ Ebbie Mae or Abby Nevada FREELAND b: 1881 in NC Cherokee, m: Abt. 1903 in
　　　　Oklahoma, d: Abt. 1911 in Sun City Kansas; Y
.......................10 Charles Clifford Charlie LAWLER b: 1902 in father, of, Denton Co., Texas
　　　　+ Hazel BOOTH b: Abt. 1904
.......................11 Dorothy May LAWLER b: Abt. 1927
　　　　+ MERRILL RUEDE ANDERSON b: Abt. 1925
.......................12 CRAIG ALAN ANDERSON b: Abt. 1950 in of Ore
　　　　+ Cathy
.......................10 Emery Warren LAWLER b: 06 Mar 1905 in McCullen, Tx, d: 12 Dec 1974 in
　　　　Oklahoma City, Okla; Y
　　　　+ Dorena Nora Woodward b: 06 Jun 1906 in Fairfew, Oklahoma
.......................11 Charles Leroy LAWLER b: 31 Jan 1926 in Fairfew, Okla, d: 1981 in Oklahoma
　　　　City, Okla; Y
　　　　+ Collene POE
.......................12 Dorthy Mae LAWLER b: 08 Sep 1948 in of, Oklahoma City, Oklahoma
　　　　+ James FURR b: 1928 in of, Oklahoma City, Oklahoma
.......................13 Brenda FURR b: 13 Mar 1967 in of, Oklahoma City, Oklahoma
.......................13 Margaret FURR b: 1969 in of, Oklahoma City, Oklahoma
.......................13 ALLEN Jay FURR b: 1970 in of, Oklahoma City, Oklahoma, d: 1971 in baby; Y
.......................13 David FURR b: Jul 1973 in of, Oklahoma City, Oklahoma, d: Dec 1991 in
　　　　Oklahoma City, Ok; Y
　　　　+ Autumn b: Abt. 1975 in of, Oklahoma City, Oklahoma

............14 Aaron FURR b: Dec 1991 in of, Oklahoma City, Oklahoma, d: 1992 in baby; Y
............13 Marcia FURR b: 1975 in of, Oklahoma City, Oklahoma
............12 Leroy ALLEN LAWLER b: 15 Oct 1950 in of, Oklahoma City, Oklahoma
+ Maida May BLAIN b: 11 Jun 1950 in of, Oklahoma City, Oklahoma, m: 28 Dec 1971
............13 Alan LAWLER b: 04 Jul 1972 in Oklahoma City, Oklahoma
+ Elizabeth LILES b: Abt. 1935 in of, Oklahoma City, Oklahoma
............12 Ebbie May LAWLER b: 1954 in of, Oklahoma City, Oklahoma, d: 1989 in Chawtal, Okla; Y
+ Michael BRYANT b: Abt. 1949 in of, Ok
+ Dean JAGGERS b: Abt. 1950 in of, Oklahoma City, Ok, m: 1980 in of, Oklahoma City, Ok
............13 Tina Michelle JAGGERS b: 19 Jul 1979 in of, Oklahoma City, Ok
............13 Kevin Dean JAGGERS b: 03 Mar 1982 in of, Oklahoma City, Ok
............12 Charles LAWLER b: 12 Mar 1967 in of, Oklahoma City, Oklahoma
+ Penny b: Abt. 1969 in of, Oklahoma City, Ok
+ Patricia Hawkins b: Abt. 1972 in of, Oklahoma City, Oklahoma, m: of, Oklahoma City, Ok
............13 Jacqueline Evelyn LAWLER b: 01 Feb 1993 in of, Oklahoma City, Oklahoma
............11 Alfred Larry LAWLER b: 1927 in Fairfew, Okla
+ Odel ASHLEY b: Abt. 1928 in of, Oklahoma City, Oklahoma, Oklahoma, m: Abt. 1945 in Oklahoma City, Oklahoma, Ok
............12 Edward Warren "Sonny" LAWLER b: Apr 1947 in of, Oklahoma City, Oklahoma, Oklahoma
+ Pat
............13 Eddie LAWLER b: 1968, d: 1984 ; Y
............12 Sue LAWLER b: Abt. 1948 in of, Oklahoma City, Oklahoma, Oklahoma, d: 1984 in of, Oklahoma City, Ok; Y
+ Dan TEDFORD b: Abt. 1946 in of, Oklahoma City, Ok
............13 Sheila TEDFORD b: Abt. 1972 in of, Oklahoma City, Oklahoma, Oklahoma, d: 1992 in of, Oklahoma City, traffic accident, Ok; Y
+ Randy SYKES b: Abt. 1972 in of, Oklahoma City, Oklahoma, Oklahoma
............14 Natasha SYKES b: Abt. 1988 in of, Oklahoma City, Oklahoma, Oklahoma, d: 1992 in traffic accident, Oklahoma City, Ok; Y
............12 Rickie LAWLER b: Abt. 1949 in of, Oklahoma City, Oklahoma, Oklahoma
............12 Evelyn LAWLER b: Abt. 1951 in of, Oklahoma City, Oklahoma, Oklahoma
............12 Janice LAWLER b: 1956 in of, Oklahoma City, Oklahoma, Oklahoma
............12 Keith LAWLER b: Abt. 1960 in of, Oklahoma City, Oklahoma, Oklahoma
............12 Roger "Sam" LAWLER b: Abt. 1970 in of, Oklahoma City, Oklahoma, Oklahoma, d: May 1993 in Oklahoma City, Ok; Y
............12 Shelly Dawn LAWLER b: 1972 in of, Oklahoma City, Oklahoma, Oklahoma
............12 Brenda LAWLER b: of, Oklahoma City, Oklahoma, Oklahoma
+ ROGERS
............11 Ebby May "SHERRY" LAWLER b: 1929 in Sun City, Kansas
+ LEONARD ROBB b: 1925 in of, Oklahoma City, Oklahoma, Oklahoma, m: Abt. 1947 in Oklahoma City, Oklahoma, divorced, abt 1958
............12 LEONARD Eugene ROBB b: 16 Oct 1948 in of, Oklahoma City, Oklahoma, Oklahoma
+ Melissa b: Abt. 1950
............13 Mistie ROBB b: 1974 in twin
............13 Mindy ROBB b: 1974 in twin
............13 AMBER ROBB
............12 Kenneth ROBB b: 08 Aug 1950 in of, Oklahoma City, Oklahoma, Oklahoma
+ Mary

.................................13 Apollo ROBB b: Abt. 1974
.................................13 Robert ROBB b: Abt. 1977
.................................13 Angella ROBB b: Abt. 1980
.................................12 Ronald Gene ROBB b: 1951 in of, Oklahoma City, Oklahoma, Oklahoma
   + Ruth FERGUSSON b: Abt. 1954 in of, Oklahoma City, Oklahoma
.................................13 Ronna ROBB b: Abt. 1985 in of, Oklahoma City, Oklahoma
.................................13 Donna ROBB b: Abt. 1985 in of, Oklahoma City, Oklahoma
   + Hersel Lee Martin b: Abt. 1939 in of, Edmond, Oklahoma, m: 1960 in of,
   Oklahoma, divorced, 1969
.................................12 Gary Lee Martin b: 1961 in Edmond, Oklahoma
   + Jennifer
.................................12 Dorena Sue Martin b: 1966 in Seminole, Oklahoma
   + Paul CATT b: Abt. 1954 in of, Oklahoma City, Oklahoma
.................................13 Shelly Jean CATT b: 1987 in Midwest City, Oklahoma
.................................13 Steven GLENN CATT b: 1990 in Midwest City, Oklahoma
   + Norman PEARCE b: Abt. 1940 in of, Oklahoma City, Oklahoma, m: Abt. 1970
.................................11 Evelyn Dorena LAWLER b: 1932 in Longdale, Okla
   + Delmar COLLETT b: Abt. 1935, m: Abt. 1955 in divorced, 1961
.................................12 Sherry Ann COLLETT b: 31 Jan 1957 in HUTCHINSON, Kansas
.................................12 Del Wayne COLLETT b: 15 Jun 1958 in Port Lyolla, French Morocco
.................................12 Ellen Jean COLLETT b: 21 Nov 1960 in Newport, RI
   + William Newton HALE b: Abt. 1940 in of, Durant, Oklahoma, m: 01 Feb 1964 in
   Durant, Oklahoma
.................................12 William Nathan HALE b: 04 Jan 1971 in Oklahoma City, Oklahoma, Oklahoma
.................................11 Emery Leon LAWLER b: 05 Nov 1939 in Oklahoma City, Okla
   + Sammie Don Rose b: Abt. 1942 in Oklahoma City, Oklahoma, Oklahoma, m:
   1955 in Oklahoma City, Okla, divorced, 1960
.................................12 Stanley Leon LAWLER b: 02 Aug 1957 in Oklahoma City, Oklahoma, Oklahoma
.................................12 Alan Dane LAWLER b: Mar 1959 in Oklahoma City, Oklahoma, Oklahoma
   + Hazel Sue JOHNSON b: 12 Feb 1945 in Oklahoma City, Oklahoma, Oklahoma,
   m: 03 May 1961 in Oklahoma City, Oklahoma, Oklahoma
.................................12 Carolyn Sue LAWLER b: 24 Sep 1961 in Oklahoma City, Oklahoma, Oklahoma
   + Phillip TEMPLETON b: Abt. 1959 in of, Oklahoma City, Oklahoma, m: Nov 1979
   in of, Oklahoma City, Div 1981, Ok
.................................13 Casey Wayne TEMPLETON b: 09 May 1980 in of, Oklahoma City, Oklahoma
   + James A Herman b: Abt. 1961 in of, Oklahoma City, Oklahoma, m: Apr 1988 in
   of, Oklahoma City, Div 1981, Ok
.................................13 Justin Dale Herman b: 26 Apr 1990 in of, Oklahoma City, Oklahoma
.................................12 Lonnie Gene LAWLER b: 29 May 1963 in Oklahoma City, Oklahoma, Oklahoma
   + Sandra MARS b: Abt. 1965 in of, Ok
.................................13 Michel LAWLER b: 1984 in of, Ok
.................................13 Melissa LAWLER b: 1989 in of, Ok
.................................12 Daryl Lynn LAWLER b: 15 Feb 1969 in Oklahoma City, Oklahoma, Oklahoma
.................................11 Charlene Veldamae LAWLER b: 03 Jun 1945 in Oklahoma City, Oklahoma,
   Oklahoma
   + John Wayne JOHNSON b: 04 Apr 1941 in Tullahma, Oklahoma, m: 26 Aug 1961
   in Oklahoma City, Oklahoma, Oklahoma
.................................12 John Wayne JOHNSON jr b: 10 May 1962 in Oklahoma City, Oklahoma,
   Oklahoma
   + Mary Ann Miller b: Abt. 1964 in Oklahoma City, Oklahoma, Oklahoma
.................................13 Alex Wayne JOHNSON b: 12 May 1991 in Oklahoma City, Oklahoma,
   Oklahoma
.................................12 Stevan Dewayne JOHNSON b: 23 Jun 1964 in Oklahoma City, Oklahoma,
   Oklahoma
   + not known m: not married

...................13 James Steven TYLER b: 27 Feb 1991 in Oklahoma City, Oklahoma, Oklahoma
...................12 David Eugene JOHNSON b: 16 Dec 1965 in Oklahoma City, Oklahoma, Oklahoma
...................12 Emery Joe JOHNSON b: 03 Feb 1968 in Oklahoma City, Oklahoma, Oklahoma
+ Gala Rena Henry b: Abt. 1970 in Oklahoma City, Oklahoma, Oklahoma
...................13 BRYAN Joseph JOHNSON b: 11 Oct 1990 in Oklahoma City, Oklahoma, Oklahoma
...................13 Nicholas Brannon JOHNSON b: 26 Mar 1991 in Oklahoma City, Oklahoma, Oklahoma
...................12 Michael Don JOHNSON b: 27 Mar 1971 in Oklahoma City, Oklahoma, Oklahoma
+ Minnie seond wife
...................9 James Wesley LAWLER b: near, Argile, Denton, Tx, d: 15 Mar 1947 in Ocona, Montague, Tx; Y
+ Lucy Mary Jones b: 13 May 1871 in of, HAYES, Tx, m: 27 Apr 1887, d: 27 Jan 1897 in Reck, Carter, Okla; Y
...................10 Oscar LAWLER b: 14 Apr 1888 in Kimbal, Tx
...................10 James Stanley LAWLER b: 11 Mar 1890 in Jack, Tx, d: 12 Nov 1965 in St Jo, Montague, Tx; Y
+ [unknown spouse]
...................11 Mildred LAWLER b: 04 Apr 1921 in Bonita, Montague, Tx
+ James Reuben CAPPS b: Abt. 1919 in of, Bonita, Montague, Tx, m: 31 May 1941 in Rhine, Ok
...................12 James William CAPPS b: 12 Mar 1942 in Belcherville, Montague, Tx
+ Nedra Fae Armstrong b: Abt. 1944 in Nacona, Montague, Tx, m: 22 Jun 1963 in Lindsey, Ok
...................12 Donald David CAPPS b: 09 Aug 1943 in Nacona, Montague, Tx
+ Nelia b: Minea valley, CA
...................13 Shelly Ann CAPPS b: 01 Jun 1965 in Odessa, Tx
+ Bliss Kay b: Abt. 1963 in of, Odessa, Tx
...................14 Tamma Lynn Kay b: 10 Aug 1966 in of, Odessa, Tx
...................13 CHRISTIE Lynn CAPPS b: 24 Sep 1967 in Odessa, Tx
+ Clay BRISCOE b: Abt. 1967 in of, Odessa, Tx
...................14 Seith BRISCOE b: Dec 1992 in Odessa, Tx, d: 1992 in infant, one, DAY; Y
...................14 PAGE Erin BRISCOE b: 04 Mar 1993 in Odessa, Tx
...................11 Vernon "Buck" LAWLER b: Abt. 1923 in of, Bonita, Montague, Tx
+ Doris ROBINSON
...................12 Michael LAWLER b: Abt. 1945 in of, Bonita, Montague, Tx
...................12 Patsey Fae LAWLER b: Abt. 1947 in of, Bonita, Montague, Tx
...................12 Shirley Ann LAWLER b: Abt. 1949 in of, Bonita, Montague, Tx
...................12 Susan LAWLER b: Abt. 1952 in of, Bonita, Montague, Tx
+ no children name not known
+ Michie b: no children
...................11 James Kornegay LAWLER b: Abt. 1925 in of, Bonita, Montague, Tx
+ Willie BEE b: Abt. 1927 in no children
...................11 Sybil LAWLER b: Abt. 1927 in of, Bonita, Montague, Tx
+ John PRICE b: Abt. 1927 in of, Montague, Tx
...................12 Steven PRICE b: Abt. 1950 in of, Montague, Tx
...................12 Roxanne PRICE b: Abt. 1955 in of, Montague, Tx
...................11 Arnold Weldon LAWLER b: Abt. 1930 in of, Bonita, Montague, Tx
...................10 Edna LAWLER b: 30 May 1893 in Kimbal, County, Tx, d: 27 Feb 1921 ; Y
...................10 William Homer LAWLER b: 27 Feb 1896 in Reck, County, Okla, d: 1974 in Montague Co., TX; Y

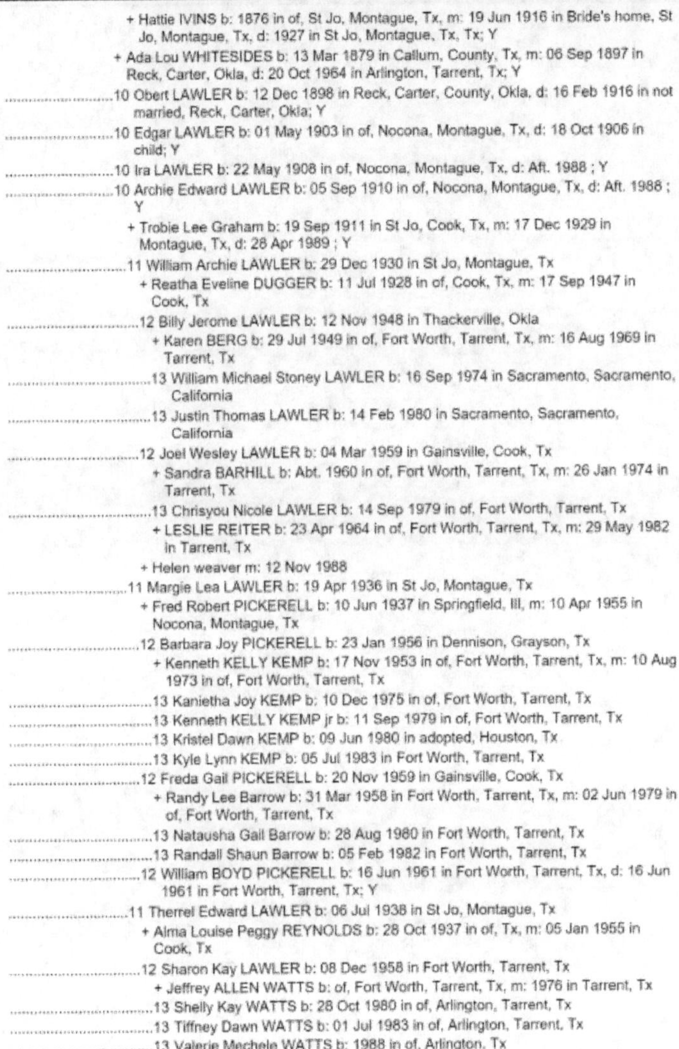

+ Hattie IVINS b: 1876 in of, St Jo, Montague, Tx, m: 19 Jun 1916 in Bride's home, St Jo, Montague, Tx, d: 1927 in St Jo, Montague, Tx, Tx; Y

+ Ada Lou WHITESIDES b: 13 Mar 1879 in Callum, County, Tx, m: 06 Sep 1897 in Reck, Carter, Okla, d: 20 Oct 1964 in Arlington, Tarrent, Tx; Y

10 Obert LAWLER b: 12 Dec 1898 in Reck, Carter, County, Okla, d: 16 Feb 1916 in not married, Reck, Carter, Okla; Y

10 Edgar LAWLER b: 01 May 1903 in of, Nocona, Montague, Tx, d: 18 Oct 1906 in child; Y

10 Ira LAWLER b: 22 May 1908 in of, Nocona, Montague, Tx, d: Aft. 1988 ; Y

10 Archie Edward LAWLER b: 05 Sep 1910 in of, Nocona, Montague, Tx, d: Aft. 1988 ; Y

+ Trobie Lee Graham b: 19 Sep 1911 in St Jo, Cook, Tx, m: 17 Dec 1929 in Montague, Tx, d: 28 Apr 1989 ; Y

11 William Archie LAWLER b: 29 Dec 1930 in St Jo, Montague, Tx

+ Reatha Eveline DUGGER b: 11 Jul 1928 in of, Cook, Tx, m: 17 Sep 1947 in Cook, Tx

12 Billy Jerome LAWLER b: 12 Nov 1948 in Thackerville, Okla

+ Karen BERG b: 29 Jul 1949 in of, Fort Worth, Tarrent, Tx, m: 16 Aug 1969 in Tarrent, Tx

13 William Michael Stoney LAWLER b: 16 Sep 1974 in Sacramento, Sacramento, California

13 Justin Thomas LAWLER b: 14 Feb 1980 in Sacramento, Sacramento, California

12 Joel Wesley LAWLER b: 04 Mar 1959 in Gainsville, Cook, Tx

+ Sandra BARHILL b: Abt. 1960 in of, Fort Worth, Tarrent, Tx, m: 26 Jan 1974 in Tarrent, Tx

13 Chrisyou Nicole LAWLER b: 14 Sep 1979 in of, Fort Worth, Tarrent, Tx

+ LESLIE REITER b: 23 Apr 1964 in of, Fort Worth, Tarrent, Tx, m: 29 May 1982 in Tarrent, Tx

+ Helen weaver m: 12 Nov 1988

11 Margie Lea LAWLER b: 19 Apr 1936 in St Jo, Montague, Tx

+ Fred Robert PICKERELL b: 10 Jun 1937 in Springfield, Ill, m: 10 Apr 1955 in Nocona, Montague, Tx

12 Barbara Joy PICKERELL b: 23 Jan 1956 in Dennison, Grayson, Tx

+ Kenneth KELLY KEMP b: 17 Nov 1953 in of, Fort Worth, Tarrent, Tx, m: 10 Aug 1973 in of, Fort Worth, Tarrent, Tx

13 Kanietha Joy KEMP b: 10 Dec 1975 in of, Fort Worth, Tarrent, Tx

13 Kenneth KELLY KEMP jr b: 11 Sep 1979 in of, Fort Worth, Tarrent, Tx

13 Kristel Dawn KEMP b: 09 Jun 1980 in adopted, Houston, Tx

13 Kyle Lynn KEMP b: 05 Jul 1983 in Fort Worth, Tarrent, Tx

12 Freda Gail PICKERELL b: 20 Nov 1959 in Gainsville, Cook, Tx

+ Randy Lee Barrow b: 31 Mar 1958 in Fort Worth, Tarrent, Tx, m: 02 Jun 1979 in of, Fort Worth, Tarrent, Tx

13 Natausha Gail Barrow b: 28 Aug 1980 in Fort Worth, Tarrent, Tx

13 Randall Shaun Barrow b: 05 Feb 1982 in Fort Worth, Tarrent, Tx

12 William BOYD PICKERELL b: 16 Jun 1961 in Fort Worth, Tarrent, Tx, d: 16 Jun 1961 in Fort Worth, Tarrent, Tx; Y

11 Therrel Edward LAWLER b: 06 Jul 1938 in St Jo, Montague, Tx

+ Alma Louise Peggy REYNOLDS b: 28 Oct 1937 in of, Tx, m: 05 Jan 1955 in Cook, Tx

12 Sharon Kay LAWLER b: 08 Dec 1958 in Fort Worth, Tarrent, Tx

+ Jeffrey ALLEN WATTS b: of, Fort Worth, Tarrent, Tx, m: 1976 in Tarrent, Tx

13 Shelly Kay WATTS b: 28 Oct 1980 in of, Arlington, Tarrent, Tx

13 Tiffney Dawn WATTS b: 01 Jul 1983 in of, Arlington, Tarrent, Tx

13 Valerie Mechele WATTS b: 1988 in of, Arlington, Tx

...................12 Melinda Fay LAWLER b: 21 May 1962 in Fort Worth, Tarrent, Tx
                + Edward LATHAM b: Abt. 1960 in of, Tarrent, Tx, m: Abt. 1982 in Tarrent, Tx
...................13 Jessie Edward LATHAM b: 05 Dec 1984 in of, Fort Worth, Tarrent, Tx
...................13 John David LATHAM b: Jun 1991
...............11 Jeral Wesley LAWLER b: 05 Jun 1947 in St Jo, Montague, Tx
                + Alice Fay MARTINDALE b: 10 Aug 1948 in of, Tarrent, Tx, m: 1963 in divorced, abt, 1968
...................12 Angie Fay LAWLER b: 18 Aug 1964 in of, Dallas, Tarrent, Tx
...................12 Larry Edward LAWLER b: 09 Apr 1966 in of, Dallas, Tarrent, Tx
                + Beverly Kay STEAL b: 13 Sep 1953 in of, Dallas, Tx
...................12 Traci Kay LAWLER b: 11 Sep 1976 in of, Fort Worth, Tarrent, Tx
...................12 LESLIE Dawn LAWLER b: 09 Oct 1978 in of, Dallas, Tx
                + Vicki Jo Jackson ERICKSON b: 22 Sep 1953 in St Sault Marie, MI, m: 14 Feb 1981 in Dennison, Tx, d: Living, 1993; Y
                + Anna Mrs Archie LAWLER m: Aft. 1990
.............10 Mittie Adelied LAWLER b: 03 Nov 1912 in St Jo, Montague, Tx, d: Aft. 1988 in of, Dale, Oklahoma; Y
                + Ralph MOLSBEE b: 04 Jan 1910 in Nocona, Montague, Tx, m: 29 Apr 1939 in Ryne, Oklahoma, d: Aft. 1988 ; Y
...............11 Anna Louise MOLSBEE b: 27 Jan 1942 in Nocona, Montague, Tx
                + James Rodney Rod HALFEN b: Abt. 1940 in of, Nocona, Montague, Tx, m: Abt. 1969 in of, Nocona, Montague, Tx, d: Aft. 1988 ; Y
...................12 Eric HALFEN b: 09 Nov 1970 in 11:55 PM, Nocona, Montague, Tx
...................12 Christopher HALFEN b: 10 Nov 1970 in 12:05 AM, Nocona, Montague, Tx
                + Charles Lester b: Abt. 1940 in of, Nocona, Montague, Tx, m: Jan 1964 in husband, terminally, Ill, d 6 mo, d: Jun 1964 in Kidney Disease; Y
...............11 Donald Kent MOLSBEE b: 17 May 1944 in Nocona, Montague, Tx
                + Judy K b: Abt. 1946 in Nocona, Montague, Tx, m: Abt. 1968 in of, Nocona, Montague, Tx
...................12 Brandett Kaye MOLSBEE b: 02 Nov 1970
                + Patricia Ann ROOKER b: 20 Jul 1934 in of, Nocona, Montague, Tx
...............11 Ernest Leo MOLSBEE b: 26 Jul 1945 in Nocona, Montague, Tx, d: Aft. 1988 ; Y
                + Peggie RICHARDSON Kimberly
...................12 Tanya Ray MOLSBEE b: 14 Dec 1966 in Longpine, Inyo, CA
                + David Wayne ARMITAGE b: Abt. 1964 in of, Shawnee. Pottowatami, Ok, m: 10 Oct 1986 in of, Shawnee, Pottowatami, Ok
...................13 Michael David MOLSBEE b: 19 Oct 1985 in of, Shawnee, Pottowatami, Ok
...................13 TYLER Ray ARMITAGE b: 04 Sep 1988 in of, Shawnee, Pottowatami, Ok
...................13 Colton Wayne ARMITAGE b: 06 Oct 1990 in of, Shawnee, Pottowatami, Ok
...................12 Tammy Ray MOLSBEE b: 15 Dec 1969 in Prague, Lincoln, Ok
                + James REMPE b: Abt. 1967 in of, Shawnee, Pottowatami, Ok
...................13 Autumn Lynn REMPE b: 15 Aug 1989 in of, Shawnee, Pottowatami, Ok
...................13 Tristin Rene' REMPE b: 06 Jul 1992 in of, Shawnee, Pottowatami, Ok
                + Karen Gardner
                + Kimberly Ann RAMSEY b: 26 Aug 1960 in of, Montague, Tx, m: Abt. 1988
...................12 Barry Franklin MOLSBEE b: 18 Jun 1983 in Midwest City, Ok, Ok
...................12 Lynsey Renee MOLSBEE b: 12 Oct 1984 in Midwest City, Ok, Ok
.............10 Herman LAWLER b: 07 Jun 1914 in of, Nocona, Montague, Tx, d: 08 Oct 1914 in age 3, Nocona, Montague, Tx; Y
.............10 Orene Ada LAWLER b: 16 Mar 1916 in of, Nocona, Montague, Tx, d: Aft. 1988 in Arlington, Tx; Y
                + Rual Carroll b: of, Montague, Tx, m: Aug 1935 in of, Montague, Tx
...............11 Melvane Carroll b: 06 Aug 1936 in Montague, Tx
                + Joe Ray Phelps b: 19 Jun 1933 in of, Montague, Tx, m: 07 Feb 1953 in Whitesboro, Tx, divorced, 1961

........................12 Beverly Dianne Phelps b: 22 Nov 1956 in Whitesboro, Sherman, Tx
    + Thomas Craig b: Feb 1955 in of, Dallas, Dallas, Tx, m: Nov 1972
........................13 Christopher Lee Craig b: 20 Jul 1973
........................13 Daniel Craig b: 10 Jul 1978
    + Henry John MALONE b: Abt. 1936 in of, Dallas, Dallas, Tx, m: 10 Jun 1966 in Fort Worth, Tarrent, divorced, Jan 1984
........................12 John Martin Gregg MALONE b: 30 Jul 1970 in Dallas, Dallas, Tx
    + Mario Caesar Moreno b: 15 Aug 1949 in Dallas, Dallas, Tx, m: Abt. 1986 in Dallas, Dallas, Tx
........................10 Juanita LAWLER b: 30 May 1919 in of, Nocona, Montague, Tx, d: Aft. 1988 ; Y
    + Karl McKenzie b: 21 Oct 1915 in of, Tx, m: 08 Dec 1936 in div 1959
........................11 Karl Leon McKenzie b: 20 Dec 1937 in Nocona, Tx
    + Sarah Joe WAGNER b: Abt. 1939 in of, Nocona, Tx, m: 15 May 1957 in Tx
........................12 BRADLEY Leon McKenzie b: 27 Oct 1959 in of, Nocona, Tx
    + Susan FLEITMAN b: 12 Jun 1965, m: 07 Oct 1989 in Muenster, Tx
........................13 Sara Morgan McKenzie b: 02 Sep 1991
........................12 Bobby Joe McKenzie b: 07 Oct 1960 in of, Nocona, Tx, d: 05 Apr 1982 ; Y
........................11 Jerry Wayne McKenzie b: 04 Jun 1942 in Nocona, Tx
    + Betty DAVIS b: 20 May 1940 in Gainsville, Cook, Tx, m: 19 Sep 1963 in Dallas, Dallas, Tx
........................12 Debbie McKenzie b: 01 Apr 1958 in adopted
    + Steve b: Abt. 1957 in of, Nocona, Tx
........................13 son
........................12 Jeffrey Karl McKenzie b: 29 Dec 1975 in 548 Sellinger, Lewisville, Tx
........................11 Karla Jean McKenzie b: 28 Jan 1947 in Nocona, Tx
    + Tony HUDSON CORLEY b: Abt. 1945
........................12 Kimberly Anita CORLEY b: 27 Aug 1965
........................12 Stacy Lynn CORLEY b: 17 Apr 1970
........................10 Ava Lee LAWLER b: 01 Apr 1922 in of, Nocona, Montague, Tx, d: 18 Jan 1988 in of, Gainsville, Cook, Tx; Y
    + Olen DAY b: 1921, d: Aft. 1988 ; Y
    + Martha Cordelia Mary TRAMEL b: 14 May 1856 in of, Denton Co., Tx, d: 21 Jun 1940 in Montague, Co., Tx; Y
........................9 Charles Charlie Walter LAWLER b: 02 Jan 1876 in near, St Jo, Montague, Tx, d: 02 Oct 1959 in North Tx State Hospital, Turberculosis; Y
    + Malinda Evaline Wilson b: Abt. 1878 in Pilot Point, or Bonita, Montague CO., TX, m: 07 Jan 1900 in St.Joe, Montague Co., TX, d: 22 Jun 1964 in Wichita Falls, Tx; Y
........................10 Ethal May (Jones) LAWLER b: 01 Apr 1901 in Wichita Falls, Tx, d: Jun 1973 in Chicago ILL; Y
    + Thomas Tommie WARE b: Abt. 1898 in of Chicago
........................11 Clem WARE b: Abt. 1925 in of Chicago, d: 1999 in of Chicago; Y
........................11 Harold WARE b: Abt. 1927 in of Chicago
........................10 Rosabelle LAWLER b: 11 Oct 1902 in Wichita Falls, Tx, d: 04 Oct 1978 in Wichita Falls, Tx; Y
    + DILSWORTH b: of Wichita Falls, Tx
........................11 Ramond Lee DILSWORTH b: Abt. 1927 in Wichita Falls, Tx
........................10 Essie B. LAWLER b: 01 Jan 1905 in Wichita Falls, Tx, d: 23 Oct 1984 in Wichita Falls, Tx; Y
    + B. C. Dewoody b: Abt. 1903 in Wichita Falls, Tx, m: Abt. 1922 in Wichita Falls, Tx
........................11 Alberta Marcille "Mickey" Dewoody b: 11 Sep 1924 in Wichita Falls, Tx
........................11 Jerrel Dewoody b: Abt. 1925 in Wichita Falls, Tx
    + Alfred Bert Crawford b: Wichita Falls, Tx, m: Abt. 1933 in Wichita Falls, Tx
........................11 Edwin Bert Crawford b: 19 Nov 1935 in Wichita Falls, Tx
........................10 Charles Henry LAWLER b: 06 Feb 1907 in Wichita Falls, Tx, d: 18 Oct 1979 in Garland Tx; Y

+ Frances
...............11 CHARLES MICHAEL LAWLER
...............10 Andrew "Chuckie" Walter LAWLER b: Abt. 1909 in Wichita Falls, Tx, d: Chicago ILL; Y
+ Julia b: Abt. 1910 in of Chicago
...............11 Eveline LAWLER b: Abt. 1930 in of Chicago
...............10 Pearl Jewel Dovey LAWLER b: 25 Aug 1913 in Wichita Falls, Tx
+ Claude Corrial PARKS b: Abt. 1911 in Wichita Falls, Tx, m: Abt. 1931 in Wichita Falls, Tx
...............11 Charles Walter PARKS b: 26 Mar 1933 in Wichita Falls, Tx, d: 17 May 1997 in Wichita Falls, Tx; Y
...............11 Rose Marie PARKS b: 18 Feb 1935 in Wichita Falls, Tx
...............11 Cecil Carrol PARKS b: 05 Dec 1938 in Wichita Falls, Tx
...............11 David Lee PARKS b: 24 Aug 1943 in Wichita Falls, Tx
...............11 Christine Louise Lois PARKS b: 26 Nov 1945
...............11 Claude Corrial "Tom Thumb" PARKS b: 05 Dec 1947 in Wichita Falls, Tx, d: 07 May 2001 ; Y
...............11 Mary Frances PARKS b: 06 Dec 1948 in Wichita Falls, Tx
...............11 Cynthia Joyce PARKS b: 02 Jun 1951 in Wichita Falls, Tx
...............10 Walter Edwin LAWLER b: Mar 1915 in Wichita Falls, Tx, d: Abt. 1935 in Wichita Falls, Tx killed by Train; Y
+ [unknown spouse]
...............11 Paul Allen "Ikie" LAWLER b: 28 Dec 1935 in of Wichita Falls, Tx., now of Ariz
+ Betty Jean BREWER b: 22 Sep 1939 in Wichita Falls, Tx, m: Abt. 1954 in Gilespie Co., TX
...............12 Annette LAWLER b: 21 Feb 1959 in Gilespie Co., TX., of Dennison Tx, Newark, Del
+ CARR
...............13 Jennifer Irene CARR b: 07 Oct 1977 in Olney Tx
...............13 Melissa Jean CARR b: 09 Dec 1979 in Alice Tx
+ SCALONE
...............13 Joann Carmella SCALONE b: 26 Sep 1996 in Wilmington DE
...............12 Walter Allen LAWLER b: 29 Oct 1995 in Gilespie Co., TX
...............9 Emma D. LAWLER b: 13 Jun 1878 in near, St Jo, Montague, Tx
+ mr PIERCE b: Abt. 1876 in near, St Jo, Montague, Tx
...............9 John PRESLEY LAWLER b: 18 Nov 1883 in near, St Jo, Montague, Tx, d: 21 Jun 1969 ; Y
+ Lucy BELL STOGNER b: 11 Nov 1888 in of, Tx, m: 21 Nov 1907 in Paris, Texas, d: 09 Jan 1962 in Magnum, Okla; Y
...............10 Bertha Cordella LAWLER b: 18 Sep 1908 in Bonita, Tx, d: Aft. 1992 in of, Houston, Tx; Y
+ Lincoln Bartow Mitchell b: 02 Aug 1904 in Wedowee, ALA, d: 1977 in Tx; Y
...............11 Eveylyn Charlene Mitchell b: 17 Aug 1927 in Burkburnett, Tx, d: 29 Sep 1932 in Tx; Y
...............11 Alma Lorraine Mitchell b: 25 Jul 1930 in Newtontown, Tx
+ WILLIS Dale HANSON
...............12 Brenda Elaine HANSON b: 29 Nov 1954 in Columbus, Mo
...............12 Laura Marie HANSON b: 26 Apr 1957 in Columbus, Mo
...............11 Sarah Helen Mitchell b: 17 Dec 1937 in Corpus Christi, Tx
+ SCOTT Stewart WINTERHALTER b: Abt. 1935 in of, Houston, Tx
...............12 SCOTT Stewart WINTERHALTER b: 22 Sep 1957 in Corpus Christi, Tx
...............12 Dareen York WINTERHALTER b: 02 Apr 1965 in Houston, Tx
...............11 Lincoln Bartow Mitchell jr b: 03 Jan 1943 in Corpus Christi, Tx
+ Deanne GABLER b: Abt. 1940 in Houston, Tx
...............12 Lincoln Bartow Mitchell III b: 31 Dec 1963 in Houston, Tx

............12 Jolene Mitchell b: 10 Feb 1968 in Houston, Tx
............12 Evangeline Mitchell b: 04 Sep 1977 in Houston, Tx
............10 Alma LAWLER b: 14 Oct 1913 in St. Jo, Tx, d: 14 Oct 1913 ; Y
............10 John William Ray LAWLER b: 29 May 1917 in St. Jo, Tx, d: 06 Nov 1976 ; Y
............+ Verba Lucille HILLIARD b: 24 Jun 1939 in Killeen, Tx
............11 Leta Rhea LAWLER b: 15 Mar 1943
............+ Bruce GOVETT b: 15 Oct 1943 in Oklahoma City, Okla, m: 17 Apr 1965 in
............Seminole, Okla
............12 David Ray GOVETT b: 27 Jul 1967 in Ada, Okla
............11 Arthur PRESLEY LAWLER b: 28 Apr 1944 in NJ
............+ Kay b: Abt. 1946 in of, Tx
............12 Shari Lyn LAWLER b: 27 Jan 1965 in Amarillo, Tx
............12 Brian LAWLER b: Abt. 1970 in of, Tx
............12 Anna Lisa LAWLER b: Mar 1989 in of, Abilene, Tx
............10 Arthur James LAWLER b: 15 Jul 1919 in St. Jo, Tx, d: 25 Nov 1943 in soldier, in,
............Italy; Y
............10 Floyd Washington LAWLER b: 24 Nov 1924 in Henrietta, Tx, d: Aft. 1992 ; Y
............+ Martha Jo LAURENCE b: 01 Jan 1927 in ARCHER, Co, Tx
............11 Linda Jean LAWLER b: 14 Mar 1947 in Wichita Falls, Texas
............+ Richard Edwin SAUNDERS b: 27 Sep 1945
............12 Melissa Ann SAUNDERS b: 21 Nov 1961 in Killeen, Tx
............+ Gregory BRUNN b: Abt. 1965 in of, Texas
............13 Brittani Danielle BRUNN b: 02 Jan 1987 in Wichita Falls
............13 Morgaine Nacole BRUNN b: 05 Feb 1990 in Treasure Island, CA
............12 Kimberly Kay SAUNDERS b: 31 Aug 1971 in Wichita Falls, Tx
............12 Deborah Deann SAUNDERS b: 06 Dec 1972 in Wichita Falls, Tx
............+ Shannon HASTINGS b: Abt. 1970 in of, Wichita Falls, Tx, m: Abt. 1989 in of,
............Wichita Falls, Tx
............13 Monika Denise HASTINGS b: 19 Jul 1990 in of, Wichita Falls, Tx
............11 Lori Carolyn LAWLER b: 03 May 1950 in Wichita Falls, Texas
............+ Jerry Lee FREEMAN b: 11 Mar 1947 in Wichita Falls, Tx
............12 Lori Jean FREEMAN b: 04 Jul 1970 in Wichita Falls, Tx
............12 David Lee FREEMAN b: 28 Dec 1973 in Wichita Falls, Tx
............11 Cathy Ann LAWLER b: 21 Jun 1954 in Loveland, Texas
............+ Paul William ROBERTS b: 18 Sep 1954 in Cinn, Ohio
............12 Michael Paul ROBERTS b: 30 Aug 1982 in Lawton, Ok
............11 Tammy Lin LAWLER b: 09 Jan 1960 in Loveland, Texas
............+ Johnnie Eugene FETSCH b: 14 May 1960 in Munday, Tx
............12 Johnica Jo FETSCH b: 17 Feb 1987 in Wichita Falls, Tx
............12 Jacob Keaton FETSCH b: 19 Jun 1989 in Wichita Falls, Tx
............11 Lauri Diane LAWLER b: 28 Jul 1963 in Loveland, Texas
............+ Arthur Henry LITTEKEN b: 05 Feb 1960 in Camp Irwin, CA
............12 Arthur Henry III LITTEKEN b: 25 Apr 1991 in Wichita Falls, Tx
............9 Willie Edyth LAWLER b: 22 Oct 1887 in Junction City, St Jo, Montague, Tx, d: 20 Aug
............1970 in Muenster, St Jo, Montague, Tx; Y
............+ Albert S. THOMPSON b: Abt. 1883 in of, Montague, County, Texas, m: 24 Jun 1906
............in Mc Collum, Montague, Tx
............10 Newell THOMPSON b: 15 Aug 1907 in Saint Jo, Montague, Tx, d: 1988 in
............Oklahoma, Tx; Y
............+ Laura b: Abt. 1912 in Saint Jo, Montague, Tx
............10 Esta Lee THOMPSON b: 21 Dec 1909 in Saint Jo, Montague, Tx
............+ S. Orvile GIDLOW b: Abt. 1910 in Saint Jo, Montague, Tx
............10 Elbert J THOMPSON b: 06 Dec 1913 in Saint Jo, Montague, Tx, d: 27 Oct 1986 in
............West Memphis, Ark; Y

+ Blanche GRUNDY b: Abt. 1912 in Saint Jo, Montague, Tx, m: 05 Apr 1934 in Ardmore, First Methodist, Ok

............11 Keith THOMPSON b: Abt. 1936 in of, Gainsville, Tx

............11 James THOMPSON b: Abt. 1938 in of, Gainsville, Tx

............11 Faye THOMPSON b: Abt. 1940 in of, Gainsville, Tx

............10 Albert THOMPSON b: 26 Dec 1917 in Saint Jo, Montague, Tx, d: 1977 in age 59, Ft Worth, Tarrent, Tx; Y

+ Juanetta b: Abt. 1912 in Saint Jo, Montague, Tx

............11 Albert III THOMPSON b: Abt. 1945 in of, Ft Worth, Tarrent, Tx

............10 Wilbur THOMPSON b: 16 Aug 1920 in Saint Jo, Montague, 7PM Cora Moore, Tx

+ Norma Kathleen CAMBRON b: 28 Jun 1920 in Cedartown, Polk, Co, Ga, m: 04 Mar 1944 in Bradington, FL, d: L-93, St Jo, Tx; Y

............11 Tommy Clark THOMPSON b: 23 Jan 1946 in Rome, Floyd, Co, Ga

+ Lillian HAVERCAMP b: Abt. 1945 in of, St Jo, Montague, Tx

+ Cindy Sue Watson b: Abt. 1949 in of, St Jo, Montague, Tx

............12 LUCAS Clark THOMPSON b: Abt. 1980 in of, St Jo, Montague, Tx

............12 Amanda Suzette THOMPSON b: of, St Jo, Montague, Tx

............11 Kenneth William THOMPSON b: 03 Feb 1959 in Cedartown, Polk, Co, Ga

............10 Orville e THOMPSON b: 21 Jul 1928 in Saint Jo, Montague, Tx

............10 Bessie Reney THOMPSON b: Saint Jo, Montague, Tx

+ Eldon RINEY b: Abt. 1912 in Saint Jo, Montague, Tx

............10 Bernice GOWER THOMPSON b: Saint Jo, Montague, Tx

+ James GOWER b: of, St Jo, Montague, Tx

............10 Joyce WHITEHEAD THOMPSON b: Saint Jo, Montague, Tx

+ Whitie WHITEHEAD b: Abt. 1910 in Saint Jo, Montague, Tx

+ Duncan PAYNE b: Abt. 1910 in of, Duncan, Ok

............9 Andrew Carroll Carol LAWLER b: 31 Mar 1891 in Junction City, Kimball Co, of Montague Co., Tx, d: 18 Oct 1979 in of, Montague Co., TX; Y

+ Pearl Mae Hogue LAWSON b: 11 Feb 1893 in Rubottom, Oklahoma, Indian Territory, m: 08 Jan 1911 in Bonita, Texas, of, Junction City, Tx, d: 06 May 1977 ; Y

............10 Lois LAWLER b: Abt. 1913 in of, Montague Co., TX

............10 Rosa Alma LAWLER b: Abt. 1915 in of, Montague Co., TX

............10 Cecil Andrew LAWLER b: Abt. 1917 in of, Montague Co., TX

............10 Floyd LAWLER b: Abt. 1922 in of, Montague Co., TX

............10 Roy William LAWLER b: Abt. 1925 in near, St Jo, Montague, Tx

+ Mary Faye DUNN b: Abt. 1927 in near, St Jo, Montague, Tx, m: 09 Feb 1947 in of, St Jo, Montague, Tx

............8 Emily C. LAWLER b: 1844 in nr Franklin, SIMPSON, Ky, d: 1875 in Denton, Denton, Tx; Y

+ John W. Prentiss b: 1845 in Tn, d: 1913 in Denton Co., Tx; Y

............9 Nancy Annie Prentiss b: 02 Nov 1869 in Denton, Denton, Tx, d: 21 Apr 1950 in Denton, Denton, Tx; Y

+ James Walker HUMPHREY b: 1844 in McCracken, Ky, m: 21 Oct 1885 in Jack, Tx, d: 05 Dec 1901 in Denton, Denton, Tx; Y

............10 Ada Florence HUMPHREY b: 07 Nov 1886 in Tarrent, Tx, d: 23 May 1964 in Olney, Young Co., TX; Y

+ George Washington WILSON b: 15 Apr 1880 in Brown CO, TX, m: 16 Mar 1903, d: 12 Apr 1951 in Electra, Wichita Co., TX; Y

............11 Howard WILSON b: 11 May 1904 in Denton, Denton Co., TX, d: 1904 in Clayton, Union Co., NM; Y

............11 John Prentiss WILSON b: 09 Sep 1906 in Denton, Denton Co., TX, d: 22 Aug 1975 in Denison, Grayson Co., TX; Y

+ MIRTY LAURA ELLISON b: 15 Apr 1910, m: 23 Dec 1928, d: 12 Aug 1998 in Denison, Grayson Co., Texas.; Y

............................11 Francis C. Frank WILSON b: 1908 in Denton, Denton Co., TX, d: 16 May 1935 in
                Abilene, Taylor CO., Tx; Y
............................11 Anna Florence WILSON b: 22 Mar 1910 in Harrold, Wilbarger Co., Tx, d: 13 Apr
                1984 in Douglas Cochise Co., AZ; Y
                + WILLIAM ANDREW BERRY b: 22 Sep 1909 in Denton, Denton Co., TX. m: 28
                Dec 1928 in Denton, Denton Co., TX, d: 24 Oct 1985 in Cassa Grande, Pinal
                CO., AZ; Y
............................12 Larry Andrew BERRY b: Abt. 1934 in Tx
                + Chsrlotte HOWELL
............................11 KIMBROUGH C. WILSON b: 12 Jun 1912 in Denton, Denton Co., TX, d: 24 Jun
                1948 in Wichita, Wichita Co., TX; Y
............................11 GEORGIA LORENE WILSON b: 17 Oct 1915 in Denton, Denton Co., TX, d: 18
                Apr 1967 in Electra, Wichita Co., TX; Y
                + JOHN EPPS REED b: 03 Feb 1904 in Miss., m: 16 Feb 1935 in OK, d: 16 Feb
                1976 in Dallas, Dallas Co., Tx; Y
                + CLARENCE ATWOOD RANKIN
                + T. L. LEVERETT b: 24 May 1912, d: 16 Jan 1995 in Electra, Wichita Co., TX; Y
............................11 ED PERSHING WILSON b: 1919 in Electra, Wichita Co., TX, d: 1919 in Electra,
                Wichita Co., TX; Y
............................11 ROSS ABNER WILSON b: 22 Jun 1922 in Electra, Wichita Co., TX, d: 27 Dec
                1977 in Electra, Wichita Co., TX; Y
                + FLORENCE EVELYN SINGLETON b: 08 Sep 1925 in Spanish Fork, Montague
                Co., TX, m: 01 Mar 1942 in Electra, Wichita Co., TX
............................11 Juaneitha WILSON b: 06 Feb 1924 in Electra, Wichita Co., Texas, d: 09 Jun 2003
                in 4541 E. Cooper, Tuscon, Arizona; Y
                + Frank Darrell WILTBANK b: 23 May 1922 in Greer, Apache, Arizona, m: 01 Jun
                1952 in Eagar, Apache, Arizona
............................12 son WILTBANK
............................12 Nancy WILTBANK
............................11 EARL LEWIS WILSON b: 03 Aug 1927 in Electra, Wichita Co., TX
                + REBECCA FAYE EDWARDS b: 21 May 1929, m: 09 Oct 1950, d: 10 Nov 2001 in
                Graham, Young Co., Tx; Y
............................10 John Finley HUMPHREY b: Abt. 1888 in Tx, d: child; Y
............................10 Gela May HUMPHREY b: 24 Dec 1890 in Denton, Denton, Tx, d: 14 Apr 1962 ; Y
                + George B. BUSH b: 22 Jul 1904, m: 22 Jul 1907
............................10 James Alvis HUMPHREY b: 14 Mar 1894 in Denton, Denton, Tx, d: 31 Jul 1946 ; Y
                + Lillian BURNS b: Abt. 1896, m: 06 Oct 1913
............................10 Clement HUMPHREY b: 11 Sep 1897 in Denton, Denton, Tx, d: 24 Mar 1922 ; Y
                + Rose BRANDENBURGER
............................9 Emily Idella Prentiss b: 07 Feb 1872 in Denton, Denton, Tx, d: 05 Aug 1926 ; Y
                + William Gay EASTON b: 02 Apr 1862 in Alabama, m: Denton, Denton, Tx, d: 05 Aug
                1926 in San Angelo, Tx; Y
............................10 Willie Mae EASTON b: 04 May 1890 in Kimbal, Kimbal, Tx
                + John Oscar TALBOTT b: Abt. 1888 in of, Kimbal, Kimbal, Tx
............................10 Prentiss Edmund EASTON b: 28 Mar 1892 in Kimbal, Kimbal, Tx
                + Jimmie Gilmore b: Abt. 1895 in of, Kimbal, Kimbal, Tx
............................10 Thomas Gay EASTON b: 12 Sep 1895 in Kimbal, Kimbal, Tx, d: 11 Sep 1911 ; Y
............................10 W. D. Jack EASTON b: 22 Feb 1899 in Sherwood, Tx
                + Mary GLENN b: Abt. 1901
............................10 Emma Jo EASTON b: 11 Apr 1906 in San Angelo, Tx
                + Euston S. WOLLARD b: Abt. 1900 in of, San Angelo, Tx
............................8 Samuel Finley LAWLER b: 14 Aug 1849 in nr Franklin, SIMPSON, Ky, d: 18 Oct 1918 in
                near, Junction, Kimble, Tx; Y
                + Martha Jane Mattie McAuley b: 01 Feb 1852 in Clairborne, parish, LA, m: 1872 in
                Denton, Denton, Tx, d: 19 Sep 1934 in Junction, Kimbal, Tx; Y

..............9 Arthur Oran LAWLER b: 02 Feb 1876 in Argyle, Denton, Tx, d: 12 Feb 1973 in San Antonio, Tx; Y

    + Olive Louise Lulu SKAGGS b: 03 Aug 1877 in Lavaca Co., Tx, m: 21 Jan 1902 in Kimbal, Tx, d: 15 Nov 1914 in near, Junction, Kimbal, Tx; Y

..............10 Oran Arthur LAWLER b: 15 Apr 1905 in near, Junction, Kimbal, Tx, d: 22 May 1908 in near, Junction, Kimbal, Tx; Y

..............10 Minnie Verena LAWLER b: 13 Feb 1909 in Junction, Kimble, Tx, d: Aft. 1999 in 106 Primera Dr, San Antonio, Tx; Y

    + WALLACE Lawrence GARVEY b: 23 Apr 1907 in San Antonio, Kimbal, Tx, m: 25 Oct 1930, d: Abt. 1986 in 106 Primera Dr, San Antonio, Tx; Y

..............11 no children

    + Willie Etta ROBBINS b: 05 Oct 1885 in of, Junction, Kimbal, Tx, m: 21 Feb 1916 in Kimbal, Tx, d: 28 Aug 1970 in San Antonio, Tx; Y

..............10 Arthur LAWLER b: 14 Aug 1918 in near, Junction, Kimbal, Tx

    + Audry June HUNTER b: Abt. 1920 in of, Junction, Kimbal, Tx, m: 09 Sep 1944

..............11 June Heather LAWLER b: 11 Jan 1953

    + Troy Wayne Lindley b: Abt. 1950 in of, Tx

..............12 David Arthur Lindley b: 20 Mar 1976 in of, Tx

..............11 Martha Lynn LAWLER b: 20 Feb 1957

..............10 William Clayton LAWLER b: 21 Nov 1921 in near, Junction, Kimbal, Tx

    + Katherine Louisa WOODS b: Abt. 1922 in of, Junction, Kimbal, Tx, m: 11 Dec 1948

..............9 Cornelia LAWLER b: Abt. 1879 in of, Coleman, Tx, d: child; Y

..............9 James Walker LAWLER b: 26 Jan 1883 in of, Kimbal, Tx, d: 06 Mar 1955 in of, Bakersfield, CA; Y

    + Laura Mae EVANS b: 05 May 1886 in of, Kimball, Co, Tx, d: 14 Feb 1975 in Bakersfield, California; Y

..............10 Harvey Willam LAWLER b: Abt. 1910 in of, Bakersfield, CA

    + [unknown spouse]

..............11 Harald H LAWLER b: Abt. 1940 in of Ca

    + [unknown spouse]

..............12 Mark LAWLER b: Abt. 1960 in CA

..............10 Giford LEONARD LAWLER b: Abt. 1911 in of, Bakersfield, CA

..............10 Alcy Rebecca LAWLER b: Abt. 1912 in of, Bakersfield, CA

..............10 Bessie Lorena LAWLER b: Abt. 1915 in of, Bakersfield, CA

..............10 Anna Lee LAWLER b: Abt. 1917 in of, Bakersfield, CA

..............10 Vena Lucy LAWLER b: Abt. 1919 in of, Bakersfield, CA

..............10 Reba Wauline LAWLER b: Abt. 1920 in of, Bakersfield, CA

..............10 Irene Victor LAWLER b: Abt. 1921 in of, Bakersfield, CA

..............10 Jennie Audrey LAWLER b: Abt. 1922 in of, Bakersfield, CA

..............9 Claude LEONARD LAWLER b: 21 Oct 1889 in of, Kimbal, Tx, d: 02 Sep 1967 ; Y

    + Mamie Mary GOODALL b: Abt. 1891 in of, Junction, Tx, m: 04 Jan 1914 in Junction, Tx

..............10 Ruby Marion LAWLER b: Abt. 1915 in of, Junction, Tx

    + Woodrow WILSON SMITH b: Abt. 1912 in of, Junction, Tx

..............11 Beverly Sue SMITH b: Abt. 1935 in of, Junction, Tx

..............11 Woodrow WILSON jr SMITH b: Abt. 1936 in of, Junction, Tx

..............11 Robert Virgil SMITH b: Abt. 1938 in of, Junction, Tx

..............11 Carroll Wayne SMITH b: Abt. 1940 in of, Junction, Tx

..............11 Gerald Lee SMITH b: Abt. 1944 in of, Junction, Tx

..............11 Patricia Ann SMITH b: Abt. 1946 in of, Junction, Tx

..............11 Wanda Gene SMITH b: Abt. 1947 in of, Junction, Tx

..............11 Marion Gene SMITH b: Abt. 1949 in of, Junction, Tx

..............10 Hugh LESLIE LAWLER b: Abt. 1917 in of, Junction, Tx

..............10 Virgil Claude LAWLER b: Abt. 1919 in of, Junction, Tx

    + Ruth ALLEN b: Abt. 1919 in of, Junction, Tx

............................11 Clyde LEONARD LAWLER b: Abt. 1941 in Roosevelt, of, Junction, Tx
        + Syliva
............................12 Tina LAWLER b: Abt. 1970 in Roosevelt, of, Junction, Tx
          + David HARTMAN b: Abt. 1972 in of New Braunfels, TX
............................13 Ian Michael HARTMAN b: Apr 1999 in of New Braunfels, TX
............................12 Kyle LAWLER b: Abt. 1975 in Roosevelt, of, Junction, Tx
          + Sharlene b: Abt. 1977 in of, Junction, Tx
............................13 Shane Brandon LAWLER b: Dec 1998 in Yuma, AZ
............................13 James Matthew LAWLER b: Feb 2000 in Yuma, AZ
............................11 Thomas Richard LAWLER b: Abt. 1944 in of, Junction, Tx
............................11 Walter ALLEN LAWLER b: Abt. 1947 in of, Junction, Tx
............................11 Sharon Jean LAWLER b: Abt. 1950 in of, Junction, Tx
............................10 Lester Robert LAWLER b: Abt. 1920 in of, Junction, Tx
          + Lena DRUMMOND b: Abt. 1920 in of, Junction, Tx
............................11 Larry Robert LAWLER b: Abt. 1940 in of, Junction, Tx
............................11 LESLIE Deanne LAWLER b: Abt. 1945 in of, Junction, Tx
............................9 Harry Hayden LAWLER b: 09 Jan 1892 in of, Kimbal, Tx
        + Edna DUNK b: Abt. 1902 in of, Junction, Kimbal, Tx, m: 1919 in Kimbal, Tx
............................10 Irma May LAWLER b: Abt. 1920 in of, Kimbal, Tx
          + Cecil Woodward b: Abt. 1908 in of, Kimbal, Tx
............................10 Mary Frances LAWLER b: Abt. 1922 in of, Kimbal, Tx
          + Thomas TOMLINSON Dr b: Abt. 1919 in of, Junction, Tx
............................11 Rebecca TOMLINSON b: Abt. 1944 in of, Junction, Tx
............................9 William LAWLER d: Bef. 1880 in child; Y
............................8 Mary Sabrina LAWLER b: 1852 in nr Franklin, SIMPSON, Ky
        + Zachary TAYLOR b: Abt. 1850, m: 27 Dec 1869 in Wise, Tx
............................9 James TAYLOR b: Abt. 1871 in of, Wise, Tx
............................8 George Henry LAWLER b: 20 Sep 1855 in near, St Jo, Montague, Tx, d: 24 Mar 1939 in
        Newark, Tx; Y
        + Sarah Rebecca Sims b: 04 Nov 1862 in Little Rock, Ark, m: 22 Dec 1888, d: 26 Sep
        1900 in Okla; Y
............................9 Leila Missouri LAWLER b: 05 May 1881 in Roanoke, Denton, Tx, d: 09 Oct 1974 in
        Odessa, Ector Co, Tx; Y
        + Amos WILSON HUDSON b: Abt. 1879 in of, Denton, Tx, m: Junction Falls, Denton,
        TX, d: Abt. 1946 in Boise, ID; Y
............................10 Donald "Jack" HUDSON b: Aug 1903 in Newark, Denton, Tx, d: Aft. 1998 ; Y
          + Eula b: Abt. 1910 in of, Tx, m: div
............................11 Daryal HUDSON b: Abt. 1935, d: of, Utah; Y
............................11 Janice HUDSON b: Abt. 1936, d: Aft. 1998 ; Y
............................11 Clark HUDSON b: Abt. 1938
          + Ivy
............................10 Clifford P HUDSON b: Abt. 1906 in Newark, Denton, Tx, d: Abt. 1986 in Parma, ID;
        Y
        + Ida Veora ALLEN b: Abt. 1909 in of, Parma, ID
............................11 John HUDSON b: Abt. 1940 in of, Parma, ID, d: Bef. 1998 ; Y
............................11 Lee HUDSON b: Abt. 1944 in of, Parma, ID, d: Aft. 1998 ; Y
............................11 Helena HUDSON b: Jan 1948 in of, Parma, ID, d: Aft. 1998 ; Y
          + SMITH
............................10 TURNER HUDSON b: Abt. 1909 in Newark, Denton, Tx
............................10 Cleo Grace HUDSON b: Oct 1912 in Newark, Denton, Tx, d: Aft. 1998 ; Y
        + Edward DOUGHTY b: Abt. 1910 in of, Tx
............................11 Larry DOUGHTY b: Abt. 1946 in of, Tx, d: Bef. 1998 in Odessa, Tx; Y
............................10 Lela Opal HUDSON b: 18 Apr 1918 in Newark, Denton, Tx, d: Aft. 1998 ; Y

+ Harold Bardon McDADE b: 20 May 1916 in Ft Worth, Tarrant, Tx, m: Fort Worth, Tarrant, Tx, d: 06 Feb 1986 in AF, ND; Y

................11 Gloria Jeanette McDADE b: 29 Jan 1938 in Ft Worth, Tarrant, Tx, d: Aft. 1998 in of, Livermore, CA, 94550; Y

+ Monte William Cook b: Abt. 1936, m: 18 May 1956 in Reno, div, Nevada

................12 Darrell William Cook b: 25 Oct 1957 in Napa, CA

................12 Neickol William Cook b: 1962

+ David DICKENSON b: 1962 in of Ca

................13 Cecelie Kassandra Jeannette Cook DICKENSON b: 1989 in of Ca

................12 still birth Cook b: 1964

................12 Darrick Jason Eugene Cook b: 29 Mar 1971 in Livermore, CA

+ Shannon JENKINS b: 1973 in of Ca

................13 Kyle William Cook b: 24 Sep 1992 in of Livermore Ca

................13 Sierra Jenkins Cook b: 24 Aug 1996 in Manteca, Ca

................13 Emely "Renee" Cook b: 24 Apr 1997 in Manteca, Ca

+ Troy SCOTT b: Abt. 1938

+ Robert Arnold PATZER b: Abt. 1921 in of, Riverside, CA, m: Abt. 1944

................11 Robert A PATZER b: 06 Dec 1946 in Riverside, CA, d: Aft. 1998 ; Y

+ Lucille m: div

+ Nancy b: of Ca (LA area), m: second, wife

................12 Megan PATZER b: Abt. 1976 in of Ca (LA area)

................11 Jerry Wayne PATZER b: 21 Oct 1947 in Almeda, Almeda, CA, d: Aft. 1998 ; Y

+ Shirleen b: Abt. 1969 in of, CA

................12 Jerrold PATZER b: Abt. 1975 in of Ca (LA area)

................12 Jeffrey PATZER b: Abt. 1977 in of Ca (LA area)

................12 Chamane PATZER b: Abt. 1979 in of Ca (LA area)

................11 Cleo Louise PATZER b: 18 Mar 1950 in Almeda, Almeda, CA, d: Aft. 1998 ; Y

+ Michael ALVARADO b: Abt. 1948 in of, Alameda, CA

................12 Miles ALVARADO b: Abt. 1973 in of Ca (LA area)

................12 Elis ALVARADO b: Abt. 1976 in of Ca (LA area)

+ PENDERS b: Abt. 1948 in of Ca (LA area)

................12 Dillon PENDERS b: Abt. 1979 in of Ca (LA area)

................12 Benjamine HANSON b: Abt. 1980 in of Ca (LA area)

................11 Shirley Ann PATZER b: 26 Aug 1951 in Almeda, Almeda, CA, d: Aft. 1998 ; Y

+ Steven DAVIS b: Abt. 1949 in of, Alameda, CA

................12 Nathan DAVIS b: Abt. 1973 in of Ca (LA area)

................12 Marla DAVIS b: Abt. 1974 in of Ca (LA area)

................12 Kyle DAVIS b: Abt. 1979 in of Ca (LA area)

..........9 Sabrina Frances LAWLER b: 15 Dec 1883 in Roanoke, Denton, Tx, d: 30 Jul 1930 in Bisbee, Ariz; Y

+ Albert BOHANNON b: Abt. 1881 in of, Denton, Tx, d: of, Bisbee, Ariz; Y

..........9 Henry Clay LAWLER b: 24 Jun 1890 in Junction, Kimbal, Tx, d: 1955 in Broken Arrow, Okla; Y

..........9 Lula Claude LAWLER b: 12 Nov 1895 in twin, Okla, d: 16 Feb 1936 ; Y

+ Luther BAYES b: Abt. 1888 in of, Denton, Tx

................10 Johnnie girl BAYES b: 1915 in of Denton, Denton, Tx

+ Ernest HILLARD b: Nov 1913 in of, Okla, m: 1933

................11 Jimmy (girl) Ruth HILLARD b: 1935

+ Evert MARTIN b: Abt. 1933, m: Jun 1954

................12 Sherri Juwan MARTIN b: 02 Nov 1956

+ Mark WIMS b: Abt. 1954 in Of Tx, m: Abt. 1974 in Tx

................13 Sara Ann WIMS b: 1975 in Of Tx

+ Kent BALLARD b: Abt. 1973 in Of Tx, m: Abt. 1995 in Tx

................14 Abby BALLARD b: Abt. 1996

...............................14 Emily BALLARD b: Abt. 1997
...............................13 Kent Ballard WIMS b: 1978 in Of Tx
...............................13 Katherine Michelle WIMS b: 1980 in Of Tx
+ Billy STARKS b: Abt. 1963 in Tx, m: Abt. 1986
...............................13 Dustin Wayne STARKS b: 1889 in Tx
...............................12 Bryan Evert MARTIN b: 11 Mar 1958
+ Sharon HASS b: Abt. 1960 in of Quitman TX, m: Abt. 1978 in Quitman TX
...............................13 Leslie MARTIN b: 1980 in of Quitman TX
...............................13 Cody MARTIN b: 1983 in of Quitman TX
...............................12 John David MARTIN twin b: 20 Sep 1972 in Mt.Vernon, Franklin, TX
+ Raimey Ann LYNCY b: Abt. 1972 in Of Tx, m: 1992 in Tx
...............................13 Lainey Alexsandra Victoria MARTIN b: 1993 in Of Tx
...............................13 Laci Ray Dawn MARTIN b: 1998 in Of Tx
...............................13 MARTIN b: Feb 2001
...............................12 Jimmy Don MARTIN twin b: 20 Sep 1972 in Mt.Vernon, Franklin, TX
+ Miranda Claborn HADDOCK b: Abt. 1980, m: 1997
...............................11 Ronnie Franklin HILLARD b: 1946
...............................10 Blanche BAYES b: Abt. 1917 in of, Okla
+ Claude BAGGET b: Abt. 1918 in Of Tx, m: Jan 1934 in Tx
...............................11 Elmer Ray BAGGET b: of, Tx, Okla
+ [unknown spouse]
...............................12 Terry Lynn BAGGET b: Abt. 1956
...............................12 son BAGGET b: Abt. 1957
...............................10 Doris Dorsey BAYES b: Abt. 1918 in of, Tx, Okla
+ Lewis NOWLIN b: Abt. 1917
...............................11 Douglas NOWLIN b: Abt. 1940
...............................11 Troy NOWLIN b: Abt. 1942
...............................10 L. C. BAYES b: Abt. 1922 in of, Okla
+ Velma
...............................10 Delma Jean BAYS b: 22 Jul 1931 in Denton, Tx, d: 31 Jan 2001 ; Y
+ John Paul MEEK b: of Wood County, Tx, m: 23 May 1951 in Dallas, Dallas, TX
...............................11 Richard Wayne MEEK b: 16 Apr 1954 in Gary AFB, San Marcos, Tx
...............................11 John Clarance MEEK b: 22 Jan 1956 in Cristobal Hsptl, Canal Zone, Panama
...............................9 Eula Maude LAWLER b: 12 Nov 1895 in twin, Okla, d: 05 Nov 1990 in Denton, Denton, Co., Tx; Y
+ Frank HARRAL b: 25 Aug 1899 in Cave City, Ark. of Denton Co Tx, m: 22 Mar 1924 in Denton, Denton Co., Tx. second husband, d: 12 May 1976 in Denton, Denton, Co., Tx; Y
...............................10 Peggy HARRAL b: 14 Nov 1924 in Denton, Denton Co., Tx., d: 10 Oct 1998 in Nixon, TX; Y
+ William A. SMITH b: Abt. 1922 in of Denton, Denton Co., Tx., m: 1943 in Denton, Denton Co., Tx., d: Denton, Denton Co., Tx.; Y
...............................11 Richard Lee SMITH b: 16 Nov 1943 in Denton, Denton Co., Tx., d: Aug 1976 in Denton, Denton Co., Tx.; Y
...............................11 William Harral SMITH b: 27 Oct 1944 in Denton, Denton Co., Tx.
...............................11 Edward Allen SMITH b: 18 Jul 1946 in Denton, Denton Co., Tx.
+ William A. ZAESKE b: Abt. 1924 in of Denton, Denton Co., Tx., m: 03 Jun 1951 in Dallas, Dallas Co., Tx, d: Nixon, TX; Y
...............................11 Billie Dell ZAESKE b: Abt. 1953 in of Denton, Denton Co., Tx.
...............................10 William Frank HARRAL b: 28 Feb 1927 in Denton, Denton Co., Tx., d: Lamar Colorado; Y
+ JoAnne Vanderbush b: Abt. 1929 in Decatur Tx, m: 26 Aug 1947 in Decatur Tx, d: Lamar Colorado; Y
...............................10 Holland ELWOOD HARRAL b: 09 Oct 1930 in Denton, Denton Co., Tx., d: 15 Aug 1998 in Denton, Denton Co., Tx.; Y

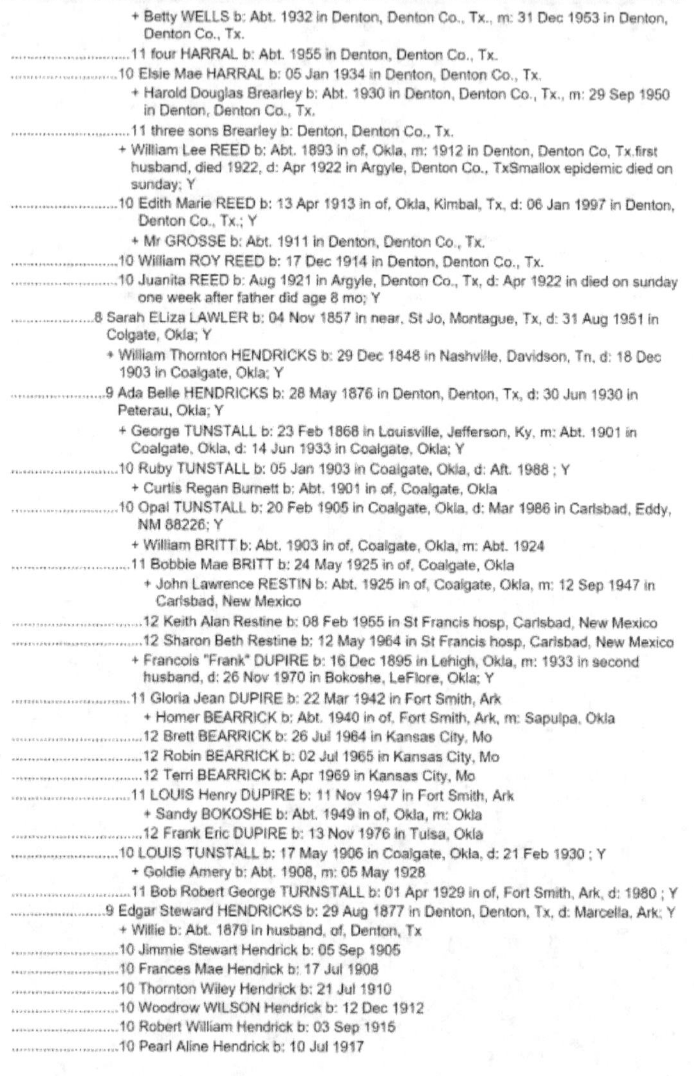

    + Betty WELLS b: Abt. 1932 in Denton, Denton Co., Tx., m: 31 Dec 1953 in Denton, Denton Co., Tx.

...............11 four HARRAL b: Abt. 1955 in Denton, Denton Co., Tx.

...............10 Elsie Mae HARRAL b: 05 Jan 1934 in Denton, Denton Co., Tx.

    + Harold Douglas Brearley b: Abt. 1930 in Denton, Denton Co., Tx., m: 29 Sep 1950 in Denton, Denton Co., Tx.

...............11 three sons Brearley b: Denton, Denton Co., Tx.

    + William Lee REED b: Abt. 1893 in of, Okla, m: 1912 in Denton, Denton Co, Tx.first husband, died 1922, d: Apr 1922 in Argyle, Denton Co., TxSmallox epidemic died on sunday; Y

...............10 Edith Marie REED b: 13 Apr 1913 in of, Okla, Kimbal, Tx, d: 06 Jan 1997 in Denton, Denton Co., Tx.; Y

    + Mr GROSSE b: Abt. 1911 in Denton, Denton Co., Tx.

...............10 William ROY REED b: 17 Dec 1914 in Denton, Denton Co., Tx.

...............10 Juanita REED b: Aug 1921 in Argyle, Denton Co., Tx, d: Apr 1922 in died on sunday one week after father did age 8 mo; Y

...........8 Sarah ELiza LAWLER b: 04 Nov 1857 in near, St Jo, Montague, Tx, d: 31 Aug 1951 in Colgate, Okla; Y

    + William Thornton HENDRICKS b: 29 Dec 1848 in Nashville, Davidson, Tn, d: 18 Dec 1903 in Coalgate, Okla; Y

...............9 Ada Belle HENDRICKS b: 28 May 1876 in Denton, Denton, Tx, d: 30 Jun 1930 in Peterau, Okla; Y

    + George TUNSTALL b: 23 Feb 1868 in Louisville, Jefferson, Ky, m: Abt. 1901 in Coalgate, Okla, d: 14 Jun 1933 in Coalgate, Okla; Y

...............10 Ruby TUNSTALL b: 05 Jan 1903 in Coalgate, Okla, d: Aft. 1988 ; Y

    + Curtis Regan Burnett b: Abt. 1901 in of, Coalgate, Okla

...............10 Opal TUNSTALL b: 20 Feb 1905 in Coalgate, Okla, d: Mar 1986 in Carlsbad, Eddy, NM 88226; Y

    + William BRITT b: Abt. 1903 in of, Coalgate, Okla, m: Abt. 1924

...............11 Bobbie Mae BRITT b: 24 May 1925 in of, Coalgate, Okla

    + John Lawrence RESTIN b: Abt. 1925 in of, Coalgate, Okla, m: 12 Sep 1947 in Carlsbad, New Mexico

...............12 Keith Alan Restine b: 08 Feb 1955 in St Francis hosp, Carlsbad, New Mexico

...............12 Sharon Beth Restine b: 12 May 1964 in St Francis hosp, Carlsbad, New Mexico

    + Francois "Frank" DUPIRE b: 16 Dec 1895 in Lehigh, Okla, m: 1933 in second husband, d: 26 Nov 1970 in Bokoshe, LeFlore, Okla; Y

...............11 Gloria Jean DUPIRE b: 22 Mar 1942 in Fort Smith, Ark

    + Homer BEARRICK b: Abt. 1940 in of, Fort Smith, Ark, m: Sapulpa, Okla

...............12 Brett BEARRICK b: 26 Jul 1964 in Kansas City, Mo

...............12 Robin BEARRICK b: 02 Jul 1965 in Kansas City, Mo

...............12 Terri BEARRICK b: Apr 1969 in Kansas City, Mo

...............11 LOUIS Henry DUPIRE b: 11 Nov 1947 in Fort Smith, Ark

    + Sandy BOKOSHE b: Abt. 1949 in of, Okla, m: Okla

...............12 Frank Eric DUPIRE b: 13 Nov 1976 in Tulsa, Okla

...............10 LOUIS TUNSTALL b: 17 May 1906 in Coalgate, Okla, d: 21 Feb 1930 ; Y

    + Goldie Amery b: Abt. 1908, m: 05 May 1928

...............11 Bob Robert George TURNSTALL b: 01 Apr 1929 in of, Fort Smith, Ark, d: 1980 ; Y

...............9 Edgar Steward HENDRICKS b: 29 Aug 1877 in Denton, Denton, Tx, d: Marcella, Ark; Y

    + Willie b: Abt. 1879 in husband, of, Denton, Tx

...............10 Jimmie Stewart Hendrick b: 05 Sep 1905

...............10 Frances Mae Hendrick b: 17 Jul 1908

...............10 Thornton Wiley Hendrick b: 21 Jul 1910

...............10 Woodrow WILSON Hendrick b: 12 Dec 1912

...............10 Robert William Hendrick b: 03 Sep 1915

...............10 Pearl Aline Hendrick b: 10 Jul 1917

........................10 Edgar Ninsuall Hendrick b: 06 Jun 1921
........................10 Tommy BRYAN Hendrick b: 17 Jun 1924
........................9 Clarence Walden HENDRICKS b: 28 Mar 1879 in Denton, Denton, Tx, d: Hot Springs, Ark; Y
    + Ava Lenore BALES b: 06 Nov 1887 in of, Bowie, Tx, m: 06 Nov 1887 in at, Bowie, Tx
........................10 Lyman Hendrick b: 22 Oct 1901 in Krebs, Okla, d: 14 Jan 1956 ; Y
    + Roxie ANDREWS b: Abt. 1903 in of, Krebs, Okla
........................10 Juanita Hendrick b: 27 Jan 1903 in Krebs, Okla, d: 22 Feb 1941 ; Y
    + Carl LaRue b: Abt. 1900 in of, Krebs, Okla
........................9 Lena Hendrick b: 21 Aug 1882 in Denton, Tx, d: 28 Aug 1960 ; Y
    + John P McGuigan b: 1879 in Indianapolis, Indiana, m: Abt. 1903 in of, Coalgate, Okla
........................10 Ina Claire McGuigan b: 26 Oct 1903 in Coalgate, Okla
    + Earl C. HOUSEWEART b: Abt. 1901 in of, Albany, Ore, m: of, Albany, Ore
........................11 Patricia McGuigan HOUSEWEART b: 24 Feb 1932 in Salem, Ore
    + Howard ALLEN Klopfenstein b: Abt. 1931 in of, Salem, Ore, m: Abt. 1954 in of, Salem, Ore
........................12 Duane ALLEN Klopfenstein b: 20 Feb 1956 in of, Salem, Ore
........................12 Dean Howard Klopfenstein b: 20 Dec 1958 in of, Salem, Ore
........................12 DOUGLAS Jon Klopfenstein b: 26 Dec 1959 in of, Salem, Ore
........................10 Marie Pearl McGuigan b: 15 Mar 1906 in Coalgate, Okla
    + Lyle COLESGROVE
........................11 Barbara Jean COLESGROVE b: 24 Jul 1931 in Spokane, Wa
    + Vincent CUPO m: divorced, no children
    + Earl JOHNSON
    + John P SHAEFER m: second husband
    + Edward H. Rolph
........................9 William Hendrick b: 1885 in DAVIS, Indian Territory, now, Okla, d: 1928 ; Y
........................9 Myrtle e Hendrick b: 02 Aug 1887 in DAVIS, Indian Territory, now, Okla, d: 11 Jan 1926 Y
    + John STECKSTOR b: Abt. 1885 in of, DAVIS, Okla
........................10 George STECKSTOR b: Abt. 1919 in of, DAVIS, Okla
........................10 Tressie STECKSTOR b: Abt. 1921 in of, DAVIS, Okla
........................10 John STECKSTOR jr b: Abt. 1923 in of, DAVIS, Okla
........................9 Maude Hendrick b: 1890 in DAVIS, Indian Territory, now, Okla, d: 1895 in child; Y
........................9 Almeida Hendrick b: Feb 1892 in Argyle, Tx, d: 10 Jan 1933 in Dallas, Dallas, Tx; Y
    + John Henry HOOE b: 09 Aug 1889 in Grapevine, Tx, m: 1911 in Kiowa, Okla
........................10 Iretta HOOE b: 18 Feb 1912 in Pittsburgh, County, Okla
    + Jack Henry ADAMS b: Abt. 1910, m: 10 Jan 1929
........................11 Jack Henry ADAMS jr b: 14 Sep 1934 in San Antonio, Bexar, Tx
    + Mary Ann ZAPALAC b: Abt. 1936
........................12 Jack Henry ADAMS III b: 23 Dec 1961 in Dallas, Dallas, Tx
........................12 ALLEN Craig ADAMS b: 08 Dec 1967 in Dallas, Dallas, Tx
........................9 Beulah May Hendrick b: 01 Jun 1894 in DAVIS, Indian Territory, now, Okla
    + Harry Ward b: Abt. 1892 in of, Shreveport, LA
........................10 Marcia Mae Ward b: 05 May 1923 in of, Shreveport, LA
    + John Noble b: Abt. 1921 in of, Shreveport, LA, m: Abt. 1941 in divorced, Shreveport, LA
........................11 Sandra Jean Noble b: 27 Nov 1942 in of, Shreveport, LA
........................11 Donna Lynn Noble b: 12 Aug 1947 in Shreveport, LA
........................11 Marcia Elaine Noble b: 12 Oct 1948 in Shreveport, LA
........................11 Johnny Arthur Noble b: 14 Aug 1951 in Shreveport, LA
........................10 Doris Elaine Ward b: 28 Sep 1925 in of, Shreveport, LA
    + Edward W BURBANK b: Abt. 1923 in of, Dallas, Dallas, Tx, m: Abt. 1945
........................11 Carol Ann BURBANK b: 08 Oct 1947 in of, Dallas, Dallas, Tx

................................11 Richard Ward BURBANK b: 01 Dec 1948 in of, Dallas, Dallas, Tx
................................11 Kenneth Rowe BURBANK b: 03 Apr 1950 in of, Dallas, Dallas, Tx
................................11 Judith Gayle BURBANK b: 23 Mar 1951 in of, Dallas, Dallas, Tx
................................11 Susan Lynn BURBANK b: 01 Aug 1952 in of, Dallas, Dallas, Tx
..............................10 Don R. Ward b: 01 Jan 1930 in of, Shreveport, LA
                + Mildred
................................11 Donna Gail Ward b: 05 Mar 1955
........................9 Pearl Hendrick b: 20 Jul 1896 in DAVIS, Indian Territory, now, Okla, d: Bef. 1986 ; Y
....................7 Silas NEELY LAWLER school teacher b: 04 Nov 1822 in nr Franklin, SIMPSON, Ky, d: 02
          Dec 1900 in to, Denton Co., Tx, abt Oct 1853; Y
                + Aletha Ann Rowland b: 1828 in of, SIMPSON, Co, Ky, m: SIMPSON, Ky, d: 24 Feb 1854
                in near Georgetown, Williamson Co., Tx; Y
..........................8 Samuel E. LAWLER b: 1850 in SIMPSON, Ky, d: 1851 in d abt 9 mo. child, SIMPSON,
          Ky; Y
..........................8 Finis Eugene LAWLER Preacher b: 04 Nov 1851 in SIMPSON, Ky, d: 17 Oct 1923 in
          Denton, Tx; Y
                + Nell Aletha Nellie Stallcup Teacher b: Abt. 1854 in born, Colorado, m: 31 Mar 1892 in
                of, Dallas, Tx
........................9 Eugene Stallcup LAWLER b: Aug 1893 in North, Dallas, Plano Rd, Tx
..........................8 Silas Micajah LAWLER b: 1852 in SIMPSON, Ky, d: 1853 in d abt 9 mo. child, SIMPSON,
          Ky; Y
..........................8 Nancy T "Mattie" LAWLER b: 02 Jan 1853 in Simpson Co. KY, d: 1918 in Los Angeles,
          Los Angeles, CA; Y
                + William King LOGAN b: Abt. 1851 in of Simpson Co. KY, m: 25 Aug 1871 in Gallatin,
                Sumner, TN
........................9 Alice Lee LOGAN b: Abt. 1872 in Denton, Denton, TX
                + John P FOWLER b: Abt. 1870 in of Wise Co. TX
..........................10 Alice Lee FOWLER b: Abt. 1900
                + Joseph Dietz b: Abt. 1900
..........................11 Joseph Dietz-Conger b: Abt. 1925
                + Dorothy HATFIELD b: Abt. 1925
..........................12 Ron Conger b: Abt. 1944
                + Carol Montgomery b: Abt. 1944
              + CONGER
              + DAVIDSON
              + Mary A. DAVIS b: Abt. 1834 in of, SIMPSON, Co, Ky, m: 27 Mar 1857 in Denton, Co, Tx
....................8 James H. LAWLER b: 16 Mar 1859 in Dallas, Dallas, Tx, d: 14 Jul 1938 ; Y
                + Lucy Edmonia Eddie PRIGMORE b: 1864, m: 22 Nov 1885, d: 16 Aug 1947 ; Y
....................9 Oliver Eugene LAWLER b: 04 Oct 1886, d: 11 Dec 1970 ; Y
                + Ella Curly PIERCE b: 01 Feb 1894, m: 29 Dec 1909, d: 27 Oct 1958 ; Y
....................9 Ben Silas LAWLER b: 1889, d: 16 Nov 1946 in Garland, RICHARDSON, Dallas, Tx; Y
....................9 Nell LAWLER b: 1892, d: 1967 ; Y
                + Joe McCallum b: 1888, d: 1963 ; Y
....................9 Archie e LAWLER b: 01 Jul 1894 in Dallas, Tx, d: 15 Apr 1951 ; Y
                + Ethel Ora b: 16 Mar 1896 in Dallas, Tx, d: 01 Apr 1970 ; Y
....................8 infant LAWLER b: Abt. Apr 1860 in Dallas, Dallas, Tx, d: Abt. Jun 1860 in Dallas, Dallas,
          Tx; Y
....................8 Pattie L. LAWLER b: Jun 1861 in Dallas, Dallas, Tx
                + George Thomas WHITFIELD b: Mar 1854 in of, Dallas, Tx, m: 14 Dec 1878
....................8 John W LAWLER b: Jun 1863 in Dallas, Dallas, Tx, d: 21 Jan 1943 in near, Garland,
          Dallas, Tx; Y
....................8 infant unnamed LAWLER b: Abt. 1866 in Denton Co., Tx
....................8 Virgil W V LAWLER b: Jan 1867 in Dallas, Dallas, Tx, d: 20 Oct 1908 in Addison, Tx; Y
                + Lou Ella MAYES b: Abt. 1869 in of, Dallas, Tx, m: 20 Oct 1908
....................8 Samuel E LAWLER b: Abt. 1869 in Dallas, Dallas, Co, Tx

................8 Caroline infant LAWLER b: Abt. 1870 in Dallas, Dallas, Co, Tx, d: child; Y
................8 Mary Belle LAWLER b: 04 Sep 1871 in Dallas, Dallas, Tx, d: 01 Jan 1936 ; Y
      + Robert Bob HUFFHINES b: Abt. 1896 in of, SIMPSON, Co, Ky, m: 27 May 1894
................9 NEELY HUFFHINES b: 28 Dec 1895 in Plano Rd, Dallas, Dallas, Tx
      + Jackie b: Abt. 1898 in Plano Rd, Dallas, Dallas, Tx
................8 Aletha Ann LAWLER b: Oct 1872 in Dallas, Dallas, Tx, d: 09 Nov 1904 ; Y
      + D. Young NEELY b: Abt. 1870 in of, Dallas, Tx, m: 09 Nov 1904
................7 Samuel Fenley LAWLER b: 1824 in nr Franklin, SIMPSON, Ky, d: 1894 in not md, Texas; Y
................7 Ann Eliza LAWLER b: 31 Oct 1826 in nr Franklin, SIMPSON, Ky, d: 19 Apr 1875 in SIMPSON, Ky; Y
      + Theopholis Robey b: 27 Feb 1823 in Lincoln, NC, m: 29 May 1853 in SIMPSON, Ky, d: 29 Nov 1885 in SIMPSON, Ky; Y
................8 Hosa E. Robey b: 10 Apr 1854 in SIMPSON, Ky, d: 11 Sep 1916 ; Y
................8 Silas VanDyke Robey b: 20 Oct 1855 in SIMPSON, Ky, d: 09 May 1945 in SIMPSON, 3 miles west, Franklin, Ky; Y
      + Mahalia HARRIS b: 12 Sep 1868 in Simpson, Co, Ky, m: 25 Feb 1886 in Franklin, Simpson Co Ky, d: 20 Jun 1940 in SIMPSON, Ky; Y
................9 Finley Ezra ROBEY b: 31 Oct 1888 in SIMPSON, Ky, d: 19 Dec 1908 in see notes bible differs; Y
................9 Annie Florence ROBEY b: 11 Jun 1891 in SIMPSON, Ky, d: 24 May 1959 in Franklin, SIMPSON, Ky; Y
      + Lloyd RALSTON HARRIS b: 1886 in Simpson Co., Ky, d: 1969 in Franklin, SIMPSON, Ky; Y
................10 William Robey HARRIS Sr. b: 1912 in homestead, near Franklin, SIMPSON, Ky, d: 1990 in Franklin, SIMPSON, Ky; Y
      + Margaret Lewis TAYLOR b: 1914 in Ohio Co.Ky, m: 1936 in BowlingGreen, Warren, Ky, d: Dec 1999 in Franklin, SIMPSON, Ky; Y
................11 Nan Lewis HARRIS b: 06 Nov 1939 in Franklin, SIMPSON, Ky
      + Jerry DOBBS
................11 William Robey HARRIS Jr b: 06 May 1943 in Franklin, SIMPSON, Ky
................11 LLoyd Taylor HARRIS b: 11 Dec 1948 in Franklin, SIMPSON, Ky
................9 Mary Ellen ROBEY b: 19 Nov 1892 in SIMPSON, Ky, d: 13 Oct 1920 in see notes; Y
................9 Eliga Dee ROBEY b: 14 Nov 1893 in Simpson, Co, Ky, d: 14 Aug 1984 in Simpson Co., Ky; Y
................9 Ida Iheda Belle ROBEY b: 01 Nov 1897 in SIMPSON, Ky
      + Roy PHILLIPS b: Abt. 1895 in of Simpson, Logan, Co, Ky, m: 23 Dec 1919 in Nashville, Davidson Co., Tenn
................9 James Peter Pete ROBEY Pete b: 08 Sep 1899 in SIMPSON, Ky
................9 Thelma E ROBEY b: 16 Aug 1904 in of, SIMPSON, Co, Ky, d: 09 Apr 1942 in SIMPSON, 3 miles west, Franklin, Ky; Y
      + A. Vernon STUART
................9 Agnes M ROBEY b: 16 Jul 1910 in Simpson, Co, Ky
      + Joe HANER
      + Hugo Byer
................9 Robert VanDyke "Dyke" ROBEY b: 18 Feb 1917 in Simpson, Co, Ky, d: 28 Jan 2002 in Franklin, Simpson CO., Ky age 84; Y
      + Lorene
................8 Lillie Belle Robey b: 03 Aug 1857 in SIMPSON, Ky, d: 16 Apr 1919 in SIMPSON, Ky; Y
................8 Stephen D. Robey b: 01 Mar 1861 in SIMPSON, Ky, d: 11 Apr 1943 in SIMPSON, Ky; Y
................8 children 8 total Roby b: Abt. 1965 in known total 8 ch, SIMPSON, Ky
................7 Newton VanDyke LAWLER b: 1828 in nr Franklin, SIMPSON, Ky
      + Caroline M. DAVIS b: 1829 in age 51 in 1880, census, Fanmin, Tx, m: 12 Jan 1850 in Russellville, Logan, Ky, d: of, Fanmin, 1872/1881, Tx; Y
................8 Nancy T LAWLER b: 1853 in 7 in 1860, Denton Co., census, Tx
................8 Margie N B LAWLER b: 1854 in 6 in 1860, census, Denton Co., Tx

...............8 Mary A LAWLER b: 1858 in 2 in 1860, census, Denton Co., Tx
...............8 Samuel Van Dyke LAWLER b: 1859 in 1 in 1860, census, Denton Co., Tx, d: 17 Jul 1917
           in Clebourn, Death Cert., 19645, Tx; Y
           + Belle LOVEN b: Abt. 1862 in of, Dallas, Dallas, Tx, m: 24 Oct 1899
           + Mary MOCKTON b: Abt. 1880 in of, Dallas, Dallas, Tx, m: 04 Apr 1914
...............8 Mollie LAWLER b: 1874 in Fanmin, Tx
...............8 Martha Mattie LAWLER b: Denton, Tx
           + J. D. DAWSON b: Abt. 1863 in of, Dallas, Dallas, Tx, m: 05 Jun 1885 in Dallas, Dallas,
           Tx
...............9 Annie DAWSON b: Dec 1888 in Dallas, Dallas, Tx
...............7 Nancy C. LAWLER b: 03 Sep 1830 in nr Franklin, SIMPSON, Ky, d: Abt. 1860 in
           SIMPSON, Ky; Y
           + Thomas Coleman COGHILL Jr b: 1828 in Simpson Co., Ky, m: 18 Jan 1848 in
           SIMPSON, Ky
...............8 Artamesa Artainsa Patsey L. COGHILL b: 1853 in Simpson Co., Ky, d: 1868 in
           SIMPSON, Ky; Y
...............8 Mary F. COGHILL b: 21 Feb 1854 in SIMPSON, Ky, d: 02 Aug 1855 in (child), nr Franklin,
           SIMPSON, Ky; Y
...............8 Eugene Spencer COGHILL b: Sep 1856 in Simpson Co., Ky
           + Sarah b: Sep 1868 in Mo
...............9 Eugene S. COGHILL b: Jun 1888 in Kansas
...............9 Thomas H COGHILL b: May 1890 in Henry Co., MO
...............8 Belle COGHILL b: Abt. 1859 in SIMPSON, Ky, d: Bef. 1874 in deed, SIMPSON, Ky; Y
...............8 Alice COGHILL b: Abt. 1861 in SIMPSON, Ky
...............8 Avolin E. Arlena A COGHILL b: SIMPSON, Ky, d: died as infant; Y
...............7 unknown son LAWLER b: Abt. 1832 in of, Franklin, SIMPSON, Ky, d: 2 died as infant; Y
...............7 unknown son LAWLER b: Abt. 1834 in of, Franklin, SIMPSON, Ky, d: known to be, 12
           children, 2 died as infant; Y
...............7 Mary E. LAWLER b: 1836 in nr Franklin, SIMPSON, Ky
           + Henry Wade b: Abt. 1834 in of, SIMPSON, Ky
...............8 Frank Wade b: Abt. 1860 in SIMPSON, Ky
           + Elizabeth Betty Roby b: 1871 in of, SIMPSON, Ky, d: 1918 in Simpson Co., Ky; Y
...............7 William H. LAWLER b: 11 Aug 1838 in Homestead, nr Franklin, SIMPSON, Ky, d: 16 Jul
           1853 in thrown by horse, Homestead, SIMPSON, Ky; Y
...............7 Henry Clay LAWLER b: 02 Oct 1840 in Farm, near Franklin, Simpson Co., Ky, d: 12 Sep
           1915 in Homestead, nr Franklin, SIMPSON, Ky; Y
           + Anthie Armeda SMITH b: 21 May 1861 in Smith farm, Clay District, Logan Co., Ky, m: 01
           Mar 1887 in Franklin, SIMPSON, Ky, d: 08 Jan 1929 in Lawler farm, nr Franklin,
           SIMPSON, Ky; Y
...............8 William Henry LAWLER b: 29 Jul 1889 in Homestead, nr Franklin, SIMPSON, Ky, d: 08
           Nov 1937 in Franklin, SIMPSON, Ky; Y
           + Bessie Lucille SPEAR b: 20 Nov 1894 in Logan, Kentucky, m: Sep 1914 in SIMPSON,
           Ky, d: 26 Dec 1972 in Portland, Tn; Y
...............9 Norman Elvis LAWLER b: 17 Sep 1915 in Franklin, SIMPSON, Ky, d: Aft. 1998 in 1924
           Montair, Long Beach, CA, 90815; Y
           + "Jane" Avanola Bernice FURTNEY b: 20 Dec 1915 in 7705 SE Tolman, Portland,
           Ore, m: 11 Jun 1939 in First Lafaytette Church, Brooklyn, Long Island, NY, d: 26 Jan
           2001 in 1924 Montair, Long Beach, CA; Y
...............10 Jean Yvonne LAWLER b: 18 Sep 1940 in Mercy Hospital, San Diego, CA, d: 27 Nov
           2002 in Scottsdale, AZ; Y
           + DOUGLAS Eugene HOOD b: Abt. 1938 in of, Long Beach, Los Angeles, CA, m: 11
           Jun 1966 in Grace, Methodist, Long Beach, CA, d: 85251, (606)945 3918; Y
...............11 Trina LaVonne HOOD b: 01 Nov 1968 in of, Scottsdale, Arizona
           + David Jonathon Weisman b: 10 Nov 1964 in NY, m: Abt. 1993 in of, Scottsdale,
           Arizona

..................................12 David Jonathon Weisman jr b: 15 Mar 1995 in Scottsdale, Arizona

..................................12 Joshua James Weisman b: 16 Feb 1998 in Scottsdale, Arizona

..................................11 Craig Eugene HOOD b: 20 Oct 1969 in of, Scottsdale, Arizona

..................................11 Lisa Suzanne HOOD b: 01 Dec 1972 in of, Scottsdale, Arizona

..................................11 Cindie Marie HOOD b: 05 Mar 1975 in of, Scottsdale, Arizona

..................................10 Marylin Jane LAWLER b: 01 Apr 1947 in Long Beach, Los Angeles, CA, d: 04 Mar 2001 in jan 2001 "gone to ID to die" in note ss#553-76-7189; Y

..................................10 Michael Roy LAWLER b: 02 Feb 1954 in Fort Clayton, Canal Zone, Panama

..................................10 Renee' Susanne LAWLER b: 25 Aug 1959 in Long Beach, Los Angeles, CA

..................................9 Clara Beatrice LAWLER b: 19 Jan 1917 in Franklin, SIMPSON, Ky, d: Aft. 1987 in of, Portland, Sumner, Tn; Y

    + WALLACE Pat Patterson STOVALL b: 12 Sep 1914 in of, Portland, Sumner, Tenn, m: Abt. 1935 in Galliton, Sumner, Tenn, d: 17 Sep 2003 in Buntin Rd, Portland, Tenn; Y

..................................10 Norman Patterson STOVALL b: 02 Jun 1936 in Portland, Sumner, Tenn, d: 03 Aug 2005 in PO Box 1496, Gallatin, TN 37066; Y

    + Bobby Lena Jones MOTT b: 09 Aug 1936 in Portland, Sumner, Tenn, m: 24 Jun 1955 in first wife

..................................11 Martha Clair STOVALL b: 20 Feb 1957 in of Portland, Sumner, TN

    + Raymond Ewing Jones b: Abt. 1955 in of, Portland, Sumner, Tenn, m: 12 Nov 1984 in Davidson Co., TN

..................................12 Jennifer Elizabeth Jones b: 16 Dec 1985 in of Portland, Sumner, TN

..................................12 Robert Ewing Jones b: 27 Jun 1988 in of Portland, Sumner, TN

..................................12 Chad Joseph Jones b: 27 Jun 1989 in of Portland, Sumner, TN

..................................11 Mary Alice STOVALL b: 20 Feb 1958 in of Portland, Sumner, TN

    + Jeffrey Lynn Keith b: 15 Apr 1954 in of, Portland, Sumner, Tenn, m: Abt. 1981 in Portland, Sumner, Tenn

..................................12 Jeffrey Brad Keith b: 13 Sep 1982 in of, Portland, Sumner, Tenn

..................................12 Greg Patterson Keith b: 25 Oct 1984 in of, Portland, Sumner, Tenn

..................................12 Beth Allison Keith b: 13 Oct 1986 in of Portland, Sumner, TN

..................................11 Robert Patterson STOVALL b: 05 Oct 1961 in of, Portland, Sumner, Tenn

    + Lorie Arlene WHITSON b: 16 Aug 1963 in of Portland, Sumner, TN, m: Abt. 1987 in Davidson Co., TN

..................................12 Daniel Patterson STOVALL b: 06 Jan 1989 in of Portland, Sumner, TN

..................................12 Graham Patterson STOVALL b: 01 Jul 1991 in of Portland, Sumner, TN

..................................12 Slater Rickerman STOVALL b: 06 Apr 1994 in of Portland, Sumner, TN

..................................12 Bowen Harrison STOVALL b: 22 Dec 1997 in of Portland, Sumner, TN

    + Cynthia Moore b: of, Portland, Sumner, Tn of Goodlettsville, Davidson Co., TN

..................................8 Ruth Estelle LAWLER b: 08 Oct 1891 in Homestead, nr Franklin, SIMPSON, Ky, d: 20 Feb 1964 in Louisville, Jefferson, Ky; Y

    + John Hubert BROWN b: 15 Apr 1893 in Louisville, Jefferson, Ky of Adairville, Logan Co., m: 29 Dec 1912 in Franklin, SIMPSON, Ky, d: 15 Apr 1972 in Louisville, Jefferson, shot 10 AM b.day, Ky; Y

..................................9 girl BROWN b: 07 Jun 1916 in Adairville, Logan, Ky, d: 07 Jun 1916 in home, Adairville, Logan, Ky; Y

..................................9 Otis LAWLER "Jack" BROWN b: 28 Jul 1918 in home, Adairville, Logan, Ky, d: 13 Mar 1996 in Nursing home, Louisville, Jefferson, Ky; Y

    + Jessie Amanda MURR b: 24 Apr 1920 in Depauw, HARRISON, Indiana, home, m: 08 Nov 1941 in St Louis, Mo, d: 31 May 1992 in 7:22 PM, Jeffersonville, Clark, Indiana; Y

..................................10 Martha Ruth BROWN b: 05 Apr 1947 in Louisville, Jefferson, Ky

..................................10 Lawrence Hubert BROWN b: 18 May 1950 in Louisville, Jefferson, Ky, d: 602-297-7597; Y

..................................8 Edward Lee LAWLER b: 28 Mar 1893 in Homestead, nr Franklin, SIMPSON, Ky, d: 21 Mar 1963 in St.Petersburg, FL; Y

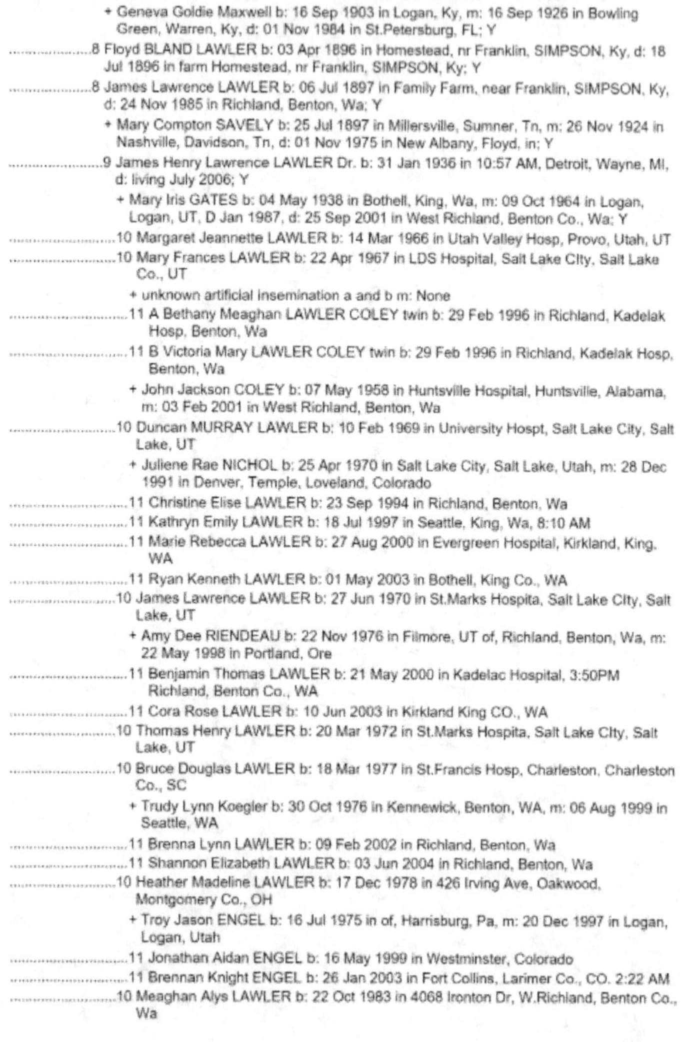

+ Geneva Goldie Maxwell b: 16 Sep 1903 in Logan, Ky, m: 16 Sep 1926 in Bowling Green, Warren, Ky, d: 01 Nov 1984 in St.Petersburg, FL; Y

........8 Floyd BLAND LAWLER b: 03 Apr 1896 in Homestead, nr Franklin, SIMPSON, Ky, d: 18 Jul 1896 in farm Homestead, nr Franklin, SIMPSON, Ky; Y

........8 James Lawrence LAWLER b: 06 Jul 1897 in Family Farm, near Franklin, SIMPSON, Ky, d: 24 Nov 1985 in Richland, Benton, Wa; Y

+ Mary Compton SAVELY b: 25 Jul 1897 in Millersville, Sumner, Tn, m: 26 Nov 1924 in Nashville, Davidson, Tn, d: 01 Nov 1975 in New Albany, Floyd, in; Y

........9 James Henry Lawrence LAWLER Dr. b: 31 Jan 1936 in 10:57 AM, Detroit, Wayne, MI, d: living July 2006; Y

+ Mary Iris GATES b: 04 May 1938 in Bothell, King, Wa, m: 09 Oct 1964 in Logan, Logan, UT, D Jan 1987, d: 25 Sep 2001 in West Richland, Benton Co., Wa; Y

........10 Margaret Jeannette LAWLER b: 14 Mar 1966 in Utah Valley Hosp, Provo, Utah, UT

........10 Mary Frances LAWLER b: 22 Apr 1967 in LDS Hospital, Salt Lake City, Salt Lake Co., UT

+ unknown artificial insemination a and b m: None

........11 A Bethany Meaghan LAWLER COLEY twin b: 29 Feb 1996 in Richland, Kadelak Hosp, Benton, Wa

........11 B Victoria Mary LAWLER COLEY twin b: 29 Feb 1996 in Richland, Kadelak Hosp, Benton, Wa

+ John Jackson COLEY b: 07 May 1958 in Huntsville Hospital, Huntsville, Alabama, m: 03 Feb 2001 in West Richland, Benton, Wa

........10 Duncan MURRAY LAWLER b: 10 Feb 1969 in University Hospt, Salt Lake City, Salt Lake, UT

+ Juliene Rae NICHOL b: 25 Apr 1970 in Salt Lake City, Salt Lake, Utah, m: 28 Dec 1991 in Denver, Temple, Loveland, Colorado

........11 Christine Elise LAWLER b: 23 Sep 1994 in Richland, Benton, Wa

........11 Kathryn Emily LAWLER b: 18 Jul 1997 in Seattle, King, Wa, 8:10 AM

........11 Marie Rebecca LAWLER b: 27 Aug 2000 in Evergreen Hospital, Kirkland, King, WA

........11 Ryan Kenneth LAWLER b: 01 May 2003 in Bothell, King Co., WA

........10 James Lawrence LAWLER b: 27 Jun 1970 in St.Marks Hospita, Salt Lake City, Salt Lake, UT

+ Amy Dee RIENDEAU b: 22 Nov 1976 in Filmore, UT of, Richland, Benton, Wa, m: 22 May 1998 in Portland, Ore

........11 Benjamin Thomas LAWLER b: 21 May 2000 in Kadelac Hospital, 3:50PM Richland, Benton Co., WA

........11 Cora Rose LAWLER b: 10 Jun 2003 in Kirkland King CO., WA

........10 Thomas Henry LAWLER b: 20 Mar 1972 in St.Marks Hospita, Salt Lake City, Salt Lake, UT

........10 Bruce Douglas LAWLER b: 18 Mar 1977 in St.Francis Hosp, Charleston, Charleston Co., SC

+ Trudy Lynn Koegler b: 30 Oct 1976 in Kennewick, Benton, WA, m: 06 Aug 1999 in Seattle, WA

........11 Brenna Lynn LAWLER b: 09 Feb 2002 in Richland, Benton, Wa

........11 Shannon Elizabeth LAWLER b: 03 Jun 2004 in Richland, Benton, Wa

........10 Heather Madeline LAWLER b: 17 Dec 1978 in 426 Irving Ave, Oakwood, Montgomery Co., OH

+ Troy Jason ENGEL b: 16 Jul 1975 in of, Harrisburg, Pa, m: 20 Dec 1997 in Logan, Logan, Utah

........11 Jonathan Aidan ENGEL b: 16 May 1999 in Westminster, Colorado

........11 Brennan Knight ENGEL b: 26 Jan 2003 in Fort Collins, Larimer Co., CO. 2:22 AM

........10 Meaghan Alys LAWLER b: 22 Oct 1983 in 4068 Ironton Dr, W.Richland, Benton Co., Wa

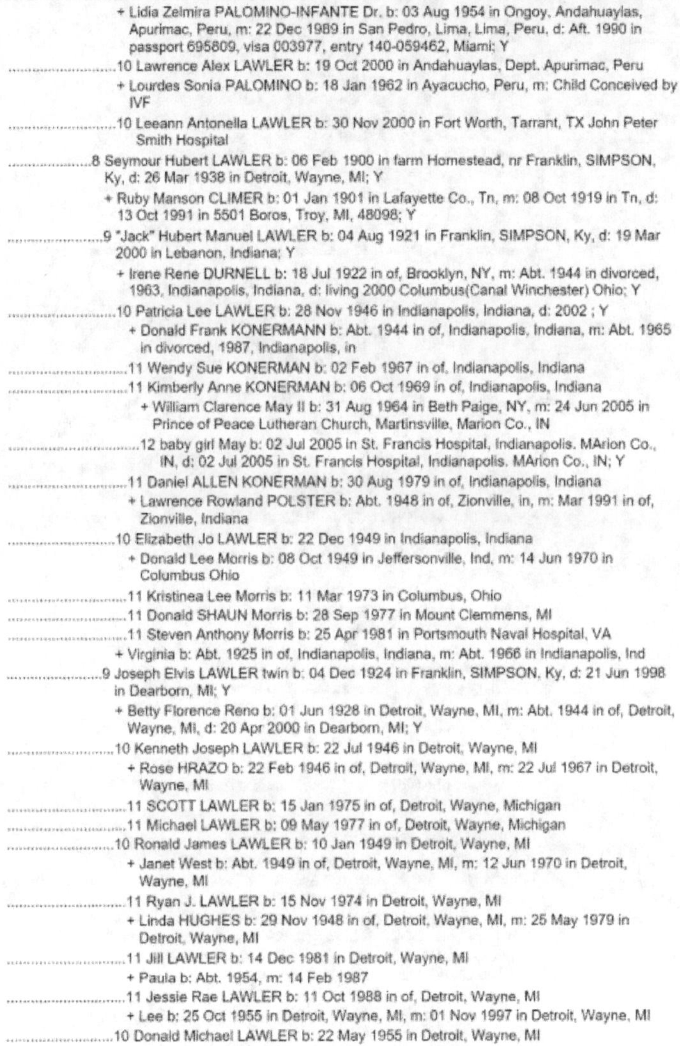

+ Lidia Zelmira PALOMINO-INFANTE Dr. b: 03 Aug 1954 in Ongoy, Andahuaylas,
  Apurimac, Peru, m: 22 Dec 1989 in San Pedro, Lima, Lima, Peru, d: Aft. 1990 in
  passport 695809, visa 003977, entry 140-059462, Miami; Y
...........10 Lawrence Alex LAWLER b: 19 Oct 2000 in Andahuaylas, Dept. Apurimac, Peru
  + Lourdes Sonia PALOMINO b: 18 Jan 1962 in Ayacucho, Peru, m: Child Conceived by
    IVF
...........10 Leeann Antonella LAWLER b: 30 Nov 2000 in Fort Worth, Tarrant, TX John Peter
  Smith Hospital
.........8 Seymour Hubert LAWLER b: 06 Feb 1900 in farm Homestead, nr Franklin, SIMPSON,
  Ky, d: 26 Mar 1938 in Detroit, Wayne, MI; Y
  + Ruby Manson CLIMER b: 01 Jan 1901 in Lafayette Co., Tn, m: 08 Oct 1919 in Tn, d:
    13 Oct 1991 in 5501 Boros, Troy, MI, 48098; Y
...........9 "Jack" Hubert Manuel LAWLER b: 04 Aug 1921 in Franklin, SIMPSON, Ky, d: 19 Mar
  2000 in Lebanon, Indiana; Y
  + Irene Rene DURNELL b: 18 Jul 1922 in of, Brooklyn, NY, m: Abt. 1944 in divorced,
    1963, Indianapolis, Indiana, d: living 2000 Columbus(Canal Winchester) Ohio; Y
...........10 Patricia Lee LAWLER b: 28 Nov 1946 in Indianapolis, Indiana, d: 2002 ; Y
  + Donald Frank KONERMANN b: Abt. 1944 in of, Indianapolis, Indiana, m: Abt. 1965
    in divorced, 1987, Indianapolis, in
...........11 Wendy Sue KONERMAN b: 02 Feb 1967 in of, Indianapolis, Indiana
...........11 Kimberly Anne KONERMAN b: 06 Oct 1969 in of, Indianapolis, Indiana
  + William Clarence May II b: 31 Aug 1964 in Beth Paige, NY, m: 24 Jun 2005 in
    Prince of Peace Lutheran Church, Martinsville, Marion Co., IN
...........12 baby girl May b: 02 Jul 2005 in St. Francis Hospital, Indianapolis. MArion Co.,
  IN, d: 02 Jul 2005 in St. Francis Hospital, Indianapolis. MArion Co., IN; Y
...........11 Daniel ALLEN KONERMAN b: 30 Aug 1979 in of, Indianapolis, Indiana
  + Lawrence Rowland POLSTER b: Abt. 1948 in of, Zionville, in, m: Mar 1991 in of,
    Zionville, Indiana
...........10 Elizabeth Jo LAWLER b: 22 Dec 1949 in Indianapolis, Indiana
  + Donald Lee Morris b: 08 Oct 1949 in Jeffersonville, Ind, m: 14 Jun 1970 in
    Columbus Ohio
...........11 Kristinea Lee Morris b: 11 Mar 1973 in Columbus, Ohio
...........11 Donald SHAUN Morris b: 28 Sep 1977 in Mount Clemmens, MI
...........11 Steven Anthony Morris b: 25 Apr 1981 in Portsmouth Naval Hospital, VA
  + Virginia b: Abt. 1925 in of, Indianapolis, Indiana, m: Abt. 1966 in Indianapolis, Ind
...........9 Joseph Elvis LAWLER twin b: 04 Dec 1924 in Franklin, SIMPSON, Ky, d: 21 Jun 1998
  in Dearborn, MI; Y
  + Betty Florence Reno b: 01 Jun 1928 in Detroit, Wayne, MI, m: Abt. 1944 in of, Detroit,
    Wayne, MI, d: 20 Apr 2000 in Dearborn, MI; Y
...........10 Kenneth Joseph LAWLER b: 22 Jul 1946 in Detroit, Wayne, MI
  + Rose HRAZO b: 22 Feb 1946 in of, Detroit, Wayne, MI, m: 22 Jul 1967 in Detroit,
    Wayne, MI
...........11 SCOTT LAWLER b: 15 Jan 1975 in of, Detroit, Wayne, Michigan
...........11 Michael LAWLER b: 09 May 1977 in of, Detroit, Wayne, Michigan
...........10 Ronald James LAWLER b: 10 Jan 1949 in Detroit, Wayne, MI
  + Janet West b: Abt. 1949 in of, Detroit, Wayne, MI, m: 12 Jun 1970 in Detroit,
    Wayne, MI
...........11 Ryan J. LAWLER b: 15 Nov 1974 in Detroit, Wayne, MI
  + Linda HUGHES b: 29 Nov 1948 in of, Detroit, Wayne, MI, m: 25 May 1979 in
    Detroit, Wayne, MI
...........11 Jill LAWLER b: 14 Dec 1981 in Detroit, Wayne, MI
  + Paula b: Abt. 1954, m: 14 Feb 1987
...........11 Jessie Rae LAWLER b: 11 Oct 1988 in of, Detroit, Wayne, MI
  + Lee b: 25 Oct 1955 in Detroit, Wayne, MI, m: 01 Nov 1997 in Detroit, Wayne, MI
...........10 Donald Michael LAWLER b: 22 May 1955 in Detroit, Wayne, MI

+ Pamela b: 19 Dec 1959 in California (where they met), m: 25 Nov 1987
...............11 Aaron LAWLER b: 04 Jun 1987 in of, Detroit, Wayne, MI
...............10 Thomas Gregory LAWLER b: 11 Oct 1957 in Detroit, Wayne, MI
+ Mary b: 19 Mar 1959 in of, Detroit, Wayne, MI, m: 11 Oct 1986
...............11 Katie LAWLER b: 18 Apr 1988 in Detroit, Wayne, MI
+ Christina b: 19 Apr 1962 in Detroit, Wayne, MI, m: 04 Apr 1994
...............11 Kelly LAWLER b: 14 Jun 1994 in Detroit, Wayne, MI
...............11 Karelyn LAWLER b: 23 May 1996 in Detroit, Wayne, MI
...............10 Debra Ann LAWLER b: 28 Jul 1959 in Detroit, Wayne, MI
+ Daniel FENNELL b: 02 Aug 1951 in Detroit, Wayne, MI, m: 22 Sep 1980 in
divorced, by, 1985
...............11 Shane Brian FENNELL b: 07 Oct 1980 in Detroit, Wayne, MI
+ Albert SCOTT b: 09 Jul 1057 in Detroit, Wayne, MI, m: 22 Mar 1994 in Detroit,
Wayne, MI
...............9 Josephine Elvin LAWLER twin b: 04 Dec 1924 in Franklin, SIMPSON, Ky
+ Donald ROSS GLISMAN b: 30 Apr 1918 in DAVENPORT, Iowa, m: 14 Oct 1940 in
Toledo, Lucas Co., Ohio, d: 23 Jan 1998 in 5501 Boros, Troy, MI, 48298; Y
...............10 Donna Karen GLISMAN b: 14 Jul 1941 in Detroit, Wayne, MI
+ Ernest Robert Ernie KNIFFEN b: 19 Sep 1938 in Detroit, Wayne, MI, m: 17 Jun
1961 in divorced Oct 1971, Detroit, Wayne, MI
...............11 Karie Lynn KNIFFEN b: 10 Jun 1963 in Gross Point, Wayne, MI
+ Curtis Alan I SEPTER b: 06 Aug 1961 in of, Detroit, Wayne, MI, m: 27 Nov 1982
in Detroit, Wayne, MI
...............12 Laura Amara SEPTER b: 30 Nov 1986 in Mobile ALA
...............12 Curtis Alan II SEPTER b: 28 Mar 1988 in WOODSTOCK, ILL
...............11 KELLY Lynn KNIFFEN b: 28 Dec 1964 in Gross Point, Wayne, MI
+ Robert Charles MOHN b: 22 Jan 1957 in McDonald, Ohio, m: 16 Feb 1985 in
Detroit, Wayne, MI, d: in 2000 resided Put-In-Bay, Ohio; Y
...............12 Allie Lynn MOHN b: 30 Mar 1988 in Cleveland, Ohio, d: 31 Mar 1988 in child,
Cleveland, Ohio; Y
...............12 Andrew Charles MOHN b: 12 Jan 1990 in Sandusky, Ohio
...............12 Dallas Jolly MOHN b: 09 Jul 1993 in Sandusky, Ohio
+ Michael Alan CENIT b: 10 May 1940 in of Brooklyn NY
...............11 David ROSS KNIFFEN b: 21 Jun 1979 in Ft Lauderdale, Broward Co., Fla
+ Sarah Kay Quick b: 14 Mar 1980 in Detroit, Wayne, MI
...............12 Aliza McKenzie QUICK b: 23 Mar 2000 in Detroit, Wayne, MI
...............10 Connie Sharon GLISMAN b: 29 Nov 1942 in Detroit, Wayne, MI
+ LEONARD Anthony KACZYNSKI KANE jr b: 28 Oct 1940 in Highland Park, Wayne,
MI, m: 16 May 1959 in Detroit, Wayne, MI
...............11 Debora Lynn KANE b: 20 Nov 1959 in Detroit, Wayne, MI
+ DOUGLAS KERNER b: Abt. 1959 in Sterling Heights, Wayne, MI, m: 24 May
1985 in Detroit, Wayne, MI
+ <No name>
...............12 Nicholas Adam KANE b: 02 Feb 1993 in Detroit, Wayne, MI
...............11 Lorrie Ann KANE b: 27 Jun 1962 in Detroit, Wayne, MI
+ James Harold GOODWIN b: 18 Apr 1961 in Detroit, Wayne, MI, m: 25 Oct 1985
in Sterling Heights, Detroit, Wayne, MI
...............12 James TYLER GOODWIN b: 08 Jan 1988 in of, Detroit, Wayne, MI
...............12 Britnie Rene GOODWIN b: 25 Sep 1990 in of, Detroit, Wayne, MI
+ James Allen MERCIER b: 02 Dec 1959, m: 01 Mar 1997
...............12 Jacob Charles MERCIER b: 02 Oct 1997
...............11 Michael Thomas KANE b: 21 Jul 1964 in Detroit, Wayne, MI
+ Robin Lewandowski b: Abt. 1970 in Roseville, Wayne, MI, m: 15 Aug 1985 in
Roseville, Detroit, Wayne, MI
...............12 Erica Ann Kelly KANE b: 06 Feb 1985 in of, Detroit, Wayne, MI

...................................11 Paul Matthew KANE b: 10 Mar 1970 in Detroit, Wayne, MI
+ Michel Lynn b: 13 Apr 1973, m: 14 Jun 1996 in Detroit, Wayne, MI
...................................12 Rachek Ann KANE b: 29 Oct 1999 in Detroit, Wayne, MI
+ Majewski b: Abt. 1966
...................................12 Cody Douglas MAJEWSKI b: 02 Oct 1992
...................................11 Cheryl Rene KANE b: 31 Dec 1972 in Warren, Wayne, MI
+ Michael John MOZAL b: 27 Jan 1966 in Detroit, Wayne, MI, m: 09 Jun 1995 in Detroit, Wayne, MI
...................................12 Renee' Danielle MOZAL b: 04 Jun 1997 in Detroit, Wayne, MI
...................................12 Justin Anthony MOZAL b: 20 Aug 1999 in Detroit, Wayne, MI
...................................10 Linda Carolyn GLISMAN b: 10 Sep 1947 in Detroit, Wayne, MI
...................................10 John Arthur GLISMAN b: 26 Oct 1958 in Gross Point, Wayne, MI
+ Sandra Lynn FORD b: 10 Dec 1962 in Detroit, Wayne, MI, m: 20 May 1982 in Detroit, Wayne, MI
...................................11 Amanda Marie GLISMAN b: 24 Mar 1987 in of, Detroit, Wayne, MI
...................................11 Jessica Kay GLISMAN b: 04 Jul 1990 in of, Detroit, Wayne, MI
...................................11 Samantha Jo GLISMAN b: 08 Nov 1992 in of, Detroit, Wayne, MI
...................................8 Jessie Herman LAWLER b: 17 Sep 1902 in Homestead, nr Franklin, SIMPSON, Ky, d: 31 May 1903 in Farm, nr Franklin, SIMPSON, Ky; Y
+ Angella Louise Holland b: 03 Sep 1843 in Logan Co., Ky, m: 24 Jan 1865 in Franklin, SIMPSON, Ky, d: 05 Apr 1883 in Lawler homestead, nr Franklin, SIMPSON, Ky; Y
...................................8 Nancy Edmonie LAWLER b: 26 Nov 1865 in Homestead, nr Franklin, SIMPSON, Ky, d: 21 Oct 1928 in Simpson Co., Ky; Y
+ William H. Maxwell b: Abt. 1859 in of Farm, Simpson Co., nr Franklin, Ky, m: Abt. 1920 in Franklin, SIMPSON, Ky, d: Abt. 1826 in Simpson Co., Ky; Y
...................................8 Mary Virginia LAWLER b: 09 Jun 1867 in Homestead, nr Franklin, SIMPSON, Ky, d: 12 Jul 1903 ; Y
+ Theodore Guy. "Bud" Little Lyttle b: 16 Nov 1871 in Walnut Flats, Lincoln Co., Kentucky, m: 13 Jul 1888 in Dennison, Grayson Co., Texas, d: 23 Mar 1934 in Denver, Denver Co., Colo; Y
...................................9 Edythe Edith Angela LYTTLE b: 11 Nov 1889 in PURCELL, Okla, d: May 1985 in San Jose, Santa Clara, California; Y
+ Lyman A. STOCKTON b: Abt. 1889, m: 1920 in Div about 1926-7, d: 16 May 1927 in Oreoff, CA; Y
...................................10 Leland WILLIS STOCKTON b: 28 Apr 1921 in Orange Co., Ca of Santa Ana, CA
+ Flora CARRIGAN b: Abt. 1923 in of, Los Angeles, CA
...................................11 Dale Neil STOCKTON b: 06 Sep 1944 in Palo Alto, CA
+ Laury W. MAJERVA b: Abt. 1925 in of, Luxumburg, Germany, m: second wife
...................................11 Barbara Joyce STOCKTON b: 02 Jul 1950 in of, Luxumburg, Germany, d: 1965 in Killed by car Barstow CA; Y
...................................11 Margaret Laurine Laurie STOCKTON b: 13 Mar 1956 in Wiesbaden, Germany
+ Kevin Buck
...................................10 ALLEN Dale STOCKTON b: 18 Aug 1925 in Orcuff, Santa Barbara Co., CA
+ Virginia HADLO b: Abt. 1927 in of, CA
+ Frederick Emery Norman STRONG b: 08 Jun 1878 in Paradise, Butte Co., Ca, m: 30 Apr 1929 in San Mateo, San Mateo, California, d: 03 Nov 1957 in San Mareo Hospital, San Mateo, Co., Ca; Y
...................................10 Edith Yvonne "Dianne" STRONG b: 28 Feb 1932 in Grigsby Hospital, Santa Maria, Santa Barbara Co., CA, d: living 2005; Y
+ Richard James KNAPP b: 30 Sep 1929 in San Mateo, San Mareo Co Ca, m: 1949 in divorced Las Vegas, remarried, 1960, d: Everett, Snohomish Co., WA; Y
...................................11 Richard James "Rick" KNAPP b: 13 Aug 1950 in Palo Alto, Santa Clara Co., CA
+ Juanita Todd b: of Clear Lake CA, m: Abt. 1967 in div 1972
...................................12 Richard James KNAPP III b: 11 May 1968 in Sequoia Hospital, Redwood City, San Mateo Co., CA

+ Deborah Swisher m: 1973 in San Carlos, San Mateo Co., CA
...........................12 Erica Rochell KNAPP b: 03 Nov 1974 in Sequoia Hospital, Redwood City, San Mateo Co., CA
    + Moshia m: 01 Oct 2005 in Capitola, Santa Cruz Co., CA
...........................11 Karen Yvonne KNAPP b: 04 Apr 1952 in Sequoia Hospital, Redwood City, San Mateo Co., CA
    + Houghhton
...........................12 Steven Daniel Robert Houghhton b: 17 Sep 1983 in Dominican Hospital, Santa Cruz, CA
    + BAGLEY
...........................12 Michael James Shawn BAGLEY b: 15 Oct 1975 in ElCamino Hospital, Mountian View, CA
    + [unknown spouse]
...........................13 Kai BAGLEY Harada b: 03 Jun 2003 in Honda, Japan
...........................11 David ALLEN KNAPP b: 29 Jul 1955 in Palo Alto, Santa Clara Co., CA
    + Sherman Earl Vanover b: 19 Jul 1922 in Calhoun, Davis Co., KY, m: 19 Jun 1960 in Carson City, NV, d: 06 Jun 1998 in Lodi, San Joaquin Co., CA; Y
...........................11 Kenneth Earl "Van" Vanover b: 28 Feb 1961 in Sequoia Hospital, Redwood City, San Mateo Co., CA
    + LORRAINE ANN MONAGHETTI m: Abt. 1978
...........................12 Joshua Vanover b: 21 Apr 1979 in ElCamino Hospital, Mountian View, Santa Clarra Co., CA
...........................12 Jennifer Vanover b: 21 Aug 1981 in Dominican Hospital, Santa Cruz Co., CA
...........................12 Jessica Coral Vanover b: 24 Apr 1988 in Dominican Hospital, Santa Cruz Co., CA
    + George J. Kaehl b: Abt. 1890 in Ohio, m: divorced late 1920
    + James Allen b: marraige annuled, m: marraige annuled 1910
...........................9 Thelma LYTTLE b: 20 Jan 1899 in Walsenburg, Colo, d: 13 Jul 1948 ; Y
    + Finis Leslie BUCKNER b: 03 Sep 1898 in MO., d: 14 Sep 1951 in San Francisco, Ca; Y
...........................10 Virginia Lena BUCKNER b: 13 Feb 1921 in Fresno, CA
    + John HARVILLE b: Abt. 1920 in of, Fresno, CA, m: Abt. 1940
...........................11 Thomas HARVILLE b: 05 Jan 1941 in of, Fresno, CA
...........................11 Richard John HARVILLE b: 17 Jun 1944 in of, Fresno, CA
...........................10 Edith Fay BUCKNER b: 17 Aug 1924 in Fresno, CA
    + John Harvil
...........................10 Thomas Harvil
...........................10 Ricky Harvil
...........................9 Regina Irene Lucille LYTTLE b: 26 May 1902 in Lajunta, Colo, d: 12 Dec 1983 in Redondo Beach, Los Angeles Co., CA; Y
    + Frank GARCIA b: Abt. 1900 in Phillappines, of Regondo Beach, CA, d: 1884 in Redondo Beach, Los Angeles Co., CA; Y
...........................10 no children
...........................8 Alice Gertrude LAWLER b: 04 Dec 1870 in Homestead, nr Franklin, SIMPSON, Ky, d: 20 Oct 1893 ; Y
    + John Richard Munday b: Abt. 1864 in Barren, Ky, m: 19 Dec 1889 in Franklin, SIMPSON, Ky, d: Abt. Oct 1893 in of, Franklin, SIMPSON, Ky; Y
...........................9 Etta Irene Munday b: Sep 1890 in Franklin, SIMPSON, Ky
    + Jepson Jessie J. Matthews b: Abt. 1890 in of, Simpson Co., Ky, m: Abt. 1911 in Franklin, SIMPSON, Ky
...........................10 Mary Lee Matthews b: 13 Oct 1913 in of, Franklin, SIMPSON, Ky
    + BYRON CONLEY b: 20 May 1903 in Lawrenceville, Lawrence Co., Ill of Franklin, SIMPSON, Ky, d: Jul 1982 in Bartow, Polk Co., Florida; Y
...........................11 Louette CONLEY b: 23 Jan 1936 in Fla
    + C.D. Moore b: Abt. 1934 in of FLA

.................................11 Homer Lee CONLEY b: 03 Jan 1937 in Fla
                    + Gayle W b: Abt. 1939 in FL, m: Abt. 1960
.................................11 Norma Jean CONLEY b: 30 Jun 1938 in Fla
.................................11 Warren CONLEY b: 30 Dec 1939 in Fla
.................................11 Mary B. CONLEY b: 27 Dec 1940 in Fla
.................................11 Paul CONLEY b: 13 Oct 1942 in Fla
.................................11 Dale CONLEY b: 18 Nov 1943 in Fla
.................................11 Jennie K. CONLEY b: 18 Dec 1944 in Fla
.................................11 Barbara CONLEY b: 15 May 1946 in Fla
.................................11 Ruth CONLEY b: 25 May 1949 in Fla
.............................10 Jessie Matthews b: 11 Apr 1915 in of, Franklin, SIMPSON, Ky
                    + Jessie GORDON b: 04 Mar 1914
.................................11 Alyce F. GORDON b: 11 Jul 1940
                    + Jack JESUP b: Abt. 1940
.................................12 Alicia Lynette Jessup b: 21 Nov 1958
.................................11 Janyee I. GORDON b: 11 Jul 1940 in twins
                    + Dean HARLOD b: Abt. 1940
.................................12 Albert Elden Dean b: 04 Oct 1958
.................................11 Patricia A. GORDON b: 22 Dec 1942
.................................11 Connie L. GORDON b: 15 Aug 1944
.............................10 Robert E. Matthews b: 05 Jan 1928 in of, Franklin, SIMPSON, Ky
                    + Iris PRICE b: Abt. 1930
.................................11 Robert E. Matthews Jr. b: 10 Dec 1949
.................................11 Raymond Matthews b: 03 Dec 1953
.................................11 Bettie Gene Matthews b: 03 Jan 1954
.................................11 Peggie A. Matthews b: 15 Sep 1955
.................................11 Brenda Q. Matthews b: 15 Jun 1957
.........................9 Ira EARL MUNDAY b: 11 Sep 1892 in Franklin, SIMPSON, Ky, d: 30 May 1971 in
                    Barren Co., Ky; Y
                    + Veda Allie PEDIGO b: 11 Feb 1897 in Barren Co., Ky, m: 1921 in Barren Co., Ky, d:
                    01 Mar 1963 in Barren Co., Ky; Y
...................8 Samuel Joseph LAWLER b: 11 Oct 1872 in Homestead, nr Franklin, SIMPSON, Ky, d: 16
                    Aug 1873 in (child), nr Franklin, SIMPSON, Ky; Y
...................8 Carrie Omega "Oma" LAWLER b: 11 Jul 1876 in Homestead, nr Franklin, SIMPSON, Ky,
                    d: 05 May 1922 in (never md), SIMPSON, Ky; Y
...................8 Bessie Ella LAWLER b: 13 Dec 1879 in Homestead, nr Franklin, SIMPSON, Ky, d: 15
                    Jan 1970 in at home dau, Murfreesboro, Tn; Y
                    + Ernest Munday b: Abt. 1881 in Slick Rock, Barren Co., Ky, m: 12 Dec 1910 in Franklin,
                    SIMPSON, Ky, d: 02 Nov 1965 in Farm, nr Franklin, SIMPSON, Ky; Y
.........................9 Gladys Munday b: nr Franklin, SIMPSON, Ky
                    + Harry Lawrence BELCHER b: 25 Oct 1914 in Simpson County, Kentucky, m: Abt.
                    1936 in Simpson Co Ky of, Murfreesboro, Tn, d: 23 Jul 1999 in Murfreesboro,
                    Rutherford Co, Tennessee; Y
.............................10 Barbara Jean BELCHER b: 11 Jan 1938 in of, Louisville, Ky
                    + Howard MARSHALL Vaughn b: 24 May 1938 in MARSHALL, Co., Tn, m: 21 Aug
                    1961
.............................10 Harry Glen BELCHER b: 30 May 1948 in of, Murfreesboro, Tn
...............6 Margery LAWLER b: 27 Oct 1796 in Mercer Co., KY, d: 15 Dec 1883 in Simpson Co., Ky; Y
                    + Francis Bell b: 01 Mar 1797 in Union Co., SC of Logan Simpson Co., KY, d: 04 Sep 1840 in
                    Simpson Co., Ky; Y
...................7 Elizabeth Bell b: 08 Dec 1824 in Simpson Co., Ky, d: 28 Jan 1825 in Simpson Co., Ky; Y
...................7 Francis Bell b: 1828 in Simpson Co., Ky
                    + Matilda b: 1838 in Simpson Co., Ky, m: Abt. 1858
...................8 Georgia Bell b: 1864 in Simpson Co., Ky
...............6 Rebecca LAWLER b: Abt. 1798 in Mercer, Ky

.............6 Mary Polly LAWLER b: 17 Aug 1800 in Mercer, Ky, d: 14 May 1874 in Farm, SIMPSON, Ky; Y
+ Samuel WILSON b: 15 Mar 1795 in SC, m: 15 Jan 1819 in Russelville, Logan, Ky, d: 04 May 1872 in Farm, Simpson Co., Ky; Y
.............7 daughter WILSON b: 1820 in 1820-30-40, Simpson Co., census, Ky
.............7 daughter WILSON b: 1821 in 1820-30-40, Simpson Co., census, Ky
.............7 Rebecca E. Wilson b: 13 Sep 1823 in Simpson Co., Ky, d: 12 Dec 1883 in Dallas, Dallas Co., Tx; Y
+ John E. Wainscott b: 16 Nov 1819 in Ky, m: 09 Oct 1843 in Sumner Co, Tn, d: 21 Feb 1900 in Dallas, Dallas Co., Tx; Y
.............8 Christopher E. or C. Wainscott b: Abt. 1845 in Ky
+ Martha b: 1849
.............8 Parlina or Pelina Wainscott b: 1846 in Ky
.............8 Charlotte Temple Wainscott b: 27 Jan 1848 in Ky, d: 24 Dec 1930 in Fort Worth, Tarrent Co, TX; Y
+ James Henry O'Shields b: 14 Apr 1848 in Laurens Co, SC, m: 27 Jan 1868 in Dallas Co, TX, d: 08 Dec 1930 in Fort Worth, Tarrent Co, TX; Y
.............9 John J. O'Shields b: 29 Oct 1869
.............9 Edward W. O'Shields b: 02 Dec 1870
.............9 *Annie May O'Shields b: 05 Jul 1872 in Plano, Dallas Co, TX, d: 27 Jun 1964 in Altus, Jackson Co, OK; Y
+ Richard Ansted b: 07 Dec 1871 in Hillsboro, Hill Co, TX, m: 01 Jun 1889 in Hillsboro, Hill Co, TX, d: 28 Nov 1959 in Elmer, Jackson Co, OK; Y
.............10 Lee Ansted b: 09 May 1891 in Willow Vale, Greer Co, Okla Territory, d: 05 Jul 1981 in Durant, OK; Y
+ Allie Smith b: 04 Feb 1896 in Delta Co, TX, d: 24 Mar 1982 in Durant OK; Y
.............11 Velma Lee Ansted b: Durant, OK
+ Van Dalton Martin
.............12 Michael Van Martin b: 06 Jun 1953 in Fort Worth, Tarrant Co, TX
+ Debra Marie Vacek b: 19 Jul 1956 in Chickasha, Grady Co, OK, m: 26 May 1979 in Garland, Dallas Co, TX
.............13 Jason Allen Martin b: 03 Oct 1986 in Dallas, Dallas Co, TX
.............13 Harrison Tyler Martin b: 12 Jun 1990 in Dallas, Dallas Co, TX
.............10 Emlie Ansted b: 09 Jun 1893 in Willow Vale, OK, d: 1897 ; Y
.............10 Mary Ansted b: 07 Dec 1894 in Hillsboro, Hill Co, TX, d: 1994 in CA; Y
+ Jack McFarland d: 1911 in Altus, OK; Y
+ Fred Bramlett
.............11 Ira Fred Bramlett d: 22 Mar 1995 in Tarrant Co, TX; Y
.............11 Mary Myrtle Bramlett b: Decater, Wise Co, TX, d: Denver, Co; Y
.............11 Emmett Bramlett b: Decater, Wise Co, TX, d: CA; Y
+ Will Franklin b: 22 Feb 1901, d: May 1968 in Vernon, Wilbarger Co, TX; Y
+ Guy
.............10 Ellen Ansted b: 07 Aug 1898 in Hillsboro, Hill Co, TX, d: 18 Nov 1989 in Riverside, CA; Y
+ Tom Quinn m: 1917
.............11 Mary Elizabeth Quinn d: May 1920 in Okla Union, TX: Y
+ Carse John Carson Hicks b: 09 Nov 1884 in Decatur, Wise County, Texas, m: Jan 1920, d: 09 Nov 1957 in Riverside, Riverside co., CA; Y
.............11 Juil Lee Hicks b: 1921 in Wellington TX
.............11 Tempa Bell Hicks b: 10 Nov 1924 in Olton, TX
.............10 Truman Jay Ansted b: 19 Jun 1900 in Grand Prairie, Dallas Co, TX, d: 25 Jul 1974 in Elizabeth, NJ; Y
+ Molly Viscount m: 1932
+ Harmine
.............11 Edward Ansted d: 16 Aug 1974 ; Y

..................10 Eddie May Ansted b: 22 Mar 1902 in Abilene, Taylor Co, TX, d: 1906 in Boggy
    Cemetery, Olustee, OK; Y
..................10 Bertha Ansted b: 04 Mar 1904 in Decatur, Wise Co, TX, d: 03 Mar 1976 in Denison,
    TX; Y
    + Ernest Coffman
..................11 Sarah May Coffman b: 24 Feb 1925 in Dallas, TX
..................11 Ernest Coffman Jr b: May 1926 in Dallas, TX
..................11 Jessie Thomas Coffman b: 1929 in Dallas, TX, d: 1995 in Mason, TX; Y
    + Framk Gibbs
    + Jack Rogers
    + Jerry Fleek
    + Sol Kaufman
    + Laird
    + Henry Ramsey
..................10 Lloyd Ansted b: 22 Apr 1906 in Olustee, OK, d: 01 Jul 1982 in Altus, OK; Y
    + Desta Canada m: 1934 in Olustee, Jackson Co, OK, d: 1974 in Elmer, Jackson Co,
    OK; Y
..................11 John Lloyd Ansted b: 1935 in Elmer, OK
..................10 Brady Albert Ansted b: 28 May 1908 in Olustee, OK, d: 21 Jul 1972 in Johnson City,
    KS; Y
    + Josephine Arminnie Copeland b: 02 Oct 1910 in Mt. Pleasent, TX
..................11 Richard Theodore Ansted b: 02 Sep 1929 in Olustee, OK, d: 21 Aug 1996 in San
    Jose, Santa Clara Co, CA; Y
    + Sheila
..................12 Melissa Ansted
..................12 Adelia Ansted
..................12 Hellen Ansted
..................11 Albert Lynn Ansted b: Jul 1942
    + Karen
..................11 Delbert Glenn Ansted b: Jul 1942 in Roswell, NM, d: Jul 1942 ; Y
..................11 Wayne Ansted b: Chickasaw, TX
    + Vesta
..................12 Calvin Ansted
..................12 Valarie Ansted
..................10 Beatrice Ansted b: 19 Sep 1909 in Olustee, Jackson Co, OK, d: 14 May 1998 in CA;
    Y
    + Orville Little b: 04 May 1908, m: 1933, d: Sep 1976 in Sacramento, CA; Y
..................11 Richard Orville Little b: 12 Nov 1934 in Pampa, TX, d: Sacramento, CA; Y
..................10 *Vesta Jane Ansted b: 11 Nov 1911 in Olustee, OK
    + William Eldon Armstrong b: 27 Feb 1916 in Duncanville, Dallas Co, TX, m: 26 Mar
    1947 in Duncanville, Dallas Co, TX, d: 06 Jan 1992 in Duncanville, Dallas Co, TX;
    Y
..................11 Fredrick William Armstrong b: 23 Feb 1948 in Dallas, TX
..................10 Kitty Oleta Ansted b: 22 Nov 1914 in Decatur, Wise Co, TX
    + Leroy Stowe m: Nov 1933 in Thanksgiving
..................11 Anna Ruth Stowe b: 26 Jan 1936 in Dallas, TX
    + Fleetwood Page m: 1941
    + Mell Benedict
    + Dean Wright
    + Roff Rasmussen m: Cal. 1961
..................10 Richard Petty Ansted Jr b: 08 Feb 1916 in Decatur, Wise Co, TX, d: 08 Aug 1916 in
    Little Bethel, Decatur, Wise Co. TX; Y
..................10 Minnie Lee Ansted b: 04 Jul 1917 in Decatur, Wise Co, TX, d: 04 Sep 1917 in Little
    Bethel, Decatur, Wise Co, TX; Y
..................9 Charles Morris O'Shields b: 07 May 1874, d: 28 Mar 1956 in Fort Worth, TX; Y

      + Nancy Ann Farmer b: 05 Feb 1881, d: Nov 1955 in Fort Worth, TX; Y
......................10 Opal O'Shields b: 18 Jan 1903, d: ARK; Y
      + Mac Maxwell
......................10 Valta O'Shields b: 21 Apr 1905 in Fort Worth, TX
......................10 Vaughn O'Shields b: 02 Apr 1907 in Fort Worth, TX
......................10 Cecil M. O'Shields b: 31 Oct 1908 in Fort Worth, TX
      + Hazel Inez Pickard
......................11 Millicent Jane O'Shields b: 24 Oct 1948 in Tarrant Co, TX
......................10 James Lewis O'Shields b: 20 Apr 1920 in Forth Worth, TX
      + Faye Lee Walker b: 02 Nov 1921 in Fort Worth, TX, m: 16 Jul 1939 in Weatherford, TX
......................11 Douglas Lee O'Shields b: 21 Aug 1942 in Fort Worth, TX, d: 03 Jan 2001 in Dallas Co, TX; Y
      + Ellen Dunigan m: 24 Nov 1972
......................12 Katie O'Shields
......................12 Luke O'Shields
......................11 Lewis "Mike" O'Shields b: 24 Nov 1948 in Fort Worth, TX
      + Mare Dale Shelton m: 29 Mar 1972
......................11 Peggy Faye O'Shields b: 26 Jun 1952 in Fort Worth, TX
      + William Roy Sims m: 29 Mar 1972
......................11 Mary "Angie" O'Shields b: 31 Dec 1957 in Fort Worth, TX
      + Craig Leon Becker m: 02 Aug 1980
......................10 Robert O'Shields b: 12 Apr 1922
......................10 Amon O'Shields
......................9 William H. O'Shields b: 27 Aug 1876, d: Sep 1876 ; Y
......................9 E. Bell O'Shields b: 19 Feb 1878, d: Abt. 196 AD ; Y
      + Al Cisco d: Abt. 1906 in CA; Y
      + John D.Parks
......................9 Ada Pearl O'Shields b: 21 Jul 1880
......................9 D. Richard "Dick" O'Shields b: 15 Sep 1882, d: 1935 ; Y
      + <No name>
......................10 Elkins Henry O'Shields d: 08 Feb 1991 in Tarrant Co, TX; Y
      + Daisy Gaynell Winn
......................11 Tommye Cue O'Shields b: 30 Jun 1930 in Wise Co, TX
      + McLemore
......................11 Sammy Drew O'Shields b: 03 Dec 1932 in Wise Co, TX, d: 23 Feb 1991 in Tarrant Co, TX; Y
......................10 Carl O'Shields
......................9 Andrew O'Shields b: 06 Apr 1884
......................9 Sarah R. O'Shields b: 09 Apr 1887
      + George J.Elsnor
......................9 Joe H. O'Shields b: 22 May 1889, d: Abt. 196 AD ; Y
......................9 Robert F. O'Shields b: 26 Apr 1891
......................8 M.A. Wainscott b: May 1849 in Ky
......................8 William J. Wainscott b: Abt. 1850 in Ky
      + Annie b: 1825 in AR
......................8 Samuel A. Wainscott b: 12 Jul 1851
......................8 Mary E. Wainscott b: Abt. 1852 in Ky
......................8 Henrietta Wainscott b: Abt. 1855 in Ky
......................8 Violet H. Wainscott b: 1857 in Ky
......................8 George Washington Wainscott b: 20 Feb 1858 in Dallas, Dallas Co., Tx, d: 20 Jul 1858 in Dallas, Dallas Co., Tx; Y
......................8 Martha J. Wainscott b: Nov 1859 in Tx

...............8 Louisa J. Wainscott b: 12 Nov 1859 in Dallas, Dallas Co., Tx, d: 23 Apr 1868 in Dallas,
Dallas Co., Tx; Y

...............8 Sarah R. Wainscott b: 1865 in Dallas, Dallas Co., Tx

...............8 R. Bell Wainscott b: 1867 in Dallas, Dallas Co., Tx

...............8 Mary R. Wainscott b: 1868 in Dallas, Dallas Co., Tx

...............7 William J. WILSON b: 15 Jul 1824 in Simpson Co., Ky, d: 30 Jul 1845 in Simpson Co., Ky;
Y

...............7 Francis A. WILSON b: 14 May 1828 in census, Simpson Co., 1850 p8 #110, Ky, d: 22 Nov
1903 in Simpson Co., Ky; Y

+ Mary R. HOLCOMB b: 12 Apr 1836 in of, SIMPSON, Ky, m: 11 Dec 1856 in SIMPSON,
Ky, d: 20 Nov 1865 in Simpson Co., Ky.; Y

...............8 Julia Frances Fannie WILSON b: 1859 in of Simpson Co., Ky.

...............8 Daniel WILSON b: 1864 in of Simpson Co., Ky.

+ Sophia C. Holland b: 03 Nov 1840 in of, SIMPSON, Ky, m: 18 Aug 1866 in SIMPSON,
Ky, d: 21 Dec 1875 in Simpson Co., Ky.; Y

...............8 John M (Minor) WILSON b: May 1867 in Simpson Co., Ky., d: 1937 in Simpson Co., Ky.;
Y

...............8 Mary Elizabeth WILSON b: 1869 in Simpson Co., Ky.

...............8 Florence (Ida Florence) WILSON b: 1871 in Simpson Co., Ky., d: 1958 in Simpson Co.,
Ky.; Y

...............8 Samuel WILSON b: 1875 in Simpson Co., Ky.

+ G. A b: 10 Dec 1851 in 1880, census, Simpson Co., Ky, m: SIMPSON, Ky, d: 20 Aug
1878 in Simpson Co., Ky.; Y

...............8 James Monroe WILSON b: 07 Dec 1877 in Simpson Co., Ky., d: 28 Nov 1921 in Simpson
Co., Ky.; Y

+ Myrtle Jones b: 10 Jul 1883 in of Simpson Co., Ky., d: 07 Oct 1905 in of Simpson Co.,
Ky.; Y

...............7 Mary C. WILSON b: 13 Apr 1830 in Simpson Co., Ky, d: 13 Mar 1885 in Dallas, Dallas
County, Texas; Y

+ George Washington Huffhines Sr. b: 21 Mar 1826 in Simpson Co., Ky, m: first husband,
SIMPSON, Ky, d: 19 Sep 1863 in Walker Co., Georgia; Y

...............8 John S HUFFHINES b: 09 Jan 1852 in SIMPSON, Co, Ky, d: 22 Jun 1929 in
RICHARDSON, Dallas Co, Tx; Y

+ Mary Ella FOX b: 07 Dec 1859 in Denton, Co, Tx, m: 24 Nov 1881 in Denton, Co, Tx, d:
14 Dec 1916 in Quanah, Tx; Y

...............9 Waldo Emmett HUFFHINES b: 1884 in Dallas, Co, Ky, d: 1886 in child; Y

...............9 Julian Sanger HUFFHINES b: 06 Nov 1887 in RICHARDSON, Dallas, Co, Tx, d: 19 Apr
1958 ; Y

+ Julia CRAWFORD b: 09 Sep 1892 in Quanah, Hardeman, Co, Tx, m: 11 May 1913 in
Quanah, Tx, d: 31 May 1966 ; Y

...............10 John Sherwood HUFFHINES b: 30 Jul 1914 in Quanah, Tx

+ Reba BARKLEY b: Abt. 1916 in of, Spearman, Tx, m: 23 Apr 1938 in Spearman, Tx

...............11 Judye Elizabeth HUFFHINES b: 13 May 1947 in Amarillo, Tx

+ Donald Cameron COOPER b: Abt. 1947 in of, Solvang, CA, m: 17 Feb 1973 in
Solvang, CA

...............12 LESLIE Megan COOPER b: 05 May 1975 in San Antonio, Tx

...............11 Reba Jan HUFFHINES b: 18 May 1949 in Amarillo, Tx

+ tom Rogers b: Abt. 1947 in Amarillo, Tx, m: 17 Oct 1970 in Amarillo, Tx

...............12 Justy Breanne Rogers b: 14 Sep 1971 in Ft Worth, Tarrent, Tx

...............12 Thomas TODD Rogers b: 11 May 1973 in Ft Worth, Tarrent, Tx

...............8 Mary Elizabeth Sis HUFFHINES b: 13 Sep 1854 in Dallas, Co, Tx, d: 13 Aug 1887 in
Rockwall Co., Texas; Y

+ Andrew Jackson Fender b: 19 Dec 1844 in of, Dallas, Co, Tx, m: 20 Jun 1872 in
Dallas, Co, Tx, d: 16 May 1918 in Rockwall, Tx; Y

...............9 George W Fender minister b: 18 Sep 1873 in Dallas, Co, Tx

+ Annie Byrd Stokes b: 15 Jan 1879 in of, Dallas, Co, Tx, m: 29 May 1899
............................10 Mary Fender b: 18 Oct 1901 in of, Dallas, Co, Tx
+ Sidney Walter Duke b: Abt. 1900 in of, Dallas, Co, Tx, m: 14 Jun 1923
............................11 Sidney Walter jr Duke b: 06 Jul 1924 in Dallas, Co, Tx
............................11 Hannah Duke b: 19 Jan 1926 in Dallas, Co, Tx
............................9 Cynthia Catherine Fender b: 11 Apr 1875 in RICHARDSON, Dallas, Co, Tx, d: 1944 in Rockwall Co., Tx; Y
+ WT William (or Willis) Terry Wade b: 1865 in Kaufman Co., of, Rockwall, Co, Tx, m: 24 Dec 1893 in Rockwall Co., Tx, d: 1927 in Rockwall Co., Tx; Y
............................10 Bonnie Wade b: 09 Jan 1896 in of, Rockwall, Co, Tx
+ W H VAUGHTER b: Abt. 1892 in of, Rockwall, Co, Tx, m: 24 Dec 1913 in Rockwall, Tx
............................11 4 children VAUGHTER
............................10 Fender Wade b: 04 Jul 1908 in of, Rockwall, Co, Tx
+ Etta PHILLIPS b: Abt. 1890 in of, Rockwall, Tx
............................10 Ruth Wade b: 13 Jul 1911 in of, Rockwall, Co, Tx
............................10 James O. Wade b: Abt. 1913 in Rockwall Co., Tx
............................9 Walter S Fender b: Abt. 1878 in of, Rockwall, Co, Tx, d: Oregon; Y
............................9 Sallie K Fender b: 05 Jan 1880 in Blackland, Co, Tx
+ ROSS C SMITH b: Abt. 1875 in of, Rockwall, Co, Tx, m: 01 Nov 1903, d: 10 Feb 1922 in of, Rockwall, Co, Tx; Y
............................10 Jeter e SMITH b: 24 Dec 1904 in Rockwall, Tx
+ Gwendolyn Miller b: Abt. 1906 in Rockwall, Tx, m: 07 Jan 1938 in Rockwall, Tx
............................10 Mary Ruth SMITH b: 01 Aug 1907 in Rockwall, Tx
+ Jewell Leon BALL b: Abt. 1905 in Rockwall, Tx, d: 18 May 1946 ; Y
............................10 Elizabeth Bess SMITH b: 18 Oct 1911 in Rockwall, Tx
+ A D COOPER b: Abt. 1910 in Rockwall, Tx, m: 17 Sep 1937 in Rockwall, Tx
............................10 Frances Irene SMITH b: 16 Aug 1914 in Rockwall, Tx
+ Maurice Eugene TETER b: 03 Apr 1913 in Rockwall, Tx, m: 04 Jun 1937 in Rockwall, Tx
............................11 Maurice Eugene jr TETER b: 11 Aug 1938 in Rockwall, Tx
+ Heather McNeill Llewellyn b: Abt. 1940 in of, Dallas, Tx, m: 25 May 1960 in Dallas, Dallas, Tx
............................12 Elizabeth Llewellyn TETER b: 16 Oct 1965 in of, Dallas, Tx
............................12 John Llewellyn TETER b: 05 Jun 1968 in of, Dallas, Tx
............................12 Katherine Llewellyn TETER b: 03 Feb 1971 in of, Dallas, Tx
............................11 William ROSS TETER b: 31 Jul 1940 in of, Rockwall, Co, Tx
+ Wyvonne Lynn WHITE b: Abt. 1942, m: 08 Feb 1974
............................12 Trevor SCOTT TETER b: 21 Nov 1975
............................11 Gayle TETER b: 24 Feb 1943 in of, Rockwall, Co, Tx
+ Alan Ray Gardner b: Abt. 1942 in of, Tx, m: 09 Sep 1973
............................12 Michael Alan Gardner b: 26 Feb 1976
............................11 Jack David TETER b: 29 Apr 1947 in of, Rockwall, Co, Tx
+ Karen Evanson b: Abt. 1949, m: 07 Feb 1976
............................10 Genevive SMITH b: 05 Dec 1915 in Rockwall, Tx
+ Darcey BROWN BOBBITT b: Abt. 1915 in of, Rockwall, Tx, m: 20 Jul 1938
............................11 Darcey BROWN jr BOBBITT b: 09 Dec 1941 in of, Rockwall, Tx
+ Shirley RENFROW b: Abt. 1943 in Tx
............................12 Lance Charles BOBBITT b: 16 Aug 1968 in of, Tx
............................11 Jay Charles BOBBITT b: 12 Jun 1949
............................10 Ida Lois SMITH b: 10 Feb 1919 in Rockwall, Tx
+ Elmer Frank CAUGHRAN b: Abt. 1917 in of, Rockwall, Tx, m: 14 Oct 1944
............................11 William Frank CAUGHRAN b: 05 Mar 1949 in of, Rockwall, Tx
+ Susan Anne Miller b: Abt. 1951 in of, Rockwall, Tx, m: 14 Aug 1971 in of, Rockwall, Tx

...........................12 Amy Suzanne CAUGHRAN b: 26 Aug 1973 in of, Rockwall, Tx
....................9 Ida Mae Fender b: 04 May 1883 in of, Blackland, Tx, d: 18 Sep 1961 ; Y
+ Charles Olin Wade b: 23 Oct 1883 in of, Rockwall, Co, Tx, m: 31 Dec 1908 in of,
Rockwall, Tx, d: 27 Feb 1954 in of, Rockwall, Co, Tx; Y
......................10 Mary Laura Wade b: 20 Sep 1910 in of, Rockwall, Co, Tx
+ Daniel Frank McInnis b: Abt. 1910 in of, Amarillo, Tx, m: 16 Aug 1934 in Amarillo,
Tx
.........................11 Amy Lynn McInnis b: 05 May 1941 in PHILLIPS, Tx
+ Delbert C jr OVERSTREET b: Abt. 1939 in of, Sweeny, Tx, m: 25 Aug 1963 in
Sweeny, Tx
.........................12 Susan Lynn OVERSTREET b: 27 Apr 1968 in Houston, Tx
.........................12 DOUGLAS Carl OVERSTREET b: 17 Jul 1970 in Houston, Tx
.........................11 Martha May McInnis b: 20 Mar 1945 in PHILLIPS, Tx
+ Edmund Vaughn III GUIDRY b: Abt. 1940 in of, Sweeny, Tx, m: 06 Sep 1970 in
Sweeny, Tx
.........................11 Marion Kay McInnis b: 20 Mar 1945 in PHILLIPS, Tx
+ David Edwin Williams b: Abt. 1943 in of, Sweeny, Tx, m: 11 Jun 1966 in Sweeny,
Tx
.........................12 Kate Wade Williams b: 07 Dec 1971 in of, Sweeny, Tx
.........................12 Keith Wade Williams b: 31 Dec 1974 in of, Sweeny, Tx
......................10 Kathlen Wade b: 15 Jun 1913 in of, Rockwall, Co, Tx
+ James NOLAND b: Abt. 1913 in of, Rockwall, Tx, m: 19 Aug 1939 in of, Rockwall,
Tx
.........................11 Joe ALLEN NOLAND b: 25 Apr 1942 in of, Rockwall, Tx
+ Cynthia Jean HUMPHREYS b: Abt. 1944 in of, Rockwall, Tx, m: 12 Sep 1964 in
of, Rockwall, Tx
.........................12 Rebecca Ann NOLAND b: 16 Apr 1965 in of, Rockwall, Tx
.........................12 Julie Christine NOLAND b: 08 May 1967 in of, Rockwall, Tx
.........................12 Tracy Michelle NOLAND b: 26 Aug 1969 in of, Rockwall, Tx
.........................11 Sally NOLAND b: 08 Jun 1946 in of, Rockwall, Tx
.........................11 Kathy Lee NOLAND b: 24 May 1950 in of, Rockwall, Tx
......................10 Marion Wade b: 04 Nov 1915 in of, Rockwall, Co, Tx
+ Lloyd Walden FARNSWORTH b: Abt. 1915 in of, Amarillo, Tx, m: Jul 1937 in
Amarillo, Tx
.........................11 Marion Elizabeth FARNSWORTH b: 18 Jan 1938 in of, Amarillo, Tx
+ Robert Clay HUMPERT b: Abt. 1937 in of, Boulder, Colorado, m: Apr 1958 in
Boulder, Colo
.........................12 Donald Eric HUMPERT b: 24 Oct 1965 in of, Boulder, Colorado
.........................12 Jennifer Lynn HUMPERT b: 13 Jan 1969 in of, Boulder, Colorado
.........................11 Virginia Anne FARNSWORTH b: 15 Sep 1940 in of, Amarillo, Tx, d: Aug 1967 ; Y
.........................11 David Lloyd FARNSWORTH b: 15 Jun 1944 in of, Amarillo, Tx
+ Alberta B BERTAPELLE b: Abt. 1946, m: Jan 1967
.........................12 Richard Lloyd FARNSWORTH b: 28 May 1969
.........................12 Jeffrey Earl FARNSWORTH b: 21 Feb 1975
.........................11 James Richard FARNSWORTH b: 21 Apr 1946 in of, Amarillo, Tx
.........................11 Stephen Wade FARNSWORTH b: 05 Jan 1948 in of, Amarillo, Tx
+ Deborah Joy SOLIS m: Feb 1969 in divorced, 1972
.........................12 Thomas Wade FARNSWORTH b: 24 Sep 1969
+ Eileen VINING b: Abt. 1952 in of, Tx, m: 1974
......................10 Virginia Anne Wade b: 15 Aug 1917 in of, Rockwall, Co, Tx
+ Maurice C Finley b: 25 Sep 1911 in of, Tx, m: 11 Nov 1939 in of, Rockwall, Tx
.........................11 Mary Lynn Finley b: 17 Oct 1946 in of, Rockwall, Tx
+ e Randolph WHITELAW b: Abt. 1944 in of, Saint Louis, Mo, m: 02 Aug 1969 in of,
Rockwall, Tx
.........................11 Richard Wade Finley b: 11 Aug 1959 in of, Rockwall, Tx

...................10 Charles Olin jr Wade b: 20 Sep 1919 in of, Rockwall, Co, Tx
      + Edith Elaine DUNN b: 04 Mar 1920 in McKinney, Tx, m: 23 Apr 1941
...................11 Jan Elaine Wade b: 28 Oct 1942 in Amarillo, Tx
      + Dwight Earl parish b: 24 Sep 1940, m: 20 Feb 1959
...................12 Lorri LEIGH parish b: 22 Nov 1959 in Amarillo, Tx
...................12 Julie Noell parish b: 23 Dec 1967 in Amarillo, Tx
...................11 Charles Christopher Wade b: 27 Feb 1952 in Amarillo, Tx
      + Connie Jo KELLY b: 19 Jan 1953 in Colorado Springs, Colo
...................10 Betty Lynn Wade b: 27 Mar 1924 in of, Rockwall, Co, Tx
...................9 Robert Newton Fender b: 04 Dec 1884 in 1 mile east, Rockwall, Blackland, Tx
      + Zoe OGDEN b: 11 May 1887 in Martinsburg, Iowa, m: 18 Dec 1909 in McMinnville, Ore, d: 29 Apr 1939 in Rockwall, Tx; Y
...................10 Dorothy Rachel Fender b: 27 Jan 1911 in McMinnville, Ore, d: 20 Jan 1914 in age 3, Rockwall, Tx; Y
...................10 Clara Elizabeth Fender b: 16 Jan 1913 in of, Rockwall, Tx
      + Henry WEBB b: 25 Jan 1911 in of, Rockwall, Tx, m: 03 Jun 1936 in Rockwall, Tx
...................11 Robert Henry WEBB b: 17 Sep 1937 in Stamford, Tx
      + Oleta BRICE b: 19 Apr 1933 in Stamford, Tx, m: 28 Nov 1958 in Stamford, Tx
...................12 James Robert Jim Bob WEBB b: 27 Oct 1960 in Stamford, Tx
...................12 Vonda Jo WEBB b: 02 Oct 1962 in Stamford, Tx
...................11 Dorothy Alice WEBB b: 03 Aug 1938 in Stamford, Tx
      + George BATTEY b: 21 Apr 1931 in of, Stamford, Tx, m: 01 Feb 1958 in Stamford, Tx
...................12 Dorothy Elizabeth BATTEY b: 14 Mar 1959 in of, Stamford, Tx
...................12 George Franklin BATTEY b: 22 May 1960 in of, Stamford, Tx
...................11 Virginia Jo WEBB b: 25 Oct 1939 in Stamford, Tx
      + Julian Newton KELLY b: 31 Dec 1939 in of, Stamford, Tx, m: 15 Oct 1960 in Stamford, Tx
...................12 Alice Kay KELLY b: 14 Oct 1961 in of, Stamford, Tx
...................12 Joe Henry KELLY b: 17 May 1963 in of, Stamford, Tx
...................11 BRYAN Lee WEBB b: 09 Dec 1943 in Stamford, Tx
...................10 Martha Fender RN b: 11 Aug 1914 in Rockwall, Tx
      + David GRANT b: Abt. 1912 in of, Rockwall, Tx, m: 08 Mar 1941 in Rockwall, Tx
...................11 Don Garland GRANT b: 13 May 1913 in Rockwall, Tx
      + Carol m: 31 Mar 1961 in Rockwall, Tx
...................12 Don Garland jr GRANT b: 09 Jan 1962 in Rockwall, Tx
...................10 Mary Emilie Fender b: Abt. 1917 in of, Rockwall, Girlhill, Tx
      + Wesley HODGE b: of, Rockwall, Tx
...................10 Sally Catherine Fender b: 27 Jul 1921 in of, Rockwall, Girlhill, Tx
      + William Leon Dudley b: 01 Apr 1919 in of, Rockwall, Tx
...................11 Elaine Dudley b: 20 Mar 1944 in of, Rockwall, Tx
      + Harry Leon Austin twin b: 27 Aug 1943 in East, Rockwall, Tx, m: 30 Nov 1962
...................12 Diedra LEIGH Austin b: 28 Feb 1964 in East, Rockwall, Tx
...................12 Jason Austin b: East, Rockwall, Tx
...................11 Zoe Dudley b: 25 Nov 1948 in of, Rockwall, Tx
      + Larry Don Austin twin b: 27 Aug 1943 in twin, Rockwall, Tx, m: 03 Aug 1963
...................12 Rhonda Gale Austin b: 01 Apr 1967 in of, Rockwall, Tx
...................12 Laura Leavin Austin b: 19 Aug 1969 in of, Rockwall, Tx
...................11 Mary Dudley b: 26 Nov 1957 in of, Rockwall, Tx
      + Rick PHARAOH b: of, Rockwall, Tx
...................12 Katie PHARAOH b: of, Crane, Tx
...................10 Ethel Joy Katie Fender b: 11 Feb 1924 in of, Rockwall, Girlhill, Tx
      + Robert Lee CARRELL b: Abt. 1922 in of, Rockwall, Tx, m: 23 Nov 1942
...................11 Betty Kay CARRELL b: 09 Dec 1947 in of, Odessa, Graham, Tx

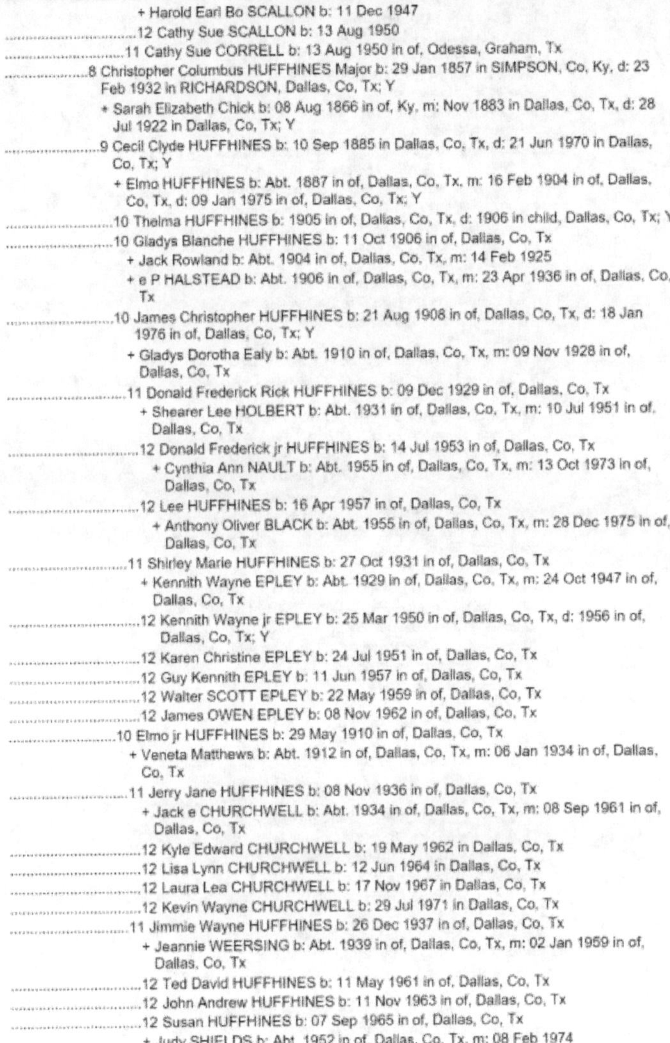

```
                    + Harold Earl Bo SCALLON b: 11 Dec 1947
...................12 Cathy Sue SCALLON b: 13 Aug 1950
.....................11 Cathy Sue CORRELL b: 13 Aug 1950 in of, Odessa, Graham, Tx
...............8 Christopher Columbus HUFFHINES Major b: 29 Jan 1857 in SIMPSON, Co, Ky, d: 23
                Feb 1932 in RICHARDSON, Dallas, Co, Tx; Y
             * Sarah Elizabeth Chick b: 08 Aug 1866 in of, Ky, m: Nov 1883 in Dallas, Co, Tx, d: 28
                Jul 1922 in Dallas, Co, Tx; Y
...................9 Cecil Clyde HUFFHINES b: 10 Sep 1885 in Dallas, Co, Tx, d: 21 Jun 1970 in Dallas,
                Co, Tx; Y
                 + Elmo HUFFHINES b: Abt. 1887 in of, Dallas, Co, Tx, m: 16 Feb 1904 in of, Dallas,
                Co, Tx, d: 09 Jan 1975 in of, Dallas, Co, Tx; Y
................10 Thelma HUFFHINES b: 1905 in of, Dallas, Co, Tx, d: 1906 in child, Dallas, Co, Tx; Y
................10 Gladys Blanche HUFFHINES b: 11 Oct 1906 in of, Dallas, Co, Tx
                 + Jack Rowland b: Abt. 1904 in of, Dallas, Co, Tx, m: 14 Feb 1925
                 + e P HALSTEAD b: Abt. 1906 in of, Dallas, Co, Tx, m: 23 Apr 1936 in of, Dallas, Co,
                Tx
................10 James Christopher HUFFHINES b: 21 Aug 1908 in of, Dallas, Co, Tx, d: 18 Jan
                1976 in of, Dallas, Co, Tx; Y
                 + Gladys Dorotha Ealy b: Abt. 1910 in of, Dallas, Co, Tx, m: 09 Nov 1928 in of,
                Dallas, Co, Tx
................11 Donald Frederick Rick HUFFHINES b: 09 Dec 1929 in of, Dallas, Co, Tx
                 + Shearer Lee HOLBERT b: Abt. 1931 in of, Dallas, Co, Tx, m: 10 Jul 1951 in of,
                Dallas, Co, Tx
................12 Donald Frederick jr HUFFHINES b: 14 Jul 1953 in of, Dallas, Co, Tx
                 + Cynthia Ann NAULT b: Abt. 1955 in of, Dallas, Co, Tx, m: 13 Oct 1973 in of,
                Dallas, Co, Tx
................12 Lee HUFFHINES b: 16 Apr 1957 in of, Dallas, Co, Tx
                 + Anthony Oliver BLACK b: Abt. 1955 in of, Dallas, Co, Tx, m: 28 Dec 1975 in of,
                Dallas, Co, Tx
................11 Shirley Marie HUFFHINES b: 27 Oct 1931 in of, Dallas, Co, Tx
                 + Kennith Wayne EPLEY b: Abt. 1929 in of, Dallas, Co, Tx, m: 24 Oct 1947 in of,
                Dallas, Co, Tx
................12 Kennith Wayne jr EPLEY b: 25 Mar 1950 in of, Dallas, Co, Tx, d: 1956 in of,
                Dallas, Co, Tx; Y
................12 Karen Christine EPLEY b: 24 Jul 1951 in of, Dallas, Co, Tx
................12 Guy Kennith EPLEY b: 11 Jun 1957 in of, Dallas, Co, Tx
................12 Walter SCOTT EPLEY b: 22 May 1959 in of, Dallas, Co, Tx
................12 James OWEN EPLEY b: 08 Nov 1962 in of, Dallas, Co, Tx
................10 Elmo jr HUFFHINES b: 29 May 1910 in of, Dallas, Co, Tx
                 + Veneta Matthews b: Abt. 1912 in of, Dallas, Co, Tx, m: 06 Jan 1934 in of, Dallas,
                Co, Tx
................11 Jerry Jane HUFFHINES b: 08 Nov 1936 in of, Dallas, Co, Tx
                 + Jack e CHURCHWELL b: Abt. 1934 in of, Dallas, Co, Tx, m: 08 Sep 1961 in of,
                Dallas, Co, Tx
................12 Kyle Edward CHURCHWELL b: 19 May 1962 in Dallas, Co, Tx
................12 Lisa Lynn CHURCHWELL b: 12 Jun 1964 in Dallas, Co, Tx
................12 Laura Lea CHURCHWELL b: 17 Nov 1967 in Dallas, Co, Tx
................12 Kevin Wayne CHURCHWELL b: 29 Jul 1971 in Dallas, Co, Tx
................11 Jimmie Wayne HUFFHINES b: 26 Dec 1937 in of, Dallas, Co, Tx
                 + Jeannie WEERSING b: Abt. 1939 in of, Dallas, Co, Tx, m: 02 Jan 1959 in of,
                Dallas, Co, Tx
................12 Ted David HUFFHINES b: 11 May 1961 in of, Dallas, Co, Tx
................12 John Andrew HUFFHINES b: 11 Nov 1963 in of, Dallas, Co, Tx
................12 Susan HUFFHINES b: 07 Sep 1965 in of, Dallas, Co, Tx
                 + Judy SHIELDS b: Abt. 1952 in of, Dallas, Co, Tx, m: 08 Feb 1974
```

...............10 Juanita Jeanette HUFFHINES b: 18 Oct 1911 in of, Dallas, Co, Tx
  + B B LAIR b: Abt. 1909 in of, Dallas, Co, Tx, m: 06 Nov 1930 in of, Dallas, Co, Tx, d: 02 Aug 1965 in of, Dallas, Co, Tx; Y
...............11 Norma Jean LAIR b: 11 Aug 1931 in of, Dallas, Co, Tx, d: 23 Sep 1960 in of, Dallas, Co, Tx; Y
  + Stephen L PLACKO b: Abt. 1929 in of, Dallas, Co, Tx, m: 18 Nov 1950 in of, Dallas, Co, Tx
...............12 Cynthia Ann PLACKO b: 26 May 1952 in of, Dallas, Co, Tx
...............12 Sherry Lynn PLACKO b: 22 Nov 1953 in of, Dallas, Co, Tx
  + Robert NORRIS MEFFORD b: Abt. 1951 in of, Dallas, Co, Tx, m: 02 Dec 1972 in of, Dallas, Co, Tx
...............12 Stephanie Dawn PLACKO b: 27 Dec 1955 in of, Dallas, Co, Tx
...............11 Ted Edward LAIR b: 04 Sep 1936 in of, Dallas, Co, Tx, d: 15 Mar 1960 in of, Dallas, Co, Tx; Y
...............11 Brian DOUGLAS LAIR b: 10 Jun 1942 in of, Dallas, Co, Tx
...............10 Ruby Elizabeth HUFFHINES b: 29 Dec 1913 in of, Dallas, Co, Tx
  + Thomas V WHEELER b: Abt. 1911 in of, Dallas, Co, Tx, m: 18 Feb 1930 in of, Dallas, Co, Tx
...............11 Thomas V jr WHEELER b: 25 Oct 1930 in of, Dallas, Co, Tx
  + Lola Mae ALDERSON b: Abt. 1932 in of, Dallas, Co, Tx, m: 04 Aug 1952 in of, Dallas, Co, Tx
...............12 DOUGLAS Edward WHEELER b: 11 Apr 1958 in of, Dallas, Co, Tx
...............12 Sandra Dawn WHEELER b: 28 Jul 1962 in of, Dallas, Co, Tx
...............10 Vivian Pearl HUFFHINES b: 19 Jan 1916 in of, Dallas, Co, Tx
  + L G HALSTEAD b: Abt. 1914 in of, Dallas, Co, Tx, m: 22 Apr 1938 in of, Dallas, Co, Tx
...............10 Oliver Mitchell HUFFHINES b: 15 Jan 1918 in of, Dallas, Co, Tx
  + Mildred Bernice Prewitt b: 20 Nov 1920 in of, Dallas, Co, Tx, m: 03 Dec 1938 in of, Dallas, Co, Tx
...............11 Rebecca Lynn HUFFHINES b: 20 Nov 1940 in of, Dallas, Co, Tx
  + Donald Joe Robertson b: 16 Jul 1939 in of, Dallas, Co, Tx
...............12 Kerry Don Robertson b: 25 Dec 1962 in of, Dallas, Co, Tx
...............12 John Michael Robertson b: 05 Sep 1964 in of, Dallas, Co, Tx
...............12 Jennifer Lynn Robertson b: 25 Apr 1968 in of, Dallas, Co, Tx
...............11 Stanley Carson HUFFHINES b: 31 Jul 1942 in of, Dallas, Co, Tx
  + Bettie Lynn Ray b: 03 Jan 1947 in of, Dallas, Co, Tx, m: Abt. 1865 in of, Dallas, Co, Tx
...............12 Craig Prewitt HUFFHINES b: 21 Nov 1967 in of, Dallas, Co, Tx
...............12 Chad Eric HUFFHINES b: 19 Jan 1970 in of, Dallas, Co, Tx
...............12 CHRISTIE Lynn HUFFHINES b: 25 Sep 1971 in of, Dallas, Co, Tx
...............11 Olivia HUFFHINES b: 13 Feb 1944 in of, Dallas, Co, Tx
  + David Lawrence HOVER b: 23 Sep 1942 in of, Dallas, Co, Tx
...............12 David SCOTT HOVER b: 24 Sep 1962 in of, Dallas, Co, Tx
...............12 Jeffrey Brian HOVER b: 28 Jul 1965 in of, Dallas, Co, Tx
...............12 TODD Michael HOVER b: 31 Dec 1970 in of, Dallas, Co, Tx
...............12 BRADLEY Lawrence HOVER b: 01 May 1973 in of, Dallas, Co, Tx
...............10 Charles HUFFHINES b: 09 Feb 1919 in of, Dallas, Co, Tx, d: 05 Jun 1972 in of, Dallas, Co, Tx; Y
  + Lucille LUTZ b: Abt. 1921 in of, Dallas, Co, Tx, m: 26 Apr 1947 in of, Dallas, Co, Tx
...............10 Eloise HUFFHINES b: 12 Feb 1921 in of, Dallas, Co, Tx
  + Ted Kenneth Bailey b: Abt. 1919 in of, Dallas, Co, Tx, m: 20 Jan 1951 in of, Dallas, Co, Tx
...............11 Michael Bailey b: 22 Mar 1946 in Dallas, Co, Tx
  + Linda DOEBECKA b: Abt. 1948 in of, Dallas, Co, Tx, m: 22 Aug 1969 in Dallas, Dallas, Co, Tx

...................................12 Michael SCOTT Bailey b: 22 Mar 1970 in Dallas, Co, Tx
..............................11 Ted Kenneth jr Bailey b: 30 Nov 1951 in Dallas, Co, Tx
            + Theresa WEBB b: Abt. 1953 in of, Dallas, Co, Tx, m: 07 Dec 1973 in Dallas,
            Dallas, Co, Tx
..............................12 Jason Kenneth Bailey b: 05 Oct 1974 in of, Dallas, Co, Tx
..............................11 Robert Elmo Bailey b: 14 Feb 1953 in Dallas, Co, Tx
            + Norma FOX b: Abt. 1955 in of, Dallas, Co, Tx, m: 16 Dec 1971 in Dallas, Dallas,
            Co, Tx
..............................12 Jon Wes Bailey b: 16 May 1972 in of, Dallas, Co, Tx
........................10 Hugh HUFFHINES b: 1923 in of, Dallas, Co, Tx, d: 1923 in baby, died, at, birth; Y
....................9 Cyrus Fields HUFFHINES b: 24 Oct 1886 in Dallas, Co, Tx, d: 14 Apr 1966 in Dallas,
            Co, Tx; Y
            + Clara Maude WRIGHT b: Abt. 1888 in of, Dallas, Co, Tx, m: 30 Oct 1907 in Dallas,
            Dallas, Co, Tx
........................10 Harold Clifton HUFFHINES b: 12 Dec 1911 in of, Dallas, Co, Tx
            + Norene MURPHY b: Abt. 1913 in of, Dallas, Co, Tx, m: 29 Apr 1944 in Dallas,
            Dallas, Co, Tx
........................10 Cecil Cyrus HUFFHINES b: 09 Oct 1914 in of, Dallas, Co, Tx
........................10 LESLIE Doris HUFFHINES b: 03 Apr 1918 in of, Dallas, Co, Tx
            + J B RICH b: Abt. 1916 in of, Dallas, Co, Tx, m: 27 Jun 1936 in Dallas, Co, Tx
..............................11 Billy Don RICH b: 15 Jul 1939 in of, Dallas, Co, Tx
            + Jo Ann DAVIS b: 05 Feb 1943 in of, Dallas, Co, Tx, m: 29 Aug 1959 in Dallas, Co,
            Tx
..............................12 Joseph Don RICH b: 24 Dec 1961 in of, Dallas, Co, Tx
..............................12 Donna Lynn RICH b: 17 Mar 1964 in of, Dallas, Co, Tx
..............................12 Donald James RICH b: 03 Feb 1966 in of, Dallas, Co, Tx
..............................12 Mitchell Dean RICH b: 14 May 1968 in of, Dallas, Co, Tx
..............................11 Jerry Lynn RICH b: 18 Feb 1942 in of, Dallas, Co, Tx
            + Millie Ann King b: 07 Nov 1946 in of, Dallas, Co, Tx, m: 13 Mar 1960 in Dallas,
            Co, Tx
..............................12 James GLENN RICH b: 09 Sep 1960 in of, Dallas, Co, Tx
..............................12 Jerry Claude RICH b: 01 Sep 1961 in of, Dallas, Co, Tx
..............................12 Sherry Lynn RICH b: 18 Apr 1963 in of, Dallas, Co, Tx
..............................12 Dianna Ann RICH b: 09 Oct 1965 in of, Dallas, Co, Tx
..............................11 Marcena Ann RICH b: 24 Nov 1943 in of, Dallas, Co, Tx
            + Travis Lynn FLOWERS b: 26 Jun 1939 in of, Dallas, Co, Tx, m: 01 Sep 1961 in
            Dallas, Co, Tx
..............................12 Terri Dwan FLOWERS b: 05 Feb 1963 in of, Dallas, Co, Tx
..............................12 Clifford Keith FLOWERS b: 20 Aug 1965 in of, Dallas, Co, Tx
..............................12 Trina Ann FLOWERS b: 06 Jan 1968 in of, Dallas, Co, Tx
........................10 Wilma Earl HUFFHINES b: 10 Oct 1923 in of, Dallas, Co, Tx
            + J T ISBON b: Abt. 1921 in of, Dallas, Co, Tx, m: 03 Jun 1939 in Dallas, Co, Tx
....................9 Emory Ward HUFFHINES b: 31 Mar 1889 in Dallas, Co, Tx, d: 25 May 1950 in Dallas,
            Co, Tx; Y
            + Fannie WHITE b: Abt. 1891 in of, Dallas, Co, Tx, m: 17 Jul 192 AD in RICHARDSON,
            Dallas, Co, Tx
........................10 Emory Lee HUFFHINES b: 14 Jun 1914 in of, Dallas, Co, Tx
            + LaVerne HARRINGTON b: Abt. 1916 in of, Dallas, Co, Tx, m: 16 Aug 1940 in
            RICHARDSON, Dallas, Co, Tx
..............................11 Judith Lee HUFFHINES b: 03 May 1942 in of, Dallas, Co, Tx
            + Robert Lee DIETZE b: Abt. 1940 in of, Dallas, Co, Tx, m: 31 Jul 1965 in of,
            Dallas, Co, Tx
..............................12 Catherine Diane DIETZE b: 29 Jun 1969 in of, Dallas, Co, Tx
..............................12 Deborah Lynn DIETZE b: 20 Nov 1973 in of, Dallas, Co, Tx
..............................11 Robert Emory HUFFHINES b: 23 Jul 1946 in of, Dallas, Co, Tx

                    + Sybil Marie Chee chee STOVALL b: Abt. 1948 in of, Dallas, Co, Tx, m: 22 Jun
                      1968
...........................11 Jonelle HUFFHINES b: 28 May 1950 in of, Dallas, Co, Tx
.......................10 Jack Erwin HUFFHINES b: 22 Jul 1918 in of, Dallas, Co, Tx, d: 16 Mar 1973 in of,
                      Dallas, Co, Tx; Y
                    + Vanara Boe DAVIS b: Abt. 1922 in of, Dallas, Co, Tx, m: 08 Dec 1945 in of, Dallas,
                      Co, Tx
...........................11 Gary Erwin HUFFHINES b: 04 Oct 1950 in of, Dallas, Co, Tx
.......................10 Frances Naomi HUFFHINES b: 27 Aug 1921 in of, Dallas, Co, Tx
                    + J Durwood HAYES b: Abt. 1918 in of, Dallas, Co, Tx, m: 09 Apr 1939 in of, Dallas,
                      Co, Tx
...........................11 Priscilla Rebecca HAYES b: 08 Feb 1940 in of, Dallas, Co, Tx
                      + James S MULDER b: Abt. 1938 in of, Dallas, Co, Tx, m: 13 Sep 1958 in of,
                        Dallas, Co, Tx
...........................12 BRYAN Mitchell MULDER b: 03 May 1960 in of, Dallas, Co, Tx
...........................12 Michael Neale MULDER b: 02 Oct 1961 in of, Dallas, Co, Tx
...........................12 Rebecca Michelle MULDER b: 27 May 1963 in of, Dallas, Co, Tx
                      + Thomas Jodie tom GALLOWAY b: Abt. 1945 in of, Dallas, Co, Tx, m: 06 Oct 1975
                        in of, Dallas, Co, Tx
...........................11 Patricia Ann HAYES b: 03 Sep 1941 in of, Dallas, Co, Tx
                      + Dennis Austin LOCKE b: Abt. 1939 in of, Dallas, Co, Tx, m: 14 Aug 1959 in of,
                        Dallas, Co, Tx
...........................12 Denise Ann LOCKE b: 26 May 1960 in of, Dallas, Co, Tx
...........................12 Johnny Austin LOCKE b: 02 Jul 1962 in of, Dallas, Co, Tx
...........................12 Dal Austin LOCKE b: 08 Aug 1964 in of, Dallas, Co, Tx
...........................11 Jacqueline Lark HAYES b: 14 Nov 1944 in of, Dallas, Co, Tx
                      + Thomas e Jeffrey b: Abt. 1942 in of, Dallas, Co, Tx, m: 05 Jun 1963 in of, Dallas,
                        Co, Tx
...........................12 Thomas Bradford Jeffrey b: 27 Apr 1967 in of, Dallas, Co, Tx
...........................11 Glenda Jill HAYES b: 31 Aug 1948 in of, Dallas, Co, Tx
                      + Joe MEEKS b: Abt. 1965 in of, Dallas, Co, Tx, m: 05 Feb 1967 in of, Dallas, Co,
                        Tx
...........................12 Joe Clayton MEEKS COVINGTON b: 25 Oct 1967 in of, Dallas, Co, Tx
                      + Steve Lynn COVINGTON b: Abt. 1948 in of, Dallas, Co, Tx, m: 15 Oct 1971 in of,
                        Dallas, Co, Tx
...........................12 Emily Lynn COVINGTON b: 22 May 1975 in of, Dallas, Co, Tx
...........................11 Mary Frances HAYES b: 16 Jul 1950 in of, Dallas, Co, Tx
.......................10 Charles Calvin HUFFHINES b: 09 Oct 1927 in of, Dallas, Co, Tx
                    + Bettie Kay SMITH b: Abt. 1929 in of, Dallas, Co, Tx, m: 11 Jul 1953 in of, Dallas,
                      Co, Tx
...........................11 Lisa Lynn HUFFHINES b: 12 Oct 1955 in of, Dallas, Co, Tx
...........................11 Stacy SMITH HUFFHINES b: 09 Feb 1958 in of, Dallas, Co, Tx
...........................11 Amy Allison HUFFHINES b: 15 Jan 1960 in of, Dallas, Co, Tx
...........................11 Hailey Hewitt HUFFHINES b: 02 Mar 1964 in of, Dallas, Co, Tx
...................9 Birdie HUFFHINES b: 27 Dec 1890
                    + Archie POPPLEWELL Dr b: Abt. 1888 in RICHARDSON, Dallas, Co, Tx, m: 17 Jul
                      1912 in RICHARDSON, Dallas, Co, Tx
.......................10 Dorothy POPPLEWELL b: 17 Apr 1913 in RICHARDSON, Dallas, Co, Tx
                    + Frank WIRTH b: Abt. 1915 in of, Hamburg, Germany, m: 17 Jul 1939 in of, Dallas,
                      Co, Tx
...........................11 Ronald WIRTH b: 28 Nov 1942 in of, Dallas, Tx
                      + Cheryl Ann BEAVERS b: Abt. 1944 in of, Dallas, Tx, m: 20 Jun 1964 in divorced,
                        1975, Dallas, Tx
                      + Maria Elena Irma Ciardonel b: Abt. 1952 in of, Cardoba, Argentina, m: 10 Apr
                        1975

...................................12 Darwin WIRTH b: 27 Dec 1975
...................................11 Larry WIRTH b: 06 Jan 1945 in of, Dallas, Tx
...................................11 Franzisca WIRTH b: 01 Sep 1948 in of, Dallas, Tx
...............................10 Archie LEONARD POPPLEWELL b: 11 Nov 1914 in RICHARDSON, Dallas, Co, Tx
    + Evelyn NEWBERRY b: Abt. 1916 in of, Dallas, Tx, m: 21 Jun 1941 in of, Dallas, Tx
...............................11 Peggy Lynn POPPLEWELL b: 31 Oct 1942 in of, Dallas, Co, Tx
    + Gerald Monroe Hannah b: Abt. 1940 in of, Dallas, Co, Tx, m: 28 Oct 1961 in of,
Dallas, Tx
...................................12 Stephen Brett Hannah b: 06 Sep 1963 in of, Dallas, Co, Tx
...................................12 Sharon Kimberly Hannah b: 28 Feb 1966 in of, Dallas, Co, Tx
...............................11 Robert Craig POPPLEWELL b: 20 Jul 1944 in of, Dallas, Co, Tx
    + Phylis WILSON b: Abt. 1946 in of, Dallas, Co, Tx, m: 15 Oct 1965 in of, Dallas, Tx
...................................12 HOLLY Paige POPPLEWELL b: 04 Jan 1967 in of, Dallas, Co, Tx
...................................12 Adam Ladd POPPLEWELL b: 26 Oct 1969 in of, Dallas, Co, Tx
...............................11 Jeanne Ruth POPPLEWELL b: 05 Aug 1947 in of, Dallas, Co, Tx
    + Dennis Lee RHOTEN b: Abt. 1964 in of, Dallas, Co, Tx, m: 05 Aug 1966 in of,
Dallas, Tx
...................................12 Lance Eric RHOTEN b: 16 Dec 1968 in of, Dallas, Co, Tx
...................................12 Wesley Wade RHOTEN b: 23 Sep 1972 in of, Dallas, Co, Tx
...................................12 Jody Lee RHOTEN b: 15 Jun 1974 in of, Dallas, Co, Tx
    + Edgar W McCollum b: Abt. 1890 in RICHARDSON, Dallas, Co, Tx, d: Feb 1971 in
RICHARDSON, Dallas, Co, Tx; Y
...........................9 Irene HUFFHINES b: 28 Aug 1892 in of, Dallas, Co, Tx
    + Lawrence Lee WHITE b: 04 Aug 1897 in of, Dallas, Co, Tx, m: 09 Sep 1914 in of,
Dallas, Tx
...............................10 Lawrence Lee jr WHITE b: 26 Aug 1915, d: killed, WW II; Y
    + Cleo JOHNSON b: 10 Aug 1915 in of, Dallas, Co, Tx, m: 27 Dec 1937 in of, Dallas,
Tx
...................................11 Barbara Ann WHITE b: 22 Oct 1938 in of, Dallas, Co, Tx
...............................10 Arthur Christopher WHITE b: 16 Jun 1922
    + Dorothy Jean GRATIGNY b: 18 Apr 1935 in Dallas, Dallas, Co, Tx, m: 28 Jun 1960
in Dallas, Dallas, Co, Tx
...................................11 Margaret Ann WHITE b: 10 Jul 1963 in Dallas, Dallas, Co, Tx
...................................11 Nancy Lee WHITE b: 31 May 1965 in Dallas, Dallas, Co, Tx
...........................9 Royce HUFFHINES b: 03 Jan 1894 in of, Dallas, Co, Tx, d: 15 Nov 1974 in of, Dallas,
Co, Tx; Y
    + Clara Maude WRIGHT b: Abt. 1888 in of, Dallas, Co, Tx, m: 1966 in widow, brother
    + Nora BELL LANE b: 19 Feb 1893 in RICHARDSON, Dallas, Co, Tx, m: 12 Dec 1914
in RICHARDSON, Dallas, Co, Tx, d: 02 Sep 1966 in RICHARDSON, Dallas, Co, Tx;
Y
...............................10 Fredna Pauline HUFFHINES b: 22 Oct 1916 in RICHARDSON, Dallas, Co, Tx
    + James Edward BOSWELL b: 30 Aug 1906 in of, Dallas, Co, Tx, m: 16 Sep 1937 in
of, Dallas, Co, Tx
...................................11 Patsey Sue BOSWELL b: 28 Sep 1939 in Dallas, Dallas, Co, Tx
...............................10 Charles Quita HUFFHINES b: 17 May 1919 in RICHARDSON, Dallas, Co, Tx
    + Charles GLENN BAKER b: 10 Dec 1915 in Noble, Okla, m: 25 Apr 1942 in of,
Dallas, Co, Tx
...................................11 Cathey Annette BAKER b: 03 Jan 1949 in Dallas, Dallas, Co, Tx
...................................11 Reginald GLENN BAKER b: 02 Feb 1951 in Dallas, Dallas, Co, Tx
    + Tanya McGuire b: 20 Nov 1951 in Dallas, Dallas, Co, Tx, m: 07 Dec 1973 in of,
Dallas, Co, Tx
...................................11 Schari Doreene BAKER b: 13 Apr 1958 in Dallas, Dallas, Co, Tx
...............................10 Malva Doren HUFFHINES b: 13 Apr 1921 in RICHARDSON, Dallas, Co, Tx
    + William Ward AYCOCK b: 15 Jul 1915 in Durant, Ok, m: 22 Sep 1939 in of, Dallas,
Co, Tx

...................10 Royce jr HUFFHINES b: 17 Jan 1923 in RICHARDSON, Dallas, Co, Tx
...................10 R L HUFFHINES b: 14 Aug 1930 in Gordonville, Dallas, Co, Tx
...................10 Parthenia Ann HUFFHINES b: 04 Oct 1937 in Grayson, Co, Tx
+ Bobby Gene LEMONS b: 16 Feb 1933 in Cooke, Co, Tx, m: 20 Mar 1953 in Durant, Ok
...................11 Ronald Gene LEMONS b: 31 Jul 1955 in Ft Worth, Tarrent, Tx
...................11 Belinda Michele LEMONS b: 28 Apr 1958 in Houma, LA
...................11 Sherry Denise LEMONS b: 28 May 1962 in Franklin, LA
...................9 Fannie Mae HUFFHINES b: 06 Jun 1897 in of, Dallas, Co, Tx
+ Charlie HUFFHINES m: 01 Apr 1932 in RICHARDSON, Dallas, Co, Tx
...................9 John S HUFFHINES Little Major b: 25 Feb 1900 in of, Dallas, Co, Tx, d: 20 Aug 1970 in Temple, Tx; Y
+ Ola Mae CHRISTIE b: 19 Nov 1902 in of, Dallas, Co, Tx
...................10 Mary Eunice HUFFHINES b: 11 Feb 1924 in of, Dallas, Co, Tx
+ J W MORROW b: 30 May 1922 in of, Dallas, Co, Tx, m: 25 Apr 1942 in RICHARDSON, Dallas, Co, Tx
...................11 Larry Edward MORROW b: 27 Feb 1946 in of, Dallas, Co, Tx
+ Nancy Gayle MASSEY b: 10 Jan 1948 in of, Dallas, Co, Tx, m: 27 Jan 1967
...................12 Eric Vincent MORROW b: 21 Dec 1967 in of, Dallas, Co, Tx
...................12 Lisa Dawn MORROW b: 30 May 1969 in of, Dallas, Co, Tx
...................11 Paul Dwayne MORROW b: 14 Apr 1947 in of, Dallas, Co, Tx
+ Janet Marie MAZINSKI b: 18 Apr 1948 in of, Dallas, Co, Tx, m: 20 Apr 1968 in RICHARDSON, Dallas, Co, Tx
...................12 Christopher Bart MORROW b: 29 Jan 1969 in of, Dallas, Co, Tx
...................12 Aaron James MORROW b: 02 Oct 1975 in of, Dallas, Co, Tx
...................11 Robert Lee MORROW b: 26 Nov 1951 in of, Dallas, Co, Tx
+ Karen EVANS b: 18 Mar 1955 in of, Dallas, Co, Tx, m: 14 Jun 1975 in of, Dallas, Co, Tx
...................10 Donald Ray HUFFHINES b: 18 Dec 1927 in of, Dallas, Co, Tx
+ Eunice Marie BULLS b: 12 Sep 1931 in of, Dallas, Co, Tx, m: 21 Dec 1947 in of, Dallas, Co, Tx
...................11 Stephen Wayne HUFFHINES b: 05 Jul 1948 in of, Dallas, Co, Tx
+ Wanda WARE b: Abt. 01 Feb 1950 in of, Dallas, Co, Tx, m: 27 Jun 1967 in of, Dallas, Co, Tx
...................12 Anthony Heath HUFFHINES b: 03 Mar 1971 in of, Dallas, Co, Tx
...................12 Jason Wayne HUFFHINES b: 10 Mar 1973 in of, Dallas, Co, Tx
...................11 Donna Marie HUFFHINES b: 25 Oct 1951 in of, Dallas, Co, Tx
+ Mike JOHNSON b: Abt. 1949 in of, Dallas, Co, Tx, m: 22 May 1976 in of, Dallas, Co, Tx
...................11 David Bruce HUFFHINES b: 16 Jan 1955 in of, Dallas, Co, Tx
+ Paula Van Winkle b: 07 Mar 1956 in of, Dallas, Co, Tx, m: 07 Mar 1974 in of, Dallas, Co, Tx
...................11 Mark Alan HUFFHINES b: 10 Dec 1956 in of, Dallas, Co, Tx
+ Deborah Lynn URBANOSKY b: Abt. 1958 in of, Dallas, Co, Tx, m: 21 Dec 1974 in of, Dallas, Co, Tx
...................11 Kenneth Ray HUFFHINES b: 12 Jun 1963 in of, Dallas, Co, Tx
...................10 Minnie Ethyl HUFFHINES b: 28 Jan 1931 in of, Dallas, Co, Tx
+ Harold B Lancaster b: 04 Apr 1921 in of, Dallas, Co, Tx, m: 10 Dec 1948 in of, Dallas, Co, Tx
...................11 Dennis Harold Lancaster b: 19 Dec 1955 in of, Dallas, Co, Tx
...................11 Jerry Neil Lancaster b: 25 Mar 1958 in of, Dallas, Co, Tx
...................9 Ophie Chick HUFFHINES b: 19 Feb 1901 in of, Dallas, Co, Tx
+ Charles Grady SMITH b: 10 Sep 1896 in Leanon, Tenn, m: 20 Nov 1919 in RICHARDSON, Dallas, Co, Tx
...................10 Charles Richard SMITH b: 24 Sep 1920 in RICHARDSON, Dallas, Co, Tx

+ Rose Ann Julian b: 15 Oct 1919 in Addison, Dallas, Co, Tx, m: 11 Mar 1944 in RICHARDSON, Dallas, Co, Tx
.............11 Charles Julian SMITH b: 14 Apr 1947 in Carrollton, Tx
..........10 Jane Elizabeth SMITH b: 17 Sep 1922 in RICHARDSON, Dallas, Co, Tx
+ Edgar Wilton COWLING b: 23 Feb 1920 in RICHARDSON, Dallas, Co, Tx, m: 25 Sep 1945 in RICHARDSON, Dallas, Co, Tx
.............11 Harriet Jane COWLING b: 17 Jul 1950 in RICHARDSON, Dallas, Co, Tx
+ David Paul GARRISON b: 03 Dec 1949 in RICHARDSON, Dallas, Co, Tx, m: 20 Jul 1968 in RICHARDSON, Dallas, Co, Tx
.............12 Wendy Gale GARRISON b: 03 Sep 1973 in Denton, Tx
.............11 Edgar Wilton jr COWLING b: 29 Jun 1951 in Bridgeport, Tx
+ Candice Sue BOWERS b: 08 Jan 1952 in of, Dallas, Co, Tx, m: 13 May 1973 in RICHARDSON, Dallas, Co, Tx
.............11 Grady Lee COWLING b: 23 Jun 1954 in Bridgeport, Tx
+ Rhonda Gail Green b: 29 Dec 1955 in of, Dallas, Co, Tx, m: 03 Aug 1974 in of, Dallas, Co, Tx
.............11 Phylis Ann COWLING b: 17 Aug 1961 in of, Bridgeport, Tx
..........9 GLENN HUFFHINES b: 21 Jul 1903 in of, Dallas, Co, Tx
+ Olena CYPHER b: Abt. 1905 in of, Dallas, Co, Tx
+ Ethyl b: Abt. 1922 in of, NY, Tx, m: 03 Apr 1942
..........10 Diane Darby HUFFHINES b: 28 Jul 1943 in Buffalo, NY
+ Gerald Raymond SANTWIRE b: Abt. 1941 in of, Bothel, Wa, m: 30 Jul 1971
.............11 Ryan GLENN SANTWIRE b: 15 Apr 1968 in Seattle, King, Wa
.............11 Renee Gerene SANTWIRE b: 17 Nov 1971 in Bellevue, King, Wa
..........9 Verna Louise HUFFHINES b: 18 Jul 1907 in of, Dallas, Co, Tx
+ Virgil ALLEN PISTOLE b: Abt. 1905 in of, Dallas, Co, Tx, m: 16 Feb 1907 in of, Dallas, Co, Tx
..........10 Sarah Elizabeth PISTOLE b: 26 Feb 1939 in of, Houston, Tx
+ LOUIS B jr BARKLEY b: 12 Jul 1936 in Lubbock, Tx, m: 02 Aug 1961 in Tx
.............11 LOUIS B III BARKLEY b: 23 Jun 1970 in Fort Hood, Tx
.............11 David Alan BARKLEY b: 17 Jun 1974 in Houston, Tx
..........10 Dorothy Allene PISTOLE b: 14 Apr 1940 in of, Dallas, Co, Tx
+ James Ivory EDLIN b: Abt. 1938 in of, Amarillo, Tx, m: 14 Jun 1958 in Amarillo, Tx
.............11 Kathryn Marie EDLIN b: 07 Aug 1959 in Amarillo, Tx
.............11 Cynthia Anne EDLIN b: 11 Aug 1961 in Amarillo, Tx
.............11 James Ivory II EDLIN b: 25 Dec 1964 in Amarillo, Tx
..........9 Raymond Earl HUFFHINES b: 04 Feb 1912 in of, Dallas, Co, Tx, d: 07 Aug 1912 in child, Dallas, Co, Tx; Y
..........8 Winfield SCOTT HUFFHINES b: 28 May 1858 in Dallas, Co, Tx, d: 17 Dec 1939 in RICHARDSON, Dallas, Co, Tx; Y
+ Frances Ann Fannie HARRIS b: 02 Jul 1867 in SIMPSON, Co, Ky, m: 20 Dec 1883 in Dallas, Co, Tx, d: 13 Dec 1902 in Godley, JOHNSON, Co, Tx; Y
..........9 Clarence Lester HUFFHINES minister b: 20 Jul 1886 in RICHARDSON, Dallas, Co, Tx, d: 17 Dec 1918 in Nicholasville, Ky; Y
+ Mabel ALLEN b: 12 Apr 1884 in RICHARDSON, Dallas, Co, Tx, m: 05 May 1909 in RICHARDSON, Dallas, Co, Tx, d: 11 May 1927 ; Y
..........10 LEONARD ALLEN HUFFHINES Lawyer b: 08 Oct 1911 in Ennis, Tx
+ Noma HARRIS m: 11 Sep 1940 in RICHARDSON, Dallas, Co, Tx
..........10 Clifford Lester HUFFHINES b: 13 May 1912 in Ennis, Tx
+ Josephine Klutts OWENS m: 14 Feb 1958 in RICHARDSON, Dallas, Co, Tx
..........10 Elsie May HUFFHINES b: 02 Sep 1915 in Rose Hill, Ky
+ John W Stanford b: 08 Nov 1901 in Dallas, Dallas, Co, Tx, m: 02 Sep 1935 in RICHARDSON, Dallas, Co, Tx, d: 30 Dec 1955 in Dallas, Dallas, Co, Tx; Y
.............11 Jerry Ann Stanford b: 03 Aug 1936 in Dallas, Dallas, Co, Tx

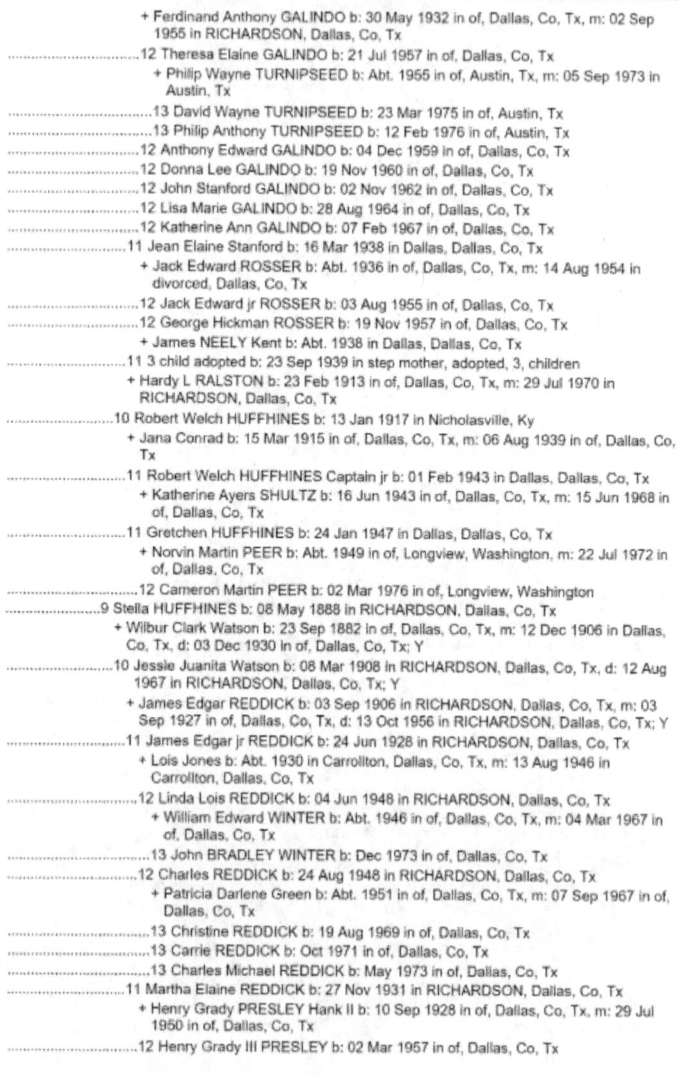

+ Ferdinand Anthony GALINDO b: 30 May 1932 in of, Dallas, Co, Tx, m: 02 Sep 1955 in RICHARDSON, Dallas, Co, Tx

............12 Theresa Elaine GALINDO b: 21 Jul 1957 in of, Dallas, Co, Tx

+ Philip Wayne TURNIPSEED b: Abt. 1955 in of, Austin, Tx, m: 05 Sep 1973 in Austin, Tx

............13 David Wayne TURNIPSEED b: 23 Mar 1975 in of, Austin, Tx

............13 Philip Anthony TURNIPSEED b: 12 Feb 1976 in of, Austin, Tx

............12 Anthony Edward GALINDO b: 04 Dec 1959 in of, Dallas, Co, Tx

............12 Donna Lee GALINDO b: 19 Nov 1960 in of, Dallas, Co, Tx

............12 John Stanford GALINDO b: 02 Nov 1962 in of, Dallas, Co, Tx

............12 Lisa Marie GALINDO b: 28 Aug 1964 in of, Dallas, Co, Tx

............12 Katherine Ann GALINDO b: 07 Feb 1967 in of, Dallas, Co, Tx

............11 Jean Elaine Stanford b: 16 Mar 1938 in Dallas, Dallas, Co, Tx

+ Jack Edward ROSSER b: Abt. 1936 in of, Dallas, Co, Tx, m: 14 Aug 1954 in divorced, Dallas, Co, Tx

............12 Jack Edward jr ROSSER b: 03 Aug 1955 in of, Dallas, Co, Tx

............12 George Hickman ROSSER b: 19 Nov 1957 in of, Dallas, Co, Tx

+ James NEELY Kent b: Abt. 1938 in Dallas, Dallas, Co, Tx

............11 3 child adopted b: 23 Sep 1939 in step mother, adopted, 3, children

+ Hardy L RALSTON b: 23 Feb 1913 in of, Dallas, Co, Tx, m: 29 Jul 1970 in RICHARDSON, Dallas, Co, Tx

............10 Robert Welch HUFFHINES b: 13 Jan 1917 in Nicholasville, Ky

+ Jana Conrad b: 15 Mar 1915 in of, Dallas, Co, Tx, m: 06 Aug 1939 in of, Dallas, Co, Tx

............11 Robert Welch HUFFHINES Captain jr b: 01 Feb 1943 in Dallas, Dallas, Co, Tx

+ Katherine Ayers SHULTZ b: 16 Jun 1943 in of, Dallas, Co, Tx, m: 15 Jun 1968 in of, Dallas, Co, Tx

............11 Gretchen HUFFHINES b: 24 Jan 1947 in Dallas, Dallas, Co, Tx

+ Norvin Martin PEER b: Abt. 1949 in of, Longview, Washington, m: 22 Jul 1972 in of, Dallas, Co, Tx

............12 Cameron Martin PEER b: 02 Mar 1976 in of, Longview, Washington

............9 Stella HUFFHINES b: 08 May 1888 in RICHARDSON, Dallas, Co, Tx

+ Wilbur Clark Watson b: 23 Sep 1882 in of, Dallas, Co, Tx, m: 12 Dec 1906 in Dallas, Co, Tx, d: 03 Dec 1930 in of, Dallas, Co, Tx; Y

............10 Jessie Juanita Watson b: 08 Mar 1908 in RICHARDSON, Dallas, Co, Tx, d: 12 Aug 1967 in RICHARDSON, Dallas, Co, Tx; Y

+ James Edgar REDDICK b: 03 Sep 1906 in RICHARDSON, Dallas, Co, Tx, m: 03 Sep 1927 in of, Dallas, Co, Tx, d: 13 Oct 1956 in RICHARDSON, Dallas, Co, Tx; Y

............11 James Edgar jr REDDICK b: 24 Jun 1928 in RICHARDSON, Dallas, Co, Tx

+ Lois Jones b: Abt. 1930 in Carrollton, Dallas, Co, Tx, m: 13 Aug 1946 in Carrollton, Dallas, Co, Tx

............12 Linda Lois REDDICK b: 04 Jun 1948 in RICHARDSON, Dallas, Co, Tx

+ William Edward WINTER b: Abt. 1946 in of, Dallas, Co, Tx, m: 04 Mar 1967 in of, Dallas, Co, Tx

............13 John BRADLEY WINTER b: Dec 1973 in of, Dallas, Co, Tx

............12 Charles REDDICK b: 24 Aug 1948 in RICHARDSON, Dallas, Co, Tx

+ Patricia Darlene Green b: Abt. 1951 in of, Dallas, Co, Tx, m: 07 Sep 1967 in of, Dallas, Co, Tx

............13 Christine REDDICK b: 19 Aug 1969 in of, Dallas, Co, Tx

............13 Carrie REDDICK b: Oct 1971 in of, Dallas, Co, Tx

............13 Charles Michael REDDICK b: May 1973 in of, Dallas, Co, Tx

............11 Martha Elaine REDDICK b: 27 Nov 1931 in RICHARDSON, Dallas, Co, Tx

+ Henry Grady PRESLEY Hank II b: 10 Sep 1928 in of, Dallas, Co, Tx, m: 29 Jul 1950 in of, Dallas, Co, Tx

............12 Henry Grady III PRESLEY b: 02 Mar 1957 in of, Dallas, Co, Tx

..............................12 Kenneth Wayne PRESLEY b: 17 Feb 1959 in of, Dallas, Co, Tx
..........................11 Sally Sue REDDICK b: 21 Nov 1940 in RICHARDSON, Dallas, Co, Tx
　　　+ James L Buddy Lenamond b: Abt. 1938 in of, Dallas, Co, Tx, m: 28 Mar 1958 in
　　　of, Dallas, Co, Tx
..............................12 Cynthia Kay Lenamond b: 28 Nov 1959 in of, Dallas, Co, Tx
..............................12 James Randall Lenamond BELL b: 05 Jun 1961 in of, Dallas, Co, Tx
　　　+ Joe William BELL b: Abt. 1943 in of, Dallas, Co, Tx, m: 28 Jan 1963 in of, Dallas,
　　　Co, Tx
..............................12 Joe William jr BELL b: 16 Sep 1963 in of, Dallas, Co, Tx
..............................12 Natalie Ann BELL b: 01 Sep 1970 in of, Dallas, Co, Tx
..........................11 Mary Frances REDDICK b: 18 Nov 1942 in RICHARDSON, Dallas, Co, Tx
　　　+ Melvin Ray BELL b: 28 Dec 1940 in of, Dallas, Co, Tx, m: 17 Mar 1962 in of,
　　　Dallas, Co, Tx
..............................12 Lisa Lynn BELL b: 26 Jan 1963 in RICHARDSON, Dallas, Co, Tx
　　　+ Clifford Osten JORDAN b: Abt. 1942 in of, Dallas, Co, Tx, m: 04 Dec 1962 in of,
　　　Dallas, Co, Tx
......................10 Chester Winfield Watson Lawyer b: 25 Sep 1909 in RICHARDSON, Dallas, Co, Tx
　　　+ Ann STARK b: Abt. 1911 in of, Dallas, Co, Tx, m: 01 Jun 1939 in Dallas, Co, Tx
..........................11 Jeannine Watson b: 27 Aug 1941 in Dallas, Dallas, Co, Tx
　　　　+ Lawrence Edward KUHLKEN b: Abt. 1938 in Dallas, Dallas, Co, Tx
..............................12 Julie Vanda KUHLKEN b: 03 Aug 1969 in Dallas, Dallas, Co, Tx
..............................12 David Lawren KUHLKEN b: 02 Sep 1972 in Dallas, Dallas, Co, Tx
......................10 Mary Frances Bunny Watson b: 12 Jul 1911 in RICHARDSON, Dallas, Co, Tx, d:
　　　Jun 1974 in RICHARDSON, Dallas, Co, Tx; Y
　　　+ Virgil McILVAN b: 03 Aug 1908 in of, Dallas, Co, Tx, m: 30 Aug 1930 in Dallas, Co,
　　　Tx
......................10 William Ardrey Watson b: 23 Sep 1922 in RICHARDSON, Dallas, Co, Tx, d: Jun
　　　1974 in of, Dallas, Co, Tx; Y
　　　+ Mary Lee COLLINS b: 28 Oct 1923 in of, Dallas, Co, Tx, m: 12 Jun 1942 in Dallas,
　　　Co, Tx
..........................11 Janet Lee Watson b: 27 Aug 1943 in of, Dallas, Co, Tx
　　　+ John BRUMMIT b: 25 Nov 1940 in of, Dallas, Co, Tx, m: 09 Apr 1960 in Garland,
　　　Tx
..............................12 John Davidson BRUMMIT b: 10 Nov 1963 in of, Dallas, Co, Tx
..............................12 Jennifer Lee BRUMMIT b: 08 Oct 1965 in of, Dallas, Co, Tx
..........................11 William Audrey jr Watson b: 11 Feb 1946 in of, Dallas, Co, Tx
　　　+ Elizabeth McAdams b: Abt. 1948 in of, Dallas, Co, Tx
..............................12 William Audrey III Watson b: 25 Jun 1970 in of, Dallas, Co, Tx
..........................11 Wilbert Watson Watson b: 23 Jun 1947 in of, Dallas, Co, Tx
..........................11 Robert Clifford Watson b: 07 Oct 1949 in of, Dallas, Co, Tx
..........................11 Michael John Elliott Watson b: 15 May 1954 in of, Dallas, Co, Tx
　　　+ WYLIE SMITH b: of, Dallas, Co, Tx, m: 03 Dec 1939 in divorced, Dallas, Co, Tx
..................9 Frank HARRIS HUFFHINES b: 05 Sep 1894 in RICHARDSON, Dallas, Co, Tx, d: 11
　　　Jan 1939 in Athens, Tx; Y
　　　+ Clifford Moses m: 15 Dec 1917 in McKinney, Tx
......................10 Ada Frances HUFFHINES b: 27 Sep 1818 in of, Dallas, Co, Tx, d: 17 Aug 1942 in
　　　of, Dallas, Co, Tx; Y
　　　+ Marvin M RHODES b: Abt. 1816 in of, Dallas, Co, Tx, m: 12 Oct 1934 in of, Dallas,
　　　Co, Tx
..........................11 Marvin HARRIS RHODES b: 25 Oct 1935 in of, Dallas, Co, Tx
　　　+ Suzanne Mitchell b: 23 Apr 1941 in of, Houston, Tx, m: 13 Jun 1959 in Houston,
　　　Tx
..............................12 Elizabeth Ann RHODES b: 28 Nov 1960 in of, Tx
..............................12 Greg Stephen RHODES b: 16 Oct 1961 in of, Tx
..............................12 Greg Stephen RHODES b: 26 Dec 1963 in of, Tx

...................10 William SCOTT HUFFHINES minister b: 05 Jan 1920 in of, Dallas, Co, Tx
          + Doris Vandine McLENDON b: Abt. 1922 in of, Dallas, Tx, m: 03 Apr 1941 in of,
             Dallas, Co, Tx
...................11 Linda Joyce HUFFHINES b: 23 Nov 1942 in of, Dallas, Tx
          + David Bruce TOON b: Abt. 1940 in of, Dallas, Tx, m: 01 Jul 1961 in of, Dallas,
             Co, Tx
...................12 David DOUGLAS TOON b: 29 Jun 1963 in of, Dallas, Tx
...................12 Donna Michelle TOON b: 18 Mar 1965 in of, Dallas, Tx
...................12 John Bruce TOON b: 02 Sep 1970 in of, Dallas, Tx
...................11 William SCOTT jr HUFFHINES b: 21 Aug 1944 in of, Dallas, Tx
          + Charlotte DUNNAVANT b: Abt. 1946 in of, Dallas, Tx, m: 16 Aug 1966 in of,
             Dallas, Co, Tx
...................12 Valerie Gay HUFFHINES b: 23 Jun 1967 in of, Dallas, Tx
...................12 Sunni Gayle HUFFHINES b: 31 May 1972 in of, Dallas, Tx
...................11 Donald Mack HUFFHINES b: 28 Jun 1946 in of, Dallas, Tx
...................11 Joe Lynn HUFFHINES b: 12 Jan 1949 in of, Dallas, Tx
          + Nancy Cullene South b: Abt. 1951 in of, Dallas, Tx, m: 01 Aug 1969 in GILMER,
             Tx
...................12 Cullen SCOTT HUFFHINES b: 29 Dec 1971 in of, Dallas, Tx
...................12 Joel Winfield HUFFHINES b: 02 Jun 1973 in of, Dallas, Tx
...................11 John Mark HUFFHINES b: 29 Aug 1951 in of, Dallas, Tx
          + Patsey HUBBARD b: Abt. 1953 in of, Dallas, Tx, m: 05 Dec 1969 in of, Dallas,
             Co, Tx
...................12 Amy Kay HUFFHINES b: 27 Dec 1974 in of, Dallas, Tx
...................12 Maranda Joyce HUFFHINES b: 17 May 1976 in of, Dallas, Tx
...................9 Vera Frances HUFFHINES b: 09 Apr 1900 in RICHARDSON, Dallas, Co, Tx, d: 20 May
             1976 in RICHARDSON, Dallas, Tx; Y
          + William Statler STRATTON b: 23 Aug 1898 in RICHARDSON, Dallas, Tx, m: 05 Nov
             1919 in RICHARDSON, Dallas, Tx, d: 16 Jan 1975 in RICHARDSON, Dallas, Co, Tx;
             Y
...................10 Stella Frances STRATTON b: 19 Aug 1928 in RICHARDSON, Dallas, Co, Tx
          + Don Lowell BELL b: 29 Sep 1926 in of, Dallas, Co, Tx, m: 06 Jun 1947 in Garland,
             Tx
...................11 Don Lowell jr BELL b: 10 Jul 1948 in of, Dallas, Co, Tx
...................11 William Raymond BELL b: 08 May 1951 in of, Dallas, Co, Tx
          + Donna Lee Martin b: Abt. 1953 in of, Dallas, Co, Tx
          + Vicki Lynn RIDDLE b: Abt. 1953 in of, Dallas, Co, Tx, m: 19 Apr 1969 in Dallas,
             Dallas, Tx
...................12 Monica Lynn BELL b: 07 Sep 1970 in of, Dallas, Co, Tx
...................11 Charles SCOTT BELL b: 11 Aug 1959 in of, Dallas, Co, Tx
...................11 Karen Frances BELL b: 10 Dec 1962 in of, Dallas, Co, Tx
...................10 William Statler II STRATTON b: 05 Sep 1932 in Dallas, Dallas, Tx
          + Margie Louise Lloyd b: Abt. 1934 in of, Dallas, Co, Tx, m: 25 Jun 1955 in Dallas,
             Dallas, Tx
...................11 Gary Dee STRATTON b: 21 Nov 1962 in of, Dallas, Co, Tx
...................11 Shelly Gay STRATTON b: 21 May 1963 in of, Dallas, Co, Tx
          + Alice Brittain b: 12 Sep 1876 in Dallas, Co, Tx, m: 05 Mar 1908 in Kaufman, Tx, d: 1951
             in Dallas, Co, Tx; Y
...................9 Mary Katheryn HUFFHINES b: 17 Dec 1909 in RICHARDSON, Dallas, Co, Tx
          + Weldon STRAWN b: 07 Dec 1907 in RICHARDSON, Dallas, Co, Tx
...................10 Mary Ann STRAWN b: 06 Feb 1934 in RICHARDSON, Dallas, Co, Tx
          + N Jack Oliver Dr b: 28 Nov 1929 in Smithfield, NC, m: 17 Feb 1956 in Houston, Tx
...................11 Sharon May Oliver b: 20 Oct 1957 in of, Tx
...................11 Michael J Oliver b: 21 Apr 1959 in of, Tx
...................11 Cynthia Ann Oliver b: 31 Dec 1962 in of, Tx

...............11 Julie Kathryn Oliver b: 02 Apr 1968 in of, Tx
..............10 Cynthia STRAWN b: 05 Jul 1943 in Milwaukee, Wis
    + Richard SHARP SNELL b: 03 Jul 1942 in of, Dallas, Co, Tx, m: 21 Aug 1965 in of,
    Dallas, Co, Tx
...............11 Richard SHARP jr SNELL b: Dec 1969 in of, Dallas, Co, Tx
...............11 Susan Elizabeth twins SNELL b: 28 Sep 1973 in of, Dallas, Co, Tx
...............11 SCOTT WOOD twins SNELL b: 29 Sep 1973 in of, Dallas, Co, Tx
............9 Brittain W HUFFHINES b: 29 May 1913 in RICHARDSON, Dallas, Co, Tx, d: 23 Sep
    1976 in Dallas, Co, Tx; Y
    + Mary BOWMAN LOVELESS m: 25 Dec 1935 in Plano, Tx
............10 Carol Jeanne HUFFHINES b: 09 Apr 1942 in RICHARDSON, Dallas, Co, Tx
    + Donald Eugene WEBB b: Abt. 1942 in of, Graham, Tx, m: 14 Aug 1965 in Co, Tx
............10 Rosemary HUFFHINES b: 21 Jun 1944 in RICHARDSON, Dallas, Co, Tx
    + Robert Lee KINSEY b: Abt. 1942 in of, Dallas, Co, Tx, m: 23 Aug 1962 in of, Dallas,
    Co, Tx
...............11 Robert Brittain KINSEY b: 01 Jan 1965 in of, Dallas, Co, Tx
...........8 George Washington Huffhines Jr. b: 14 Sep 1859 in Dallas, Dallas County, Texas, d: 01
    Oct 1938 in RICHARDSON, Dallas, Co, Tx; Y
    + Mary WRIGHT b: 11 Apr 1869 in Barren, or, Warren, Ky, m: 17 Oct 1888 in Dallas, Co,
    Tx, d: 07 Aug 1894 in Dallas, Co, Tx; Y
............9 Eula Bess HUFFHINES b: 01 Aug 1891 in RICHARDSON, Dallas, Co, Tx, d: 16 Dec
    1947 in RICHARDSON, Dallas, Co, Tx; Y
    + Oliver HARBEN b: Abt. 1889 in RICHARDSON, Dallas, Co, Tx
............10 Margaret HARBEN b: 03 Jan 1913 in RICHARDSON, Dallas, Co, Tx
    + Lloyd SLATON b: Abt. 1910 in of, Dallas, Co, Tx, m: 18 Nov 1938 in
    RICHARDSON, Dallas, Co, Tx, d: 16 Mar 1965 in of, Dallas, Co, Tx; Y
............9 Mary WRIGHT HUFFHINES b: 14 May 1894 in RICHARDSON, Dallas, Co, Tx
    + John Henson Jackson b: Abt. 1880 in of, Dallas, Co, Tx, d: 10 Apr 1954 in of, Dallas,
    Co, Tx; Y
............10 Jeanette Jackson b: 12 Jun 1917 in of, Dallas, Co, Tx
    + H. C JOHNSON b: Abt. 1915 in Dallas, Dallas, Tx, m: 08 Sep 1939 in Dallas,
    Dallas, Co, Tx
...............11 Linda Jeanette JOHNSON b: 18 Nov 1944 in Dallas, Dallas, Tx
    + Philip Weston SHARP b: Abt. 1942 in Dallas, Dallas, Tx, m: 10 Aug 1975 in
    Dallas, Dallas, Co, Tx
...............11 Harold Lee JOHNSON b: 29 Jan 1948 in Dallas, Dallas, Tx
    + Kathleen Telitha WILSON b: Abt. 1950 in of, Dallas, Tx
............10 Hazel Elizabeth Jackson b: 10 Dec 1918 in of, Dallas, Co, Tx
    + Raymond C BROUGHTON b: Abt. 1916 in of, Dallas, Tx, m: 06 Jul 1950 in Dallas,
    Dallas, Co, Tx
............10 John Henson jr Jackson b: 30 Sep 1921 in of, Dallas, Co, Tx
    + Beatrice Luella MORGOTCH b: Abt. 1923 in of, Dallas, Tx, m: 02 Sep 1950 in
    Dallas, Dallas, Co, Tx
...............11 Linda Marie Jackson b: 07 Aug 1953 in of, Dallas, Tx
...............11 James DOUGLAS Jackson b: 10 Mar 1957 in of, Dallas, Tx, d: 10 Mar 1957 in
    same day, Dallas, Co, Tx; Y
...............11 Margaret Kay Jackson b: 23 Feb 1960 in of, Dallas, Tx
............10 Everts Earl Jackson b: 30 Sep 1927 in Dallas, Dallas, Tx, d: Aft. 1991 in 311 S.
    Texas, RICHARDSON, Tx, 75081; Y
............10 Patricia Joyce Jackson b: 29 Feb 1932 in Dallas, Dallas, Tx
    + Minnie Estelle FOX b: 28 May 1870 in Denton, Co, Tx, m: 18 Nov 1897 in Lewisville,
    Dallas, Co, Tx, d: 17 Oct 1909 in RICHARDSON, Dallas, Co, Tx; Y
............9 LeElla HUFFHINES b: 10 Aug 1899 in RICHARDSON, Dallas, Co, Tx, d: 12 Oct 1963
    in of, Irvine, Tx; Y
    + Wesley A VEACH b: Abt. 1897 in of, Irvine, Tx

...........................11 Julie Kathryn Oliver b: 02 Apr 1968 in of, Tx
...........................10 Cynthia STRAWN b: 05 Jul 1943 in Milwaukee, Wis
+ Richard SHARP SNELL b: 03 Jul 1942 in of, Dallas, Co, Tx, m: 21 Aug 1965 in of, Dallas, Co, Tx
...........................11 Richard SHARP jr SNELL b: Dec 1969 in of, Dallas, Co, Tx
...........................11 Susan Elizabeth twins SNELL b: 28 Sep 1973 in of, Dallas, Co, Tx
...........................11 SCOTT WOOD twins SNELL b: 29 Sep 1973 in of, Dallas, Co, Tx
...........................9 Brittain W HUFFHINES b: 29 May 1913 in RICHARDSON, Dallas, Co, Tx, d: 23 Sep 1976 in Dallas, Co, Tx; Y
+ Mary BOWMAN LOVELESS m: 25 Dec 1935 in Plano, Tx
...........................10 Carol Jeanne HUFFHINES b: 09 Apr 1942 in RICHARDSON, Dallas, Co, Tx
+ Donald Eugene WEBB b: Abt. 1942 in of, Graham, Tx, m: 14 Aug 1965 in Co, Tx
...........................10 Rosemary HUFFHINES b: 21 Jun 1944 in RICHARDSON, Dallas, Co, Tx
+ Robert Lee KINSEY b: Abt. 1942 in of, Dallas, Co, Tx, m: 23 Aug 1962 in of, Dallas, Co, Tx
...........................11 Robert Brittain KINSEY b: 01 Jan 1965 in of, Dallas, Co, Tx
...........................8 George Washington Huffhines Jr. b: 14 Sep 1859 in Dallas, Dallas County, Texas, d: 01 Oct 1938 in RICHARDSON, Dallas, Co, Tx; Y
+ Mary WRIGHT b: 11 Apr 1869 in Barren, or, Warren, Ky, m: 17 Oct 1888 in Dallas, Co, Tx, d: 07 Aug 1894 in Dallas, Co, Tx; Y
...........................9 Eula Bess HUFFHINES b: 01 Aug 1891 in RICHARDSON, Dallas, Co, Tx, d: 16 Dec 1947 in RICHARDSON, Dallas, Co, Tx; Y
+ Oliver HARBEN b: Abt. 1889 in RICHARDSON, Dallas, Co, Tx
...........................10 Margaret HARBEN b: 03 Jan 1913 in RICHARDSON, Dallas, Co, Tx
+ Lloyd SLATON b: Abt. 1910 in of, Dallas, Co, Tx, m: 18 Nov 1938 in RICHARDSON, Dallas, Co, Tx, d: 16 Mar 1965 in of, Dallas, Co, Tx; Y
...........................9 Mary WRIGHT HUFFHINES b: 14 May 1894 in RICHARDSON, Dallas, Co, Tx
+ John Henson Jackson b: Abt. 1880 in of, Dallas, Co, Tx, d: 10 Apr 1954 in of, Dallas, Co, Tx; Y
...........................10 Jeanette Jackson b: 12 Jun 1917 in of, Dallas, Co, Tx
+ H. C JOHNSON b: Abt. 1915 in Dallas, Dallas, Tx, m: 08 Sep 1939 in Dallas, Dallas, Co, Tx
...........................11 Linda Jeanette JOHNSON b: 18 Nov 1944 in Dallas, Dallas, Tx
+ Philip Weston SHARP b: Abt. 1942 in Dallas, Dallas, Tx, m: 10 Aug 1975 in Dallas, Dallas, Co, Tx
...........................11 Harold Lee JOHNSON b: 29 Jan 1948 in Dallas, Dallas, Tx
+ Kathleen Telitha WILSON b: Abt. 1950 in of, Dallas, Tx
...........................10 Hazel Elizabeth Jackson b: 10 Dec 1918 in of, Dallas, Co, Tx
+ Raymond C BROUGHTON b: Abt. 1916 in of, Dallas, Tx, m: 06 Jul 1950 in Dallas, Dallas, Co, Tx
...........................10 John Henson jr Jackson b: 30 Sep 1921 in of, Dallas, Co, Tx
+ Beatrice Luella MORGOTCH b: Abt. 1923 in of, Dallas, Tx, m: 02 Sep 1950 in Dallas, Dallas, Co, Tx
...........................11 Linda Marie Jackson b: 07 Aug 1953 in of, Dallas, Tx
...........................11 James DOUGLAS Jackson b: 10 Mar 1957 in of, Dallas, Tx, d: 10 Mar 1957 in same day, Dallas, Co, Tx; Y
...........................11 Margaret Kay Jackson b: 23 Feb 1960 in of, Dallas, Tx
...........................10 Everts Earl Jackson b: 30 Sep 1927 in Dallas, Dallas, Tx, d: Aft. 1991 in 311 S. Texas, RICHARDSON, Tx, 75081; Y
...........................10 Patricia Joyce Jackson b: 29 Feb 1932 in Dallas, Dallas, Tx
+ Minnie Estelle FOX b: 28 May 1870 in Denton, Co, Tx, m: 18 Nov 1897 in Lewisville, Dallas, Co, Tx, d: 17 Oct 1909 in RICHARDSON, Dallas, Co, Tx; Y
...........................9 LeElla HUFFHINES b: 10 Aug 1899 in RICHARDSON, Dallas, Co, Tx, d: 12 Oct 1963 in of, Irvine, Tx; Y
+ Wesley A VEACH b: Abt. 1897 in of, Irvine, Tx

...............8 Mattie Arwin Jasper b: Jul 1871 in Dallas, Co., Tx, d: 1901 in Dallas, Dallas, Tx; Y
                    + Robert Lee Chick b: 1864 in Dallas, Co., Tx, m: Abt. 1890 in Dallas, Co, Tx, d: 11 Mar
                       1940 in age 76, Dallas, Tx; Y
...............9 Audrey Lee McCollum Chick b: 1891 in Washburn, Tx
                       + Edgar McCollum b: Abt. 1890 in of, RICHARDSON, Tx, m: 1910 in RICHARDSON,
                          Tx
...............10 child McCollum b: Abt. 1912 in of, RICHARDSON, Tx, d: Bef. 1929 in child; Y
...............10 child McCollum b: Abt. 1915 in of, RICHARDSON, Tx, d: Bef. 1929 in child; Y
...............9 Willie Mae Chick b: Abt. 1894 in of, Dallas
                       + Roy DALTON
...............9 LESLIE e Chick b: of, Dallas
...............9 Jack W Chick b: of, Dallas
...............9 GORDON R Chick b: of, Dallas
...............7 Larkin. WILSON b: 1832 in census, Simpson Co., 1850, Ky
...............7 Samuel Lee WILSON b: 08 Jan 1832 in Simpson Co., Ky, d: 31 Dec 1865 in Simpson Co.,
                    Ky; Y
...............7 Winnie Melvina WILSON b: 06 Jan 1834 in Simpson Co., Ky, d: 04 Nov 1865 in Simpson
                    Co., Ky; Y
                    + William Newton. PISTOLE b: 17 Jul 1834 in Smith Co., Tn of, Simpson Co., Ky, m: 17
                       Sep 1857 in Franklin, SIMPSON, Ky, d: 21 Aug 1895 in Simpson Co., Ky.; Y
...............8 Samuel William PISTOLE b: 01 Jul 1858 in Simpson Co., Ky., d: 1929 in Seymour, Baylor
                    County, TX; Y
                    + Martha Ann Mattie Harris b: Apr 1865 in Pilot Knob, Simpson Co., Ky, m: Abt. 1888
...............9 Eschol Harris PISTOLE b: Sep 1887, d: 1918 in accidentally shot himself, Seymour,
                    Baylor County, TX; Y
                    + Lorina DEATS b: Ky
...............10 Harry PISTOLE b: 12 Oct 1916 in Seymour, Baylor County, TX, d: 10 Sep 1979 in
                    Houston, Harris Co., Texas; Y
...............8 Mary A. PISTOLE b: 28 Mar 1861 in Simpson Co., Ky., d: 09 Apr 1964 in Simpson Co.,
                    Ky.; Y
...............8 Lucy Ann PISTOLE b: 16 Dec 1864 in Simpson Co., Ky., d: 11 Aug 1897 in Simpson Co.,
                    Ky.; Y
...............8 Angie Lucy PISTOLE b: 25 Jul 1865 in Simpson Co., Ky, d: 04 Jul 1952 ; Y
                    + James Isaac DENNIS b: 30 Mar 1862, m: Abt. 1885
...............7 Louisa WILSON b: 1835 in 1840, census, SIMPSON, Co.
                    + Aspley
...............7 Henry Jason Jackson WILSON b: 05 Jul 1837 in Simpson Co., Ky, d: 02 Sep 1916 in
                    Simpson Co., Ky; Y
                    + Lou Ella TRIBBLE b: 1851 in Simpson Co., Ky, m: 20 Sep 1875 in Franklin, SIMPSON,
                       Ky, d: 1928 in Simpson Co., Ky.; Y
...............8 Clarence WILSON b: Oct 1876 in Simpson Co., Ky., d: 1953 in Simpson Co., Ky.; Y
...............8 Ivan WILSON b: Nov 1881 in Simpson Co., Ky., d: 1953 in Simpson Co., Ky.; Y
...............8 Bertha WILSON b: Dec 1882 in Simpson Co., Ky., d: 1967 in Simpson Co., Ky.; Y
...............7 Martha Jane WILSON b: 02 Oct 1839 in Simpson Co., Ky, d: 13 Feb 1914 in Pilot Knob,
                    Simpson Co., Ky; Y
                    + Vernal King Reeder b: 10 Mar 1844 in Simpson Co., Ky, m: 1864 in Franklin, SIMPSON,
                       Ky, d: 07 Aug 1913 in Pilot Knob, Simpson Co., Ky; Y
...............8 Reeder b: 28 Aug 1865 in Pilot Knob, Simpson Co., Ky, d: 28 Aug 1865 in Pilot Knob,
                    Simpson Co., Ky; Y
...............8 Henry J Reeder b: 30 Aug 1866 in Pilot Knob, Simpson Co., Ky, d: 13 Jul 1927 in
                    Simpson Co., Ky.; Y
                    + Massie C b: 12 Nov 1865 in Simpson Co., Ky., d: 27 Aug 1938 in Simpson Co., Ky.; Y
...............8 Samuel Thomas Reeder b: Abt. 1868 in Pilot Knob, Simpson Co., Ky, d: Abt. 1868 in
                    Same year, Simpson CO., Ky; Y

.................8 Mary Louella Reeder b: 22 Jul 1871 in Pilot Knob, Simpson Co., Ky, d: 21 Jun 1898 in Simpson Co., Ky.; Y

+ James STAGNER b: 10 Jul 1851 in Simpson Co., Ky., d: 07 Oct 1913 in Simpson Co., Ky.; Y

.................8 Laura Jane Reeder b: 1873 in Pilot Knob, Simpson Co., Ky, d: 1946 in Simpson Co., Ky.; Y

+ William Sanford ROANK b: 1869 in Simpson Co., Ky., d: 1939 in Simpson Co., Ky.; Y

.................8 Charles K Reeder b: 03 Mar 1875 in Pilot Knob, Simpson Co., Ky, d: 03 Jun 1925 in Simpson Co., Ky.; Y

.................8 Florence E Reeder b: Nov 1877 in Pilot Knob, Simpson Co., Ky, d: 1960 in Simpson Co., Ky.; Y

.................8 Joseph Vinson "Vince" Reeder b: 12 Feb 1879 in Pilot Knob, Simpson Co., Ky, d: 05 Aug 1956 in Simpson Co., Ky.; Y

.................8 Pelhari Lewis "Lowie" Reeder b: Nov 1880 in Pilot Knob, Simpson Co., Ky

.................8 Maggie L "Leona" Reeder b: 1884 in Pilot Knob, Simpson Co., Ky, d: 1964 in Simpson Co., Ky.; Y

+ James Clark Pistole b: 03 Apr 1836 in Smith Co., TN, m: 01 Aug 1859 in Simpson Co., Ky, d: 17 Feb 1930 ; Y

.................7 John M. WILSON b: 14 Aug 1844 in Simpson Co., Ky, d: 19 May 1921 in Dallas, Dallas, Tx; Y

+ America E. STAHL b: 19 Oct 1850 in Simpson Co., Ky, m: Franklin, SIMPSON, Ky, d: 23 Dec 1915 in Dallas. Dallas Co., TX; Y

.................8 Vinson WILSON b: Sep 1864 in Simpson Co., Ky., d: 13 Oct 1917 in Dallas. Dallas Co., TX; Y

+ Priscilla

.................8 Amanda Belle WILSON b: Abt. 1866 in Simpson Co., Ky.

.................8 Edna Myrtle WILSON b: 19 May 1874 in Ky, d: 18 Jul 1961 in San Antonio, Tx; Y

+ BYRD

+ J.E. Boyd b: Abt. 1870 in of Dallas. Dallas Co., TX

.................8 John Ellington WILSON b: Jan 1878 in Simpson Co., Ky.

.................8 Edgar L WILSON b: 1880 in Simpson Co., Ky.

.................8 Claude WILSON b: 1880 in Simpson Co., Ky.

+ Maud b: 1883 in of Dallas. Dallas Co., TX, d: 1960 in of Dallas. Dallas Co., TX; Y

.................8 Opha CLyde WILSON b: 01 Nov 1887 in Dallas. Dallas Co., TX, d: 14 Jul 1967 in Dallas. Dallas Co., TX; Y

+ P.W. Brooks b: Abt. 1885 in of Dallas. Dallas Co., TX

+ Ross C HEATH b: 16 Aug 1885 in of Dallas. Dallas Co., TX, d: 25 Jul 1962 in Dallas. Dallas Co., TX; Y

.................8 Amelia E WILSON

.................7 Perhars Larkin WILSON b: census, Simpson Co., Ky

+ [unknown spouse]

.................8 two sons WILSON b: Abt. 1850 in Simpson Co., Ky

.........4 John Lee Major b: Abt. 1739/40 in Richmond, King and Queen, Co, Va, d: Leesville, Campbell, Co, Va; Y

+ Susannah Guthrie b: Abt. 1735 in of, Cumberland, Campbell, Va, m: Abt. 1765, d: Abt. 1788 in of, Cumberland, Campbell, Va; Y

.............5 Sarah Guthrie Lee b: Abt. 1766 in Campbell, Co, Va

+ Samuel Alexander Lee b: Abt. 1770 in of, Bedford, Campbell, Va, m: 07 Mar 1795 in license 4 March, Campbell, Co, Va, d: Tazewell, Russell, Co, Va; Y

.................6 Elvira Lee b: 1812 in of, Bedford, Campbell, Va

.................6 Elizabeth Lee b: 1820 in of, Bedford, Campbell, Va

.................6 William Lee b: 1825 in of, Bedford, Campbell, Va

.................6 Robert R. Lee b: 08 Mar 1829 in of, Bedford, Campbell, Va, d: Abt. 1858 in Died crossing a river in TN; Y

+ Margaret T. Barber b: 12 Mar 1829 in of Limestone Co., ALABAMA, m: 22 Jul 1849 in Limestone Co., ALABAMA

.............7 Sarah Jane Lee b: 15 Jun 1850 in Limestone Co., ALABAMA

.............7 Nancy Elizabeth Lee b: 08 Jul 1851 in Limestone Co., ALABAMA, d: 27 Sep 1919 in Ellis Co. TX; Y

   + F. H. BRAZIER b: Abt. 1849 in Tn

.............8 son BRAZIER b: Abt. 1873 in Tx

.............8 Charles Alexander BRAZIER b: Abt. 1875 in Tx, d: 1966 in Tx; Y

.............8 son also BRAZIER b: Abt. 1877 in Tx

.............7 Mary Lee b: 1853 in Limestone Co., ALABAMA

...........6 James M. Lee b: 1835 in of, Bedford, Campbell, Va

...........5 Burwell Lee b: Abt. 1767 in Campbell, Co, Va, d: 15 Nov 1825 in Campbell, Co Va; Y

   + Rebecca Nancy (Ann) ARNOLD b: Abt. 1770 in Cumberland Co., VA, m: 06 Sep 1788 in Campbell, Co, Va

...........6 Ann Lee b: Abt. 1794 in Campbell Co., VA

   + John Anderson b: Abt. 1792 in Campbell Co., VA, m: 30 Apr 1828 in Campbell Co., VA

...........6 Susanah G. Lee b: Abt. 1796 in Campbell Co., VA, d: Abt. 1870 in Campbell Co., Va; Y

   + Beverly ARNOLD b: 27 May 1797 in Campbell Co., Va, m: 16 Dec 1822 in Campbell Co., Va, d: May 1862 in Campbell Co., VA; Y

.............7 Alexander A. ARNOLD b: 30 Nov 1823 in Campbell Co., Va

.............7 Fletcher ARNOLD b: 18 May 1834 in Campbell Co., Va

...........6 Burwell Lee Jr. b: Abt. 1800 in Campbell Co., VA, d: 1872 in Pittsylvania Co., Va; Y

   + Matilda Arnold b: 18 Nov 1801 in Campbell Co., VA, m: 25 Mar 1822 in Campbell Co., Va, d: Abt. 1842 in Campbell Co., VA; Y

.............7 Angelina Catherine Lee b: 15 Jun 1823 in Campbell Co., Va

   + Washington Arnold b: 16 Jan 1816 in Oglethorpe Co., GA, m: 09 Oct 1843 in Campbell Co., VA, d: 16 Nov 1898 ; Y

.............7 Martha (Ann) Lee b: Abt. 1828 in Campbell Co., Va

.............7 Edward Price Lee Jr. b: Abt. 1830 in Campbell Co., Va, d: 14 Jul 1864 in Hospital Civil War, Petersburgh, VA; Y

   + Hardinia B. DUKE b: 1833 in Campbell Co., Va, m: 14 Jan 1851 in Campbell Co., Va, d: 1851 in Campbell Co., Va; Y

   + Affiah Susan ARNOLD b: 18 Dec 1827 in Bedford Co., VA, m: 16 Sep 1852 in LaFayette Co., MO

.............8 Anna Florence Lee b: 19 Jun 1853 in near Wellington, MO

   + Barry Clay Collins b: Jul 1841 in in KY, m: 13 Jan 1875 in Lafayette Co., .MO

.............8 Mosby Arnold Lee b: 28 Jul 1855 in Odessa, LaFayette Co., MO

   + Anna (Lydia) B. Jones b: Jan 1863 in in IA, m: 1888

.............9 Hazel Ena Lee b: Feb 1889 in Mo

.............8 Walter Selwyn Lee b: 02 Jun 1857 in Pittsylvania Co., Va

.............8 Edward Price Lee b: 13 Mar 1858 in LaFayette Co., MO

.............8 Eugene Leslie Lee b: 20 Dec 1860 in Pittsylvania Co., Va

   + Mary Laura Keene b: Abt. 1869 in MT, m: 1886 in Canton, Montana

.............9 Harriett Lee b: 1887 in Montana

.............9 Annie Laura Lee b: 1889 in Montana

.............9 Flavius Olin Lee b: Dec 1890 in Near Dernesville, Kalispel, Co., Montana

.............9 Eugene Leslie Lee b: 1892 in Near Dernesville, Kalispel, Co., Montana

.............9 Gertrude May Lee b: 27 Dec 1893 in Townsend, MT

.............9 Jesse W. Lee b: Jun 1895 in Townsend, MT

.............9 daughter Lee b: 24 Dec 1899 in Montana

.............9 Thomas Arnold Lee b: 1903 in Canton, Montana

.............9 Mary Lee b: Abt. 1906 in Montana, d: portland, OR E; Y

   + GALLOWAY

.............8 Gertrude Lee b: 1863 in Pittsylvania Co., Va

.............7 Julianna A. Lee b: Abt. 1832 in Campbell Co., Va

...............7 Jeremiah A. Lee b: 27 Sep 1833 in Campbell Co., Va
+ Medora C. Lee b: 17 May 1846 in MS, m: 30 Dec 1867 in Lafayette Co., MO
...............7 Robert Austin Lee b: 25 Dec 1835 in Campbell Co., Va, d: 16 Apr 1918 in Motley, Pittsylvania Co., VA; Y
+ Martha Kerziah ARNOLD b: 02 Jul 1840 in near Leesville, Campbell Co., Va, m: 02 Jul 1856 in Campbell Co., Va
...............8 Lelia E. Lee b: 13 Sep 1861 in Pittsylvania Co., Va
...............8 Margaret Eudalia "Dolly" Lee b: 25 Sep 1866 in Pittsylvania Co., Va
...............8 Ella V. Lee b: 29 Aug 1869 in Motley, Pittsylvania Co., VA
...............8 Robert Austin Lee Jr. b: 1872 in Motley, Pittsylvania Co., VA, d: 1937 in WVa; Y
+ Lillian Pearl Foster b: Abt. 1872 in NC, m: 26 Dec 1894 in Campbell Co., VA
...............9 Emma P. Lee b: Abt. 1899 in NC
...............9 Russell Lee b: Abt. 1902 in NC
...............9 Robert A. Lee b: Abt. 1904 in NC
...............9 Keziah "Kizzie" Lee b: Abt. 1906 in NC, d: Bef. 1910 in child NC; Y
...............9 Audrey Lee b: Abt. 1908 in NC
...............9 Burdette Lee b: Abt. 1913 in NC
...............9 Jack Lee b: 1915 in NC
...............8 Mary Matilda (Molly) Lee b: Abt. 1875 in Pittsylvania Co., Va
...............7 Chestina Lee b: Abt. 1838 in Campbell Co., Va, d: 18 Sep 1866 in Pittsylvanias Co., VA; Y
+ Elizabeth S. PURCELL b: Abt. 1820 in Bedford Co., VA, m: 27 Nov 1843 in Campbell Co., Va
...............7 Virginia T. Jennie Lee b: Abt. 1845 in Campbell Co., VA, d: 02 Sep 1875 in Pittsylvania Co., VA; Y
...............7 Alonzo H. Lee b: Abt. 1850 in Campbell Co., VA
...............7 Lucy E. Lee b: Apr 1854 in Campbell Co., VA
+ George Austin b: Mar 1848 in Orange Co., VA, m: 13 Jan 1876 in Pittsylvania Co., VA
...............8 Mary Austin b: Jun 1880 in Alabama
+ Mildred (Dillard) Doyle b: 1813 in of Pittsylvanias Co., VA, m: 12 Oct 1857 in Pittsylvanias Co., VA
...............6 Permelia G. Lee b: Abt. 1800 in Campbell Co., VA, d: 1841 in Campbell Co., VA; Y
...............6 Tabitha Lee b: Abt. 1802 in Campbell Co., VA, d: Bef. 02 Dec 1842 in Campbell Co., VA; Y
...............6 Jane Lee b: Abt. 1804 in Campbell Co., VA
+ Caleb Witt b: Abt. 1802 in Campbell Co., VA, m: 26 Sep 1830 in Bedford Co., VA
...............6 Martha Lee b: Abt. 1806 in Campbell Co., VA
+ James Anthony b: Abt. 1795, m: 26 Mar 1820 in Campbell Co., VA
...............6 William A. Lee b: Abt. 1808 in Campbell Co., VA, d: Amherst Co., VA; Y
+ Mildred BROOKS b: Abt. 1807 in Campbell Co., Va, m: 20 Dec 1831 in Campbell Co., Va
...............7 Hezekiah B. LEE b: Abt. 1833 in Campbell Co., Va
+ Jane
...............7 Ann Elizabeth LEE b: 12 Jul 1835 in Campbell Co., Va, d: 15 Sep 1918 ; Y
+ Alexander T. Ward b: 18 Apr 1829 in Campbell Co., VA, m: 01 Oct 1851 in Campbell Co., VA
...............7 Frances Virginia LEE b: Abt. 1837 in Campbell Co., Va
+ William M. Withers b: Abt. 1835 in Campbell Co., VA, m: 30 Nov 1852 in Campbell Co., VA
...............8 Ward A. Withers b: Abt. 1853 in Campbell Co., VA
...............8 L. L. Withers b: Abt. 1855 in Campbell Co., VA
...............7 Sarah A. LEE b: 1843 in Campbell Co., Va
...............7 Cora A. LEE b: Abt. 1847 in Campbell Co., Va
...............7 Mary W. LEE b: Abt. 1849 in Campbell Co., Va
...............7 U. L. D. LEE b: 1851 in Campbell Co., Va
...............6 Doshia A. Lee b: Abt. 1812 in Campbell Co., VA
+ Isaac WILSON b: Abt. 1810 in Campbell Co., Va, m: 15 Dec 1832 in Campbell Co., Va
...............7 Catherine C. WILSON b: Abt. 1833 in Morgan Co., KY

+ Abijah B. WILSON b: Abt. 1824 in Morgan Co. Ky, m: 05 Dec 1848 in Morgan Co. Ky
........8 Mary WILSON b: 1850 in Licking, Morgan Co. Ky
........8 Tabitha WILSON b: 28 Jan 1852 in Licking, Morgan Co. Ky
........8 Anna L. WILSON b: 20 Apr 1853 in Licking, Morgan Co. Ky
........8 William WILSON b: 07 Oct 1855 in Licking, Morgan Co. Ky, d: 04 Apr 1908 in Bath
County, KY; Y
........8 Willard or Millard WILSON b: Abt. 1857 in Licking, Morgan Co. Ky, d: Bef. 1870 in
Morgan Co. Ky; Y
........8 Jeremiah WILSON b: Abt. 1860 in Licking, Morgan Co. Ky
........8 Isaac WILSON b: Abt. 1864 in Licking, Morgan Co. Ky
........8 Lander or Laura WILSON b: Abt. 1870 in Licking, Morgan Co. Ky
........8 Lucinda WILSON b: Abt. 1874 in Licking, Morgan Co. Ky
........7 Sarah Jane WILSON b: Abt. 1834 in Morgan Co., KY
+ Isaiah WILSON b: Abt. 1829 in Morgan Co. Ky, m: 17 Mar 1851 in Morgan Co. Ky
........7 William WILSON b: Abt. 1837 in Morgan Co., KY
........7 Frances WILSON b: Abt. 1842 in Morgan Co., KY, d: 24 Aug 1853 in Lik, Morgan Co. Ky.; Y
........7 Louisa WILSON b: Abt. 1845 in Morgan Co., KY
........7 Jacob WILSON b: Abt. 1847 in Morgan Co., KY
........7 Caroline WILSON b: Abt. 1852 in Morgan Co., KY
........5 Patty Lee b: 14 Aug 1769 in Campbell, Co, Va, d: 16 Jan 1840 in Campbell, Co Va; Y
+ John Arnold b: 08 Aug 1768 in Cumberland Co., VA, m: 19 Dec 1788 in Campbell, Co, Va, d:
20 Feb 1834 in Campbell Co., VA; Y
........6 Mosby Arnold b: 03 Feb 1790 in Campbell, Co, Va, d: 18 Feb 1876 in Lafayette Co., Mo.; Y
+ Ann Dabbs ANDREWS b: 17 Mar 1790 in Bedford Co., VA, m: 02 Sep 1813 in Bedford Co.,
VA, d: 07 Jun 1868 in Lafayette Co., Mo.; Y
........7 Almary Coke Arnold b: 05 Jan 1821 in Bedford Co., VA, d: 31 Oct 1877 in Lafayette Co.,
MO; Y
+ Richard Lee b: 18 Sep 1810 in Campbell Co., Va, m: 05 Dec 1840 in Bedford Co., VA
........8 John Mosby Lee b: 14 Dec 1842 in Campbell Co., VA, d: 19 Feb 1843 in Lynch Station,
Campbell Co., VA; Y
........8 Ethelbert Thomas Lee b: 18 Dec 1843 in Campbell Co., VA
+ Amanda Allen b: 18 Feb 1845 in Lafayette Co., MO, m: 22 Nov 1866 in Lafayette Co.,
MO
........9 Elmore Lee b: May 1863 in Lafayette Co., MO
........9 Edward A. Lee b: Nov 1867 in Lafayette Co., MO
+ Manor S. PAGE b: Sep 1870 in Lafayette Co., MO, m: 09 Sep 1891 in Lafayette Co.,
MO
........10 Sophia M. Lee b: 18 Jan 1893 in Lafayette Co., MO
........10 Marquerite Lee b: 18 Jun 1894 in Lafayette Co., MO
........9 infant girl Lee b: 01 Jun 1869 in Lafayette Co., MO, d: 01 Jun 1869 in Lafayette Co.,
MO; Y
........9 Lucy Lee b: Oct 1873 in Lafayette Co., MO
........8 Medora C. Lee b: 17 May 1846 in MS
+ Jeremiah A. Lee b: 27 Sep 1833 in Campbell Co., Va, m: 30 Dec 1867 in Lafayette Co.,
MO
........8 Anna Eliza Lee b: 26 Sep 1848 in Lafayette Co., MO, d: 03 Sep 1850 in Napoleon,
Lafayette Co., MO; Y
........8 Sarah Virginia Lee b: Abt. 1852 in Lafayette Co., MO, d: 1901 in Bedford Co., VA; Y
+ Edwin James Lee b: 26 Aug 1846 in Bedford Co., VA, m: Abt. 1874
........9 baby boy Lee b: Abt. 1778 in Bedford Co., VA
........9 eleven total see notes unk boy Lee b: Abt. 1875 in Bedford Co., VA
........9 Edwin Cecil Lee b: Mar 1876 in Bedford Co., VA
........9 infant boy Lee b: Abt. 1880 in Bedford Co., VA
........9 Samuel Hunt Lee b: Feb 1882 in Bedford Co., VA
........9 Gilmer Lee b: May 1886 in Bedford Co., VA

....................9 Kirtley Lee b: Jun 1886 in Bedford Co., VA
....................9 Booker Lee b: Aug 1888 in Bedford Co., VA
....................9 Susan Adeline Lee b: Feb 1890 in Bedford Co., VA
....................9 Robert Fitzhugh Lee b: Nov 1891 in Bedford Co., VA
....................9 Carmi Lee b: May 1898 in Bedford Co., VA
....................8 Leila C. Lee b: 28 Sep 1853 in Lafayette Co., MO, d: 26 Feb 1882 in Lafayette Co., MO;
        Y
....................8 Alonzo Hunt Lee b: 18 Jun 1856 in Lafayette Co., MO
....................8 Ida May Lee b: 08 Sep 1858 in Lafayette Co., MO
....................8 Richard Henry Lee b: Abt. 1860 in Lafayette Co., MO
....................8 Clara A. Lee b: 27 Apr 1862 in Lafayette Co., MO, d: 19 Jan 1864 in Lafayette Co., MO;
        Y
....................8 two boy infants Lee b: Lafayette Co., MO
..............6 Elizabeth N. "Betsy" Arnold b: 09 Apr 1791 in Campbell Co., VA, d: 19 Dec 1869 ; Y
..............6 Susannah G. Arnold b: 09 Apr 1791 in Campbell Co., VA
..............6 Sarah G. (Sally) Arnold b: 02 Dec 1792 in Campbell Co., VA
..............6 John Arnold b: 11 Feb 1794 in Campbell Co., VA
..............6 Ann G. (Nancy) Arnold b: 29 Sep 1795 in Campbell Co., VA, d: Pittsylvanias Co., VA; Y
..............6 Beverly ARNOLD b: 27 May 1797 in Campbell Co., Va, d: May 1862 in Campbell Co., VA; Y
      + Susanah G. Lee b: Abt. 1796 in Campbell Co., VA, m: 16 Dec 1822 in Campbell Co., Va, d:
        Abt. 1870 in Campbell Co., Va; Y
....................7 Alexander A. ARNOLD b: 30 Nov 1823 in Campbell Co., Va
....................7 Fletcher ARNOLD b: 18 May 1834 in Campbell Co., Va
..............6 Tabitha Arnold b: 11 Aug 1798 in Campbell Co., VA
..............6 Martha (Patsy) Arnold b: 03 Apr 1800, d: 1883 in Campbell Co., VA; Y
..............6 Matilda Arnold b: 18 Nov 1801 in Campbell Co., VA, d: Abt. 1842 in Campbell Co., VA; Y
      + Burwell Lee Jr. b: Abt. 1800 in Campbell Co., VA, m: 25 Mar 1822 in Campbell Co., Va, d:
        1872 in Pittsylvania Co., Va; Y
....................7 Angelina Catherine Lee b: 15 Jun 1823 in Campbell Co., Va
        + Washington Arnold b: 16 Jan 1816 in Oglethorpe Co., GA, m: 09 Oct 1843 in Campbell
         Co., VA, d: 16 Nov 1898 ; Y
....................7 Martha (Ann) Lee b: Abt. 1828 in Campbell Co., Va
....................7 Edward Price Lee Jr. b: Abt. 1830 in Campbell Co., Va, d: 14 Jul 1864 in Hospital Civil War,
        Petersburgh, VA; Y
        + Hardinia B. DUKE b: 1833 in Campbell Co., Va, m: 14 Jan 1851 in Campbell Co., Va, d:
         1851 in Campbell Co., Va; Y
        + Affiah Susan ARNOLD b: 18 Dec 1827 in Bedford Co., VA, m: 16 Sep 1852 in LaFayette
         Co., MO
....................8 Anna Florence Lee b: 19 Jun 1853 in near Wellington, MO
        + Barry Clay Collins b: Jul 1841 in in KY, m: 13 Jan 1875 in Lafayette Co., .MO
....................8 Mosby Arnold Lee b: 28 Jul 1855 in Odessa, LaFayette Co., MO
        + Anna (Lydia) B. Jones b: Jan 1863 in in IA, m: 1888
....................9 Hazel Ena Lee b: Feb 1889 in Mo
....................8 Walter Selwyn Lee b: 02 Jun 1857 in Pittsylvania Co., Va
....................8 Edward Price Lee b: 13 Mar 1858 in LaFayette Co., MO
....................8 Eugene Leslie Lee b: 20 Dec 1860 in Pittsylvania Co., Va
        + Mary Laura Keene b: Abt. 1869 in MT, m: 1886 in Canton, Montana
....................9 Harriett Lee b: 1887 in Montana
....................9 Annie Laura Lee b: 1889 in Montana
....................9 Flavius Olin Lee b: Dec 1890 in Near Dernesville, Kalispel, Co., Montana
....................9 Eugene Leslie Lee b: 1892 in Near Dernesville, Kalispel, Co., Montana
....................9 Gertrude May Lee b: 27 Dec 1893 in Townsend, MT
....................9 Jesse W. Lee b: Jun 1895 in Townsend, MT
....................9 daughter Lee b: 24 Dec 1899 in Montana
....................9 Thomas Arnold Lee b: 1903 in Canton, Montana

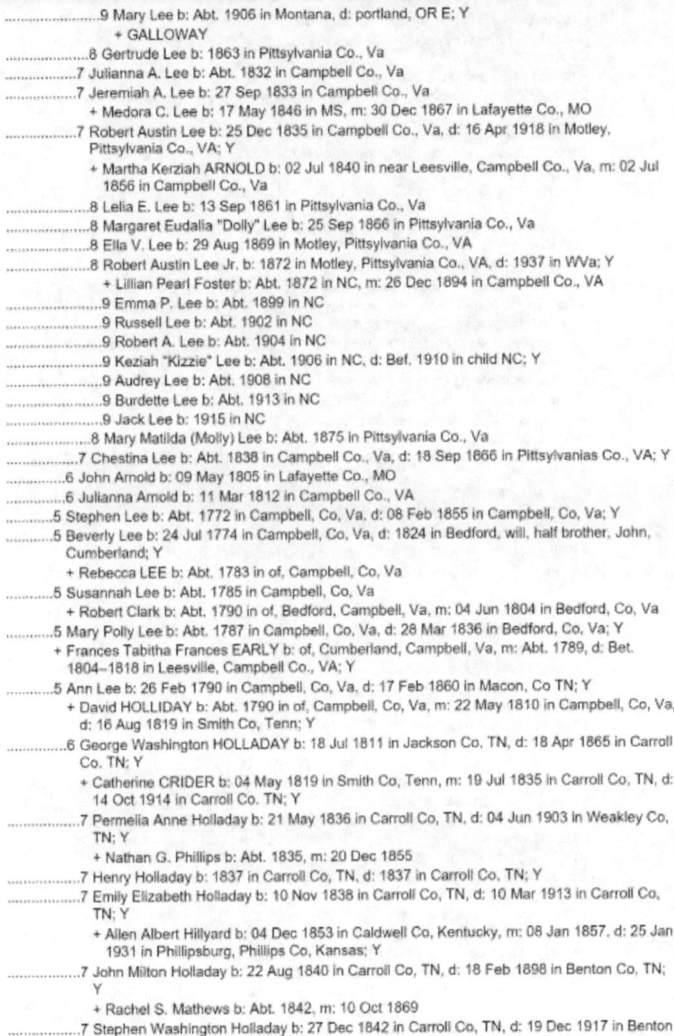

......................9 Mary Lee b: Abt. 1906 in Montana, d: portland, OR E; Y
    + GALLOWAY
......................8 Gertrude Lee b: 1863 in Pittsylvania Co., Va
......................7 Julianna A. Lee b: Abt. 1832 in Campbell Co., Va
......................7 Jeremiah A. Lee b: 27 Sep 1833 in Campbell Co., Va
    + Medora C. Lee b: 17 May 1846 in MS, m: 30 Dec 1867 in Lafayette Co., MO
......................7 Robert Austin Lee b: 25 Dec 1835 in Campbell Co., Va, d: 16 Apr 1918 in Motley, Pittsylvania Co., VA; Y
    + Martha Kerziah ARNOLD b: 02 Jul 1840 in near Leesville, Campbell Co., Va, m: 02 Jul 1856 in Campbell Co., Va
......................8 Lelia E. Lee b: 13 Sep 1861 in Pittsylvania Co., Va
......................8 Margaret Eudalia "Dolly" Lee b: 25 Sep 1866 in Pittsylvania Co., Va
......................8 Ella V. Lee b: 29 Aug 1869 in Motley, Pittsylvania Co., VA
......................8 Robert Austin Lee Jr. b: 1872 in Motley, Pittsylvania Co., VA, d: 1937 in WVa; Y
    + Lillian Pearl Foster b: Abt. 1872 in NC, m: 26 Dec 1894 in Campbell Co., VA
......................9 Emma P. Lee b: Abt. 1899 in NC
......................9 Russell Lee b: Abt. 1902 in NC
......................9 Robert A. Lee b: Abt. 1904 in NC
......................9 Keziah "Kizzie" Lee b: Abt. 1906 in NC, d: Bef. 1910 in child NC; Y
......................9 Audrey Lee b: Abt. 1908 in NC
......................9 Burdette Lee b: Abt. 1913 in NC
......................9 Jack Lee b: 1915 in NC
......................8 Mary Matilda (Molly) Lee b: Abt. 1875 in Pittsylvania Co., Va
......................7 Chestina Lee b: Abt. 1838 in Campbell Co., Va, d: 18 Sep 1866 in Pittsylvanias Co., VA; Y
......................6 John Arnold b: 09 May 1805 in Lafayette Co., MO
......................6 Julianna Arnold b: 11 Mar 1812 in Campbell Co., VA
......................5 Stephen Lee b: Abt. 1772 in Campbell, Co, Va, d: 08 Feb 1855 in Campbell, Co, Va; Y
......................5 Beverly Lee b: 24 Jul 1774 in Campbell, Co, Va, d: 1824 in Bedford, will, half brother, John, Cumberland; Y
    + Rebecca LEE b: Abt. 1783 in of, Campbell, Co, Va
......................5 Susannah Lee b: Abt. 1785 in Campbell, Co, Va
    + Robert Clark b: Abt. 1790 in of, Bedford, Campbell, Va, m: 04 Jun 1804 in Bedford, Co, Va
......................5 Mary Polly Lee b: Abt. 1787 in Campbell, Co, Va, d: 28 Mar 1836 in Bedford, Co, Va; Y
    + Frances Tabitha Frances EARLY b: of, Cumberland, Campbell, Va, m: Abt. 1789, d: Bet. 1804–1818 in Leesville, Campbell Co., VA; Y
......................5 Ann Lee b: 26 Feb 1790 in Campbell, Co, Va, d: 17 Feb 1860 in Macon, Co TN; Y
    + David HOLLIDAY b: Abt. 1790 in of, Campbell, Co, Va, m: 22 May 1810 in Campbell, Co, Va, d: 16 Aug 1819 in Smith Co, Tenn; Y
......................6 George Washington HOLLADAY b: 18 Jul 1811 in Jackson Co, TN, d: 18 Apr 1865 in Carroll Co. TN; Y
    + Catherine CRIDER b: 04 May 1819 in Smith Co, Tenn, m: 19 Jul 1835 in Carroll Co, TN, d: 14 Oct 1914 in Carroll Co. TN; Y
......................7 Permelia Anne Holladay b: 21 May 1836 in Carroll Co, TN, d: 04 Jun 1903 in Weakley Co, TN; Y
    + Nathan G. Phillips b: Abt. 1835, m: 20 Dec 1855
......................7 Henry Holladay b: 1837 in Carroll Co, TN, d: 1837 in Carroll Co, TN; Y
......................7 Emily Elizabeth Holladay b: 10 Nov 1838 in Carroll Co, TN, d: 10 Mar 1913 in Carroll Co, TN; Y
    + Allen Albert Hillyard b: 04 Dec 1853 in Caldwell Co, Kentucky, m: 08 Jan 1857, d: 25 Jan 1931 in Phillipsburg, Phillips Co, Kansas; Y
......................7 John Milton Holladay b: 22 Aug 1840 in Carroll Co, TN, d: 18 Feb 1898 in Benton Co, TN; Y
    + Rachel S. Mathews b: Abt. 1842, m: 10 Oct 1869
......................7 Stephen Washington Holladay b: 27 Dec 1842 in Carroll Co, TN, d: 19 Dec 1917 in Benton Co, TN; Y

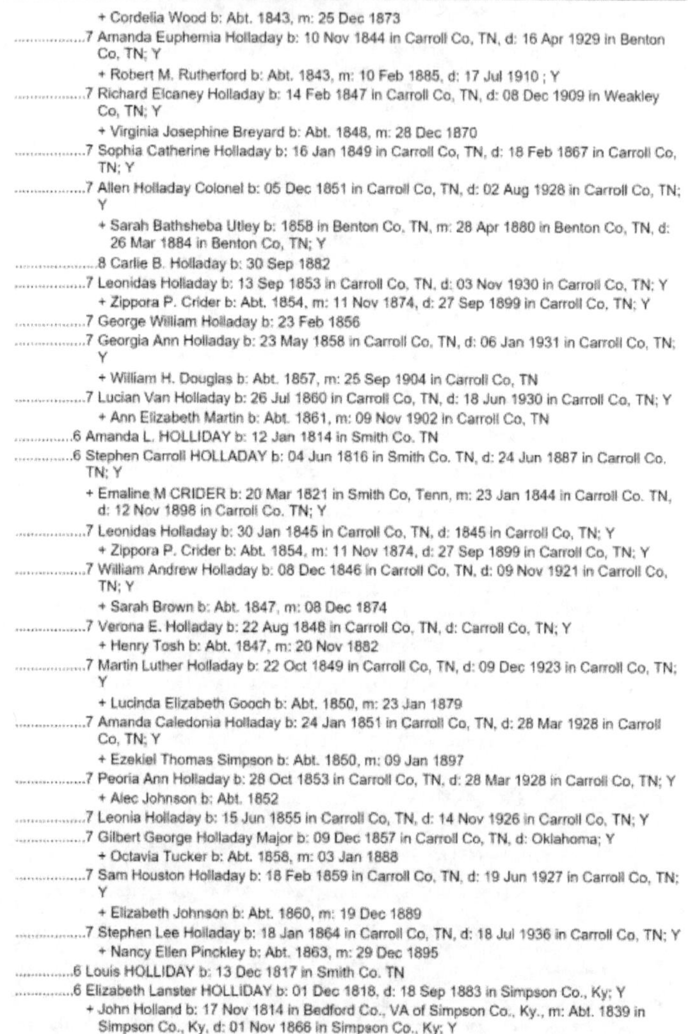

           + Cordelia Wood b: Abt. 1843, m: 25 Dec 1873

.................7 Amanda Euphernia Holladay b: 10 Nov 1844 in Carroll Co, TN, d: 16 Apr 1929 in Benton Co, TN; Y

           + Robert M. Rutherford b: Abt. 1843, m: 10 Feb 1885, d: 17 Jul 1910 ; Y

.................7 Richard Elcaney Holladay b: 14 Feb 1847 in Carroll Co, TN, d: 08 Dec 1909 in Weakley Co, TN; Y

           + Virginia Josephine Breyard b: Abt. 1848, m: 28 Dec 1870

.................7 Sophia Catherine Holladay b: 16 Jan 1849 in Carroll Co, TN, d: 18 Feb 1867 in Carroll Co, TN; Y

.................7 Allen Holladay Colonel b: 05 Dec 1851 in Carroll Co, TN, d: 02 Aug 1928 in Carroll Co, TN; Y

           + Sarah Bathsheba Utley b: 1858 in Benton Co, TN, m: 28 Apr 1880 in Benton Co, TN, d: 26 Mar 1884 in Benton Co, TN; Y

.................8 Carlie B. Holladay b: 30 Sep 1882

.................7 Leonidas Holladay b: 13 Sep 1853 in Carroll Co, TN, d: 03 Nov 1930 in Carroll Co, TN; Y

           + Zippora P. Crider b: Abt. 1854, m: 11 Nov 1874, d: 27 Sep 1899 in Carroll Co, TN; Y

.................7 George William Holladay b: 23 Feb 1856

.................7 Georgia Ann Holladay b: 23 May 1858 in Carroll Co, TN, d: 06 Jan 1931 in Carroll Co, TN; Y

           + William H. Douglas b: Abt. 1857, m: 25 Sep 1904 in Carroll Co, TN

.................7 Lucian Van Holladay b: 26 Jul 1860 in Carroll Co, TN, d: 18 Jun 1930 in Carroll Co, TN; Y

           + Ann Elizabeth Martin b: Abt. 1861, m: 09 Nov 1902 in Carroll Co, TN

.................6 Amanda L. HOLLIDAY b: 12 Jan 1814 in Smith Co. TN

.................6 Stephen Carroll HOLLADAY b: 04 Jun 1816 in Smith Co. TN, d: 24 Jun 1887 in Carroll Co. TN; Y

           + Emaline M CRIDER b: 20 Mar 1821 in Smith Co, Tenn, m: 23 Jan 1844 in Carroll Co. TN, d: 12 Nov 1898 in Carroll Co. TN; Y

.................7 Leonidas Holladay b: 30 Jan 1845 in Carroll Co, TN, d: 1845 in Carroll Co, TN; Y

           + Zippora P. Crider b: Abt. 1854, m: 11 Nov 1874, d: 27 Sep 1899 in Carroll Co, TN; Y

.................7 William Andrew Holladay b: 08 Dec 1846 in Carroll Co, TN, d: 09 Nov 1921 in Carroll Co, TN; Y

           + Sarah Brown b: Abt. 1847, m: 08 Dec 1874

.................7 Verona E. Holladay b: 22 Aug 1848 in Carroll Co, TN, d: Carroll Co, TN; Y

           + Henry Tosh b: Abt. 1847, m: 20 Nov 1882

.................7 Martin Luther Holladay b: 22 Oct 1849 in Carroll Co, TN, d: 09 Dec 1923 in Carroll Co, TN; Y

           + Lucinda Elizabeth Gooch b: Abt. 1850, m: 23 Jan 1879

.................7 Amanda Caledonia Holladay b: 24 Jan 1851 in Carroll Co, TN, d: 28 Mar 1928 in Carroll Co, TN; Y

           + Ezekiel Thomas Simpson b: Abt. 1850, m: 09 Jan 1897

.................7 Peoria Ann Holladay b: 28 Oct 1853 in Carroll Co, TN, d: 28 Mar 1928 in Carroll Co, TN; Y

           + Alec Johnson b: Abt. 1852

.................7 Leonia Holladay b: 15 Jun 1855 in Carroll Co, TN, d: 14 Nov 1926 in Carroll Co, TN; Y

.................7 Gilbert George Holladay Major b: 09 Dec 1857 in Carroll Co, TN, d: Oklahoma; Y

           + Octavia Tucker b: Abt. 1858, m: 03 Jan 1888

.................7 Sam Houston Holladay b: 18 Feb 1859 in Carroll Co, TN, d: 19 Jun 1927 in Carroll Co, TN; Y

           + Elizabeth Johnson b: Abt. 1860, m: 19 Dec 1889

.................7 Stephen Lee Holladay b: 18 Jan 1864 in Carroll Co, TN, d: 18 Jul 1936 in Carroll Co, TN; Y

           + Nancy Ellen Pinckley b: Abt. 1863, m: 29 Dec 1895

.................6 Louis HOLLIDAY b: 13 Dec 1817 in Smith Co. TN

.................6 Elizabeth Lanster HOLLIDAY b: 01 Dec 1818, d: 18 Sep 1883 in Simpson Co., Ky; Y

           + John Holland b: 17 Nov 1814 in Bedford Co., VA of Simpson Co., Ky., m: Abt. 1839 in Simpson Co., Ky, d: 01 Nov 1866 in Simpson Co., Ky; Y

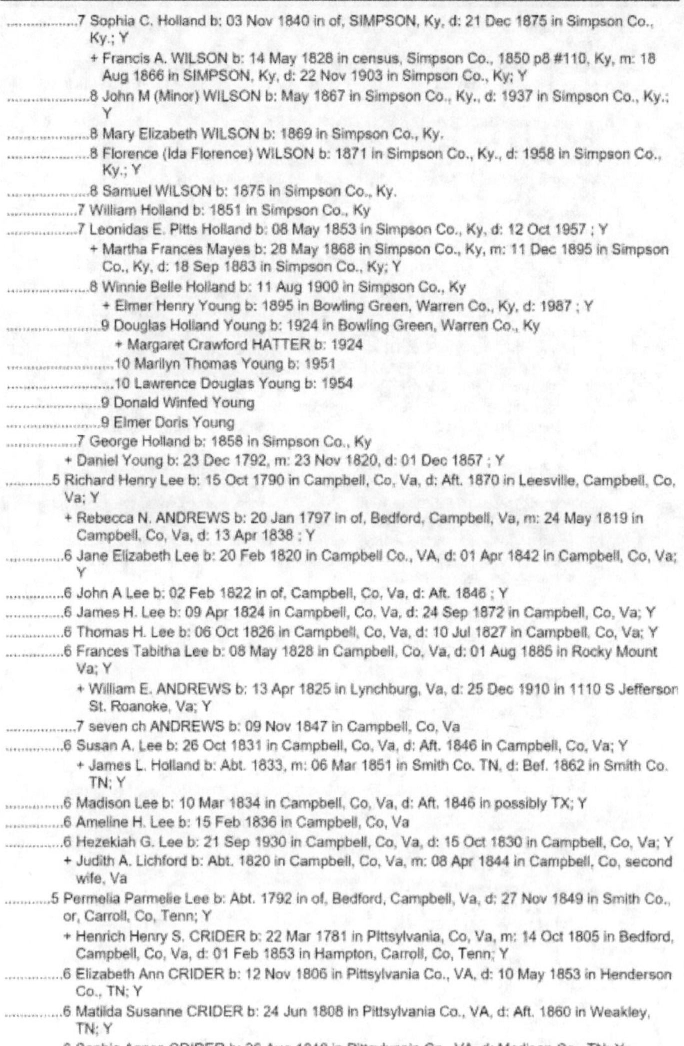

```
.................7 Sophia C. Holland b: 03 Nov 1840 in of, SIMPSON, Ky, d: 21 Dec 1875 in Simpson Co.,
                 Ky.; Y
                     + Francis A. WILSON b: 14 May 1828 in census, Simpson Co., 1850 p8 #110, Ky, m: 18
                       Aug 1866 in SIMPSON, Ky, d: 22 Nov 1903 in Simpson Co., Ky; Y
.....................8 John M (Minor) WILSON b: May 1867 in Simpson Co., Ky., d: 1937 in Simpson Co., Ky.;
                 Y
.....................8 Mary Elizabeth WILSON b: 1869 in Simpson Co., Ky.
.....................8 Florence (Ida Florence) WILSON b: 1871 in Simpson Co., Ky., d: 1958 in Simpson Co.,
                 Ky.; Y
.....................8 Samuel WILSON b: 1875 in Simpson Co., Ky.
.................7 William Holland b: 1851 in Simpson Co., Ky
.................7 Leonidas E. Pitts Holland b: 08 May 1853 in Simpson Co., Ky, d: 12 Oct 1957 ; Y
                     + Martha Frances Mayes b: 28 May 1868 in Simpson Co., Ky, m: 11 Dec 1895 in Simpson
                       Co., Ky, d: 18 Sep 1883 in Simpson Co., Ky; Y
.................8 Winnie Belle Holland b: 11 Aug 1900 in Simpson Co., Ky
                     + Elmer Henry Young b: 1895 in Bowling Green, Warren Co., Ky, d: 1987 ; Y
.................9 Douglas Holland Young b: 1924 in Bowling Green, Warren Co., Ky
                     + Margaret Crawford HATTER b: 1924
.....................10 Marilyn Thomas Young b: 1951
.....................10 Lawrence Douglas Young b: 1954
.................9 Donald Winfed Young
.................9 Elmer Doris Young
.................7 George Holland b: 1858 in Simpson Co., Ky
                     + Daniel Young b: 23 Dec 1792, m: 23 Nov 1820, d: 01 Dec 1857 ; Y
...........5 Richard Henry Lee b: 15 Oct 1790 in Campbell, Co, Va, d: Aft. 1870 in Leesville, Campbell, Co,
                 Va; Y
                     + Rebecca N. ANDREWS b: 20 Jan 1797 in of, Bedford, Campbell, Va, m: 24 May 1819 in
                       Campbell, Co, Va, d: 13 Apr 1838 ; Y
.............6 Jane Elizabeth Lee b: 20 Feb 1820 in Campbell Co., VA, d: 01 Apr 1842 in Campbell, Co, Va;
                 Y
.............6 John A Lee b: 02 Feb 1822 in of, Campbell, Co, Va, d: Aft. 1846 ; Y
.............6 James H. Lee b: 09 Apr 1824 in Campbell, Co, Va, d: 24 Sep 1872 in Campbell, Co, Va; Y
.............6 Thomas H. Lee b: 06 Oct 1826 in Campbell, Co, Va, d: 10 Jul 1827 in Campbell, Co, Va; Y
.............6 Frances Tabitha Lee b: 08 May 1828 in Campbell, Co, Va, d: 01 Aug 1885 in Rocky Mount
                 Va; Y
                     + William E. ANDREWS b: 13 Apr 1825 in Lynchburg, Va, d: 25 Dec 1910 in 1110 S Jefferson
                       St. Roanoke, Va; Y
.................7 seven ch ANDREWS b: 09 Nov 1847 in Campbell, Co, Va
.............6 Susan A. Lee b: 26 Oct 1831 in Campbell, Co, Va, d: Aft. 1846 in Campbell, Co, Va; Y
                     + James L. Holland b: Abt. 1833, m: 06 Mar 1851 in Smith Co. TN, d: Bef. 1862 in Smith Co.
                       TN; Y
.............6 Madison Lee b: 10 Mar 1834 in Campbell, Co, Va, d: Aft. 1846 in possibly TX; Y
.............6 Ameline H. Lee b: 15 Feb 1836 in Campbell, Co, Va
.............6 Hezekiah G. Lee b: 21 Sep 1930 in Campbell, Co, Va, d: 15 Oct 1830 in Campbell, Co, Va; Y
                     + Judith A. Lichford b: Abt. 1820 in Campbell, Co, Va, m: 08 Apr 1844 in Campbell, Co, second
                       wife, Va
...........5 Permelia Parmelie Lee b: Abt. 1792 in of, Bedford, Campbell, Va, d: 27 Nov 1849 in Smith Co.,
                 or, Carroll, Co, Tenn; Y
                     + Henrich Henry S. CRIDER b: 22 Mar 1781 in Pittsylvania, Co, Va, m: 14 Oct 1805 in Bedford,
                       Campbell, Co, Va, d: 01 Feb 1853 in Hampton, Carroll, Co, Tenn; Y
.............6 Elizabeth Ann CRIDER b: 12 Nov 1806 in Pittsylvania Co., VA, d: 10 May 1853 in Henderson
                 Co., TN; Y
.............6 Matilda Susanne CRIDER b: 24 Jun 1808 in Pittsylvania Co., VA, d: Aft. 1860 in Weakley,
                 TN; Y
.............6 Sophia Agnes CRIDER b: 26 Aug 1810 in Pittsylvania Co., VA, d: Madison Co., TN; Y
```

...........6 William Aire CRIDER b: 10 Nov 1812 in Pittsylvania Co., VA, d: 05 Oct 1884 in Carroll Co.
TN; Y
...........6 Narcissus CRIDER b: 1814 in Pittsylvania Co., VA, d: 1814 in Pittsylvania Co., VA; Y
...........6 Belbederra CRIDER b: 14 Feb 1815 in Pittsylvania Co., VA, d: 15 Mar 1817 in Smith Co,
Tenn; Y
...........6 Richard Henry CRIDER b: 07 Aug 1817 in Smith Co, Tenn, d: 12 Nov 1903 in Carroll, Co,
Tenn; Y
        + Margaret WHITE b: Abt. 1818 in Smith Co. TN, m: 02 Jul 1854
...........7 Zippora P. Crider b: Abt. 1854, d: 27 Sep 1899 in Carroll Co, TN; Y
        + Leonidas Holladay b: 30 Jan 1845 in Carroll Co, TN, m: 11 Nov 1874, d: 1845 in Carroll
        Co, TN; Y
...........7 Hatton H. CRIDER b: 1858 in Carroll Co. TN, d: 22 Nov 1859 in Carroll Co. TN; Y
        + Eady BRINKLEY b: 19 May 1819 in North Carolina, m: Jan 1837 in Carroll Co. TN, d: 27
        Nov 1852 in Carroll Co. TN; Y
...........7 Richard CRIDER b: Nov 1837 in Carroll Co. TN, d: 1840 in Carroll Co. TN; Y
...........7 Felix Henry CRIDER b: 19 Oct 1838 in Carroll Co. TN, d: 19 Sep 1924 in Carroll Co. TN; Y
        + Larcenia Eliz LAYCOOK b: 07 May 1845 in Carroll Co. TN, m: 1861 in Carroll Co. TN, d:
        08 Jan 1925 in Carroll Co. TN; Y
...........8 Edie A CRIDER b: 10 Mar 1862 in Carroll County, Tennessee, d: 02 Nov 1921 in
        Huntingdon, Carroll County, Tennessee; Y
        + John HILL b: Abt. 1862, m: 25 Feb 1882
...........9 Sammy HILL b: Abt. 1883, d: Abt. 1894 in Huntingdon, Carroll County, Tennessee; Y
...........9 Nettie HILL b: 16 Jul 1888, d: 11 Oct 1959 ; Y
        + J.W. McADOO b: 21 Jan 1880, m: 11 Dec 1904, d: 11 Jan 1962 ; Y
...........10 Mae McADOO b: 28 Oct 1905
...........8 Frances Isabella CRIDER b: 18 Aug 1864 in Carroll County, Tennessee, d: 01 Jul 1942 in
        Huntingdon, Carroll County, Tennessee; Y
        + Louis VICKERS b: 25 Mar 1866, m: 16 Nov 1890, d: 31 Mar 1931 ; Y
...........8 Richard Samuel CRIDER b: 24 Nov 1868 in Carroll County, Tennessee, d: 23 Dec 1934
        in Hardin County, Tennessee; Y
        + Martha Belle KING b: 07 Oct 1871, m: 05 Nov 1891
...........9 Walter CRIDER b: Aug 1893 in Carroll County, Tennessee
...........9 Joseph CRIDER b: Feb 1894 in Carroll County, Tennessee
...........9 Ivie Mae CRIDER b: Sep 1896 in Carroll County, Tennessee
...........9 Carrie CRIDER b: 1899
...........9 Gracie CRIDER b: 1904
...........8 Exie Louise * CRIDER b: 28 Jun 1870 in Carroll Co. TN
        + Robert BEDWELL
...........9 Vernice Alford BEDWELL b: Abt. 1894 in Carroll Co. TN
        + Mary Ethel KELLY b: Aug 1894, m: 14 Nov 1911 in Carroll County, Tennessee
...........10 Robert H. Bedwell b: 08 Jan 1913 in Carroll Co. TN, d: 19 Mar 1993 in Carroll Co.
        TN; Y
        + Ree BAKER
...........11 Ella MAE Bedwell b: Abt. 1935
        + Dave LAWSON
...........10 Nannie Lee BEDWELL
...........10 Vera BEDWELL
...........10 Charles BEDWELL
...........10 Willie G. BEDWELL
        + J.A. HALL
...........9 Henry HALL
...........8 Richard Albert CRIDER b: 02 Jun 1877 in TENNESSEE, d: 23 Oct 1952 in Carroll
        County, Tennessee; Y
        + Mary MORGAN b: 26 Oct 1876, m: 11 Feb 1900 in Carroll County, Tennessee, d: 17
        Jan 1962 in Carroll County, Tennessee; Y

................9 Essie Mae CRIDER b: 17 Jun 1901, d: 30 Jun 1983 ; Y
            + William Ray WHITE Sr. b: 02 May 1902, m: 16 Mar 1923, d: 24 Apr 1963 ; Y
..................10 William Ray WHITE Jr. b: 11 Jan 1926, d: 23 Oct 1984 ; Y
..................10 Maribelle Gwendolyn WHITE b: 03 Jan 1929
..................10 Living WHITE
................9 Carmack Graydon CRIDER b: 13 Sep 1903, d: 08 Dec 1959 ; Y
            + Hattie ROWLAND b: 09 Jun 1908, d: 11 Jul 1974 ; Y
..................10 James Albert CRIDER b: 12 May 1928, d: Aug 1985 ; Y
................9 Orville G. CRIDER b: 02 Nov 1905
            + James Priestly WYATT
..................10 Living WYATT
..................10 Living WYATT
................9 Ida L. CRIDER b: 24 Sep 1909, d: 11 Apr 1977 ; Y
            + Henry Nathan MEBANE b: 21 Oct 1906, d: 28 Nov 1978 ; Y
................9 Minnie Lillian CRIDER b: 24 Jul 1914, d: 01 Mar 1995 ; Y
            + Alton HOLLAND
..................10 Living HOLLAND
            + Dameron DAY
..................10 Patricia DAY b: 10 Jul 1935, d: 06 Jan 1990 ; Y
................9 Roy Albert CRIDER b: 21 May 1921, d: 23 May 1980 ; Y
            + Fay McALPINE
..................10 Living CRIDER
..................10 Living CRIDER
................8 Mary Etta CRIDER b: 24 Jul 1879 in Carroll County, Tennessee, d: 24 May 1972 in
            Carroll County, Tennessee; Y
            + John William DILL b: 05 Nov 1870 in Carroll County, Tennessee, m: 28 Dec 1898, d: 01
            Aug 1961 ; Y
................9 Floyd Austin DILL b: 28 Oct 1899, d: 13 Sep 1985 ; Y
            + Florence DAVIS
..................10 Floyd Davis DILL b: 07 Apr 1926
................9 Ovie Elizabeth DILL b: 06 Nov 1901, d: 29 Jan 1972 ; Y
            + Ernest VICKERS Sr. b: 28 Aug 1896, m: 31 Oct 1920
..................10 Ernest VICKERS Jr. b: 18 Aug 1921
..................10 Mary Aline VICKERS b: 10 Dec 1924
..................10 Living VICKERS
................9 Homer Collee DILL b: 18 Aug 1904 in Carroll County, Tennessee
            + Louisa Gertrude HOOD b: 06 Jun 1906, m: Abt. 1925
................9 Carlos DeWhitt DILL b: 22 Mar 1907 in Carroll County, Tennessee, d: 18 Oct 1982 ; Y
            + Willie Bevia PARRISH b: 12 Feb 1918, m: 11 Jul 1941
..................10 Living DILL
................9 Fred Houston DILL b: 27 Aug 1910 in Carroll County, Tennessee, d: 16 Dec 1975 ; Y
            + Lous Marie BRADSHAW b: 06 Jun 1916, m: 28 Jul 1937
..................10 Living DILL
..................10 Living DILL
................9 Hulon Cox DILL b: 17 Apr 1913 in Carroll County, Tennessee, d: 11 Sep 1999 in
            Huntingdon, Carroll County, Tennessee; Y
            + Roberta Nell BENNETT b: 18 Dec 1914, m: 24 Nov 1933
..................10 Living DILL
..................10 Living DILL
................9 Eulon Grey DILL b: 17 Apr 1913 in Carroll County, Tennessee, d: 12 Aug 1981 ; Y
            + Clara Ardelle JOHNSON b: 12 Sep 1918, m: 06 Nov 1937
..................10 Living DILL
            + Dorothy Oberton HOPPER b: 07 Apr 1925 in Yuma, Carroll County, Tennessee
................9 Mary Odean DILL b: 05 Sep 1920

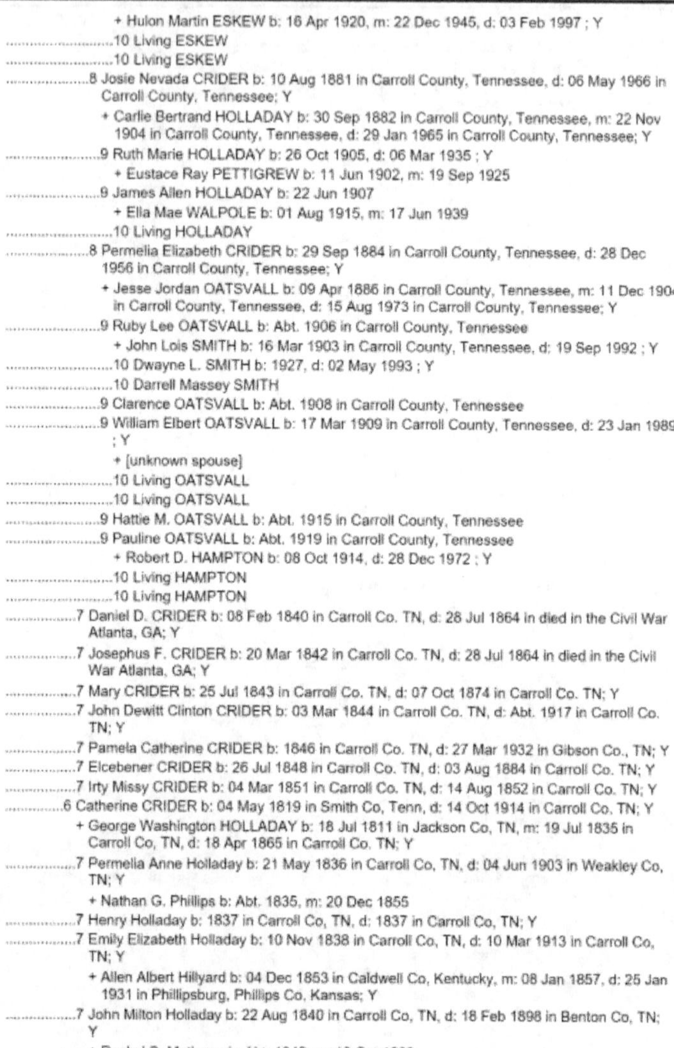

```
                        + Hulon Martin ESKEW b: 16 Apr 1920, m: 22 Dec 1945, d: 03 Feb 1997 ; Y
......................10 Living ESKEW
......................10 Living ESKEW
..................8 Josie Nevada CRIDER b: 10 Aug 1881 in Carroll County, Tennessee, d: 06 May 1966 in
                  Carroll County, Tennessee; Y
                        + Carlie Bertrand HOLLADAY b: 30 Sep 1882 in Carroll County, Tennessee, m: 22 Nov
                        1904 in Carroll County, Tennessee, d: 29 Jan 1965 in Carroll County, Tennessee; Y
..................9 Ruth Marie HOLLADAY b: 26 Oct 1905, d: 06 Mar 1935 ; Y
                        + Eustace Ray PETTIGREW b: 11 Jun 1902, m: 19 Sep 1925
..................9 James Allen HOLLADAY b: 22 Jun 1907
                        + Ella Mae WALPOLE b: 01 Aug 1915, m: 17 Jun 1939
......................10 Living HOLLADAY
..................8 Permelia Elizabeth CRIDER b: 29 Sep 1884 in Carroll County, Tennessee, d: 28 Dec
                  1956 in Carroll County, Tennessee; Y
                        + Jesse Jordan OATSVALL b: 09 Apr 1886 in Carroll County, Tennessee, m: 11 Dec 1904
                        in Carroll County, Tennessee, d: 15 Aug 1973 in Carroll County, Tennessee; Y
..................9 Ruby Lee OATSVALL b: Abt. 1906 in Carroll County, Tennessee
                        + John Lois SMITH b: 16 Mar 1903 in Carroll County, Tennessee, d: 19 Sep 1992 ; Y
......................10 Dwayne L. SMITH b: 1927, d: 02 May 1993 ; Y
......................10 Darrell Massey SMITH
..................9 Clarence OATSVALL b: Abt. 1908 in Carroll County, Tennessee
..................9 William Elbert OATSVALL b: 17 Mar 1909 in Carroll County, Tennessee, d: 23 Jan 1989
                  ; Y
                        + [unknown spouse]
......................10 Living OATSVALL
......................10 Living OATSVALL
..................9 Hattie M. OATSVALL b: Abt. 1915 in Carroll County, Tennessee
..................9 Pauline OATSVALL b: Abt. 1919 in Carroll County, Tennessee
                        + Robert D. HAMPTON b: 08 Oct 1914, d: 28 Dec 1972 ; Y
......................10 Living HAMPTON
......................10 Living HAMPTON
..............7 Daniel D. CRIDER b: 08 Feb 1840 in Carroll Co. TN, d: 28 Jul 1864 in died in the Civil War
              Atlanta, GA; Y
..............7 Josephus F. CRIDER b: 20 Mar 1842 in Carroll Co. TN, d: 28 Jul 1864 in died in the Civil
              War Atlanta, GA; Y
..............7 Mary CRIDER b: 25 Jul 1843 in Carroll Co. TN, d: 07 Oct 1874 in Carroll Co. TN; Y
..............7 John Dewitt Clinton CRIDER b: 03 Mar 1844 in Carroll Co. TN, d: Abt. 1917 in Carroll Co.
              TN; Y
..............7 Pamela Catherine CRIDER b: 1846 in Carroll Co. TN, d: 27 Mar 1932 in Gibson Co., TN; Y
..............7 Elcebener CRIDER b: 26 Jul 1848 in Carroll Co. TN, d: 03 Aug 1884 in Carroll Co. TN; Y
..............7 Irty Missy CRIDER b: 04 Mar 1851 in Carroll Co. TN, d: 14 Aug 1852 in Carroll Co. TN; Y
............6 Catherine CRIDER b: 04 May 1819 in Smith Co, Tenn, d: 14 Oct 1914 in Carroll Co. TN; Y
                  + George Washington HOLLADAY b: 18 Jul 1811 in Jackson Co, TN, m: 19 Jul 1835 in
                  Carroll Co, TN, d: 18 Apr 1865 in Carroll Co. TN; Y
..............7 Permelia Anne Holladay b: 21 May 1836 in Carroll Co, TN, d: 04 Jun 1903 in Weakley Co,
              TN; Y
                  + Nathan G. Phillips b: Abt. 1835, m: 20 Dec 1855
..............7 Henry Holladay b: 1837 in Carroll Co, TN, d: 1837 in Carroll Co, TN; Y
..............7 Emily Elizabeth Holladay b: 10 Nov 1838 in Carroll Co, TN, d: 10 Mar 1913 in Carroll Co,
              TN; Y
                  + Allen Albert Hillyard b: 04 Dec 1853 in Caldwell Co, Kentucky, m: 08 Jan 1857, d: 25 Jan
                  1931 in Phillipsburg, Phillips Co, Kansas; Y
..............7 John Milton Holladay b: 22 Aug 1840 in Carroll Co, TN, d: 18 Feb 1898 in Benton Co, TN;
              Y
                  + Rachel S. Mathews b: Abt. 1842, m: 10 Oct 1869
```

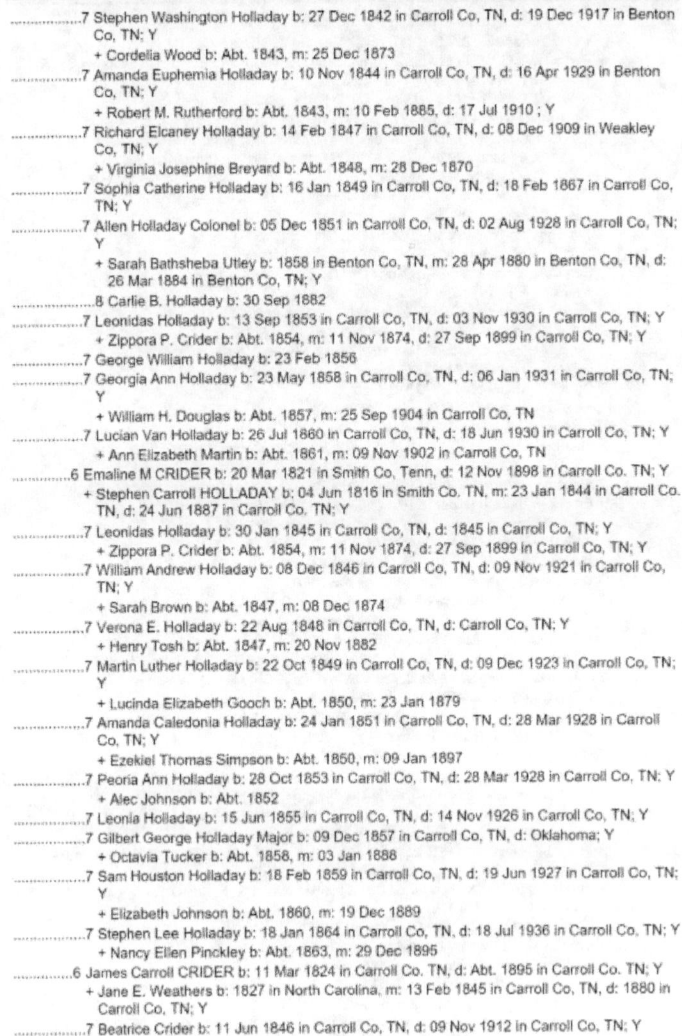

....7 Stephen Washington Holladay b: 27 Dec 1842 in Carroll Co, TN, d: 19 Dec 1917 in Benton Co, TN; Y

    + Cordelia Wood b: Abt. 1843, m: 25 Dec 1873

....7 Amanda Euphemia Holladay b: 10 Nov 1844 in Carroll Co, TN, d: 16 Apr 1929 in Benton Co, TN; Y

    + Robert M. Rutherford b: Abt. 1843, m: 10 Feb 1885, d: 17 Jul 1910 ; Y

....7 Richard Elcaney Holladay b: 14 Feb 1847 in Carroll Co, TN, d: 08 Dec 1909 in Weakley Co, TN; Y

    + Virginia Josephine Breyard b: Abt. 1848, m: 28 Dec 1870

....7 Sophia Catherine Holladay b: 16 Jan 1849 in Carroll Co, TN, d: 18 Feb 1867 in Carroll Co, TN; Y

....7 Allen Holladay Colonel b: 05 Dec 1851 in Carroll Co, TN, d: 02 Aug 1928 in Carroll Co, TN; Y

    + Sarah Bathsheba Utley b: 1858 in Benton Co, TN, m: 28 Apr 1880 in Benton Co, TN, d: 26 Mar 1884 in Benton Co, TN; Y

....8 Carlie B. Holladay b: 30 Sep 1882

....7 Leonidas Holladay b: 13 Sep 1853 in Carroll Co, TN, d: 03 Nov 1930 in Carroll Co, TN; Y

    + Zippora P. Crider b: Abt. 1854, m: 11 Nov 1874, d: 27 Sep 1899 in Carroll Co, TN; Y

....7 George William Holladay b: 23 Feb 1856

....7 Georgia Ann Holladay b: 23 May 1858 in Carroll Co, TN, d: 06 Jan 1931 in Carroll Co, TN; Y

    + William H. Douglas b: Abt. 1857, m: 25 Sep 1904 in Carroll Co, TN

....7 Lucian Van Holladay b: 26 Jul 1860 in Carroll Co, TN, d: 18 Jun 1930 in Carroll Co, TN; Y

    + Ann Elizabeth Martin b: Abt. 1861, m: 09 Nov 1902 in Carroll Co, TN

....6 Emaline M CRIDER b: 20 Mar 1821 in Smith Co, Tenn, d: 12 Nov 1898 in Carroll Co. TN; Y

    + Stephen Carroll HOLLADAY b: 04 Jun 1816 in Smith Co, TN, m: 23 Jan 1844 in Carroll Co. TN, d: 24 Jun 1887 in Carroll Co. TN; Y

....7 Leonidas Holladay b: 30 Jan 1845 in Carroll Co, TN, d: 1845 in Carroll Co, TN; Y

    + Zippora P. Crider b: Abt. 1854, m: 11 Nov 1874, d: 27 Sep 1899 in Carroll Co, TN; Y

....7 William Andrew Holladay b: 08 Dec 1846 in Carroll Co, TN, d: 09 Nov 1921 in Carroll Co, TN; Y

    + Sarah Brown b: Abt. 1847, m: 08 Dec 1874

....7 Verona E. Holladay b: 22 Aug 1848 in Carroll Co, TN, d: Carroll Co, TN; Y

    + Henry Tosh b: Abt. 1847, m: 20 Nov 1882

....7 Martin Luther Holladay b: 22 Oct 1849 in Carroll Co, TN, d: 09 Dec 1923 in Carroll Co, TN; Y

    + Lucinda Elizabeth Gooch b: Abt. 1850, m: 23 Jan 1879

....7 Amanda Caledonia Holladay b: 24 Jan 1851 in Carroll Co, TN, d: 28 Mar 1928 in Carroll Co, TN; Y

    + Ezekiel Thomas Simpson b: Abt. 1850, m: 09 Jan 1897

....7 Peoria Ann Holladay b: 28 Oct 1853 in Carroll Co, TN, d: 28 Mar 1928 in Carroll Co, TN; Y

    + Alec Johnson b: Abt. 1852

....7 Leonia Holladay b: 15 Jun 1855 in Carroll Co, TN, d: 14 Nov 1926 in Carroll Co, TN; Y

....7 Gilbert George Holladay Major b: 09 Dec 1857 in Carroll Co, TN, d: Oklahoma; Y

    + Octavia Tucker b: Abt. 1858, m: 03 Jan 1888

....7 Sam Houston Holladay b: 18 Feb 1859 in Carroll Co, TN, d: 19 Jun 1927 in Carroll Co, TN; Y

    + Elizabeth Johnson b: Abt. 1860, m: 19 Dec 1889

....7 Stephen Lee Holladay b: 18 Jan 1864 in Carroll Co, TN, d: 18 Jul 1936 in Carroll Co, TN; Y

    + Nancy Ellen Pinckley b: Abt. 1863, m: 29 Dec 1895

....6 James Carroll CRIDER b: 11 Mar 1824 in Carroll Co. TN, d: Abt. 1895 in Carroll Co. TN; Y

    + Jane E. Weathers b: 1827 in North Carolina, m: 13 Feb 1845 in Carroll Co, TN, d: 1880 in Carroll Co, TN; Y

....7 Beatrice Crider b: 11 Jun 1846 in Carroll Co, TN, d: 09 Nov 1912 in Carroll Co, TN; Y

    + Eli Daniel Brown b: Abt. 1845, m: 08 Nov 1862

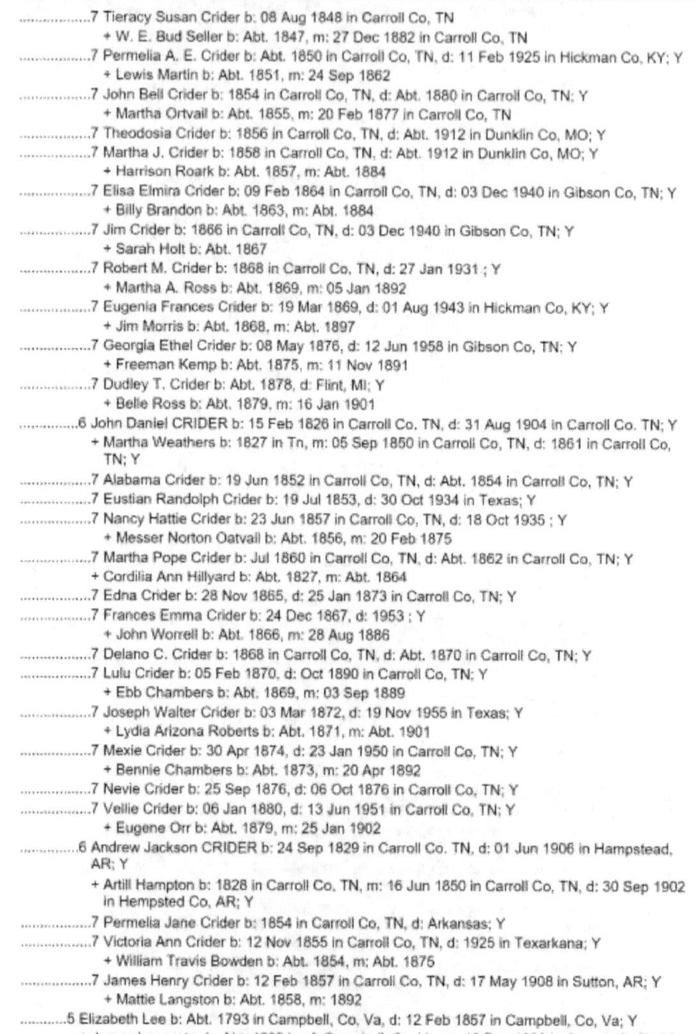

.......................7 Tieracy Susan Crider b: 08 Aug 1848 in Carroll Co, TN
         + W. E. Bud Seller b: Abt. 1847, m: 27 Dec 1882 in Carroll Co, TN
.......................7 Permelia A. E. Crider b: Abt. 1850 in Carroll Co, TN, d: 11 Feb 1925 in Hickman Co, KY; Y
         + Lewis Martin b: Abt. 1851, m: 24 Sep 1862
.......................7 John Bell Crider b: 1854 in Carroll Co, TN, d: Abt. 1880 in Carroll Co, TN; Y
         + Martha Ortvail b: Abt. 1855, m: 20 Feb 1877 in Carroll Co, TN
.......................7 Theodosia Crider b: 1856 in Carroll Co, TN, d: Abt. 1912 in Dunklin Co, MO; Y
.......................7 Martha J. Crider b: 1858 in Carroll Co, TN, d: Abt. 1912 in Dunklin Co, MO; Y
         + Harrison Roark b: Abt. 1857, m: Abt. 1884
.......................7 Elisa Elmira Crider b: 09 Feb 1864 in Carroll Co, TN, d: 03 Dec 1940 in Gibson Co, TN; Y
         + Billy Brandon b: Abt. 1863, m: Abt. 1884
.......................7 Jim Crider b: 1866 in Carroll Co, TN, d: 03 Dec 1940 in Gibson Co, TN; Y
         + Sarah Holt b: Abt. 1867
.......................7 Robert M. Crider b: 1868 in Carroll Co, TN, d: 27 Jan 1931 ; Y
         + Martha A. Ross b: Abt. 1869, m: 05 Jan 1892
.......................7 Eugenia Frances Crider b: 19 Mar 1869, d: 01 Aug 1943 in Hickman Co, KY; Y
         + Jim Morris b: Abt. 1868, m: Abt. 1897
.......................7 Georgia Ethel Crider b: 08 May 1876, d: 12 Jun 1958 in Gibson Co, TN; Y
         + Freeman Kemp b: Abt. 1875, m: 11 Nov 1891
.......................7 Dudley T. Crider b: Abt. 1878, d: Flint, MI; Y
         + Belle Ross b: Abt. 1879, m: 16 Jan 1901
...............6 John Daniel CRIDER b: 15 Feb 1826 in Carroll Co. TN, d: 31 Aug 1904 in Carroll Co. TN; Y
         + Martha Weathers b: 1827 in Tn, m: 05 Sep 1850 in Carroll Co, TN, d: 1861 in Carroll Co,
         TN; Y
.......................7 Alabama Crider b: 19 Jun 1852 in Carroll Co, TN, d: Abt. 1854 in Carroll Co, TN; Y
.......................7 Eustian Randolph Crider b: 19 Jul 1853, d: 30 Oct 1934 in Texas; Y
.......................7 Nancy Hattie Crider b: 23 Jun 1857 in Carroll Co, TN, d: 18 Oct 1935 ; Y
         + Messer Norton Oatvail b: Abt. 1856, m: 20 Feb 1875
.......................7 Martha Pope Crider b: Jul 1860 in Carroll Co, TN, d: Abt. 1862 in Carroll Co, TN; Y
         + Cordilia Ann Hillyard b: Abt. 1827, m: Abt. 1864
.......................7 Edna Crider b: 28 Nov 1865, d: 25 Jan 1873 in Carroll Co, TN; Y
.......................7 Frances Emma Crider b: 24 Dec 1867, d: 1953 ; Y
         + John Worrell b: Abt. 1866, m: 28 Aug 1886
.......................7 Delano C. Crider b: 1868 in Carroll Co, TN, d: Abt. 1870 in Carroll Co, TN; Y
.......................7 Lulu Crider b: 05 Feb 1870, d: Oct 1890 in Carroll Co, TN; Y
         + Ebb Chambers b: Abt. 1869, m: 03 Sep 1889
.......................7 Joseph Walter Crider b: 03 Mar 1872, d: 19 Nov 1955 in Texas; Y
         + Lydia Arizona Roberts b: Abt. 1871, m: Abt. 1901
.......................7 Mexie Crider b: 30 Apr 1874, d: 23 Jan 1950 in Carroll Co, TN; Y
         + Bennie Chambers b: Abt. 1873, m: 20 Apr 1892
.......................7 Nevie Crider b: 25 Sep 1876, d: 06 Oct 1876 in Carroll Co, TN; Y
.......................7 Veilie Crider b: 06 Jan 1880, d: 13 Jun 1951 in Carroll Co, TN; Y
         + Eugene Orr b: Abt. 1879, m: 25 Jan 1902
...............6 Andrew Jackson CRIDER b: 24 Sep 1829 in Carroll Co. TN, d: 01 Jun 1906 in Hampstead,
         AR; Y
         + Artill Hampton b: 1828 in Carroll Co. TN, m: 16 Jun 1850 in Carroll Co, TN, d: 30 Sep 1902
         in Hempsted Co, AR; Y
.......................7 Permelia Jane Crider b: 1854 in Carroll Co, TN, d: Arkansas; Y
.......................7 Victoria Ann Crider b: 12 Nov 1855 in Carroll Co, TN, d: 1925 in Texarkana; Y
         + William Travis Bowden b: Abt. 1854, m: Abt. 1875
.......................7 James Henry Crider b: 12 Feb 1857 in Carroll Co, TN, d: 17 May 1908 in Sutton, AR; Y
         + Mattie Langston b: Abt. 1858, m: 1892
............5 Elizabeth Lee b: Abt. 1793 in Campbell, Co, Va, d: 12 Feb 1857 in Campbell, Co, Va; Y
         + James Lancaster b: Abt. 1800 in of, Campbell, Co, Va, m: 13 Dec 1802 in Campbell, Co, Va

............5 John Lee b: Abt. 1796 in Campbell, Co, Va, d: Bef. 26 Feb 1830 in will probate, Rustburg,
Cumberland, Va; Y

............5 Matilda Lee b: Abt. 1798 in Campbell, Co, Va

+ Drury Holland b: Abt. 1791 in Bedford Co., Virginia, m: 03 Feb 1817 in Campbell, Co, Va, d:
Abt. 1841 in Smith Co., Tennessee; Y

............6 Richard Lee Holland b: 1818 in Smith Co. TN, d: Civil War; Y

+ Alethea Dean b: Abt. 1822, m: 1842

............6 Elizabeth Ann Holland b: 1820, d: 1867 ; Y

+ A. H. Pistole b: 1818, d: Civil War; Y

............6 Judith Emiline Holland b: 27 Jan 1824 in Campbell Co., VA, d: 21 Oct 1912 in Simpson Co.,
Ky; Y

+ James Lee Kirby b: Abt. 1811 in Tn, m: Abt. 1838 in Smith Co. TN, d: Abt. 1862 in Simpson
Co., Ky; Y

............6 Sophia Agnes Holland b: 11 Aug 1827, d: 13 May 1929 in Smith Co. TN; Y

............6 Charles William Holland b: 01 Jun 1830, d: 28 Sep 1869 ; Y

............6 James L. Holland b: Abt. 1833, d: Bef. 1862 in Smith Co. TN; Y

+ Susan A. Lee b: 26 Oct 1831 in Campbell, Co, Va, m: 06 Mar 1851 in Smith Co. TN, d: Aft.
1846 in Campbell, Co, Va; Y

............6 Stephen Monroe Holland b: Abt. 1836 in Smith Co. TN

+ Lucy E. Butler b: Abt. 1838 in Simpson Co., Ky, m: 30 Apr 1857 in Simpson Co., Ky

............6 George Milton Holland b: Abt. 1838 in Smith Co. TN

............5 Agness Aggie Lee b: Abt. 1799 in Campbell, Co, Va, d: Franklin, Co Va; Y

+ Richard BOOTH Jr. b: Abt. 1795 in Campbell, Co, Va, m: 11 Mar 1819 in Campbell, Co, Va

............6 John H. BOOTH b: 1820 in Franklin Co., Va

............6 Almira BOOTH b: Abt. 1822 in Franklin Co., Va

............6 James Callihill BOOTH b: 05 Sep 1823 in Franklin Co., Va, d: 10 Nov 1885 in Boone Co.,
MO; Y

............6 Sophia BOOTH b: 20 May 1825 in Franklin Co., Va, d: 1906 ; Y

............6 William BOOTH b: Abt. 1827 in Franklin Co., Va

............6 Matilda BOOTH b: Abt. 1830 in Franklin Co., Va

............5 Sophie Lee b: Abt. 1800 in Campbell, Co, d: Franklin, Co Va; Y

+ Isaac WILSON b: Abt. 1810 in Campbell, Co, Va

............5 Mary Lee b: Abt. 1801 in Campbell, Co, Va

+ Daniel YOUNG b: Abt. 1800 in of, Campbell, Co, Va

............6 William Lee YOUNG b: 16 Aug 1821

............6 Leonidas D. YOUNG b: 28 Sep 1823, d: 05 Feb 1866 ; Y

............6 John Milton YOUNG b: 10 Jul 1825, d: 15 Aug 1880 ; Y

............6 Francis C. YOUNG b: 22 Mar 1827

............6 Richard H. YOUNG b: 04 Feb 1829, d: 03 Jul 1862 ; Y

............6 Emily YOUNG b: 04 Jul 1830, d: 04 Jul 1830 ; Y

............6 Milton D. YOUNG b: 09 Sep 1832

..........4 Joseph Dabbs Lee b: Abt. 1741 in Richmond, King and Queen, Co, Va, d: Cumberland, Co, will
probate, Va; Y

+ Nancy Anne NOEL or Newell b: Abt. 1743 in of, Cumberland, Co, Va

............5 Keziah Lee b: Abt. 1762 in of, Cumberland, Co, Va

+ William COX b: Abt. 1765 in Cumberland, Co, Va, m: 08 Feb 1785 in Cumberland, Co, Va

............5 Ann Lee b: Abt. 1765 in of, Cumberland, Co, Va

............5 Sarah Lee b: Abt. 1766 in of, Cumberland, Co, Va

............5 Joseph Dabbs Lee Jr b: Abt. 1768 in of, Cumberland, Co, Va

............5 Seymore or Saymore Lee b: 15 Jun 1769 in of, Cumberland, Co, Va, d: 23 Sep 1830 in
Oglethorpe County, Georgia; Y

+ Nancy Anne Woodruff b: 13 Aug 1770 in of Cumberlabd Co., Va, m: 18 Dec 1790 in
Cumberlabd Co., Va, d: Aft. 1840 in Oglethorpe County, Georgia; Y

............6 Dabbs Lee b: 1790

+ Sussanna Pierce

............6 Joseph Dabbs Lee b: 29 Oct 1791 in Littleton Parish, Cumberlabd Co., Va, d: 21 Sep 1853 in Natchitoches Parish, La.; Y

+ Frances Keenion Taylor m: 16 Dec 1812

............6 Huldy W. Lee b: 28 Jan 1794 in Littleton Parish, Cumberlabd Co., Va

+ James Nowell m: 30 Aug 1811

............6 Permula Ann Lee b: 19 Jan 1796 in Cumberlabd Co., Va

............6 William Barnet Lee b: 09 Oct 1797 in Cumberlabd Co., Va, d: 23 Apr 1798 in Oglethorpe County, Georgia; Y

............6 John Garnet Lee b: 25 Jul 1799 in Cumberlabd Co., Va, d: 25 Oct 1871 ; Y

+ Polly Lewis b: Abt. 1801 in VA

..............7 Nancy Lee b: Abt. 182 AD in VA

..............7 William Dabbs Lee b: Abt. 1823 in VA

..............7 E.A. Lee b: Abt. 1825 in VA

..............7 Polly Lee b: Abt. 1827 in VA

..............7 Anson Pollen Lee b: Abt. 1831 in VA

+ Arabella Nicholson Bedwell b: Abt. 1835 in VA, m: 1857

..............8 John Grimes Lee b: 1858 in Hinds County, Mississippi

..............8 Olivia Lee b: 1861

..............8 Seymore Lee b: 1865

..............8 Garnett Lee b: 1867

..............8 Maggie Lee b: 1869

..............8 Robert B. Lee b: 1870

..............8 Mary Avaline Lee b: 15 Dec 1871, d: Apr 1962 in Drew County Arkansas, Pairie Grove Cemetery; Y

+ Phillip Zadock Wolfe b: 1867, d: 1939 in Drew County Arizona, Pairie Grove Cemetery; Y

..................9 Eudora Pearl Wolfe b: 1894, d: 25 Mar 1980 ; Y

+ Carrol Deal b: 1886, d: 1996 ; Y

..................10 Ernest Deal b: 17 Dec 1909

..................10 Hallie Deal b: 20 Oct 1910

..................10 Madie Deal b: 1912, d: 1957 ; Y

..................10 infant Deal b: 27 Sep 1916

..................10 Mary Katherine Deal b: 08 Jan 1924

..................10 Jewel Deal

..................10 Margie Deal

..................10 Norwood Lee Deal

..................9 Robert Lee Wolfe b: 16 Dec 1895, d: 19 Sep 1910 ; Y

..................9 Dan Bull Wolfe b: 24 Aug 1901, d: 08 Jan 1989 ; Y

+ Maggie Elizabeth Lagrone

..................9 Jesse Young Wolfe b: 1903, d: 1957 ; Y

+ Hazel Etta Mullins b: 1912, d: 1990 ; Y

..................9 Clarence Albert Wolfe b: 17 Jul 1906, d: 04 Nov 1924 ; Y

..................9 Minnie Mary Wolfe b: 1906

+ Cylde Talbot Stauber

..................10 Living Stauber

..................9 Benjamin Franklin Wolfe b: 12 Jul 1911, d: 01 Dec 1997 ; Y

+ Edna Louise Wolfe b: 24 Jul 1916, m: 09 Oct 1932, d: 03 May 1997 ; Y

..................10 Frankie Wayne Wolfe b: 14 Nov 1933, d: 14 Nov 1933 ; Y

..................10 Living Wolfe

..................9 Columus Patton Wolfe b: 11 Mar 1914, d: 03 Mar 1935 ; Y

..................9 Scharlotte Wolfe

..................9 Leta Bell Wolfe

+ George Mansfield

..................9 Anson Philip Wolfe

+ Lottie Chapman
..................10 A.P. Wolfe
..................10 Irving Wolfe
..................10 Mildred Wolfe
..................10 Eunice Wolfe
................9 Willie Claud Wolfe
+ Luna Bell Johnson
..................10 Ella Mae Wolfe
..................10 Claude Bell Wolfe
..................10 Marie Wolfe
..................10 Marcilla Wolfe
................8 Maggie B. Lee b: 1872
................8 Eudora Lee b: 1873
................8 Donald Bedwell Lee b: 1874
................8 William A. Lee b: 1875
................8 Eric Lee b: 1877
................8 Enoch Lee b: 1878
+ Mary F. Ferguson
................8 Alma Lee b: 1869
................8 Elma Lee b: 1870
..............6 Temprerance Lawrence Lee b: 15 Jul 1801 in Cumberlabd Co., Va
+ Thomas Farrer m: 24 May 1817
..............6 Charles Henry Lee b: 31 Mar 1803 in Cumberlabd Co., Va
+ Mary Ann HAWKINS b: Abt. 1808 in Oglethorpe County, Georgia, m: 13 Nov 1828 in
Oglethorpe County, Georgia
+ Eliza Andrews b: Abt. 1805 in Oglethorpe County, Georgia, m: 16 Feb 1825 in Oglethorpe
County, Georgia
+ Ann A. Arnold b: Abt. 1819 in of Oglethorpe County, Georgia, m: 05 Feb 1839 in
Oglethorpe County, Georgia
..............6 Elizabeth Pearce Lee b: 28 Mar 1806 in Cumberlabd Co., Va
+ Richard Ready m: 28 Mar 1822
..............6 Robert Wilborn Lee b: 31 Oct 1808 in Cumberlabd Co., Va, d: 1894 ; Y
..............6 Joel Allen Lee b: 18 Jun 1811 in Cumberlabd Co., Va, d: 25 Dec 1836 ; Y
............5 Elizabeth Lee b: Abt. 1770 in of, Cumberland, Co, Va, d: 15 Aug 1867 in Marshall, Co TN; Y
+ John B FOWLER b: Abt. 1778 in of, Bedford, Co, Va, m: 23 Sep 1805 in Cumberland, Co,
Va, d: Marshall, Co TN; Y
............5 Mary LEE b: Abt. 1772 in of, Cumberland, Co, Va
............5 William Noel Lee b: Abt. 1773 in of, Cumberland, Co, Va
............5 Charles Barnett Lee b: 1784 in Cumberland Co., VA, d: 12 Nov 1863 in Grimes Co., Texas; Y
+ Sarah Coyners YOUNG b: 20 Dec 1785 in Union County, SC, m: 12 Dec 1803 in Oglethorpe,
Co Ga, d: 10 Sep 1847 in Monroe Co., MS (now the area is part of Clay Co., MS); Y
..............6 George Henderson Lee b: 27 Nov 1804 in Oglethorpe Co., GA, d: 12 Jul 1871 in Lowndes
(now Clay) Co., MS; Y
+ Mary Ann Hawkins b: 06 Jan 1803 in Oglethorpe Co. (?), GA, m: 13 Nov 1828 in
Oglethorpe Co., GA, d: 10 May 1856 in Lowndes (now Clay) Co., MS; Y
..................7 Nancy Susan Lee b: 29 May 1829 in Oglethorpe Co., GA, d: 15 Jul 1852 in Clay Co., MS;
Y
+ James H. Curry m: 22 Jan 1850 in Lowndes Co., MS
..................7 John Barnett Lee b: 09 Jul 1830 in Oglethorpe Co., GA, d: 1886 in Clay Co., MS; Y
+ Frances E. McDaniel b: 1840, m: 29 Jun 1856 in Lowndes Co., MS, d: 1905 in Clay Co.,
MS; Y
....................8 John B. Lee b: 1863 in Clay Co., Mississippi
....................8 William T. Lee b: 1865 in Clay Co., Mississippi
+ Carrie or Caroline Aycock b: Ogelthorp County, Georgia, d: Clay Co., Mississippi; Y
....................9 Will Henderson Lee

....................9 Aubrey McDaniel Lee
....................8 Franklin Lee b: 1867 in Clay Co., Mississippi
....................8 George F. Lee b: Abt. 1868 in Pheba, MS, d: 1931 ; Y
     + Ella b: 1874, d: 1951 ; Y
....................9 John Barney Lee b: 1899 in Pheba, MS, d: 1960 ; Y
....................9 Catherine M. Lee b: 1901, d: 1980 ; Y
....................8 Robert E. Lee b: 1869 in Clay Co., Mississippi
....................8 Oneta Lee b: 1874 in Clay Co., Mississippi
....................8 Emmett D. Lee b: 1876 in Clay Co., Mississippi
....................8 Annie Lee b: 1878 in Clay Co., Mississippi
....................7 Sarah Hawkins Lee b: 07 Sep 1833 in Oglethorpe Co., GA, d: 17 Jul 1895 in Cedar Bluff, MS; Y
     + Joseph Watson Joiner* b: 17 Sep 1830 in Fairfield Co., SC, m: 14 Jul 1856 in "Waverly", Lowndes County, MS (now Clay County), d: 06 Aug 1901 in Cedar Bluff, MS; Y
....................8 Henderson Lee Joiner b: 04 Oct 1857 in Oktibbeha County, MS, d: 07 Feb 1916 in West Point, MS; Y
     + Margaret Robinson m: 15 Mar 1897 in West Point, MS
....................9 Margaret Joiner b: Abt. 1900
     + C. J. Robb
....................10 Peggy Robb b: 1929
....................8 Anna C(atherine?) Joiner b: 08 Jun 1859 in Oktibbeha County, MS, d: 19 Jul 1943 in Ferraday, LA; Y
     + James Manley Rife m: 18 Oct 1883 in Clay County, MS (Tampico?)
....................8 John Claude Joiner b: 18 May 1862 in Oktibbeha County, MS, d: 18 Mar 1921 ; Y
     + Willie Sanford m: 18 Oct 1897 in Noxubee Co, MS, book 10, p. 32
....................9 Edward Joiner b: Abt. 1899
....................8 Katie Lee Joiner b: 01 Sep 1864
....................8 Ed(mund) Joiner* b: 24 Mar 1866 in Oktibbeha Co., MS, d: 09 Jun 1938 in West Point, MS; Y
     + Marcella Rose Wilsford* b: 02 Jun 1876 in LaGrange, AR, m: 24 Jun 1896 in M. E. Church S., West Point, MS, d: 15 Jan 1973 in West Point, MS; Y
....................9 Claude Wilsford Joiner b: 14 Apr 1897 in West Point, MS, d: May 1987 in Lookout Mountain, TN; Y
     + Sadie Alice Davis m: 02 Aug 1921 in West Point, MS
....................10 Claude Wilsford Joiner
....................10 Edward Homer Joiner
....................10 Living Joiner
....................10 Living Joiner
....................9 Joseph Granville Joiner b: 22 Jan 1899 in West Point, Mississippi, d: Dec 1965 in Sumter, South Carolina; Y
     + Margaret Durant
....................9 Sara Evelyn Joiner* b: 17 May 1904 in West Point, MS, d: 09 Mar 1984 in Vicksburg, MS; Y
     + Newton Thomas Baggett* Jr b: 27 Dec 1896 in Rolling Fork, MS, m: 07 Jun 1927 in Memphis, TN, d: 08 Jan 1974 in Indianola, MS; Y
....................10 Marcella Wilsford Baggett b: 09 Jun 1928 in West Point, MS, d: 12 Feb 1987 in Thibodeaux, LA; Y
     + Lee Robinson Jr. b: 12 Mar 1927 in Hickory, MS, m: 10 Jun 1950 in Sumter, SC, d: 10 Jul 1974 in Indianola, MS; Y
....................11 Thomas Lee Robinson b: 11 Mar 1951 in Sumter, SC, d: 23 Dec 1965 in Indianola, MS; Y
....................11 Living Robinson
....................11 Living Robinson
....................10 Living Baggett*

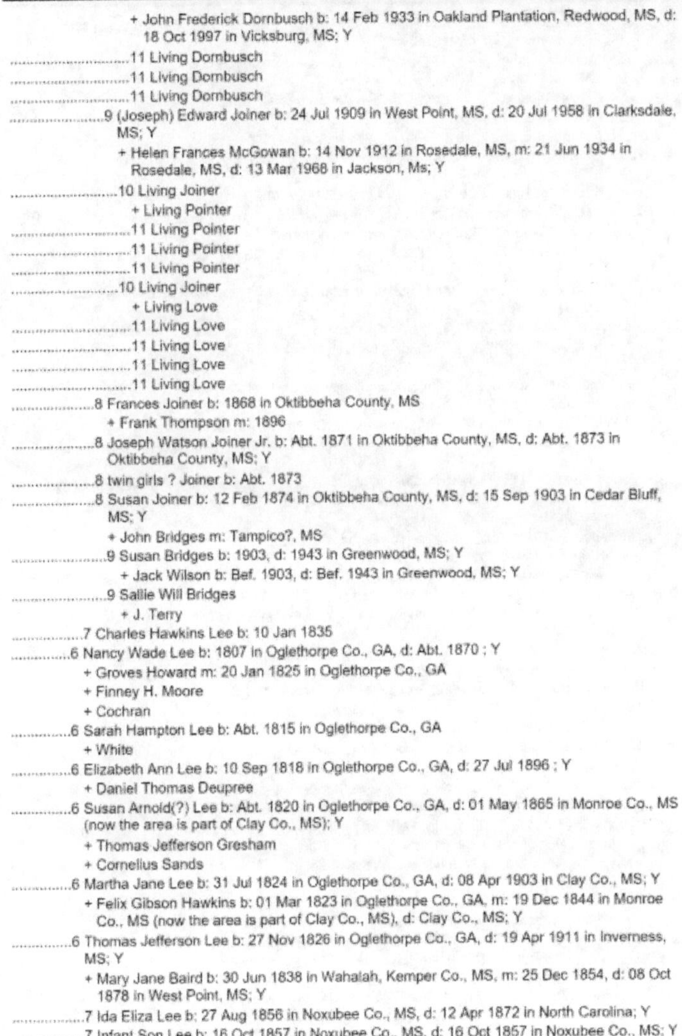

............................+ John Frederick Dornbusch b: 14 Feb 1933 in Oakland Plantation, Redwood, MS, d:
                18 Oct 1997 in Vicksburg, MS; Y
.............................11 Living Dornbusch
.............................11 Living Dornbusch
.............................11 Living Dornbusch
.............................9 (Joseph) Edward Joiner b: 24 Jul 1909 in West Point, MS, d: 20 Jul 1958 in Clarksdale,
                MS; Y
............................+ Helen Frances McGowan b: 14 Nov 1912 in Rosedale, MS, m: 21 Jun 1934 in
                Rosedale, MS, d: 13 Mar 1968 in Jackson, Ms; Y
.............................10 Living Joiner
                + Living Pointer
.............................11 Living Pointer
.............................11 Living Pointer
.............................11 Living Pointer
.............................10 Living Joiner
                + Living Love
.............................11 Living Love
.............................11 Living Love
.............................11 Living Love
.............................11 Living Love
.............................8 Frances Joiner b: 1868 in Oktibbeha County, MS
                + Frank Thompson m: 1896
.............................8 Joseph Watson Joiner Jr. b: Abt. 1871 in Oktibbeha County, MS, d: Abt. 1873 in
                Oktibbeha County, MS; Y
.............................8 twin girls ? Joiner b: Abt. 1873
.............................8 Susan Joiner b: 12 Feb 1874 in Oktibbeha County, MS, d: 15 Sep 1903 in Cedar Bluff,
                MS; Y
                + John Bridges m: Tampico?, MS
.............................9 Susan Bridges b: 1903, d: 1943 in Greenwood, MS; Y
                + Jack Wilson b: Bef. 1903, d: Bef. 1943 in Greenwood, MS; Y
.............................9 Sallie Will Bridges
                + J. Terry
.............................7 Charles Hawkins Lee b: 10 Jan 1835
.............................6 Nancy Wade Lee b: 1807 in Oglethorpe Co., GA, d: Abt. 1870 ; Y
                + Groves Howard m: 20 Jan 1825 in Oglethorpe Co., GA
                + Finney H. Moore
                + Cochran
.............................6 Sarah Hampton Lee b: Abt. 1815 in Oglethorpe Co., GA
                + White
.............................6 Elizabeth Ann Lee b: 10 Sep 1818 in Oglethorpe Co., GA, d: 27 Jul 1896 ; Y
                + Daniel Thomas Deupree
.............................6 Susan Arnold(?) Lee b: Abt. 1820 in Oglethorpe Co., GA, d: 01 May 1865 in Monroe Co., MS
                (now the area is part of Clay Co., MS); Y
                + Thomas Jefferson Gresham
                + Cornelius Sands
.............................6 Martha Jane Lee b: 31 Jul 1824 in Oglethorpe Co., GA, d: 08 Apr 1903 in Clay Co., MS; Y
                + Felix Gibson Hawkins b: 01 Mar 1823 in Oglethorpe Co., GA, m: 19 Dec 1844 in Monroe
                Co., MS (now the area is part of Clay Co., MS), d: Clay Co., MS; Y
.............................6 Thomas Jefferson Lee b: 27 Nov 1826 in Oglethorpe Co., GA, d: 19 Apr 1911 in Inverness,
                MS; Y
                + Mary Jane Baird b: 30 Jun 1838 in Wahalah, Kemper Co., MS, m: 25 Dec 1854, d: 08 Oct
                1878 in West Point, MS; Y
.............................7 Ida Eliza Lee b: 27 Aug 1856 in Noxubee Co., MS, d: 12 Apr 1872 in North Carolina; Y
.............................7 Infant Son Lee b: 16 Oct 1857 in Noxubee Co., MS, d: 16 Oct 1857 in Noxubee Co., MS; Y

...............7 Sallie Alice Lee b: 07 Aug 1859 in Crawfordville, Lowndes Co., MS, d: 11 Aug 1860 in
           Crawfordville, Lowndes Co., MS; Y
...............7 James Barnett Lee b: 17 Oct 1861 in Inverness, Washington Co., (now Sunflower Co.),
           MS, d: Marigold, MS; Y
...............7 Annie Victoria Lee b: 29 Mar 1864 in Washington Co., MS
...............7 William Henry Lee b: 04 Oct 1865
...............7 Mary Edna Lee b: 18 Jul 1867 in Washington Co., MS
...............7 Thomas Henderson Lee b: 17 Jul 1869 in Washington Co., MS, d: 11 Jun 1915 in
           Washington Co., MS; Y
...............7 Joseph Lamar Lee b: 17 Jul 1871 in West Point, MS
...............7 Mary Baird Lee b: 05 Oct 1878 in West Point, MS
           + L. R. Early m: 30 Jun 1880 in Meridian, Lauderdale Co., MS
...............7 Sallie Young Lee b: 12 Apr 1881 in Sunflower Co., MS, d: 22 Jul 1882 in Sunflower Co.,
           MS; Y
...............7 Sallie Lee b: 13 Feb 1884 in Sunflower Co., MS, d: 01 Dec 1886 in Sunflower Co., MS; Y
...............7 Nellie C. Lee b: 27 Dec 1885
           + Anne Eleanore SCOTT b: Abt. 1820 in Monroe, Co, MS, m: 06 Jul 1848 in Monroe, Co, MS
.........4 Richard Lee b: Abt. 1742 in Richmond, King and Queen, Co, Va, d: 1811 in Cumberland, Co, Va;
       Y
           + Tabitha ANDREWS b: 1757 in of, Cumberland, Campbell, Va, m: 1777, d: 1828 ; Y
.........4 Keziah Lee b: Abt. 1745 in Cumberland, Co, Va
           + William COX b: Abt. 1743 in of, Cumberland, Co, Va, m: Abt. 1768 in Va
......3 Anne Lee b: Abt. 1707 in Richmond, Co, Va, d: Aft. 1747 in will, grandmother, Elizabeth, TAYLOR;
       Y
......3 Richard Lee b: 1711 in Richmond, Co, Va, d: Aft. 1747 in will, grandmother, Elizabeth, TAYLOR; Y
......3 John Lee b: 11 Oct 1713 in Richmond, Co, Va, d: 12 Dec 1722 in N. Farnham, parish, register,
       Richmond Co. Va.; Y
           + Elizabeth PAGE b: Abt. 1715 in of, Richmond, Co Va
......3 Joseph Lee b: 1714/15 in York, Co, Va
......3 Elizabeth Betsey Lee b: Abt. 1715 in Richmond, Co, Va, d: Aft. 1747 in will, grandmother, Elizabeth,
       TAYLOR; Y
......3 Sarah Lee b: Abt. 1716 in Richmond, Co, Va, d: Aft. 1747 in will, grandmother, Elizabeth, TAYLOR;
       Y
...2 John Lee Major b: Abt. 1682 in Surry, County, Va, d: 05 Oct 1731 in of, Surry, King and Queen, Va; Y
       + Anne* TAYLOR twin b: 12 Jan 1683/84 in Hare Forest, New Kent Co, Va, m: Abt. 1699 in
       Richmond, Co, Va, d: 1731 in St. George Parish, Spotsylvania Co., VA; Y
......3 John Lee jr b: 01 Sep 1700 in Richmond, Co, Va, d: Orange, Co, Va; Y
           + Ann Carter b: Abt. 1695 in of, Spotsylvania, King and Queen, Va, d: later, Orange, Co, Va; Y
.........4 William Lee b: Abt. 1718 in King and Queen, Co, Spotsylvania, Va
           + Sarah b: Abt. 1716 in King and Queen, Co, Spotsylvania, Va
......3 Catherine Lee b: Abt. 1702 in King and Queen Co., Va
           + George PRIDDY b: Abt. 1700 in King and Queen Co., Va, m: 1725 in first husband
         ' + Richard SHACKLEFORD b: Abt. 1710, m: Abt. 1730 in second husband
......3 Ferdinand Leigh b: Abt. 1704 in Surry Co., VA of Warwick Co., VA, d: Dinwiddie, Virginia, USA; Y
           + Mary Martha Cole b: 1711 in Boldrup, Warwick County, VA, m: Abt. 1731 in Surry Co., VA, d: Abt.
           1750 ; Y
.........4 Mary Lee Leigh b: Abt. 1733 in Surry Co., VA
           + William Claiborne b: Abt. 1731 in Surry Co., VA, m: 03 Nov 1753 in Surry Co., VA
.........4 William Leigh b: 1747, d: 14 Sep 1787 in Chesterfield, Virginia, USA; Y
......3 Elizabeth Lee b: 1706 in Richmond, Co, Va, d: Apr 1750 in Orange Co., VA; Y
           + Benjamin TAYLOR b: Abt. 1699 in Wicomico Pa. Northumberland Co. VA, m: Abt. 1736 in
           Northumberland Co., VA, d: 18 Jul 1748 in Northumberland Co., VA; Y
.........4 Winifred TAYLOR b: 1737 in Rapidan, Orange Co, Va
.........4 Hannah TAYLOR b: 1739 in Rapidan, Orange Co, Va
.........4 Elizabeth TAYLOR b: 1741 in Rapidan, Orange Co, Va

..........4 Richard TAYLOR b: 22 Mar 1743/44 in Rapidan, Orange Co, Va, d: 19 Jan 1829 in Louisville,
        Jefferson Co, Ky; Y
      + Sarah Pannill Dabney STROTHER b: 11 Dec 1760 in Rapidan, Orange Co, Va, m: 20 Aug
        1779 in Orange, Virginia, d: 13 Dec 1822 in Louisville, Jefferson Co, Ky; Y
..........5 Zackary TAYLOR b: Abt. 1769 in Of, Virginia
..........5 Mary TAYLOR b: 1781 in Orange, Virginia
..........5 Hancock TAYLOR b: 29 Jan 1781 in Possibly, Orange, Va, d: 29 Mar 1841 in Louisville,
        Jefferson Co, Ky; Y
..........5 William Dabney Strother TAYLOR b: 1782 in Rapidan, Orange Co, Va, d: 03 Jun 1808 in
        Louisville, Jefferson Co, Ky; Y
..........5 Zachary TAYLOR b: 24 Nov 1784 in Montebello, Orange, Va, d: 09 Jul 1850 in Washington,
        District Of, Columbia; Y
..........5 Elizabeth TAYLOR b: 1788 in Oldham, Kentucky
..........5 Sally TAYLOR b: 1790 in <, Oldham, Kentucky>
..........5 Daughter TAYLOR b: Aft. 1790 in <, Oldham, Kentucky>
..........5 Daughter TAYLOR b: Aft. 1791 in <, Oldham, Kentucky>
      + Judith BATAILLE b: Abt. 1739 in <, Lancaster, Va>, m: 1759
..........5 Richard TAYLOR b: 10 Dec 1760 in Winchester, Frederick, Va, d: 09 Dec 1843 in Ohio,
        Kentucky; Y
..........5 Elizabeth TAYLOR b: 07 Sep 1762 in Orange, Virginia, d: 03 Jul 1832 in Fauquier, Va; Y
..........5 John Young TAYLOR b: 11 Jul 1765 in Lancaster, Va, d: 06 Oct 1845 in Greensburg, Green,
        Kentucky; Y
..........5 Nancy TAYLOR b: 1766 in Lancaster, Va, d: Aft. 1781 ; Y
.......4 Mary TAYLOR b: 1745 in Rapidan, Orange Co, Va
.......4 Frances TAYLOR b: 1748 in Rapidan, Orange Co, Va
......3 William Lee Lea b: 1710 in King and Queen Co., Va of Richmond, Co, Va, d: 10 Mar 1784 in
      Leesburg, Caswell Co., also Orange Co., NC 1755 moved, Leesburg, NC; Y
      + Frances WHITE b: Abt. 1717 in Richmond, Co, Va, m: Abt. 1737 in Spotsylvania, King and
        Queen, Richmond, Va, d: Aft. 1758 in South Hico, Caswell, Co, NC; Y
.........4 James Lee b: 1738 in Leesburgh, Caswell Co., NC
.........4 George Lee b: 16 Jan 1739 in Richmond Co., Va
.........4 Zachary Lee b: Abt. 1740 in Richmond, Co, Va
.........4 Sarah Lee b: 1741 in Richmond, or, Spotsylvania, Va, d: Orange, Co, NC; Y
.........4 Henry Lee b: Abt. 1746 in Richmond, Co, Va
.........4 Elizabeth Betty Lee b: Abt. 1746 in Richmond, Co, Va
.........4 Barnett Lee b: Abt. 1748 in Richmond, Co, Va
      + Catherine b: second wife, Caswell, NC, m: Aft. 1758 in Caswell, NC
......3 James Lee b: Abt. 1713 in Surry Co., Va. of Richmond, Co, Va, d: 1791 in Bedford, Co, Va; Y
      + Mary CLARKE Garnett b: 1718 in daughter, William, Garnett, Essex Co., Va, m: Abt. 1737, d:
        1794 ; Y
.........4 John Lee b: 1738 in later, of, Bedford, Va, d: 1818 in of, Campbell, Bedford, Va; Y
      + Sarah Tobitha PRICE b: 1747 in of, Bedford, Co, Va, m: 1769, d: 1818 in of, Bedford,
        Campbell, Va; Y
..........5 Tobitha Lee b: 1770 in of, Bedford, Campbell, Va, d: father, will probate, Campbell, Va; Y
        + mr ANDERSON b: Abt. 1770 in of, Campbell, Bedford, Va
..........5 Nancy Lee b: 1771 in of, Bedford, Campbell, Va, d: father, will probate, Campbell, Va; Y
        + mr ANDERSON b: Abt. 1770 in of, Campbell, Bedford, Va
..............6 John ANDERSON b: Abt. 1795
..........5 Stephen Lee b: Abt. 1775 in of, Bedford, Campbell, Va
        + Sarah Roach see = 71403 b: Abt. 1777 in of, Campbell, Co, Va, m: 01 Sep 1804 in
         Washington, Co, Va
..........5 Patty Lee b: Abt. 1777 in of, Bedford, Campbell, Va
        + James Anthony b: Abt. 1775 in of, Campbell, Co, Va, m: Abt. 1800 in Campbell, Co, Va
..........5 Susannah Lee b: Abt. 1779 in of, Bedford, Campbell, Va
        + Robert Lancaster b: Abt. 1777 in of, Campbell, Co, Va, m: Abt. 1800 in Campbell, Co, Va

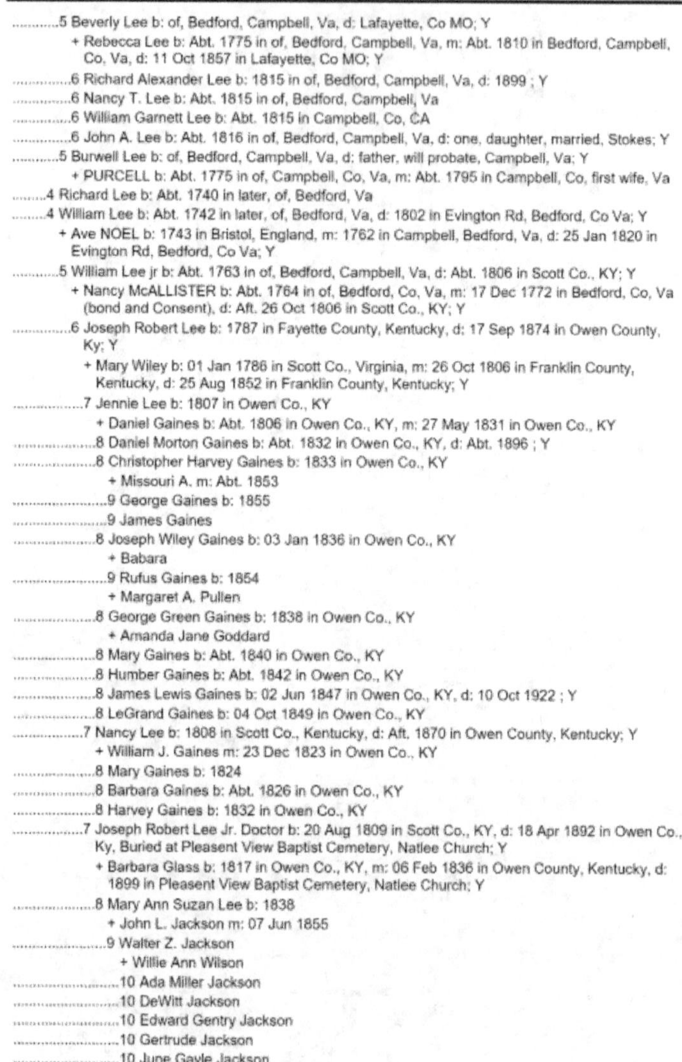

............5 Beverly Lee b: of, Bedford, Campbell, Va, d: Lafayette, Co MO; Y
    + Rebecca Lee b: Abt. 1775 in of, Bedford, Campbell, Va, m: Abt. 1810 in Bedford, Campbell, Co, Va, d: 11 Oct 1857 in Lafayette, Co MO; Y
..............6 Richard Alexander Lee b: 1815 in of, Bedford, Campbell, Va, d: 1899 ; Y
..............6 Nancy T. Lee b: Abt. 1815 in of, Bedford, Campbell, Va
..............6 William Garnett Lee b: Abt. 1815 in Campbell, Co, CA
..............6 John A. Lee b: Abt. 1816 in of, Bedford, Campbell, Va, d: one, daughter, married, Stokes; Y
............5 Burwell Lee b: of, Bedford, Campbell, Va, d: father, will probate, Campbell, Va; Y
    + PURCELL b: Abt. 1775 in of, Campbell, Co, Va, m: Abt. 1795 in Campbell, Co, first wife, Va
.........4 Richard Lee b: Abt. 1740 in later, of, Bedford, Va
.........4 William Lee b: Abt. 1742 in later, of, Bedford, Va, d: 1802 in Evington Rd, Bedford, Co Va; Y
    + Ave NOEL b: 1743 in Bristol, England, m: 1762 in Campbell, Bedford, Va, d: 25 Jan 1820 in Evington Rd, Bedford, Co Va; Y
............5 William Lee jr b: Abt. 1763 in of, Bedford, Campbell, Va, d: Abt. 1806 in Scott Co., KY; Y
    + Nancy McALLISTER b: Abt. 1764 in of, Bedford, Co, Va, m: 17 Dec 1772 in Bedford, Co, Va (bond and Consent), d: Aft. 26 Oct 1806 in Scott Co., KY; Y
..............6 Joseph Robert Lee b: 1787 in Fayette County, Kentucky, d: 17 Sep 1874 in Owen County, Ky; Y
    + Mary Wiley b: 01 Jan 1786 in Scott Co., Virginia, m: 26 Oct 1806 in Franklin County, Kentucky, d: 25 Aug 1852 in Franklin County, Kentucky; Y
..................7 Jennie Lee b: 1807 in Owen Co., KY
    + Daniel Gaines b: Abt. 1806 in Owen Co., KY, m: 27 May 1831 in Owen Co., KY
........................8 Daniel Morton Gaines b: Abt. 1832 in Owen Co., KY, d: Abt. 1896 ; Y
........................8 Christopher Harvey Gaines b: 1833 in Owen Co., KY
    + Missouri A. m: Abt. 1853
........................9 George Gaines b: 1855
........................9 James Gaines
........................8 Joseph Wiley Gaines b: 03 Jan 1836 in Owen Co., KY
    + Babara
........................9 Rufus Gaines b: 1854
    + Margaret A. Pullen
........................8 George Green Gaines b: 1838 in Owen Co., KY
    + Amanda Jane Goddard
........................8 Mary Gaines b: Abt. 1840 in Owen Co., KY
........................8 Humber Gaines b: Abt. 1842 in Owen Co., KY
........................8 James Lewis Gaines b: 02 Jun 1847 in Owen Co., KY, d: 10 Oct 1922 ; Y
........................8 LeGrand Gaines b: 04 Oct 1849 in Owen Co., KY
..................7 Nancy Lee b: 1808 in Scott Co., Kentucky, d: Aft. 1870 in Owen County, Kentucky; Y
    + William J. Gaines m: 23 Dec 1823 in Owen Co., KY
........................8 Mary Gaines b: 1824
........................8 Barbara Gaines b: Abt. 1826 in Owen Co., KY
........................8 Harvey Gaines b: 1832 in Owen Co., KY
..................7 Joseph Robert Lee Jr. Doctor b: 20 Aug 1809 in Scott Co., KY, d: 18 Apr 1892 in Owen Co., Ky, Buried at Pleasent View Baptist Cemetery, Natlee Church; Y
    + Barbara Glass b: 1817 in Owen Co., KY, m: 06 Feb 1836 in Owen County, Kentucky, d: 1899 in Pleasent View Baptist Cemetery, Natlee Church; Y
........................8 Mary Ann Suzan Lee b: 1838
    + John L. Jackson m: 07 Jun 1855
........................9 Walter Z. Jackson
    + Willie Ann Wilson
..........................10 Ada Miller Jackson
..........................10 DeWitt Jackson
..........................10 Edward Gentry Jackson
..........................10 Gertrude Jackson
..........................10 June Gayle Jackson

```
.....................10 Ward B Jackson
.....................10 John B. Jackson
.....................10 Walter Jackson
.....................10 Stella Bernice Jackson
.....................9 John C. Jackson
                      + Florence Pense?
.....................10 Lewis Porter Jackson
.....................10 Mary Lizzie Jackson
                         + Lotus Curtis
.....................11 Juanita Curtis
.....................9 Alice Miller Jackson
                      + William Anderson
.....................10 Iva Lee Anderson
                         + Nudger Glass
.....................11 Alice Elizabeth Glass
.....................10 John L. Anderson
.....................9 America Ellen Jackson
                      + John D. White
.....................10 Mary Edna White
                         + Ford Adkins
.....................11 Ana Miller Adkins
.....................10 Annie Florence White
                         + Sanford Wiggington
.....................11 William Wiggington
.....................8 Robert Belfield Lee b: 29 Jul 1842, d: 16 Apr 1906 ; Y
                      + Cornelia Smith b: 24 Apr 1853 in Owen County, d: 09 Feb 1925 ; Y
.....................9 Cora Dean Lee b: 16 Sep 1874, d: 29 Apr 1952 ; Y
                      + L. F. Aulick
.....................10 Louis Dean Aulick
                         + Evelyn Carrol
.....................11 Living Aulick
.....................11 Lewis Howard Aulick
.....................11 Lynn Carrol Aulick
.....................10 Robert Belfield Aulick
.....................10 Jennie Lee Aulick
                         + Irvan Wesley
.....................11 Robert Lester Wesley
.....................11 Betty Jean Wesley
.....................9 John Howard Lee
.....................8 Letitia Laititia J. Lee b: 1844, d: New Columbus, KY; Y
                      + William J. Hughes m: 11 Dec 1861
.....................9 Annie Craig Hughes b: 1863
                      + Winslow Robinson m: 13 Jan 1881
.....................10 Elizabeth Ellen Robinson
.....................10 Armon Winslow Robinson
.....................10 Calvin Ward Robinson
.....................10 Leona Robinson
.....................10 Hansley Todd Robinson
.....................10 Kelly Earl Robinson
.....................10 Verna Vendetta Robinson
.....................10 Irene Robinson
.....................10 Zola Belfield Robinson
.....................10 Audrey Lee Robinson
.....................9 Morilla Hughes b: 1864
```

```
                              + Jeff Lee
......................10 Isobella Lee
......................10 Beckham Lee
......................9 Mary Barbara Hughes b: 1866
......................9 Eliza Hughes
                              + Lina Fightmaster
......................10 Vicroy Fightmaster
......................9 Agnes Hughes
                              + Emmanuel Dempsey
......................10 Latitia Dempsey
......................10 Armel Dempsey
                                  + Eva Rose
......................11 Living Dempsey
......................9 Isobelle Hughes
......................9 Laura Hughes
                              + Clarence Smith
......................9 Ethel Hughes d: 02 Dec 1961 ; Y
                              + Emma Basset
......................9 Willie Hughes
......................9 Owen Hughes
......................8 James Monday Lee b: 01 Dec 1846 in Owen County, Kentucky, d: 24 Dec 1926 in Owen
                         County, Kentucky; Y
                              + Elvira Smith b: 14 Jul 1845 in Owen County, Kentucky, m: 19 Nov 1866, d: 12 Jan 1883
                                in Owen County, Kentucky; Y
......................9 Jefferson Craig Lee b: 1867 in Owen County, Kentucky, d: 1945 ; Y
                              + Nancy Wilson
......................10 Walter Lee
                              + Viola Smith
......................11 Omer B. Lee
......................11 Louise Lee
......................10 James Monday Lee II
                              + Naomi Lamay
......................11 Phyllis Lamay
                              + Dora Mae Sargent
......................11 Scotty Sargent
......................10 C.T. Lee
                              + Beaulah Barker
......................11 Clarence B. Lee
......................11 Living Lee
......................11 Living Lee
......................11 Carl Lee
......................11 James Thomas Lee
......................10 Stella Lee
                              + Leightan Gillespie
......................11 Charles Gillespie
......................11 Alma Mae Gillespie
                              + Simmie Barnetta
......................10 Roy Lee
                              + Mabel McFarland
......................11 Otis Lee
......................11 James Walker Lee
......................11 Estill Lee
......................11 Arnetta Lee
......................11 Roy Everett Lee
```

.................9 Ella Barbara Lee b: 09 Nov 1869 in Owen County, Kentucky, d: 17 Nov 1953 in Scott, Co., KY; Y
....................+ William Ashberry Marshall b: 02 Jun 1849 in Scott, Co., KY, m: 11 Apr 1889 in Porter, Scott, Co., KY, d: 27 Oct 1916 in Scott, Co., KY; Y
.................10 Humphrey Marshall b: 21 Apr 1891 in Porter, Scott, Co., KY
....................+ Sarah Wright
.................11 Living Marshall
.................11 Ina Marshall
.................11 Ada Marshall
.................11 Elaine Marshall
.................11 William Marshall
.................10 Lew Wallace Marshall b: 20 Feb 1893 in Porter, Scott, Co., KY
....................+ Stella Vance
.................11 Dorothy Marshall
.................11 Algena Marshall
.................11 Mary Ella Marshall
.................11 Robert Marshall
.................11 Aliene Marshall
.................9 Joseph Anderson Lee b: 1875 in Owen County, Kentucky, d: 1953 ; Y
....................+ Sarah Elizabeth Kelly
.................10 Alma Irene Lee
....................+ Alonzo Ralston
.................11 Everett Franklin Ralston
.................11 Frances Mae Ralston
.................11 Living Ralston
.................11 Alonzo Ralston Jr.
.................11 Doris Jean Ralston
.................10 Ona Lancaster Lee
....................+ Willie Mae Pugh
.................11 Agnes Elizabeth Lee
.................11 Ona Lancaster Lee d: Korea; Y
.................10 Essie Mae Lee
....................+ Atmore Jackson
.................11 Joseph Davis Jackson
.................11 Flora Kathleen Jackson
.................11 Imogene Jackson
.................10 Elvira Frances Lee
....................+ Edgar Conner Wright
.................11 Sarah Opal Wright
.................11 Wilbur Conner Wright
.................11 Elena Gay Wright
.................11 Ruby Lee Wright
.................10 Eugene Earl Lee
.................9 Elisha Lee b: 1881 in Owen County, Kentucky
....................+ Grace Truman Vance
.................10 Edith J. Lee b: 02 Dec 1907
....................+ James Thomas Wright
.................10 James Roscoe Lee
.................9 Dozia Lee
.................9 James M. Lee
.................9 Benjamin Lee
....................+ Maggie Sweeney
.................9 Ben Franklin Lee
....................+ Stella Covington

...................9 Dozier Belfield Lee
            + Orna Ruthledge
...................10 Opal Lee
            + Wm Whitlock
...................11 Helen Jean Whitlock
            + J.B. Foust
...................10 Gladys Lee
            + Julius Schrieber
...................11 Living Schrieber
...................11 Karen Schrieber
...................11 Patricia Ann Schrieber
...................11 Living Schrieber
...................10 Annie Laurie Lee
            + Charles Lynn
...................11 Living Lynn
...................11 Living Lynn
...................10 Sylvia Lee
            + Thomas Marshall
...................11 Jane Carol Marshall
...................11 Living Marshall
...................8 America Lee b: 1849 in Owen County, Kentucky
...................8 William Brackenridge Lee b: 06 Jul 1852 in Owen County, Kentucky
            + [unknown spouse]
...................9 Eural Lee
...................9 Willie T. Lee
...................8 Benjamin Franklin Lee b: 1856 in Owen County, Kentucky
            + Susan b: 1861 in Owen County, Kentucky
...................9 Bessie Lee b: Abt. 1880 in Owen County, Kentucky
...................9 Ina Lee b: Abt. 1885 in Owen County, Kentucky
...................9 Jack Lee b: Abt. 1888 in Owen County, Kentucky
...................9 Maggie B. Lee b: Owen County, Kentucky
...................9 Essie Lee b: Owen County, Kentucky
...................8 John Henry Lee b: Owen County, Kentucky, d: 1909 in Frankfort, Franklin Co., Kentucky; Y
            + Mary Elizabeth Walker b: 13 Nov 1845 in Owen County, Kentucky, m: 24 Sep 1862 in Owen County, Kentucky, d: 20 Jul 1930 in Frankfort, Franklin Co., Kentucky; Y
...................9 Robert E. Lee b: Jun 1865 in Owenton, Owen County, Kentucky
            + Hallie McQueen b: Jun 1869 in Owen County, Kentucky, m: 18 Oct 1887 in Owen County, Kentucky
...................10 Dallas B. Lee b: Abt. 1888 in Owen County, Kentucky
...................10 Earl Lee b: Abt. 1890 in Owen County, Kentucky
            + Mary Ann Duke
...................11 Doris Lee
...................11 Fanny Lee
...................10 Talmage Wellington Lee b: Abt. 1892 in Owen County, Kentucky
            + Aulene Jones
...................11 Cornelia Lee
...................11 Clara Lee
...................11 Eugene Lee
...................11 Walter Lee
...................10 Fanny Lee b: Abt. 1894 in Owen County, Kentucky
...................10 Arnetta Lee b: Abt. 1896 in Owen County, Kentucky
            + Wm. K. Juett
...................11 Edward Lee Juett

....................11 William K. Juett Jr.
....................11 Nell Louise Juett
....................11 Gene Juett
....................10 Robert Walker Lee b: Abt. 1898 in Owen County, Kentucky
          + Sudie Morgan
....................11 Donald Morgan Lee
....................10 Cornell Lee b: Abt. 1900 in Owen County, Kentucky
          + Paul Thompson
....................11 Living Lee
....................11 Robert Paul Lee
....................11 Living Lee
....................11 Living Lee
....................11 Living Lee
....................9 Allen J. Lee b: Abt. 1867 in Owen County, Kentucky
....................9 Crawford Lee b: 20 Mar 1868 in Owen County, Kentucky, d: 22 Dec 1935 in Frankfort
          Cemetery, Frankfort, Kentucky; Y
          + Annie Belle Duvall b: 09 Jul 1872, m: Abt. 1892 in Franklin County, Kentucly, d: 27
          Oct 1952 in Frankfort, Kentucky, Frankfort Cemetery; Y
....................10 Estill HM. Lee b: Abt. 1893 in Franklin County, Kentucly
....................10 Kelly C. Lee b: Abt. 1895 in Franklin County, Kentucly
....................10 Arthur Marion Lee b: 15 Sep 1897 in Franklin County, Kentucly, d: 29 Dec 1958 in
          Fayette County, Kentucky, Interment at Frankfort Cemetery, Frankfort, Ky; Y
....................10 Neville Garrett Lee b: Abt. 1899 in Franklin County, Kentucly
....................10 Cleora Grace Lee b: 13 Oct 1902 in Franklin County, Kentucky, d: 22 Jul 1976 in
          Franklin County, Kentucky, interned at Sunset Memorial Gardens; Y
          + Guy E. Franks b: 12 Oct 1892 in Grant County, Kentucky, d: 25 Oct 1958 in
          Franklin County, Kentucky, interned at Sunset Memorial Gardens; Y
....................11 John Leonard Franks b: 30 Oct 1925
....................11 Jane Franks b: 05 Aug 1931, d: 18 Jun 1982 in City of Faith Hospital in Tulsa,
          Okla., buried on June 23, 1982 in Resthaven Cemetery, Sperry, Okla; Y
          + Charles R. Robinett
....................11 Dan A. Franks
....................11 Helen Franks
....................11 Sue Franks
....................11 Shirley Franks
....................9 Wellington T. Lee b: 1872 in Owen County, Kentucky, d: 21 Oct 1943 in Frankfort,
          Franklin Co., Kentucky; Y
          + Clementine Roberson
....................10 Wellington Vernon Lee
....................10 John Franklin Lee
....................10 Charles Clay Lee
....................10 Leo Harold Lee
....................9 Lewis Mason Lee b: 1874 in Saltville, Washington Co., Va, d: Oct 1953 in Owen
          County, Kentucky; Y
          + Lena Webster b: Abt. 1876 in Owen County, Kentucky, m: Abt. 1894, d: Abt. 1898 in
          Owen County, Kentucky; Y
....................10 Carrie Lucille Lee b: Abt. 1894 in Owen County, Kentucky, d: Of Lexington Ky; Y
          + Anderson
....................10 Myra Lee b: Abt. 1896, d: Of Miami, FL; Y
          + Anderson
....................10 Lewis Mason Lee Jr. b: Abt. 1897 in Owen County, Kentucky, d: Of Louisville,
          Jefferson Co., Ky; Y
....................10 Will Lee b: Abt. 1898 in Owen County, Kentucky, d: Of Louisville, Jefferson Co., Ky;
          Y

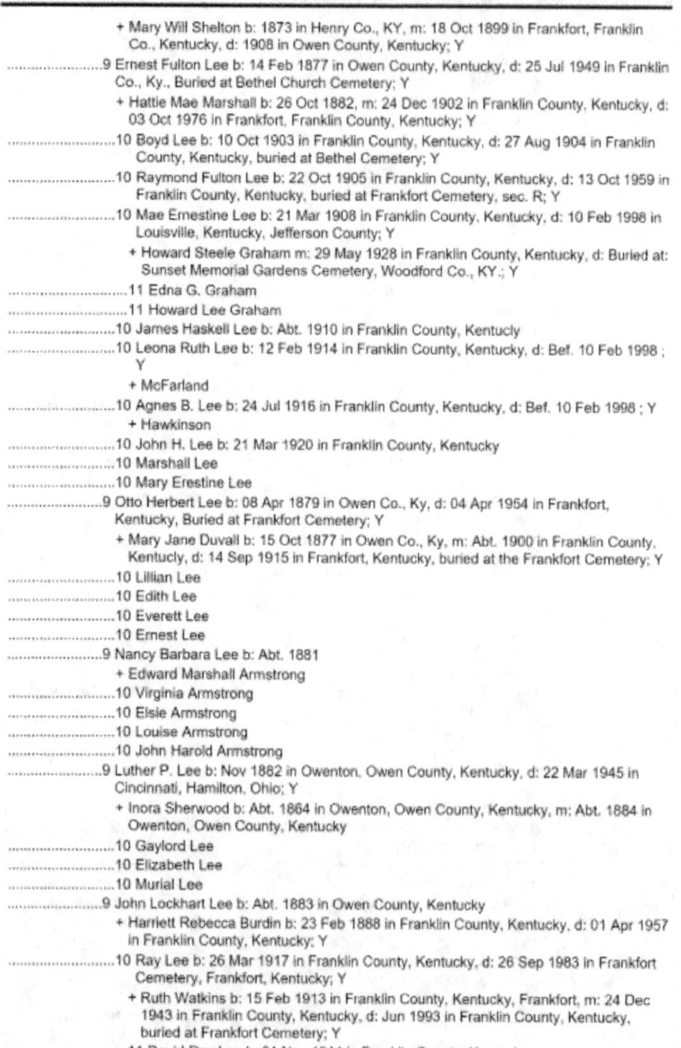

+ Mary Will Shelton b: 1873 in Henry Co., KY, m: 18 Oct 1899 in Frankfort, Franklin Co., Kentucky, d: 1908 in Owen County, Kentucky; Y

.........................9 Ernest Fulton Lee b: 14 Feb 1877 in Owen County, Kentucky, d: 25 Jul 1949 in Franklin Co., Ky., Buried at Bethel Church Cemetery; Y

+ Hattie Mae Marshall b: 26 Oct 1882, m: 24 Dec 1902 in Franklin County, Kentucky, d: 03 Oct 1976 in Frankfort, Franklin County, Kentucky; Y

.........................10 Boyd Lee b: 10 Oct 1903 in Franklin County, Kentucky, d: 27 Aug 1904 in Franklin County, Kentucky, buried at Bethel Cemetery; Y

.........................10 Raymond Fulton Lee b: 22 Oct 1905 in Franklin County, Kentucky, d: 13 Oct 1959 in Franklin County, Kentucky, buried at Frankfort Cemetery, sec. R; Y

.........................10 Mae Ernestine Lee b: 21 Mar 1908 in Franklin County, Kentucky, d: 10 Feb 1998 in Louisville, Kentucky, Jefferson County; Y

+ Howard Steele Graham m: 29 May 1928 in Franklin County, Kentucky, d: Buried at: Sunset Memorial Gardens Cemetery, Woodford Co., KY.; Y

.........................11 Edna G. Graham

.........................11 Howard Lee Graham

.........................10 James Haskell Lee b: Abt. 1910 in Franklin County, Kentucly

.........................10 Leona Ruth Lee b: 12 Feb 1914 in Franklin County, Kentucky, d: Bef. 10 Feb 1998 ; Y

+ McFarland

.........................10 Agnes B. Lee b: 24 Jul 1916 in Franklin County, Kentucky, d: Bef. 10 Feb 1998 ; Y

+ Hawkinson

.........................10 John H. Lee b: 21 Mar 1920 in Franklin County, Kentucky

.........................10 Marshall Lee

.........................10 Mary Erestine Lee

.........................9 Otto Herbert Lee b: 08 Apr 1879 in Owen Co., Ky, d: 04 Apr 1954 in Frankfort, Kentucky, Buried at Frankfort Cemetery; Y

+ Mary Jane Duvall b: 15 Oct 1877 in Owen Co., Ky, m: Abt. 1900 in Franklin County, Kentucly, d: 14 Sep 1915 in Frankfort, Kentucky, buried at the Frankfort Cemetery; Y

.........................10 Lillian Lee

.........................10 Edith Lee

.........................10 Everett Lee

.........................10 Ernest Lee

.........................9 Nancy Barbara Lee b: Abt. 1881

+ Edward Marshall Armstrong

.........................10 Virginia Armstrong

.........................10 Elsie Armstrong

.........................10 Louise Armstrong

.........................10 John Harold Armstrong

.........................9 Luther P. Lee b: Nov 1882 in Owenton, Owen County, Kentucky, d: 22 Mar 1945 in Cincinnati, Hamilton, Ohio; Y

+ Inora Sherwood b: Abt. 1864 in Owenton, Owen County, Kentucky, m: Abt. 1884 in Owenton, Owen County, Kentucky

.........................10 Gaylord Lee

.........................10 Elizabeth Lee

.........................10 Murial Lee

.........................9 John Lockhart Lee b: Abt. 1883 in Owen County, Kentucky

+ Harriett Rebecca Burdin b: 23 Feb 1888 in Franklin County, Kentucky, d: 01 Apr 1957 in Franklin County, Kentucky; Y

.........................10 Ray Lee b: 26 Mar 1917 in Franklin County, Kentucky, d: 26 Sep 1983 in Frankfort Cemetery, Frankfort, Kentucky; Y

+ Ruth Watkins b: 15 Feb 1913 in Franklin County, Kentucky, Frankfort, m: 24 Dec 1943 in Franklin County, Kentucky, d: Jun 1993 in Franklin County, Kentucky, buried at Frankfort Cemetery; Y

.........................11 David Ray Lee b: 01 Nov 1944 in Franklin County, Kentucky

+ Anne Gentry Barnett m: 20 Aug 1966 in Mercer County, Kentucky
...............11 John Bruce Lee b: 03 Aug 1946 in Frankfort, Franklin County, Kentucky
+ Judy Ann Arnold m: 19 Jun 1970 in Frankfort, Franklin County, Kentucky
...............11 Willis Allen Lee b: 25 Jun 1947 in Bowling Green, Warren County, Kentucky
+ Anne Carol Holder m: 07 Aug 1972 in Franklin County, Kentucky
+ Teresa Falk m: 16 Aug 1991 in Franklin County, Kentucky
...............12 Willis Mathew Lee b: 18 Feb 1996 in Lexington, Fayette County, Kentucky
...............12 Jonathan Grady Lee b: 14 Mar 1998 in Lexington, Fayette County, Kentucky
...............11 Carol Todd Lee b: 30 Oct 1949 in Frankfort, Franklin County, Kentucky
+ Donna Jean Whiston m: 16 Mar 1973 in Frankfort, Franklin County, Kentucky
...............11 Barry Stuart Lee b: 07 May 1956 in Frankfort, Franklin County, Kentucky
+ Joy Lynn Haering m: 23 Jun 1979 in Lorriane, Ohio
...............10 John L. Lee b: Abt. 1922 in Franklin County, Kentucky, d: Abt. 27 May 1994 in
Phoneix, Arizona; Y
+ Ophenia Plunkett
...............10 Rachel Lee b: Abt. 1925 in Anderson County, Kentucky, d: Abt. 11 May 1995 in
Marathon, Florida; Y
+ Fred Caldwell
...............10 Elmer Nixon Lee b: Abt. 1932, d: Abt. 31 Jan 1997 ; Y
...............10 Anna Lee
...............10 Sarah Kath. Lee
...............10 Sally B. Lee
...............10 Mary Walker Lee
...............10 Paul Lee
...............10 Rebecca Lee
...............10 Billie Jean Lee
...............10 Alice Lee
...............10 Harry Clifton Lee
...............10 Lewis Lockhart Lee
...........7 Christopher Lee b: 11 Apr 1811 in Scott Co., Kentucky, d: 01 Mar 1852 in Franklin County,
Kentucky; Y
+ Nancy Witherspoon b: 27 Apr 1803, m: Abt. 1833, d: 05 Mar 1852 ; Y
...............8 William J. Lee b: 1839, d: 1901 ; Y
+ Elizabeth Duvall b: 1843 in Franklin County, Kentucky, m: 30 Mar 1864 in Frankfort,
Kentucky, Franklin Co., d: 1867 ; Y
+ Sarah C. Duvall b: 02 Mar 1851 in Franklin Co., Kentucky, m: 11 May 1870 in Franklin
County, Kentucky, d: 10 Jul 1909 ; Y
...............9 Marietta Lee b: 17 May 1871
...............8 Joseph Robert Lee b: 1840 in Frankfort, Franklin Co., Kentucky, d: 1852 ; Y
...............8 Lewis J. Lee b: 1842 in Scott Co., KY
...............8 Martha Lee b: 1844 in Owen Co., KY, d: Abt. 1852 ; Y
...............8 Mary Lee b: Abt. 1846, d: 1852 ; Y
...........7 Cecelia Lee b: 22 May 1813 in Scott County, Kentucky, d: 21 Aug 1897 in Frankfort,
Franklin Co., Kentucky; Y
+ Francis Asbury Duvall b: 12 Feb 1808 in Frankfort, Kentucky, m: 04 Feb 1834 in Franklin
Co., Kentucky, d: 05 Aug 1858 in Frankfort, Franklin Co., Kentucky; Y
...............8 Charles Duvall b: 18 Jan 1835 in Franklin Co., Kentucky, d: 27 Aug 1865 in Lexington,
Kentucky; Y
+ Susan A. Luckett b: 1843 in Franklin County, Kentucky, m: 15 Mar 1859
...............9 Martha F. Duvall b: Apr 1861
...............8 Mary Jane Duvall b: 1836 in Franklin Co., Kentucky
+ Moses Harrod m: 15 Nov 1855 in Franklin Co., Ky
...............8 Francis Marion Duvall b: 15 Nov 1838 in Franklin Co., Kentucky, d: 14 Dec 1917 in
Franklin Co., Kentucky, Buried at Bethel Church Cemetery, Franklin Co., Ky.; Y

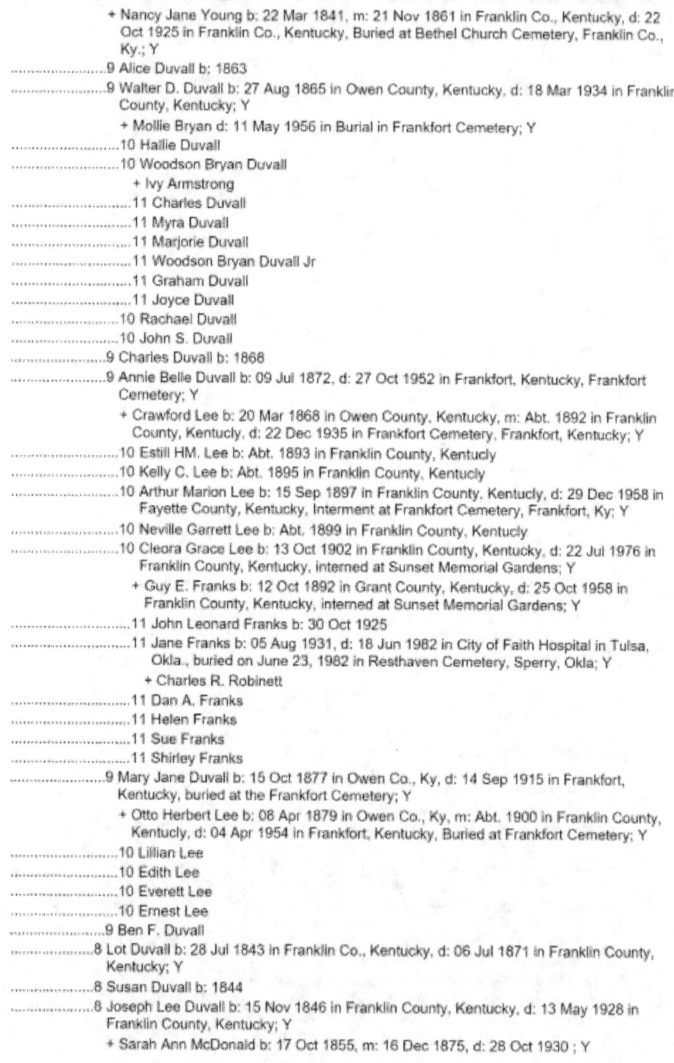

+ Nancy Jane Young b: 22 Mar 1841, m: 21 Nov 1861 in Franklin Co., Kentucky, d: 22 Oct 1925 in Franklin Co., Kentucky, Buried at Bethel Church Cemetery, Franklin Co., Ky.; Y

.........................9 Alice Duvall b: 1863

.........................9 Walter D. Duvall b: 27 Aug 1865 in Owen County, Kentucky, d: 18 Mar 1934 in Franklin County, Kentucky; Y

+ Mollie Bryan d: 11 May 1956 in Burial in Frankfort Cemetery; Y

.........................10 Hallie Duvall

.........................10 Woodson Bryan Duvall

+ Ivy Armstrong

.........................11 Charles Duvall

.........................11 Myra Duvall

.........................11 Marjorie Duvall

.........................11 Woodson Bryan Duvall Jr

.........................11 Graham Duvall

.........................11 Joyce Duvall

.........................10 Rachael Duvall

.........................10 John S. Duvall

.........................9 Charles Duvall b: 1868

.........................9 Annie Belle Duvall b: 09 Jul 1872, d: 27 Oct 1952 in Frankfort, Kentucky, Frankfort Cemetery; Y

+ Crawford Lee b: 20 Mar 1868 in Owen County, Kentucky, m: Abt. 1892 in Franklin County, Kentucly, d: 22 Dec 1935 in Frankfort Cemetery, Frankfort, Kentucky; Y

.........................10 Estill HM. Lee b: Abt. 1893 in Franklin County, Kentucly

.........................10 Kelly C. Lee b: Abt. 1895 in Franklin County, Kentucly

.........................10 Arthur Marion Lee b: 15 Sep 1897 in Franklin County, Kentucly, d: 29 Dec 1958 in Fayette County, Kentucky, Interment at Frankfort Cemetery, Frankfort, Ky; Y

.........................10 Neville Garrett Lee b: Abt. 1899 in Franklin County, Kentucly

.........................10 Cleora Grace Lee b: 13 Oct 1902 in Franklin County, Kentucky, d: 22 Jul 1976 in Franklin County, Kentucky, interned at Sunset Memorial Gardens; Y

+ Guy E. Franks b: 12 Oct 1892 in Grant County, Kentucky, d: 25 Oct 1958 in Franklin County, Kentucky, interned at Sunset Memorial Gardens; Y

.........................11 John Leonard Franks b: 30 Oct 1925

.........................11 Jane Franks b: 05 Aug 1931, d: 18 Jun 1982 in City of Faith Hospital in Tulsa, Okla., buried on June 23, 1982 in Resthaven Cemetery, Sperry, Okla; Y

+ Charles R. Robinett

.........................11 Dan A. Franks

.........................11 Helen Franks

.........................11 Sue Franks

.........................11 Shirley Franks

.........................9 Mary Jane Duvall b: 15 Oct 1877 in Owen Co., Ky, d: 14 Sep 1915 in Frankfort, Kentucky, buried at the Frankfort Cemetery; Y

+ Otto Herbert Lee b: 08 Apr 1879 in Owen Co., Ky, m: Abt. 1900 in Franklin County, Kentucly, d: 04 Apr 1954 in Frankfort, Kentucky, Buried at Frankfort Cemetery; Y

.........................10 Lillian Lee

.........................10 Edith Lee

.........................10 Everett Lee

.........................10 Ernest Lee

.........................9 Ben F. Duvall

.........................8 Lot Duvall b: 28 Jul 1843 in Franklin Co., Kentucky, d: 06 Jul 1871 in Franklin County, Kentucky; Y

.........................8 Susan Duvall b: 1844

.........................8 Joseph Lee Duvall b: 15 Nov 1846 in Franklin County, Kentucky, d: 13 May 1928 in Franklin County, Kentucky; Y

+ Sarah Ann McDonald b: 17 Oct 1855, m: 16 Dec 1875, d: 28 Oct 1930 ; Y

...............9 Claude Duvall b: 29 Jun 1876 in Franklin County, Ky., d: 14 Feb 1950 in Louisville, Ky.,
Buried at Bethel Church Cemetery, Franklin County, Kentucky; Y
+ Mildred Peffer
...............10 Clara M. Duvall b: 21 Jan 1900 in Frankfort, Ky., Franklin County, d: 05 Jan 1975 in
Bagdad, Kentucky, Shelby County; Y
+ Thomas Grant Smither m: 19 Nov 1921 in Shelbyville, Ky., Shelby County
...............11 Romayne Smither b: 26 Jul 1922 in Frankfort, Ky., Franklin County, d: 1975 in
Riverside, California; Y
+ John Isaac Dehart Jr m: Abt. 1942
...............12 John Isaac Dehart III b: 08 Apr 1944
+ Sherly Audeen McCracken m: Aug 1962
...............12 Thomas Grant Dehart b: 12 Feb 1946
+ Lisa
+ Priscilla
+ Shelia
...............12 Romayne Yvonne Dehart b: 15 Jul 1950 in Portsmouth, Ohio
+ Gerald Batross m: 08 Nov 1968 in San Bernardino, California
+ Jim Madden m: 08 Mar 1980 in San Bernardino, California
+ James J. Benadom m: 07 Mar 1987 in Phelan, California
...............12 Dale Rene' Dehart b: 26 Feb 1952 in Pasadena, California
+ Lynne Marie Nosser m: 28 Aug 1973 in Riverside, California
+ Tamma Maurisolette Davis m: 08 Feb 1997 in St. Helena, California
...............12 Darryl Lee Dehart b: 22 Aug 1956 in Anaheim California, Orange Coounty
+ Arthur Tharaldson m: Abt. 1965 in Riverside, California
...............10 Joseph Lee Duvall b: 24 Jul 1913 in Frankfort, Ky., Franklin County
...............9 Edna Duvall b: 25 Dec 1877, d: 05 Jan 1914 ; Y
...............9 Elvira Duvall b: 1878
...............9 John W. Duvall Sr. b: 05 Oct 1880, d: 12 Apr 1970 in Buried at Frankfort Cemetery; Y
+ [unknown spouse]
...............10 John W. Duvall Jr
...............9 Samuel J. Duvall b: 15 Jan 1889 in Kentucky, d: 23 Jan 1978 in Marian Co., Indiana,
buried at George Washington Park East in Indianapolis, Ind.; Y
...............9 Carrie Lee Duvall b: 16 May 1891 in Franklin County, Kentucly, d: 29 Sep 1969 in
Frankfort, Kentucky, buried in the Lawerance Plot, Frankfort Cemetery; Y
+ Duard Miles Lawrence b: 17 Jan 1887, m: 16 Dec 1908, d: 29 Jun 1949 ; Y
...............10 Gladys M. Lawrence
+ Charles Roth
...............10 Edna Louise Lawrence
+ Robert Harry Devine
...............11 Lynne Devine
...............10 Edith Lee Lawrence
+ Charles Burns
...............8 Cynthia Ellen Duvall b: 1847 in Franklin Co., Kentucky, d: Abt. 1942 ; Y
+ Bill Dinkle
...............9 Benjamin F. Dinkle b: 1872
...............9 Fanny Dinkle b: 1874
...............8 John E. Duvall b: 05 Feb 1851 in Franklin Co., Kentucky, d: 20 Feb 1871 in Frankfort,
Franklin County, Kentucky; Y
...............8 Edward Morton Duvall Sr b: 11 Mar 1853 in Franklin Co., Kentucky, d: 02 Jan 1933 in
Franklin Co., Kentucky, Buried at Bethel Cemt.; Y
+ Mary Catherine Pfeiffer b: 20 Jul 1862 in Owenton Road, Franklin Co., Kentucky, m: 13
Mar 1881 in his House, soon to be shared by Mary, d: 02 Apr 1911 in Frankfort,
Kentucky, Buried at Bethel Cemt.; Y
...............9 William Samuel Duvall b: Sep 1885, d: 1964 in Frankfort, Kentucky; Y
+ May Reese

...................10 Thomas Duvall
                + Margaret McQueen
                + Olivia Louise Gartin
...................10 Ann Mary Duvall
                + Thompson
                + Jerry Combs
...................10 Barbara Duvall
                + Jack Capsel
...................10 Agnes Pearl Duvall
...................10 John Claude Duvall
...................9 Jennie Lind Duvall b: Apr 1886, d: Abt. 1968 ; Y
                + Grover C. Phillips
...................10 Mary Phillips
                + W. T. Caillouette
...................11 Diane Caillouette
...................11 Thomas Caillouette
...................9 Ella Duvall b: 03 Apr 1886, d: 07 Mar 1981 in Louisville, Jefferson Co., Kentucky; Y
                + Frank Robert Fromang b: 10 Jan 1886, m: 02 Sep 1912 in Church of Good
                  Shephard, Frankfort, Ky., d: 28 Oct 1917 ; Y
...................10 Elinor Elizabeth Fromang b: 11 Jun 1913
                + Joseph Edward Maloney m: Abt. 1933
...................11 Joseph Edward Maloney Jr. b: 13 Jul 1935
                + Yvonne Bushong b: 1940, m: 1961
...................12 Mary Elinor Maloney
...................12 Melissa Maloney
...................11 Patrick Frank Maloney b: 04 Dec 1937
                + Helen Magers m: 1961
...................12 Michael Edward Maloney
...................12 Martha Maloney
...................12 John Maloney
...................12 Matthew Maloney
...................12 Sarah Ann Maloney
                + Jason L. Stepp m: 04 Sep 1998 in St. Gabriel Catholic Ch., Louisville, Ky
...................10 Mary Virginia Fromang b: 17 Jan 1916 in Louisville, Jefferson Co., Kentucky, d: 07
                  Jun 1993 in Louisville, Jefferson Co., Kentucky; Y
                + Austin L. Smith m: 08 Dec 1934
...................11 Charles Austin Smith b: 12 Sep 1935
                + Barbara Ballenger m: 1962
...................12 Hillary Elizabeth Smith
...................12 Mereddith Elaine Smith
                + Charloette Byrd
...................11 Linda Jane Smith b: 05 Dec 1938
                + Behrle W. Hubbuch II
...................12 Robin Lynn Hubbuch
...................12 Behrle W. Hubbuch III
...................12 John Austin Hubbuch
...................12 Jennifer Wren Hubbuch
...................12 Jordan Peter Hubbuch
...................11 Mary Ann Smith b: 31 Jul 1941
                + Richard J. Ronconi m: 1966
...................12 Matthew Angelo Ronconi
...................12 Amanda Duvall Ronconi
                + James Robert Williams m: 1920
...................10 William Robert Williams b: 24 Mar 1924, d: Aug 1976 ; Y

+ Barbara Stover
............................11 James Williams
............................11 Michael Lee Williams
............................11 Laura Lynn Williams
............................11 Tony Williams
............................11 Sylvia Williams
............................9 Houston T. Duvall b: 11 Jun 1888 in Franklin County, Kentucky, d: 03 Nov 1959 in
          Buried at Frankfort Cemetery, Frankfort, Kentucky; Y
          + Margaret Smith b: 17 Jun 1890, d: 07 Jun 1982 in Frankfort Cemetery, Frankfort,
              Kentucky; Y
............................10 Jessie Thomas Duvall
............................9 Sallie Duvall b: Jul 1890, d: 1952 ; Y
          + Jessie Leslie Miles
............................10 Francis M. Miles
............................9 Eugene Duvall b: 13 Jun 1892, d: 18 Sep 1893 ; Y
............................9 Bessie Duvall b: Nov 1894, d: 1929 ; Y
          + [unknown spouse]
............................10 James Edward Peffer b: 01 Apr 1918 in Kenton County, Kentucky
          + Virgie
............................11 James Alfred Peffer b: 1954
............................10 Sarah Helen Peffer b: 12 Jan 1921 in Kenton County, Kentucky
          + Dick Foster
............................11 Linda Peffer
          + Ted Volpenheim
............................12 Timmy Volpenheim
............................12 Traci Volpenheim
............................9 Nellie Ann Duvall b: Sep 1896
          + Louis B. Harrod
............................10 Lillian Harrod
............................9 Mary Elizabeth Duvall b: 29 Jul 1903 in Frankfort, Kentucky, d: Jul 1993 ; Y
          + Julius E. Stivers
............................10 Eugene Stivers
............................10 Frank Stivers
............................9 Mable Duvall b: 1906, d: 07 Jul 1998 in Cincinnati, Ohio, abt 0300 am, Entombed at
          Blanchchester, Ohio; Y
          + Maynard Kirk
............................9 Edward Morton Duvall Jr. b: 22 Apr 1910 in Frankfort, Kentucky, d: 28 Jan 1985 in
          Louisville, Jefferson Co., Kentucky; Y
          + Della Lee Henderson b: 02 Jun 1916 in Scott Co., KY, m: 16 Jun 1934 in
              Jeffersonville, Indiana, d: 01 Jul 1984 in Louisville, Jefferson Co., Kentucky; Y
............................10 Edward McDowell Duvall b: 11 Jan 1936 in Frankfort, Kentucky
          + Fabia Harlene Johnson b: 24 May 1943 in Bowling Green, Kentucky, m: 04 Jun
              1960 in Louisville, Kentucky, d: Sep 1996 in Panama City, Florida; Y
............................11 Jackqueline Marie Duvall b: 14 Nov 1960 in Louisville, Kentucky
          + Harry Coy m: Bef. 1988
............................12 Melissa Dorothy Higgins b: Sep 1988
............................12 Matthew Higgins
          + Lynn Higgins m: Bef. 1981
............................12 Tina Higgins b: 1981
............................11 James Edward Duvall b: 03 May 1962 in Biloxi, Mississippi
          + Denise
............................11 Anthony Mark Duvall b: 20 Jul 1963 in Savannah, Georgia
          + Iris Marlynn Rogers b: 05 Dec 1959 in Picayunne, Mississippi, m: 20 Jul 1988 in
              Galianburg, Tennessee
............................12 Britney Elizabeth Duvall b: 30 Jan 1989

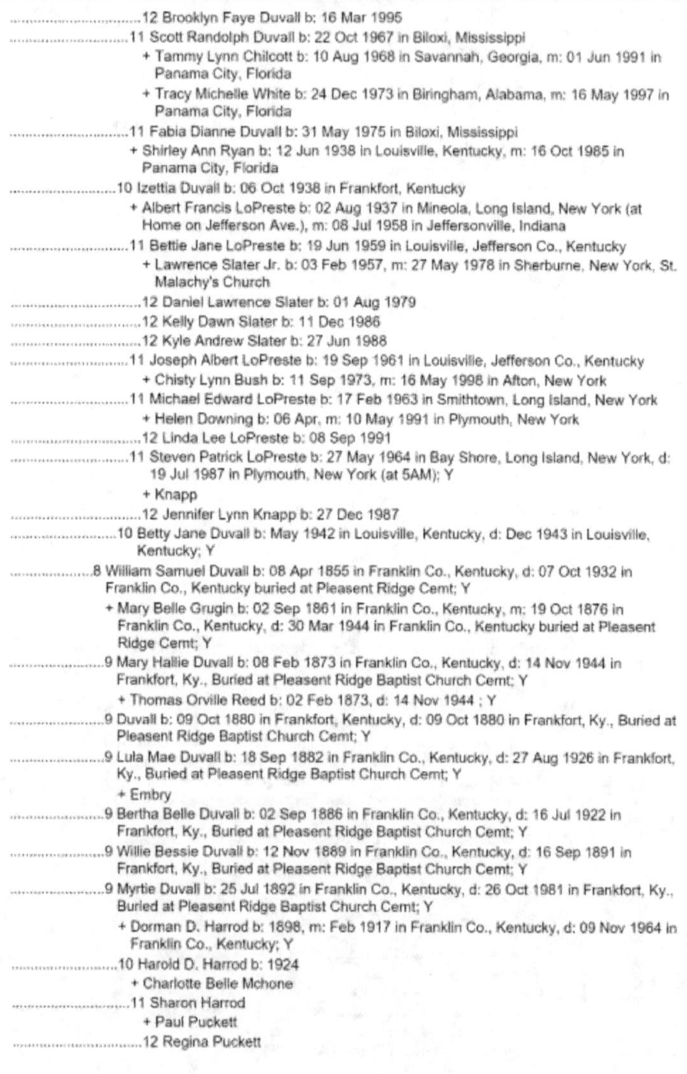

...................................12 Brooklyn Faye Duvall b: 16 Mar 1995
...................................11 Scott Randolph Duvall b: 22 Oct 1967 in Biloxi, Mississippi
+ Tammy Lynn Chilcott b: 10 Aug 1968 in Savannah, Georgia, m: 01 Jun 1991 in Panama City, Florida
+ Tracy Michelle White b: 24 Dec 1973 in Biringham, Alabama, m: 16 May 1997 in Panama City, Florida
...................................11 Fabia Dianne Duvall b: 31 May 1975 in Biloxi, Mississippi
+ Shirley Ann Ryan b: 12 Jun 1938 in Louisville, Kentucky, m: 16 Oct 1985 in Panama City, Florida
...................................10 Izettia Duvall b: 06 Oct 1938 in Frankfort, Kentucky
+ Albert Francis LoPreste b: 02 Aug 1937 in Mineola, Long Island, New York (at Home on Jefferson Ave.), m: 08 Jul 1958 in Jeffersonville, Indiana
...................................11 Bettie Jane LoPreste b: 19 Jun 1959 in Louisville, Jefferson Co., Kentucky
+ Lawrence Slater Jr. b: 03 Feb 1957, m: 27 May 1978 in Sherburne, New York, St. Malachy's Church
...................................12 Daniel Lawrence Slater b: 01 Aug 1979
...................................12 Kelly Dawn Slater b: 11 Dec 1986
...................................12 Kyle Andrew Slater b: 27 Jun 1988
...................................11 Joseph Albert LoPreste b: 19 Sep 1961 in Louisville, Jefferson Co., Kentucky
+ Chisty Lynn Bush b: 11 Sep 1973, m: 16 May 1998 in Afton, New York
...................................11 Michael Edward LoPreste b: 17 Feb 1963 in Smithtown, Long Island, New York
+ Helen Downing b: 06 Apr, m: 10 May 1991 in Plymouth, New York
...................................12 Linda Lee LoPreste b: 08 Sep 1991
...................................11 Steven Patrick LoPreste b: 27 May 1964 in Bay Shore, Long Island, New York, d: 19 Jul 1987 in Plymouth, New York (at 5AM); Y
+ Knapp
...................................12 Jennifer Lynn Knapp b: 27 Dec 1987
...................................10 Betty Jane Duvall b: May 1942 in Louisville, Kentucky, d: Dec 1943 in Louisville, Kentucky; Y
...................................8 William Samuel Duvall b: 08 Apr 1855 in Franklin Co., Kentucky, d: 07 Oct 1932 in Franklin Co., Kentucky buried at Pleasent Ridge Cemt; Y
+ Mary Belle Grugin b: 02 Sep 1861 in Franklin Co., Kentucky, m: 19 Oct 1876 in Franklin Co., Kentucky, d: 30 Mar 1944 in Franklin Co., Kentucky buried at Pleasent Ridge Cemt; Y
...................................9 Mary Hallie Duvall b: 08 Feb 1873 in Franklin Co., Kentucky, d: 14 Nov 1944 in Frankfort, Ky., Buried at Pleasent Ridge Baptist Church Cemt; Y
+ Thomas Orville Reed b: 02 Feb 1873, d: 14 Nov 1944 ; Y
...................................9 Duvall b: 09 Oct 1880 in Frankfort, Kentucky, d: 09 Oct 1880 in Frankfort, Ky., Buried at Pleasent Ridge Baptist Church Cemt; Y
...................................9 Lula Mae Duvall b: 18 Sep 1882 in Franklin Co., Kentucky, d: 27 Aug 1926 in Frankfort, Ky., Buried at Pleasent Ridge Baptist Church Cemt; Y
+ Embry
...................................9 Bertha Belle Duvall b: 02 Sep 1886 in Franklin Co., Kentucky, d: 16 Jul 1922 in Frankfort, Ky., Buried at Pleasent Ridge Baptist Church Cemt; Y
...................................9 Willie Bessie Duvall b: 12 Nov 1889 in Franklin Co., Kentucky, d: 16 Sep 1891 in Frankfort, Ky., Buried at Pleasent Ridge Baptist Church Cemt; Y
...................................9 Myrtie Duvall b: 25 Jul 1892 in Franklin Co., Kentucky, d: 26 Oct 1981 in Frankfort, Ky., Buried at Pleasent Ridge Baptist Church Cemt; Y
+ Dorman D. Harrod b: 1898, m: Feb 1917 in Franklin Co., Kentucky, d: 09 Nov 1964 in Franklin Co., Kentucky; Y
...................................10 Harold D. Harrod b: 1924
+ Charlotte Belle Mchone
...................................11 Sharon Harrod
+ Paul Puckett
...................................12 Regina Puckett

...............................12 Michael Puckett
..........................10 Flora Mae Harrod
                    + Bill Burnett
..........................10 Gladys Harrod d: 1955 ; Y
                    + Bud Rogers
..........................10 Helen Harrod d: 1984 ; Y
                    + Bud Rogers
.........................9 Lillian T. Duvall b: 16 Feb 1895 in Franklin Co., Kentucky, d: 28 Feb 1895 in Frankfort,
                    Ky., Buried at Pleasent Ridge Baptist Church Cemt; Y
.........................9 Orville Ransford Duvall Sr b: 22 Nov 1902 in Franklin Co., Kentucky, d: 03 Aug 1978 in
                    Frankfort, Ky., Buried at Pleasent Ridge Baptist Church Cemt; Y
                    + Mary Geraldine Gaines b: 22 Dec 1903 in Franklin Co., Kentucky, m: Dec 1926 in
                       Franklin Co., Kentucky, d: 13 Sep 1947 in Frankfort, Ky., Buried at Pleasent Ridge
                       Baptist Church Cemt; Y
...........................10 Orville Ransford Duvall Jr b: 08 Feb 1928 in Franklin Co., Kentucky
                    + Elizabeth Brown m: Bef. 1954
.............................11 Teresa S. Duvall b: 16 Nov 1954 in Franklin County, Kentucky
.............................11 Beverly A. Duvall b: 27 Jul 1956 in Franklin County, Kentucky
.............................11 Julia K. Duvall b: 29 Apr 1960
.............................11 Geralden Duvall b: 30 Oct 1966 in Franklin County, Kentucky
...........................10 William Gaines Duvall Sr. b: 01 Feb 1930 in Franklin Co., Kentucky
                    + Nancy Shearer m: Bef. 1954
.............................11 William Gaines Duvall Jr. b: 19 Jan 1954
.............................11 Christopher Duvall
...........................10 Cecil Thomas Duvall b: 15 Jan 1931 in Franklin Co., Kentucky
                    + Eloise Hutcherson
...........................10 Patricia Ann Duvall b: 19 Oct 1934 in Franklin Co., Kentucky
                    + Wilbert Perkins m: Bef. 1953
.............................11 Linda Perkins b: 10 Apr 1953 in Franklin County, Kentucky
.............................11 Roger Perkins b: 24 Apr 1954 in Franklin County, Kentucky
.............................11 Clara Deana Perkins b: 12 Oct 1963 in Franklin County, Kentucky
...........................10 Mary Susan Duvall b: 22 Feb 1946 in Frankfort, Kentucky
                    + Charles Kenneth Foster b: 05 Jan 1944 in Shelby Co., Kentucky, m: 25 Sep 1965
                       in Frankfort Ky., Pleasent Ridge Baptist Church
.............................11 Kenneth Foster b: 08 Apr 1971
.............................11 Julienne Foster b: 15 May 1974
                    + Ada Moore O'Nan m: Aft. 1947
.........................9 Duward Duvall d: Dec 1980 ; Y
                    + Lucy Niles
.....................8 Cordelia Duvall b: 11 Dec 1857 in Franklin Co., Kentucky, d: 04 Jan 1921 in Frankfort,
                    Ky., Buried at Pleasent Ridge Baptist Church Cemt; Y
                    + Nunley m: Aft. 1880, d: Frankfort, Ky., Buried at Pleasent Ridge Baptist Church Cemt; Y
                    + James C. Marshall d: Frankfort, Ky., Buried at Pleasent Ridge Baptist Church Cemt; Y
.........................9 Hattie Mae Marshall b: 26 Oct 1882, d: 03 Oct 1976 in Frankfort, Franklin County,
                    Kentucky; Y
                    + Ernest Fulton Lee b: 14 Feb 1877 in Owen County, Kentucky, m: 24 Dec 1902 in
                       Franklin County, Kentucky, d: 25 Jul 1949 in Franklin Co., Ky., Buried at Bethel
                       Church Cemetery; Y
...........................10 Boyd Lee b: 10 Oct 1903 in Franklin County, Kentucky, d: 27 Aug 1904 in Franklin
                    County, Kentucky, buried at Bethel Cemetery; Y
...........................10 Raymond Fulton Lee b: 22 Oct 1905 in Franklin County, Kentucky, d: 13 Oct 1959 in
                    Franklin County, Kentucky, buried at Frankfort Cemetery, sec. R; Y
...........................10 Mae Ernestine Lee b: 21 Mar 1908 in Franklin County, Kentucky, d: 10 Feb 1996 in
                    Louisville, Kentucky, Jefferson County; Y

+ Howard Steele Graham m: 29 May 1928 in Franklin County, Kentucky, d: Buried at: Sunset Memorial Gardens Cemetery, Woodford Co., KY.; Y
................................11 Edna G. Graham
................................11 Howard Lee Graham
..............................10 James Haskell Lee b: Abt. 1910 in Franklin County, Kentucly
..............................10 Leona Ruth Lee b: 12 Feb 1914 in Franklin County, Kentucky, d: Bef. 10 Feb 1998 ; Y
    + McFarland
..............................10 Agnes B. Lee b: 24 Jul 1916 in Franklin County, Kentucky, d: Bef. 10 Feb 1998 ; Y
    + Hawkinson
..............................10 John H. Lee b: 21 Mar 1920 in Franklin County, Kentucky
..............................10 Marshall Lee
..............................10 Mary Erestine Lee
..........................9 Marshall
    + James L Baker d: Frankfort, Ky., Buried at Pleasent Ridge Baptist Church Cemt; Y
......................8 Eveline Duvall b: 1859 in Franklin County, Kentucky, d: 1894 in Owen County, Kentucky; Y
..................7 William Will Lee b: 1815 in Scott Co., Kentucky, d: 1854 in Killed on trip to Mo; Y
    + Lizzie b: 11 Apr 1813, d: 13 Feb 1862 ; Y
......................8 Mary F Lee b: 1842 in Scott Co., KY, d: 1854 in Killed on trip to Mo; Y
......................8 Sarah A. Lee b: 1844 in Scott Co., KY, d: 1854 in Killed on trip to Mo; Y
......................8 John H. Lee b: 1847 in Scott Co., KY, d: 1854 in Killed on trip to Mo; Y
......................8 Polly Lee b: Abt. 1852 in Scott Co., KY
..................7 John William Lee b: 20 Feb 1817 in Franklin Co., Ky, d: 15 Mar 1898 in near Glenco., Gallatin Co., KY; Y
    + Ellen Berry b: Abt. 1819 in Owen County, Kentucky, m: Abt. 1835 in Owen County, Kentucky, d: Abt. 1837 ; Y
    + Susan E. Glass b: Abt. 1818, m: 05 Jan 1838
    + Susannah Ringo b: 01 Sep 1824, m: Abt. 1845 in Gallatin Co., KY, d: 25 Jul 1858 in Gallatin Co., KY; Y
    + Georgie C b: Abt. 1835 in of Gallatin Co., KY, m: Abt. 1860 in Gallatin Co., KY
..................7 Elizabeth Lee b: 1821 in Owen County, Kentucky
    + James Penn b: Abt. 1819, m: Abt. 1841
......................8 Mattie Penn b: 1862 in Frankfort, Franklin Co., Kentucky
......................8 Annie Penn b: 1869 in Frankfort, Franklin Co., Kentucky
......................8 Charles Penn b: 1949
    + Margaret b: 1845
..........................9 Alice Penn b: 1879 in Frankfort, Franklin Co., Kentucky
..................7 Robert M. or W. Lee b: 16 Apr 1822 in Owen County, Kentucky, d: 25 Aug 1863 in Camp Chase, Franklin County, Ohio; Y
    + Appaline D. F. Ward m: 24 Jul 1843 in Owen County, Kentucky, d: 30 May 1847 in Owen Co., KY; Y
......................8 ? M. Martha Lee b: 25 Dec 1845 in Owen Co., KY
......................8 Cynthia Cintha Appalene Lee b: 26 Feb 1847 in Owen Co., KY, d: 05 May 1907 in Owenton, Owen, Kentucky; Y
    + William Richard Bourne b: 16 Apr 1843 in of Owen Co., Ky, m: 25 Sep 1865, d: 24 Oct 1915 in Owenton, Owen Co., Ky; Y
..........................9 Ella Bourne b: 1867 in Owenton, Owen Co., Ky
..........................9 Allice Bourne b: 1869 in Owenton, Owen Co., Ky
..........................9 Robert Davis Bourne b: 04 Mar 1871 in Owenton, Owen, Kentucky, d: 01 Apr 1908 ; Y
..........................9 Maranda Marandy Bourne b: 1874 in Owenton, Owen Co., Ky
..........................9 William Rolland Bourne b: 26 Feb 1876 in Owenton, Owen, Kentucky, d: 23 Feb 1955 in Owenton, Owen, Kentucky; Y
..........................9 Nannie C. Bourne b: 09 Aug 1878 in Owenton, Owen, Kentucky, d: 20 Jan 1964 in Owenton, Owen, Kentucky; Y

................9 Thomas Edwin Bourne b: 31 Mar 1881 in Owenton, Owen, Kentucky, d: 19 Jul 1895 in Owenton, Owen, Kentucky; Y
................9 Mason Cull Bourne b: 07 Dec 1886 in Owen, Kentucky, d: 19 Jan 1957 ; Y
         + Mary America Wingate b: of Owen Co., Ky, m: 17 Oct 1853 in Owen County, Kentucky, d: Owen Co., KY; Y
................8 Fred Lee b: Abt. 1854 in Owen County, Ky
................8 Charles Lee b: Abt. 1856 in Owen County, Ky
................8 Salin Lee b: Abt. 1858 in Owen County, Ky
................8 America Lee b: Abt. 1860 in Owen County, Ky
         + Amanda Pence b: this marr may be in error dates do not fit, m: 1848 in Owen Co., KY
................7 Nathaniel Wylie Lee b: 14 Jan 1825 in Franklin Co., Ky, d: 25 Aug 1891 in Owen Co., KY; Y
         + Lucy Arnold b: 1832, m: 25 Nov 1874, d: 1888 ; Y
................8 four ch Lee
         + Francis Abott b: 1829, m: 05 Mar 1846, d: 1872 ; Y
................8 John Lee b: Abt. 1847 in Owen Co., KY
................8 Sarah Lee b: Abt. 1850 in Owen Co., KY
................8 Willis (Pink) Lee b: Abt. 1852 in Owen Co., KY
            + Susan Ireland
................9 Roberta Lee
................9 Allie T. Lee
................9 Willis A. Lee USN
................9 Lucy (Lutie) Lee
................9 Curtis Lee
................8 America Lee b: Abt. 1854 in Owen Co., KY
................8 William W. Lee b: 1856 in Owen Co., KY
            + Mollie b: 1861 in Owen Co., KY
................9 Stella Lee b: 1877 in Owen Co., KY
................8 Emma Lee b: Abt. 1858 in Owen Co., KY
................8 Jefferson Davis Lee b: 1860 in Owen Co., KY, d: 1918 ; Y
................8 Francis Lee b: Abt. 1862 in Owen Co., KY
................8 James Lee b: 1864 in Owen Co., KY
................8 Robert Edward Lee b: 1866 in Owen Co., KY
            + Mary Stevenson Gano m: Abt. 1890 in Owen Co., KY
................9 Edward Gano Lee b: 1891
................9 Owen Scott Lee b: 1893
................9 Frances Elizabeth Lee b: 1904
................9 Lee
................8 B.M. Lee b: 1869 in Owen Co., KY
................8 Rivera Lee b: Owen Co., KY
................8 Mary A. Lee b: Owen Co., KY
................8 A. J. Lee b: Owen Co., KY
         + Molly Reed m: 28 Sep 1889
................8 Lucas Lee b: 1890 in Owen Co., KY, d: 1946 ; Y
            + Hazel
................9 Loring Wiley Lee
................9 Phyllis Lee
................9 Lois Lee
................7 Grandison R. Lee Doctor b: 29 Aug 1827 in Near Leestown, Franklin Co., Ky., d: 30 Sep 1905 in Scott County, Ky., Buried at Pleasent View Baptist Cemetery, Natlee Church; Y
         + Cynthia Powell b: 23 Aug 1831 in Ky, m: 15 Oct 1849, d: 12 Oct 1854 in Pleasent View Baptist Cemetery, Natlee Church; Y
................8 Mary E. Lee b: 1850
................8 Francis C. Lee b: 1852
................8 Melinda Lee b: 30 Mar 1853

+ Nathaniel Daniel REDDING
+ Sarah Ann Yarbough b: 1840 in New Albany, Floyd Co., Indiana (In or around), m: 27 Jan 1859 in Owen Co., KY, d: 14 Jul 1922 in Pleasent Ridge Baptist Church Cemetery; Y
.................8 Samuel Kelly Sam Lee b: 03 Jan 1860 in Ky
.................8 Nannie Gran Lee b: 06 Sep 1861 in Owen Co., KY
.................8 Robert Morgan Lee b: 21 Mar 1864 in Owen Co., KY
.................8 John Alfred Lee b: 28 Apr 1866 in Owen Co., KY
.................8 Millie Stevenson Lee b: 31 Mar 1868 in Owen Co., KY
.................8 James Russell Lee b: 09 May 1869 in Owen Co., KY
.................8 Amanda Adaline Addie Lee b: 05 Jul 1870 in Owen Co., KY
.................8 Quincy Edward Lee b: 09 Dec 1872 in Owen Co., KY
.................8 Grand Quincy Lee b: 04 Aug 1874 in Owen Co., KY
.................8 Samuel Jefferson Jeff Lee b: 25 Nov 1876 in Owen Co., KY
.................8 Sallie Gaines Lee b: 07 Aug 1879 in Owen Co., KY
.................8 Joseph Blackburn Lee b: 08 Dec 1882 in Owen Co., KY
.................8 Gilby Gilba Kelly Lee b: 09 Oct 1885 in Owen Co., KY
.................8 Joe Buchner Lee b: Owen Co., KY
.................7 Cynthia Lee b: 1832 in Owen Co., KY
 + Julia Ann Wylie m: 27 Jan 1852 in Owen County, Kentucky
.................7 Mary Lee b: 09 Feb 1853 in Owen County, Kentucky
.................7 Martha Lee b: Abt. 1855
...........6 Richard Lee b: Abt. 1791 in of, Bedford, Co, Va
...........6 Robert Lee b: 18 Mar 1793 in Scott County, Kentucky, d: 06 Dec 1877 in Buried at St. Francis Mission, White Sulphur, Scott Co., Ky., in the Lee plot.; Y
 + Martha Susan Powell b: 28 Apr 1804 in Woodford Co., KY, m: 13 Sep 1819 in Scott Co., Kentucky, d: 20 Feb 1880 ; Y
.................7 Willis A. Lee b: 18 Aug 1822 in Scott Co., Kentucky, d: 04 Nov 1847 in In a Catholic Seminary; Y
.................7 Benedict Joseph Lee b: 12 Oct 1823 in Scott Co., Kentucky, d: 05 Sep 1904 ; Y
 + Jane Elizabeth Easley m: 05 May 1859 in Scott Co., Kentucky
.................8 Robert Lee
.................8 Mattie Lee
.................8 William Lee
.................8 Benidict Lee
.................8 Emma Lee
.................8 Elizabeth Lee
.................8 Ruth Lee
.................7 Jonathan E. Lee b: 04 Sep 1825 in Scott Co., Kentucky, d: 26 Oct 1847 in Scott Co., KY; Y
.................7 Robert (W. or M.) Lee b: 04 Apr 1827 in Scott Co., KY, d: 19 Nov 1875 ; Y
 + Malerma Pence
.................8 Mary Elizabeth Lee b: 1851, d: 23 Jan 1917 ; Y
 + Virgil Willis Easly m: 08 Sep 1869
.................8 Frank Lee d: Falmouth; Y
.................8 Robert M. Lee
.................7 Mary Catherine Kate Lee b: 21 Dec 1829 in Scott Co., KY
 + Phillip Barthlemew Shepherd
.................8 John Shepherd b: 1853
.................8 Mollie Shepherd
.................8 Lulu Shepherd
.................8 Jim Shepherd
.................8 Teresa Shepherd
.................8 Owen Shepherd
.................7 George Frank Lee b: 04 Sep 1831, d: Killed Civil War CSA; Y
.................7 Anne Eliza Lee b: 05 Aug 1832 in Scott Co., Kentucky, d: 12 Mar 1905 ; Y

```
                    + John Glass
..................8 Catherine Glass
..................8 Wallace Glass
..................8 John Glass
..................8 George Glass
..................8 Ophilia Glass
..................8 Jefferson Glass
..................8 Lizzie Glass
..................8 Robert Glass
..................8 Owen Glass
..................7 Rebecca Ophelia Lee b: 24 Dec 1834 in Scott Co., Kentucky
                    + A.J. Gano
..................8 Rose Gano
..................8 William Gano
..................8 Robert Gano
..................8 Carrie Gano
..................8 Fannie Gano
..................7 Martha Lee b: 24 Jan 1837 in Scott Co., KY
..................7 Christopher Columbus Lee b: 23 Jan 1839 in Scott Co., Kentucky, d: 24 Jun 1882 ; Y
                    + America L. J. Glass m: 16 Sep 1862 in Owen County, Kentucky
..................8 Martha Rose Lee b: Abt. 1765
..................8 John Lee b: Abt. 1863
..................8 Ann Catherine Lee
..................8 Jane Veronica Lee d: 21 Mar 1961 ; Y
                      + Lewis Bramlett
..................9 Bramlett
                      + Noah Thomas
..................9 W.F. Bramlett
..................8 Teresa Lee
..................8 Margaret Mary Lee
..................8 Agnes Lee
..................8 Betty K. Lee
..................7 James Cyrillus (Janus C.) Lee b: 03 Jul 1840 in Scott Co., KY, d: 02 Jul 1841 in Scott Co.,
                    KY; Y
..................7 Theodore Lee b: 08 Feb 1842 in Scott Co., KY
                    + Annie
..................7 Mary R. Lee b: 02 Jan 1843 in Scott Co., Kentucky
                    + Benard J. Laughlin
                    + Thomas Callahan
..................7 Elizabeth Lee b: 05 Mar 1848 in Scott Co., Kentucky, d: 28 Oct 1870 ; Y
                    + Owen Laughlin
..............6 John A. Lee b: 1794 in of, Bedford, Co, Va
..............6 Elizabeth Lee b: 25 May 1799 in Forks of the Elkhorn, Franklin Co. Ky, d: 28 Sep 1880 in
                    Switzerland Co, Indiana; Y
                    + Charles NEAL b: 20 Feb 1790 in Culpeper Co., Va, m: 23 Dec 1814 in Georgetown, KY, d:
                    27 Aug 1831 ; Y
..................7 William E. Neal b: 12 Dec 1815, d: 10 Dec 1869 ; Y
                    + Phebe
..................8 Neal
..................8 Neal
..................8 Neal
..................8 Neal
..................8 Neal
..................8 Neal
```

.................7 Robert Henry Neal b: 25 Dec 1817, d: 09 Aug 1863 in St Lmer, Indiana; Y
            + Lucy Ann Wells m: 19 Nov 1843 in Scott Co, Ky, d: St. Lmer, Indiana; Y
.................8 George W. Neal
.................8 Minerva Ann Neal
.................8 Mariah Elizabeth Neal
.................8 Robert Henry Neal Jr.
.................8 Charles W. Neal
.................8 martha Suzan Neal
.................7 Martha Suzan Neal b: 16 Dec 1853
            + Benjamin E. Reese
.................8 Olga Ona Reese b: 31 Oct 1876, d: 01 Jan 1880 ; Y
.................8 Vera Reese b: 27 Mar 1881
            + Ira W. Tranter
.................7 Thomas Neal
            + Sarah Burgess
.................8 Sarah Neal
.................8 Jown W. Neal
.................8 Thomas Neal
.................8 Preston Neal
.................8 Jacob Neal
.................7 Nancy Neal
            + Robert Jones
.................7 Eliza Neal
            + William Jones
.................7 John C. Lee Neal
            + Harrie Marcus
.............6 Nancy Lee b: Abt. 1800 in Va
...........5 Tabitha Lee b: 31 Oct 1765 in of, Bedford, Campbell, Va, d: 09 Nov 1832 in Bedford Co., VA; Y
        + Thomas N. ANDREWS b: 12 Dec 1761 in son, Mark, Grandson, John, m: Abt. 1784, d: 31
        Aug 1853 in Bedford Co., VA; Y
.............6 Avie S. ANDREWS b: 17 Oct 1788 in Bedford Co., Va., d: Bef. 31 Mar 1846 ; Y
.............6 Ann Dabbs ANDREWS b: 17 Mar 1790 in Bedford Co., VA, d: 07 Jun 1868 in Lafayette Co.,
        Mo.; Y
            + Mosby Arnold b: 03 Feb 1790 in Campbell, Co, Va, m: 02 Sep 1813 in Bedford Co., VA, d:
            18 Feb 1876 in Lafayette Co., Mo.; Y
.................7 Almary Coke Arnold b: 05 Jan 1821 in Bedford Co., VA, d: 31 Oct 1877 in Lafayette Co.,
        MO; Y
            + Richard Lee b: 18 Sep 1810 in Campbell Co., Va, m: 05 Dec 1840 in Bedford Co., VA
.................8 John Mosby Lee b: 14 Dec 1842 in Campbell Co., VA, d: 19 Feb 1843 in Lynch Station,
            Campbell Co., VA; Y
.................8 Ethelbert Thomas Lee b: 18 Dec 1843 in Campbell Co., VA
            + Amanda Allen b: 18 Feb 1845 in Lafayette Co., MO, m: 22 Nov 1866 in Lafayette Co.,
            MO
.................9 Elmore Lee b: May 1863 in Lafayette Co., MO
.................9 Edward A. Lee b: Nov 1867 in Lafayette Co., MO
            + Manor S. PAGE b: Sep 1870 in Lafayette Co., MO, m: 09 Sep 1891 in Lafayette Co.,
            MO
.................10 Sophia M. Lee b: 18 Jan 1893 in Lafayette Co., MO
.................10 Marquerite Lee b: 18 Jun 1894 in Lafayette Co., MO
.................9 infant girl Lee b: 01 Jun 1869 in Lafayette Co., MO, d: 01 Jun 1869 in Lafayette Co.,
            MO; Y
.................9 Lucy Lee b: Oct 1873 in Lafayette Co., MO
.................8 Medora C. Lee b: 17 May 1846 in MS
            + Jeremiah A. Lee b: 27 Sep 1833 in Campbell Co., Va, m: 30 Dec 1867 in Lafayette Co.,
            MO

.............8 Anna Eliza Lee b: 26 Sep 1848 in Lafayette Co., MO, d: 03 Sep 1850 in Napoleon,
          Lafayette Co., MO; Y
.............8 Sarah Virginia Lee b: Abt. 1852 in Lafayette Co., MO, d: 1901 in Bedford Co., VA; Y
          + Edwin James Lee b: 26 Aug 1846 in Bedford Co., VA, m: Abt. 1874
.............9 baby boy Lee b: Abt. 1778 in Bedford Co., VA
.............9 eleven total see notes unk boy Lee b: Abt. 1875 in Bedford Co., VA
.............9 Edwin Cecil Lee b: Mar 1876 in Bedford Co., VA
.............9 infant boy Lee b: Abt. 1880 in Bedford Co., VA
.............9 Samuel Hunt Lee b: Feb 1882 in Bedford Co., VA
.............9 Gilmer Lee b: May 1886 in Bedford Co., VA
.............9 Kirtley Lee b: Jun 1886 in Bedford Co., VA
.............9 Booker Lee b: Aug 1888 in Bedford Co., VA
.............9 Susan Adeline Lee b: Feb 1890 in Bedford Co., VA
.............9 Robert Fitzhugh Lee b: Nov 1891 in Bedford Co., VA
.............9 Carmi Lee b: May 1898 in Bedford Co., VA
.............8 Leila C. Lee b: 28 Sep 1853 in Lafayette Co., MO, d: 26 Feb 1882 in Lafayette Co., MO;
          Y
.............8 Alonzo Hunt Lee b: 18 Jun 1856 in Lafayette Co., MO
.............8 Ida May Lee b: 08 Sep 1858 in Lafayette Co., MO
.............8 Richard Henry Lee b: Abt. 1860 in Lafayette Co., MO
.............8 Clara A. Lee b: 27 Apr 1862 in Lafayette Co., MO, d: 19 Jan 1864 in Lafayette Co., MO;
          Y
.............8 two boy infants Lee b: Lafayette Co., MO
.............6 William Wyatt ANDREWS b: 17 Mar 1792 in Bedford Co., Va., d: 13 Dec 1871 ; Y
          + Elizabeth P. PRICE b: Abt. 1792 in Va., m: 13 Dec 1814 in Bedford Co., VA
.............7 William Wyatt ANDREWS Jr b: Abt. 1816 in Bedford Co., VA
.............6 Elizabeth L. ANDREWS b: 18 Jul 1794 in Bedford Co., Va., d: Bef. 31 Mar 1846 ; Y
.............6 Thomas ANDREWS b: 1796 in of, Bedford, Campbell, Va
          + Patsey ARNOLD b: Abt. 1800 in Campbell Co Va, m: 23 Feb 1823 in Campbell Co Va
.............6 Rebecca N. ANDREWS b: 20 Jan 1797 in of, Bedford, Campbell, Va, d: 13 Apr 1838 ; Y
          + Richard Henry Lee b: 15 Oct 1790 in Campbell, Co, Va, m: 24 May 1819 in Campbell, Co,
          Va, d: Aft. 1870 in Leesville, Campbell, Co, Va; Y
.............7 Jane Elizabeth Lee b: 20 Feb 1820 in Campbell Co., VA, d: 01 Apr 1842 in Campbell, Co,
          Va; Y
.............7 John A Lee b: 02 Feb 1822 in of, Campbell, Co, Va, d: Aft. 1846 ; Y
.............7 James H. Lee b: 09 Apr 1824 in Campbell, Co, Va, d: 24 Sep 1872 in Campbell, Co, Va; Y
.............7 Thomas H. Lee b: 06 Oct 1826 in Campbell, Co, Va, d: 10 Jul 1827 in Campbell, Co, Va; Y
.............7 Frances Tabitha Lee b: 08 May 1828 in Campbell, Co, Va, d: 01 Aug 1885 in Rocky Mount
          Va; Y
          + William E. ANDREWS b: 13 Apr 1825 in Lynchburg, Va, d: 25 Dec 1910 in 1110 S
          Jefferson St. Roanoke, Va; Y
.............8 seven ch ANDREWS b: 09 Nov 1847 in Campbell, Co, Va
.............7 Susan A. Lee b: 26 Oct 1831 in Campbell, Co, Va, d: Aft. 1846 in Campbell, Co, Va; Y
          + James L. Holland b: Abt. 1833, m: 06 Mar 1851 in Smith Co. TN, d: Bef. 1862 in Smith
          Co. TN; Y
.............7 Madison Lee b: 10 Mar 1834 in Campbell, Co, Va, d: Aft. 1846 in possibly TX; Y
.............7 Ameline H. Lee b: 15 Feb 1836 in Campbell, Co, Va
.............7 Hezekiah G. Lee b: 21 Sep 1930 in Campbell, Co, Va, d: 15 Oct 1830 in Campbell, Co, Va;
          Y
.............6 Mark ANDREWS b: 06 Oct 1799 in Bedford Co., Va.
          + Sally S "Sarah" PRICE b: Abt. 1804 in Bedford Co., VA, m: 12 Aug 1822 in Bedford Co., VA
.............6 John ANDREWS b: 24 Dec 1801 in Bedford Co., Va., d: 1885 in Campbell, Co, Va; Y
          + Martha ARNOLD b: 30 Apr 1800 in Campbell, Co, Va, m: 12 Feb 1823 in Campbell, Co, Va,
          d: 1883 in Campbell, Co, Va; Y
.............6 Mary ANDREWS b: 24 Feb 1805 in Bedford Co., Va.

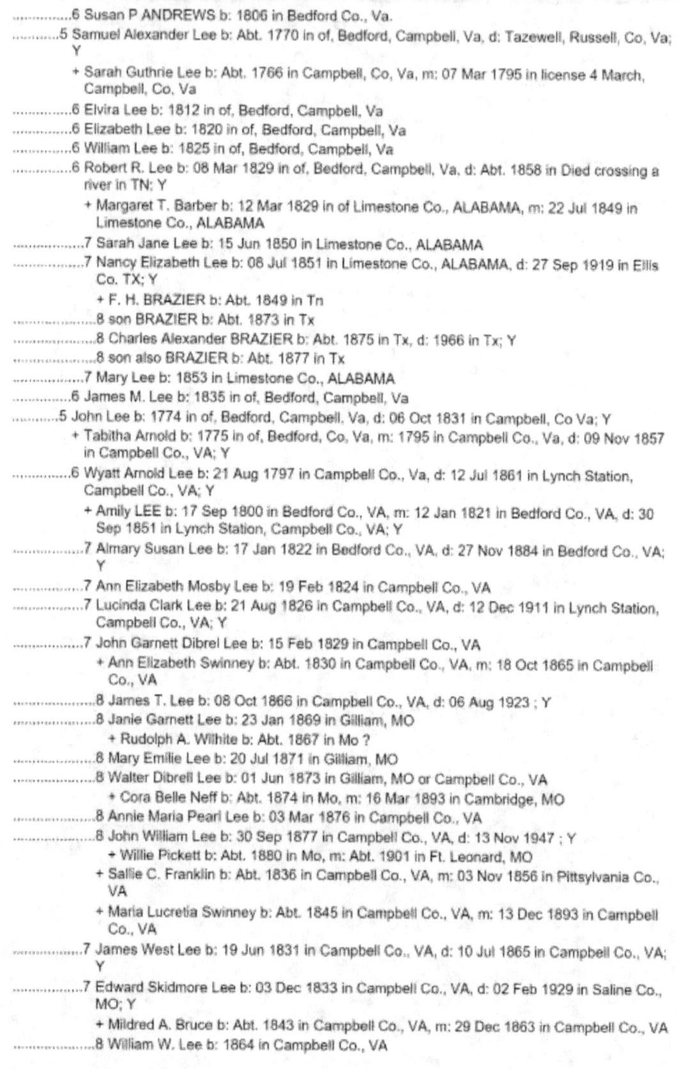

..............6 Susan P ANDREWS b: 1806 in Bedford Co., Va.

............5 Samuel Alexander Lee b: Abt. 1770 in of, Bedford, Campbell, Va, d: Tazewell, Russell, Co, Va; Y

    + Sarah Guthrie Lee b: Abt. 1766 in Campbell, Co, Va, m: 07 Mar 1795 in license 4 March, Campbell, Co, Va

..............6 Elvira Lee b: 1812 in of, Bedford, Campbell, Va

..............6 Elizabeth Lee b: 1820 in of, Bedford, Campbell, Va

..............6 William Lee b: 1825 in of, Bedford, Campbell, Va

..............6 Robert R. Lee b: 08 Mar 1829 in of, Bedford, Campbell, Va, d: Abt. 1858 in Died crossing a river in TN; Y

    + Margaret T. Barber b: 12 Mar 1829 in of Limestone Co., ALABAMA, m: 22 Jul 1849 in Limestone Co., ALABAMA

..................7 Sarah Jane Lee b: 15 Jun 1850 in Limestone Co., ALABAMA

..................7 Nancy Elizabeth Lee b: 08 Jul 1851 in Limestone Co., ALABAMA, d: 27 Sep 1919 in Ellis Co. TX; Y

    + F. H. BRAZIER b: Abt. 1849 in Tn

..................8 son BRAZIER b: Abt. 1873 in Tx

..................8 Charles Alexander BRAZIER b: Abt. 1875 in Tx, d: 1966 in Tx; Y

..................8 son also BRAZIER b: Abt. 1877 in Tx

..................7 Mary Lee b: 1853 in Limestone Co., ALABAMA

..............6 James M. Lee b: 1835 in of, Bedford, Campbell, Va

............5 John Lee b: 1774 in of, Bedford, Campbell, Va, d: 06 Oct 1831 in Campbell, Co Va; Y

    + Tabitha Arnold b: 1775 in of, Bedford, Co, Va, m: 1795 in Campbell Co., Va, d: 09 Nov 1857 in Campbell Co., VA; Y

..............6 Wyatt Arnold Lee b: 21 Aug 1797 in Campbell Co., Va, d: 12 Jul 1861 in Lynch Station, Campbell Co., VA; Y

    + Amily LEE b: 17 Sep 1800 in Bedford Co., VA, m: 12 Jan 1821 in Bedford Co., VA, d: 30 Sep 1851 in Lynch Station, Campbell Co., VA; Y

..................7 Almary Susan Lee b: 17 Jan 1822 in Bedford Co., VA, d: 27 Nov 1884 in Bedford Co., VA; Y

..................7 Ann Elizabeth Mosby Lee b: 19 Feb 1824 in Campbell Co., VA

..................7 Lucinda Clark Lee b: 21 Aug 1826 in Campbell Co., VA, d: 12 Dec 1911 in Lynch Station, Campbell Co., VA; Y

..................7 John Garnett Dibrel Lee b: 15 Feb 1829 in Campbell Co., VA

    + Ann Elizabeth Swinney b: Abt. 1830 in Campbell Co., VA, m: 18 Oct 1865 in Campbell Co., VA

..................8 James T. Lee b: 08 Oct 1866 in Campbell Co., VA, d: 06 Aug 1923 ; Y

..................8 Janie Garnett Lee b: 23 Jan 1869 in Gilliam, MO

    + Rudolph A. Wilhite b: Abt. 1867 in Mo ?

..................8 Mary Emilie Lee b: 20 Jul 1871 in Gilliam, MO

..................8 Walter Dibrell Lee b: 01 Jun 1873 in Gilliam, MO or Campbell Co., VA

    + Cora Belle Neff b: Abt. 1874 in Mo, m: 16 Mar 1893 in Cambridge, MO

..................8 Annie Maria Pearl Lee b: 03 Mar 1876 in Campbell Co., VA

..................8 John William Lee b: 30 Sep 1877 in Campbell Co., VA, d: 13 Nov 1947 ; Y

    + Willie Pickett b: Abt. 1880 in Mo, m: Abt. 1901 in Ft. Leonard, MO

    + Sallie C. Franklin b: Abt. 1836 in Campbell Co., VA, m: 03 Nov 1856 in Pittsylvania Co., VA

    + Maria Lucretia Swinney b: Abt. 1845 in Campbell Co., VA, m: 13 Dec 1893 in Campbell Co., VA

..................7 James West Lee b: 19 Jun 1831 in Campbell Co., VA, d: 10 Jul 1865 in Campbell Co., VA; Y

..................7 Edward Skidmore Lee b: 03 Dec 1833 in Campbell Co., VA, d: 02 Feb 1929 in Saline Co., MO; Y

    + Mildred A. Bruce b: Abt. 1843 in Campbell Co., VA, m: 29 Dec 1863 in Campbell Co., VA

..................8 William W. Lee b: 1864 in Campbell Co., VA

....................8 Robert Lee b: Abt. 1866 in Campbell Co., VA
....................8 John O. Lee b: Abt. 1870 in Campbell Co., VA
....................8 Cora S. Lee b: Nov 1872 in Campbell Co., VA
....................8 Charles Lee b: Abt. 1874 in Campbell Co., VA
....................8 Edward Skidmore Lee b: Abt. 1876 in Campbell Co., VA
....................8 Leanna Lee b: 1878 in Campbell Co., VA
....................8 West Lee b: Abt. 1880 in Campbell Co., VA
....................8 Sally Bruce Lee b: Jul 1884 in Campbell Co., VA
....................8 Howard C. Lee b: Feb 1887
....................7 Robert C. Lee b: Jul 1839 in Campbell Co., VA
　　　　+ Mary Hassie Pearman b: 21 Apr 1850 in Campbell Co., VA, m: 04 Mar 1874 in Campbell
　　　　　　Co., VA
....................7 Abner T. Lee b: 25 Nov 1840 in Campbell Co., VA, d: 24 Sep 1845 in Campbell Co., VA; Y
................6 Ann D. Lee b: 12 Nov 1799 in Campbell Co., Va, d: 06 Oct 1870 in Napoleon, Lafayette Co.,
　　　　MO; Y
................6 John Lee Jr. b: Abt. 1800 in Bedford Co., VA, d: 1827 in Campbell Co., VA; Y
................6 Elizabeth Betsy Noel Lee b: 25 Jun 1801 in Campbell Co., Va
　　　　+ John Wesley Laughon b: 23 Oct 1801 in Bedford Co., VA, m: 08 Nov 1830 in Campbell
　　　　　　Co., VA
....................7 John E. Laughon b: Abt. 1831 in Lynch Station, Campbell Co., VA
....................7 James W. Laughon b: Abt. 1833 in Lynch Station, Campbell Co., VA
....................7 Tabitha A. Laughon b: Abt. 1835 in Lynch Station, Campbell Co., VA
....................7 William A. Laughon b: Abt. 1838 in Lynch Station, Campbell Co., VA
....................7 Mary E. Laughon b: 1840 in Lynch Station, Campbell Co., VA
....................7 Teriza W. Laughon b: Abt. 1843 in Lynch Station, Campbell Co., VA
................6 William Lee b: 27 Apr 1805 in Campbell Co., Va, d: 18 Apr 1854 in Lafayette Co., MO; Y
................6 Garnett Lee b: 1806 in Campbell Co., Va, d: Bef. 1843 in Mo; Y
　　　　+ Charlotte Dobyns b: Abt. 1808, m: 17 Oct 1826 in Bedford Co., VA
....................7 son Lee b: Abt. 1825 in Campbell Co., VA
................6 Moses A. Lee b: 17 Sep 1807 in Campbell Co., Va
　　　　+ Lydia A. Farley b: Abt. 1813 in Campbell Co., VA, m: 24 Nov 1835 in Campbell Co., VA
....................7 Sarah Ann Lee b: 1836 in Campbell Co., VA
　　　　+ A. L. Trundle b: Abt. 1824, m: 06 May 1856 in Lafayette Co., MO
....................7 Mildred Catherine Lee b: Abt. 1838 in Campbell Co., VA
　　　　+ David W. Trudle b: Abt. 1836 in Campbell Co., VA
....................7 Susan P Lee b: Abt. 1840 in Campbell Co., VA, d: of Lafayette Co., MO; Y
　　　　+ Edward Penick Arnold b: 1835 in Lafayette Co., MO, m: 09 Nov 1860 in Lafayette Co.,
　　　　　　MO
................6 Richard Lee b: 18 Sep 1810 in Campbell Co., Va
　　　　+ Almary Coke Arnold b: 05 Jan 1821 in Bedford Co., VA, m: 05 Dec 1840 in Bedford Co.,
　　　　　　VA, d: 31 Oct 1877 in Lafayette Co., MO; Y
....................7 John Mosby Lee b: 14 Dec 1842 in Campbell Co., VA, d: 19 Feb 1843 in Lynch Station,
　　　　　　Campbell Co., VA; Y
....................7 Ethelbert Thomas Lee b: 18 Dec 1843 in Campbell Co., VA
　　　　+ Amanda Allen b: 18 Feb 1845 in Lafayette Co., MO, m: 22 Nov 1866 in Lafayette Co.,
　　　　　　MO
....................8 Elmore Lee b: May 1863 in Lafayette Co., MO
....................8 Edward A. Lee b: Nov 1867 in Lafayette Co., MO
　　　　+ Manor S. PAGE b: Sep 1870 in Lafayette Co., MO, m: 09 Sep 1891 in Lafayette Co.,
　　　　　　MO
....................9 Sophia M. Lee b: 18 Jan 1893 in Lafayette Co., MO
....................9 Marquerite Lee b: 18 Jun 1894 in Lafayette Co., MO
....................8 infant girl Lee b: 01 Jun 1869 in Lafayette Co., MO, d: 01 Jun 1869 in Lafayette Co., MO;
　　　　Y
....................8 Lucy Lee b: Oct 1873 in Lafayette Co., MO

....................7 Medora C. Lee b: 17 May 1846 in MS
    + Jeremiah A. Lee b: 27 Sep 1833 in Campbell Co., Va, m: 30 Dec 1867 in Lafayette Co., MO
....................7 Anna Eliza Lee b: 26 Sep 1848 in Lafayette Co., MO, d: 03 Sep 1850 in Napoleon, Lafayette Co., MO; Y
....................7 Sarah Virginia Lee b: Abt. 1852 in Lafayette Co., MO, d: 1901 in Bedford Co., VA; Y
    + Edwin James Lee b: 26 Aug 1846 in Bedford Co., VA, m: Abt. 1874
....................8 baby boy Lee b: Abt. 1778 in Bedford Co., VA
....................8 eleven total see notes unk boy Lee b: Abt. 1875 in Bedford Co., VA
....................8 Edwin Cecil Lee b: Mar 1876 in Bedford Co., VA
....................8 infant boy Lee b: Abt. 1880 in Bedford Co., VA
....................8 Samuel Hunt Lee b: Feb 1882 in Bedford Co., VA
....................8 Gilmer Lee b: May 1886 in Bedford Co., VA
....................8 Kirtley Lee b: Jun 1886 in Bedford Co., VA
....................8 Booker Lee b: Aug 1888 in Bedford Co., VA
....................8 Susan Adeline Lee b: Feb 1890 in Bedford Co., VA
....................8 Robert Fitzhugh Lee b: Nov 1891 in Bedford Co., VA
....................8 Carmi Lee b: May 1898 in Bedford Co., VA
....................7 Leila C. Lee b: 28 Sep 1853 in Lafayette Co., MO, d: 26 Feb 1882 in Lafayette Co., MO; Y
....................7 Alonzo Hunt Lee b: 18 Jun 1856 in Lafayette Co., MO
....................7 Ida May Lee b: 08 Sep 1858 in Lafayette Co., MO
....................7 Richard Henry Lee b: Abt. 1860 in Lafayette Co., MO
....................7 Clara A. Lee b: 27 Apr 1862 in Lafayette Co., MO, d: 19 Jan 1864 in Lafayette Co., MO; Y
....................7 two boy infants Lee b: Lafayette Co., MO
    + Sarah E. BELL m: 20 Oct 1874 in Lafayette Co., MO
..............6 Tabitha A. Lee b: Abt. 1812 in Campbell Co., Va
    + Boler Cocke b: Abt. 1816 in Campbell Co., VA, m: Abt. 1837 in Campbell Co., VA
....................7 Thomas W. Cocke b: 1838 in Campbell Co., VA
....................7 Virginia Cocke b: Abt. 1840 in Campbell Co., VA
....................7 Mariah L. Cocke b: Abt. 1842 in Campbell Co., VA
....................7 Lelia Gustus Cocke b: Abt. 1846 in Campbell Co., VA
....................7 RObert S. Cocke b: Abt. 1850 in Campbell Co., VA
..............6 Tariza W. Lee b: 15 Sep 1819 in Campbell Co., Va
..........5 Richard Lee b: Abt. 1774 in of, Bedford, Campbell, Va, d: Bedford, Co VA; Y
    + Tabitha
..........5 Rebecca Lee b: Abt. 1775 in of, Bedford, Campbell, Va, d: 11 Oct 1857 in Lafayette, Co MO; Y
    + Beverly Lee b: of, Bedford, Campbell, Va, m: Abt. 1810 in Bedford, Campbell, Co, Va, d: Lafayette, Co MO; Y
..............6 Richard Alexander Lee b: 1815 in of, Bedford, Campbell, Va, d: 1899 ; Y
..............6 Nancy T. Lee b: Abt. 1815 in of, Bedford, Campbell, Va
..............6 William Garnett Lee b: Abt. 1815 in Campbell, Co, CA
..............6 John A. Lee b: Abt. 1816 in of, Bedford, Campbell, Va, d: one, daughter, married, Stokes; Y
..........5 James Garnett Early Lee b: 23 Feb 1777 in Cumberland, Co Va, d: 01 Sep 1862 in Bedford, Co VA; Y
    + Polly ROBINSON b: Abt. 1790 in of, Bedford, Co, Va, m: 11 Jun 1811 in of, Bedford, Co, Va
    + Elvira PRICE THORP b: Abt. 1800 in of, Bedford, Co, Va, m: 25 Apr 1820 in of, Bedford, Co, Va
..............6 Lafayette Lee
    + Charlotte DOBYNS b: Abt. 1800 in of, Bedford, Co, Va, m: 13 Oct 1826 in third wife, Bedford, Co, Va
..........5 Ave or Ava Lee b: 05 May 1782 in of, Bedford, Campbell, Va, d: Bedford; Y
    + William HICKS b: Abt. 1790 in of, Bedford, Co, Va, m: 21 Dec 1804 in Bedford, Co, Va
..........5 Ann Lee b: Abt. 1784 in of, Bedford, Campbell, Va, d: 1879 in Bedford, Co VA; Y
    + Nathaniel PRICE b: Abt. 1790 in of, Bedford, Co, Va, m: 26 Mar 1812 in Bedford, Co, Va

......3 James Lee b: 1715 in King and Queen Co., Va of Richmond, Co, Va, d: Caswell, Co, NC; Y
 + Ann Tolbert HERNDON b: Abt. 1717 in Richmond, Co, Va, m: Abt. 1739 in Caswell Co., NC, d: 1777 in Caswell, Co, NC; Y
.........4 Luke LEA or Lee b: 26 Dec 1739 in St. Georges Par., Spotsylvania Co., VA, d: 04 May 1813 in St Tammany Parish, LA; Y
 + ELizabeth WILSON b: 26 Nov 1749 in Newville, Cumberland Dist., Pennsylvania, m: 04 May 1759 in Caswell County, North Carolina, d: 1792 in Campbell, Tennessee; Y
.........5 James M LEA b: 03 Apr 1760 in Orange Co. NC (present day Caswell Co.), d: 07 Apr 1823 in Amite Co., Ms; Y
 + Elizabeth RODDYE b: 1767 in Tennessee, m: Abt. 1785, d: 1823 in Amite Co., Ms; Y
.............6 Squire LEA b: 1786 in Knoxville, Jefferson Co., Tennessee, d: Manchac, Louisiana; Y
.............6 Cecelia LEA b: 06 May 1789 in Knoxville, Jefferson Co., Tennessee, d: 28 Apr 1819 ; Y
.............6 Franklin LEA b: Abt. 1791 in Knoxville, Jefferson Co., Tennessee
.............6 Alexander LEA b: 25 Oct 1792 in Knoxville, Jefferson Co., Tennessee, d: 01 Feb 1814 in Tx; Y
.............6 Sarah Ann LEA b: 23 Sep 1794 in Knoxville, Jefferson Co., Tennessee, d: 21 Jun 1873 in New Orleans, Orleans, Louisiana; Y
.............6 George Roddy LEA b: 10 Nov 1796 in Knoxville, Jefferson Co., Tennessee, d: 01 Mar 1869 ; Y
.........5 William Wilson LEA b: 21 Feb 1762 in Orange Co. NC (present day Caswell Co.), d: 1823 in Amite Co., Ms; Y
.........5 Joseph LEA b: 04 Feb 1764 in Orange Co. NC (present day Caswell Co.), d: Dec 1769 in Caswell Co., Nc; Y
.........5 John LEA b: 24 Feb 1765 in Orange Co. NC (present day Caswell Co.), d: Dec 1769 in Caswell Co., Nc; Y
.........5 Mary Elizabeth LEA b: 31 Jul 1767 in Orange Co. NC (present day Caswell Co.)
.........5 Joseph Lea b: 13 May 1769 in Orange Co. NC (present day Caswell Co.), d: 14 Feb 1811 in Amite County, Mississippi; Y
 + Amy Barton b: Abt. 1779 in of Jefferson, TN, m: Abt. 1798 in Jefferson, Tennessee
...............6 Major Lea b: Abt. 1800 in Summit, Mississippi
...............6 Barton Lea b: Abt. 1802 in Summit, Mississippi
 + Matilda Burkhead
...............6 Elizabeth Lea b: Abt. 1804 in Summit, Mississippi
 + Joseph Gibson
...............6 Elceba Lea b: Abt. 1806 in Summit, Mississippi
 + Wiley P. Harris Hon. b: Jackson, Mississippi
...............6 Lavinia Lea b: 1808 in Summit, Mississippi, d: 1871 ; Y
 + Joseph Newsome b: Abt. 1804, m: 1826
..................7 Newsome b: Summit, Mississippi
...............6 Luke Lea b: 1809
 + Nancy East m: Abt. 1831
 + M. A. Williams
...............6 Noble Lea b: 1810 in Summit, Mississippi
 + Sophronia b: 1818, d: 1884 ; Y
.........5 Major LEA b: 21 May 1771 in Surry Co, North Carolina, d: 16 Jul 1822 in Grainger Co, Tennessee; Y
 + Lavinia JARNAGIN b: 02 Oct 1770 in Tn, m: 17 Nov 1793 in Jefferson Co, Tennessee, d: 17 Mar 1849 in Grainger Co, Tennessee; Y
.............6 Pryor LEA b: 13 Aug 1794 in Grainger Co., TN, d: 14 Sep 1880 in Goliad, Goliad Co., Tx; Y
 + Mary (Perkins) b: Abt. 1798 in Grainger Co., TN, m: Abt. 1815 in Grainger Co., TN
 + Maria KENNEDY b: 27 Jan 1799 in Knoxville, Knox Co., Tn, m: 06 Oct 1818 in Knoxville, Knox Co., Tn, d: 11 Mar 1828 in Knoxville, Knox Co., Tn; Y
..................7 James Kennedy LEA b: 27 Nov 1819 in Knoxville, Knox Co., Tn, d: 21 Oct 1852 in Carrollton, Ms; Y

.................7 Lavinia Jarnagin LEA b: Abt. 1822 in Knoxville, Knox Co., Tn, d: 15 Oct 1908 in Jackson, Rankin Co., Ms; Y

.................7 Sarah Stephenson LEA b: 03 Apr 1825 in Knoxville, Knox Co., Tn, d: 27 Feb 1869 in Charleston, Tallahatchie Co., Ms; Y

          + Minerva HEARD b: Abt. 1810 in <Knoxville, Knox Co., Tn>, m: Abt. 1830 in Knoxville, Knox Co., Tn, d: May 1866 in Goliad, Goliad Co., Tx; Y

.................7 Abrahm LEA b: Abt. 1831 in Knoxville, Knox Co., Tn, d: Abt. 1860 in Golaid, Golaid Co., Tx; Y

.................7 Nannie LEA b: Abt. 1833 in Knoxville, Knox Co., Tn

.................7 Julia LEA b: Abt. 1835 in Knoxville, Knox Co., Tn, d: Macon, Jones Co., Ga; Y

.................7 Eliza Cynthia LEA b: 15 Mar 1837 in Macon, Jones Co., Ga, d: 18 Dec 1912 in Oxford, Lafayette Co., Ms; Y

.................7 Pryor LEA b: Abt. 1839 in Jackson, Hinds CO., MS

.............6 William Wilson LEA b: 09 Apr 1796 in Grainger Co., Tn, d: 14 Feb 1878 in Fulton, Tipton Co., Tn; Y

          + Martha (Corprew) NEWTON b: Abt. 1800 in Fulton, TN, m: 1854 in Fulton, TN

          + Elizabeth Augusta LEWIS b: Abt. 1800 in Grainger Co., TN, m: 21 Dec 1821 in Grainger Co., TN

.................7 Mary Louise LEA b: Abt. 1828 in <, Grainger Co., Tn>, d: Abt. 1878 ; Y

.................7 Joel Lewis LEA b: 13 Apr 1837 in <, Grainger Co., Tn>

.............6 Anderson LEA b: 04 Feb 1798 in Grainger Co., Tn, d: 1807 ; Y

.............6 Thomas Jarnagin LEA b: 11 Nov 1799 in Grainger Co., Tn, d: 06 Oct 1838 in Knox Co., Tn; Y

          + Mary Carper TALBOT b: Abt. 1803 in <, Davis Co., Ky>, m: 27 Sep 1821 in Knoxville, Knox Co., Tn, d: Davis Co., Ky; Y

.................7 Martha LEA b: Abt. 1822 in <Knoxville, Knox Co., Tn>

.................7 Williston LEA b: Abt. 1824 in <Knoxville, Knox Co., Tn>

.................7 Elizabeth Houston LEA b: Abt. 1825 in <Knoxville, Knox Co., Tn>

.................7 Sarah LEA b: Abt. 1828 in <Knoxville, Knox Co., Tn>

.................7 Major LEA b: Abt. 1830 in <Knoxville, Knox Co., Tn>

.............6 John Hampton LEA b: 12 Oct 1801 in Grainger Co., Tn

          + Eliza Ann MARTIN b: Abt. 1805 in <, Grainger Co., Tn>

.................7 Edward LEA b: Abt. 1823 in <, Grainger Co., Tn>

.................7 Major LEA b: Abt. 1825 in <, Grainger Co., Tn>

.................7 Cynthia LEA b: Abt. 1828 in <, Grainger Co., Tn>

.................7 Sarah LEA b: Abt. 1830 in <, Grainger Co., Tn>

.................7 Annie LEA b: Abt. 1832 in <, Grainger Co., Tn>

.............6 Cynthia Ann LEA b: 31 Aug 1803 in Grainger Co., Tn, d: 31 Jul 1890 in Grainger Co., Tn; Y

          + Elihu MILLIKAN b: Abt. 1799 in <, Grainger Co., Tn>, m: 02 Feb 1838, d: 20 Dec 1864 ; Y

.................7 Lavinia Lea MILLIKAN b: Abt. 1839 in <, Grainger Co., Tn>

.............6 Harmon Graves LEA b: 24 Aug 1805 in Grainger Co., Tn, d: 06 Feb 1887 ; Y

          + Johanna SHIELDS b: 28 Jan 1808 in <, Chester Co., Pa.>, m: 02 Oct 1827, d: 09 Nov 1883 ; Y

.................7 Major LEA b: 1771 in <Midway, Tn., Shields Cem.>, d: 1822 ; Y

.............6 Cecilia LEA b: 02 May 1807 in <, Grainger Co., Tn>, d: Jun 1807 ; Y

.............6 Albert Miller LEA b: 23 Jul 1808 in Grainger Co., Tn, d: 30 Jan 1891 in Corsicana, Navarro Co., Tx; Y

          + Catherine Sarah Davey HEATH b: Abt. 1809 in <, Grainger Co., Tn>, m: 30 Sep 1845, d: 10 Apr 1884 in Corsicana, Navarro Co., Tx; Y

.................7 Alexander Mckim LEA b: 27 Dec 1847 in <, Grainger Co., Tn>

.................7 Eliza Lavinia LEA b: 19 Aug 1848 in <, Grainger Co., Tn>, d: Abt. 1938 in Corsicana, Navarro Co., Tx; Y

.................7 Luke LEA b: Abt. 1849 in <, Grainger Co., Tn>

.................7 Albert Heath LEA b: 26 Jun 1850 in <, Grainger Co., Tn>

          + Ellen SHOEMAKER b: Abt. 1814 in <, Grainger Co., Tn>, m: 05 May 1836, d: Feb 1840 ; Y

.................7 Edward LEA b: 31 Jan 1837 in <, Grainger Co., Tn>, d: 01 Jan 1863 ; Y

............6 Luke LEA b: 16 Nov 1810 in Grainger Co., Tn, d: 14 May 1898 in Vicksburg, Warren Co., MS;
           Y
           + Mary Mayrant SMITH b: 1826 in Tennessee, m: Abt. 1848, d: At Arkansas; Y
..................7 Albert Major LEA b: Abt. 1849 in <, Grainger Co., Tn>
..................7 Mary E. LEE b: Abt. 1851 in Tennessee
..................7 Norvelle LEA b: Abt. 1853 in <, Grainger Co., Tn>
............6 James LEA b: 22 May 1814 in <, Grainger Co., Tn>, d: 07 Jul 1814 ; Y
..........5 John LEA b: 08 Mar 1773 in Wilkes Co., Nc, d: 1830 in Rhea Co., Tenn.; Y
           + Ann RODDY b: Abt. 1796 in <, Nc>, m: 08 Oct 1805
..............6 Pleasant Miller LEA b: 06 Feb 1806 in Powell's Valley, Sevier, Tn, d: 1866 in Bradley, Tn; Y
..............6 Thomas LEA b: Abt. 1808 in <Powell's Valley, Sevier, Tn>
..............6 John LEA b: Abt. 1810 in <Powell's Valley, Sevier, Tn>, d: Louisiana; Y
..............6 James LEA b: Abt. 1812 in <Powell's Valley, Sevier, Tn>
..............6 Luke LEA b: Abt. 1814 in <Powell's Valley, Sevier, Tn>, d: 1856 in Fl; Y
..............6 Franklin LEA b: Abt. 1816 in <Powell's Valley, Sevier, Tn>, d: 1835 in Mo; Y
..............6 Susan LEA b: 1817 in Tennessee
..............6 Isaac R LEA b: Abt. 1820 in <Powell's Valley, Sevier, Tn>
..........5 Zachariah LEA b: 18 Jan 1776 in Wilkes Co. NC later of Surrey, North Carolina, d: 05 Feb 1845
           in Amite, Mississippi; Y
           + Sabrina CLAY b: 14 Jan 1783 in Chesterfield, Virginia, m: 19 Jan 1802 in Lea Springs,
           Granger, Tn, d: 11 Aug 1842 in Amite, Mississippi; Y
..............6 Elizabeth LEA b: 22 Nov 1802 in Lea Springs, Grainger, Tennessee, d: 06 Jan 1878 in Amite,
           Mississippi; Y
..............6 Lucinda Clay LEA b: 01 Mar 1805 in Grainger, Tennesee, d: 17 Dec 1886 in Amite,
           Mississippi; Y
..............6 Isabella LEA b: 01 Mar 1805 in Grainger, Tennesee, d: 22 Dec 1877 ; Y
..............6 Alfred Mead LEA b: 1809 in Amite, Mississippi, d: 1883 in Jackson, Louisiana; Y
..............6 Hampton Muse LEA b: 05 Oct 1810 in Amite, Mississippi, d: 19 Aug 1886 in Amite,
           Mississippi; Y
..............6 Nancy LEA b: 07 Mar 1814 in Amite, Mississippi, d: 06 Feb 1846 in Amite, Mississippi; Y
..............6 Wilfred LEA b: 27 Dec 1816 in Amite, Mississippi, d: 20 Dec 1906 in Amite, Mississippi; Y
..............6 James Everett LEA b: 28 Jul 1819 in Amite, Mississippi, d: 25 Apr 1878 in Amite, Mississippi;
           Y
..............6 Iverson Green LEA b: 16 Aug 1822 in Amite, Mississippi, d: 16 Apr 1864 in Amite, Mississippi;
           Y
..............6 Margaret A LEA b: 31 Jan 1826 in <Amite, Mississippi>, d: 22 May 1851 ; Y
..........5 Jesse Jefferson LEA b: 30 Nov 1777 in Wilkes Co. NC later of Surrey, North Carolina, d: 25
           Dec 1830 in Amite Co., Ms; Y
           + Elizabeth TAYLOR b: Abt. 1781 in Amite, Ms, m: 16 Aug 1825 in Amite, Ms
           + Elizabeth FARLEY b: 16 May 1780 in Amelia County, Virginia, m: 21 Apr 1798 in Jefferson,
           Tn, d: 1824 in Darling Creek, St. Helena Parish, Louisiana; Y
..............6 Jesse Jefferson LEA b: 17 Nov 1799 in Knox County, Tennessee, d: 1863 in Livingston,
           Livingston Parish, Louisiana; Y
           + Anderson m: St. Helena Parish, Louisiana
..............6 Caswell LEA b: 31 Mar 1801 in Knox, Tennessee
           + Mariah "Mary" Kinchen m: 03 Sep 1829 in St. Helena Parish, Louisiana
..............6 Matilda LEA b: 01 Dec 1803 in Amite County, Mississippi, d: Aft. 1850 ; Y
           + William (Martin or R.) Naul b: Abt. 1797 in Mercer County, Kentucky, m: 06 Jul 1826 in St.
           Helena Parish, Louisiana, d: Bef. 23 Apr 1836 in Baywood, East Baton Rouge Parish,
           Louisiana; Y
..................7 Caswell James Naul Sr. b: Abt. 1827 in Louisiana
           + Ursula Ewell b: Abt. 1832 in Mississippi, m: 04 Dec 1858 in Amite County, Mississippi
......................8 Martha Naul b: Abt. Dec 1859 in Mississippi
               + Thomas Newman
..........................9 Cora Newman

```
                        + Hooper
.................9 Lula Newman
.................9 Grady Newman
.............8 Caswell James "Jim" Naul b: Sep 1862 in Mississippi
                + Elva E. Waller b: 19 Aug 1872 in Louisiana, m: Abt. 1892
.................9 Alla Elizabeth Naul b: 08 Jan 1894 in Mississippi
.................9 Frances Martha "Fannie" Naul b: May 1895 in Mississippi
                  + Odon Edward Loper Sr. b: Abt. 1888 in Arkansas
..................10 Odon E. Loper Jr. b: Abt. 1920 in Mississippi
.................9 Lillie Corine Naul b: Jan 1900 in Louisiana
.................9 Elva Naul b: Abt. 1903 in Louisiana
.............8 Candace Elizabeth "Tweet" Naul b: Abt. 1865 in Mississippi
                + A. S. Cook m: 30 Apr 1889 in Amite County, Mississippi
.............8 Francis "Fannie" Naul b: Abt. 1867 in Mississippi
...........7 Nicholson Jefferson Naul b: 02 Oct 1829 in Louisiana, d: 01 Jan 1865 in Goodman,
                Mississippi; Y
                + Elizabeth Lee b: 16 Aug 1829 in Louisiana, m: 09 Dec 1852, d: 15 Mar 1861 ; Y
.............8 William Jefferson Naul b: 20 Sep 1853, d: Bet. 1935–1936 ; Y
.............8 Martin Lafayette Naul b: 04 Aug 1855, d: 01 Jun 1928 ; Y
                + Amanda Jane "Mandy" Frazier b: Sep 1857, m: 12 Oct 1874 in St. Helena Parish,
                  Louisiana, d: 23 Apr 1876 ; Y
.................9 Nickles J. Naul b: 07 Sep 1875, d: 15 Sep 1875 ; Y
                + Alice Frances Wilson b: 03 Jun 1866, m: 23 Jul 1877, d: 26 Dec 1933 ; Y
.................9 Frances Amanda Naul b: 30 Apr 1888, d: 11 Mar 1945 ; Y
                + Will A. Tidwell m: 1907, d: 13 Jun 1961 ; Y
..................10 Mattie Alice Tidwell b: 05 Oct 1918
..................10 James Lafayette Tidwell b: 30 Dec 1921
..................10 Anna Elizabeth Tidwell b: 03 Mar 1926
.................9 Jesse Frederick Naul b: 23 Jul 1890, d: 04 Jul 1951 ; Y
                + Eva Womack b: Abt. 1902 in Louisiana, m: 01 Jul 1930
.................9 William Martin Naul b: 24 Nov 1892, d: 31 Aug 1931 ; Y
                + Ada Prime m: 22 Aug 1920
.................9 Maggie Elizabeth Naul b: 20 May 1894, d: 1965 ; Y
                + Oscar Green Barlow b: Abt. 1886 in Monroe, Louisiana, m: 23 Nov 1919
..................10 Martin Barlow b: Abt. 1921
..................10 May Barlow b: Abt. 1924
..................10 Alfred Barlow b: Abt. Jan 1929
.................9 Mary Corrinne Naul b: 01 Sep 1895
                + Elmer F. Dykes m: 16 Sep 1923, d: 20 Aug 1960 ; Y
.................9 (twin) Naul b: 1897, d: 1897 ; Y
.................9 (twin) Naul b: 1897, d: 1897 ; Y
.............8 Leroy Brown Naul b: 15 Oct 1857, d: 16 Aug 1862 ; Y
.............8 Margaret Ann Naul b: 30 Mar 1859 in Mississippi, d: 1912 ; Y
                + Orril Clarence "Bud" Cox b: 1866, d: 1940 ; Y
                + James Alexander T. Taylor b: 05 May 1852 in Louisiana, m: 09 Jan 1879 in St. Helena
                  Parish, Louisiana, d: 04 Jan 1885 ; Y
.................9 Maggie Taylor b: 30 Nov 1879, d: 05 Dec 1879 ; Y
.................9 Jimmy Taylor b: 30 Nov 1879, d: 30 Nov 1879 ; Y
.................9 Elizabeth Lee Taylor b: 12 Oct 1880, d: 08 Sep 1963 ; Y
                + Rennie Schwartz
.................9 Rutha Mary Jane Taylor b: 27 Sep 1882, d: 07 Sep 1889 ; Y
.................9 Cora Taylor b: 06 Oct 1884
.............8 Jesse Thomas Naul b: 24 Feb 1861, d: 14 Dec 1861 ; Y
...........7 Franklin M. Naul b: Abt. 1831 in Louisiana
```

+ <No name>
........8 Isaac N. "Ike" Naul b: 07 Jan 1864, d: 30 Aug 1934 ; Y
........8 Cora Naul
........8 Charlie Naul
........7 Jesse Washington Naul Sr. Dr. b: 02 Jun 1833 in Louisiana, d: 25 Dec 1909 ; Y
+ Mary Jane Alford b: 09 Nov 1846, m: 21 Dec 1865 in St. Helena Parish, Louisiana, d: 23 Dec 1923 ; Y
........8 Tillie Matilda Ann Naul b: 04 May 1867 in Louisiana, d: 11 Jan 1932 ; Y
+ S. S. Stebbins b: Abt. 1863 in Mississippi, m: 28 Jan 1891, d: Bef. Jan 1920 ; Y
........9 Freddy Stebbins b: Abt. 1891
........9 Sam J Stebbins b: Abt. 1893
........9 Carrie Stebbins b: Abt. 1895
........9 Pearl Stebbins b: Abt. 1897
........8 Nicholas Jefferson "Nick" Naul b: 18 Jun 1869, d: 30 Aug 1935 ; Y
........8 Julius Alford "Jules" Naul b: 27 Oct 1871, d: 01 Feb 1931 ; Y
+ Anna Whittington m: 20 Dec 1899
........9 Mary Lee Naul b: 31 Dec 1900
........9 Julius Alford Naul Jr. b: 30 May 1902
........8 Ida Augusta Naul b: 24 Sep 1875, d: 13 Dec 1875 ; Y
........8 Mary Elizabeth "Mollie" Naul b: 15 Dec 1876, d: 18 Jan 1899 ; Y
........8 Jesse Washington Naul Jr. b: 20 Jul 1879, d: 29 Oct 1947 ; Y
+ Lilah Belle Kent m: 26 Dec 1917
........9 Jesse Washington Naul III b: 25 Jan 1921
+ Sarah Ellen Tycer
........8 William Martin Naul b: 26 Jun 1884, d: 11 Aug 1886 ; Y
........8 Lea Gill Naul Sr. b: 16 Dec 1886
+ Wilna Magee
........9 Lea Gill Naul Jr. b: 03 May 1925
+ Eleanor Idella Bond b: 1927 in Louisiana
........8 Pearla Belle Naul b: 04 Jul 1889
........7 Candace Naul b: Abt. 1834 in Mississippi
........6 LEA b: Abt. 1805 in Amite County, Mississippi
........6 Mahulda Lea b: 1806 in Amite, Mississippi, d: Aft. 1850 ; Y
........6 Sheppard LEA b: 20 Apr 1808 in St. Helena Parish, Louisiana
........6 Mariah "Maria" LEA b: 03 Aug 1810 in St. Helena Parish, Louisiana
+ Thomas Oliver Garner m: 05 Jun 1837 in Amite County, Mississippi
+ James Tate
........6 Tennessee LEA b: 20 Apr 1815 in St. Helena Parish, Louisiana, d: 28 Mar 1859 ; Y
+ James Tate b: 18 Mar 1809 in Orange County, North Carolina, m: 09 Mar 1836 in Kentwood, St. Helena (Tangipahoa) Parish, Louisiana, d: 04 Oct 1855 in Louisiana; Y
........7 Martha Ann Elizabeth Tate b: 20 Jan 1837 in Kentwood, Louisiana
+ Emanuel Cutrer b: Abt. 1831 in Mississippi, m: 17 Jun 1856 in St. Helena Parish, Louisiana
........8 O. E. Cutrer b: Abt. 1857 in Mississippi
........8 J. J. Cutrer b: Abt. Oct 1859 in Mississippi
........7 Ann Cassander Tate b: 06 Mar 1839 in Kentwood, Louisiana, d: 10 Jul 1847 ; Y
........7 Nicholas Bayfies "Nick" Tate b: 19 Dec 1839 in Louisiana
+ Julia E. b: Abt. 1845 in Mississippi
........8 Charlie Tate b: Abt. 1871 in Mississippi
........7 Thomas Scott Tate b: 15 May 1843
........7 Jesse Naul Tate b: 11 Mar 1845 in Louisiana
+ Elizabeth "Lizzie" Carruth b: 25 Apr 1846 in Louisiana, m: 10 Jun 1880 in St. Helena Parish, Louisiana, d: 20 Apr 1918 ; Y
+ Martha E. Wall b: Abt. 1845 in Mississippi, m: 05 Jan 1865, d: Bef. 1880 ; Y

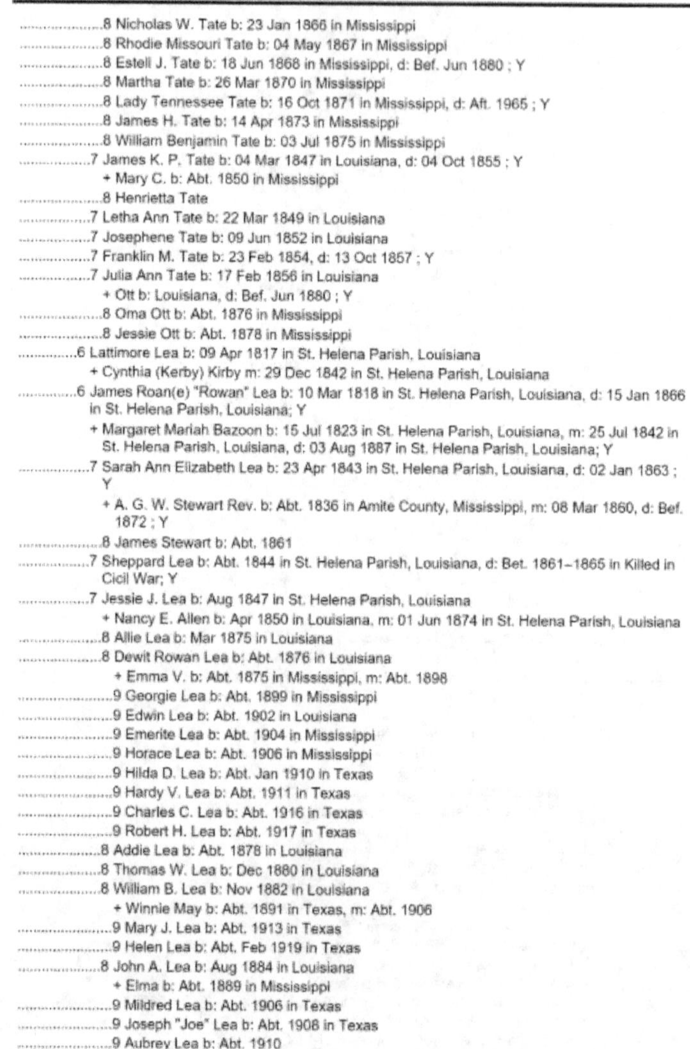

.................8 Nicholas W. Tate b: 23 Jan 1866 in Mississippi
.................8 Rhodie Missouri Tate b: 04 May 1867 in Mississippi
.................8 Estell J. Tate b: 18 Jun 1868 in Mississippi, d: Bef. Jun 1880 ; Y
.................8 Martha Tate b: 26 Mar 1870 in Mississippi
.................8 Lady Tennessee Tate b: 16 Oct 1871 in Mississippi, d: Aft. 1965 ; Y
.................8 James H. Tate b: 14 Apr 1873 in Mississippi
.................8 William Benjamin Tate b: 03 Jul 1875 in Mississippi
.................7 James K. P. Tate b: 04 Mar 1847 in Louisiana, d: 04 Oct 1855 ; Y
        + Mary C. b: Abt. 1850 in Mississippi
.................8 Henrietta Tate
.................7 Letha Ann Tate b: 22 Mar 1849 in Louisiana
.................7 Josephene Tate b: 09 Jun 1852 in Louisiana
.................7 Franklin M. Tate b: 23 Feb 1854, d: 13 Oct 1857 ; Y
.................7 Julia Ann Tate b: 17 Feb 1856 in Louisiana
        + Ott b: Louisiana, d: Bef. Jun 1880 ; Y
.................8 Oma Ott b: Abt. 1876 in Mississippi
.................8 Jessie Ott b: Abt. 1878 in Mississippi
.............6 Lattimore Lea b: 09 Apr 1817 in St. Helena Parish, Louisiana
        + Cynthia (Kerby) Kirby m: 29 Dec 1842 in St. Helena Parish, Louisiana
.............6 James Roan(e) "Rowan" Lea b: 10 Mar 1818 in St. Helena Parish, Louisiana, d: 15 Jan 1866
        in St. Helena Parish, Louisiana; Y
        + Margaret Mariah Bazoon b: 15 Jul 1823 in St. Helena Parish, Louisiana, m: 25 Jul 1842 in
        St. Helena Parish, Louisiana, d: 03 Aug 1887 in St. Helena Parish, Louisiana; Y
.................7 Sarah Ann Elizabeth Lea b: 23 Apr 1843 in St. Helena Parish, Louisiana, d: 02 Jan 1863 ;
        Y
        + A. G. W. Stewart Rev. b: Abt. 1836 in Amite County, Mississippi, m: 08 Mar 1860, d: Bef.
        1872 ; Y
.................8 James Stewart b: Abt. 1861
.................7 Sheppard Lea b: Abt. 1844 in St. Helena Parish, Louisiana, d: Bet. 1861–1865 in Killed in
        Cicil War; Y
.................7 Jessie J. Lea b: Aug 1847 in St. Helena Parish, Louisiana
        + Nancy E. Allen b: Apr 1850 in Louisiana, m: 01 Jun 1874 in St. Helena Parish, Louisiana
.................8 Allie Lea b: Mar 1875 in Louisiana
.................8 Dewit Rowan Lea b: Abt. 1876 in Louisiana
        + Emma V. b: Abt. 1875 in Mississippi, m: Abt. 1898
.................9 Georgie Lea b: Abt. 1899 in Mississippi
.................9 Edwin Lea b: Abt. 1902 in Louisiana
.................9 Emerite Lea b: Abt. 1904 in Mississippi
.................9 Horace Lea b: Abt. 1906 in Mississippi
.................9 Hilda D. Lea b: Abt. Jan 1910 in Texas
.................9 Hardy V. Lea b: Abt. 1911 in Texas
.................9 Charles C. Lea b: Abt. 1916 in Texas
.................9 Robert H. Lea b: Abt. 1917 in Texas
.................8 Addie Lea b: Abt. 1878 in Louisiana
.................8 Thomas W. Lea b: Dec 1880 in Louisiana
.................8 William B. Lea b: Nov 1882 in Louisiana
        + Winnie May b: Abt. 1891 in Texas, m: Abt. 1906
.................9 Mary J. Lea b: Abt. 1913 in Texas
.................9 Helen Lea b: Abt. Feb 1919 in Texas
.................8 John A. Lea b: Aug 1884 in Louisiana
        + Elma b: Abt. 1889 in Mississippi
.................9 Mildred Lea b: Abt. 1906 in Texas
.................9 Joseph "Joe" Lea b: Abt. 1908 in Texas
.................9 Aubrey Lea b: Abt. 1910

.................9 Philip Lea b: Abt. 1912
.................9 Elizabeth Lea b: Abt. 1914
.................9 Elina Lea b: Abt. 1918
   + Emily Adaline "Addie" Williams
.................7 Lavania Lea b: 29 Aug 1849 in St. Helena Parish, Louisiana, d: 27 Feb 1928 ; Y
   + Thomas Warner "T.W." Hurst b: Abt. 1841 in Louisiana
.................8 Richard Henry Hurst b: 10 Oct 1870 in Louisiana, d: 08 Mar 1954 ; Y
   + Minnie Eudora McCoy b: 19 Jun 1878 in Mississippi, m: 27 Oct 1895 in St. Helena
     Parish, Louisiana, d: 11 Jan 1952 ; Y
.................9 Nannie Hurst b: 05 Nov 1896 in Louisiana, d: 01 Feb 1975 ; Y
   + Thomas E. Carruth b: 17 May 1911 in Louisiana, d: 11 Nov 1981 ; Y
.................9 Walter Hurst b: Aug 1897 in Louisiana, d: Bef. Jan 1992 ; Y
.................9 Lavania Hurst b: May 1900 in Louisiana, d: 1901 ; Y
.................9 Willie Hurst b: Abt. 1901 in Louisiana, d: Bef. Jan 1992 ; Y
.................9 (unnamed) Hurst b: 15 May 1904, d: 15 May 1904 ; Y
.................9 (unnamed) Hurst b: 15 May 1904, d: 15 May 1904 ; Y
.................9 (unnamed) Hurst b: 15 May 1904, d: 15 May 1904 ; Y
.................9 Henry Hurst b: Abt. 1906 in Louisiana, d: Bef. Jan 1992 ; Y
.................9 Toler Hurst b: 07 Feb 1909 in Lookout, Louisiana, d: 31 Jan 1992 in Baton Rouge
    General Medical Center, Baton Rouge, Louisiana; Y
   + Hazel Hutchinson b: 16 Aug 1909 in Liverpool, St. Helena Parish, Louisiana, m: Abt.
     1934, d: 03 Apr 1999 in St. Helena Parish Nursing Home, Greensburg, St. Helena
     Parish, Louisiana; Y
.................10 Living Hurst
   + Living McKnight
.................10 Living Hurst
   + Living Dyer
.................11 Living Dyer
   + Living Reeves
.................12 Living Reeves
.................9 James Brown "J.B." Hurst b: Abt. 1911 in Louisiana, d: Bef. Jan 1992 ; Y
   + Allie Dee Doughty b: Abt. 1917 in St. Helena Parish, Louisiana, m: 09 Dec 1935 in St.
     Helena Parish, Louisiana, d: 04 Jun 1995 in her residence in Jackson, East Feliciana
     Parish, Louisiana; Y
.................10 Carlton Seville Hurst d: Bef. Jun 1995 ; Y
   + Living Palmer
.................11 Living Hurst
   + Living Flood
.................12 Living Hurst
.................12 Living Hurst
.................11 Michael Bryan Hurst d: Bef. Jun 1995 ; Y
.................11 Living Hurst
   + Living Flood
   + Iona b: Abt. 1913 in Louisiana, m: Abt. 1929
.................10 Living Hurst
.................9 Minnie Lovie Hurst b: Abt. 1914 in Louisiana, d: Bef. Jan 1992 ; Y
   + Wales
.................10 Russell Wales d: Bef. Jan 1992 ; Y
.................9 Helen Hurst b: Abt. 1917 in Louisiana
   + Leo Hall Doughty b: 14 Sep 1911 in St. Helena Parish, Louisiana, m: Abt. 1936, d: 23
    Oct 1994 in St. Helena Parish Hospital, Greensburg, St. Helena Parish, Louisiana; Y
.................10 Living Doughty
   + Living Ray
.................10 Living Doughty
   + Living Armstrong

..........................11 Living Armstrong
..........................11 Living Armstrong
..........................10 Living Doughty
                    + Living Kirby
..........................8 Roan Lea Hurst b: Feb 1872 in Louisiana, d: Bef. Dec 1999 ; Y
                    + Clara Talbert b: Jul 1878 in Louisiana, m: Abt. 1895, d: Bef. Dec 1999 ; Y
..........................9 (infant) Hurst b: 10 Nov 1896, d: 10 Nov 1896 ; Y
..........................9 Hurst b: Mar 1898 in Louisiana, d: Bef. Apr 1910 ; Y
..........................9 Emma Lorena Hurst b: 17 Mar 1900 in Louisiana, d: Jun 1983 ; Y
                    + DeLee
..........................9 Bessie Hurst b: Abt. 1901 in Louisiana, d: Bef. Dec 1999 ; Y
                    + Hogan
                    + Kennedy
..........................9 Bythel Hurst b: 02 Oct 1906 in Louisiana, d: Jan 1986 ; Y
..........................9 Cornelia Hurst b: Abt. 1910 in Louisiana
                    + Bond
..........................9 (infant) Hurst b: 21 Feb 1913, d: Jun 1913 ; Y
..........................9 Claudia Grace Hurst b: 10 Jan 1915 in St. Helena Parish, Louisiana, d: 25 Dec 1999 in
                    St. Helena Parish Hospital, Greensburg, St. Helena Parish, Louisiana; Y
                    + Clayton C. Strickland b: Abt. 1915 in Louisiana, m: 22 Jun 1934 in St. Helena Parish,
                    Louisiana, d: Bef. Dec 1999 ; Y
..........................10 Robert C. "Bobby" Strickland b: 31 Dec 1947, d: 01 Apr 1969 ; Y
..........................10 Living Strickland
                    + Living Devall
..........................11 Living Devall
..........................11 Living Devall
..........................10 Living Strickland
                    + Living Dean
..........................11 Living Strickland
..........................11 Living Strickland
..........................9 Lea Fulton Hurst b: Abt. 1917 in Louisiana
..........................9 Ruby Blanch Hurst b: Abt. 1921 in Louisiana
                    + Roberts
..........................8 Emma Estell Hurst b: Abt. 1873 in Louisiana, d: 1896 ; Y
..........................8 Mary Susan Hurst b: Jun 1875 in Louisiana, d: 1915 ; Y
                    + Thomas Ervin Frazier b: Dec 1864 in Louisiana, d: Bef. Jun 1995 ; Y
..........................9 Amanda "Mandy" Frazier b: Jan 1899, d: Bef. Jun 1995 ; Y
                    + Bean
..........................9 Lottie Frazier b: Abt. 1900, d: Bef. Jun 1995 ; Y
                    + Caston
..........................9 Morris Frazier b: Abt. 1902, d: Bef. Jun 1995 ; Y
..........................9 Alex Frazier b: 28 May 1903, d: 08 Jan 1906 ; Y
..........................9 Maggie Lee Frazier b: 04 Aug 1905, d: Apr 1979 ; Y
                    + Carl Miller Bellue b: 08 Jul 1907 in Louisiana, m: 15 Sep 1927, d: 18 Feb 1947 ; Y
..........................10 Emeral Dewey Bellue b: 03 Jul 1928, d: 24 Jul 1928 ; Y
..........................10 Patsy Ann Bellue b: 22 Feb 1942, d: 06 May 1949 ; Y
..........................10 Living Bellue
                    + Living Winters
..........................11 Living Bellue
..........................11 Living Bellue
..........................10 Living Bellue
                    + Living Hamby
..........................11 Living Bellue
..........................11 Living Bellue

......................11 Living Bellue
......................11 Living Bellue
......................10 Living Bellue
              + Living Roussell
......................11 Living Roussell
......................11 Living Roussell
......................11 Living Roussell
......................10 Living Bellue
              + Wilton Rudolph Jenkins b: 15 Jul 1925
......................11 Living Jenkins
              + Living Alford
......................12 Living Jenkins
......................11 Living Jenkins
              + Living Rhodes
......................12 Living Rhodes
......................12 Living Rhodes
......................11 Living Jenkins
              + Living Alford
......................12 Living Jenkins
......................12 Living Jenkins
......................10 Living Bellue
              + Living Rawls
......................11 Living Rawls
......................11 Living Rawls
......................11 Living Rawls
......................11 Living Rawls
......................9 Ervena Frazier b: 05 Aug 1907 in St. Helena Parish, Louisiana, d: 26 Jun 1995 in Lane Memorial Hospital, Zachary, East Baton Rouge Parish, Louisiana; Y
              + Perry Lea "Pete" Allen b: 11 Sep 1910 in St. Helena Parish, Louisiana, m: 15 Oct 1927 in St. Helena Parish, Louisiana, d: 07 Aug 1995 in Lane Memorial Hospital, Zachary, East Baton Rouge Parish, Louisiana; Y
......................10 Iva Lea Allen b: Abt. Sep 1929, d: Bef. 2005 ; Y
              + James S. Williams b: Abt. Apr 1928 in Glen, Alcorn County, Mississippi, d: 09 Apr 2005 in his residence in Jackson, East Feliciana Parish, Louisiana; Y
......................11 Perry Wayne Williams b: 13 May 1951 in McComb, Pike County, Mississippi, d: 06 Dec 1990 in his residence in Denham Springs, Livingston Parish, Louisiana; Y
              + Living Goza
......................12 Living Williams
              + Living
......................12 Living Williams
......................9 Nicholas Nelf Frazier Sr. b: 26 Mar 1911, d: Dec 1983 ; Y
              + Albertine Porshe d: Bef. Mar 2001 ; Y
......................10 Jerry J. Frazier Sr. b: 17 Oct 1940 in Liverpool, St. Helena Parish, Louisiana, d: 01 Mar 2001 in his home in Bringhurst, Carroll County, Indiana; Y
              + Living
......................11 Living Frazier
              + Living (M-unknown)
......................12 Living Frazier
......................12 Living Frazier
......................11 Living Frazier
              + Living
......................12 Living Frazier
......................12 Living Frazier
......................12 Living Frazier
......................11 Living Frazier

...........................11 Living Frazier
                          + Yvonne (L-unknown)
...........................12 Living Frazier
...........................12 Living Frazier
                          + Living Taylor
........................10 Living Frazier
........................10 Living Frazier
                          + Living LeTard
........................10 Living Frazier
........................10 Living Frazier
........................10 Living Frazier
........................10 Living Frazier
......................9 Irene Frazier b: 18 Oct 1913, d: 22 Feb 1988 ; Y
                          + Dickerson
....................8 Nancy Jane "Nannie" Hurst b: Feb 1877 in Louisiana, d: 1907 ; Y
                          + Harris Waller "H.W." Powell b: Jul 1875 in Louisiana, m: 08 Apr 1894 in St. Helena
                             Parish, Louisiana
......................9 Geneva Powell b: Feb 1895 in Louisiana
......................9 Felder Powell b: Nov 1896 in Louisiana
......................9 Percer Powell b: Nov 1898 in Louisiana
......................9 Lewis Powell b: Abt. 1900 in Louisiana
......................9 Hallery Powell b: Abt. 1902 in Louisiana
......................9 Burnell Powell b: Abt. 1903 in Louisiana
....................8 James Joseph "Jim" Hurst b: 1878 in Louisiana, d: Bef. Nov 2002 ; Y
                          + Annie Victoria Leonard b: Abt. 1884, m: Abt. 1902, d: Bef. Nov 2002 ; Y
......................9 Mazie Hurst b: Abt. 1903, d: Bef. Jan 2002 ; Y
                          + White
......................9 Thomas Linton Hurst Sr. b: 12 Jun 1905, d: 22 Oct 1987 ; Y
......................9 Dollie E. "Geneva" Hurst b: 10 Dec 1909, d: 04 Feb 1997 ; Y
                          + Freeman
......................9 Annie Marie Hurst b: 08 Jan 1913, d: Sep 1990 ; Y
                          + Massey
......................9 Zelma Lea Hurst b: 19 Jul 1915 in Osyka, Pike County, Mississippi, d: 29 Nov 2002 in
                             Summit Hospital in Baton Rouge, East Baton Rouge Parish, Louisiana; Y
                          + Earl C. Rosevear b: 15 Aug 1909 in Missouri, d: Feb 1986 ; Y
........................10 Living Rosevear
                          + Living Wall
...........................11 Living Wall
                          + Living Young
...........................12 Living Young
...........................12 Living Young
...........................11 Living Wall
                          + Living Williams
...........................12 Living Williams
...........................12 Living Williams
                          + Living Babcock
...........................11 Living Babcock
...........................11 Living Babcock
                          + Living Nall
...........................12 Living Nall
...........................12 Living Nall
........................10 Living Rosevear
                          + Living
...........................11 Living Rosevear

```
                          + Living Pourciau
.........................12 Living Pourciau
.........................12 Living Pourciau
.........................11 Living Rosevear
                          + Living
.........................12 Living Rosevear
.........................12 Living Rosevear
.........................12 Living Rosevear
.........................9 Kathryn "Aunt Kat" Hurst b: 08 Mar 1919 in Osyka, Pike County, Mississippi, d: 30 Jan
                           2002 in her residence in Greensburg, St. Helena Parish, Louisiana; Y
                          + Lathan Powers Bridges b: 16 Apr 1918, d: 25 Oct 1994 ; Y
.........................10 Living Bridges
                          + Living Campo
.........................11 Living Campo
.........................11 Living Campo
.........................11 Living Campo
                          + Living
.........................12 Living Campo
.........................11 Living Campo
.........................9 James R. "Jimbo" Hurst b: Abt. 1923 in Mississippi
.........................9 Hazel (infant) Hurst d: Bef. Jan 2002 ; Y
.........................8 Thomas Warner Hurst Jr. b: 22 Nov 1880, d: 1951 ; Y
.........................8 Saluda Angelina "Ludia" Hurst b: Abt. 1882 in Louisiana
                          + Harris Waller "H.W." Powell b: Jul 1875 in Louisiana, m: 06 Sep 1908 in St. Helena
                           Parish, Louisiana
.........................9 Creson Powell b: Abt. 1910 in Louisiana
.........................9 Printis Powell b: Abt. 1911 in Louisiana
.........................9 Clara Mae Powell b: Abt. 1913 in Louisiana
.........................9 Clayton Powell b: Abt. 1915 in Louisiana
.........................8 Margaret Winifred "Maggie Winne" Hurst b: 14 Mar 1884 in Louisiana, d: 03 Jun 1966 ; Y
                          + Major Wellington "M.W." Carter b: 27 Jan 1875 in Louisiana, m: 20 Nov 1912 in St.
                           Helena Parish, Louisiana, d: 07 Jan 1928 ; Y
.........................9 Wellington Warner Carter b: Abt. Feb 1914
.........................9 Roberta Lee "Robbie" Carter b: Abt. 1917 in St. Helena Parish, Louisiana, d: 31 Oct
                           1999 in St. Helena Parish Nursing Home, Greensburg, St. Helena Parish, Louisiana; Y
                          + Roscoe G. Brecheen b: 26 Feb 1909, d: 26 Dec 1997 ; Y
.........................10 Living Brecheen
                          + Living
.........................11 Living Brecheen
                          + Living Fournet
.........................12 Living Fournet
.........................12 Living Fournet
.........................11 Living Brecheen
.........................11 Living Brecheen
.........................9 Robert Frieler Carter b: Abt. 1919
.........................8 Lavinia Hurst b: Abt. 1888, d: 1916 ; Y
                          + John S. White b: Abt. 1884
.........................9 Alina M. White b: Abt. 1907
.........................9 Winnie L. White b: Abt. 1908
.........................9 Mattie White b: Abt. 1913
.........................8 Jesse Bazoon Hurst d: 1916 ; Y
                          + Bessie Stewart Williams
.................7 Matilda Angeline Lea b: 06 Sep 1851 in St. Helena Parish, Louisiana, d: 10 Nov 1861 ; Y
.................7 Nicholas B. Lea b: Nov 1853 in Louisiana
```

+ Lorraine Elizabeth Susan Carruth b: Jan 1855 in Louisiana, m: 09 Feb 1876 in St. Helena Parish, Louisiana
........8 John S. Lea b: Aug 1880
........8 Minnie Alice Lea b: 04 May 1884 in Kentwood, Tangipahoa Parish, Louisiana, d: 15 Sep 1921 in Kentwood, Tangipahoa Parish, Louisiana; Y
+ Thomas Lawrence Hughes Sr. b: 29 Jul 1878 in Amite County, Mississippi, d: 24 Aug 1960 in New Orleans, Orleans Parish, Louisiana; Y
........9 Olivia Hughes b: 15 Feb 1903 in Kentwood, Tangipahoa Parish, Louisiana, d: 02 Nov 1971 in New Orleans, Orleans Parish, Louisiana; Y
+ John Henserling
........9 Beatrice Hughes b: Oct 1904 in Kentwood, Tangipahoa Parish, Louisiana, d: 13 Apr 1989 ; Y
+ Jack Earles
........9 Ruby Lee Hughes b: 05 Feb 1909 in Kentwood, Tangipahoa Parish, Louisiana, d: 11 Mar 1976 in Kentwood, Tangipahoa Parish, Louisiana; Y
+ Frederick Gustav [Grigaitis] Gregot b: 25 Oct 1903 in Taliusaiciai Village, Taurage Region, Russia (Lithuania), m: New Orleans, Orleans Parish, Louisiana, d: 02 Jan 1990 in McComb, Pike County, Mississippi; Y
........10 Gloria Mae (infant) [Grigaitis] Gregot b: 26 Feb 1928 in New Orleans, Orleans Parish, Louisiana, d: 12 Feb 1929 in New Orleans, Orleans Parish, Louisiana; Y
........10 Norma Althea [GrigatGrigaitis] Gregot b: 20 Jan 1937 in New Orleans, Orleans Parish, Louisiana, d: 02 Jan 1990 in McComb, Pike County, Mississippi; Y
+ Living Day
........11 Living Day
+ Living Maloley
........10 Living Gregot
+ Herbert Lewis b: Kentwood, Tangipahoa Parish, Louisiana
........11 Living Lewis
+ Living Crawford
........12 Living Crawford
........12 Living Crawford
+ Living Stoudenmier
........12 Living Stoudenmier
........9 Lenarda Hughes b: Abt. 1911, d: New Orleans, Orleans Parish, Louisiana; Y
+ Lucille
........9 Edna Hughes b: 24 Oct 1914, d: 15 Apr 1994 ; Y
+ William S. Earles
........9 Arnell Leigeton Hughes b: 04 Sep 1916 in Kentwood, Tangipahoa Parish, Louisiana, d: 28 May 1922 in Kentwood, Tangipahoa Parish, Louisiana; Y
........9 Minnie Hughes b: Abt. Mar 1929
+ Musgrove
........8 Homer A. Lea Sr. b: Jul 1895
+ <No name>
........9 Homer A. Lea b: 29 Jul 1923, d: 29 Aug 1988 ; Y
+ Living Anders
........10 Living Lea
+ Living Rhodus
........11 Keith Rhodus b: Abt. 1969 in Baton Rouge, East Baton Rouge Parish, Louisiana, d: 26 Oct 1993 in Hammond, Tangipahoa Parish, Louisiana; Y
........11 Living Rhodus
+ Living
........12 Living Rhodus
........12 Living Rhodus
........11 Living Rhodus
........9 Robert Lea

.............7 Winniford (Winfred) Agnes "Winnie" Lea b: 30 Apr 1857 in St. Helena Parish, Louisiana, d:
             09 Feb 1917 ; Y
                + John Preston Strickland b: 07 Apr 1852 in Louisiana, m: 09 Apr 1874 in St. Helena
                  Parish, Louisiana, d: 25 Sep 1915 ; Y
.............8 Maggie Strickland b: Abt. 1875
.............8 Ella Strickland b: Abt. 1877
                + J. W. Lee
.............8 Elizabeth "Lizzie" Strickland b: Jan 1879
                + David Gordon Lee b: 17 Feb 1875 in Louisiana
.............8 Clara May Strickland b: 20 May 1883 in Louisiana, d: 11 Oct 1968 ; Y
                + Leslie Self "Les" Harvell b: 13 Apr 1878 in Louisiana, m: 15 Jun 1905 in St. Helena
                  Parish, Louisiana, d: 30 Nov 1957 ; Y
.............9 Bettye Doris Harvell b: 23 Aug 1907, d: 27 Feb 1918 in Grangeville, St. Helena Parish,
             Louisiana; Y
.............9 Leslie Lea Harvell b: 18 May 1908
                + Nettie Mae Dunn m: 15 Apr 1933 in Greensburg, St. Helena Parish, Louisiana
.............9 Ethel Bankston Harvell b: 24 Jan 1911
                + Joseph Emmerson Dunn m: 05 Jul 1936 in Denham Spring, Livingston Parish,
                  Louisiana
.............9 Edith Day Harvell b: 24 Jan 1911 in Louisiana
                + Gus R. Hartner b: Abt. 1906 in Louisiana, m: 17 Apr 1927 in St. Francisville, West
                  Feliciana Parish, Louisiana
.............8 Mary Strickland b: Jan 1885
.............8 Olivia Strickland b: Nov 1887
.............8 Lois Strickland b: 06 Aug 1888, d: 22 Jun 1948 in Jackson, East Feliciana Parish,
             Louisiana; Y
                + Thomas Christian Haggadore b: 22 Feb 1876, d: 25 Nov 1924 ; Y
.............9 Elizabeth "Bobbie" Haggadore b: 13 Sep 1910 in McComb, Mississippi, d: 01 Aug 1971
             in Lane Memorial Hospital, Zachary, Louisiana; Y
                + Mally Wesley Day b: 18 Jan 1920 in Greensburg, St. Helena Parish, Louisiana, d: 19
                  Aug 1997 in Our Lady of the Lake Regional Medical Center, Baton Rouge, Louisiana;
                  Y
                + Fred Allen "Freddie" Daniel b: 1907 in Arkansas, d: 1966 in Memphis, Shelby County,
                  Tennessee; Y
.............10 Freddie Haggadore Daniel b: 23 Dec 1929 in Memphis, Tennessee
                + Living Schelling
.............11 Living Daniel
.............11 Living Daniel
.............11 Living Daniel
.............10 Gerald "Jerry" (infant) Daniel b: 1934 in Memphis, Tennessee, d: 1934 in Memphis,
             Tennessee; Y
.............10 Living Daniel
                + Living Morgan
.............11 Living Daniel
                  + Living Clouatre
.............12 Living Daniel
.............11 Living Daniel
.............9 Margaret Nell Haggadore b: 31 Oct 1915 in Natalbany, Tangipahoa Parish, Louisiana,
             d: 11 Jan 1996 in her residence in Greenwell Springs, Louisiana; Y
                + Arthur E. White d: Bef. Jan 1996 ; Y
.............10 Carol Elizabeth White b: 03 Sep 1944, d: 19 Aug 1959 ; Y
.............10 Living Palmer
                + Clyde J. Lemoine b: 29 Aug 1939 in Big Bend, Avoyelles Parish, Louisiana, d: 07
                  Oct 1998 in his home in Jackson, East Feliciana Parish, Louisiana; Y
                + Living Tinkler

........................11 Living Tinkler
........................11 Living Tinkler
........................11 Living Tinkler
........................11 Living Tinkler
                    + Living Thomas
........................11 Living Tinkler
                    + Living Johnston
....................10 Living Palmer
                    + Living Johnson
                    + Henry Earl "Red" Palmer b: 14 Nov 1913 in Jackson, East Feliciana Parish,
                        Louisiana, d: 28 Oct 1991 in Lane Memorial Hospital, Zachary, East Baton Rouge
                        Parish, Louisiana; Y
....................10 Living Palmer
                    + Living Guillory
....................10 Living Palmer
                    + Living Harvey
..................9 Clara Mae "Dit" Hagadore b: 02 Feb 1918, d: 18 May 1979 ; Y
                    + Allen
................8 Lottye Strickland b: Sep 1890
                    + F. W. Loving m: 24 Jun 1909 in St. Helena Parish, Louisiana
................8 Effie Belle Strickland b: 28 Nov 1892 in Louisiana
                    + George Otis Venable b: 18 Dec 1885 in Greensburg, Louisiana, m: 16 Sep 1914 in
                        Greensburg, St. Helena Parish, Louisiana, d: 26 Jul 1948 ; Y
..................9 Effie Cewilla Venable b: 11 Sep 1915 in Tangipahoa, Tangipahoa Parish, Louisiana, d:
                        31 Oct 1993 in Hood Memorial Hospital, Amite, Tangipahoa Parish, Louisiana; Y
                    + Rembert A. Carloss b: 25 Jan 1909, m: 16 Jun 1936, d: 24 Feb 1998 ; Y
....................10 Living Carloss
                    + Living Gray
....................11 Living Gray
                        + Living
....................12 Living Gray
....................12 Living Gray
..................9 Ouida Blakeman Venable b: 27 Aug 1918 in Hammond, Tangipahoa Parish, Louisiana,
                        d: 04 Jul 1999 in Summit Hospital, Baton Rouge, Louisiana; Y
                    + Carl M. Hutchinson b: 12 Apr 1914, m: Aug 1935, d: 17 Feb 1991 ; Y
....................10 Ouida Carleen Hutchinson b: 02 Oct 1937 in Beaumont, Jefferson County, Texas, d:
                        02 May 2001 in Summit Hospital, Baton Rouge, East Baton Rouge Parish,
                        Louisiana; Y
                    + Living Holshouser
....................10 Rita Janelle Hutchinson b: 16 Oct 1939, d: 09 Jun 1999 ; Y
                    + Living Green
..................9 George Otis Venable Jr. b: 16 Aug 1921 in Louisiana
                    + Sibil Gotts
....................10 Living Venable
....................10 Living Venable
....................10 Living Venable
....................10 Living Venable
....................10 Living Venable
                    + Living Dequeant
....................11 Living Dequeant
..................9 Nelda Venable b: 07 Dec 1922 in Louisiana
                    + Ben Dameron Carloss m: Bet. 10 Sep 1939–1950, d: Bef. Nov 1999 ; Y
....................10 Living Carloss
....................10 Living Carloss
..................9 Living Venable

```
                        + Living Cox
..........................10 Living Venable
..........................10 Living Venable
......................8 Lona Strickland b: Jan 1895
......................8 Willis C. Strickland b: Jun 1897
..................7 Josephine Lea b: Abt. 1859 in Louisiana
                    + Alexander Andrew "Alex" Frazier b: Abt. 1859
..................7 Aurelia Cecelia Lea b: 19 Apr 1860 in St. Helena Parish, Louisiana, d: 27 Jul 1927 ; Y
                    + James Allen Carruth b: 13 Feb 1853 in Louisiana, m: 12 Apr 1876 in St. Helena Parish,
                      Louisiana, d: 25 Dec 1893 ; Y
......................8 Jessie Clinton Carruth b: 13 Oct 1877, d: 17 Jun 1939 ; Y
                        + Nancy Allen b: 13 Jul 1879, m: 14 Dec 1899 in St. Helena Parish, Louisiana, d: 12 Nov
                          1964 ; Y
......................9 Dillon Carruth b: 24 Sep 1900, d: May 1981 ; Y
                        + Ella Sanders m: 23 Jan 1921 in St. Helena Parish, Louisiana
......................9 D. P. Carruth b: 1907, d: 1907 ; Y
......................9 Nettles Carruth b: 06 Nov 1908, d: Aug 1988 ; Y
......................9 O. D. Carruth b: 25 Jun 1911 in St. Helena Parish, Louisiana, d: 29 Jul 1993 in St.
                        Helena Parish Hospital, Greensburg, Louisiana; Y
                        + Irma McCoy b: 26 May 1917 in St. Helena Parish, Louisiana, d: 22 Nov 1995 in Our
                          Lady of the Lake Regional Medical Center, Baton Rouge, Louisiana; Y
..........................10 Living Carruth
..........................10 Living Carruth
                            + Living Frohn
..........................11 Living Carruth
                              + Living
..........................12 Living Carruth
..........................12 Living Carruth
..........................11 Living Carruth
                              + Living
......................9 Addie Marie Carruth b: 01 Nov 1914 in St. Helena Parish, Louisiana, d: 01 Dec 1996 in
                        North Oaks Medical Center, Hammond, Tangipahoa Parish, Louisiana; Y
                        + Virgil Lee Allen b: 30 Oct 1915 in Louisiana, m: 15 Apr 1938, d: 03 Oct 1973 ; Y
..........................10 Living Allen
                            + Living Lee
..........................11 Living Lee
                              + Living Taylor
..........................11 Living Lee
..........................11 Living Lee
                              + Living Erdey
..........................10 Living Allen
                            + Living Wallace
..........................11 Living Wallace
..........................11 Living Wallace
..........................11 Living Wallace
                            + Living Crayton
..........................10 Living Allen
                            + Living Strong
..........................11 Living Strong
..........................11 Living Strong
..........................11 Living Strong
..........................11 Living Strong
..........................10 Living Allen
```

+ Robert Earl Tarver b: 25 May 1934 in Magnolia, Pike County, Mississippi, d: 16 Mar 2001 in Veterans Affairs Medical Center, Jackson, Hinds County, Mississippi; Y
..............................11 Living Tarver
..............................11 Living Tarver
+ Living Butler
+ Living Williams
..............................11 Living Williams
+ Living Pouncey
..............................11 Living Williams
..............................11 Living Williams
+ Living Coon
..............................11 Living Williams
+ Clyde Blades b: 11 May 1964, d: 30 May 1985 ; Y
..............................12 Living Blades
+ Living Dean
..............................12 Living Dean
+ Living Zeigler
..............................10 Living Allen
+ Living Labry
..............................11 Brandon Lee Allen b: 02 Nov 1974, d: 03 Nov 1974 ; Y
..............................11 Living Allen
..............................11 Living Allen
..............................11 Living Allen
..............................9 Amy Carruth b: 10 Oct 1917, d: Jun 1985 ; Y
+ McNabb
..............................9 Minnie Carruth d: Bef. Dec 1996 ; Y
+ Fleming
..............................9 William Carruth d: Bef. Jul 1993 ; Y
..............................9 Elton Carruth d: Bef. Jul 1993 ; Y
..............................8 Sarah Elizabeth "Bessie" Carruth b: 01 Mar 1880 in Louisiana, d: 27 Nov 1938 ; Y
+ James Benton "Bran" Frazier b: 29 Nov 1869 in Louisiana, m: 04 Jul 1895 in St. Helena Parish, Louisiana, d: 23 Nov 1947 ; Y
..............................9 Eual Frazier Sr. b: May 1896, d: Bef. Feb 1992 ; Y
+ Nettie Travis
..............................10 Eual Frazier Jr. b: 13 May 1933, d: 11 Jun 1988 ; Y
+ Living Birch
..............................11 Living Frazier
+ Living Peterson Dr.
+ Living Navin
..............................12 Living Navin
..............................12 Living Navin
+ Living Meyer
..............................12 Living Meyer
..............................11 Living Frazier
..............................9 John Hugh Frazier b: Jun 1897, d: Bef. Feb 1992 ; Y
..............................9 Arneter "Needa" Frazier b: 01 Jan 1899 in St. Helena Parish, Louisiana, d: 07 Feb 1992 in Lane Memorial Hospital Nursing Home, Louisiana; Y
+ Allen Q. Smith b: 27 Mar 1896 in Louisiana, m: 23 Nov 1919 in St. Helena Parish, Louisiana, d: 26 Sep 1956 ; Y
..............................10 James L. Smith b: Abt. 1922, d: Bef. Feb 1992 ; Y
..............................10 Roy Louis Smith b: 06 Jan 1924 in Greensburg, St. Helena Parish, Louisiana, d: 15 Sep 2002 ; Y
+ Bennie Mae Easley b: Jan 1925, m: Abt. 1942
..............................11 Living Smith

+ Living Stark
............................12 Living Smith
............................12 Living Smith
............................12 Living Smith
........................11 Living Smith
+ Living Elizey
............................12 Living Elizey Lt.
............................12 Living Elizey
............................12 Living Elizey
........................11 Living Smith
....................10 Wilma Smith b: Abt. 1926
+ Maxwell "Max" McDaniel
....................10 Lee Joe Smith b: Abt. 1932 in Greensburg, St. Helena Parish, Louisiana, d: 21 Dec
2002 in Greensburg, St. Helena Parish, Louisiana; Y
+ Living Duncan
....................10 Living Smith
+ Gerald Norman "Buddy" Birch b: 29 Apr 1928
........................11 Living Birch
+ Living Beasley
............................12 Living Beasley
........................11 Living Birch
+ Living Bearden
........................11 Living Birch
+ Living Pray
............................12 Living Birch
............................12 Living Birch
....................10 Living Smith
+ Living Chapman
+ Joe Strickland d: Bef. Feb 1992 ; Y
................9 James Benton Frazier Jr. b: Abt. 1901 in Louisiana, d: Bef. Feb 1992 ; Y
+ Lonie Mae Travis b: 03 Jun 1906 in Louisiana, m: 15 Oct 1921 in St. Helena Parish,
Louisiana, d: 14 Sep 1988 ; Y
....................10 Bessie B. Frazier b: Abt. 1923
................9 Annie Mae Frazier b: Abt. 1906 in Louisiana
+ Louis P. Harrell b: Abt. 1899 in Louisiana, m: 17 May 1924 in St. Helena Parish,
Louisiana
....................10 Louis Harrell b: Abt. Apr 1925
....................10 William Harrell b: Abt. Mar 1927
....................10 Donald Harrell b: Abt. Jul 1929
................9 Jessie Frazier b: 18 Jun 1908 in St. Helena Parish, Louisiana, d: 11 Dec 1967 ; Y
+ Willie Travis Woodard b: 03 Dec 1903 in St. Helena Parish, Louisiana, m: 14 Apr
1928, d: 20 Mar 1986 ; Y
....................10 Nicholas Leroy Woodard b: 10 Jan 1929
+ Living Summral
........................11 Living Woodard
........................11 Living Woodard
........................11 Living Woodard
+ Living Spears
........................11 Living Woodard
....................10 Dewey Wilton Woodard b: 31 Jul 1931, d: 25 Dec 1946 ; Y
....................10 Living Woodard
+ Living Hickman
........................11 Thomas Wilton Hickman b: 22 Nov 1953, d: 03 Jun 1972 ; Y
........................11 Kenneth Roy Hickman b: 18 Sep 1957, d: 03 Jun 1972 ; Y

........................9 Mamie Frazier b: 20 Oct 1910 in Louisiana, d: 06 Apr 2003 in St. Helena Parish Hospital, Greensburg, St. Helena Parish, Louisiana; Y
    + John Vernon Kirby b: Abt. 1910, m: Abt. 1928, d: Bef. Apr 2003 ; Y
........................10 Bobby Lee Kirby b: Abt. Sep 1929
    + Living Willis
........................10 Zellon Quin Kirby d: Bef. Apr 2003 ; Y
........................10 Johnny Edward Kirby d: Bef. Apr 2003 ; Y
........................9 Olevia Frazier b: Abt. 1912
    + Welch
........................9 Minnie Frazier b: Abt. 1914, d: Bef. Feb 1992 ; Y
    + Lee
........................9 John A. Frazier b: Abt. 1919, d: Bef. Feb 1992 ; Y
........................9 Nannie Frazier b: Abt. 1921, d: Bef. Feb 1992 ; Y
    + Lee
    + Alford
........................8 Nicholas Bazoon "Nick" Carruth b: 20 May 1882 in Louisiana, d: Nov 1968 ; Y
    + Rena M. b: Abt. 1892 in Mississippi, m: Abt. 1910
........................9 Doris Carruth
    + Rufus Pittman
........................10 Russell Douglas "Buddy" Pittman b: Abt. 1940, d: 07 Nov 2003 ; Y
    + Living Brock
........................10 Living Pittman
    + Living Gill
........................11 Living Gill
    + Living Dykes
........................11 Living Gill
    + Living McCoy
........................12 Living McCoy
........................11 Living Gill
    + Living Woodard
........................12 Living Gill
........................8 Roener(Rowena) Estelle "Stella" Carruth b: 11 Mar 1884 in Louisiana
    + John L. Sanders b: Abt. 1880 in Louisiana, m: 14 Sep 1900 in St. Helena Parish, Louisiana
........................9 Minerva Sanders b: Abt. 1901
........................9 Myrtis Sanders b: Abt. 1903
........................9 J. Y. Sanders b: Abt. 1907
........................9 John Lafayette "Fat" Sanders b: Abt. 1909
........................9 Edgar Sanders b: Abt. 1911
........................9 Lorena Sanders b: Abt. 1913
........................9 Herbert Sanders b: Abt. 1914
........................8 Minnie Mot Carruth b: 05 Feb 1886 in Louisiana
    + Lawrence Johnston b: McComb, Mississippi
........................8 Addie Mariah Carruth b: 02 Dec 1887 in Louisiana, d: Nov 1968 ; Y
    + Obie Lester Simmons b: 08 Oct 1877, m: 02 Jun 1921, d: 10 Feb 1948 ; Y
........................9 Aurelia Elizabeth Simmons b: 23 Nov 1925
    + Harold Fenn Douglass b: Ponchatoula, Louisiana, m: 24 Aug 1947
........................8 Viola "Violer" May Carruth b: 07 Dec 1889 in Louisiana, d: Sep 1963 ; Y
    + J. H. Williams b: Baton Rouge, Louisiana
........................8 James Edgar Carruth b: 16 Dec 1892 in Louisiana, d: 29 Jun 1955 ; Y
    + Hattie Copes b: 20 Oct 1898, d: Oct 1973 ; Y
........................9 Dorothy Carruth
........................9 LaNell Carruth
    + Willard Varnado

......................9 James Carruth
......................7 James Roane Lea Jr. b: 15 Aug 1866 in Louisiana
          + Nancy Prudence "Nanny" Wall b: 29 Mar 1869 in Near Gillsburg, Mississippi, m: 17 Dec
             1885, d: 30 Aug 1954 ; Y
......................8 Edgar B. Lea b: Feb 1887 in Mississippi
          + Laura b: Abt. 1893 in Louisiana
......................9 Rubie L. Lea b: Abt. 1926 in Louisiana
......................8 Tate B. Lea b: Jan 1889 in Mississippi
......................8 Jessie N. Lea b: Mar 1891 in Mississippi
          + Lilly b: Abt. 1893 in Mississippi, m: Abt. 1912
......................9 Jessie Williamson Lea b: 1917 in Mississippi
......................9 Nannie May Lea b: 15 Mar 1919 in Mississippi, d: Mar 1980 ; Y
          + John Edwads Wales Sr. b: Abt. 1912 in Greensburg, Louisiana, d: 17 Jan 1984 in
             Lane Memorial Hospital, Zachary, Louisiana; Y
......................10 John Edward "Johnny" Wales b: Abt. 1943, d: 07 Apr 2005 in his home in Zachary,
             East Baton Rouge Parish, Louisiana; Y
          + Living Canezaro
......................11 Living Wales
          + Living
......................11 Living Wales
          + Living Patin
......................11 Living Wales
          + Living
......................10 Living Wales
          + Living
          + Mixon
......................9 Roan Lea b: Abt. 1920 in Mississippi
......................9 Fred Lea b: Abt. 1922 in Mississippi
......................9 Louise Lea b: Abt. 1927 in Mississippi
......................9 Bettie J. Lea b: Abt. 1929 in Mississippi
......................8 Lester R. Lea b: Sep 1893 in Mississippi
......................8 William O. Lea b: Aug 1896 in Mississippi
          + Stella b: Abt. 1900 in Oklahoma, m: Abt. 1923
......................9 Billie Mamie Lea b: Abt. 1929 in Louisiana
......................8 Bonnie M. Lea b: Nov 1898 in Mississippi
          + W. W. Morris b: Amite, Louisiana
......................8 Fitzhugh Lea b: Abt. 1901 in Mississippi
......................8 Iley D. Lea b: Abt. 1903 in Mississippi
          + Alma b: Abt. 1908 in Mississippi
......................9 James I. Lea b: Abt. 1927 in Illinois
......................9 Evelyn D. Lea b: Abt. 1929 in Illinois
......................8 Rayborn Lea b: Abt. 1907 in Louisiana
          + Lizzie L. b: Abt. 1907 in Mississippi, m: Abt. 1925
......................9 Armond Lea b: Abt. 1926 in Louisiana
......................9 Adrian Lea b: Abt. 1929 in Louisiana
......................8 T. L. [Tate Lester?] Lea b: Abt. 1911 in Louisiana
......................6 Lavinia Lea b: 21 Jan 1822 in St. Helena Parish, Louisiana, d: 03 Mar 1908 in Amite County,
             Mississippi; Y
          + John Joseph Travis b: 04 Aug 1818, m: 28 Dec 1840, d: 20 Feb 1905 in Amite County,
             Mississippi; Y
......................5 David LEA b: 02 Dec 1779 in Surrey, North Carolina, d: 05 Dec 1844 in Amite, Mississippi; Y
          + Nancy CLAY b: 22 Jan 1781 in Chesterfield, Va, m: 02 Feb 1802 in Lea Springs, Grainger
             County, Tennessee, d: 13 Oct 1858 in Amite, Mississippi; Y
......................6 Margaret Muse LEA b: 02 Jan 1803 in Amite, Mississippi, d: 10 Sep 1945 in Amite,
             Mississippi; Y

...............6 Wesley Wilson LEA b: 17 Nov 1804 in Amite, Mississippi, d: 24 Jun 1860 in Amite, Mississippi; Y
...............6 William Dixon LEA b: 28 Jan 1807 in Amite, Mississippi, d: 04 May 1849 in Clinton, Louisiana; Y
...............6 Winchester Muse LEA b: 11 Aug 1809 in Amite, Mississippi, d: 21 Nov 1809 in Amite, Mississippi; Y
...............6 Landon Ludwell LEA b: 16 Oct 1810 in Amite, Mississippi, d: 08 Jul 1890 in Amite, Mississippi; Y
...............6 Melissa LEA b: 18 Feb 1813 in Amite, Mississippi, d: 19 Sep 1882 in Bayou Gross Tete, Point Coupee, Louisiana; Y
...............6 James Monroe LEA b: 16 May 1815 in Amite, Mississippi, d: Oakland College, Ms; Y
...............6 Robert Montgomery LEA b: 07 Oct 1817 in Amite, Mississippi, d: 30 Aug 1855 ; Y
...............6 Mary Reed LEA b: 06 Feb 1820 in Amite, Mississippi, d: 14 Sep 1884 ; Y
...............6 David Clay LEA b: 04 Nov 1821 in Amite, Mississippi, d: 04 Oct 1847 ; Y
...............6 Julia Clay LEA b: 16 Oct 1823 in Amite, Mississippi, d: 05 Dec 1840 in Amite, Mississippi; Y
...............6 Charles Clinton LEA b: 12 Nov 1827 in Amite, Mississippi, d: Oakland College, Ms; Y
............5 Luke LEA b: 26 Jan 1782 in Surey Co., NC, d: 17 Jun 1851 in Leavenworth Co., Ks; Y
            + Susan Wells MCCORMICK b: Abt. 1786 in <, Surry, Nc>, m: Abt. 1815
...............6 James Armstrong LEA b: Abt. 1816 in <Knoxville, Tn>
...............6 John Mccormick LEA b: 25 Dec 1818 in Knoxville, Tn
...............6 Francis Wells LEA b: Abt. 1820 in <Knoxville, Tn>
...............6 William Park LEA b: Abt. 1822 in <Knoxville, Tn>
...............6 Ann E LEA b: Abt. 1824 in <Knoxville, Tn>
...............6 Susan Jane LEA b: Abt. 1826 in <Knoxville, Tn>
...............6 Lavinia LEA b: Abt. 1828 in <Knoxville, Tn>
...............6 Margaret LEA b: 1831 in <Knoxville, Tn>
...............6 Luke LEA b: Abt. 1833 in <Knoxville, Tn>
            + Nancy Roberts JOHNSON
..........4 Major Lee b: Abt. 1743 in of, Caswell, Co, NC, d: 19 Nov 1842 in Powell's Valley, Tennessee; Y
            + Elizabeth HERNDON b: Abt. 1742 in Caroline Co. VA, m: Abt. 1763 in Caswell Co., NC, d: Abt. 1764 in Caswell Co., NC; Y
..........4 William Lee b: Abt. 1745 in Caswell Co., NC
            + Catherine 'Caty' Van Hook b: Abt. 1739, m: 1759 in Caswell Co., NC
..........4 Lucinda Lee b: Abt. 1746 in of, Caswell, Co, NC
            + Joseph Patterson b: Abt. 1745 in Caswell Co., NC, m: 1766 in Orange Co., NC
..........4 Nancy Lee b: Abt. 1747 in of, Caswell, Co, NC
            + Paul Harrelson b: 1722 in New Kent, Virginia
..........4 James Lee b: Abt. 1748 in Leesburgh, Caswell Co., NC, d: Bef. 1830 ; Y
..........4 Delphia Lee b: Abt. 1750 in of, Caswell, Co, NC
            + Joseph Henderson m: Abt. 1772 in of, Caswell, Co, NC
..........4 John Lee b: Abt. 1752 in of, Caswell, Co, NC
..........4 Mary Polly Lee b: Abt. 1754
            + James SERGEANT b: Abt. 1748 in Caswell Co., NC, m: Abt. 1774 in Caswell Co., NC
..............5 Phoebe SERGEANT b: Abt. 1776 in Caswell Co., NC
..........4 Phoebe Lee b: Abt. 1755 in Leesburgh, Caswell Co., NC
            + Thomas Kilgore b: Abt. 1751 in Caswell Co., NC, m: 02 Jan 1786 in Caswell Co., NC
..........4 Gabriel Lee b: Abt. 1756 in Leesburgh, Caswell Co., NC, d: 1839 ; Y
            + Elizabeth Ashburne b: Abt. 1758 in Leesburgh, Caswell Co., NC

www.ingramcontent.com/pod-product-compliance
Lightning Source LLC
Chambersburg PA
CBHW072207150726
48002CB00005B/1703